BIRDS OF AUSTRALIA

A Summary of Information

BIRDS
OF AUSTRALIA

A Summary of Information

J. D. MACDONALD
with contribution by D. L. Serventy

Illustrated by
PETER SLATER

REED

First published 1973
Revised and reprinted 1978
Revised and reprinted 1984
Revised and reprinted 1988
This edition reprinted 1992

REED
Part of William Heinemann Australia
Level 9, North Tower
1–5 Railway Street
Chatswood NSW 2067

National Library of Australia
Cataloguing in Publication data

Macdonald, J.D. (James David), 1908–
    Birds of Australia: a summary of information.

    Includes index.
    ISBN 0 7301 0385 4.

    1. Birds – Australia – Identification. I. Serventy, D.L. (Dominic
    Louis), 1904–   . II. Slater, Peter, 1932–   . III. Title.
598.2994

Printed in Singapore
for Imago Productions (F.E.) Pte Ltd

HAROLD WESLEY HALL, OBE, MC

Much of the information recorded in this book was obtained on the five expeditions from the British Museum (Natural History) made possible by the generosity of Harold Hall or as a result of studies stimulated by them.

Harold Hall was born in Melbourne and educated in England. He gave distinguished service in World War I. His father was responsible for the development of the Mount Morgan Mining Company. His uncle founded the Walter and Eliza Hall Institute in which Major Hall maintained a generous interest. After World War II he bought a diesel-engined trawler with which he did several years research for the British Museum, culminating in voyages to the Gulf of Aquaba and the Red Sea.

Major Hall came to Australia expressly to join the first of his expeditions but much to his regret was unable to take part. By good fortune a new species was discovered in southern Queensland which now bears his name, Hall Babbler, *Pomatostomus halli*.

CONTENTS

Preface to this Edition

SINCE THE PREVIOUS FAIRLY EXTENSIVE REVISION very little has occurred to affect the main purpose of this book, namely the identification of Australia's largely unique bird fauna. The quota of species remains much the same, with two doubtful reservations. There is no record of action being taken, with either positive or negative results, to investigate the probable existence of a distinct species of quail, referred to in the Addenda as 'Red-rumped Quail'. Conversely, a field party spent some time attempting to confirm the validity of a claim that the Paradise Parrot was seen in central Queensland, although believed to be extinct for some time. If there is any substance in either claim it may be that the few birds seen were a disappearing remnant. To remain viable a species requires an adequate population.

When the First Fleet arrived in 1788 the Emu was common in the vicinity of Botany Bay. Only two hundred years later it would be a rare event to find one anywhere in the metropolitan area of Sydney. The continual seepage of urban development into surrounding bushland has adversely affected many native species, but regrettably benefitted some less welcome introduced birds. Land use, the continual alteration and destruction of habitats, the use of insecticides, the bulldozing of mulga to feed stock and many other human activities have taken a sad toll on bird inhabitants. Worse still, the uncontrolled and perhaps uncontrollable existence of feral cats will inevitably reduce the numbers of certain species to the level of no return. This far from desirable process has been offset to some extent — not nearly enough — by increases in the number and variety of nature reserves, and government action to protect endangered species.

There has been a recent major revision of the phylogeny and classification of birds based on DNA hybridisation studies. Although it would cause a number of changes in the concept of relationships indicated here it is unlikely to be generally adopted for some considerable time. In any case methods of identification would be very little affected, and of course birds live and behave in a manner regardless of how we classify and name them.

INTRODUCTION

THERE IS A GROWING INTEREST in Australian birds and in the need for their conservation. Protective measures are only effective when based on correct identification, on knowledge of where and how birds live, and how they fit into their environment, and an understanding of their biology. The purpose of this book is to provide for the first essential —identification—and to summarise as many of the main facts about each species as can be contained within a volume of reasonable size. There are many birds whose life histories are not well known, indeed some species have rarely been seen and perhaps there are others still to be discovered. There are opportunities therefore to add to knowledge by careful observation and record keeping.

Australia has good reason to be concerned about conservation. We have one of the richest bird faunas in the world, not perhaps in diversity of kinds, or even in abundance of individuals, but certainly in the many peculiar and strikingly distinctive species which are found nowhere else. Certain unique birds like the Emu and Kookaburra—or Laughing Jackass—are common and well known in many literary contexts outside Australia, and of course the Budgerigar is a domestic pet in most countries. At the other extreme of recognition is the very rare Noisy Scrub-bird which attracted attention in the world press only when preservation of the remnants of its population meant the abandonment of plans to build houses on part of what is thought to be its last refuge. Over 60 per cent of species which breed in Australia are unique to the continent; they are indicated in the text as endemic species. Some are common and widespread like the Mudlark or Peewee but a large number are not well known and survive precariously in restricted areas or special habitats. It is a curious fact, for instance, that most of the endemic birds of prey are the least well known. It is outside the scope of this book to make special reference to endemic species or their plight but the point can be made that there is need for detailed life history studies to ensure effective protective measures.

Australia has about 745 kinds or species of birds. The number is not precise for two reasons. One is that new birds are still being found, like the Hall Babbler and Grey Grasswren, which have always been here but passed unnoticed; others occur as non-breeding visitors which may have extended their ranges or have been overlooked because of close resemblance to similar species, as in the case of some shore birds. Also people who are interested in relationships (taxonomists) find it difficult to decide, or agree among themselves, whether certain kinds are species in their own right or merely variants of some other species as in the case of the Spurwing and Masked Plovers.

Of the 745 species listed twenty have been introduced and 125 do not breed in Australia. They come from other countries, mainly in the northern hemisphere. These non-breeding visitors consist largely of the 'wader' assemblage—of all the family Scolopacidae recorded not one breeds here—but there are also rarer occurrences of pelagic petrels and subantarctic penguins and others. The few breeding species which migrate north and leave the continent, rarely completely, are regarded as residents.

There are then about 600 resident species. Of these 383 are truly Australian. They do not occur anywhere else, except as regular migrants or occasional vagrants (about fifteen), a few may have established small colonies in southeast New Guinea. Some are closely related to species outside the continent but many are quite unique. The origins of the latter lie deep in Australia's past, perhaps they are ancient settlers whose relatives elsewhere have long since disappeared, or who have modified and adapted in the peculiar conditions of the Australian environment beyond recognition of their ancestry. Some indeed have thrived so well that overflow populations have emigrated and formed colonies in adjacent countries. These and other matters relating to the origin and structure of the Australian bird fauna are discussed by Dr D. L. Serventy in a special section.

The text is as concise as possible. Statements are made mostly without reference to source, perhaps giving the impression that they are from personal knowledge. This is not so. Many data have been obtained from observations made by others which is published in various forms, or has readily been given for the asking. Much literature has been sifted through and the information used is largely first-hand. To all these numerous people, known and unknown, whose statements have been accepted and used, grateful thanks is given. The author's qualifications are a life-long interest in birds and a professional life devoted to their study. More to the point, specimens of every Australian species have been examined so that descriptions are original. Much first-hand knowledge of birds was obtained in connection with the Harold Hall expeditions and extensive travel in Australia since retirement.

The author has had the privilege of long acquaintance with D. L. Serventy, an Australian ornithologist whose views are widely known and respected. His enthusiasm and support made the Harold Hall expeditions possible at a time when their objectives were misunderstood. This long association, in which similar and conflicting views have been discussed and warmly debated, resulted in his agreeing to read the text and contribute on a subject on which he is a recognised authority. It is fortunate also that Peter Slater agreed to co-operate despite pressure of other work. He is a bird artist of considerable ability and has studied and photographed many species in various parts of the continent. His knowledge of Australian birds of prey is unique.

This close liaison with two experienced ornithologists has improved the usefulness of the information, but the author is entirely responsible for what is written. It is not claimed that this summary is infallible; it is certain that some important data have been overlooked and that what is stated here is far from complete or completely accurate. The reader could contribute to the improvement of a later edition by pointing out faults and providing new data.

NOTES ON THE TEXT

AREA

Included in the area covered are adjacent seas of undefined limits, some of whose oceanic birds may never come within sight of or 'set foot' on land, except as storm victims, but which can be seen from ships plying in Australian waters. The only land masses of importance which are omitted and which are politically part of Australia are Lord Howe, Norfolk and Macquarie Islands.

SYSTEMATIC ARRANGEMENT

Systematic arrangement is the sequence in which species are listed in groups of similar kinds, like genera and families. The criterion of similarity could be anything. In birds it is relationship and sequences usually begin with the oldest or least specialised forms. Unfortunately neither affinity nor age have been determined with certainty for all bird species. Views on both are constantly changing in the light of new facts and in the opinions of various taxonomists, so that sequences vary greatly.

Ornithologists in many countries make the best use of available information, according to their views, in preparing systematic arrangements or 'checklists' as guides for local use in various contexts. But many species have connections far beyond political boundaries, and people's interests are now wider, so the best course seems to be to conform as far as possible with some more general arrangement. With this in mind the sequence of families and species used here is based on the *Checklist of Birds of the World* begun by J. L. Peters, now frequently referred to as 'Peters Checklist' or 'World Checklist'.

Some divergence is necessary because of recent research and to suit this book. The latter is of little importance for it only means that in a group of very similar species, the commonest is listed first and others are compared with it. Research causes more complex changes by revealing previously unknown relationships. Thus the unique Australian or Inland Dotterel, *Peltohyas australis,* was thought to belong to the courser family, Glareolidae, but now it is believed to have close affinity with the genus *Charadrius* in the family Charadriidae— incidentally confirming John Gould's conclusion when he placed it near the European Dotterel. There is a current opinion that the Mudlark might belong to the wagtail family. Changes are inevitable and will continue unless some arbitrary method of listing can be accepted.

SYSTEMATIC CATEGORIES

There is a great variety of relationships, comparable with first cousins, second cousins and so on in human relationships. The more distant they are, the less obviously discernible they are, except in the case of very distinct groups like parrots. The many degrees of affinity have to be fitted into a limited number of categories, of which the primary ones are Species, Genus, Family, Order and Class. The only categories included here are Species, Genus and Family. When there is more than one genus in a family the oldest provides the family name, thus *Malurus* makes Maluridae. It is a tradition that only generic and specific names are printed in italics, that the genus begins with a capital letter but not the species part, even if it is a proper noun. Genera are frequently regarded as no more than convenient assemblages of related forms—they may be first cousins or tenth cousins or anything else.

The species name is essentially a combination of a noun and an adjective. It is comparable with the name of a person when in two parts, like John Smith, but it is written reversed *Smith john*. Species names are authenticated by author and date. When the name of the author is in brackets it means that the original genus was different to the one shown. Thus *Myzantha flavigula* Gould 1840 is now *Manorina flavigula* (Gould) 1840 — both of which mean White-rumped Miner.

The categories superspecies and subspecies are referred to in the text, the latter as races in the subhead 'variation'. Subspecies are populations of species which have more or less distinct features but which intergrade with others. As these forms occupy separate areas they are also known as geographical races or simply races. An example is found in the Pale-yellow Robin on Plate 16. The bird shown has buff coloured lores characteristic of northern populations; southern birds have white lores. It is indicated by a third name, *nana*, tacked on to the species name. Geographical variation is an important aspect of bird life but for most purposes the species is the important unit; subspecies can be named blindly on geographical location.

In cases where populations are clearly different and separate from the rest of the species and it is difficult to decide if they should be regarded as races or species they are often given the intermediate rank of semispecies. A group of semispecies make a superspecies. An example is in the fairy-wrens. Across the continent from east to west the Blue Wren is replaced by the Black-backed Wren, which in turn is replaced by the Turquoise Wren, and finally the Banded Wren (see Map 140). Each has distinctive features and separate distributions but all are basically similar and originated from the same once-uniform stock. Australia is rich in such groups.

COMMON NAMES

Unfortunately both common and scientific names are inherently unstable, and for simple reasons. Many common names originate in everyday speech. Birds are frequently referred to by different names derived from different characteristics noticed by different people in different places. The same bird may have a white throat, white in its tail, a distinctive voice and a habit of spreading its tail and may therefore become known as White-fronted Fantail, White-tailed Fantail, Cranky Fan, or just Fanny.

Inconsistency becomes a problem when it is necessary to select one name for use in writing. It is like deciding on a name in which to register a person who has no birth certificate and has already acquired several nicknames. In the case of little-known species the problem scarcely arises, for common names are often derived from scientific ones, like White-quilled Rock Pigeon for *Petrophassa albipennis*, which is suitable, if cumbersome — there are some odd cases, like *nigra* belonging to a white bird. But it is difficult when *Eolophus roseicapilla,* the Rose-breasted Cockatoo, becomes Galah in popular language, and *Dacelo gigas* is called Kookaburra, instead of Giant Kingfisher. It can be even more difficult when popular names are misapplied. There are several groups of Australian 'wrens' which are doubtfully related and not at all to the original Jenny Wren of Britain. Other misused names are 'robin', 'magpie' and 'treecreeper'. They can be misleading, even if like the ambiguous 'dollar' they are qualified as 'Australian Magpie' and 'European Magpie'.

Some names are inaccurate descriptions, the worst being intentional. At one time words like 'rump' and 'belly' were not considered polite and were altered to 'back' or 'tail', 'chest' or 'breast', usually with misleading results. The White-breasted Whistler of current usage, for example, has a black breast and white belly; it was previously named White-bellied Whistler and is so listed here. Attempts to stabilise common names meet with little success. People in certain regions as well as older naturalists resent the non-use of their own familiar names, and others with more tolerant outlooks get confused with alternatives. There might be better prospects of stability if it were accepted that verbal names or nicknames will always be used and new ones will evolve. Then it might be possible to agree to formal names. The names used here will not suit everyone. As far as possible names in the CSIRO Index* have been adopted with reference also made to notes on the draft revision of the Royal Australasian Ornithologists Union Checklist which have kindly been made available.

SCIENTIFIC NAMES

Scientific names should be more stable than common ones for they are unique, like car registration numbers. But they are bedevilled by many upsetting factors. It might transpire that a bird thought to be a new species had already been named in some other part of its range. For example, the Bushlark of Australia, named *Mirafra horsfieldi* by Gould in 1847, is now considered to be the same species as the Java Bushlark named *Mirafra javanica* in 1821. By an agreed law of priority the older name takes precedence and Gould's name disappears. But such superceded names or synonyms usually remain dormant, for in certain circumstances they can be revived. In the example used, Gould's name reappears in a lower rank because Australian birds are racially distinct and they have the name *Mirafra javanica horsfieldi*. Species are sometimes named inadvertently several times, the oldest perhaps overlooked in some obscure publication, like the recently discovered *Dacelo novaeguineae* for the Kookaburra (older than *Dacelo gigas*). The adoption of such names in preference to long established ones causes confusion, but fortunately there is now an internationally agreed rule that names in long use can be retained.

But the main cause of confusion is the fact that a scientific name is not only a 'registration number' but an index of relationship. It follows that changing concepts of affinity can cause havoc. It is no discredit to early taxonomists, faced with a wealth of new birds to name, that they should place some in the wrong genus or family, on present understanding of their affinities. Even current conclusions, often based on intensive research, are constantly being modified in the light of new information.

Some of the complexities of both scientific and common names are illustrated by the two Stilts in Australia. Gould named one *Himantopus leucocephalus*, White-headed Stilt. A current view is that it is not entitled to species rank but is a race of the widespread old-world species *Himantopus himantopus* whose name in Europe is Black-winged Stilt. Both names are descriptively accurate. The situation is further complicated by the second Australian Stilt, an endemic species. It was named *Leptorhynchus pectoralis* (the genus is now *Clado-*

---

* *An Index of Australian Bird Names*, CSIRO, Canberra, 1969.

rhynchus), drawing attention to the chestnut pectoral band and giving rise to the name Banded Stilt. Subsequently it was found that it had been named earlier as *Recurvirostra leucocephala*, White-headed Stilt, which is also appropriate, for the Banded Stilt is more extensively white on the head than the White-headed Stilt. So the Australian Stilts are (1) either Black-winged Stilt or White-headed Stilt and (2) either White-headed Stilt or Banded Stilt. The problem has been resolved (or further complicated) in New Zealand by using the name Pied Stilt for the former, and that solution is adopted here—with Banded Stilt for the latter. Incidentally, there would be further difficulties, which the reader may wish to explore, if it is decided that *Cladorhynchus* is not a valid genus distinct from the older *Himantopus*. It is unfortunate that scientific names are so wedded to taxonomy.

ILLUSTRATIONS
Illustrations have been selected to supplement the text. Apart from considerations of cost it is not necessary to illustrate each species and every variant of it when there are detailed descriptions and keys to identification. Where groups of species are basically similar, as in the male malurids, only one of each group is shown. Illustrations are sometimes restricted to distinctive features, especially in the head region; bills of waders for instance can be important in identification. The selection of species on the plates shows the wide range of colour and colour-pattern in Australian birds. In all, 467 species of the 745 listed here are illustrated in one form or another.

DISTRIBUTION
The distributions of species as indicated here on maps must be regarded as simplified patterns of very complex situations. The areas show where birds have been recorded at one time or another throughout the year and over a period of time. Maps are based on the evidence of collected specimens and reliable sight identifications. A sight record may be suspect if it is made far outside limits already known, but it could be valid, for the distributions of many species are uncertain or may fluctuate. In the arid interior, where rain seldom falls in the same places in successive years, species have a nomadic distribution pattern. Birds like the Flock Pigeon and *Polytelis* parrots may be well known in one area for several years then suddenly disappear, to reappear again later—they go 'flyabout'. In years of great drought, some dry country species invade coastal districts but do not settle there. Individual birds are known to get 'lost', probably meaning that whatever instinct holds them to a certain range ceases to function and they wander long distances. It is not always possible to know which records are of vagrants and where to draw the distribution limit. In species whose populations have shrunk, the known range in historic time is illustrated, as in the Paradise Parrot and Noisy Scrub-bird, and others. Where birds are increasing their range, like the Little Corella, the distribution limit may be different by the time this book is published.

Not only are limits uncertain and boundaries unstable but few populations are distributed evenly. Most occur in patches depending on the availability of preferred habitats. The wide range of the Painted Finch in the northwest consists of scattered groups associated with permanent waterholes in rocky localities. Many groups are far removed from each other and may never come in contact. The Painted Finch has what amounts to a discontinuous distribution of numerous populations, but it is not practicable (though possible) to map it in that form. This pattern, usually in less extreme form, is more common than might be expected, especially among sedentary species.

Migration also influences distribution patterns. Some species breed in one area and move to another when not breeding, like the Grey Teal which travels from inland to coastal waters. The distance travelled varies between species and in populations of the same species. The principal migratory pattern is that birds are mainly breeding visitors in the southern part of their range and non-breeding visitors in the northern sector, usually with a broad area in between where they are present at all seasons, but the same birds are not necessarily in any one place. The Swift Parrot breeds in Tasmania and then moves to the mainland as far north as the tropic; the White-winged Triller breeds mainly south of the tropic and then moves north, a few reaching New Guinea; the Koel travels a relatively long distance beyond the continent. But migration in the southern hemisphere is not on the same extensive scale as in the northern. Breeding and non-breeding ranges have not been clearly defined for most migratory species and little attempt is made to indicate any here.

KEYS AND RECOGNITION

Keys are signposts to identity which help to head the searcher in the right direction. The signposts are contrasting features. For instance in the case of the *Gerygone* warblers (page 328) there are two groups of species, one with 'breast and belly yellow' and the other with 'breast and belly white'. If the bird seen has a white breast and belly it is in the group 7–13. Numbers 7 and 8 indicate that it may or may not have a white base to the tail. If the latter then it should have one of three features indicated in the group 9–11. If the back and crown are brownish with white on the face then it lies in the group 12–13. If the white on the face is a white eyebrow and there is white on the forehead, the bird should be a Mangrove Warbler.

Keys are kept as concise and uncomplicated as possible. An inherent limitation is that different observers may notice different features and the ones selected here may seem less important than others or may be used in the wrong sequence. One pitfall is ambiguity in a group of contrasting features (where a bird seems to fit more than one group) and if this happens near the beginning of a long key there are grounds for condemning it as useless. The fault may lie with the key-maker but also it may be due to immature plumages or seasonal variations. This is a risk that has to be taken in constructing a key for it would be cumbersome indeed to include all plumage stages. In the case of 'difficult' identifications, a useful policy is to see if there are other similar birds nearby which are more easily identifiable. Immature birds are often in the company of their parents and frequently solicit food.

The subheading 'recognition' is a summary of salient characteristics. In some keys 'male' and 'female' are indicated by the ancient symbols ♂ and ♀, the shield and spear of Mars and the looking-glass of Venus.

DESCRIPTION

When several species are very similar, full notes are given only for the first; notes on others are abbreviated to principal differences and are listed under the subheading 'recognition'. Size is important. Precise dimensions are of little use, except with birds in the hand, but they provide standards for comparison and convey more exact information than 'large' and 'small'. Total length is given as an index of size, and when bills and tails differ from the average they are referred to separately, either as part of the total or in addition to it. In some cases wingspans are noted, but they are often less useful than wing shape and the angle of the wings in flight.

For the rest, descriptions are of colours and colour patterns. Shades of colour intermediate with the primary ones are difficult to describe, and descriptions often mean different things to different people, like 'rufous' for example. There are various colour standards in use but the 'describer' and the 'described to' have to use the same one for any sense to be conveyed. It helps if the describer always uses the same one, and in this instance it is the *Colour Atlas*.* It consists of 7279 shades arranged in thirty-eight hues which are subdivided on the basis of two co-ordinates: lightness value and degree of chromaticity. The authors related popular colour names to Atlas shades, not all of which are named, and these are used here, or at least those likely to be reasonably well known which are as near as possible to precise shades.

The sexes are described as 'alike' when differences are only minor ones of size or colour shade; otherwise they are 'different' or 'very different'. Sometimes there are two kinds of plumage in the course of a year, usually confined to males. When this occurs the general rule is that some feathers are replaced by more brightly coloured ones about the beginning of the breeding season. They are lost again during the complete moult of both sexes after breeding. There are many variations on this theme. Moult sequences are not well known for most Australian birds, especially changes from nestling to adult. Breeding and non-breeding plumages are briefly described but not those of immature birds, except for a few species.

VARIATION

Reference has already been made to subspecies or races under the subheading 'Systematic Categories'.

HABITAT

It has been noted that the distribution of species is mainly determined by the availability of preferred habitats. These are environments in which each kind of bird is most secure from enemies, where food and water are available (the latter is not always required) and where the birds can successfully compete with other species. Food requirements or the method of obtaining it can be so specialised that several species apparently with similar needs (insect eaters for example) can live together without competing.

Some birds live in a variety of environments like the Willie Wagtail which may be found almost anywhere except in rain forest. Others have more specialised requirements and may be confined to mangrove swamps or mallee or porcupine grass or gibber desert. The restricting factor or factors may be the need for certain kinds of food or places suitable for nesting such as the amount and depth of water or its rise and fall in the case of some water birds. Habitats are described according to the various more or less distinctive types into which vegetation is classified. The terms used here are self-explanatory.

HABITS

Observers can often identify birds by their behaviour. But as with other characteristics there are many similarities between closely related species as well as much variation in the habits of a single species, both in one area and throughout its range. The extent to which a bird can modify its habits shows how adaptable it is and what its chances of survival are in a changing environment. A number of species have readily adapted to human settlement, many others have not.

---

*C. and J. Villalobos, *Colour Atlas*, Libreria El Ateneo Editorial, Buenos Aires, 1947.

Most birds can be classified according to whether they are arboreal, terrestrial or aquatic, but with the qualification 'usually' or 'mostly' or some such term. Some are mostly arboreal but feed on the ground, or sometimes feed on the ground, or rarely feed on the ground. There are many habit characteristics, like the way a bird flies and the way it perches, whether it runs or hops, and so on. The association of individuals of the same species is described broadly by the terms 'solitary' or 'gregarious'; in this instance solitary is used to mean individuals or mated pairs. But there are many kinds of association, often in the same species. A male or female may be entirely alone, especially when immature, but frequently the sexes form pairs even when not breeding, for example, magpies. Some young stay in the company of their parents until the next breeding season or longer, or when there are several broods in one season all may keep together, like sittellas, forming family parties of varying size. Others, like the Apostlebird, form small close-knit communal units which remain together at all seasons. Some are solitary when breeding and band into flocks at other times, or they may feed together. There are many variations.

Movements of birds are also varied and complex. There are sedentary species in which individuals may never move outside a small area. At the other extreme there are the fully migratory kinds which breed in one region and then move to an entirely different one, the movement being mostly between north and south. But even at these extremes some individuals of a sedentary species may move, possibly as a result of overcrowding—in certain circumstances large numbers may break away or 'irrupt' into new areas—and numbers of a migratory species (usually sexually undeveloped birds) may stay behind in one area or the other. In between there are many variations. A usual pattern is that a bird breeds where there is likely to be an adequate supply of food for nestlings. When not tied to a nest, local food becomes less important and birds may wander, often in parties or flocks, in search of other sources, like flocks of lorikeets on the hunt for flowering eucalypts. Such nomadic movements may be restricted to a small area or may cover long distances, they may affect only a few members or a large population, perhaps sometimes a whole species as is thought to be the case of some arid country birds like the Alexandra Parrot. Movements of many species are not well known but are becoming clearer as data accumulate from recoveries of banded birds.

BREEDING

A number of species, or at least certain populations of them, have a clearly defined breeding period. The Short-tailed Shearwater or Muttonbird arrives on Fisher Island in the Bass Strait during the last week of September and thereafter follows a precisely-timed sequence of events. Similar patterns are sometimes recorded by observers for local populations of many birds, but over the range of a species there can be wide variation in the breeding period, even to the extent of being in different seasons. In the south, breeding takes place in the spring but elsewhere it may be anytime depending on various factors. Rainfall is important in arid regions and a number of Australian species are unique in that they can delay breeding (apparently even after gonads have matured) until rains come or until they discover an area where rains have fallen. Some species find conditions suitable for continuous breeding, probably different pairs at different times, while others extend or contract the period, or lay more or fewer eggs depending on circumstances.

A few birds are relatively unselective in where they place their nests but most have fairly definite requirements. It may be holes in banks with an unlined chamber or a chamber containing a fully formed and domed nest. Nests may be on the ground or in a variety of forms attached to or suspended from all kinds of vegetation, or anything to keep them off the ground. The position and form of nests is largely determined by the importance of concealment. Hawks and eagles have little need to hide and their nests are often large exposed platforms of sticks. In the same category are nests suspended from slender twigs in outer foliage whose protection lies in the difficulty a predator such as snake or goanna would have in reaching them. But for many species concealment is important and the form this takes is characteristic of various groups. Parrots and kingfishers make nests in holes in trees or holes drilled in termite mounds. Two groups of pardalotes are distinguished by one nesting mainly in holes in trees and the other in holes in banks. Nests on or near the ground may be concealed by elaborate construction or by none at all, as in the case of many waders who lay their eggs among stones or ground litter with little semblance of a formed nest. In the latter instance eggs and precocious nestlings have camouflage patterns. Australia's largest bird, the Emu, has the largest eggs, one of the largest clutches and even so a ground nest that is among the most difficult to find.

Eggs laid in concealed places, including domed nests, are protected by being out of sight and are usually white, while eggs in open and otherwise exposed nests are often patterned in protective colours. Eggs and the make of nest they are placed in as well as the location of the nests are distinctive for each species, and usually have certain characteristics common to related groups. In closely related species, distinction is often difficult but sometimes there are clear differences in nearly identical species, as in the two cisticolas.

VOICE

Many birds, especially small or elusive ones, are often identified more by what they say than by what they look like. The Bellbird's tinkling notes are known to many who have not seen the dark green bird camouflaged among the foliage. Although the sounds birds make are characteristic, they are mostly difficult to describe in writing. Various descriptive methods have been used including musical notation but they seldom convey much meaning to anyone who has not already heard the sound. It is difficult to imagine what is meant by the 'raucous laughter' of the Kookaburra but once heard it is easily identified and readily remembered.

Most birds have a small vocabulary of notes and phrases. They are used more often by males than females but sometimes by both together as in the duetting of magpies, or alternately to form a continuous phrase as in whipbirds. Important vocal functions are to proclaim territory ownership and to attract a mate. Such notes are often in the form of loud phrases and, as many are pleasing to the human ear, they are labelled as songs. Other uses of vocal sounds are danger warnings, harsh and sometimes not easily located sounds, and contact notes, the continuous 'chatter' of flocks dispersed while feeding which are important for keeping them together. Similar contact sounds are used between parents and young, like the clucking of a domestic hen and responding cheep of the chicks.

The language of birds is a complex and vastly interesting subject but for most species it is not well known or understood in human terms. One observer at least has translated the meaning of about twenty phrases of the Noisy Miner. It should be added that sounds may vary from place to place for birds are as prone to regional dialects as humans. Also it has been established in the case of one individual of one species that a phrase was modified slightly from year to year so that the extremes were very different. All that is attempted here is to give some brief indication of the main sounds uttered by each species either in descriptive terms or some phonetic rendering.

FOOD

Much of the information under this heading is relatively uninformative. About all that can be said on the matter of bird food in a short space is that one species may live mainly on vegetable material, seeds or fruit or honey or such like, and that another lives on animal food of one kind or another, including insects. Many eat both animal and vegetable, either at all times or special times—finches nurture their young on insect protein until their digestive systems are fit to cope with hard seeds. Some species seem to be very adaptable and feed on almost anything they can get. The food requirements of a number of birds have been studied in detail but for most it is not known whether their diet is a narrowly restricted one, like tubers of bulguru sedge required by the Brolga (but now being replaced by cereal crops) or whether a wide range of food items is acceptable. What seems to be least well known about bird food is the kind eaten by each species when a number of birds with apparently similar requirements live together. For example, several species of insectivorous birds can be found feeding together in the same tree and the question is if they compete for the same insects or specialise, one taking ants, another beetles (perhaps one species of beetle) and another lerps? The probability is that they specialise, that they are non-competitive in the matter of food and therefore tolerant of each other. Members of the same species have the same food requirements and are highly competitive; they will battle for ownership of an area over which they claim sole feeding rights. There is much to be learned.

STATUS

Status is used here to refer to the abundance of a species and whether it is resident or visitor. Populations of species are not known with certainty except perhaps those of very rare ones, like the Noisy Scrub-bird. Abundance can only be estimated in very general terms. Some species are obviously common over a wide area but there may be other species equally common but more furtive in their habits and more remote in their habitats and therefore seen less often. Most species, even the rarest, are common somewhere. Information under this heading therefore should be regarded as very rough estimates.

TAXONOMY

This is a brief summary of the relationship of each species to others of similar kind and of its distribution.

As a final comment on taxonomy and in summary of what has been said in the foregoing notes, the number of species listed here may not be the same as numbers listed elsewhere on good authority. The discrepancy is not due to some species being overlooked or new ones discovered (although both could happen) but because it is difficult to decide if certain forms are races or species. The notion that each kind of bird was specially created, and therefore a true entity, is not now widely held although perhaps tacitly accepted by those who have had no reason to give the matter thought.

It is important also to note that scientific names are affected by changing views on relationships. Contrary to what Linnaeus may have intended they are rather loose pegs, to the exasperation of naturalists who want to hang their information on something stable. This is an unfortunate situation but one likely to continue for a long time.

ORIGIN AND STRUCTURE
OF AUSTRALIAN BIRD FAUNA
by D. L. Serventy

ORIGIN OF THE FAUNA—THE OLDER EXPLANATION

HOW AUSTRALIA RECEIVED ITS bird population is now a subject of lively and interesting controversy. This continent was believed to have been isolated from the Afro-Asian land masses since Mesozoic time, when modern-type birds were thought not to exist. So, until recently, ornithologists who speculated on the origin of our avifauna agreed that, in the words of Professor Ernst Mayr, it must have been produced by 'continuous single origin colonisation from Asia', the process taking place by 'island-hopping' across the narrow seaways between northern Australia and southeastern Asia. This view was supported by the undoubted fact that the ancestors of those Australian birds whose overseas affinities are fairly obvious could only have reached Australia by this route. Their relatives are clearly Palaearctic and Oriental forms. And, because of the orthodox geological views on past land connections, or lack of them, this compelled acceptance of the belief that the ancestors of the older Australian endemic families, whose nearest relatives were unknown, had almost certainly colonised Australia in a similar manner. There appeared no need, therefore, to invoke the theory of continental drift in explaining the origins of the Australian bird fauna, though as early as 1926 Professor Launcelot Harrison, of the University of Sydney, had suggested that there was enough plausible evidence to warrant its serious consideration.

In 1944 Ernst Mayr* gave the first clear indication how this colonising process from southeast Asia may have occurred. He pointed out that on the basis of relative age, and consequentially, the degree of later differentiation, there were probably five major layers of colonists. The most recent of these consisted of some forty species that can only be subspecifically separated from their old world derivatives. The next oldest was a group of over sixty species which had diverged to species status since their arrival, the date of which Mayr would place at late Pliocene or early in the Pleistocene. The third oldest group were members of endemic genera which are obviously related to old world genera, and whose ancestors were thought to have arrived mainly in the Pliocene and perhaps also in the Miocene. The fourth oldest layer was a group of families and subfamilies, of presumed early or middle Tertiary origin, which are more or less clearly related to old world families. Finally we have the most interesting assemblage of all, distinctive families of Australian birds, many of which have captured the popular imagination, and which have been in Australia so long, and under isolation have differentiated so markedly, that their affinities are shrouded in obscurity. These include the Dromaiidae (emus), Megapodiidae (mound-birds), Podargidae (frogmouths), several Parrot groups (Loriniinae, Cacatuinae, Platycercinae), Menuridae (lyrebirds), Atrichornithidae (scrub-birds), Grallinidae (mudlarks), Meliphagidae (honeyeaters), Ptilono-

Emu, 1944, 44:113.

rhynchidae (bowerbirds), Paradisaeidae (birds of paradise) and Cracticidae (Australian 'magpies').

IMPLICATIONS OF CONTINENTAL DRIFT

However modern geological and palaeontological researches have questioned the plausibility of this explanation, and though the history of the more recent immigrants, as just outlined, is undoubtedly true, an alternative explanation for the origin of the more archaic, and more distinctive forms may have to be sought.

It had been traditionally held that the break-up of continents was exclusively a phenomenon of the Mesozoic, pre-dating the evolution and expansion of modern birds, and so could be only of academic interest to the student of bird zoogeography. However a considerable amount of recent geological investigation has shown that the movements of continents relative to one another have been such that the Australian block remained closer to its southern African and Antarctic neighbours for a longer period than had formerly been admitted. The technical geological evidence has been lucidly summarised for ornithologists by Stephen Marchant.* The dismemberment of the continents began in the Triassic but the divergence between them remained slight until the early Tertiary. The water gap between the Australian and Asiatic continental blocks was much wider than it is today, and Australia has moved progressively northward from Antarctica. The warning implications of this to those zoogeographers who still wish to derive the whole of the Australian avifauna from the north are stated in a later essay by Marchant.

> If you agree that there has been a measure of ocean floor spreading and yet want to introduce flora and fauna into Australia by island-hopping in an orthodox manner from the north, remember this. You are denied the opportunity to do so certainly before the Tertiary, probably before the Miocene and perhaps before the Pliocene. In other words you have at most 65 million years, but probably less than 20 million years, perhaps much less, for a lot of evolution in some groups.†

The difficulty has been compounded for the upholders of a wholly northern origin by palaeontological findings of a longer fossil history of modern-type birds than was previously realised. Professor Robert W. Storer has reminded us that several groups of water birds are known to have evolved in the Cretaceous, including the first representatives of swans and ducks, flamingos and cormorants and their allies. He believed that the early Tertiary was probably a period of major radiation of birds and by the close of the Eocene a wide variety of modern-type families was in existence, including early forms of song-birds. Of particular Australian interest is the recent discovery of three fossil bird feathers from the Koonwarra claystones in southern Gippsland, Victoria. This deposit is regarded as of Lower Cretaceous age (about 130 millions of years old), but may even be older, perhaps of Upper Jurassic age according to Professor J. Warren, of Monash University. The feathers cannot be identified as of any particular bird group but are exciting enough in themselves as proving that birds *of some kind* existed in Australia at a very early stage in bird evolution. The Koonwarra feathers may be of an age approximating that of the earliest known bird, the reptile-like *Archaeopteryx* from the Upper Jurassic of Bavaria. Significant discoveries bearing on

---

*Ibis, 1972, 114:219.

†Emu, 1972, 72:189.

Australian bird evolution are hopefully expected from current investigations in these beds. Other evidence of early birds comes from New Zealand. Near Christchurch, in the South Island, a partial skull and toothed jaws of an archaic pelecaniform bird, *Pseudodontornis*, was recently found, whose allies were previously only known from the Eocene of Europe and North America. The New Zealand fossils were found in deposits of Pliocene age but could have been derived from older Lower Miocene formation.

GONDWANALAND ORIGINS OF SOME AUSTRALIAN BIRDS

All these data compel a reconsideration of the history of the older Australasian birds. Some of these older elements may well have reached Australia via Africa and Antarctica, or were locally evolved in parts of this earth block, during the earlier stages of fragmentation of Gondwanaland—the name given to the southern land masses when they were united. One group of birds almost certainly in this category is that of the Ratites (including the Australian emus and cassowaries and the New Zealand kiwis and moas), now generally accepted as having a common ancestry. Others may have been the parrot assemblage. Also warranting consideration, from this standpoint, is the primitive Pied Goose *(Anseranas)*, the megapodes, lyrebirds, scrub-birds and perhaps others of the peculiar Australian passerine families. Stephen Marchant has published a case for including the bronze cuckoos *(Chrysococcyx)* in this category too.

One argument against the idea that Australia had a close contact with other earth masses, when bird groups were able to radiate freely, was the absence of so many widespread families —such as the old world vultures *(Aegyptinae)*, pheasants *(Phasianus)*, skimmers *(Rhynchopidae)*, sandgrouse *(Pteroclinae)*, trogons *(Trogonidae)*, barbets *(Capitonidae)*, woodpeckers *(Picidae)*, broadbills *(Eurylaemidae)*, the true finches *(Fringillidae)*, and hornbills *(Bucerotidae)*—absences which point to the comparatively unbalanced composition of the existing Australian avifauna and so provide an indication that it was comprised essentially of elements capable of sea crossings. The flamingos were formerly placed in this category, too, until the unexpected finds in 1961 and 1962 by Alden H. Miller of the fossil remains of four species in the Lake Eyre basin, ranging in age from at least the late Oligocene to the end of the Pleistocene. Accepting the thesis that the Australian Ratites, parrots and (now extinct) flamingos were elements of an archaic fauna dating from an Africa-Antarctica colonisation route, we cannot exclude the possibility that other widespread families—such as some of the absentees just enumerated—may also have been present and have since become lost to the fauna. This pauperisation of what may originally have been a more balanced avifauna may have been due to the combined effects of climatic change, habitat alteration by early man, and competition by more recent types colonising from the southeastern Asia sector.

AUSTRALIA IN THE TERTIARY

This old Australia, part of a block which fragmented from Africa in the Mesozoic and became reduced in size by rifting off, successively from Antarctica and then New Zealand by the early Tertiary, was a very different continent climatically both from what it became in the Pleistocene and what it is today. When Australia separated off from the rest of Gondwanaland, or in the earlier stages of drift, its archaic fauna must have included birds, as we know from the Koonwarra fossil feathers just mentioned. Its climate was equable and humid and large parts of the continent were vegetated by a broad-leafed mesophytic flora, characterised by such types as the southern beeches *(Nothofagus)*, which are now restricted to subtropical and temperate rain-forest pockets in eastern Australia. There were extensive freshwater lakes. A change to strongly marked seasonal climates began in the Upper Miocene, with a rise in the dominance of more xerophyllous genera like *Eucalyptus* and *Acacia*. In the later Tertiary extensive mountain-building began, continuing into the Pleistocene, producing the Great Dividing Range, Mt Lofty and the Flinders Range. The extreme of climatic changes took place during the Pleistocene Ice Ages, when, though there were no extensive glaciations, there were marked pluvial periods alternating with intervals of intense aridity, and the great Australian deserts developed.

These formidable climatic and topographic changes must undoubtedly have led to the disappearance of much of the older fauna, though fossil evidence at present is limited to the flamingos. The present-day relict ranges of the primitive Passerines, *Atrichornis* and *Menura* in Australia and *Xenicus* in New Zealand suggest that others may have vanished earlier. Avian palaeontological studies in the future may provide as exciting discoveries as those already made by Alden Miller. There is another important implication arising from a consideration of these great physical changes.

BEGINNINGS OF CHANGE

One of the most important factors for successful entry to a new area by animal species is the existence of unstable scattered habitats: this is now admitted by ecologists to be a necessary precondition for successful colonisation. Throughout most of the Tertiary, Australia would have offered little capacity for immigrants to capitalise on this situation. In the lush forests of its long-continued mild climate, undoubtedly harbouring a rich biota, there would have been a considerable resistance to an invader. But later in the Tertiary, and particularly in the Pleistocene, the disturbed environments, extreme variations in climate, and the rapidly altering topography, would have combined to offer ideal situations for opportunistic colonisers from southeastern Asia—particularly after Continental Drift had moved Australia nearer the Asiatic block. It was then, probably, that the majority of the northern island-hoppers were able to establish a bridge-head. With their successful entry, many members of the archaic fauna, particularly those which had lost ecological resiliency and had become intimately and irreversibly adapted to the equable conditions of pre-Oligocene Australia, must have suffered elimination.

The physiographical and climatic upheavals in the later Tertiary and in the Pleistocene probably introduced the first barriers disrupting the distribution of the pan-Australian fauna —the 'older' Australian forms as well as the newer immigrants from Asia. The previous uniform and mild conditions over a vast area of continental Australia, combined with low relief, enduring until the late Tertiary, would not have provided much in the way of isolating mechanisms to cause speciation. What species transformation did occur would be that known as phyletic evolution, producing chrono-clines or even chrono-species. Geographic isolation is necessary to produce additional species. Thus active speciation could only become general after the varied effects of climate, topography and vegetation disrupted the continuity of populations from the Pliocene onwards.

DIFFERENTIATION OF AUSTRALIAN FAUNAS

The Great Dividing Range was probably the first considerable barrier. It split the pan-Australian fauna into two great assemblages, permitting independent evolution within each.

The development of the central arid area was of equal potency in shaping the later Tertiary, Pleistocene and Recent faunal distribution pattern. This fluctuated in size and position during the Pleistocene and divided off a northern (tropical) fauna from most of the rest of Australia. The periodic expansion of the arid centre, with its intensification into desert conditions during Pleistocene and Recent time, has been perhaps the major causative factor in recent speciation by isolating fragments of formerly continuous populations into humidity refuges. Thus an 'archipelago effect' was created within the continent and the pockets of isolated populations differentiated from each other at all levels, from subspecies to full species (semispecies).

The physical and climatic barriers just discussed produced a faunal distribution pattern which has long attracted the attention of zoogeographers. The first rational subdivision of the higher vertebrates into natural geographical units was proposed in 1896 by Professor W. Baldwin Spencer, of the University of Melbourne, when he analysed the results of the Horn Scientific Expedition into central Australia, which he led. Though he was indebted to earlier proposals by the botanist Professor Ralph Tate and the malacologist Charles Hedley, whose arrangements he had to modify considerably, Spencer showed a remarkably perceptive insight into the distribution problems. His three natural regions (see map), of Torresian,

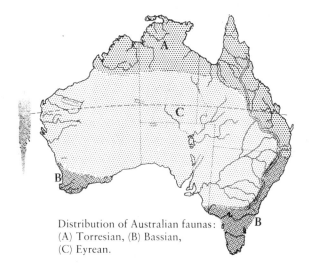

Distribution of Australian faunas:
(A) Torresian, (B) Bassian,
(C) Eyrean.

Bassian and Eyrean, have stood the test of time despite several later suggestions for amendment. It was undoubtedly the formation of the Great Dividing Range which led to the separation of the fauna into the Bassian and the Eyrean, and the development of the central desert (the 'dead heart' of Australia) separated the northern Torresian from the Eyrean, which because of climatic selection pressure evolved into a dry-adapted avifauna. The Bassian fauna continued to enjoy humid conditions, and the Torresian had to adapt to monsoonal summer rains and, mostly, winter drought.

The more important modifications to Spencer's faunal arrangements had to do with resolving an apparently anomalous situation in southwestern Australia, which had been left by Spencer as part of the Eyrean Region. In 1928 Tom Iredale proposed dividing off the southwest as a separate region, the Leeuwinian with Bassian affinities. From a study of other fauna Professor G. E. Nicholls, of the University of Western Australia, confirmed this separation in 1932, also recognising its relation with the Bassian, but he proposed an alternative name, the Hesperonotian Region.

Serventy and Whittell* eliminated the difficulty of the southwest by altering Spencer's original notion of fixed faunal regions by invoking Ernst Mayr's concept of fluid faunas (which he stated in 1946). It was necessary to abandon the old ideas of a static zoogeography and to think instead of Torresian, Bassian and Eyrean *faunas* not *regions*. Elements of these faunas were able to transgress average faunal boundaries (set up originally by physiography and climate) and to invade neighbouring areas inhabited largely by an 'alien' fauna. This is what happened in the southwest. It was originally Bassian, but had been isolated from the southeastern Bassian by the periodic encroachments of the desert in Pleistocene times, aided by the down-faulting which produced the Great Australian Bight either in the late Pliocene or early Pleistocene. Climatic deterioration led to its receiving many Eyrean invaders, so many that the region became an intimate intermingling of two faunas, Eyrean and Bassian, on a scale which was unparalleled elsewhere in Australia. A lesser degree of intermingling occurs in many other transitional areas at faunal boundaries. Thus Francis Ratcliffe and John Calaby in their analysis of the Canberra fauna, in 1954, showed that though this fauna was predominantly Bassian there was a substantial representation of Eyrean forms, as well as a small Torresian element.

A recent study of the distribution of Australian land-birds by Jiro Kikkawa and Kay Pearce,† by the modern method of numerical analysis by computer, has confirmed the validity of the Spencer and Serventy-Whittell arrangements. They have proposed an alteration of the nomenclature of some of the faunas, which is scarcely warranted. Of greater merit, however, is their subdivision of the Torresian into two faunas, by separating out a western component, which they term the Timorian, from the eastern Torresian.

Many members of the Eyrean avifauna have differentiated into eastern and western forms, some so strongly marked that they now form good species. In the east, moreover, several species have evolved which are peculiar to the region, including the Desert Chat, Hall Babbler, Chestnut-crowned Babbler and Grey Grasswren. The isolating barrier which produced this differentiation has been suggested by the herpetologist Arnold Kluge (who in 1967 recognised its importance for reptile speciation), as the great Pleistocene Lake Dieri (now represented by its saline remnants, Lakes Eyre, Frome and Torrens), as well as by the Flinders Range and the sea bight to the south which existed at the heightened sealevels during interglacial maxima.

A slighter differentiation in the western Eyrean fauna can also be detected. Thus there are differences between the Western Australian and central Australian forms of Spotted Bowerbird, in whitefaces of the respective regions, in forms of the Cinnamon Quail-thrushes and the Banded Wren. The barrier in this case is probably the desert belt (Great Sandy, Gibson's and Victoria Deserts) separating some elements of the central Australian and more western faunas. Ameliorating conditions are bringing some forms into secondary contact and hybrid zones are developing (as in the case of the Turquoise and Banded Wrens).

The repeated waxing and waning of the dry centre, due to the alteration of dry and pluvial periods, caused periodic connections and interruptions between the eastern and

---

*D. L. Serventy and H. M. Whittell, *Handbook of the Birds of Western Australia*, Patersons Press Ltd, Perth, 1948.
†*Australian Journal of Zoology*, 1969, 821.

western Bassian, the southern Eyrean and even the western and eastern Torresian faunas. At the present time a climatic barrier, referred to by J. D. Macdonald* as the 'Carpentaria Barrier', still partially separates many elements of the Torresian fauna at the south of the Gulf of Carpentaria. From the standpoint of Eyrean birds, this barrier may be looked on as a 'salient', as it has enabled many Eyrean species to penetrate to the northern seaboard, and is the only place where they do so (see for example, the distribution maps in the body of this book of the Spiny-cheeked Honeyeater, White-plumed Honeyeater, Grey-headed Honeyeater, Black Honeyeater and the Yellow-tailed Thornbill (race *normantoni*)).

These fluctuations in the size of the arid centre have also provided opportunities for double or multiple invasions from the eastern Bassian west to the Bassian outlier in south-western Australia. In the yellow robin group, for example, an earlier invasion led to the differentiation of the White-breasted Robin, characterised by the loss of all yellow pigments on the underparts. A second invasion from the east seems to be producing a similar result, for in the Western Yellow Robin the yellow colouring has disappeared from the chest and upper breast. The three chestnut-shouldered blue wrens of the southwest are also the product of multiple invasions due to climatic oscillations and other instances are noted by Serventy and Whittell in the *Birds of Western Australia*.

RELATIONS WITH NEIGHBOURING ISLANDS

Tasmania is analogous to southwestern Australia in being an outlier of the Bassian fauna, in this case the intermittent existence of Bass Strait separating the faunas instead of a desert land barrier. Some insular differentiation has similarly taken place (outstanding examples being the Yellow Wattle-bird, a derivative of the mainland Red Wattle-bird, and the Yellow-throated Honeyeater, with similar relations to the mainland White-eared Honeyeater; the Scrubtit appears to be the insular differentiation of a stock allied to the mainland Large-billed Scrubwren). And, as in southwestern Australia, there are interesting examples of double invasions (in the genera *Acanthiza* and *Pardalotus*).

With regard to New Zealand there is geological evidence that it remained in contact or very close to Australia, as a remnant of rifting Gondwanaland, until the Upper Cretaceous, and it may not have drifted away so very far before the end of the Eocene. It is, therefore, not so difficult to explain peculiar elements in the New Zealand avifauna, such as the extinct moas, the kiwis and the primitive passerines (the New Zealand wrens) as originating from that ancient land connection. Other distinctive forms are allied to groups otherwise now restricted to Australia and may have had a similar origin or may be the descendants of later trans-Tasman Sea crossings. These include the owl-parrots (Strigopinae) allied to the Austra-lian Night Parrot, and possibly the New Zealand wattlebirds (Callaeidae) which may be the derivatives of a form from which the Australian Apostlebird also descended. Most of the land birds of New Zealand are clearly the results of age-long colonisations across the Tasman Sea, a process which is still going on.

Sir Robert Falla has pointed out that in Pleistocene and Recent times a fairly rich water-fowl and open-country fauna allied to Australian types flourished in New Zealand and then died out, possibly because of the onset of arid cycles. These included a swan allied to the Australian Black Swan, a large eagle, a coot, a corvid and representatives of two Australian monotypic ducks (the Musk Duck and the Pink-eared Duck).

Emu, 1967, 66:341.

New Guinea is a well marked subregion of the Australasian fauna, characterised by several striking locally-evolved groups, such as the birds of paradise, the crowned pigeons (*Goura*) and the cassowaries. It is a mountainous land of far more varied topography than Australia, and because of the consequently greatly increased opportunities for isolation of populations, it now contains about as many species of birds as the whole of Australia, though it is only one-tenth its size.

The other islands in the nearer Pacific region have been bird-colonised by sea crossings from either New Guinea or Australia, and in some cases from New Zealand. Thus the parakeets of the genus *Cyanorhamphus* (allied to the Australian *Psephotus* group) have dispersed from New Zealand northwards to New Caledonia, as far east as the Society Islands, south to Macquarie Island and west to Lord Howe Island. The Chestnut Teal from Australia colonised New Zealand, where it evolved into the form known there as the Brown Teal, which from New Zealand entered the Auckland and Campbell Islands, differentiating into local, flightless races.

Mention may finally be made of some old world forms, colonising the Australian region by island-hopping from southeastern Asia, which have spread fairly widely but have by-passed Australia, or failed to establish a bridge-head there. One of the hornbills (Bucerotidae) has spread to New Guinea and the Solomons. One of the shrikes (Laniidae) has reached New Guinea but no further. One of the widespread thrush genus, *Turdus*, has established itself not only in New Guinea and some of the Pacific Islands, but also on Lord Howe and Norfolk Islands, between Australia and New Zealand.

SYSTEMATIC ACCOUNT
OF FAMILIES

Australian birds are an integral part of the world of birds. It adds interest to the study of them to make some reference to their kith and kin elsewhere. This is done in several ways. There is a note at the head of each family of the total number of species (number in brackets, and so far as known) in relation to the number occurring in Australia. Also the distribution of each family in the world is either briefly described or illustrated on a map. Further, there are a few comments on the composition and characteristics of each family and genus, and other references to forms related to listed species under the heading 'taxonomy'. Finally, there is an analysis in tabular form of the composition of families represented in Australia in terms of native and visiting species, together with notes on some salient features which the analysis reveals.

Family CASUARIIDAE

Cassowaries and Emu

2(4) species : 1 endemic

CASSOWARIES BELONG TO THE tropical rain forests of north Queensland and New Guinea. Like other large flightless birds which do not thrive in competition with man, cassowaries are shrinking in range and numbers. Their heyday was in earlier times—in wetter periods when forests were more extensive.* Features of the head, especially the large bony protuberance or casque, seem to be related to life in forests and the habit of pushing through dense undergrowth, or crashing blindly through undergrowth with head lowered

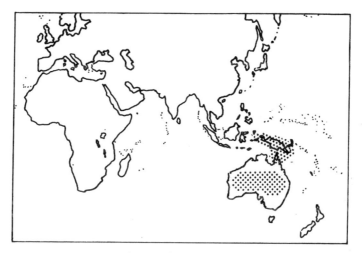

Distribution of CASUARIIDAE

and neck extended when in a hurry, as observers report. Wings are rudimentary and legs are relatively short and thick. The plumage is black in adults and brown in immatures, the feathers long and drooping. Eggs are light green and usually rough. The voice is loud and booming.

The Emu, second largest of the world's flightless birds, has been placed in a unique family of its own, but it has so many features closely resembling those of cassowaries that there is little doubt it originated as an offshoot from an early cassowary stock which left a forest environment and learned to live in open country. Such adaptation to dry habitats, necessitated by widespread shrinkage of rain forests, is typical of several other Australian groups. Only found in Australia the Emu is widespread and fairly numerous in spite of certain restrictive measures. It thrives in thinly populated areas and has a high reproductive rate.

*In Pleistocene times the Dwarf Cassowary, *Casuarius bennetti*, now restricted to New Guinea and islands, ranged as far south as the Wellington Valley in New South Wales.

1 SOUTHERN CASSOWARY *Casuarius casuarius* (Linnaeus) 1758

Distribution: Map 1.

RECOGNITION: *large and flightless and confined to rain forests in north Queensland; large protuberance on head.*

DESCRIPTION: 1·5m from head to tail, stands nearly 1m to centre of back and 1·5m to top of head. Wings rudimentary with feather shafts bare and resembling porcupine quills. Sexes alike. Plumage black in adults, brown in immatures; head and neck bare; casque, bill and face in front of eye blackish; remainder of head and front and sides of neck bright blue; streak on hind neck bright red; wattles red; eyes blue-black; legs grey-green.

HABITAT: tropical rain forests. HABITS: terrestrial, shy but fiercely aggressive and dangerous if cornered, more likely to be heard than seen; usually in pairs or small family parties; probably sedentary but may wander far in search of food; follows regular tracks and rests in sunny places during middle of day. BREEDING: July and August; nest a roughly cleared space on forest floor; three to four eggs, light green; 14 by 9·5cm. VOICE: harsh 'heugh-heugh' and deep booming. FOOD: seeds, fruits and vegetable material.

STATUS: Fairly common. TAXONOMY: endemic race *(johnsonii)* of species extending to New Guinea and adjacent islands.

Cassowary (1)   Emu (2)

2 EMU *Dromaius novaehollandiae* (Latham) 1790

Distribution: throughout, except in northeast forests, heavily populated areas, Tasmania and Kangaroo Island.

RECOGNITION: *the only large flightless bird outside rain forests.*

DESCRIPTION: 2m from head to tail; stands 1·25m to centre of back and 2m to top of head. Sexes alike, except in voice. Wings vestigial. Feathers long and double (due to development of aftershaft). Plumage dark grey-brown with a whitish ruff at base of neck, especially in old birds; feathers on head and neck thin and wispy; face and throat bare and pale grey-blue; bill blackish; eyes reddish-brown; legs dark grey-brown.

HABITAT: woodlands to semi-deserts, especially savanna. HABITS: in pairs or small scattered parties; sedentary and nomadic, depending on water and food supply; runs at speeds of up to thirty miles per hour. BREEDING: April–November; nests on open ground or under bush or tree, a rough circle of stones or sticks and other vegetation; six to eleven eggs, dark grey-green, 13.5cm by 9cm. VOICE: in male harsh and guttural, in female booming. FOOD: green vegetable matter and fruits, also insects, including caterpillars.

STATUS: common to abundant. TAXONOMY: endemic species, genus and family.

Family STRUTHIONIDAE

Ostrich

Introduced
2A OSTRICH *Struthio camelus* Linnaeus

INTRODUCED FROM AFRICA and farmed for plumes in South Australia and central Queensland; now only a small feral population south of Flinders Ranges. Flightless; stands 3–3½m; plumage black or brown with white on wings and tail; head, neck and legs bare.

Family SPHENISCIDAE

Penguins

9(18) species

Distribution: subantarctic seas.

PENGUINS HAVE EVOLVED FROM flying ancestors but are now completely flightless and largely aquatic. Wings are modified for swimming although they carry the components which once enabled them to fly; they are now better described as flippers. Penguins are torpedo shaped, like miniature seals, with thick necks and short legs set far back on the body, which cause them to stand upright on land or to slide along on their bellies; they are blackish above and white below with varying amounts of black and white on the throat and face, and sometimes have a colourful decoration of yellow plumes above the eyes. They live in antarctic and adjacent seas; the normal range does not extend north of the equator and only in one instance north of the southern tropic. Several species belong to Australian and New Zealand seas. Although small and nondescript, one of them, the Little or Fairy Penguin, is an appealing attraction near Melbourne during the period of its terrestrial breeding cycle. The other species included here are uncommon or rare non-breeding visitors to southern coastal waters. It is quite likely that they occur more frequently than records admit and the following aids to identification may help to increase the numbers of certain records.

Key to SPHENISCIDAE

1 Head plumed	3–6	
2 Head not plumed	7–12	
3 Plumes meet on forehead; throat white	Royal Penguin	No 8
4 Plumes do not meet; throat black	5–6	
5 Plumes yellow, long and drooping	Rockhopper Penguin	No 7
	Thick-billed Penguin	No 9
6 Plumes golden yellow, short and stiff	Erect-crested Penguin	No 10
7 Less than 45cm	Little Penguin	No 11
8 Over 60cm	9–12	
9 Orange patch on side of head	King Penguin	No 3
10 White band on crown	Gentoo Penguin	No 4
11 White ring around eye	Adelie Penguin	No 6
12 Black band on white throat	Chinstrap Penguin	No 5

Genus APTENODYTES

The two largest penguins, standing 90–130cm, make up this genus. Only the King Penguin, the smaller one, has been recorded in Australian seas. Large size, long slender bill and patch of orange-yellow on side of neck are distinctive features.

3 KING PENGUIN   *Aptenodytes patagonica*   Miller 1778

Distribution: southeastern seas; recorded from Tasmania.

RECOGNITION: 90cm; bill 13cm from angle of mouth. Black of chin extends to sharp point in centre of throat, bordered by *orange-yellow extending from patch on side of neck* and merging with pale yellow of foreneck and upper breast; bill blue-black with patch of reddish-orange at base of lower mandible.

STATUS: rare; non-breeding straggler.

Genus PYGOSCELIS

Three medium-sized penguins, about 75cm, without head plumes but having some other distinctive head features. Bills are more slender than in the plumed species. All three have been recorded in Australian seas.

4 GENTOO PENGUIN   *Pygoscelis papua*   (Forster) 1781

Distribution: southeastern seas; recorded from Tasmania.

RECOGNITION: 75cm; bill fairly slender. *White band extending from above eye across crown;* chin black; bill yellow to reddish-orange with black streak on top. Back visible when swimming.

STATUS: rare; non-breeding straggler.

5 CHINSTRAP PENGUIN   *Pygoscelis antarctica*   (Forster) 1781

Distribution: southeastern seas; recorded from Tasmania.

RECOGNITION: like Gentoo but throat white with thin *blackish 'chinstrap'*; no white band on crown; bill black.

STATUS: rare; non-breeding straggler.

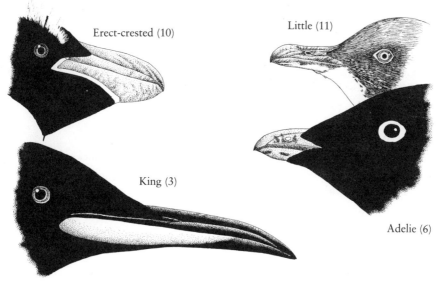

Erect-crested (10)

Little (11)

King (3)

Adelie (6)

PENGUIN BILLS

6 ADELIE PENGUIN *Pygoscelis adeliae* (Hom. & Jacq.) 1841

Distribution: southern seas; records uncertain.

RECOGNITION: like Gentoo with black throat but distinguished by *white ring around eye*; no white band on crown; bill reddish with black tip and feathered on basal half. Back not visible when swimming.

STATUS: uncertain.

Genus EUDYPTES

Plumed penguins; four of the five species have been recorded in Australian seas. The feathers at the edge of the crown above the eye are extended to varying lengths and are brightly coloured in shades of yellow. Chins are usually black, white only in the Royal, and there are different amounts of white and black on the underside of the flippers.

7 ROCKHOPPER PENGUIN *Eudyptes chrysocome* (Forster) 1781

Distribution: southern seas, as far north as Fremantle and mid-New South Wales.

RECOGNITION: 60cm; *yellow plumes 8cm, drooping and do not meet on forehead*; throat black; flippers have narrow white margins front and rear; bill reddish-orange. Hops.

STATUS: fairly common; non-breeding visitor.

8 ROYAL PENGUIN *Eudyptes chrysolophus* (Brandt) 1837

Distribution: southeastern seas; recorded in Tasmania and South Australia.

RECOGNITION: like other plumed species but *plumes orange-yellow and meet on forehead*; face grey or white; throat white; bill brown and angle of mouth pinkish-brown.

STATUS: rare; non-breeding straggler.

9 FIORDLAND PENGUIN *Eudyptes pachyrhynchus* Gray 1845

Distribution: southern seas, especially near Tasmania.

RECOGNITION: like other plumed species; plumes 6cm, droop and do not meet on forehead, yellow; throat black; *flippers have narrow white rear margin only*; bill reddish-brown. Back not visible when swimming.

STATUS: fairly common; non-breeding visitor.

10 ERECT-CRESTED PENGUIN *Eudyptes sclateri* Buller 1888   Fig p 35

Distribution: southeastern seas; recorded Tasmania to New South Wales.

RECOGNITION: like other plumed species but *plumes short and stiff*, golden-yellow and do not meet on forehead; throat black; flippers have broad white rear margin.

STATUS: occasional; non-breeding visitor.

Genus EUDYPTULA

Two of the smallest penguins, less than 45cm, make up this genus. Both are confined to Australian and New Zealand seas. The underparts are wholly white, and so is the extremely small tail which is nearly hidden by the upper tail coverts. The Little Penguin is the only penguin breeding in Australia.

11 LITTLE PENGUIN *Eudyptula minor* (Forster) 1871

Distribution: temperate coasts from Fremantle to southern Queensland.

RECOGNITION: *small with wholly white underparts and no distinctive markings on head.*

DESCRIPTION: 38–43cm. Sexes alike. Upperparts shiny blue-grey; underparts white; tail very short, white and nearly covered by upper tail coverts; bill brownish-black; eyes whitish; legs pinkish-white.

HABITAT: coastal seas, nesting on offshore islands and sometimes mainland. HABITS: aquatic except when breeding and moulting; gregarious; mainly sedentary, but wanders along coasts; comes ashore to breeding colonies after dark and leaves before dawn, some remain in burrows during day; walks upright but slides on belly when in a hurry. BREEDING: mainly August–November, sometimes as late as March; nests in burrows up to 2m in length or in hollows under bushes and ledges, a bed of seaweed or grass; two white eggs. VOICE: dog-like bark. FOOD: squid and fish.

STATUS: common. TAXONOMY: endemic race *(novaehollandiae)* of species extending to New Zealand and Chatham Is.

Little Penguin (11)

Family DIOMEDEIDAE
Albatrosses and Mollymawks
9(13) species

Distribution: subantarctic and temperate seas.

ALBATROSS IS A NAME suitable for all members of this family although some of the smaller and darker species are sometimes referred to as mollymawks. Their haunts are the southern oceans with northern limit roughly 20 degrees south latitude, except for three species which occur in the north Pacific. Life on the high seas, where they range widely in search of food, is made possible by their skill in gliding. Wind energy is used to conserve their own; they rise into the wind on motionless wings, sweep round and down gaining speed, bank almost vertically with a wingtip nearly cutting the water, then climb again. An important feature of a glider is long thin wings and an albatross' wings look excessively long in relation to body size. The Wandering Albatross with body size of 130cm has wingspan of up to 4m, the largest among all birds. Albatrosses may remain at sea for several years, until the urge to breed brings them to land, usually on remote islands. The only Australian breeding species, the White-capped Albatross, nests on islands around Tasmania. The other eight species listed here regularly visit or occasionally wander into Australian seas. Most albatrosses are white with varying amounts of black on wings and back, but a few are sooty black. Bills are large and strongly hooked and constructed of separate plates whose detailed pattern is distinctive for most species; the nostrils are separate small tubes at the sides of the bill, not united into a single large tube at the top of the bill as in petrels. Legs of species occurring in or near Australia are flesh-coloured. Only adult features are given in the following notes. Bill colours especially in immatures are frequently different.

Key to DIOMEDEIDAE

1 White with varying amounts of black, especially on wing; tail rounded	3–8 *(Diomedia)*	
2 Blackish; tail wedge-shaped	9–10 *(Phoebetria)*	
3 Black wing tips	*Wandering Albatross	No 14
	Royal Albatross	No 15
4 Blackish on upper wings and centre of back (forming continuous black bar); dusky eye patch	5–8	
5 Underwing with black tip and narrow black margin	*Shy Albatross	No 12
	Buller's Albatross	No 13
6 Underwing with broad black margin	7–8	
7 Bill yellow	Black-browed Albatross	No 16
8 Bill black	*Yellow-nosed Albatross	No 17
	Grey-headed Albatross	No 18
9 Sooty brown, yellow line on lower mandible	Sooty Albatross	No 20
10 Grey-brown, purplish line on lower mandible	Light-mantled Albatross	No 19

*These pairs distinguished mainly by details of bill structure.

Genus DIOMEDEA

Predominantly white with varying amounts of black on wings and back. Tails are relatively short and rounded. All are large birds, varying in length from ·75 to 1·25m with wingspans from 2 to 4m. This group includes the only albatross breeding in Australia, the White-capped.

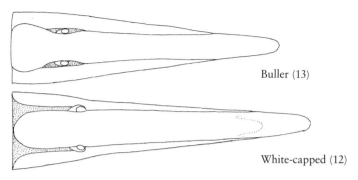

Buller (13)

White-capped (12)

ALBATROSS BILLS—DORSAL VIEW

12 SHY ALBATROSS *Diomedea cauta* Gould 1841   Pl 1

Distribution: breeding on islands around Tasmania, dispersing in coastal waters to about Fremantle and Sydney.

RECOGNITION: *white 'cap' emphasised by dark band above eye and grey nape, white underwing with broad black tip and very narrow black edges.*

DESCRIPTION: 1m; wingspan 2·5–2·75m. Sexes alike. White except for dusky band from base of bill to above eye; back and upper wing dark brown; tip of underwing and narrow edge black; tail grey-brown above and dark brown below; bill pinkish-brown, yellow on upper ridge; eyes dark brown; legs blue-grey.

VARIATION: local form as above (race *cauta*); New Zealand form may also occur; bill bluish-grey, 'cap' greyer and nape and neck grey (race *salvini*).

HABITAT: coastal islands and waters, pelagic but rarely at great distance from land. HABITS: glides and banks in albatross fashion, flaps more frequently than larger species and keeps fairly close to surface; normally does not range very far; may follow ships. BREEDING: September and October; nests on flat ground and cliff ledges, conical mound of grass, earth and excreta, size depending on how often used; one egg, white lightly flecked with reddish-brown. VOICE: cackling noises during display and breeding. FOOD: fish, squid, crustacea and offal.

STATUS: common. TAXONOMY: endemic race *(cauta)* of species extending to New Zealand and Chatham Is.

13 BULLER'S ALBATROSS *Diomedea bulleri* Rothschild 1893

Distribution: southeast seas.

RECOGNITION: like White-capped Albatross, but slightly smaller, *black margins of white underwing broad on leading edge and narrow on trailing edge;* in the hand, base of upper mandible wider.

STATUS: rare non-breeding visitor.

14 WANDERING ALBATROSS *Diomedea exulans* Linnaeus 1758

Distribution: southern seas, north to about Fremantle and Whitsunday I.

RECOGNITION: *outstanding large size, white with black wingtip.*

DESCRIPTION: 1·25 m; wingspan up to 4m. Sexes alike. White with black wing tips and varying amounts of black mottling on back and tail, depending on age; bill usually yellowish or pink with yellow tip. Very like Royal Albatross, distinguished with certainty only at close quarters by absence of black on cutting edge of bill.

HABITS: consistent follower of ships, settles on water to feed.

STATUS: fairly common; non-breeding visitor.

15 ROYAL ALBATROSS *Diomedea epomophora* Lesson 1825

Distribution: southern seas; very few records.

RECOGNITION: like Wandering Albatross; distinguished mainly by *black cutting edge of bill*, also more likely to frequent waters closer to land.

STATUS: rare; non-breeding visitor.

16 BLACK-BROWED ALBATROSS *Diomedea melanophris* Temminck 1828 Pl 1

Distribution: southern seas north to about Fremantle and Rockhampton.

RECOGNITION: *broad black margins to both edges of white underwing, yellow bill with orange or red on upper side.*

DESCRIPTION: 1m; wingspan 2·25−2·75m. Sexes alike. White with dark slate-grey back, upper wings and tail; diffuse area of dark grey in front of and behind eye, forming 'black brow'; underwing with broad black margins, the leading black margin merging diffusely with white centre; bill yellow with orange, pink or red culmen; eyes brown; legs shades of pinkish-white to pinkish-grey.

HABITS: follows ships, settles on water to feed, makes shallow dives from surface.

STATUS: common; non-breeding visitor.

17 YELLOW-NOSED ALBATROSS *Diomedea chlororynchos* Gmelin 1789

Distribution: southern seas, north on west coast to about Pt Cloates and on east coast to about Fraser I; from May to October.

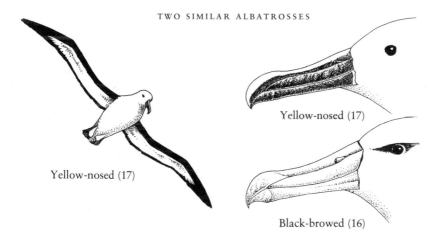

TWO SIMILAR ALBATROSSES

Yellow-nosed (17)

Yellow-nosed (17)

Black-browed (16)

RECOGNITION: *black margins to both edges of white underwing, narrowest on trailing edge, black bill with orange tip and yellow streak on top edge.*

DESCRIPTION: like Black-browed Albatross but smaller, length 75cm; wingspan 2–2·25m; narrow black margins on underwing clearly defined from white centre; bill black with orange tip and yellow streak on culmen; legs bluish or pinkish-blue.

HABITS: sometimes in flocks or small groups where abundant; less attracted to ships than Black-browed.

STATUS: common to abundant in southwest seas; non-breeding visitor.

18 GREY-HEADED ALBATROSS   *Diomedea chrysostoma*   Forster 1785

Distribution: southern seas, north to about Shark Bay and New South Wales coast.

RECOGNITION: like Yellow-nosed Albatross but head darker, pale bluish-grey, and small patch of white behind eye; bill black without yellow tip but with *bright yellow or orange streak on culmen and base of lower mandible.*

STATUS: fairly common in southwest seas, uncommon to rare in southeast; non-breeding visitor.

Genus PHOEBETRIA

The two members of this genus are blackish-brown except for white shafts to the flight feathers (there is also some white on the necks of young birds). Tails are longer than in the previous genus and distinctly pointed. Bills are black with a coloured groove on the lower mandible, either yellow or purple. They do not regularly or commonly visit Australian seas.

19 LIGHT-MANTLED ALBATROSS   *Phoebetria palpebrata*   (Forster) 1785

Distribution: southern seas, north to the tropic.

RECOGNITION: *paler on back than Sooty Albatross, purple groove on lower mandible of black bill.*

DESCRIPTION: 75cm; wingspan 2–2·25m; long wedge-shaped tail. Blackish, but distinctly greyer on back emphasising dark crown; flight feathers have white shafts; bill black with purple groove on lower mandible; eyes brown; legs pinkish-grey.

STATUS: rare straggler; non-breeding.

20 SOOTY ALBATROSS   *Phoebetria fusca*   (Hilsenberg) 1822

Distribution: southern seas.

RECOGNITION: like Light-mantled Albatross, but back darker, more uniform in colour with crown, and *black bill has yellow groove on lower mandible.*

STATUS: rare straggler; non-breeding.

Family PROCELLARIIDAE

Petrels, Shearwaters, Prions

36*(60) species: 1 endemic

Distribution: worldwide.

THIS LARGE FAMILY CONSISTS of pelagic species which range widely over all the oceans and come to land only to breed. They are completely adapted to life at sea and ill-suited to conditions on land where they are clumsy and vulnerable to predators. Survival on land depends on various protective habits such as nesting on small islands and remote mainland localities, concealing nests in burrows and in crevices among rocks (except the fulmars which use open ledges) and visiting their nests during the hours of darkness. They are less than 60cm in length, except the Giant Petrel which compares in size with some of the smaller albatrosses but it is clumsier in appearance and less graceful in flight. Most plumages are blackish or black and white but prions have delicate blue-grey upperparts—they are sometimes known as dove prions. Bills have a deeply curved 'nail' on the upper mandible, a shallow saddle and nostrils located in a single prominent tube. The tube is divided by a septum, a feature which distinguishes this family from the storm petrels (family Hydrobatidae) in which the nostril tube is not divided. Most species are sociable and go about in flocks. In flight they are accomplished gliders but on the whole less graceful in their movements than the albatrosses. Some of the smallest species, prions and gadfly petrels, have a rapid erratic flight. Only six of the thirty-five species listed here breed in Australia. Few of the others come within sight of land for their haunts are the open seas, but they qualify for inclusion because they occur as storm casualties among the jetsam of ocean beaches, and also have been observed from ships plying in what might be regarded as Australian waters.

Key to PROCELLARIIDAE

1 Length 1m; wholly black or white...................	Giant Petrel	No 21
2 Length less than 65cm............................	3–12	
3 Back dappled black and white.....................	Cape Petrel	No 25
4 Back silver-grey, wingtips black...................	Antarctic Fulmar	No 23
5 Upperparts brown and white, tail white tipped brown ..	Antarctic Petrel	No 24
6 Upperparts blue-grey.............................	8–9	
7 Wholly black or black above white below	10–12	
8 Tail grey with white tip	Blue Petrel	No 37
9 Tail grey with black tip..........................	*Pachyptila*	Nos 38–43
10 Bill long and thick	*Procellaria*	Nos 44–47
11 Bill long and slender	*Puffinus*	Nos 48–55
12 Bill short, thick or slender	*Pterodroma*	Nos 26–36

*See Fig page 42.

Genus MACRONECTES

Giant petrel. Two species are now recognised but are only likely to be distinguished by experienced observers. The more common one in Australian waters occurs in two forms, white and dark brownish-grey. They are similar to a medium-sized albatross in body length, but the wings are shorter and thicker and the general appearance in flight is less graceful, an effect emphasised by the large, pale clumsy looking bill. They are attracted to ships.

---

*Tahiti Petrel in Addenda.

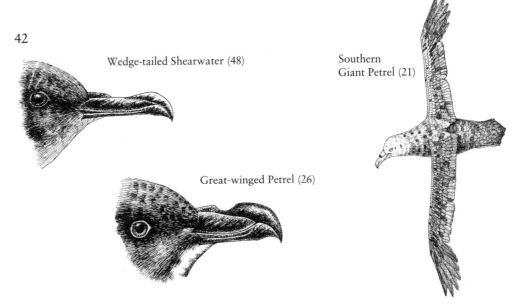

Wedge-tailed Shearwater (48)

Southern
Giant Petrel (21)

Great-winged Petrel (26)

BILLS OF PUFFINUS AND PTERODROMA

21 SOUTHERN GIANT PETREL *Macronectes giganteus* (Gmelin) 1789

Distribution: southern seas, north to about the tropic on both sides of continent.

RECOGNITION: *large, wholly dark or white, long head and neck with large pale bill, green at tip.*
1m; wingspan 2–2·25m; dimorphic. White phase: distinguished from albatrosses by having black spots and lacking black wing tips. Dark phase: wholly sooty brown when young and greying with age, foreparts and leading edge of wing mottled white, head sometimes wholly white; distinguished from dark-coloured juvenile albatrosses by lack of white on underwing. White phase seems to be less common; less than 10 percent.

STATUS: fairly common, especially after storms; non-breeding visitor from antarctic seas, usually June–September.

22 NORTHERN GIANT PETREL *Macronectes halli* Mathews 1912

Distribution: southeastern seas.

RECOGNITION: smaller than southern species, dark sooty brown, or dark grey with *light edges to feathers producing freckled appearance*; never white; bill pinkish at tip.

STATUS: birds marked in breeding grounds, mostly islands south of New Zealand, have been recorded in Australian waters; possibly occurs fairly frequently, but difficult to identify.

Genus FULMARUS

This genus consists of two similar species, one frequenting arctic seas and the other antarctic. They are mainly whitish and gull-like (except that the northern species has a dark phase) but the whole of the flight feathers are black.

23 ANTARCTIC FULMAR *Fulmarus glacialoides* (Smith) 1840

Distribution: southern seas, north to mid-Western Australia and southeast Queensland.

RECOGNITION: *whitish with black flight feathers.* 50cm; wingspan 1·5m. Silvery-grey and white (looking all white at a distance) with main flight feathers black; bill pink. Like a gull but open wings are held more stiffly and flight includes long periods of gliding; open wings also show pure white areas not found in gulls.

STATUS: uncommon; non-breeding visitor from antarctic seas.

Genus THALASSOICA

The Antarctic Petrel has, among other features, twelve tail feathers instead of the more usual fourteen in related species and is put in a genus of its own.

24 ANTARCTIC PETREL *Thalassoica antarctica* (Gmelin) 1789
Distribution: southern seas

RECOGNITION: *white tail tipped with brown.* 50cm. Upperparts, face and throat are brown with trailing edge of wing white tipped with brown; belly white; bill brown; legs yellowish.

STATUS: rare; non-breeding straggler from antarctic seas.

Genus DAPTION

The Cape Petrel, sometimes known as Cape Pigeon, is the only species in this genus. It is a regular follower of ships on southern oceans and easily identified by its pigeon-like appearance and chequered upperparts.

25 CAPE PETREL *Daption capensis* (Linnaeus) 1785   Pl 1
Distribution: southern seas, north to about the tropic.

RECOGNITION: *pied back with large white wing patches.* 40cm; wingspan 1m. Head and neck black; upperparts chequered black and white with two large patches of white on each wing; underparts white; bill and legs black. Stiff-winged flap and glide flight; patters along surface when feeding.

STATUS: common; non-breeding visitor from subantarctic.

Genus PTERODROMA

Members of this genus are frequently referred to as 'gadfly petrels'. Opinions vary on the number of species, but there are between twenty and thirty, of which eleven have been identified in the vicinity of Australia. Two of these, the Great-winged Petrel and Gould Petrel, have breeding colonies on coastal islands, the former in Western Australia and the latter only on Cabbage Tree I north of Sydney. These petrels can be distinguished from shearwaters by their relatively short bills, short nasal tubes tilted slightly up, and broader wings and longer tails. They are either wholly dark or dark above and white below, although the rarely recorded Trinidad Petrel may be either. The White-headed Petrel is rather like one of the black-backed gulls. They are 25–40cm in length and belong to tropical and subtropical seas.

Key to PTERODROMA

1 Underparts mainly dark	3–8	
2 Underparts mainly white	9–16	
3 Underwing with white patch	5–6	
4 Underwing without white patch	7–8	
5 Upperparts blackish	Kermadec Petrel	No 30
	Trinidad Petrel	No 29

26 GREAT-WINGED PETREL *Pterodroma macroptera* (Smith) 1840   Fig p 42

Distribution: southern seas to about the tropic.

RECOGNITION: *blackish; distinguished from dark shearwaters by short, thick bill, and from similar Providence Petrel by lack of white on underwing.*

DESCRIPTION: 40cm; wingspan 1m. Sexes alike. Brownish-black with blacker patch in front of eye, sometimes a little white on forehead and chin; bill and legs black.

HABITAT: coastal islands and adjacent seas. HABITS: pelagic except when nesting; gregarious; disperses widely when not breeding—birds occurring in eastern seas may have bred in New Zealand; flight swift and often high and with swept-back appearance; walks with clumsy waddle. BREEDING: mainly March–August; nests among rocks and tree roots and in burrows, lined with local vegetation; one white egg. VOICE: various squeaking notes, like 'kee-ik' and 'kik', also hoarse 'quaw-er'. FOOD: squid.

STATUS: common. TAXONOMY: race (*albini*, and *gouldi* in the east) of subantarctic species.

27 PROVIDENCE PETREL *Pterodroma solandri*   (Gould) 1844

Distribution: southeast seas as far as south Queensland.

RECOGNITION: like Great-winged Petrel but distinguished by *white patch on underwing,* speckled white on forehead and chin, and greyer general appearance.

STATUS: rare, less than ten records; non-breeding visitor from south Pacific seas.

28 WHITE-HEADED PETREL *Pterodroma lessonii*   (Garnot) 1826

Distribution: southern seas north to about the tropic.

RECOGNITION: *head white* (actually pale grey) with black mark through eye; underparts white; back grey; tail white; bill black; legs pinkish.

STATUS: fairly common; non-breeding visitor from subantarctic seas.

29 TRINIDAD PETREL *Pterodroma arminjoniana* (Gig. & Salv.) 1869

[*Note:* The varied plumages of the Trinidad and Kermadec Petrels make it practically impossible to distinguish them in the field.]

Distribution: recorded from Raine I, off northeast Queensland, and Burleigh Heads, southeast Queensland.

RECOGNITION: 40cm. Either wholly black or black above and varying from white below to brown and white, usually with dusky breast and *white patch on underwing.*

STATUS: very rare; non-breeding visitor from tropical seas.

29A TAHITI PETREL *Pterodroma rostrata* (Pele) 1848

Distribution: recorded south Queensland coast.

RECOGNITION: like Trinidad and Kermadec Petrels but lower breast and belly white and *sharply defined* from dark throat and upper breast; no white patch on underwing.

STATUS: rare; vagrant from southwest Pacific.

30 KERMADEC PETREL *Pterodroma neglecta* (Schlegel) 1863

Distribution: east coast seas.

RECOGNITION: 38cm. Either wholly brownish, darker above and lighter below with *white patch on underwing*, or brown with white head and underparts and freckled brown on forehead.

STATUS: rare; non-breeding visitor from tropical and subtropical seas.

31 KERGUELEN PETREL *Pterodroma brevirostris* (Lesson) 1831

Distribution: southern seas to about the tropic.

RECOGNITION: like other small petrels *dark above and below but no white patch on underwing*. 33cm. Brownish-grey, speckled whitish on forehead and chin.

STATUS: uncommon; non-breeding visitor from subantarctic seas.

32 MOTTLED PETREL *Pterodroma inexpectata* (Forster) 1844

Distribution: southeast seas as far north as Sydney.

RECOGNITION: *diagonal black streak on underwing*. 35cm. Upperparts grey, darker on head, centre of shoulders and tips of wings; forehead and face mottled brown and white; underparts white, mottled brown on breast.

STATUS: rare; non-breeding visitor from New Zealand seas.

33 SOFT-PLUMAGED PETREL *Pterodroma mollis* (Gould) 1841

Distribution: southern seas, especially southwest.

RECOGNITION: *white underparts with dark underwing and dark patches on sides of breast*. 33–35cm. Upperparts blue-grey, mottled with white on forehead; face white with dark patch in front of eye; underbody white with incomplete blackish band on breast; underwing dark grey with narrow white central streak.

STATUS: fairly common; non-breeding visitor from southern Atlantic and Indian oceans.

THREE SMALL PETRELS

The following three small petrels are very alike. They have on their upperparts in flight a more or less distinct flattened or expanded 'M' pattern formed by a dark leading margin of the outer wing continuous with a diagonal dark band across the inner wing to the rump. The species most likely to be seen in the vicinity of Australia, in southeastern seas, is Gould Petrel (sometimes called White-winged Petrel) and it is readily distinguished by its black crown and nape which contrast with its grey back.

34 GOULD PETREL *Pterodroma leucoptera* (Gould) 1844

Distribution: southeastern seas north to southeast Queensland; breeding on Cabbage Tree I, Port Stephens, New South Wales.

RECOGNITION: *small, black crown and nape, black 'M' on upperparts.*

DESCRIPTION: 30cm. Sexes alike. Crown and nape black; remainder of upperparts dark grey, blacker on leading margin of outer wing and diagonally across inner wing; forehead mottled black and white; face below eye and underparts white with dusky margins; bill black; legs and feet blue-grey.

HABITAT: tropical and subtropical seas, breeding on small islands. HABITS: pelagic except when breeding; gregarious; probably not dispersing very far from breeding grounds. BREEDING: November and December; nests in cavities formed by loose boulders and fallen palm fronds, among gullies overgrown with vegetation; one white egg. VOICE: a pleasant piping 'tee-tee'. FOOD: squid.

STATUS: fairly common. TAXONOMY: race *(leucoptera)* of species ranging widely over tropical and subtropical Pacific.

35 COOK PETREL *Pterodroma cookii* (Gray) 1843

Distribution: southeastern seas.

RECOGNITION: like Gould Petrel but *crown and nape grey,* uniform with back, and *narrower dark edges to underwing.*

STATUS: rare; non-breeding visitor probably from New Zealand.

36 BLACK-WINGED PETREL *Pterodroma nigripennis* (Rothschild) 1893

Distribution: southeastern seas, north to southeast Queensland.

RECOGNITION: like Cook Petrel but upperwings darker and *dark edges of white underwing more pronounced.*

STATUS: rare; non-breeding visitor probably from New Zealand.

Genus HALOBAENA

The Blue Petrel is like the prions but is unique in having a broad white tip to its nearly square tail; for this and other reasons it is put in a separate genus.

37 BLUE PETREL *Halobaena caerulea* (Gmelin) 1789

Distribution: southern seas, mainly in the southwest.

RECOGNITION: 30cm. Upperparts pale blue-grey, *tail broadly tipped with white;* forehead, face and underparts white.

STATUS: uncommon; non-breeding visitor from subantarctic.

Genus PACHYPTILA

Known as prions or whalebirds. Six are currently regarded as species, all of which are included here mainly because of their occurrence as jetsam on sea beaches. The only resident is the Fairy Prion which breeds in the southeast. Prions are so alike as to be indistinguishable except perhaps to experienced observers or on examination in the hand when beak shape is diagnostic. They are about 30cm in length with wingspan of 75cm. Wings are long and pointed, as in terns, and also like terns their flight is rapid and erratic. However they do not hover and dive as terns do but fly low over the water, sometimes skimming the surface with bills submerged to sieve plankton through lamellae at the sides of the mouth. Upperparts are blue-grey (dove grey) with a black M-shaped pattern on back and wings and a black tip to the wedge-shaped tail; the crown is darker than the back which emphasises a broad white streak above the eye and broad black streak through the eye.

Key to PACHYPTILA
(Based on features of bills)

1 Bill less than 25mm; nail well developed and broad near tip   *Fulmar Prion .... No 39
Fairy Prion .... No 38

2 Bill over 25mm; nail not well developed............... 3–4

3 Bill very wide; lamellae visible....................... Broad-billed Prion...... No 40
Medium-billed Prion.... No 41

4 Bill moderately wide; lamellae not visible .... Thin-billed Prion....... No 43
Antarctic Prion .... No 42

*These two species also have tails with broad black tips; the others have narrow black tips.

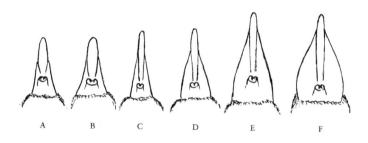

PRION BILLS—DORSAL VIEW
A Fulmar (39) B Fairy (38) C Thin-billed (43) D Antarctic (42) E Medium-billed (41)
F Broad-billed (40)

38 FAIRY PRION *Pachyptila turtur* (Kuhl) 1820

Distribution: breeding on islands in Bass St and dispersing in adjacent seas as far as south Western Australia and southern Queensland.

RECOGNITION: *relatively wide black tail band, over 35mm; nail of bill large and wide; bill less than 25mm.*

DESCRIPTION: 25–28cm; wingspan 75cm. Sexes alike. Upperparts and broad band below eye blue-grey (dove grey); broad band above eye and underparts white, except for tinge of blue-grey on sides of breast and flanks; broad band of brownish-black extending from shoulders across inner wing and lower back, forming a dark 'M' in flight; edges of outer flight feathers and tip of tail black.

HABITAT: southern oceans; breeding on islands. HABITS: pelagic; gregarious; dispersing from breeding grounds; flight swift and erratic, often skimming low over surface of sea. BREEDING: September–January; nests in burrows in soft soil or concealed clefts among rocks, lined with leaves; one white egg. VOICE: harsh cries, at nest soft coo-ing notes. FOOD: crustacea and other surface organisms, including small fish.

STATUS: fairly common. TAXONOMY: variable species with wide extralimital distribution.

39 FULMAR PRION *Pachyptila crassirostris* (Mathews) 1912

Distribution: southern seas; very few records.

RECOGNITION: *almost impossible to distinguish from Fairy Prion except by shape of bill, which is shorter and thicker.*

STATUS: rare; non-breeding visitor from subantarctic seas.

40 BROAD-BILLED PRION *Pachyptila vittata* (Forster) 1777

Distribution: southern seas to south Western Australia and mid-New South Wales.

RECOGNITION: like other prions but bill large and wide at base; like Medium-billed Prion in having visible lamellae at edge of mouth; terminal black tail band less than 30mm.

STATUS: rare; non-breeding visitor from subantarctic seas.

41 MEDIUM-BILLED PRION *Pachyptila salvini* (Mathews) 1912

Distribution: southern seas from south Western Australia to south Queensland.

RECOGNITION: like Broad-billed Prion in having broad bill with exposed lamellae but slightly narrower.

STATUS: fairly common; non-breeding visitor from subantarctic seas.

42 ANTARCTIC PRION *Pachyptila desolata* (Gmelin) 1789

Distribution: southern seas as far as south Western Australia and southern Queensland.

RECOGNITION: like other prions but with longer and wider bill and unexposed mouth lamellae.

STATUS: fairly common; non-breeding visitor from subantarctic seas.

43 THIN-BILLED PRION *Pachyptila belcheri* (Mathews) 1912

Distribution: southern seas to south Western Australia and south Queensland.

RECOGNITION: like Antarctic Prion except for minor differences in bill shape.

STATUS: uncommon; non-breeding visitor from subantarctic seas.

Genus PROCELLARIA

Relatively large petrels, nearly 60cm in length, with fairly heavy bills. The Pediunker or Grey Petrel is sometimes put in a separate genus *Adamastor*, having among other features white underparts, whereas the others are mostly brownish-black, except for varying amounts of white on the chin. Also there are opinions that at least the Black and Westland Petrels, which breed in New Zealand, and possibly also the Shoemaker, are all variants of a single species.

Key to PROCELLARIA

1 Underparts white	Pediunker	No 44
2 Wholly black, sometimes white on chin and face	Shoemaker	No 45
	Black Petrel	No 46
	Westland Black Petrel	No 47

44 PEDIUNKER *Procellaria cinerea* (Gmelin) 1789

Distribution: southern seas to south Western Australia and Victoria.

RECOGNITION: 50cm; wingspan 130cm; tail wedge-shaped. Upperparts dark grey-brown, paler on neck emphasising dark crown; *underparts white with under wing and under tail coverts ashy brown.* Flight consists of alternating long glides and rapid wing beats; dives into water from flight and swims below surface.

STATUS: rare; non-breeding visitor from subantarctic seas.

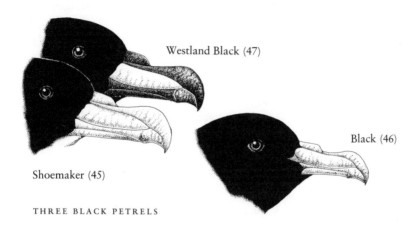

Westland Black (47)

Shoemaker (45)

Black (46)

THREE BLACK PETRELS

THREE BLACKISH PETRELS

Of the three following species the Shoemaker or White-chinned Petrel is the one most likely to be seen following ships, except possibly in the Tasman Sea; the other two are almost impossible to distinguish in the field except by experienced observers.

45 SHOEMAKER *Procellaria aequinoctialis* Linnaeus 1758   Pl 1
Distribution: southern seas to south Western Australia and southern Queensland.
RECOGNITION: nearly 60cm; wingspan 150cm. *Wholly brownish-black* usually with *white on chin* and sometimes on face; bill pale bluish or greenish-brown. Follows ships.
STATUS: uncommon (except on southern route from Fremantle to Cape Town where it is common); non-breeding visitor from subantarctic seas.

46 BLACK PETREL *Procellaria parkinsoni* Gray 1862
Distribution: southeastern seas north to Sydney.
RECOGNITION: almost impossible to distinguish from Shoemaker except by *smaller and thicker bill;* usually lacks white on chin and face.
STATUS: rare; non-breeding visitor from New Zealand seas.

47 WESTLAND BLACK PETREL *Procellaria westlandica* Falla 1946
Distribution: southeastern seas.
RECOGNITION: smaller (including bill) version of the Black Petrel.
STATUS: only recorded near Sydney; non-breeding visitor from New Zealand.

Genus PUFFINUS

Shearwaters are a numerous and successful group. They range widely over all the oceans. Close similarities between species in opposite hemispheres suggest origins from common stocks; for instance the Fluttering Shearwater of Australia, and elsewhere, resembles the Manx Shearwater of Europe which occasionally straggles as far as Australia. Shearwaters are small to medium in size, 25–50cm, and are either wholly dark or dark above and white below. Bills are typically long and slender, which distinguishes them from the gadfly petrels in which the bills are short and thick. Wings are long and narrow and birds in flight often glide as well as flutter. Four species have breeding grounds on Australian coasts and one of these, the Short-tailed Shearwater, is of economic importance as a source of food. It is sometimes better known as 'mutton-bird', a name shared with the less common Sooty Shearwater which is also eaten in New Zealand.

Key to PUFFINUS

1 Mainly dark	3–7
2 Dark above, white below	8–11
3 White area on underwing	Sooty Shearwater ...... No 51
4 No white on underwing	5–7
5 Short rounded tail, dark bill and legs	Short-tailed Shearwater No 50
6 Long wedge-shaped tail, dark bill, pale legs...........	Wedge-tailed Shearwater No 48
7 Long rounded tail, pale bill and legs.................	Fleshy-footed Shearwater No 49
8 Black of crown extends below eye, legs pinkish-brown and brown	
Wing 180–221mm	Fluttering Shearwater ... No 53
Wing 232–246mm	Manx Shearwater ...... No 54
9 Black of crown extends to eye	10–11
10 Back black, legs bright blue	Little Shearwater .... No 52
11 Back grey contrasting with black crown, tail wedge-shaped	Buller's Shearwater ... No 55

48 WEDGE-TAILED SHEARWATER
Puffinus pacificus (Gmelin) 1789   Pl 1   Fig p 42

Distribution: northern coastal waters, south to near Fremantle in west; and Montague I in east; breeds on coastal islands.

RECOGNITION: *wholly dark, long wedge-shaped tail, dark bill.*

DESCRIPTION: 40–46cm; tail 15cm; wingspan 1m. Sexes alike. Brownish-black, darker on upperparts, blacker on wings and tail, paler on throat and foreneck (rarely, underparts white); bill dark blue-grey; eyes brown; legs buff-pink.

HABITAT: pelagic and offshore waters of tropical and subtropical seas. HABITS: pelagic, landing only to breed; gregarious; mainly sedentary, dispersing near breeding grounds; flight a fast glide and slow deep wing beat. BREEDING: October–April; nests in burrows and concealed rock crevices, sometimes hollow trunks and under bushes; one white egg. VOICE: low gasping 'koo-er' or 'kuk-oo-kuk', also cat-like cries. FOOD: squid, fish, crustacea.

STATUS: common. TAXONOMY: species extending to tropical and subtropical Indian and Pacific Oceans.

49 FLESHY-FOOTED SHEARWATER *Puffinus carneipes* (Gould) 1844   Pl 1
Distribution: subtropical seas, breeding on islands of south Western Australia; birds in eastern seas come from breeding colonies on Lord Howe Island.

RECOGNITION: *wholly dark, pale bill, long fan-shaped tail, or like blunted wedge.*

DESCRIPTION: like Wedge-tailed Shearwater but of stouter build and tip of tail rounder, not as distinctly wedge-shaped; bill pale pinkish-brown; legs and feet buff-pink.

HABITAT: pelagic and offshore waters of temperate and subtropical seas; tropical seas during migration. HABITS: pelagic, landing only to breed; gregarious, congregates in large 'rafts' while waiting to land on breeding grounds after sunset; migratory—Australian breeding populations apparently travel to north Indian Ocean, other breeding groups to north Pacific; flight heavy with rapid shallow wing beats and short glides; deep dives. BREEDING: November–April; nests in burrows or concealed among rocks and under dense ground cover, lined with dry vegetation; one white egg. VOICE: high-pitched sharp notes, also series of low hoarse notes ending in scream and splutter. FOOD: squid, fish, crustacea.

STATUS: fairly common. TAXONOMY: Australian breeding populations belong to typical form (race *carneipes*); birds occurring in eastern waters apparently belong to New Zealand form (race *hullianus*).

50 SHORT-TAILED SHEARWATER *Puffinus tenuirostris* (Temminck) 1835 Pl 1

Distribution: coasts from Nuyt's Archipelago, opposite Ceduna, South Australia, to Broughton I, north of Newcastle, New South Wales, Tasmania, and in coastal waters from about Hopetoun in western Australia to central Queensland.

RECOGNITION: *wholly dark, short rounded tail with feet projecting in flight, dusky underwing; bill less than 35mm (in the hand).*

DESCRIPTION: 40–43cm; tail under 10cm; wingspan 96cm. Sexes alike. Brownish-black, paler on underparts; underwing brownish-grey; bill blue-grey; eyes brown; legs dark grey-brown.

HABITAT: coastal islands and offshore and pelagic waters of temperate and tropical seas. HABITS: pelagic, landing only to breed; gregarious, assemble in large 'rafts' until dusk when they fly to breeding grounds; migratory, depart from breeding grounds in late April–early May for north Pacific and return on precise dates at end of September; fly fast and direct with rapid wingbeats interspersed with glides. BREEDING: mid-November–April; nests in burrows, chamber lined with dry vegetation; one white egg. VOICE: asthmatical crooning and wailing, usually uttered by birds on breeding grounds. FOOD: crustacea, fish and squid.

STATUS: abundant. TAXONOMY: endemic breeding species.

51 SOOTY SHEARWATER *Puffinus griseus* Gmelin 1789

Distribution: southeast coast from southern Queensland to Tasmania, and adjacent seas.

RECOGNITION: *mainly dark with central area of underwing white, short rounded tail with feet barely projecting in flight; (in hand) bill over 40mm.*

DESCRIPTION: 46–51cm; tail under 10cm; wingspan 105cm. Sexes alike. Brownish-black, paler on underbody and very pale on chin and throat; underwing grey with large central area whitish; bill blackish; eyes dark brown; legs blackish-brown.

HABITAT: coastal islands and offshore and pelagic waters of temperate and tropical seas. HABITS: pelagic, landing only to breed; gregarious, feeds offshore in scattered flocks and forms 'rafts' before flying to breeding grounds after dark; migratory, leaves breeding grounds about March–April for north temperate seas, returning late September. BREEDING: mid-

November–April; nests in burrows among tussocks high up on hillsides, chamber lined with dry vegetation; one white egg. VOICE: asthmatic crooning. FOOD: crustacea, fish, squid. STATUS: common. TAXONOMY: species widely distributed in southern oceans.

52 LITTLE SHEARWATER *Puffinus assimilis* Gould 1838 Pl 1

Distribution: coasts from Abrolhos Is to Recherche Archipelago of Western Australia and coastal waters from mid-Western Australia to southern Queensland, northern limit about 25 degrees S.

RECOGNITION: *black above and white below, black of crown only reaches eye level; legs pale blue.*

DESCRIPTION: 25–30cm; wingspan 60cm. Sexes alike. Upperparts blue-black, black on crown not extending below eye level; underparts white; bill dark-grey; eyes dark brown; legs blue. HABITAT: coastal islands and offshore and pelagic waters of subtropical seas. HABITS: pelagic but attached to breeding grounds for longer than nesting season; gregarious; sedentary, dispersing to local pelagic feeding grounds; very fast wingbeats in flight interspersed with short glides; feeds on surface but can dive. BREEDING: June–October; nests in burrows or under rocks, sometimes lined with dry vegetation; one white egg. VOICE: throaty asthmatic sounds. FOOD: squid and fish.

STATUS: fairly common. TAXONOMY: endemic race *(tunneyi)* of species widely distributed in southern oceans.

53 FLUTTERING SHEARWATER *Puffinus gavia* (Forster) 1844

Distribution: southern seas to south Western Australia and southern Queensland.

RECOGNITION: like Little Shearwater but slightly larger, length 33–38cm, also *upperparts brownish-black, dark area of crown extends below eye level,* feathers in axil of underwing brown with white tips.

STATUS: fairly common; non-breeding visitor. TAXONOMY: birds occurring west of Victoria show differences which indicate that they belong to a different race or perhaps species and have been given the name *huttoni.* The distinctive features are only likely to be recognised in the hand and by experienced observers.

54 MANX SHEARWATER *Puffinus puffinus* (Brunnich) 1764

Distribution: one certain record; bird banded in Britain recovered at Venus Bay, Eyre Peninsula, South Australia.

RECOGNITION: like Little Shearwater in having blue-black upperparts but about size of Fluttering Shearwater, although actual wing length is distinctly greater (range 232–246 as against 180–221mm) and similar in having dark area of crown extending below eye level.

STATUS: very rare; non-breeding visitor.

55 BULLER'S SHEARWATER *Puffinus bulleri* Salvin 1888

Distribution: southeastern seas; mainly New South Wales and southern Queensland.

RECOGNITION: large, 46cm, *back grey, distinctly contrasting with black head,* wings and tail; black area of crown extends to eye level.

STATUS: fairly regular; non-breeding visitor from New Zealand.

There are also rare records of HUTTON'S SHEARWATER *Puffinus huttoni* and AUDUBON'S SHEARWATER *Puffinus lherminieri.*

Family HYDROBATIDAE

Storm-petrels
7(21) species

Distribution: worldwide.

THE VERY SMALL PETRELS in this group, less than 25cm in length, are only doubtfully separated as a distinct family from their larger relatives in the Procellariidae. Their main distinctive feature is an anatomical one, an undivided nasal tube, but this is also present to some extent in the fulmar group of petrels. Bills and legs are black and relatively slender, especially the legs which are also long and are characteristically held dangling when the birds flutter and patter low over the water, as they are often seen to do when following in the wake of ships. Storm-petrels are pelagic species and range widely over all the oceans. At one time they were superstitiously regarded as harbingers of storms but now they are more affectionately accepted as 'Mother Carey's Chickens'. The White-faced Storm-petrel is the only species breeding in Australia. It nests on southern coastal islands where, in spite of its great abundance, it is rarely seen as it only comes to land after dark and disperses far out to sea before dawn.

Key to HYDROBATIDAE

1	Tail deeply forked, rump like back	*Oceanodroma*	Nos 61–62
2	Tail square, rump grey	4–5	
3	Tail square, rump white	6–7	
4	Throat white	White-faced Storm-petrel ..	No 56
5	Throat black...............................	Grey-backed Storm-petrel .	No 57
6	Belly black	Wilson Storm-petrel	No 58
7	Belly white or pied...........................	*Fregetta*.................	Nos 59–60

Genus PELAGODROMA

The single species in this genus, the White-faced Storm-petrel, is the only member of the family entirely white on the underparts, the white being continued on to most of the face and forehead. It is found throughout the Pacific, Indian and Atlantic Oceans and breeds in countless numbers on the southern coastal islands of Australia.

56 WHITE-FACED STORM-PETREL *Pelagodroma marina* (Latham) 1790 Pl 1

Distribution: breeding southern coasts from Abrolhos Is to near Newcastle, migrating north to the tropic.

RECOGNITION: *white underparts, white forehead and face with black patch below eye, whitish rump contrasting with blackish tail.*

DESCRIPTION: 20cm; wingspan 40cm; tail square. Sexes alike. Upperparts dark grey-brown, darker on crown, wings and tail; rump and upper tail coverts pale grey; forehead and broad band above eye white; patch below eye black; underparts white except for black wingtips; bill black; eyes reddish-brown; legs and toes black, webs yellow.

HABITAT: coastal and pelagic waters of tropical and subantarctic seas. HABITS: pelagic except when breeding; gregarious, usually in small scattered parties at sea but sometimes single; migratory, moving at least to the northern Indian Ocean, and possibly elsewhere, in the non-

breeding season; weaving flight in wake of ships, low over water with legs dangling. BREED-
ING: October–January; nests in burrows, usually concealed among thick vegetation, lined
with dry grass; one white egg. VOICE: described as mournful 'wooo' and mouse-like squeak.
FOOD: surface plankton.
STATUS: abundant. TAXONOMY: endemic race *(dulciae)* of wide ranging species.

Genus GARRODIA

The single species in this genus belongs to the subantarctic, breeding as far north as New
Zealand and apparently rarely visiting Australian seas. The grey of the back is more diffuse
than in the White-faced Storm-petrel and head and throat are black.

57 GREY-BACKED STORM-PETREL *Garrodia nereis* (Gould) 1841

Distribution: southeastern seas, from Tasmania to southern Queensland.
RECOGNITION: *grey rump* less clearly defined than in the White-faced, diffusing on to lower
back and base of tail; whole *head, throat, breast and tip of tail black; belly white.* Tail square.
STATUS: rare; non-breeding straggler from subantarctic.

Genus OCEANITES

Two species with white upper and under tail coverts, one of which, Wilson Storm-petrel, is a
common non-breeding visitor to Australian seas during its seasonal migrations across the
tropic, and one of the commonest species in all the oceans.

58 WILSON STORM-PETREL *Oceanites oceanicus* (Kuhl) 1820

Distribution: all Australian seas.
RECOGNITION: black with *white upper and under tail coverts and rear flanks; pale grey band
on wing;* square tail 15cm; wingspan 40cm. Commonly following in wake of ships, weaving
and pattering low over water; often alone or in small scattered parties.
STATUS: common; readily overlooked because of small size and low flying habits; non-
breeding visitor usually on passage migration.

Genus FREGETTA

Two white-rumped species with variable underparts. In certain phases they are practically
indistinguishable in the field but readily identified in the hand. One keeps mainly to subantarctic and the other to subtropical seas; both have been recorded in the vicinity of Australia.

59 BLACK-BELLIED STORM-PETREL *Fregetta tropica* (Gould) 1844

Distribution: southern oceans, north to tropic.
RECOGNITION: like Wilson Storm-petrel in having a white rump but *flanks wholly white*
leaving a *broad black streak in centre of belly* (but see note below); centre of underwing white.
STATUS: fairly common; non-breeding visitor from subantarctic.
[Note. Some races of this species (not recorded from Australian seas) have a wholly white
belly, and are therefore similar to the White-bellied species, but all races of both species can
be distinguished in the hand as follows: *tropica*—legs and feet longer, extending beyond

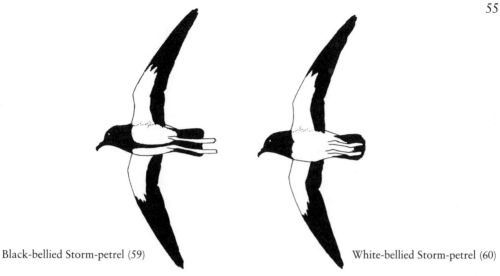

Black-bellied Storm-petrel (59)   White-bellied Storm-petrel (60)

tail, central toe about 30mm; *grallaria*—legs and feet shorter, not extending beyond tail, central toe about 20mm.]

60 WHITE-BELLIED STORM-PETREL *Fregetta grallaria* (Vieillot) 1818
Distribution: northeastern seas.
RECOGNITION: *like the Black-bellied Storm-Petrel but belly wholly white, also most of breast* (see note above).
STATUS: rare; non-breeding visitor from tropical seas (breeds on Lord Howe I).

Genus OCEANODROMA
A group of about ten species belonging mainly to the northern hemisphere and distinguished by forked tails, longer wings and more slender appearance. Two species have been identified as rare stragglers in Australian seas.

61 BLACK STORM-PETREL *Oceanodroma matsudairiae* Kuroda 1922
Distribution: a few records from northern seas.
RECOGNITION: like Wilson Storm-petrel, brownish-black with white upper tail coverts, but much larger, *tail distinctly forked and pale diagonal bar on wing.*
STATUS: rare; non-breeding straggler from islands in the north Pacific.

62 LEACH'S STORM-PETREL *Oceanodroma leucorhoa* (Vieillot) 1818
Distribution: one record from west Victoria.
RECOGNITION: like Black Storm-petrel but smaller: *leucorhoa*—wing 150–165mm, tail 73–87mm, bill 13–16mm; *matsudariae*—wing 178–194mm, tail 90–115mm, bill 16–19mm.

Diving Petrel (63)

Family PELECANOIDIDAE
Diving Petrels
2(4) species

Distribution: subantarctic seas.

MEMBERS OF THIS UNIQUE small family are stumpy little petrels 15–25cm in length, with relatively short tails, short pointed wings, and legs placed well to the rear; they are black above and white below. Thus in general appearance and also in behaviour they closely resemble the Little Auk of arctic latitudes. But they have a number of distinct anatomical features, such as nasal apertures in the form of slits opening vertically in a common protuberance at the base of the upper mandible, and a pouch suspended from the lower mandible which can be extended like a bellows. These small petrels are equipped to swim under water using wings as paddles, like penguins, but they make the most of both elements for they can emerge from the water directly into flight, thus rapidly changing the function of the wings. But this dual function reduces the effectiveness of wings in the air and flights are short with very rapidly beating wings. Only one of the four species breeds in Australia.

63 DIVING PETREL *Pelecanoides urinatrix* (Gmelin) 1789
Distribution: islands in Bass St and coastal waters of Victoria and Tasmania.
RECOGNITION: *small, stumpy, black and white; emerges from water like a flying fish and flies for short distance with rapid wing beats. In the hand, distinctive slit nostrils and pouch under bill.*
DESCRIPTION: 20cm. Sexes alike. Upperparts, including face, wings and tail shiny black; sides of throat, foreneck and breast, also flanks and underwing mottled dark grey and white; chin, breast, belly and under tail coverts white; bill black, pale grey at edge of pouch on lower mandible; eyes brown; legs pale blue, webs black.
HABITAT: coastal and pelagic waters of subantarctic. HABITS: pelagic except when breeding, perhaps also roosting on land; gregarious breeding; at sea usually in small parties; movements unknown, perhaps not dispersing far from breeding grounds; visit nesting area at night; flight swift and direct with rapid wingbeats. BREEDING: July–December; nests in tunnels among tussock grass; one white egg. VOICE: loud nasal braying and moaning whistle.
FOOD: small crustacea.

STATUS: common. TAXONOMY: race *(belcheri)* of wide ranging species extending to New Zealand.

Diving Petrel (63)   Georgian Diving Petrel (64)

DIVING PETREL BILLS—VENTRAL VIEW

64 GEORGIAN DIVING PETREL *Pelecanoides georgicus* Murphy & Harper 1916
Distribution: southeastern seas; recorded near Sydney.
RECOGNITION: identical with common species except for shape of bill (as illustrated).
STATUS: rare; non-breeding straggler from subantarctic.

Family PODICIPEDIDAE
Grebes
3(20) species: 1 endemic

Distribution: worldwide.

MEMBERS OF THIS FAMILY are highly adapted to aquatic habitats, but they keep almost entirely to fresh water, sometimes brackish in the non-breeding season. In Australia they are found on the still waters of lakes and billabongs, especially where there are reedy margins and floating vegetation, and even on small pools and dams if food can be found there. Grebes are stumpy in appearance, largely because tails are so short as to be invisible, and legs are placed far back on the body. They are clumsy out of water, which they leave with reluctance and then only to climb on to their nests. Although they are accomplished swimmers and divers they are not web-footed but the toes are fringed with broad paddles. Of the three Australian species two are small, 20–23cm, and the Crested Grebe much larger, 43cm. They are dark above and silky white below, with head adornments in the breeding season. Wings are relatively short and have a patch of white which becomes visible when the wings are extended. Nests are anchored to reeds in shallow water or on a platform of floating vegetation. The Hoary-headed Grebe is found only in Australia, the other two are found elsewhere in similar or closely related forms.

Key to PODICIPEDIDAE

1 Head crested, ruff on neck; 45cm	Crested Grebe	No 67
2 No crest or ruff; 20cm..........	3–6	
3 Foreneck dark	Little Grebe (Breeding)	No 65
4 Foreneck light..........	5–6	
5 White patch on face..........	Little Grebe (Non-breeding) ...	No 65
6 No white patch on streaked face	Hoary-headed Grebe..........	No 66

65 LITTLE GREBE *Podiceps novaehollandiae* Stephens 1826
Distribution: throughout.

RECOGNITION: *small and dumpy, apparently tailless, floating high on water and diving frequently, white patch on face.*

DESCRIPTION: 23cm. Sexes alike. *Breeding:* upperparts brownish-black; chin, throat and hind neck black; sides of neck bright chestnut; breast and flanks mottled grey-brown and white; lower breast and belly silky white; inner wing white, a conspicuous white band on inner trailing edge of extended wing; bill black, tip white; bare skin in front of eye pale greenish-yellow (whitish at a distance); eyes pale yellow; legs olive green. *Non-breeding:* black throat and chestnut on neck change to white; underparts less mottled.

HABITAT: still inland waters of almost any size, even small dams, but with a preference for permanent deep waters. HABITS: aquatic; solitary, but several pairs may nest on the same small pond or lake; sedentary and nomadic, sometimes dispersing to brackish coastal waters when not breeding, or any waters in unfavourable conditions, usually travelling at night; swims, often with head and neck erect, dives and swims long distances under water; very clumsy on land. BREEDING: mainly August–May; nests in shallows anchored to reeds or on floating vegetation made into a raft; five to six eggs, white, but often stained. VOICE: loud shrill 'chee-ee-ee'. FOOD: aquatic insects and plants.

STATUS: common. TAXONOMY: monotypic species extending to Papuan area, closely related to widespread *Podiceps ruficollis*.

Little Grebe (65) *breeding*

Hoary-headed Grebe (66) *breeding*

66 HOARY-HEADED GREBE *Podiceps poliocephalus* Jard. & Selby 1837

Distribution: mainly south of tropic, apparently vagrant north of tropic.

RECOGNITION: *distinguished from breeding plumage of Little Grebe by white throat, and from non-breeding plumage by white streaks on side of head and neck and lack of white patch in front of eye; when together looks greyer and has longer and more upright neck.*

DESCRIPTION: 28–30cm. Sexes alike. *Breeding:* upperparts dark grey-brown, blackish from crown to nape; forehead and side of head and neck finely streaked with white; underparts white, pale buffy-brown on breast; concealed patch of white in wing becomes broad white band on inner trailing edge of expanded wing; bill blackish; eyes brownish-yellow; legs olive green. *Non-breeding:* upperparts become greyer, white lines on head less distinct and breast loses buff colour.

HABITAT: similar to Little Grebe but perhaps more frequently on brackish water, also at breeding time seems to have a preference for shallow temporary water. HABITS, etc: similar to Little Grebe but almost voiceless except for soft notes near nest; three to five eggs, pale bluish-white.

STATUS: apparently much less common than Little Grebe but readily overlooked because of similarity. TAXONOMY: endemic species.

67 CRESTED GREBE *Podiceps cristatus* (Linnaeus) 1758   Pl 2

Distribution: Map 1.

RECOGNITION: *stumpy body, long neck with black and rufous ruff, crested head.*

DESCRIPTION: 43cm. Sexes alike. Upperparts blackish-brown; black of forehead and crown continued into a long double crest; feathers of upper neck extended into a long cinnamon rufous ruff tipped with black; face and underparts silky white; white on inner shoulder and inner wing become conspicuous white margins on extended wing; bill reddish, brown above; eyes red; legs dark greenish-olive.

HABITAT: large areas of still open waters well margined with water vegetation, sheltered lagoons and brackish estuaries. HABITS: aquatic; solitary, but several pairs may be on same large lake; nomadic or migratory, apparently some regular north and south seasonal movement; swims and dives, also submerges body when alarmed; has unique elaborate mating *displays.* BREEDING: August–February; nest on water attached to reeds or a floating platform of water vegetation; five to seven eggs, greenish-white, dulled with stain. VOICE: very varied; shrill, barking, rattling, whirring, moaning calls. FOOD: aquatic animals and vegetation.

STATUS: uncommon, but likely to be found wherever there are suitable habitats. TAXONOMY: endemic race *(christiani)* of cosmopolitan species.

Pelican (68)

Family PELECANIDAE

Pelicans

1(8) species: endemic

PELICANS MUST BE AMONG the best known of birds for they are found in many countries and their features are striking. The long bill with suspended pouch for scooping up fish give these large black and white birds a peculiarly grotesque appearance. The heavy body is carried on short stumpy legs and large webbed feet. The single Australian species is equally at home on fresh and salt water, but the principal habitats are estuaries, lagoons and large lakes and billabongs. They fish in the shallows and preen and sun themselves on mud banks and islands.

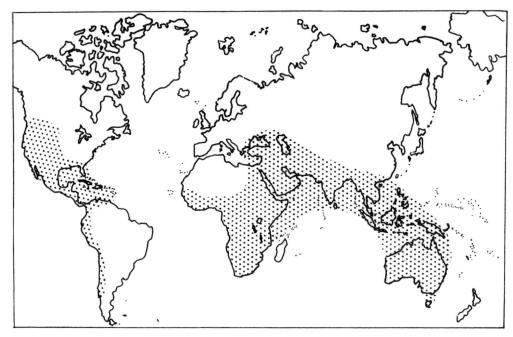

Distribution of PELECANIDAE

68 PELICAN   *Pelecanus conspicillatus*   Temminck 1824
Distribution: throughout.

RECOGNITION: *large, black and white, long bill with suspended pouch; in flight, head drawn in to body.*

DESCRIPTION: 1·75–2m; wingspan 2·75–3m; feet webbed. Sexes alike. Mainly white; crest or short 'mane' at back of head pale grey; flight feathers black; upperparts in flight show large black 'V' pattern formed by black leading edge of wing continuous with black on sides of back and meeting on rump; tail black; bare skin around eyes yellow; bill and pouch pale pinkish-brown; eyes brown; legs dark blue-grey.

HABITAT: coastal and inland waters. HABITS: aquatic when feeding, nests and roosts on land, sometimes roosts in trees on margins of inland waters; gregarious, but in dispersed flocks when feeding; nomadic, sometimes dispersing widely in non-breeding period but apparently no regular movement pattern; feeds from surface; in flight, head drawn in to body. BREED-ING: variable, in southeast mainly September–February, in west mainly March–August, inland when water conditions suitable; nests on small islands and other protected places, a scrape in the ground usually built up with sticks and other vegetation; two to three white eggs. VOICE: hoarse grunt, but rarely used. FOOD: fish and crustacea.

STATUS: common. TAXONOMY: endemic breeding species with vagrant occurrences in southern New Guinea.

Family SULIDAE

Gannets and Boobies

4(9) species

Distribution: worldwide.

THIS SMALL BUT DISTINCT family ranges widely throughout temperate and tropical regions of the world. It belongs to the shallower waters of coastal shelves rather than to the deep seas, which are the special haunts of albatrosses and petrels. The names gannet and booby are used in different context for the same birds. The course adopted here is a usual one, gannet for the temperate zone species of the genus *Morus*, and booby for the tropical species of the genus *Sula*. All four species found in Australia breed on coastal islands. They are mainly white with black areas in the wings, and sometimes tail, or mainly black with white belly; they have large pointed bills and usually long pointed tails. But they are best identified at a distance by their habit of plummeting vertically into the sea from heights of up to 20m or more, the resulting impacts producing great splashes which sometimes attract attention before the birds themselves do. A curious feature, which immediately identifies the skull of a gannet or booby, is the lack of the orthodox nasal opening; in compensation the mouth is extended backward beyond the level of the eye and the extra length is covered by a section of the horny bill which remains open to permit breathing.

Key to SULIDAE

1 Upperparts wholly black...................... Brown Booby............... No 72
2 Back dark, tail white........................ Red-footed Booby............ No 70
3 Upperparts mainly white 4–6
4 Tail white, crown buffy...................... Red-footed Booby............ No 70
5 Centre of tail black, crown buffy............... Gannet .... No 69
6 Tail wholly black, crown white................ Masked Booby.............. No 71

Genus MORUS

Three isolated temperate zone populations, two in the southern hemisphere and one in the northern, are very alike and have a common origin; they may be races but are currently regarded as species, or semispecies. They differ from a group of tropical species in a number of anatomical details, such as structure of throat feathers and scales on toes, and are put in a separate genus.

69 GANNET *Morus serrator* (Gray) 1843   Pl 1

Distribution: coastal islands of Victoria and Tasmania and seas north to tropic.

RECOGNITION: *white with wingtips and half trailing edge black, black central tail feathers and buffy head.*

DESCRIPTION: 1m; wingspan 1·75m. Sexes alike. Mainly white, forehead to nape dull buffy-yellow; main flight feathers and tip of inner feathers black; central tail feathers black; bill and bare skin of throat blue-grey; eyes pale grey; legs grey.

HABITAT: coastal and offshore waters of temperate and subtropical seas. HABITS: aquatic, nesting and often roosting on land; gregarious, breeding in large colonies or 'gannetries' and usually feeding in flocks although solitary birds may be seen; sedentary and migratory, some flocks remaining in vicinity of breeding grounds and returning there to roost, others disperse up to at least 600–800km, returning seasonally to breed; flight vigorous and direct; feeds by diving into sea from heights up to 20m. BREEDING: September–April; nests on ground, a mound of vegetation, earth and excreta; one egg, white but usually nest-stained. VOICE: harsh discordant 'urrah', and various squeaking, guttural and barking sounds. FOOD: fish. STATUS: common. TAXONOMY: species extending to New Zealand of superspecies found also in South Africa and north Atlantic.

Genus SULA

Consists of six species frequenting tropical seas and generally known as boobies. They have a number of distinct anatomical and behavioural features. Three species have small breeding colonies on several Australian coastal tropical islands. They are white, with black on wings or tail or mainly brown.

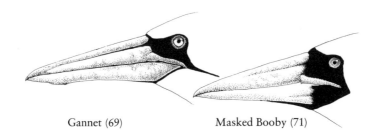

Gannet (69)   Masked Booby (71)

70 RED-FOOTED BOOBY *Sula sula* (Linnaeus) 1766

Distribution: tropical seas, especially northeast, breeding on Raine I and islands in Coral Sea.

RECOGNITION: *slender build, long pointed white tail, black wingtips, red legs.*

DESCRIPTION: 75cm; wingspan 1·5m. Sexes alike. Dimorphic. (1) Mainly white tinged with yellow-buff on head and neck; main flight feathers black, giving broad black tip to open wing; bill and bare skin of face blue, skin of chin black; legs red. (2) Mainly brown with white tail and belly.

HABITAT: offshore and pelagic waters of tropical and subtropical seas. HABITS: aquatic, nesting and roosting in trees and bushes, sometimes on land; gregarious; sedentary, seldom far from breeding and roosting grounds; dives into sea from a height. BREEDING: June–January; nests on ground or in trees and bushes, made of sticks and local vegetation; one white egg. VOICE: single 'krerk' or 'krok', also loud crackling sounds. FOOD: squid and fish.

STATUS: fairly common. TAXONOMY: race *(rubripes)* of species with pantropical distribution.

71 MASKED BOOBY *Sula dactylatra* Lesson 1829

Distribution: tropical seas, breeding on islands in Dampier Archipelago and Coral Sea.

RECOGNITION: *white with black tail and wings, except for white shoulders.*

DESCRIPTION: 76–86cm; wingspan 1·75m. Sexes alike. Body white; wing with white shoulders and all flight feathers black; tail black; bill bright yellow (♂) or dull greenish-yellow (♀); base of bill and bare skin of face and chin bluish-black; eyes golden-yellow; legs blue-grey.

HABITAT: outer limits of offshore waters in tropical and subtropical seas. HABITS: aquatic, but nesting and usually roosting on land; gregarious; perhaps sedentary but with extensive dispersal movements; dives into sea from a height. BREEDING: continuous, with spring and autumn peaks; nests on ground in unlined depressions or on rough accumulations of vegetation; two eggs, bluish-white. VOICE: whistling 'pseep' and resonant 'kerk'. FOOD: fish, especially flying fish, and squid.

STATUS: fairly common. TAXONOMY: race *(personata)* of species with pantropical distribution.

72 BROWN BOOBY *Sula leucogaster* (Boddaert) 1783

Distribution: tropical seas south to northern New South Wales, breeding on coastal islands and islands of Coral Sea.

RECOGNITION: *blackish with white belly and centre of underwing.*

DESCRIPTION: 75cm; wingspan 1·5m. Sexes differ in colour of bare skin of face and legs. Mainly dark brown except lower breast, belly and centre of underwing white, bill grey tinged with yellow or green; base of bill and bare skin of face and chin blue in male, buffy-yellow in female; eyes yellow or brown; legs pale greenish in male, buffy-yellow in female.

HABITAT: mainly offshore waters of tropical and subtropical seas. HABITS: aquatic but nests and roosts on land; gregarious; apparently sedentary but may have extensive dispersal movements; dives into sea from a height. BREEDING: continuous, with spring and autumn peaks; nests on ground, shallow scrapes or substantial structures of local vegetation; two eggs, greenish-white. VOICE: a resonant 'kruk'. FOOD: fish.

STATUS: fairly common. TAXONOMY: race *(plotus)* of species with pantropical distribution.

Family PHALACROCORACIDAE

Cormorants and Darter

6(31) species: 1 endemic

Distribution: worldwide.

CORMORANTS ARE SOMETIMES CALLED shags, especially among fishermen; the names are interchangeable. It is convenient to include the Darter with cormorants for taxonomists are divided on its entitlement to family status. Probably the Darter is a cormorant offshoot with a rather specialised way of living, and it is a very successful one for the two species (some would have six and others only one) share the tropical world between them, one in the eastern hemisphere and one in the western. Cormorants are also successful for they are numerous and widespread with habitats in most coastal and inland waters. They feed by diving, usually from the surface, and swimming under water for periods of up to half a minute or more propelled by large webbed feet. Fish of various kinds are their principal food. Legs are placed far back on the body so that when perched they have to stand nearly upright, like penguins, to maintain balance. Although water is their natural element, it is curious that their plumage is not waterproof, like most aquatic species, and a distinctive feature of cormorants is the habit of drying their feathers by standing for long periods with wings extended. Tails are long with feather shafts hard, almost spiky. Bills are long and slender and sharply hooked, but not in the Darter which has a spear-shaped bill and narrow head, and a long thin snake-like neck with a permanent kink in the middle. Cormorants are frequently black (in some languages they are called sea-crows) or black with some white on the underparts. There are three pied species in Australia and two wholly black, plus the Darter.

Key to PHALACROCORACIDAE

1 Bill pointed	Darter	No 78
2 Bill hooked at tip	3–10	
3 Black above and below	5–6	
4 Black above, white below	7–10	
5 White on face and chin; 1m	Black Cormorant.............	No 73
6 Wholly black; 60cm........................	Little Black Cormorant........	No 74
7 Thighs white..............................	Little Pied Cormorant (Ad)	No 76
8 Thighs black	9–10	
9 Facial skin orange; 75cm	Yellow-faced Cormorant	No 75
10 Facial skin black; 60cm....................	Black-faced Cormorant	No 77
	Little Pied Cormorant (Imm)...	No 76

73 BLACK CORMORANT *Phalacrocorax carbo* (Linnaeus) 1758

Distribution: throughout.

RECOGNITION: *black with bright orange bare skin on face and chin.*

DESCRIPTION: 75cm–1m; wingspan 1·25–1·65m; fairly distinct erectile crest. Sexes alike, but female smaller. Mainly black with greenish sheen; narrow white border to bare skin of face and chin, which is bright orange; in breeding season white patch on thighs and numerous white lines on neck; bill dark grey; eyes green; legs black.

HABITAT: mainly inland waters, occasionally coastal. HABITS: feeds in water, nests and roosts in trees; both solitary and gregarious, sometimes in very large flocks, sometimes flocks take communal action to herd shoals of fish into shallow water; nomadic. BREEDING: variable, but mainly between March and November, perhaps with peaks in spring and autumn; nests

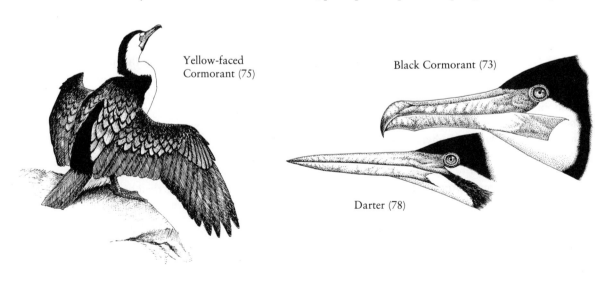

Yellow-faced
Cormorant (75)

Black Cormorant (73)

Darter (78)

in trees, usually high up, or on rocky ledges of river gorges, often mixed with nests of other species competing for similar sites, a substantial structure of sticks and twigs lined with soft bark; three to four eggs, bluish-white. VOICE: apparently not recorded, largely silent. FOOD: fish and crustacea.

STATUS: common. TAXONOMY: endemic race *(novaehollandiae)* of species extending throughout most of the northern hemisphere.

74 LITTLE BLACK CORMORANT *Phalacrocorax sulcirostris* (Brandt) 1837
Distribution: throughout.

RECOGNITION: *black, smaller than Black Cormorant and no white on face and chin.*

DESCRIPTION: 60cm. Sexes alike. Wholly black; bare skin of face purplish-grey; bill black above, dark grey below; eyes green; legs black.

HABITAT: mainly inland waters but sometimes on coasts when not breeding. HABITS: feeds in water, nests and roosts in trees; solitary and gregarious, sometimes feeds in large companies by herding fish into shallow waters; sedentary and nomadic. BREEDING: variable, but mainly March–November; nests in deeper parts of swamps, in trees, like paperbark thickets, usually high up, made of sticks and lined with strips of bark; three to five eggs, greenish-white. VOICE: various creaking sounds, but usually silent. FOOD: fish and crustacea.

STATUS: common. TAXONOMY: species extending to New Zealand and Borneo.

75 YELLOW-FACED CORMORANT *Phalacrocorax varius* (Gmelin) 1789
Distribution: throughout except Tasmania.

RECOGNITION: *white underparts with black thighs, white above eyes, orange patch in front of eyes.*

DESCRIPTION: 75cm; wingspan 1·25m. Sexes alike, but female smaller. Upperparts black with bronze-green sheen; face from above eye and underparts white; thighs black; bare skin of face orange and of chin greenish-blue; bill dark pinkish-brown; eyes bright green; legs black.

HABITAT: coastal lagoons, estuaries and lakes, large inland swamps and rivers. HABITS: feeding in water in large estuaries and bays, nesting and roosting in trees; solitary and gregarious, sometimes in enormous flocks when roosting and nesting; sedentary with limited dispersal movements; flight direct and strong and low over water. BREEDING: on coasts September–November, also March–May, inland between September and May in favourable conditions; nests on islands in estuaries and lagoons, often on ground or low bushes, or in mangroves and other trees, or high in trees on inland waters, made of branches and twigs and local vegetation cemented together with excreta; two to three eggs, pale blue. VOICE: mechanical 'tok-tok'. FOOD: fish and crustacea.

STATUS: common. TAXONOMY: endemic race *(perthi)* of species extending to New Zealand.

76 LITTLE PIED CORMORANT *Phalacrocorax melanoleucos* (Vieillot) 1817
Distribution: throughout.

RECOGNITION: *white underparts with white thighs, yellow bill and bare skin of face and chin.*

DESCRIPTION: 60cm; wingspan 1m. Sexes alike. Upperparts black; face from above eye, and underparts including thigh, white; bare skin of face and chin yellow; bill yellow, dark brown on top; eyes grey-brown; legs black. *Immature*: black to below eye, thighs black (like Black-faced Cormorant but upperparts sooty brown).

HABITAT: mainly inland waters, often small patches of water, pools in creeks, dams, small billabongs, sometimes coastal waters when not breeding. HABITS: feeding in water, nesting and roosting in trees; solitary or gregarious; sedentary and nomadic, especially in unfavourable conditions; dives for food. BREEDING: variable, in most months in some part of range, but mainly February–September; nests in trees and bushes usually in deeper parts of swamps, made of sticks often lined with green bark; three to five eggs, greenish or bluish-white. VOICE: various croaking sounds. FOOD: various small aquatic animals, including fish.

STATUS: common. TAXONOMY: race *(melanoleucos)* extending to Celebes and Solomon Is of species also extending to New Zealand.

77 BLACK-FACED CORMORANT *Phalacrocorax fuscescens* (Vieillot) 1817

Distribution: south coast from Hopetoun to Israelite Bay, Western Australia, and Ceduna to Cape Hope and Tasmania.

RECOGNITION: *white underparts with black thighs, black of crown extends below eye, naked skin of face and chin black. (Like immature Little Pied but upperparts shiny black.)*

DESCRIPTION: 60cm; wingspan 1·15m. Sexes alike. Upperparts shiny black with numerous fine white lines on neck; face below eye and underparts white; thighs black; bare skin of face and chin black; bill dark grey; eyes bright green; legs black.

HABITAT: coastal waters, rarely inland. HABITS: feeding in water, nesting and roosting on land; gregarious; sedentary; dives for food. BREEDING: variable, but mainly September–January; nests on bare rocks near sea, made of seaweed and other vegetation; two to four eggs, pale dull green. VOICE: no information. FOOD: fish.

STATUS: common. TAXONOMY: endemic species.

Genus ANHINGA

Superficially like a cormorant, the Darter (there are anything from one to six species) is often placed in a separate family. Its principal feature is the curious adaptation of head and neck into a flexible spear. The long thin neck has a special mechanism, identified by a natural kink in the vertebrae, whose purpose is to project the spear-shaped bill and head, the latter so narrow as to seem part of the bill. In the water darters usually swim with body submerged and only head and neck, like a snake, visible above the surface.

78 DARTER *Anhinga rufa* (Daudin) 1842 Fig p 64

Distribution: throughout, except Tasmania.

RECOGNITION: *very long thin neck and apparent lack of head, male wholly black, female has white underparts.*

DESCRIPTION: 1m; head and neck 40cm, body 30cm, tail 20cm. Sexes different. *Male*: mainly black, brownish on head and neck; black feathers of shoulders and edge of back have buffy-white centres; dark cinnamon brown streak on foreneck; broad white band from below eye for about 10cm along side of neck; lower part of face and narrow margin of chin white; bill yellow; eyes yellow; legs pinkish-brown. *Female*: differs in having head to upper back mottled, sooty black and buffy-white, white band on side of neck bordered with black, underparts white.

HABITAT: inland and coastal waters, preferably large swampy areas. HABITS: feeds in water, nests and roosts in trees; usually solitary but often nests in colonies and among other species with similar nesting habits; apparently sedentary; dives and swims under water when feeding, or swims with body submerged and only long sinuous neck visible; sometimes circles high up in the air for long periods. BREEDING: varies according to locality but usually between October and March; nests in remotest parts of swamps, in trees or bushes standing in water or overhanging water, at various heights, made of a platform of sticks lined with twigs and replenished each season with fresh green leaves; three to five eggs, greenish-white. VOICE: loud raucous staccato cackle. FOOD: fish and other aquatic animals.

STATUS: fairly common. TAXONOMY: race *(novaehollandiae)*, sometimes regarded as a species, extending to New Guinea, of species ranging widely throughout the old world.

Family FREGATIDAE

Frigatebirds

2(6) species

Distribution: pantropical.

FRIGATEBIRDS HAVE EARNED THEIR name from their piratical habits of forcing other birds to disgorge food, a practice shared by the quite unrelated skuas of colder seas; they also obtain food by the more orthodox means of catching it for themselves, which they do from the surface of the water while still in flight, for they rarely alight on the water. They are skilled in all the arts of flying and, like swifts, spend much of their life in the air, so much so that legs are degenerate and birds have to alight on land in places from which take off is easy, as on trees, where they nest and lay their single white egg. Frigatebirds are of medium size with long thin wings, long forked tail, long hooked bill and mainly black plumage; males have a large patch of bare skin on the throat which can be inflated into a large pouch. Two species frequent Australian tropical waters and one breeds on coastal islands.

Key to FREGATIDAE

1 Wholly black	(♂)	Greater Frigatebird	No 80
2 Black with white patches	3–5		
3 White patch on flanks	(♂)	Lesser Frigatebird	No 79
4 White breast, black throat	(♀)	Lesser Frigatebird	No 79
5 White breast, grey throat	(♀)	Greater Frigatebird	No 80

79 LESSER FRIGATEBIRD *Fregata ariel* (Gray) 1845   Pl 1

Distribution: tropical seas, breeding on coastal islands, rare south of tropic.

RECOGNITION: *black, slender, long wings and forked tail, white patch on flanks; female has white breast.*

DESCRIPTION: 75cm; forked tail 30cm; slender hooked bill 8cm; female slightly larger. Sexes different. *Male:* black with white patch on flanks; bare skin of throat bright red and extendible into large pouch; bare skin around eye black; bill blue-grey; eyes brown; legs black or dark reddish-brown. *Female:* breast and upper flanks white, continuous with pale collar; bare skin around eye red; bill pale bluish-grey; legs red.

HABITAT: offshore and pelagic waters of tropical and subtropical seas, breeding on islands. HABITS: feeds at sea but does not alight on water; solitary and gregarious, nesting in colonies; probably mainly sedentary but records of birds far from breeding grounds; flight graceful and acrobatic, consisting of leisurely deep wingbeats and frequent soaring and gliding; forces other birds to disgorge food or takes food from surface while still in flight. BREEDING: May–December; nests in trees and shrubs and on ground, made of sticks and grass and bound with excreta; one white egg. VOICE: a deep 'kukukuk'. FOOD: fish and squid.

STATUS: common. TAXONOMY: western Pacific race *(ariel)* of species extending to Indian and South Atlantic Oceans.

80 GREATER FRIGATEBIRD   *Fregata minor*   (Gmelin) 1789

Distribution: tropical seas.

RECOGNITION: like Lesser Frigatebird but larger, 1m. *Male: black with inconspicuous dark brown shoulder bar* which may show in flight as a light bar on upper side of inner wing; bare skin around eye black; bill blue-grey; legs black or dark brown. *Female:* larger, *white of breast connected with a light grey area on throat;* bill pale purplish-grey; legs pink.

HABITAT etc: similar to Lesser Frigatebird.

STATUS: uncommon; non-breeding visitor (nearest breeding grounds in Coral Sea islands and Christmas and Cocos Is).

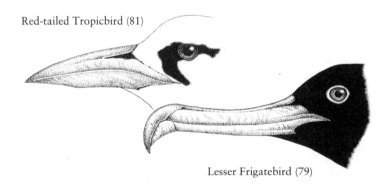

Red-tailed Tropicbird (81)

Lesser Frigatebird (79)

Family PHAETHONTIDAE

Tropicbirds

2(3) species

Distribution: pantropical.

THE THREE SPECIES OF this small family are mainly white, about the size and general appearance of the larger terns, but they do not have a black cap and the tail is wedge-shaped, not forked. In mature birds, the two central tail feathers are greatly extended. Tropicbirds generally fly high, not low over the water, and they are readily attracted to ships. Only the Red-tailed Tropicbird breeds in the Australian area; it nests on Raine I in the northeast and on Sugarloaf Rock, near Cape Naturaliste, in the southwest.

Key to PHAETHONTIDAE

1 Black bar on inner wing, bill yellow . . . .   White-tailed Tropicbird . . . . No 82
2 No bar on inner wing, bill red . . . .   Red-tailed Tropicbird . . . . No 81

81 RED-TAILED TROPICBIRD *Phaethon rubricauda* Boddaert 1783   Pl 1

Distribution: tropical seas and south at least to Abrolhos Is on west coast, rare in south and southeast; breeding on coastal islands.

RECOGNITION: *white, pointed tail with long red 'streamers', thick red bill.*

DESCRIPTION: 45cm, plus tail streamers 30cm; wingspan 1·15m. Sexes alike. Silky white with pale rose-red tinge on back and shoulders; black U-shaped patch beside eye; feathers of inner wing and flanks have black centres; two long narrow central tail feathers red; bill coral red; eyes brown; legs blue-grey.

HABITAT: offshore and pelagic waters of tropical and subtropical seas. HABITS: feeds at sea by diving into water from heights of up to 14m; usually solitary but loosely gregarious when breeding; disperses widely when not breeding but pattern of movement not well known; flutter-and-glide flight; attracted to ships but rarely accompanying for long periods. BREEDING: most months but mainly between November and March in southern breeding grounds; nests on ground in open or under shelter of bushes and rocks, an unlined depression; one egg, colour variable but often grey-brown or whitish with dull purplish markings. VOICE: harsh guttural and rattling calls. FOOD: squid and fish.

STATUS: fairly common. TAXONOMY: race *(westralis)* of species extending from western Indian Ocean to Hawaiian Is.

82 WHITE-TAILED TROPICBIRD *Phaethon lepturus* (Daudin) 1802

Distribution: northern and northeastern seas.

RECOGNITION: like Red-tailed species but smaller, conspicuous *black bar on upper side of inner wing,* black on outer webs of outer flight feathers, *white tail streamers,* white parts often tinged with reddish-yellow (apricot), yellow bill.

STATUS: rare; non-breeding visitor.

Family ARDEIDAE

Bitterns, Herons, Egrets

15(64) species: 1 endemic

Distribution: worldwide.

THIS FAMILY HAS TWO main divisions or subfamilies, one consisting of bitterns and the other of herons and egrets. Both range widely throughout the world. Bitterns are noted for being heard more often than seen. They are shy denizens of marshy places, living deep among reeds and grasses; when disturbed they 'freeze' in an upright posture and their soft plumage of mottled and streaked buffs and browns makes a perfect match with the partly dried reed stems and leaves; long necks and long sharp bills are pointed to the sky, but the eyes are curiously placed to give them horizontal vision. Legs are short. Voices are loud and of a booming or braying quality and carry far across the marshes. They are solitary and largely nocturnal. Three species normally occur in Australia; one additional species has been found and may be a rare vagrant.

There are eleven herons and egrets of which the White-necked Heron is the only endemic species. Most are about 45–60cm in length except the White Egret and Great-billed Heron which are much larger. Legs and necks are usually long and bills spear-shaped. The four species with 'egret' in their name are white, and the Reef Heron is either white or black. A distinctive feature of some members of this group is the various plumes which decorate the graceful figures of both sexes in the breeding season, especially the beautiful aigrette feathers which appear on the back of *Egretta* species. Other plumes occur on the crown and nape and the base of the foreneck, where they hang down over the breast. In contrast to plumage, the voices are unattractive, being harsh and croaky. Herons and egrets are usually found in wet or moist places but the Cattle Egret, a recent colonist, may be far from water and in the company of grazing animals. Unlike the bitterns, most are gregarious, especially when breeding. All fly with long necks folded back to the body.

Key to ARDEIDAE

[*Note:* The white species of this family, four egrets and the white phase of the Reef Heron, can be difficult to distinguish. There are confusing statements regarding colours of bills and legs, which in some cases differ in the same species between breeding and non-breeding seasons, with transitional stages adding to the confusion. The problem was resolved by Hindwood and others, 1969, *South Australian Ornithologist*, 25:95, and their conclusions are incorporated in the following keys.]

White species

Breeding

1 Over 1m, plumes on back only	White Egret	No 94
2 About 60cm, plumes on back and breast	3–8	
3 Plumes buff-orange	Cattle Egret	No 88
4 Plumes white	5–8	
5 Legs greenish-yellow; rocky coasts	Reef Heron	No 91
6 Legs blackish	7–8	
7 Bill black, two long plumes on nape	Little Egret	No 92
8 Bill orange-yellow, no plumes on nape	Plumed Egret	No 93

Non-breeding

 1 Legs yellow . . . . Reef Heron . . . . No 91
 2 Legs blackish 3–8

 3 Bill black 5–6
 4 Bill yellow 7–8

 5 Over 1m . . . . White Egret . . . . No 94
 6 Under 60cm . . . . Little Egret . . . . No 92

 7 Grey above 'knee'; associated with cattle . . . . Cattle Egret . . . . No 88
 8 Often some yellow above 'knee' . . . . Plumed Egret . . . . No 93

Other species

 1 White head and neck . . . . White-necked Heron . . . . No 96
 2 White throat and neck . . . . Pied Heron . . . . No 90
 3 White face and throat . . . . White-faced Heron . . . . No 95
 4 Mottled dark brown and buff . . . . Brown Bittern . . . . No 83
 5 Mainly black or blackish 7–10
 6 Black crown 11–14

 7 Over 1·25m . . . . Great-billed Heron . . . . No 97
 8 Less than 60cm 9–10

 9 White chin . . . . Reef Heron . . . . No 91
10 Buff on sides of neck . . . . Black Bittern . . . . No 85

11 Back black . . . . (♂) Little Bittern . . . . No 84
12 Back greenish-black* . . . . Mangrove Heron . . . . No 89
13 Back chestnut . . . . Night Heron . . . . No 87
14 Back yellowish-brown . . . . Yellow Bittern . . . . No 86
                                                              (♀) Little Bittern . . . . No 84

*Some variants are rufous brown but can be distinguished by long hackles on back and lack of long white plumes on nape.

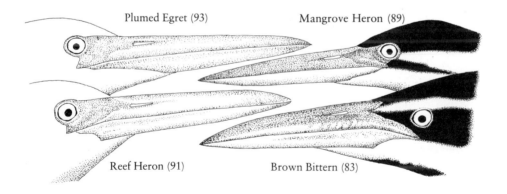

Plumed Egret (93)   Mangrove Heron (89)

Reef Heron (91)   Brown Bittern (83)

ARDEIDAE BILLS

Genus BOTAURUS

The four species which make up this genus are very alike and replace each other throughout the world. Although now isolated it seems certain that they had a common origin. Currently they are regarded as component species of a superspecies. They are large birds mottled dark brown and buff with broad blackish streaks.

83 BROWN BITTERN   *Botaurus poiciloptilus*   (Wagler) 1827   Fig p 71

Distribution: Map 2.

RECOGNITION: *large, 1m, mottled dark brown and buff with blackish streaks; loud booming and croaking voice.*

DESCRIPTION: stands 1m with neck extended. Sexes alike, but female slightly smaller. Crown, nape and lower face blackish-brown (umber); upper face and streak above eye cinnamon-buff; remainder of upperparts blackish-brown mottled with cinnamon-buff; scapulars mainly blackish; underparts pale buff broadly streaked with dark brown, especially on neck, and mottled and barred with dark brown on flanks and underwings; bare skin of face pale green; bill brown above, yellow below; eyes yellow or reddish-yellow; legs green.

HABITAT: dense beds of reeds and other swamp vegetation on borders of fresh and brackish waters. HABITS: terrestrial, sometimes roosting on horizontal branches near or overhanging water; solitary and territorial; nocturnal; apparently sedentary but probably also nomadic and flying at night; when flushed, flies low with legs dangling and head drawn in. BREEDING: October–February; nests in dense swamp vegetation, a platform of trampled vegetation which stands just above water level; five to six eggs, greenish-brown. VOICE: hoarse croaking or barking—also loud booming (possibly the origin of the bunyip legend). FOOD: frogs, crustacea and fish.

STATUS: fairly common. TAXONOMY: species extending to New Zealand of worldwide superspecies.

Genus IXOBRYCHUS

Two of the eight species in this worldwide genus are fairly common breeding species in Australia: the Little Bittern, not more than 30cm in length, and the larger Black or Mangrove Bittern. Both have much black in the plumage. The Little Bittern shows fairly distinct sexual dimorphism which is unusual in this family. A third species, the Yellow (or Chinese Least) Bittern has been found once; it may have been a straggler.

84 LITTLE BITTERN   *Ixobrychus minutus*   (Linnaeus) 1766   Pl 2

Distribution: Map 3.

RECOGNITION: *small, about 30cm, only crown and back black.*

DESCRIPTION: 30cm, with neck extended. Sexes slightly different. *Male:* forehead to nape, back and tail umber-black; margin of black crown, hind neck, tip and edge of shoulders dark reddish-brown (burnt sienna), grading to cinnamon rufous on face and sides of neck; streak from chin to breast cinnamon rufous bordered with buffy-white; breast mottled dark and light cinnamon rufous grading to pale cinnamon on belly and white on vent and under tail coverts; large area of shoulder cinnamon; outer flight feathers dark grey, inner black; bill umber-black above (like crown), remainder buffy-yellow; eyes buffy-yellow; legs pale greenish-yellow. *Female:* generally duller, browner on back and more heavily streaked.

HABITAT: reeds, rushes and other dense vegetation in swamps, marshes and river margins. HABITS: terrestrial; solitary; sedentary or nomadic, disperse at least when habitats dry out; when disturbed stands erect with head and neck fully stretched vertically; largely nocturnal. BREEDING: October–December; nests in swamp vegetation made of reeds or rushes often bent onto some leaning limb and built up with short pieces of vegetation and lined with finer pieces; four white eggs. VOICE: various deep croaking notes. FOOD: small water animals.

STATUS: uncertain, probably fairly common. TAXONOMY: endemic race *(dubius)* of species extending to New Zealand and throughout much of the old world.

85 BLACK BITTERN   *Ixobrychus flavicollis*   (Latham) 1790

Distribution: Map 4.

RECOGNITION: *60cm, almost wholly black.*

DESCRIPTION: 60cm, with neck extended. Sexes alike, but female more brownish than bluish-black. Mainly black, upperparts with slight bluish sheen; throat and foreneck mottled black and buffy-white; sides of neck buff; bare skin of face dull yellow; bill brown, blackish above and pinkish below; eyes light brown; legs dark olive brown.

HABITAT: apparently prefers thick vegetation along coastal stretches of river banks, like paperbark and mangroves. HABITS: terrestrial but sometimes roosts in trees and may nest fairly high up; solitary; movements uncertain but possibly sedentary unless forced to move; mainly nocturnal; when disturbed stands erect with neck stretched and bill pointing upwards. BREEDING: September–January; nests in trees on horizontal branches at varying heights close to or overhanging water, made of sticks; three to five eggs, greenish-white. VOICE: soft 'coo-oor' and sharp repeated 'eh-he'. FOOD: fish, crustacea, frogs.

STATUS: uncertain, but possibly fairly common. TAXONOMY: race *(gouldi)* extending to New Guinea of species widespread in eastern Asia.

86 YELLOW BITTERN   *Ixobrychus sinensis*   (Gmelin) 1789

Distribution: to date, one record from Kalgoorlie.

RECOGNITION: 30cm. Crown black; hind neck reddish-brown; back yellowish-brown; rump grey; underparts white; bill, eyes and legs yellow like female Little Bittern but distinguished in the hand by bill shape (see Boles *Corella* 1977: 33).

STATUS: very rare; non-breeding visitor.

Black
Bittern (85)

Night Heron (87)

Genus NYCTICORAX

The night feeding herons of this group are found throughout the world. They are stumpy in build with short legs, short thick bills and long plumes on the nape. Five species are currently recognised but the (Nankeen) Night Heron of Australia and elsewhere, so-called because of its colour, may only be a race of, or at most a semispecies with the very similar and much more widespread Black-crowned Night Heron. Immature plumages are very different from that of adults.

87 NIGHT HERON *Nycticorax caledonicus* (Gmelin) 1789   Fig p 73

Distribution: throughout.

RECOGNITION: *black cap, chestnut back and two long white plumes on nape.*

DESCRIPTION: 60cm. Sexes alike but immature very different. Forehead to nape black, nape with two long white lanceolate plumes; remainder of upperparts chestnut; white streak from forehead to above eye; face, side of neck and side of breast pale pinkish-cinnamon shading to buffy-white on remainder of underparts; bare skin of face bright greenish-yellow; bill black above, greenish-yellow below; eyes bright yellow; legs pale green. *Immature:* blackish-brown above, white below heavily spotted and streaked with buffy-white.

HABITAT: margins of swamps and rivers and sheltered inlets of sea with reed beds and similar ground vegetation and trees, sometimes in suburbs providing suitable conditions. HABITS: feeds on ground, roosts and nests in trees, or on ground in situations where trees not available and predation negligible, as on small islands; usually gregarious at all seasons but sometimes solitary; apparently sedentary; nocturnal, roosting in daytime in thick foliage; flies with head retracted. BREEDING: most months somewhere, but mainly between October and March; nests on horizontal branches of trees preferably standing in or overhanging water, roughly made of sticks; two to five eggs, bluish-green. VOICE: harsh croak or quack. FOOD: small aquatic animals and insects.

STATUS: fairly common. TAXONOMY: race *(hilli)* extending to New Guinea of species ranging as far as Solomon and Philippine Is.

Genus ARDEOLA

The Cattle Egret is sometimes placed in this genus along with the squacco herons and sometimes in a genus of its own, *Bubulcus*, principally because of its habit of accompanying grazing animals, to feed on the insects which they disturb. It is a white bird with a hunched or dejected appearance. This egret is a recent colonist. Some claim that the present very large population stems from eighteen birds liberated at Derby in 1933, others that it arrived of its own accord. The Cattle Egret has been extending its range in many directions in other parts of the world; it is an interesting example of a species in an 'explosive' phase of its evolution.

88 CATTLE EGRET *Ardeola ibis* (Linnaeus) 1758

Distribution: widespread, especially in coastal areas of north, west and east, and continually spreading.

RECOGNITION: *white, blackish legs, yellow or reddish-orange bill, orange-buff plumes in breeding season; often with cattle.*

DESCRIPTION: 46cm with neck extended. Sexes alike. *Breeding:* white with orange-buff plumes on crown, back and breast; bare skin of face pinkish; bill reddish-orange with yellow tip; eyes reddish-orange; legs dark olive, pink or red above 'knee'. *Non-breeding:* white without plumes; face skin, bill and eyes yellow; legs dark olive, grey above 'knee'.

HABITAT: various kinds of savanna from wet to dry, preferably where there is short grass and grazing animals. HABITS: feeds on ground often among grazing cattle and horses, perching on their backs; roosting and nesting in trees and bushes; usually gregarious, sometimes in large flocks, sometimes nesting among colonies of other species; sedentary and nomadic, readily settling in new localities. BREEDING: October–December (at least); nests in trees and thickets, on horizontal forks and up to at least 16m, well made of sticks and lined with fine twigs; three to six eggs, greenish-blue. VOICE: various croaking notes. FOOD: insects.

STATUS: common, increasing. TAXONOMY: race *(coromandus)* of species ranging widely throughout the world.

Genus BUTORIDES

The green herons which form this worldwide group have a number of distinct features: plumage with dark green gloss, blackish crown with rear feathers extended (nuchal crest), a contrasting streak from throat to breast, short legs, stocky build; also they are usually solitary in habits. In many ways they resemble bitterns. Three species are currently recognised, of which the Mangrove Heron, occurring in coastal Australia, is very variable in body colour. Numerous races are named, some frequently listed as species, throughout its very wide range.

89 MANGROVE HERON *Butorides striatus* (Linnaeus) 1758   Fig p 71

Distribution: northern coastal localities south to Shark Bay in the west and to south of Sydney in the east.

RECOGNITION: *black crown, short yellow legs, long hackles on usually greenish back, frequenting mangroves and mud flats, solitary.*

DESCRIPTION: 40–46cm, including bill 7·5cm. Sexes alike. Crown to nape black with greenish gloss, nape feathers extended; remainder of upperparts, except neck, varying from rufous brown to dark green, usually glossy, with feathers of upper back extended into long hackles, and shoulder feathers edged with buff; face below eye, neck and underparts varying from grey with very little brown to brown with very little grey; streak from throat to upper breast white mottled with dark brown; bare skin of face dull greenish-yellow; bill reddish-brown above, greenish below; eyes yellow; legs bright orange-yellow.

VARIATION: general pattern: east coast, darker and greener (races, south *macrorhynchus*, north *littleri*); north coast, paler and browner (race *stagnatalis*); extreme west, rufous (race *rogersi*).

HABITAT: coastal swamp vegetation, especially mangroves, and adjacent moist savanna woodland, rarely far inland. HABITS: feeds on ground, often on mud flats, nests and roosts in trees, sometimes dives into water; keeps head retracted in hunched attitude except when shot out to catch prey; solitary; sedentary with some nomadic or dispersal movements. BREEDING: September–December; nests in forks in mangrove and other swamp trees, up to 10m, a platform of sticks lined with fine twigs; three to four eggs, greenish-blue. VOICE: harsh squawk resembling 'tch-aah' and explosive 'hoo'. FOOD: fish and small animals from intertidal zone.

STATUS: fairly common. TAXONOMY: various endemic races of variable species with wide distribution.

Genus HYDRANASSA

The five species included in this group extend from the Australian region to central America. They are difficult to define on the basis of common features but they are connected by species showing similarities with each other. The Pied Heron of Australia, for example, has affinities with the Black Heron of tropical Africa, both having the same pattern of long ornamental plumes.

90 PIED HERON *Hydranassa picata* (Gould) 1845

Distribution: Map 5.

RECOGNITION: *black with white throat and neck, long plumes on nape, back and foreneck.*

DESCRIPTION: 45cm. Sexes alike. Mainly black with dull slate-blue sheen; white throat and foreneck; feathers of nape and upper back extended into long plumes, some white and black feathers of foreneck extended into long hackles; bare skin of face dark grey-brown; bill yellow; eyes yellow; legs greenish-yellow.

HABITAT: salt and fresh water coastal swamps and adjacent grasslands. HABITS: feeds on ground and shallow water, roosts and nests in trees, especially mangroves; usually gregarious, sometimes in flocks of up to 100, nests often among those of other species with similar habits; sedentary and nomadic, perhaps migratory; recorded at regular periods as non-breeding visitor (e.g., Innisfail, October–February); pugnacious, attacking other species, sometimes forcing them to disgorge food. BREEDING: September–November (at least); nests in trees in and around swampy places, in forks up to 5m, made of sticks and fine twigs; three to four eggs, blue-green. VOICE: soft cooing at nest and loud 'ohrk'. FOOD: varied, almost any animal and insect food available by hunting, scavenging and pillage from other birds.

STATUS: common. TAXONOMY: species extending to Celebes.

Genus EGRETTA

Members of this genus are the only species of the family which have filamentous ornamental plumes, or aigrettes, in the breeding season, hence the name 'egret' used for most. Also they are white or have a white phase, as in the Reef Heron. (The Cattle Egret, a recent colonist, is also white and has plumes but the plumes are not filamentous.) There are eight species in this worldwide group of which four occur in Australia.

91 REEF HERON *Egretta sacra* (Gmelin) 1789   Fig p 71

Distribution: throughout in suitable coastal localities.

RECOGNITION: *frequenting rocky coasts; yellow legs, crest of filamentous plumes when breeding; similar white and dark birds often together.*

DESCRIPTION: 60cm. Sexes alike. Dimorphic. *Breeding* (both phases): similar to non-breeding plumage with the addition of long filamentous plumes on nape, upper back and base of foreneck. *Non-breeding:* (1) white; bare skin of face greenish-yellow; bill yellow; eyes yellow; legs greenish-yellow; (2) head, neck and upperparts brownish-black with grey-blue gloss; chin and throat white; breast and belly dark grey-brown; bill grey-brown.

[*Note.* White phase gets increasingly common towards north and rare towards south; the two phases freely interbreed.]

HABITAT: rocky shores and reefs of mainland and coastal islands. HABITS: mainly terrestrial, feeding among intertidal rocks and reefs, roosting and nesting on rocky islets; solitary or loosely gregarious; sedentary; stands in hunched attitude singly or in pairs when not feeding; flies with head retracted. BREEDING: most months but mainly September–January; nests on ground and rocky ledges, sometimes in low bushes, made of sticks and twigs; two to five eggs, pale green. VOICE: harsh croak. FOOD: small marine animals.

STATUS: fairly common. TAXONOMY: species extending to New Zealand and southeast Asia.

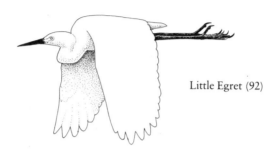

Little Egret (92)

92 LITTLE EGRET *Egretta garzetta* (Linnaeus) 1766
Distribution: Map 6.

RECOGNITION: *bill and legs black, unlike larger and often more common White Egret; distinguished in breeding plumage by breast plumes and long slender plumes on nape; usually more active than the larger species.*

DESCRIPTION: 56–60cm. Sexes alike. *Breeding:* white; two long slender plumes on nape; plumes at base of foreneck; plumes on back, extending about 5cm beyond tail; bare skin of face yellow; bill black, yellow at base; eyes yellow; legs black, underside of toes greenish-yellow. *Non-breeding:* similar but without plumes.

HABITAT: mainly coastal waters, foreshores, margins of tidal pools, swamps, less frequently inland lakes and river margins. HABITS: feeds in shallow water, sandy beaches, tidal pools, mud flats, sometimes 'puddling'; roosts and nests in trees in or near water; usually gregarious, often in company with other species, especially White Egret; sedentary and nomadic or migratory, travelling considerable distances; flies with head retracted. BREEDING: October–May; nests in trees of swamps and water margins, usually high up when with other species, made of sticks and twigs; four to five eggs, bluish-green. VOICE: harsh croak. FOOD: fish, crustacea, insects.

STATUS: uncommon, rare in south. TAXONOMY: race (*nigripes*) extending to Philippine Is of species widespread in old world.

93 PLUMED EGRET *Egretta intermedia* (Wagler) 1829   Fig p 71
Distribution: Map 7.

RECOGNITION: *bill yellow, legs blackish; breeding, plumes on back and breast but not on nape; bill orange.*

DESCRIPTION: 56–60cm. Sexes alike. *Breeding:* white; filamentous plumes on upper back, extending about 15cm beyond tail; plumes at base of foreneck; facial skin bright green; bill orange-red, yellow at tip; eyes reddish-orange; legs blackish with some red above 'knee'. *Non-breeding:* similar but plumes lost, also facial skin, bill and eyes become yellow.

HABITAT: inland and coastal waters, swampy margins of rivers and lakes, generally less common on coasts. HABITS: feeds along margins of swamps and adjacent grasslands, roosts and nests in trees; sometimes solitary but usually gregarious, often nesting with other species of similar habits; sedentary and nomadic, sometimes dispersing widely; flies with head retracted. BREEDING: October–May; nests in trees in or near water, at varying heights, frequently between 3–6m, made of sticks and twigs; three to four eggs, pale green. VOICE: various hoarse croaking sounds. FOOD: small animals, fish and insects.

STATUS: fairly common, rare in south. TAXONOMY: race *(plumifera)* extending to New Guinea of species widespread in southern Asia and Africa.

94 WHITE EGRET *Egretta alba* (Linnaeus) 1758

Distribution: throughout.

RECOGNITION: *bill and legs yellow, unlike smaller and usually less common Little Egret; distinguished in breeding plumage by plumes on back only.*

DESCRIPTION: over 1m, with neck extended. Sexes alike. *Breeding:* white; filamentous plumes on upper back extending well beyond tail; facial skin greenish; bill yellow; eyes reddish; legs black, reddish-brown above 'knee'. *Non-breeding:* similar but plumes lost; facial skin, eyes and bill yellow; legs above 'knee' dull grey or yellowish.

HABITAT: coastal and inland waters, muddy and swampy margins of lagoons, estuaries, rivers, lakes. HABITS: feeds on mud banks, shallow waters, floating vegetation on swamps, moist grasslands; nests and roosts in trees; often solitary when feeding, or in small parties, gregarious when nesting, usually in mixed colonies with species of similar habits; sedentary and nomadic; moves rather slowly and deliberately, like *Ardea* species; flies with head retracted. BREEDING: October–March; nests in trees 3–10m, or in topmost branches of mangroves, made of sticks and twigs; three to four eggs, pale bluish-green. VOICE: hoarse croak. FOOD: fish, small animals, insects.

STATUS: common. TAXONOMY: race *(modestus)* extending to India and east Asia of world-wide species.

Genus ARDEA

Eleven species are distinguished in this group of herons and they are found throughout the temperate and tropical regions of the world. Three are in Australia and of these the White-necked is found nowhere else. A feature of the group is the long lanceolate feathers, or 'hackles' which appear in the breeding season. Two Australian species are common and widespread; they have fairly slender bills and the main flight feathers are darker than the rest of the wing. In the Great-billed Heron, a species confined to north of the tropic, the bill is thicker and wing feathers are uniformly coloured.

95 WHITE-FACED HERON *Ardea novaehollandiae* Latham 1790   Pl 2

Distribution: throughout.

RECOGNITION: *blue-grey with white face and throat.*

DESCRIPTION: 60cm, with neck extended. Sexes alike. *Breeding:* long hackle feathers on lower foreneck and edge of back (scapular); forehead, face and throat white; remainder of upperparts mainly shades of dark blue-grey, blackish on crown and main flight feathers; paler on breast, belly and undershoulders, tinged with cinnamon-brown on hackle feathers and sometimes on belly; facial skin blue-grey; bill black, pale grey at base of lower mandible; eyes pale greenish-yellow; legs yellow. *Non-breeding:* similar but all ornamental hackles lost.

HABITAT: coastal and inland swamps, mud flats, shallow bays, wet grasslands. HABITS: feeds in shallow waters, intertidal zones, moist pastures, nests and roosts in trees; sometimes solitary or in pairs away from water but often feeding at all seasons in large flocks on tidal flats and estuaries; apparently sedentary apart from nomadic feeding movements; often 'puddles' pools to stir up food; flies with head retracted. BREEDING: most months but mainly July–April; nests in trees, sometimes up to a kilometre or so from water, a rough platform of sticks and twigs; three to five eggs, pale green. VOICE: a loud harsh croak. FOOD: small crustacea, frogs, insects.

STATUS: common. TAXONOMY: species extending to New Zealand and New Guinea.

96 WHITE-NECKED HERON *Ardea pacifica* Latham 1801 Pl 2

Distribution: throughout.

RECOGNITION: *white head and neck on otherwise blackish body.*

DESCRIPTION: 75cm, with neck extended; wingspan 1·6m. Sexes alike. *Breeding:* feathers at edge of back (scapulars) and lower foreneck extended into long hackles; head and neck white, lower neck hackles maroon; remainder of upperparts mainly black with bluish-green sheen; breast and belly brownish-grey with broad white central streaks; broad band of white at edge of shoulder; facial skin greenish-yellow; bill black, base of lower mandible yellow; eyes pale green to greenish-yellow; legs blackish. *Non-breeding:* similar but without ornamental hackles.

HABITAT: fresh water localities, seldom on coasts; moist grasslands, near dams and waterholes, edges of marshes and creeks. HABITS: feeds on ground, nests and roosts on trees and cliffs; usually solitary at all seasons but sometimes breeding in small colonies; sedentary and nomadic, occasionally subject to irruptions; flies with head retracted. BREEDING: mainly September–April and sometimes depending on rains; nests in trees, small or large, sometimes on sides of cliffs, made of sticks and twigs; four eggs, green. VOICE: harsh croak. FOOD: various small animals and insects.

STATUS: common. TAXONOMY: near endemic species; few in south New Guinea.

97 GREAT-BILLED HERON *Ardea sumatrana* Raffles 1822

Distribution: Map 8.

RECOGNITION: *very large, all dark; coastal swamps of the north.*

DESCRIPTION: 1·5m, with neck extended; bill 18cm. Sexes alike. *Breeding:* feathers at edge of back (scapulars) and lower foreneck extended into short hackles; upperparts blackish-brown with slight purple sheen, feathers of nape slightly extended and with white shafts; underparts grey-brown, whitish mottled with brown on chin and throat, hackle feathers darker and streaked with white, paler on belly and edge of shoulder; facial skin yellow; bill black, tip of lower mandible yellow; eyes yellow; legs brownish-black. *Non-breeding:* similar but lacking hackle feathers of back and breast.

HABITAT: coastal swamps, rarely inland except along lower reaches of large rivers. HABITS: feeds on mud flats and along shallow margins of lagoons and estuaries, nests and roosts in trees; apparently solitary at all seasons; apparently sedentary; movements slow and deliberate. BREEDING: probably extended, records from July, November, February, April; nests in trees over or near water, a rough platform of sticks; two eggs, pale blue-green. VOICE: deep guttural roar repeated several times, mostly at night. FOOD: various aquatic animals.

STATUS: rare and apparently shrinking in numbers. TAXONOMY: species extending to Burma; perhaps race of, or at least semispecies with two other species in southern Asia and Africa.

Family CICONIIDAE

Storks

1(17) species

STORKS ARE LARGE BIRDS with long necks and legs, stout bills, broad wings and short tails. In spite of their size they are strong fliers, some species travelling very long distances. Plumages are white with black areas on head, wings and tail. Storks are more clumsy in

Distribution of CICONIIDAE

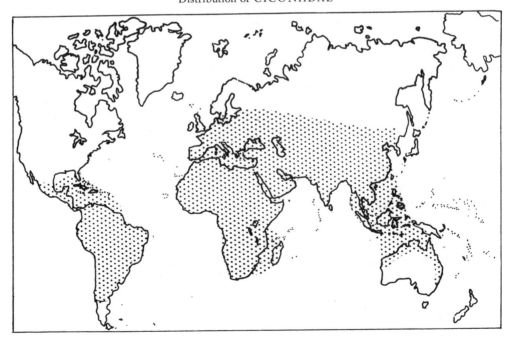

appearance than the graceful cranes which are of the same general size and proportions, but typically grey. The single stork representative in Australia is commonly called Jabiru, a name first given to a related species in South America and used also for other species. The alternative name of Blacknecked Stork for the Australian bird would be more specific.

98 JABIRU *Xenorhynchus asiaticus* (Latham) 1790

Distribution: Map 9.

RECOGNITION: *large size; white with black head and neck, black tail, white wingtips, long bill, long red legs; flies with neck extended.*

DESCRIPTION: 120cm, with neck extended and including bill 30cm; stands 120cm on 60cm legs; wingspan 2·2m. Sexes alike. Head and neck black with dark green sheen and patch of glossy purplish-bronze on nape; body white; wing white with broad black band on shoulders; tail black with green sheen; bill black; eyes white, yellow or reddish; legs deep pink.

HABITAT: coastal and inland waters, rivers and creeks with small pools as well as large estuaries and lagoons. HABITS: feeds on ground, nests and roosts in trees; often solitary but naturally gregarious; sedentary with strong nomadic tendencies. BREEDING: variable, but usually March–June in the north and August–April in the south; nests in trees, as high as possible, loosely made of sticks and twigs and lined with grass and strips of bark; four to six eggs, whitish. VOICE: probably booming, but rarely used or heard; loud clappering sounds made by bill. FOOD: fish and various small aquatic animals and insects.

STATUS: rare to uncommon, locally fairly common. TAXONOMY: species extending to southeast Asia and India.

Glossy Ibis (101)

Jabiru (98)

Family THRESKIORNITHIDAE

Ibises, Spoonbills

5(32) species: 2 endemic

IBISES AND SPOONBILLS ARE considered to be divisions of the same family in spite of the great disparity in the shapes of their bills. Both are widely distributed in tropical and temperate regions of the world, usually frequenting the vicinity of fresh water. Ibises are more common in number of species (26); three occur in Australia and of these the Straw-necked Ibis is peculiar to the continent, apart from a few birds which straggle across Torres St into southern New Guinea. Ibises are rather more or rather less than sixty centimetres in length with long necks, extended in flight, and long thin decurved bills which are stouter than those of curlews which are about the same size. Plumages vary from wholly white to wholly dark, sometimes glossy; head and neck are sometimes bare. Spoonbills are similar in size but plumages are usually white. Of the six species, two are common in Australia and the Yellow-billed is endemic. Bills are unique and unmistakable features; they are long and stout and end in a wide flat 'spoon' whose function is to sift small organisms when the bill is swept from side to side through the surface of the water.

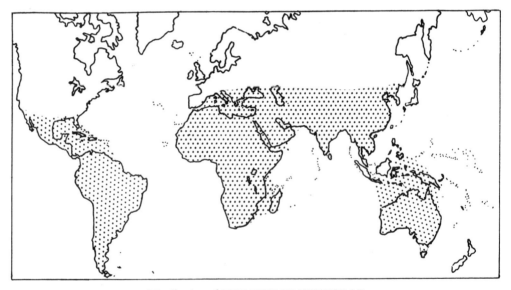

Distribution of THRESKIORNITHIDAE

Key to THRESKIORNITHIDAE

1 Bill spoon-shaped.............................. 3–4 (Spoonbills)
2 Bill long and decurved......................... 5–7 (Ibises)

3 Bill and legs black .... Royal Spoonbill.......... No 102
4 Bill and legs yellow .... Yellow-billed Spoonbill .... No 103

5 White with black on tail and wings............... White Ibis............. No 99
6 Black above with white tail, white below.......... Straw-necked Ibis .... No 100
7 Wholly dark .... Glossy Ibis .... No 101

Genus THRESKIORNIS

A group of four white birds with at least head and neck and wingtips black. The typical member of the group is the Sacred Ibis of Africa to which the Australian White Ibis bears a close resemblance. The Straw-necked Ibis is sometimes put in a separate genus because of the spiny feathers of the neck. Currently it is included with the others and there seems little doubt that it is related.

99 WHITE IBIS *Threskiornis molucca* (Cuvier) 1829
Distribution: Map 10.

RECOGNITION: *white with bald black head and half neck, black wingtips.*

DESCRIPTION: 75cm, with down-curved bill 15–18cm. Sexes alike. Mainly white; head and half neck bare and black, with pinkish scoring on nape and pinkish-brown half-moon under eye; main flight feathers tipped black with dull greenish sheen; some feathers of inner wing mottled greenish-black and a few are elongated and fanned out; bare skin at base of under-wing red; bill black; eyes dark brown; legs purplish-brown, pinkish above 'knee'.

HABITAT: fresh water, sometimes brackish and salt water, swamps and creeks, small pools and dams. HABITS: feeds and nests mainly on ground, roosts and sometimes nests in trees; gregarious, nesting in colonies; sedentary, extensively nomadic in relation to flood waters, probably at least partial north–south migration; stirs shallow water with open bill. BREEDING: variable, depending on flood waters, but mainly September–December in the south and February–June in the north; nests in flood water areas, on any vegetation strong enough to hold nests a metre or so above water level, occasionally in trees, a platform of trampled reeds strengthened with sticks; three to four white eggs. VOICE: grunts. FOOD: small animals, crustacea, insects.

STATUS: common. TAXONOMY: species extending to New Guinea, closely related to and forming superspecies with two others, or perhaps the three are races of a single species.

100 STRAW-NECKED IBIS *Threskiornis spinicollis* (Jameson) 1835   Pl 2
Distribution: throughout.

RECOGNITION: *mainly black above and white below with white tail, yellow 'straws' on foreneck.*

DESCRIPTION: 75cm, with down-curved bill 15–18cm. Sexes alike. Head, throat and upper neck bare and black with pink half-moon patch below eye; white collar; foreneck and upper breast black streaked with long yellow bare feather shafts; back and wings brownish-black glossed with bronze, green and purple; lower breast, belly and tail white; bare skin at angle of underwing yellow; bill black; eyes dark brown; legs black, reddish above 'knee'.

HABITAT: inland waters and adjacent grasslands. HABITS: feeds and nests on or near ground, roosts and sometimes nests in trees; gregarious, often seen in flocks feeding in or flying over pastoral land; sedentary, nomadic in relation to flood waters, perhaps also partially migratory as long distance south–north movements are recorded. BREEDING: variable, depending on flood waters but mainly September–January in south and April–June in north; nests in reed beds and other swamp vegetation, occasionally on open ground and in trees, made of trampled down vegetation and sticks; three to four white eggs. VOICE: grunts. FOOD: aquatic and terrestrial small animals, crustacea, insects—especially grasshoppers.

STATUS: very common. TAXONOMY: near endemic species; few in south New Guinea.

Genus PLEGADIS

Glossy Ibises are found from Australia to south Europe, Africa and South America. Although many populations are isolated by long distances, the current opinion is that they differ so slightly they can only be regarded as one species. The genus therefore consists of a single uniform species. It differs from other ibises not only in its glossy black plumage but in having dark green, instead of white, eggs.

101 GLOSSY IBIS *Plegadis falcinellus* (Linnaeus) 1766   Fig p 81

Distribution: throughout.

RECOGNITION: *blackish with long down-curved bill.*

DESCRIPTION: 56cm, with bill 13–15cm. Sexes alike. Head, neck, upper back, inner shoulders and underparts dark red-brown (maroon); back, tail and inner wings black with purplish gloss; wingtips black with oily green sheen; facial skin blue-green; bill greenish-brown, darker at base; eyes brown; legs black.

HABITAT: mostly inland waters and wet grasslands.

HABITS: feeds on ground, nests and roosts in bushes and trees; gregarious, usually nesting among other ibises and herons; sedentary and nomadic, possibly also regular seasonal movements between breeding and non-breeding areas. BREEDING: few data, but apparently October–February, possibly at other times depending on conditions; nests in bushes and trees, usually low down and above water, in forks or among branches, made of twigs often with leaves attached, sometimes old nests adapted; three to four eggs, dark greenish-blue. VOICE: various low harsh sounds. FOOD: small aquatic and terrestrial animals and insects.

STATUS: mostly rare but locally fairly common, as in northern Northern Territory. TAXONOMY: typical form of cosmopolitan species.

Genus PLATALEA

All spoonbills, of which six are currently recognised, are now placed in one genus, and in a subfamily (sometimes family) separate from the ibises. The curious shape of their bills, highly specialised for feeding, is probably one of the best known features of birds. The two Australian species are easily distinguished, one having black bill and legs and the other yellow. They differ also in that the Yellow-billed has filamentous plumes on the inner flight feathers in the breeding season whereas the Royal has ornamental plumes on the nape. Both are characteristically seen in shallow waters sweeping their bills for small aquatic organisms.

102 ROYAL SPOONBILL *Platalea regia* Gould 1838

Distribution: Map 11.

RECOGNITION: *white with long straight bill, wide and flat at the tip; bill and legs black.*

DESCRIPTION: 75cm, with bill 18–20cm, flat and very wide at tip. Sexes alike. *Breeding:* white; feathers of nape extended about 15cm to form an ornamental nuchal crest; facial skin black with small patches of reddish-orange on forehead and above and below eye; bill black; eyes dark red; legs black. *Non-breeding:* similar but without nape plumes.

HABITAT: coastal and inland swamps and marshes. HABITS: feeds and nests on or near ground, roosts and nests in trees; gregarious; sedentary and nomadic; when feeding on small aquatic organisms sweeps bill through water from side to side. BREEDING: variable, according to rains, but mainly between October and April; nests in swamp vegetation, bushes and sometimes trees, made of trampled vegetation and twigs, in trees at varying heights, sometimes right on top and made of broken green twigs; three to five white eggs. VOICE: low grunt; sounds also made by bill clappering. FOOD: small aquatic animals and insects and small organisms sifted from water.

STATUS: fairly common. TAXONOMY: species extending to New Zealand, New Guinea and Celebes, forming a superspecies with other forms in southern Asia and Africa.

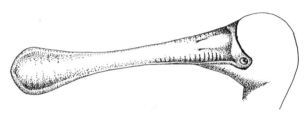

Yellow-billed Spoonbill (103)

103 YELLOW-BILLED SPOONBILL   *Platalea flavipes*   Gould 1838

Distribution: Map 12.

RECOGNITION: *white with long straight bill, wide and flat at tip, bill and legs yellow.*

DESCRIPTION: just under 1m, with bill 18–20cm, flat and very wide at tip. Sexes alike. *Breeding:* white with long hackle feathers on lower foreneck, some main flight feathers narrowly tipped with black, tip of some inner flight feathers black and frayed out into a curled spray; facial skin lilac-blue with narrow black margin; bill yellow; eyes pale yellow or whitish; legs yellow. *Non-breeding:* similar but without ornamental plumes.

HABITAT: coastal and inland swamps and marshes, also temporarily flooded areas (probably because more nomadic than the Royal). HABITS: feeds on water margins, nests among water vegetation, roosts and nests in trees; gregarious, sometimes nesting in mixed flocks with other species; sedentary and nomadic, probably more so than the Royal; sifts small organisms from water by sweeping tip of bill from side to side along the surface. BREEDING: variable, according to rains, records for most months; nests in swamp vegetation, bushes and trees in swamps, at varying heights in trees depending on associated species, made of trampled vegetation supported with sticks and twigs; three to five white eggs. VOICE: low grunt; clappering sounds with bill. FOOD: small aquatic animals and insects, and small organisms sifted from water.

STATUS: fairly common. TAXONOMY: endemic species.

Family ANATIDAE

Swans, Geese, Ducks

23 (147) species: 10 endemic, 2 introduced

Distribution: worldwide.

THE TERM WATERFOWL IS sometimes popularly used for members of this family but it is a restricted definition as many birds in other families could be included in the full sense of the word. The Anatidae are distinguished by such features as webbed feet, large bills often flattened and sometimes spatulate, stout bodies, necks usually fairly long to very long, eggs mainly white and unspotted. The numerous species are widely distributed throughout the world in aquatic habitats, largely inland waters and coastal estuaries and lagoons, less frequently in salt water and rarely far from land. They are mainly vegetarian, the swans and ducks being 'wet' feeders, browsing in water shallow enough to plumb with long necks and by up-ending like a sinking ship, or by diving to graze in deeper waters; a few species like the spatulate-billed ducks, the Pink-eared Duck and Shoveler, are non-vegetarian, their diet being various water insects and small organisms. The true geese, which are not represented in Australia, are 'dry' feeders and graze like sheep, usually in pastures close to water; their place is taken here by the Wood Duck and Cape Barren Goose. The family is divided into three main sections. One consists solely of the Pied Goose, peculiar to Australia, which has many features not found in other members of the family. Perhaps it is an early offshoot from primitive Anatidae stock which survived and evolved in isolation, as did many other Australian birds and animals. Another subfamily consists of swans and geese and the less well known treeducks or whistleducks; included with them are two other distinctive endemic species, the Freckled Duck and Cape Barren Goose, whose true relationships are not easily determined. A common factor at least in all members of this section is that males and females are similarly plumaged. The third subfamily consists of numerous species collectively known as ducks. In most species the sexes are more or less differently plumaged and males have an annual 'eclipse' phase when they change to the subdued colours of the females, apart from some distinctive markings. Included here is another unique and peculiarly Australian species, the Musk Duck, whose sexual difference is not in plumage but in the presence or absence of a distinct lobe under the bill.

Key to ANATIDAE

[*Note:* Species in square brackets are of rare or uncertain occurrence.]

1 Over 1m, long S-shaped neck.
  Black with white wingtips . . . . Black Swan . . . . No 107
    White . . . . White Swan . . . . No 108
2 1m, uniformly grey . . . . Cape Barren Goose . . . . No 110
3 75cm, black and white, long neck . . . . Pied Goose . . . . No 104
4 60cm or under, variously coloured 5–36
5 Head and underparts white, thin black bib. (Note: male Cotton Teal looks similar but has dark crown and is much smaller.) . . . . Burdekin Shelduck . . . . No 112
6 Plain reddish-brown, white bar on wing, white under-wing (male has white eye) . . . . White-eyed Duck . . . . No 121
7 Head and upper back light brownish-grey, long buff upturned flank feathers . . . . Grass Whistleduck . . . . No 106

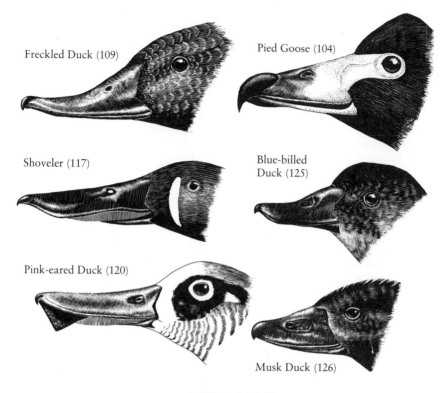

Freckled Duck (109)

Pied Goose (104)

Shoveler (117)

Blue-billed
Duck (125)

Pink-eared Duck (120)

Musk Duck (126)

ANATIDAE BILLS

8 Underparts barred brown and white, dark patch on eye, spatulate bill	Pink-eared Duck .... No 120	
9 Head and neck blackish, contrasting with back	13–21	
10 Back black, glossed green	22–25	
11 Upperparts blackish, no conspicuous markings.....	26–29	
12 Upperparts blackish, scalloped with white or cinnamon, conspicuous markings..................	30–36	
13 Breast speckled (♂, distinct 'mane')	Wood Duck .... No 122	
[Breast white, bill spatulate .... (♂)	Northern Shoveler........ No 118]	
14 Breast shades of brown	15–21	
15 White neck ring	17–18	
16 No white neck ring	19–21	
17 Bill black, body black	Mountain Shelduck....... No 111	
18 Bill yellow, body greyish..................... (♂)	Mallard.................. No 116	
19 Bill spatulate, white bar on face.............. (♂)	Shoveler .... No 117	
20 Bill blue-grey, no white on face .... (♂)	Chestnut Teal .... No 115	
21 Bill blue, body light chestnut .... (♂)	Blue-billed Duck .... No 125	
22 Neck black, glossed green.................... (♂)	Green Pygmy Goose .... No 123	
23 Neck white, black 'necklace' .... (♂)	Cotton Teal .... No 124	
24 Inconspicuous white superciliary.............. (♀)	Green Pygmy Goose .... No 123	
25 Conspicuous white superciliary .... (♀)	Cotton Teal .... No 124	
26 Plumage speckled white, long saddle-shaped bill ...	Freckled Duck .... No 109	

27 Plumage finely barred with white   28–29
28 Bill wedge-shaped (♂, lobe under bill) ....   Musk Duck .... No 126
29 Bill saddle-shaped .... (♀)   Blue-billed Duck .... No 125
30 Shoulders and belly chestnut ....   Water Whistleduck .... No 105
31 Iridescent speculum in wing   32–37
32 Speculum purple, edged white .... (♀)   Mallard.................. No 116
33 Speculum green, shoulders blue .... (♀)   Shoveler .... No 117
    [Speculum green, pale superciliary........... (♀)   Garganey .... No 119]
    [Same but with shoulders blue-grey.......... (♂)   Garganey (eclipse) .... No 119]
34 Speculum green, edged black   35–36
35 Face and throat whitish ....   Grey Teal .... No 114
36 Face and throat dark........................ (♀)   Chestnut Teal .... No 115

Genus ANSERANAS

The features of the Pied Goose are so unique that it is placed in a subfamily of its own; some authorities would have it in a separate family. Among other things the toes are only partly joined by a web (hence the *semipalmata* in its scientific name), the plumage is boldly pied, neck and legs are long and there is a distinct bony protuberance on the crown; also it can fly even when the wing quills are being moulted. It is a peculiarly Australian species except for erratic occurrences in New Guinea, suggesting that it may be extending its range.

104 PIED GOOSE *Anseranas semipalmata* (Latham) 1798   Fig p 87

Distribution: Map 13.

RECOGNITION: *large and pied; white body with long black neck, black tail and wingtips.*

DESCRIPTION: 75cm in length and height, with head and neck 30cm; top of skull extended into bony knob. Sexes nearly alike, female smaller with less distinct knob. Black parts are head and neck, wings except edge of shoulder, tail and thighs; remainder white; bill and facial skin reddish-brown; eyes brown; legs bright yellow.

HABITAT: swamps and marshy borders of lagoons and rivers. HABITS: terrestrial and aquatic, also perches and roosts in trees; gregarious at all seasons; nomadic. BREEDING: irregular, determined by rains; nests among tall reeds in shallow water, made of swamp vegetation; six to ten white eggs, glossy and pitted. VOICE: shrill trumpet or honking calls, soft whistles and grunting cackles (voices are different in males and females). FOOD: vegetable material.

STATUS: locally abundant in north, becoming less common in south. TAXONOMY: unique species, genus and subfamily, extending into southeast New Guinea.

Genus DENDROCYGNA

The eight species of whistleducks, pantropic in range, have features which are characteristic of both swans and geese, short stumpy bodies and fairly long necks and legs. The flank feathers are sometimes extended into ornamental plumes. The sexes are alike. Although often called treeducks they are on the whole less arboreal than some other members of the family. The two Australian species are found mainly in northern regions. Whistleducks are usually in dense flocks, on water or land, and swim or stand very erect with necks stretched up, and maintain a constant whistling. The Grass Whistleduck feeds mainly on land and the Water Whistleduck on the water, where it dives constantly.

105 WATER WHISTLEDUCK *Dendrocygna arcuata* (Horsfield) 1837   Pl 2

Distribution: Map 14.

RECOGNITION: *blackish upperparts, chestnut shoulders and belly, black legs, closely packed flocks.*

DESCRIPTION: 46cm. Sexes alike. Upperparts brownish-black, feathers of back barred and tipped with cinnamon-rufous, upper tail coverts white; shoulders dark chestnut; face and sides of neck buff-brown, paler shade on throat; lower foreneck and breast cinnamon-brown speckled with black; belly cinnamon-rufous; elongated feathers on flanks broadly streaked black and pale buff; bill black; eyes reddish-brown; legs black.

HABITAT: mainly permanent lagoons and swamps in coastal areas. HABITS: feeds by diving, nests and roosts on ground, rarely roosts in trees; gregarious, typically congregating in large close-packed flocks; sedentary with local movements associated with feeding. BREEDING: December–April, depending on rains; nests on ground among grass near or some distance from water, a scrape usually lined with grass; about twelve eggs, creamy. VOICE: shrill whistle. FOOD: water vegetation.

STATUS: abundant locally in north, rare and declining in south. TAXONOMY: race *(australis)* extending to New Guinea of variable species ranging throughout much of Papuan region.

106 GRASS WHISTLEDUCK *Dendrocygna eytoni* (Eyton) 1838   Pl 2

Distribution: Map 15.

RECOGNITION: *barred breast, very elongated flank plumes, pink legs, upright posture, close-packed flocks.*

DESCRIPTION: 43cm. Sexes alike. Crown and hind neck yellowish-brown; back and wings grey-brown; rump and tail black, separated by pale buff upper tail coverts; face and sides of neck buff-brown; throat and upper breast pale buff-brown; lower breast cinnamon barred with black; belly white; elongated and wide upturned flank feathers buff, edged with black; bill mottled pink and black; eyes orange; legs pink.

HABITAT: grasslands bordering inland waters, sometimes coasts. HABITS: mainly terrestrial, feeds, nests and roosts on land at water margins, merely using water for alighting; gregarious, forming large flocks in special 'camp' areas; sedentary with local dispersal and concentration movements in relation to breeding and feeding, also nomadic in relation to drought and rains. BREEDING: associated with rains, mainly February–April in the north and August–October in the south; nests on ground, rough scrape lined with grass; about twelve white eggs. VOICE: shrill whistle. FOOD: land vegetation, mainly grasses.

STATUS: common and thriving. TAXONOMY: endemic species, except for sporadic occurrence in southeast New Guinea.

Genus CYGNUS

Swans inhabit temperate and subarctic regions, five kinds in the northern hemisphere and two in the southern, one in South America and the other the endemic Black Swan of Australia. The Mute Swan of Europe has been introduced. Swans are among the largest, or heaviest, of flying birds. Their long necks are extended in flight, and legs are short. They are clumsy on land but graceful on water, where they browse on vegetation obtained at depths within reach of their long necks, and by up-ending. The sexes are alike in plumage.

107 BLACK SWAN *Cygnus atratus* (Latham) 1790

Distribution: Map 16, but also elsewhere in suitable habitats.

RECOGNITION: *large and black with white wingtips, long curved neck extended in flight.*

DESCRIPTION: body 60cm, neck and head 45cm. Sexes alike. Black with grey edges to back feathers and main flight feathers white, usually only visible in flight; bill reddish-orange with white bar near tip; eyes red or white; legs dark grey.

HABITAT: aquatic, feeding in shallow water with head submerged and by up-ending; mainly gregarious but less so when breeding; sedentary and nomadic, moving at night more than by day and in V-shaped skeins; flight strong and direct with outstretched neck. BREEDING: variable, determined by rains; nests in dense water vegetation, or on ground, but apparently only on islands, a rough platform of sticks and vegetation; five to ten eggs, pale green. VOICE: high pitched and flute-like. FOOD: water vegetation.

STATUS: abundant and thriving. TAXONOMY: endemic species. (Introduced to New Zealand.)

Introduced species

108 MUTE SWAN *Cygnus olor* (Gmelin) 1789

Distribution: restricted mainly to ornamental waters; a few feral colonies in Tasmania and extreme southwest.

RECOGNITION: *like Black Swan but white; juveniles grey.*

Genus STICTONETTA

Taxonomists are still puzzled to find the correct place of the Freckled Duck in this family. Its relationships are obscure and it is placed in a genus of its own, although it has features, mainly anatomical, which connect it with several major groups; a current opinion is that it may be closest to the geese and swans. It has a uniformly speckled appearance, no iridescent patch on the wing and the sexes are alike in plumage. It would seem to belong to some ancient, probably primitive stock which has survived, like many other Australian forms, because of isolation and perhaps minimal human interference.

109 FRECKLED DUCK *Stictonetta naevosa* (Gould) 1840   Fig p 87

Distribution: throughout.

RECOGNITION: *uniformly dark, speckled with white, lacking distinctive markings except red base of bill in breeding male.*

DESCRIPTION: 56cm. Sexes nearly alike, female paler and lacks red base of bill. Head, neck and upperparts marbled blackish-brown and dark grey-brown and speckled with white, darker on crown, paler on throat and foreneck and buffier on lower foreneck; breast and belly brownish-white speckled with dark brown; under shoulders marbled brown and white; bill dark blue-grey, reddish at base when breeding, flattened and wider at tip and slightly upturned; eyes brown; legs blue-grey.

HABITAT: fresh water with thick vegetation, especially 'cumbungi and tea-tree swamps'. HABITS: mainly aquatic, feeds in shallow water by up-ending, usually at night, roosts during day in dense cover or far out in open water; gregarious, but in small parties and frequently mixed in flocks of other ducks; sedentary, with strong nomadic tendencies. BREEDING: variable, depending on suitable water level, but usually September–December; nests on water margins in bushes or flood debris, or on leaning tree limbs, a shallow cup of twigs and sticks lined with fine twigs and down; five to nine eggs, dull white or cream. VOICE: various flute-like notes and piping calls. FOOD: aquatic vegetation.

STATUS: rather uncommon and possibly declining. TAXONOMY: unique endemic species.

Genus CEREOPSIS

The relationships of the Cape Barren Goose, the sole member of this genus, are uncertain, like many other unique Australian forms; an extinct relative has been recorded from New Zealand. Superficially at least it has some goose-like characteristics—plump body, fairly long neck, short bill, strong legs—but these are features which could have evolved because of similar grazing habits. The current opinion is that it belongs in the 'duck' subfamily near the shelducks and may be a primitive link with the 'goose' subfamily.

110 CAPE BARREN GOOSE *Cereopsis novaehollandiae* Latham 1801

Distribution: coastal islands and sometimes mainland from Cape Leeuwin to Bass St and New South Wales border.

RECOGNITION: *large and grey, black tail (above) and black trailing edge to wings in flight, short thick bill.*

DESCRIPTION: 1m; stands 85cm. Sexes alike. Ash-grey with white crown and scattered black spots on shoulders; tail black above, grey below; tip of all flight feathers black making black rear margin to wings in flight; bill black and almost covered by yellowish-green cere; eyes reddish-brown; legs dull pink, feet black.

HABITAT: grasslands. HABITS: terrestrial, seldom on water, sometimes nests in trees; gregarious, but fairly dispersed when breeding, at other times forming small or large flocks depending on numbers available; sedentary with local dispersals from breeding grounds to feeding areas. BREEDING: apparently between May and December; nests on ground, sometimes in

Cape Barren Goose (110)

Mountain Shelduck (111)

bushes and dense tree thickets, sometimes exposed rocky ledges, made of grass and other local vegetation, lined with down; four to five white eggs. VOICE: 'low-pitched grunt'; also (males only) 'high-pitched rapid honking'. FOOD: vegetation, mainly grasses.

STATUS: total population small, perhaps increasing. TAXONOMY: unique endemic species and genus.

Genus TADORNA

The species which comprise this genus, of which there are seven widely scattered throughout the old world, are commonly known as shelducks or, less frequently now, as sheldrakes. It would indicate their affinities if the two Australian species had 'shelduck' instead of 'duck' in their names, as used here. Shelducks are considered to be a link between the goose and duck subfamilies, and to outward appearance at least they seem to have features of both; they have moderately long necks and sturdy legs and sexes are similar in plumage.

111 MOUNTAIN SHELDUCK   *Tadorna tadornoides*   (Jar. & Selb.) 1828   Fig p 91
Distribution: Map 17.

RECOGNITION: *black head, neck and bill, white shoulders above and below in flight, male has white neck ring, female white eyering.*

DESCRIPTION: 60cm. Sexes slightly different. *Male:* head and upper neck black; narrow white collar; lower neck, upper breast and upper back rufous-brown; lower back, lower breast and belly blackish-brown finely mottled with white; rump and tail black; shoulders above and below white; inner wing chestnut; centre of wing black, glossed dull green; main flight feathers black; bill black; eyes dark brown; legs black. *Female:* similar but with white ring around eye, white at base of bill and lacking white collar.

HABITAT: coastal waters, preferably salt or brackish, and inland waters, sometimes up to high altitudes, especially when not breeding. HABITS: aquatic and terrestrial, often wandering some distance from water to feed and nest, sometimes nesting in trees; gregarious when not breeding, especially on open waters during moult, dispersing in isolated pairs to breed; more or less sedentary apart from dispersal movements; flies in V-shaped skeins. BREEDING: mainly January–September; nests in holes in trees up to about 16m, or in holes and crevices on ground; six to ten creamy eggs. VOICE: a deep honk. FOOD: aquatic and terrestrial vegetation and insects.

STATUS: common. TAXONOMY: endemic species.

112 BURDEKIN SHELDUCK   *Tadorna radjah*   (Garnet) 1828
Distribution: Map 17.

RECOGNITION: *white head and underparts with narrow chestnut band on breast.*

DESCRIPTION: 50cm. Sexes alike. Head, neck and underparts white; narrow chestnut band on upper breast and continued on to sides of back; remainder of upperparts and tail black; shoulders white, central feathers with narrow chestnut bar near tip; main flight feathers black, inner flight feathers dull glossy green with white tips and innermost feathers black with a broad streak of dark chestnut; bill pinkish-white; eyes white; legs pinkish-white.

HABITAT: brackish coastal waters, sometimes moving up river systems in dry periods and when not breeding, rarely more than a few yards from water edge. HABITS: feeds along water margins on foot, roosts and nests in water timber; gregarious; sedentary with local dispersal movements; flies swiftly and noisily through timber. BREEDING: April–July; nests in holes in trees, on bare wood or lined with down; six to twelve eggs, creamy white. VOICE: 'hoarse whistle' (male); 'harsh rattling' (female). FOOD: small aquatic animals and vegetation.

STATUS: fairly common but much affected by human interference. TAXONOMY: endemic race (*rufitergum*) of species extending to New Guinea and adjacent islands.

Genus ANAS

This is the main group of dabbling or surface-feeding ducks, as distinct from diving ducks; they feed on water margins or in shallow water by up-ending. The group is worldwide and consists of about thirty-five species, depending on certain isolated forms which could be species or races; associated with this group are a number of apparently aberrant forms which are put in separate genera. These ducks are squat, short-necked and short-legged, rather clumsy on land but gracefully buoyant on water; bills are fairly long and flattened, some excessively so as in the case of the shovellers. A feature of most species is a marked degree of sexual dimorphism and an annual 'eclipse' phase in males when they moult out of their bright colours into the more subdued patterns of the females. The genus is poorly represented in Australia by only four species and two are sexually dimorphic. The Chestnut Teal is endemic. Another species, the Garganey, has been recorded a number of times and perhaps occurs fairly frequently; it is a regular winter visitor to the Papuan area from breeding grounds in the northern hemisphere.

Key to ANAS

1 Crown blackish, two white and one black streak on face	Black Duck	No 113
2 Whole head blackish, contrasting with back	4–6	
3 Head relatively pale	7–11	
4 Vertical white streak on face (♂)	Shoveler	No 117
5 White collar (♂)	Mallard	No 116
6 No white on face or neck (♂)	Chestnut Teal	No 115
7 Shoulder pale blue		
Bill spatulate, common (♀)	Shoveler	No 117
Bill not spatulate, rare	Garganey	No 119
8 Speculum purple, underwing white (♀)	Mallard	No 116
9 Speculum green, underwing dark	10–11	
10 Face and throat whitish	Grey Teal	No 114
11 Face and throat dark (♀)	Chestnut Teal	No 115

113 BLACK DUCK *Anas superciliosa* (Gmelin) 1789   Fig p 96

Distribution: throughout.

RECOGNITION: *mottled brown, blackish on crown, bold white and black streaks on face, relatively long neck, body thicker at rear.*

DESCRIPTION: 50cm. Sexes alike. Body dark brown thinly scalloped with buffy-white; crown and upper face blackish with two broad white and black streaks on face; lower face and throat pale buff; wing speculum dark green or purple bordered with black; underwing white, dusky at tip; bill greenish-grey; eyes brown; legs yellowish-green.

HABITAT: most kinds of coastal and inland waters, including city lakes and ponds. HABITS: mainly aquatic, feeding in shallow margins, rarely far from water except when nesting, sometimes nesting in trees; solitary and gregarious; sedentary with more or less regular dispersal movements. BREEDING: variable, depending on rains but usually March–October in north and January–May in south; nests on ground, in bushes and tree stumps, and in holes in trees, a scrape on ground or well constructed of available vegetation, lined with down; eight to ten eggs, white or pale buff. VOICE: high-pitched whistle (male); loud quack (female). FOOD: aquatic vegetation with some animal material.

STATUS: very common. TAXONOMY: race *(rogersi)* extending to New Guinea of species widespread in southwest Pacific, including New Zealand.

114 GREY TEAL *Anas gibberifrons* Muller 1842   Pl 2

Distribution: throughout.

RECOGNITION: *relatively pale head, almost white face and throat, white edge to speculum and white bar in centre of wing in flight.*

DESCRIPTION: 40cm. Sexes alike. Upperparts dark brown, scalloped with buffy-white on upper back, paler and speckled on crown; face and throat buffy-white; breast and belly mottled light and dark brown; feathers in centre of wing tipped white and forming a white bar in flight; speculum dull black with glossy green centre and with broad white forward margin; underwing blackish with small central patch of white; bill black; eyes reddish-brown; legs black.

HABITAT: most kinds of coastal and inland waters. HABITS: mainly aquatic, feeding on shallow margins and open water, rarely far from water except when nesting; solitary and gregarious, often in very large flocks; sedentary and nomadic, regular movements between inland breeding areas and coastal feeding grounds. BREEDING: variable, depending on rainfall; nests usually fairly high up in holes in trees in or near water, also in tall grass, unformed except for some down; six to ten eggs, creamy white. VOICE: soft peep (male); loud rapid quack (female). FOOD: vegetation, mainly aquatic, and small aquatic animals, especially molluscs when feeding in open coastal waters.

STATUS: very common. TAXONOMY: race *(gracilis)* extending to New Zealand and New Guinea of species ranging to Java and Celebes.

115 CHESTNUT TEAL *Anas castanea* (Eyton) 1838   Pl 2

Distribution: Map 18.

RECOGNITION: *male has black head and neck with green sheen, mottled body with chestnut breast, white patch on rear flanks; female has dark face and throat, not whitish as in similar Grey Teal.*

DESCRIPTION: 43cm. Sexes different. *Male:* head and neck black with green sheen; remainder of upperparts brownish-black, feathers of upper back edged with cinnamon-buff; breast and belly chestnut brown, darkest at base of neck and spotted with black; patch of white on rear flanks; speculum dull black glossed green, edged in front with broad band of white and at rear with narrow band of buff; patch of white in centre of underwing; undertail black; bill blue-grey; eyes reddish-brown; legs grey-green. *Female:* mottled shades of brown, no chestnut; like Grey Teal but darker, especially on face and throat.

HABITAT: preferably brackish coastal waters but also some inland waters. HABITS: mainly aquatic, feeding in shallow margins, seldom far from water except on islands, sometimes nesting in trees; solitary or gregarious, in small flocks, in Tasmania often large flocks, and frequently mixed with Grey Teal; mainly sedentary with local dispersal movements. BREED-ING: uncertain, apparently variable depending on locality and conditions, records between July and December; nests variable, scrapes on ground to holes in trees; seven to ten creamy eggs. VOICE: soft peep (male); loud repeated quack (female). FOOD: mostly aquatic vegetation.

STATUS: common. TAXONOMY: endemic species.

Introduced species

116 MALLARD *Anas platyrhynchos* Linnaeus 1758

RECOGNITION: 56cm. Sexes different. *Male: head and neck black glossed green and purple with narrow white collar*; body greyish with black rump and tail, the latter with a curl of upturned feathers; *purple speculum* bordered with white; breast purplish-brown. *Female*, and male eclipse: like Black Duck but browner and *lacks conspicuous black and white streaked pattern on face.*

STATUS: introduced and kept in domestication or semidomestication on ornamental waters. Some feral birds may be found, probably mixed with other species. Interbreeds freely, especially in domestication, and hybrids are likely to be seen.

117 SHOVELER *Anas rhynchotis* Latham 1801   Fig p 87
Distribution: Map 19.

RECOGNITION: *dark glossy head with vertical white streak in front of bright yellow eye; female—blue shoulders and white underwing.*

DESCRIPTION: 51cm, bill 7·5cm and expanded at tip. Sexes different. *Male:* crown and base of bill blackish-brown; face and neck blue-grey glossed green; vertical white crescent streak in front of eye; base of neck and upper back blackish-brown, feathers edged with buffy-white; lower back and tail black; breast, belly and flanks dark chestnut mottled with black; patch of white on rear flanks; scapulars (edge of back) extended and streaked pale blue, black and white; shoulders pale blue; white in centre of wing; speculum glossy green; under shoulders white, remainder black; bill greenish-brown; eyes yellow; legs yellow. *Male eclipse:* like female but wings brighter coloured and underparts more chestnut. *Female:* mottled blackish-brown and buff, finely streaked on face and neck and scalloped on back, darkest on crown and back, blackish on rump and tail, palest on underparts; shoulders dull blue; speculum dark grey with slight greenish sheen; bill black; eyes dark brown; legs dark grey.

HABITAT: coastal and inland waters, especially swamps. HABITS: mainly aquatic but sometimes nests away from water; solitary and gregarious, usually in very small parties, rarely large flocks and often mixed with other species; sedentary but nomadic when conditions unfavourable. BREEDING: variable, depending on rains but frequently August–December; nests usually on ground, a scrape lined with vegetation and down; nine to eleven creamy eggs. VOICE: inclined to be silent but male utters a soft 'took-took' and female quacks rather quietly. FOOD: aquatic vegetation and small animal life.

STATUS: uncommon and possibly declining. TAXONOMY: endemic race *(rhynchotis)* of species extending to New Zealand.

118 NORTHERN SHOVELER   *Anas clypeata*

This species was recorded by Gould in 1834 but the collected specimen was lost; the species has not been recorded since. It is not recorded south of Burma and southern China.

119 GARGANEY   *Anas querquedula*   Linnaeus 1758

Distribution: scattered records.

RECOGNITION: 38cm. Sexes different. *Male:* dark head with *curved white stripe from above eye to side of neck,* blue-grey shoulders, sharply contrasting brown breast and white belly. *Female* and male eclipse: like Grey Teal but darker head with fairly distinct pale *eyestripe, blue-grey shoulders.*

STATUS: rare; non-breeding visitor from northern hemisphere.

Genus MALACORHYNCHUS

Consists only of the unique Australian Pink-eared Duck. The affinities of this duck have not been determined with certainty but it is judged to be an aberrant, or very specialised form of a section of the subfamily of dabbling ducks. As well as its peculiar plumage pattern and skin-like flaps at the tip of the bill it has a white, not iridescent, speculum and the sexes are alike. It feeds on microscopic organisms sifted from water by hair-like fringes on the edges of the bill.

120 PINK-EARED DUCK   *Malacorhynchus membranaceus*   (Latham) 1801 Fig p 87

Distribution: throughout.

RECOGNITION: *head seems much larger than body and has large dark patch over eye, barred underparts, especially flanks.*

DESCRIPTION: 40cm, bill 6·5cm, wide at tip and extended with soft flaps. Sexes alike. Forehead pale grey-brown shading to darker on crown and back; rump and tail blackish with white upper tail coverts; dark brown patch on face continued as broad streak to hind neck; small patch of bright pink behind dark eye patch; narrow white ring around eye; remainder of face, neck and underparts white barred with brown, bars thin on neck and broad on breast and flanks; inner flight feathers tipped with white giving a narrow white inner trailing margin in flight; bill blue-grey; eyes brown; legs blue-grey.

HABITAT: inland waters, especially temporary shallow waters; uncommon in coastal localities.

HABITS: aquatic, feeding in shallow water with bill or head and neck immersed; gregarious,

Wood Duck (122)

Black Duck (113)

sometimes in large flocks; sedentary and nomadic. BREEDING: variable, depending on falling water level, but mainly August–October in south and March–May in north; nests in bushes and holes in trees, usually under 3m and over water, lined with down; five to seven eggs, creamy white. VOICE: recorded as a 'chirrup' and 'continuous trill'. FOOD: microscopic animals and plants obtained by sifting water through lamellae along edge of bill.

STATUS: very common. TAXONOMY: endemic species of not very certain relationships.

Genus AYTHYA

This is a section of a small worldwide group of mainly freshwater diving ducks. They have short stout bodies, large heads and big feet. Sexes are usually distinctly but not very strikingly different. The White-eyed Duck, the only Australian representative, is one of four old world species distinguished, among other things, by white eyes, only in males. They form a super-species if not races of one species.

121 WHITE-EYED DUCK *Aythya australis* (Eyton) 1838

Distribution: throughout.

RECOGNITION: *uniform dark upperparts with white patch on wing forming a conspicuous white bar on extended upper wing, white underwing, white eye in male only.*

DESCRIPTION: 51cm. Sexes slightly different. *Male:* upperparts dark red-brown (liver brown) shading to paler on flanks and lower belly; white patch in centre of wing which becomes broad white bar on open wing; underwing and undertail white; bill black with broad tip of pale blue-grey; eyes white; legs blue-grey. *Female:* paler than male; eyes red-brown; less pale blue-grey at tip of bill.

HABITAT: fresh water, preferably large stretches of open water, still or running. HABITS: mainly aquatic, feeds from surface and by diving; gregarious, often in large flocks; sedentary, nomadic if conditions are unfavourable—when very unfavourable flocks may suddenly depart and travel long distances outside their normal range (probably the origin of colonies far outside Australia, some of which may only have a temporary existence, as in New Zealand) BREEDING: variable, coinciding with end of flood periods; nests in water vegetation and over water in bushes and trees, neat and well formed of trodden-down vegetation and lined with down; nine to twelve eggs, creamy white. VOICE: inclined to be silent but male has a low whistle and female a harsh call. FOOD: mainly aquatic vegetation.

STATUS: common to uncommon and apparently declining. TAXONOMY: essentially endemic but irrupting externally and establishing populations which are doubtfully permanent.

Genus CHENONETTA

The Wood Duck, the sole member of this genus, is placed in an assemblage of species and genera collectively known as perching ducks. The Wood Duck is unique to Australia, other perching ducks are found in several continents. The alternative name of Maned Goose describes its appearance rather than affinities. The male has an extension of feathers of the nape, like a mane, slightly resembling its more flamboyant relative the Mandarin Duck. Goose-like features are short thick bill and fairly long neck and legs. These are derived from similar terrestrial grazing habits. The Wood Duck perches and nests in trees. Although equally at home in dry and wet areas, it requires open water, if only creek pools and stock dams, however small.

122 WOOD DUCK *Chenonetta jubata*   (Latham) 1801   Fig p 96

Distribution: throughout.

RECOGNITION: *short bill, fairly long neck and sturdy legs, dark head with 'mane' in male, speckled breast; often near dams, grazing or roosting on rim.*

DESCRIPTION: 48cm. Sexes different. *Male:* head, neck and 'mane' dark brown; upper back brownish-grey mottled with black; lower back and tail black; foreneck and breast boldly mottled buffy-white and blackish-brown; centre of belly and under tail black; flanks grey finely vermiculated; shoulders brownish-grey; speculum bright glossy green bordered with white, the broad rear edge becomes conspicuous white band in flight; main flight feathers black; under shoulders white; bill dark brown; eyes brown; legs dark greenish-brown. *Female:* head lighter brown than in male; face has two white bands separated by dark band through eye; upper back mainly white; upper tail coverts white between black rump and tail; breast and flanks mottled brown and white; centre of belly and undertail white.

HABITAT: mostly savanna woodlands with open water. HABITS: largely terrestrial, grazing and roosting on ground, seldom on water for long periods, nesting in trees; solitary when breeding, at other times gregarious and often in large flocks localised on a fixed roosting 'camp'; sedentary and nomadic; mostly feeding at night. BREEDING: variable, depending on new grass after rains, but mainly September–October in south and January–March in north; nests in holes in trees, lined with down; nine to eleven eggs, creamy white. VOICE: high-pitched mew and low cluck, also sound described as loud 'gnaroo'. FOOD: terrestrial green vegetation, mainly grasses.

STATUS: common, benefiting from land development in spite of heavy predation and extending in range and distribution in the southwest. TAXONOMY: endemic species and genus.

Genus NETTAPUS

A group of four species considered to belong to the assemblage of perching ducks. They range from Africa through India to Australia where there are two species in north and northeastern coastal areas. Collectively they are known as pygmy geese because of their small size—they are among the smallest members of the family—and because of the stumpy goose-like shape of their bills. These dumpy little ducks are quite distinctive in their glossy green and white plumages. They are almost entirely aquatic, rarely venturing on land where they move with difficulty, but perch, swim and dive well.

123 GREEN PYGMY GOOSE *Nettapus pulchellus*   (Gould) 1842   Pl 2

Distribution: Map 20.

RECOGNITION: *small, short goose-like bill; dark glossy green head with white face patch and white inner trailing edge of wing; among thick vegetation of tropical lagoons.*

DESCRIPTION: 33cm. Sexes slightly different. *Male:* head and upperparts glossy dark green with large patch of white on face below eye and small patch at base of bill; lower neck, flanks and upper tail coverts barred white and glossy green; breast and belly white; inner flight feathers white showing as white inner trailing edge of open wing; main flight feathers black; bill greenish-grey above, pinkish below; eyes dark brown; legs greenish-grey. *Female:* differs in having most of neck barred white and dark brown, white face and chin speckled with dark brown, indistinct pale eyebrow, very little barring on crown.

HABITAT: large permanent lakes and lagoons with swamp vegetation, especially water-lilies. HABITS: aquatic, feeds on surface and in short shallow dives, rarely on land where it is clumsy; nests in trees; solitary breeding but largely gregarious at other times, flocks usually small; sedentary but dispersing to breed in the 'wet' and collecting in flocks in the 'dry'. BREEDING: apparently between December and March; nest and eggs not well known, sites recorded in holes in trees standing in water and containing down; probably about eight to twelve creamy white eggs. VOICE: shrill musical whistles. FOOD: aquatic vegetation.

STATUS: common. TAXONOMY: species extending into southeast New Guinea.

124 COTTON TEAL *Nettapus coromandelianus* (Gmelin) 1789

Distribution: Map 21.

RECOGNITION: *small and squat, frequenting swampy lakes and lagoons, white head with dark streak from forehead to nape, short thick bill, male has narrow dark 'necklace', female has dark streak through eye.*

DESCRIPTION: 35cm. Sexes different. *Male:* narrow band from forehead to nape brown edged glossy green; remainder of head and underparts white with narrow dark glossy green band on breast; back, wings and tail black glossed with glints of green and bronze; centre of outer flight feathers and tip of inner feathers white, forming a broad white band in flight; flanks and upper tail coverts speckled brownish-grey; bill black; eyes bright red; legs olive green. *Female:* upperparts mostly dark brown with little green sheen; face, neck and upper breast dull white speckled dull brown; dark streak through eye, emphasising white streak above eye; eyes brown.

HABITAT: lakes and lagoons with dense growth of water lilies and other plants. HABITS: aquatic, feeding on surface, not known to dive; has curious habit of jerking head and neck; solitary breeding and gregarious at other times, flocks usually quite small; apparently sedentary with seasonal dispersal inland to breed during the 'wet' and congregating near coast in the 'dry'. BREEDING: (not much data) probably December–March where there are summer rains; nests recorded in holes in trees, high up and near water, lined with down; apparently up to about twelve eggs, off-white. VOICE: male, a rattling staccato cackle; female, a soft quack. FOOD: aquatic vegetation.

STATUS: fairly common. TAXONOMY: endemic race *(albipennis)* of species extending to Indo-Malaysia.

Cotton Teal (124)

Genus OXYURA

The stifftail ducks which form this group have a number of unusually distinctive features but it is not clear where they should be placed in the duck family. The shafts of the tail feathers are thick and hard, as in cormorants, bills of males are bright blue and bodies are mainly chestnut-coloured in the breeding season. Six species are recognised, ranging over several continents and commonest in the new world. The Blue-billed Duck of Australia is curiously isolated. It is an entirely freshwater duck and is completely aquatic.

125 BLUE-BILLED DUCK *Oxyura australis*   Gould 1837   Fig p 87
Distribution: Map 22.

RECOGNITION: *squat patternless body, blue bill and chestnut body of breeding male, stiff tail held erect in display, dives.*

DESCRIPTION: 40cm; tail has hard stiff shafts and narrow webs. Sexes different. *Male:* head and neck glossy black; body mainly chestnut, blacker on rump and buffy-white in centre of belly; wings and tail grey-brown; bill bright blue; eyes dark brown; legs grey. *Male eclipse:* head dull black speckled with grey; breast mottled grey and brown; back mottled dark and light brown; bill dull blue-grey. *Female:* mainly blackish-brown finely barred with buffy-white, whiter on throat and belly; bill and legs grey-brown.

HABITAT: rivers and permanent fresh water lakes with swamp vegetation. HABITS: aquatic, seldom and clumsy on land, dives for food, and to escape in preference to flying; dispersing to breed, at other times gregarious, often in large flocks; sedentary, nomadic and apparently with some regular seasonal movements. BREEDING: October–March; nests in and made from water vegetation, a rough cup-shaped depression usually containing down; five to six eggs, pale green. VOICE: male, 'a rapid low-pitched rattling note'; female, a 'weak quack'; but usually silent. FOOD: aquatic vegetation and insects.

STATUS: common. TAXONOMY: endemic species.

Genus BIZIURA

The Musk Duck is our only other member of the stifftail group and because of its unique features is placed in a genus of its own. There is little or no sexual difference in colour but the male is larger, has a conspicuously much larger lobe under the bill and a musky odour.

126 MUSK DUCK *Biziura lobata*   (Shaw) 1796   Fig p 87
Distribution: Map 23.

RECOGNITION: *uniformly blackish, short bill with dependent lobe in male, stiff spiked tail held erect in display.*

DESCRIPTION: male 65cm, female 56cm; shafts of tail thick and hard and webs narrow. Sexes alike except for size, conspicuous lobe under bill of male, and musky odour when breeding. Crown and hind neck black; remainder of upperparts, face, foreneck and flanks black finely barred with grey, greyer on face and foreneck; breast and belly white slightly mottled and barred with brownish-black; wings dark grey-brown; tail black; eyes dark brown; legs blackish.

HABITAT: deep permanent swamps, lakes, lagoons and estuaries. HABITS: aquatic, dives to feed; disperses to breed, gregarious at other times, usually small flocks; sedentary with nomadic tendencies, reluctant to fly and apparently does so mainly at night. BREEDING: August–December; nests in water vegetation, especially bushy tea-trees, made of vegetation, cup-shaped and lined with down; one to three eggs, greenish white. VOICE: piercing whistle, also a non-vocal 'plonk' sound. FOOD: aquatic animals and insects, some vegetation.

STATUS: fairly common. TAXONOMY: endemic species and genus.

BIRDS OF PREY

IN ITS WIDEST SENSE it could be said any bird that takes live food is a bird of prey. This definition would include a great number of species in many families, like butcherbirds, kookaburras and frogmouths. In a less general sense, it is sometimes used with the qualifications 'diurnal' for the various eagles, hawks and falcons, and 'nocturnal' for the owls. Unqualified it is usually intended to mean the former, the large assemblage included in the order Falconiformes, although the term 'raptor' for such 'diurnal birds of prey' is now often used. The Australian raptors consist of twenty-four species in the families Accipitridae, Falconidae and Pandionidae—the last a single cosmopolitan species, the fish-eating Osprey. A typical feature of these birds is a short thick curved bill, hooked at the tip for tearing up prey, with a fleshy cere at the base in which the nostrils are situated. They are not the only birds with this design for parrots also have hooked bills and use them for obtaining other kinds of food. An unusual characteristic common in birds of prey, but again not peculiar to them, is that the female is usually larger, sometimes much larger, than the male. The female Wedge-tailed Eagle, for example, is among the world's largest birds with an impressive wingspan of close to 2·5m and a length of over 1m. The smallest members are the male Sparrowhawk and the dainty and nearly ubiquitous Kestrel, both about 30cm in length.

GUIDE TO FAMILIES

ACCIPITRIDAE: wings straight and held at right angles to body, broad and rounded or 'fingered' at tip (except in Black-shouldered and Letter-winged Kites which have pointed wings); often soar and glide at varying heights and for long periods.

FALCONIDAE: wings narrow and pointed and bent in middle (swept-back); flight usually in swift sudden bursts and of short duration; face often black or with black 'side-burns'.

PANDIONIDAE: wings slightly swept-back and slightly fingered; mainly white below with black tail tip and black 'necklace'; dives into water from a height and carries fish in talons.

Wedge-tailed Eagle (142)

102

Family ACCIPITRIDAE
Hawks and Eagles
17(217) species: 5 endemic

Distribution: worldwide.

A s w e l l a s h a w k s and eagles there are kites, goshawks and harriers among the Australian members of this family. Of the four endemic species the Square-tailed Kite and Black-breasted Buzzard belong to unique genera. The Accipiters are essentially 'hawkers', as distinct from the 'hunting' falcons, although the goshawks are also of the hunting kind. The usual habit of the hawkers is to soar and glide for long periods, keeping a lookout for food that can be picked up fairly easily—a dead animal in the case of the carrion feeders, like the Black and Whistling Kites, or some weakling or unwary animal on which to pounce, as in the case of goshawks. Broad wings which are held straight out from the body with tips of flight feathers open, giving a 'fingered' appearance, are associated with hawking habits. But in the goshawks the wings are more rounded and are not distinctly fingered, and in the two kites of the genus *Elanus* the wings are pointed as in falcons, perhaps because they hover like kestrels. Tails are more variable in shape and possibly related to various aspects of stability and manoeuvrability peculiar to different species. They can be long and rounded as in the goshawks, short and square as in the Black-breasted Buzzard, long and forked as in the Black Kite, or long and wedge-shaped as in the Wedge-tailed Eagle. Many hawks and eagles are dull in colour, shades of blackish-brown, sometimes relieved with splashes of golden-yellow, or much white as in the sea eagles. Identification by colour can be difficult for distinct immature plumages sometimes persist for several years; young Wedge-tailed Eagles for example may be more reddish-brown than black. A few species, notably one of the goshawks, add to the difficulty by having two colour phases (dimorphic) each with a separate name, Grey Goshawk and White Goshawk.

Key to ACCIPITRIDAE

1	Wholly white	White ⎫	
	(or) grey above, white below	Grey ⎬ Goshawk .... No 141	
2	Whitish with black on shoulders	8–9	
3	Head white, back dark	10–11	
4	Underparts barred	12–13	
5	Underparts brown spotted white.................	Spotted Harrier .... No 136	
6	Brownish above, whitish below	14–15	
7	Mainly shades of brown	16–22	
8	Underwings with black patch....................	Black-shouldered Kite...... No 128	
9	Underwings with black 'V'	Letter-winged Kite .... No 129	
10	Underparts mainly white	White-breasted Sea Eagle ... No 135	
	[*Note:* osprey has black tail tip]		
11	Throat and breast white	Brahminy Kite .... No 134	
12	Short black crest	Crested Hawk .... No 127	
13	No crest.....................................	Brown Goshawk .... No 139	
		Collared Sparrowhawk .... No 140	
14	Legs short and feathered.......................	Little Eagle (pale form)..... No 143	
15	Legs long and bare, upper tail coverts white	Swamp Harrier .... No 137	
16	Underwing has large white spot.................	Black-breasted Buzzard .... No 132	
17	Tail long and forked	Black Kite................ No 130	
18	Tail long and wedge-shaped....................	Wedge-tailed Eagle .... No 142	

19 Tail long and rounded........................	Whistling Kite	No 133
20 Tail square	Little Eagle (dark form)	No 143
21 Wings upswept in flight, folded wings longer than tail	Square-tailed Kite	No 131
22 Folded wings shorter than tail	Red Goshawk	No 138

(See also key on page 108)

Genus AVICEDA

A group of five species found in Malaysia, India, Australia and Africa. The only Australian species also occurs in New Guinea. These hawks are distinguished by a small but easily visible crest, an unusual feature in birds of prey. The belly is broadly barred and the tail long and barred. The cutting edge of the bill is serrated to form two 'teeth'. They are mainly insectivorous.

127 CRESTED HAWK *Aviceda subcristata* (Gould) 1838   Pl 3

Distribution: Map 24.

RECOGNITION: *short black crest, boldly barred belly, bright yellow eye.*

DESCRIPTION: 35–40cm, with tail 17–20cm. Sexes nearly alike, female larger and paler. Upperparts mainly dark bluish-grey with upper back and scapulars chestnut brown, hind neck paler and contrasting with short black crest; face, throat and upper breast grey; lower breast and belly white tinged with cinnamon brown and boldly barred with blackish-brown; under shoulders, vent and under tail coverts cinnamon brown; under flight feathers and under tail pale grey barred with black; tail broadly tipped with black; bill bluish-black, cere blue; eyes and eyelids bright yellow; legs pale grey. *Immature:* browner, especially on head and neck; barring on wings and tail more distinct; eyes whitish.

VARIATION: east and north larger and paler (race *subcristata*); Kimberley area smaller and darker (race *njikena*).

HABITAT: well wooded areas. HABITS: usually high up in trees; solitary; sedentary with nomadic tendencies; sometimes 'tumbles' in flight. BREEDING: September–December; nests in tree forks or horizontal branches, loosely made of green twigs, which birds obtain by clutching in claws and fluttering around until broken off; three to four eggs, greenish or bluish-white, sometimes lightly blotched with brown. VOICE: loud musical 'ee-choo' and soft warbling whistle. FOOD: mainly large insects, like stick insects and cicadas, obtained under tree canopies.

STATUS: uncommon to fairly common. TAXONOMY: endemic races of variable species extending to eastern Indonesia, New Guinea and Solomon Is.

Genus ELANUS

Although the genus ranges widely throughout the old and new worlds, it consists of only four species, two of which are endemic to Australia. They are small, about the size of a Kestrel, and have the Kestrel's habit of hovering when hunting. They are whitish, almost like a tern, and have conspicuous black patches on shoulders and underwings. They are roughly complementary in breeding distribution, with the Letter-winged Kite mostly confined to the Barkly Tableland and Channel Country but irrupting widely in conditions of abundant food supply.

128 BLACK-SHOULDERED KITE *Elanus notatus* Gould 1838

Distribution: throughout.

RECOGNITION: *pearly white with black shoulders and black patch on underwing; hawks over open ground and hovers.*

DESCRIPTION: 35cm, with tail 15cm. Sexes alike. Upperparts pale grey, whitish on forehead and tail; underparts white; face white with black half ring above and behind eye; shoulders black; under shoulders white with black patch; underside of flight feathers dark grey; bill black, cere yellow or greenish; eyes red (and relatively large); legs light yellow. *Immature:* crown and back brownish; breast tinged with brown and thinly streaked with black; feathers of wings and lower back tipped with white.

HABITAT: wooded savannas. HABITS: hawks and hovers when hunting ground prey; solitary; nomadic, sometimes irrupting into certain areas in large numbers. BREEDING: May–September; nests in forked branches of tree canopies, roughly made of twigs and sticks and lined with leaves; three to four eggs; bluish or buffy-white streaked with shades of dark brown. VOICE: musical high-pitched 'tew'. FOOD: small ground animals and insects.

STATUS: fairly common. TAXONOMY: endemic species.

Black-shouldered
Kite (128)

Letter-winged Kite (129)

129 LETTER-WINGED KITE *Elanus scriptus* Gould 1842

Distribution: Map 25.

RECOGNITION: like Black-shouldered Kite but differs in *shape of black on white underwing, which is a broad bent streak* (together vaguely resembling a rather wide and broken 'M' or 'W' on underside of bird in flight); *black in front of eye but not behind*; eyes reddish-orange and relatively large; legs whitish and very large.

HABITAT: tree and shrub savannas. HABITS: hawks low over ground in circles and hovers briefly; fairly gregarious, even when breeding, and wandering in loose companies of about twenty birds, or in larger numbers where there are rat plagues; active only from dusk to dawn; nomadic; flight rather laboured when hunting low. BREEDING: variable, on Barkly Tableland usually March–September; nests high in tree forks, roughly made of twigs and lined with fur;

four to five eggs, bluish, or buffy-white marked with shades of reddish-brown. VOICE: loud screaming 'chirp' and harsh 'kar'. FOOD: small ground animals, sometimes exclusively rats.

STATUS: uncommon, but perhaps more common than records suggest. TAXONOMY: endemic species.

Genus MILVUS

A genus of two species, frequently known as Red Kite and Black Kite, which range widely throughout the old world. The commoner Black Kite, or Fork-tailed Kite, is the only one occurring in Australia. Drab brown colours and long forked tail, which is swivelled in flight, are as distinctive as its habit of forming wheeling flocks over dead animals and town dumps. The somewhat similar but less common Square-tailed Kite belongs to the next genus.

130 BLACK KITE   *Milvus migrans*   (Boddaert) 1783

Distribution: widespread in north and east, rare in south and west.

RECOGNITION: *wholly dark drab brown with long tail, deeply forked when nearly closed but almost square when fully open.*

DESCRIPTION: 56cm, with forked tail 28cm; tail longer than folded wings. Sexes alike. Shades of grey-brown, sometimes almost black, sometimes paler on head and neck and streaked with black; pale grey on shoulders and cinnamon brown on belly; bill blackish, yellow at base and on cere; eyes dark brown; legs yellow.

HABITAT: wooded savannas. HABITS: arboreal, but mainly terrestrial scavenging feeder; gregarious; nomadic with some regular movements associated with rains; slow wheeling gliding flight with tail constantly fanned and rotated. BREEDING: variable, but mainly September–November in south and March–May in north; nests in forks in trees, often old ones refurbished, roughly made of sticks and lined with wool or fur; two to three eggs, whitish, sparsely marked with reddish-brown at wide end. VOICE: plaintive mewing. FOOD: small animals and insects, sometimes obtained at edge of bush fires, also carrion and domestic food refuse.

STATUS: common. TAXONOMY: race *(affinis)* extending to New Guinea, of wide ranging species.

Genus LOPHOICTINIA

The unique Australian Square-tailed Kite is put in a genus of its own, though perhaps it might be included in *Milvus*. It is similar in general appearance to the Black Kite but is more the reddish-brown colour of the Red Kite of Europe. It is not well known.

Black Kite (130)

Square-tailed Kite (131)

131 SQUARE-TAILED KITE *Lophoictinia isura* (Gould) 1838

Distribution: throughout, except extreme southeast and Tasmania.

RECOGNITION: *tail square, whitish patches on underside of upswept wings, solitary and flying high round tree canopies.*

DESCRIPTION: 51–56cm, with tail 23–25.5cm; tail nearly square and 5cm shorter than folded wings. Sexes alike. Upperparts brownish-black; crown, neck and underparts cinnamon, streaked with black; forehead, face and chin whitish; under shoulders cinnamon; base of under flight feathers white, tip grey barred with black; undertail grey with blackish tip; cere and base of bill yellowish-brown, tip black; eyes white or pale yellow; legs yellowish-brown. *Immature:* cinnamon head and underparts, much less streaked with black; feathers of upperparts, especially back and shoulders, tipped with cinnamon; rump whitish; eyes grey-brown; legs whitish.

HABITAT: well wooded areas near open country. HABITS: (not well known) arboreal; solitary; possibly nomadic; hawks for insects round tree canopies and over open ground; BREEDING: September–November; nests in horizontal forks and branches of tree canopies, made of large sticks and lined with leaves and strips of bark; two eggs, buffy-white freckled and blotched with reddish-brown. VOICE: not recorded. FOOD: small birds and animals, also insects.

STATUS: rare, perhaps commoner than records suggest. TAXONOMY: endemic species of endemic genus.

Genus HAMIROSTRA

The relationships of the Black-breasted Buzzard (or Kite) are uncertain. In appearance and behaviour it somewhat resembles the true buzzards, genus *Buteo* (not represented in Australia) and the Square-tailed Kite. But it has several unusual anatomical features and is placed in a genus of its own. It is endemic and one of the few species which have two colour phases (dimorphic), one dark and one light.

132 BLACK-BREASTED BUZZARD *Hamirostra melanosternon* (Gould) 1841 Pl 3

Distribution: throughout, scattered records except from Tasmania.

RECOGNITION: *short rounded tail, large white patch on underside of upswept wings.*

DESCRIPTION: 58cm; folded wings extend 5cm beyond relatively short tail. Sexes alike. Plumage in varying amounts of black and rufous brown, but base of flight feathers always white and forming large white patch on underside of extended wing, and tail always grey; otherwise apparently two main phases: (1) head, back, wings and breast mainly black, remainder rufous brown; (2) mainly rufous brown with black centres to feathers on upper-parts and black streaks on breast; in both phases bill pinkish-brown, black at tip and cere pale grey; eyes reddish-brown; legs yellow.

HABITAT: open woodlands and wooded savannas. HABITS: (not well known) arboreal, but mainly feeding on ground; slow wheeling flight. BREEDING: records between August and November; nests in horizontal forks in trees, large loose structure of sticks; two eggs, whitish with dark brown and purplish markings. VOICE: 'between a whistle and a scream'. FOOD: small animals, rarely carrion.

STATUS: rare; few scattered records. TAXONOMY: endemic species of endemic genus.

Genus HALIASTUR

Only the Whistling Kite and Brahminy Kite (or Red-backed Sea Eagle) make up this genus and both occur in Australia, but not exclusively. Although very different in adult plumage pattern they have a number of common features which show their close affinity. They have the appearance and scavenging habits of many kites.

133 WHISTLING KITE *Haliastur sphenurus* (Vieillot) 1818   Pl 3

Distribution: throughout, rarely Tasmania.

RECOGNITION: *long rounded tail pale and unbarred, pale and lightly streaked underparts; lazy wheeling flight on bowed wings.*

DESCRIPTION: 53–58cm, with tail about half, narrow and rounded. Sexes alike. Head and neck cinnamon buff to buffy-white streaked dark brown; back and shoulders grey-brown; underparts pale grey-brown streaked and mottled buffy-white; outer flight feathers black, inner buffy; tail pale grey-brown; bill and cere brown; eyes dark brown; eyelids bluish-white; legs white. *Immature:* upperparts spotted buffy-white.

VARIATION: there is some variation, especially on underparts, but it does not appear to be correlated with distribution.

HABITAT: coastal forests to dry inland savannas. HABITS: arboreal but feeds mainly on ground, a scavenger; gregarious, sometimes in large numbers where food is plentiful; nomadic; flight often in slow wheeling glides with fingered wingtips. BREEDING: most months, even in one area; nests in tree forks as high as possible, made of sticks—size depends on how often same nest has been used—and lined with fresh green leaves; two eggs, bluish or greenish-white, sometimes marked with reddish-brown. VOICE: loud shrill tremulous whistle. FOOD: carrion, sickly small animals and insects.

STATUS: common. TAXONOMY: species extending to New Guinea and New Caledonia.

134 BRAHMINY KITE *Haliastur indus* (Boddaert) 1783   Pl 3

Distribution: northern coasts, south to Gascoyne River and Clarence River.

RECOGNITION: *white head and breast, rufous back and tail, black wingtips.*

DESCRIPTION: 48cm, with tail 23cm. Sexes alike. Head, neck and breast white; remainder of upperparts, belly and under shoulders cinnamon rufous; under flight feathers pinkish-cinnamon tipped with black; under tail pinkish-cinnamon; bill yellow, base blue-grey; eyes yellowish; legs yellow. *Immature:* like Whistling Kite but tail shorter and wings broader; head and underparts buffy streaked with brown; upperparts black with whitish spots and blotches; bill bluish-black; eyes and legs grey.

HABITAT: coastal timber including mangroves. HABITS: arboreal but feeds mainly on ground and shallow waters, a scavenger; solitary; nomadic; slow wheeling flight. BREEDING: June–September; nests high up in forks of trees bordering estuaries and coastal swamps, made of twigs and lined with seaweed and other soft materials; two eggs, bluish-white, plain or marked with reddish-brown spots and vermiculations. VOICE: loud trembling 'pee-ah-h-h'. FOOD: live or dead animals, including fish.

STATUS: fairly common. TAXONOMY: race (*girrenera*) extending throughout Papuan region, of wide ranging species.

Genus HALIAEETUS

Eight species of nearly worldwide distribution, characterised by large size, broad fingered wings and short wedge-shaped tails with varying amounts of white. They frequent sea coasts and coastal islands, are sometimes found inland on large waterways, and hawk for any kind of animal food, live or dead. Represented in Australia by the White-breasted Sea Eagle.

135 WHITE-BREASTED SEA EAGLE   *Haliaeetus leucogaster*   (Gmelin) 1788

Distribution: throughout, mainly in coastal localities.

RECOGNITION: *broad white tip of wedge-shaped tail.*

DESCRIPTION: 75cm–1m, with wedge-shaped tail 25–30cm; wingspan 2–2·3m. Sexes alike, but female distinctly larger. Head and underparts white; remainder grey, except tail broadly tipped with white; bill blue-grey, cere brownish; eyes brown; legs (not feathered) yellowish-white. *Immature:* crown and neck blackish-brown like back; face and chin cinnamon; breast and belly grey-brown; tail pale grey, darker at tip.

HABITAT: coasts and coastal islands, sometimes far inland on large rivers. HABITS: arboreal, or terrestrial on treeless islands, feeds mainly on ground; solitary; sedentary but ranging widely; flight a lazy flap and glide. BREEDING: May–October; nests in forks of large trees or on rocks and stones on treeless islands, made of branches and lined with small twigs, sometimes very large when used repeatedly; two eggs, dull white. VOICE: loud cackling or honking, almost like Pied Goose. FOOD: most animals, live or dead.

STATUS: fairly common. TAXONOMY: uniform species ranging from Indian coasts to western Polynesia.

HAWKS WITH LONG YELLOW LEGS

Australian hawks of the following three genera, *Circus, Erythriotriorchis* and *Accipiter,* are all fairly slender in build with long yellow legs (greenish-yellow in the Swamp Harrier) and fairly long tails. They 'hawk' low, lower than the Whistling Kite, quartering the ground with a lazy flap and glide flight. They do not hover like the Kestrel and the two grey kites. They can be identified as follows.

1 White or grey	White Goshawk . . . . No 141
	Grey Goshawk . . . . No 141
2 Shades of brown	3–5
3 Underparts with white spots	Spotted Harrier . . . . No 136
4 Underparts with dark streaks	6–7
5 Underparts barred	
Tail round	Brown Goshawk . . . . No 139
Tail square	Collared Sparrowhawk . . . . No 140
6 Underside of tail plain	Swamp Harrier . . . . No 137
7 Underside of tail barred	
Legs massive	Red Goshawk . . . . No 138
Legs slender	Spotted Harrier (Imm) . . . . . No 136

Genus CIRCUS

Two of this distinctive group of about ten species, known as harriers, occur widely in Australia but are not peculiar to it. Harriers are readily distinguished by long tails and wings, long thin legs and a curious owl-like facial disc. They have a lazy gliding flight as they quarter low over open country in search of small prey, but they do not hover. The Spotted Harrier keeps to dry haunts and the Swamp Harrier, as its name suggests, to wetter places.

136 SPOTTED HARRIER *Circus assimilis*   Jardine & Selby 1828   Pl 3

Distribution: throughout, but mainly dry interior.

RECOGNITION: *white spotted underparts, long barred tail, long yellow legs.*

DESCRIPTION: 50–60cm, tail about half. Sexes alike, but female distinctly larger. Head russet streaked with dark grey on crown; back brownish-grey; inner margins of shoulders russet, remainder of shoulders spotted with pale grey; upper tail coverts and tail broadly barred light and dark grey; most of underparts, including under shoulders, walnut brown boldly spotted with white, less spotted and tinged with grey on foreneck; inner flight feathers pale pink narrowly barred with dark grey and tipped with black; bill black; eyes yellow; legs yellow. *Immature*: cinnamon brown streaks on crown; underparts buffy-white streaked with dark brown.

HABITAT: dry plains country, but sometimes encroaching on wetter haunts of Swamp Harrier. HABITS: arboreal but feeds mainly on ground; solitary; flight a lazy flap and glide low over ground. BREEDING: August–October; nests in trees and bushes at various heights, made of large sticks and lined with green leaves; two to four eggs, bluish-white. VOICE: shrill tremulous cry or 'whicker'. FOOD: small birds and animals up to size of rabbit.

STATUS: uncommon. TAXONOMY: species which occurs also on Sunda I and Celebes.

137 SWAMP HARRIER *Circus approximans*   Peale 1848   Pl 3

DISTRIBUTION: throughout, but mainly in coastal areas.

RECOGNITION: *white below with dark streaks on breast, white band on rump, long greenish-yellow legs.*

DESCRIPTION: 50–56cm, tail about half. Sexes nearly alike, female larger, slightly browner and more streaked below. Upperparts brownish-black with head and neck streaked black

Brown
Goshawk (139)

White-breasted
Sea Eagle (135)

and buff; upper tail coverts white, making conspicuous white band at base of tail; underparts whitish with dark brown streaks on breast; tail faintly barred above but below pale grey without bars; bill bluish-black, brown at base; eyes yellow; legs yellow. *Immature:* darker, lacks streaks on head, has less white at base of tail, upperparts dusky russet without streaks.

HABITAT: swampy grasslands and reed beds, rarely far from water. HABITS: mainly terrestrial; solitary; sedentary or nomadic, sometimes disappears from certain areas when not breeding, migrates from Tasmania to mainland; flight a lazy flap and glide low over ground with high upswept wings. BREEDING: September–January; nests in swamp vegetation and low bushes, made of reed stalks and twigs, lined with grasses; three to five eggs, dull white with pale blue or pink tinge. VOICE: short harsh scream and high-pitched single whistle. FOOD: small animals.

STATUS: fairly common. TAXONOMY: race (*gouldi*) extending to New Guinea of southwest Pacific species, which is sometimes considered to be a race of European Marsh Harrier, *C. aeruginosus.*

Genus ERYTHRIOTRIOCHIS

The Red Goshawk is considered sufficiently distinct to have a genus of its own. Its nearest relatives are probably the wide-ranging accipiter goshawks, of which it may be an offshoot which in isolation evolved distinctive features, such as rather shorter tail, longer wings and unusually long curved claws.

138 RED GOSHAWK *Erythriotriorchis radiatus* (Latham) 1801
Distribution: Map 26.

RECOGNITION: *reddish-brown with black streaks, boldly barred tail, long massive yellow legs.*
DESCRIPTION: 45–50cm, tail about half. Sexes alike, but female larger. Upperparts reddish-brown streaked and mottled with black, boldly streaked on crown; face and throat whitish to pale buff finely streaked with black; breast and belly pale reddish-brown streaked with black, but sometimes almost white on breast and under tail coverts; under shoulders reddish-brown streaked with black, remainder of underwing grey, faintly barred; upper tail coverts reddish-brown, sometimes tinged with grey; tail grey-brown boldly barred with black; bill black; cere, eyes and legs yellow.

HABITAT: open forests and woodlands. HABITS: (not well known) arboreal; solitary; sedentary; lazy gliding flight. BREEDING: August–November; nests in tree forks, made of sticks and lined with soft twigs and leaves; two to three eggs, bluish-white, sometimes marked with dark brown. VOICE: high-pitched chatter. FOOD: small animals, sometimes as large as Black Duck, nestlings of other birds.

STATUS: Rare. TAXONOMY: Endemic species of endemic genus.

Genus ACCIPITER

The goshawks and sparrowhawks make up this worldwide group of some fifty species, of which three occur in Australia. They are slender hawks with long tails and long yellow legs, relatively small heads with bright red or yellow eyes and short rounded wings. Their hunting tactics are to swoop suddenly from some vantage point or to appear unexpectedly from behind trees and bushes to snatch unsuspecting prey on the wing or on the ground. The

Brown Goshawk and Collared Sparrowhawk are almost identical in appearance and have similar distributions (sibling species). The following notes may help to identify them.

BROWN GOSHAWK AND COLLARED SPARROWHAWK

The Brown Goshawk is about 40–50cm in length and the Collared Sparrowhawk 30–38cm, the females being larger than the males. Therefore a distinctly large bird with description to fit either species is almost certain to be a female Brown Goshawk and a distinctly small bird a male Collared Sparrowhawk. Male Goshawk and female Sparrowhawk are about the same size but the Goshawk is rather more coarsely barred on the underparts. In flight the Goshawk shows a rounded tail and the Sparrowhawk a square one. In the hand a bird of tail length less than 18cm is almost certain to be a Collared Sparrowhawk and over 18cm a Brown Goshawk.

139 BROWN GOSHAWK *Accipiter fasciatus* (Vig. & Horsf.) 1827 Fig p 109
Distribution: throughout but rare in extreme north.

RECOGNITION: *lightly barred underparts, round ended tail (for comparison with similar Collared Sparrowhawk, see above).*

DESCRIPTION: 40–50cm, with tail 20–25 cm; wingspan 75cm–1m. Sexes nearly alike, female larger and has narrower bars. Upperparts dark grey-brown, darker on crown and pale rufous brown on hind neck; underparts, including underwing and under tail coverts, barred white and dark grey-brown, tinged with rufous on thighs; undertail barred light and dark grey, bars faint on upper tail; bill blackish-brown, cere greenish-yellow; eyes yellow; legs yellow. *Immature:* more rufous on upperparts, especially on crown and hind neck; underparts more boldly marked with broad bars and streaks.

VARIATION: throughout most of country, as above (race *fasciatus*); extreme north, greyer with more rufous bars (race *didimus*).

HABITAT: forests and woodlands, patches of tall timber in dry areas. HABITS: mainly arboreal but in very open country often rests on ground; solitary; mainly sedentary; hunts in swift bursts of flight catching prey by sudden attack and agility. BREEDING: August–December; nests in trees often in horizontal forks high up, well made of sticks and lined with green leaves, sometimes mistletoe; three to five eggs, bluish-white lightly marked with spots and streaks of brown. VOICE: various high-pitched chattering notes. FOOD: mainly birds, up to quite large size, but also ground animals.

STATUS: fairly common. TAXONOMY: species ranging to Christmas I and Fiji.

140 COLLARED SPARROWHAWK *Accipiter cirrhocephalus* (Vieillot) 1817 Pl 3
Distribution: throughout.

RECOGNITION: *lightly barred underparts, square ended tail (for comparision with similar Brown Goshawk, see above).*

DESCRIPTION: 30–38cm, with tail 15–18cm. Sexes alike but female larger. Upperparts dark grey-brown with band of russet on hind neck; underparts, including under shoulders, finely barred white and cinnamon brown, speckled grey on throat; remainder of underwing and undertail broadly barred light grey and grey-brown; bill black, cere yellow; eyes and legs yellow. *Immature:* upperparts more rufous and collar less distinct; underparts boldly streaked on throat and foreneck, barred on breast and belly.

HABITAT: forests and woodlands, well timbered margins of rivers and creeks. HABITS: arboreal; solitary; sedentary; flight swift and agile, often in sudden dashes from some vantage place to catch unwary prey. BREEDING: August–December; nests in trees, usually in forks high up, made of thin dry twigs and lined with green leaves; three to four eggs, greenish or bluish-white. VOICE: shrill chatter. FOOD: small birds and other animals.

STATUS: fairly common. TAXONOMY: species extending to New Guinea.

Grey Goshawk (141)

141 GREY GOSHAWK or
WHITE GOSHAWK   *Accipiter novaehollandiae*   (Gmelin) 1788

Distribution: Map 27.

RECOGNITION: *Plain grey above and white below, or wholly white; like Grey Falcon but extended wings broad and rounded and when folded much shorter than tail.*

DESCRIPTION: 40–50cm, with tail 18–23cm. Sexes alike but female larger. Dimorphic: (1) pure white; (2) upperparts plain bluish-grey with faint bars on tail; underparts white with varying amounts of narrow grey bars on breast; bill black, cere and ring around eye yellow; eyes dark red; legs yellow.

VARIATION: colour phases were often regarded as two species but there is plenty of evidence that they interbreed freely and have offspring of either colour; white phase is predominant in Tasmania and Kimberley area.

HABITAT: forests of various kinds. HABITS: arboreal but takes food on ground; solitary; sedentary; hawking owl-like flight with swift dash to secure prey. BREEDING: August–December; nests in trees high up in horizontal forks, made of sticks and lined with green leaves; two to four eggs, bluish-white faintly marked with blotches and spots of purplish-brown. VOICE: fairly soft 'queet' repeated and shrill cackle. FOOD: birds and other animals.

STATUS: fairly common. TAXONOMY: endemic race *(novaehollandiae)* of variable species extending to eastern Indonesia, New Guinea and Solomon Is.

Genus AQUILA

One of several genera of large predatory birds of aggressive habits and fierce appearance — the lions and tigers among birds. They can be distinguished by their feathered legs, sometimes described as having 'trousers', unlike the sea eagles which have bare legs. Both this and the next genus belong to this assemblage. *Aquila* consists of about nine species ranging over most parts of the world. The only representative in Australia is the Wedge-tailed Eagle. With a wingspan of up to 2·5m it ranks among the largest of flying birds.

142 WEDGE-TAILED EAGLE   *Aquila audax*   (Latham) 1801   Fig p 101

Distribution: throughout.

RECOGNITION: *large with long wedge-shaped tail and upswept wings when soaring, black or black and reddish-brown.*

DESCRIPTION: 1–1·2m, with wedge-shaped tail 40–46cm; wingspan 2–2·5m; legs feathered. Sexes alike, but female larger. Black with pale reddish-brown patch on nape and hind neck and on shoulders; usually a light patch in centre of underwing. This plumage takes about six years to become established; first *immature* plumage is reddish-brown with black flight and tail feathers; the brown areas are gradually replaced with black, except on hind neck and shoulders. Bill pinkish-brown, black at tip, cere whitish; eyes buff or brown in immature, yellow in adult; feet whitish.

VARIATION: throughout mainland, as described (race *audax*); in Tasmania, upperparts less buff in immature stages, in adult pale areas buffy-white (race *fleayi*).

HABITAT: most kinds. HABITS: perches and roosts on trees, bushes, rocks and crags; solitary; sedentary but ranges widely when hunting; soars to great heights and swoops on prey at great speed. BREEDING: mainly April–September; nests in trees and bushes at varying heights, sometimes near ground, usually quite conspicuous, made of sticks and twigs and lined with leaves, grass and feathers, becomes large structure when used repeatedly; two eggs (usually only one chick survives), dull white, one with little or no markings and the other heavily blotched and spotted with purplish-brown. VOICE: loud piercing whistle. FOOD: birds and other animals up to size of wallaby and lamb, also carrion.

STATUS: fairly common. TAXONOMY: species with slight extension into New Guinea; formerly placed in separate genus *Uroaetus*.

Genus HIERAAETUS

A group of five species ranging widely in the old world. They are relatively small but have the feathered legs of the true eagles. Some members have two plumage phases (dimorphic) and this is a feature of the only Australian representative, the Little Eagle.

143 LITTLE EAGLE *Hieraaetus morphnoides* (Gould) 1841   Pl 3

Distribution: throughout, except Tasmania.

RECOGNITION: *feathered legs, square tail, crown feathers sometimes erected into short crest; either dark brown above and below or dark above and white below.*

DESCRIPTION: 45–53cm, with square tail 20–23cm; wingspan 1·2–1·5m; erectile crown feathers; legs feathered. Sexes alike but female larger. Dimorphic: (1) head and neck pale cinnamon buff; back mottled shades of dusky brown, pale patch on shoulders, flight feathers black; underparts buffy-white with thin black streaks; underwing brownish-grey with large white patch in centre and flight feathers barred black at tip; undertail pale grey with faint bars. *Immature:* head, neck and underparts reddish-brown. (2) back, wings and tail similar but with pale areas darker; head, neck and underparts dark rufous brown, underparts streaked with black. *Immature:* dark rufous brown with little or no pale colour on shoulders. Both adult forms: bill blue-grey, tip black, cere grey; eyes reddish-brown; feet yellowish-white.

HABITAT: forests and woodlands. HABITS: arboreal; solitary; sedentary. BREEDING: July–October; nests in tree forks high up, often old nests of other species, made of sticks and lined with leaves; two eggs, bluish-white faintly marked with blotches and streaks of reddish-brown. VOICE: shrill treble whistle, also rapid succession of loud 'cuks'. FOOD: small animals.

STATUS: uncommon to fairly common. TAXONOMY: endemic race (*morphnoides*) of species extending to New Guinea.

Family PANDIONIDAE

Osprey

1(1) species

Distribution: worldwide.

THE COSMOPOLITAN OSPREY, or Fish-hawk, does not seem to have any very close relatives. It has a number of distinctive characteristics, mainly anatomical, and it is placed in a family of its own, usually between the Hawks and Falcons. The Osprey on the Australian coasts is little different to those in other parts of the world and all are considered to belong to a single species. It lives exclusively on fish which it catches by diving feet first, sometimes with such force as to be carried under water. Fish are held in the feet by sharp hooked talons and toes equipped on the underside with spiny projections.

144 OSPREY *Pandion haliaetus* (Linnaeus) 1758

Distribution: throughout in coastal areas.

RECOGNITION: *white underparts and black tail; coastal; dives from a height and holds fish in its feet.*

DESCRIPTION: 50–60cm; wingspan 1·75m; folded wings reach tip of tail; sturdy legs with large toes and talons. Sexes alike but female larger. Head mainly white, crown and nape sometimes flecked with black, black streak through eye to side of neck; remainder of upperparts brownish-black; underparts white with dusky band or 'necklace' on foreneck; underwing white with a few dark bars, small black patch at angle of shoulders and black tips; tail brownish-black; bill black, cere blue-grey; eyes orange; feet creamy-white.

HABITAT: coasts and coastal islands, lower reaches of large rivers. HABITS: arboreal and terrestrial but aquatic feeder, plunges into water from a height; solitary; sedentary. BREEDING: May–September; nests on ground, on rocky ledges, or in mangrove and other trees, sometimes large bare trees, made of sticks and seaweed, sometimes built up over years into large tower-like structures; three eggs, pale buff blotched with reddish-purple. VOICE: peeping whistle. FOOD: fish.

STATUS: fairly common. TAXONOMY: race *(cristatus)* extending throughout Papuan region, of cosmopolitan species.

Osprey (144)

Family FALCONIDAE

Falcons

6(61) species: 2–3 endemic

Distribution: worldwide.

THE FEW SPECIES OF this family in Australia belong to the genus *Falco*, of which there are thirty-seven species throughout the world. A typical Falcon, as exemplified by the Peregrine, is robust, smoothly contoured, with narrow pointed swept-back wings—adaptations for swift flight. Such falcons are 'hunters', as distinct from the 'hawking' accipiters, and take birds by outflying them or by diving or 'stooping' on them at very high speeds. The prey is grasped with the talons or stunned by a blow of the closed foot. Exception to this behaviour is found in the Kestrel and Brown Falcon, both of which hunt more in the manner of hawks, taking small mammals and insects on the ground by swooping from a stance or by hovering. For this and other reasons they are sometimes placed in other genera but current opinion is that they should be included in *Falco*. The Black Falcon and Grey Falcon belong only to Australia. The Little Falcon also might be regarded as an endemic species for its linkage at race level with a related form in Timor is doubtfully valid. Falcons are lazy nest builders, favouring holes in trees or utilising suitable unused nests of other species, or sometimes usurping used ones.

Key to FALCONIDAE

1 Mainly blackish-brown
  Centre of underwing dark .... Black Falcon .... No 147
  Centre of underwing pale .... Brown Falcon .... No 146
2 Upperparts shades of dark brown, underparts mottled
  brown and white .... Brown Falcon............. No 146
3 Upperparts reddish-brown
  Black band at tip of tail....................... Kestrel.................. No 145
  No black band on tail......................... Brown Falcon .... No 146
4 Upperparts blue-grey........................... 5–8
5 Crown and face pale grey....................... Grey Falcon .... No 148
6 Crown and face black 7–8
7 Belly barred black .... Peregrine Falcon .... No 150
8 Belly rufous.................................. Little Falcon............. No 149

145 KESTREL *Falco cenchroides* Vig. & Horsf. 1827   Pl 3

Distribution: throughout.

RECOGNITION: *cinnamon brown back; long tail with black subterminal bar, grey in male, barred in female; hovers.*

DESCRIPTION: 30–36cm, with tail 15–18cm. Sexes different. *Male:* crown and nape blue-grey finely streaked with black; back and shoulders shades of cinnamon brown with varying amounts of triangular black marks; rump and tail blue-grey, tail with broad subterminal black bar and white tip; face and underparts, including wings and tail, buffy-white with black patch below eye ('moustache' or 'sideburns') and thin black streaks on breast; main flight feathers blackish-brown above; bill blue-black, cere yellow; eyes dark brown, eyelids greenish-yellow; legs yellow. *Female:* crown, rump and tail light brown uniform with back; tail has narrow black bars in addition to broad subterminal bar and white tip.

HABITAT: various kinds of open country, sometimes treeless. HABITS: arboreal and terrestrial, hawks and frequently hovers when hunting, or pounces from stance in trees or often telegraph poles and wires; solitary but sometimes in scattered flocks when not breeding; sedentary and nomadic, apparently travelling long distances, perhaps migratory. BREEDING: August–November; nests in trees, in hollows or suitable old nests, or in caves and blow-holes; four to five eggs, white or buff, densely blotched with reddish-brown. VOICE: shrill 'kee' rapidly repeated, also low clucking. FOOD: ground animals and insects, especially grasshoppers.

STATUS: very common. TAXONOMY: race *(cenchroides)*, endemic but with stragglers to Moluccas, New Zealand and New Guinea; one other race in New Guinea.

146 BROWN FALCON   *Falco berigora*   Vig. & Horsf. 1827

Distribution: throughout.

RECOGNITION: *variable; reddest form like female Kestrel but larger and no black band at tip of tail; blackest form like Black Falcon but underside of flight feathers always pale; tarsus long (over 6cm) and not covered by thigh feathers; hovers and glides with upswept wings.*

DESCRIPTION: 40–50cm, with tail 15–20cm. Sexes alike but female larger. Plumage variable (there does not seem to be distinct colour phases as there are various degrees of difference between one extreme and the other; the only fairly constant difference is that thighs are either brown or rufous): upperparts vary from blackish-brown to pale reddish-brown, but in darkest forms there is usually some russet or tan on crown or edges of back feathers or as indistinct bars on flight and tail feathers, and in even palest forms wingtips are blackish; in most forms barring on wings and tail is quite pronounced; underparts vary from dusky brown to brown, reddish-brown, buff or buffy-white, in different proportions and usually with dark streaks; thighs brown or rufous and base of flight feathers on underwing pale; face blackish round eye and edge of chin, most distinct in pale forms; bill grey-brown, cere blue-grey; bare skin round eye bluish-white; eyes reddish-brown; legs pale blue-grey.

VARIATION: among races described are: Tasmania, smaller (race *tasmanica*); central areas, paleness predominates (race *centralia*); humid north, mostly dark (race *melvillensis*); and ill-defined variant in Western Australia (race *occidentalis*).

HABITAT: most kinds of open grass country. HABITS: arboreal but feeds mainly on ground, watches for prey from vantage points, often telegraph poles, hovers, but not as frequently as Kestrel, sometimes at bush fires; solitary; mainly sedentary. BREEDING: variable, but mainly between May and December; nests in holes in trees, tree forks or cross pieces of telegraph poles, frequently unused nests of other species scraped out and lined with green leaves; two to three eggs, variable in colour and markings, even in same clutch, but usually buffy-white blotched with reddish-brown. VOICE: loud cackling. FOOD: small animals, perched birds and nestlings, insects, sometimes associated with grasshopper plagues.

STATUS: very common. TAXONOMY: very variable species with one race in New Guinea.

147 BLACK FALCON   *Falco subniger*   Gray 1843

Distribution: throughout except Tasmania.

RECOGNITION: *sooty black, whitish on chin; like darkest form of Brown Falcon but dark on underside of flight feathers, tarsus short (under 5cm) and more or less covered by thigh feathers; does not hover, glides with horizontal wings.*

DESCRIPTION: 45–50cm. Sexes alike but female larger. Brownish-black, whitish on chin and indistinct whitish bars on underside and base of main flight feathers and on outer tail feathers; bill blue-grey, black at tip; cere and bare skin around eye bluish-white; eyes brown; legs pale blue-grey.

HABITAT: woodlands. HABITS: arboreal, sometimes feeds on ground but usually takes prey on wing by sudden bursts of speed; solitary, sometimes one or two may be with Black Kites, which they resemble in colour but not in outline; movements apparently unknown. BREEDING: variable, but mainly June–December; nests in trees usually high up, probably always old nests re-used or suitable unused nests of other species; two to four eggs, buff spotted with shades of brown. VOICE: cackling 'gak-gak' also soft whistle. FOOD: mainly birds, said to have preference for quail, also takes dead meat.

STATUS: rare to uncommon. TAXONOMY: endemic species.

148 GREY FALCON   *Falco hypoleucos*   Gould 1841   Fig p 118
Distribution: throughout except Tasmania.

RECOGNITION: *pale blue-grey above, white below, black flight feathers, rather like Grey Goshawk but face white with dark 'moustache', extended wings long and pointed and folded wings reach tip of tail.*

DESCRIPTION: 33–41cm; wingspan 75cm–1m. Sexes alike but female larger. Upperparts light blue-grey with thin black streaks; face and underparts buffy-white, face with dusky 'moustache' and underparts with thin black streaks; underwing and undertail lightly but distinctly barred; main flight feathers black; bill dark grey; cere and bare skin around eye yellow; eyes brown; legs yellow. *Immature:* upperparts darker blue-grey, blackish on crown, more streaked and spotted below.

HABITAT: drier kinds of open timbered country. HABITS: arboreal but feeds on ground as well as on wing; apparently solitary; movements little known; considered to be less speedy in flight than other falcons. BREEDING: July–November; nests in trees, same nests used repeatedly or old nests of other species taken over and repaired; two to four eggs, buffy-white spotted and blotched with shades of brown. VOICE: loud 'kek' repeated rapidly. FOOD: small birds and other animals.

STATUS: apparently uncommon. TAXONOMY: endemic species.

149 LITTLE FALCON   *Falco longipennis*   Swainson 1837   Pl 3
Distribution: throughout.

RECOGNITION: *blue-grey with black crown and face and rufous underparts.*

DESCRIPTION: 30–35cm. Sexes alike but female larger. Upperparts dark blue-grey with black crown and face, broken white hind collar and blackish-brown flight feathers; throat and foreneck creamy white blending into shades of light and dark cinnamon on breast and belly with varying amounts of black streaks and blotches; underwings and undertail barred cinnamon or buff; bill blue-grey, tip black; cere blue; eyes dark brown; legs yellow. *Immature:* upperparts blackish-brown with rufous edges to feathers and rufous crown; underparts as in adult but less densely marked with black.

VARIATION: over much of continent and in more humid areas, darker (race *longipennis*); central area extending to northwest and in more arid areas, paler (race *murchisonianus*).

HABITAT: open and lightly timbered country. HABITS: arboreal; feeds on wing, outflying or diving ('stooping') on prey at great speed; solitary; sedentary and nomadic, possibly regular seasonal movements (migration) to Indonesia. BREEDING: September–December; nests in high tree forks, made of sticks and twigs and lined with fresh leaves, or takes over unused nests of other species; two to three eggs, buff, spotted and blotched with shades of red. VOICE: short high-pitched chatter or twitter. FOOD: birds and insects taken in flight, sometimes kills birds larger than itself.

STATUS: fairly common. TAXONOMY: endemic races of species with doubtful extralimital racial connections.

150 PEREGRINE FALCON   *Falco peregrinus*   Tunstall 1771

Distribution: throughout.

RECOGNITION: *blue-grey with black crown and face, buff to rufous below with black bars on belly.*

DESCRIPTION: 38–46cm. Sexes alike but female larger. Crown, nape and face black, shading to blue-grey on back, shoulders and tail; underparts creamy white or buff or cinnamon rufous, plain or speckled with black on breast and barred with black on belly and under-wing; tail barred with black; bill blue-black, cere greenish-yellow; eyes brown; legs yellow. *Immature:* upperparts blackish-brown; underparts buff densely streaked with black; legs yellow.

VARIATION: over much of continent, underparts paler (race *macropus*); southwest, underparts more richly coloured (race *submelanogenys*). These are poorly defined variants.

HABITAT: most kinds, but especially hilly and mountainous country with rocks and cliffs. HABITS: mainly arboreal but also uses cliffs and rocky ledges, catches prey by overtaking in flight or swooping, 'stooping', at great speed from high vantage points on trees or cliffs, prey killed with blow from closed foot; solitary; sedentary and possibly nomadic. BREEDING: August–December; nests on rocky ledges, in holes in trees or old nests of other species; two to three eggs, buffy-white blotched with reddish-brown. VOICE: loud chattering 'kek' and various screaming calls. FOOD: mainly birds, usually large like ducks.

STATUS: fairly common. TAXONOMY: endemic races of variable worldwide species.

Peregrine Falcon (150)

Brush Turkey (152)

Grey Falcon (148)

Family MEGAPODIIDAE
Mound-birds
3(13) species: 2 endemic

THE MOUND BUILDING BIRDS, now commonly referred to as megapodes, are related to the gallinaceous birds, of which the Domestic Fowl is an example. This affinity is suggested at least by the short thick curved bill, plump body and mainly terrestrial habits. But the striking characteristic of megapodes, which has given them a prominent place in scientific

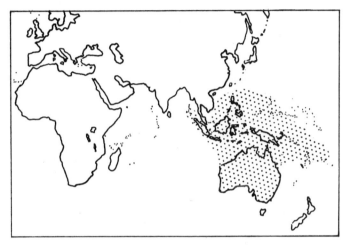

Distribution of MEGAPODIIDAE

and popular writing, is their divergence from the normal habit of incubating eggs by sitting on them. Body heat is replaced by the heat of rotting vegetation, occasionally sun heat and volcanic heat. This lack of direct attention to eggs once laid might seem to reflect the primitive reproductive behaviour of reptiles, from which birds evolved, but in fact in most cases continuous and very active care is taken to maintain a constant incubating temperature. Eggs are placed on top of vegetation gathered into a hole excavated in the ground and then covered over with loose sandy soil, the resulting structure being a mound averaging about 3m across and 1·5m in height. The temperature is regulated by adding or removing top cover, the 'thermometer' apparently being the bird's tongue or the skin on the underside of the bill. This attentive behaviour is usual but some birds, outside Australia, do in fact leave their eggs unattended in sun-warmed sand and in volcanically heated ground. Regardless of whether eggs are cared for or not the parents take no interest in the chicks which emerge from eggs and mound unassisted, fully fledged and capable of looking after themselves. This feature is unique among birds. Of the three species which are found in Australia, the Scrub Fowl is widely distributed in the Papuan area and the other two are endemic species of endemic genera. Megapodes are mainly forest birds but the Mallee Fowl has adapted to dry habitats and acquired cryptic plumage.

Key to MEGAPODIIDAE

1 Inhabiting dry woodlands of south . . . .   Mallee Fowl . . . . No 153
2 Inhabiting forests of east and north.   3–4

3 Brown and grey, head feathered . . . .   Scrub Fowl . . . . No 151
4 Black, head bare and brightly coloured . . . .   Brush Turkey . . . . No 152

Genus MEGAPODIUS

This is the largest megapode group consisting of many forms currently assembled into three species and extending from northern Australia to Nicobar I, the Philippines and central Polynesia. In colour they are shades of brown above and grey below with a distinct crest on the nape. Only one wide-ranging and variable species reaches the north and northeast coasts of Australia where it has differentiated into three races.

Mallee Fowl (153)   Scrub Fowl (151)

151 SCRUB FOWL *Megapodius freycinet* Gaimard 1823   Pl 4

Distribution: Map 28.

RECOGNITION: *about the size of an average Domestic Fowl, usually on ground in dense forests near water but flying into trees when disturbed, brown above and grey below with crest on nape.*

DESCRIPTION: 40cm. Short crest on nape. Sexes alike. Upperparts, except hind neck, shades of brown, darker on crown and nape, more rufous on upper and under tail coverts and blacker on tail; hind neck and underparts shades of blue-grey; bill reddish-brown; eyes shades of brown; legs bright orange.

VARIATION: Northern Territory, back olive-brown, underparts dark blue-grey (race *tumulus*); Cape York to Cooktown, back cinnamon-brown, underparts pale blue-grey (race *yorki*); Cairns southwards, back chestnut-brown, underparts dark blue-grey (race *castanotus*).

HABITAT: dense thickets near coasts and along banks of rivers and creeks, coastal islands. HABITS: terrestrial but flying into trees when disturbed where crouches with head and neck outstretched horizontally; solitary but in scattered colonies; movements unknown; flight laboured and for short distances, with legs dangling. BREEDING: August–March; nests are mounds basally consisting of inorganic material and topped with rotting vegetable mould in which eggs are laid in deep holes and incubated by fermentation heat; average mound may be over 3m across and 1·5m high but when used many times can grow to structures 15m across and 4m high, eggs buried as much as 2m from surface; so far as is known up to fifteen eggs laid over a long period, white with easily detached epidermis stained reddish-brown. VOICE: clucking like domestic fowl ending in loud scream. FOOD: berries, seeds, roots, insects, grubs.

STATUS: fairly common. TAXONOMY: endemic races of wide-ranging species.

Genus ALECTURA

A separate genus for the unique Brush Turkey. Bare head and neck with wattles in the breeding male and other features are distinctive. Although different in outward appearance to the Mallee Fowl, it has some similarities and it is possible that they originated from the same, not very ancient, forest stock.

152 BRUSH TURKEY *Alectura lathami* Gray 1835   Pl 4   Fig p 118
Distribution: Map 29.

RECOGNITION: *much larger than Domestic Fowl, terrestrial forest dweller, blackish with bare head and neck bright red.*

DESCRIPTION: 70cm, broad vertically folded tail 25cm. Sexes alike except that male only has wattle at base of neck in breeding season. Skin of head and neck bright red and sparsely covered with black hair-like feathers, base of neck and wattles yellow or purplish-white; upperparts black; underparts brownish-black mottled with buffy-white; bill black; eyes and legs dull brown.

VARIATION: over greater part of range base of neck and wattles yellow (race *lathami*); at Cape York, base of neck and wattles purplish-white (race *purpureicollis*).

HABITAT: forests of various kinds, from coastal rain forest to drier inland brigalow and mulga.
HABITS: terrestrial but flying into trees when disturbed and to roost; solitary but claimed that several females may use same nest mound; movements unknown; sometimes wanders into clearings and outside forests and visits homesteads near forests. BREEDING: August–December, but probably longer (mated female in captivity laid over a period of seven months); nests are mounds, at least 1m high by 3m across, consisting of vegetable material in various stages of decay—the outer cover being most recently gathered, mounds made and attended by male who 'mulches' them over and ensures that fermentation is taking place before eggs laid; thirty or more eggs, laid over extended period; perhaps, but not certainly, laid by more than one female (mated female in captivity laid fifty-six eggs in seven months). VOICE: loud clucking, grunting, muffled 'mooruk'. FOOD: fruit, berries, insects.

STATUS: fairly common. TAXONOMY: endemic species and genus.

Genus LEIPOA

The Mallee Fowl is unique and placed in a genus of its own. It is the only megapode living in arid country, presumably by adaptation from a forest ancestor, perhaps shared with the Brush Turkey, and it has acquired a camouflage plumage pattern.

153 MALLEE FOWL *Leipoa ocellata* Gould 1840   Pl 4
Distribution: Map 29.

RECOGNITION: *larger than Domestic Fowl with boldly mottled back and broad black streak from throat to breast; on ground in arid woodlands, such as mallee.*

DESCRIPTION: 60cm, broad tail 23cm. Sexes alike except that female has mottled under side of outer web of flight feathers. Crown and nape blackish-brown; hind neck and upper back blue-grey slightly barred light brown; back and wings boldly mottled black, white and brown; rump grey-brown; centre of tail barred grey-brown, buffy-white and black, outer tail dusky brown broadly tipped buffy-white; throat streaked buffy-white and dark brown; broad streak from centre of foreneck to breast black mottled buffy-white; sides of breast blue-grey; remainder of underparts buffy-white; facial skin grey, blue-grey below eye; bill dark grey; eyes light reddish-brown; legs blue grey.

VARIATION: western birds darker (race *ocellata*); eastern birds paler (race *rosinae*).

HABITAT: fairly dense arid woodlands with good cover of shrubs and fairly light soil, like most mallee. HABITS: terrestrial but roosting in trees and bushes; solitary but several pairs may be found feeding in close proximity when not breeding; sedentary with nomadic movements within a restricted area; flight heavy and for short distances, but seldom flies. BREEDING: September–April; nests are holes in ground filled and mounded up with vegetation and covered with loose earth where eggs are incubated by heat of fermentation; mounds made and heat regulated by male, average mound 1·5m high and 4m across but when used many times may grow to much larger dimensions; twenty or more eggs laid over an extended period, pale pink but become white and stained with vegetation. VOICE: loud booming and quieter grunting sounds. FOOD: buds, flowers, fruits, seeds, insects.

STATUS: fairly common. TAXONOMY: endemic species of endemic genus.

Stubble Quail (154)

Family PHASIANIDAE

Pheasants, Quails, etc.

7(165) species: 1 endemic: 4 introduced

Distribution: worldwide except southern South America.

THIS LARGE FAMILY CONSISTS of numerous pheasants, quails, partridges, jungle-fowl, including the progenitor of the Domestic Fowl (but not the Scrub Fowl—see Megapodiidae) and other named groups. It is represented in Australia by only three species of quails of which the Stubble Quail is endemic. Other species have been introduced for various reasons and some have become established in limited areas in the wild: the Californian Quail, Ring-necked Pheasant and Peafowl; also the Domestic Fowl lives in a wild state on the Capricorn Is. Quails, like other members of the family, are terrestrial. They frequent various types of grassy habitats from wet swamps to dry plains and savanna woodlands. They are small plump birds with very short tails and rounded wings. The sexes are slightly different, or very different as in the case of the King Quail. They are well camouflaged by the pattern of their plumage, are difficult to flush from the long grass and usually fly with whirring flight for only a short distance; but in spite of their apparent reluctance to fly they are strong on the wing, as long distance migration is a feature of many species. These quails are very similar in appearance and habits to the more numerous buttonquails, family Turnicidae, with which they are sometimes found in company, and also the curious Plain Wanderer, family Pedionomidae (or sub-family of Turnicidae) but they are basically different and, in the case of Australian species, can be distinguished as follows.

TRUE QUAILS: small hind toe. Underparts boldly streaked or barred with black or mainly plain with black and white throat (♂King Quail).

BUTTONQUAILS: no hind toe. Underparts mainly plain whitish or buffy and sometimes faintly barred or blotched, or black spotted with white (♀ of forest-dwelling Black-breasted Quail).

PLAIN WANDERER: small hind toe. Wide collar chequered in black and white (♀), black scalloping on back.

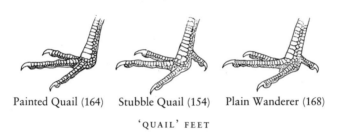

Painted Quail (164)   Stubble Quail (154)   Plain Wanderer (168)

'QUAIL' FEET

Key to PHASIANIDAE

1 Upperparts greyish, underparts streaked black .... Stubble Quail .... No 154
2 Upperparts brownish, underparts barred black .... Brown Quail .... No 155
3 Upperparts blackish, underparts barred black (♀) or multi-
   coloured (♂) .... King Quail .... No 156

Genus COTURNIX

This genus is based on a group of three species, including the Stubble Quail endemic to Australia, replacing each other throughout most of the old world, thus forming a large superspecies. Other closely related genera are *Synoicus,* one species, and *Excalfactoria,* two species, but it has been claimed, on good authority, that there are no satisfactory reasons for recognising them; there seems to be some reluctance in accepting this view. These quails are small and plump with tails so reduced as to seem absent. They have camouflage plumages and sexual dimorphism to varying degrees, and a small hind toe.

154 STUBBLE QUAIL   *Coturnix pectoralis*   Gould 1837

Distribution: Map 30

RECOGNITION: *general appearance greyish above and streaked below.*

DESCRIPTION: 15–18cm. Sexes different. *Male:* upperparts brownish-grey mottled with black and broadly streaked with buffy-white; crown and nape brownish-black with buffy-white central streak and on edge of crown above eye; throat cinnamon buff; upper breast mainly black mottled with white; centre of breast and belly whitish streaked with black; side of breast and flanks mottled black and cinnamon and broadly streaked with white; bill brownish-black; eyes light brown; legs pinkish-buff. *Female:* throat white, very little black on upper breast and very little cinnamon anywhere on underparts.

VARIATION: central and eastern populations lighter (race *pectoralis*); western populations darker (race *praetermissa*).

HABITAT: grasslands, cereal crops especially when in stubble, margins of swamps. HABITS: terrestrial; gregarious; sedentary and nomadic. BREEDING: mainly October–February; nests among grass, a scrape roughly lined with grass; seven to ten eggs, yellowish blotched with olive green. VOICE: a sharp high-pitched 'two-to-weep'. FOOD: grass seeds and insects.

STATUS: fairly common to common, rare in Tasmania. TAXONOMY: endemic species, probably semispecies of wide-ranging old world superspecies.

155 BROWN QUAIL   *Coturnix ypsilophorus*   Bosc 1792   Pl 5
Distribution: throughout.

RECOGNITION: *general appearance brownish above and barred below.*

DESCRIPTION: 15–20cm. Sexes different. *Male:* crown and nape blackish-brown with whitish central streak; remainder of upperparts greyish-brown lightly mottled with black and thinly streaked with white; throat pale buff; remainder of underparts cinnamon buff barred with blackish double-crescent markings (like birds in flight); bill dark grey above, blue-grey below; eyes red-brown; legs yellow. *Female:* upperparts thickly blotched with black.

VARIATION: large (20cm) and small (15cm) birds occur in Tasmania; their relationships are uncertain, sometimes they are regarded as species, sometimes races occupying different habitats and sometimes as one species of variable size; the large bird is the nominate form (race *ypsilophorus*); the small bird also occurs throughout the continent (race *australis*); other races have been named but they do not seem to be well defined.

HABITAT: grassy areas especially in swamp localities. HABITS: terrestrial; gregarious, in loose companies; sedentary and nomadic, moving about to suitable feeding grounds. BREEDING: throughout the year; nests among grass on ground in shallow depression lined with grass and leaves and often with grass blades bent over to form sides and canopy; up to twelve eggs, dull white or bluish-white lightly spotted with light brown. VOICE: a high-pitched short-long whistle, like 'fee-weep'. FOOD: grass seeds and insects.

STATUS: apparently fairly common, perhaps common. TAXONOMY: species (perhaps two species, one endemic to Tasmania) extending to New Guinea and adjacent islands.

156 KING QUAIL   *Coturnix chinensis*   (Linnaeus) 1766   Pl 5
Distribution: Map 31.

RECOGNITION: *blackish above; male has blue-grey breast, chestnut belly and under tail coverts; female underparts barred with black.*

DESCRIPTION: 15–18cm. Sexes very different. *Male:* upperparts dark brown blotched with black and slightly streaked with buffy-white; face below eye, and throat black bordered with white and with white 'moustache'; face above eye, side of neck, breast and flanks dark blue-grey; centre of breast and belly dark chestnut; bill black; eyes red-brown; legs yellow.

Female: upperparts similar to male; face cinnamon buff except for black streak from angle of mouth; throat white; remainder of underparts buffy-white densely barred with black.

VARIATION: several races have been described but they do not seem to be clearly defined.

HABITAT: grassy swamps and other wet grasslands. HABITS: (not well known) terrestrial; solitary or loosely gregarious, in small flocks; probably sedentary and nomadic. BREEDING: apparently most months; nests among grass tussocks, a depression in the ground lined with fine grass and roofed with bent over grasses; six to eight eggs, pale brown spotted with dark brown. VOICE: a two to three note high-pitched whistle, also clucking sounds, especially by female. FOOD: grass seeds and insects.

STATUS: uncertain, possibly fairly common. TAXONOMY: race *(australis)* of species extending to India and south China.

Introduced species

157 CALIFORNIAN QUAIL *Lophortyx californicus* (Shaw) 1798

Distribution: lives wild on King I, Bass St, and parts of coastal Victoria.

RECOGNITION: like male King Quail but about twice size and with *striking forward curved crest*; mainly greyish-brown with *black throat circled with white* and white forehead continued as streak over and behind eye; breast blue-grey. Female lacks black throat.

['RED-RUMPED QUAIL' An unidentified quail distinguished by a bright red rump has been recorded in southeast Queensland. For details see ADDENDA p. 487]

Introduced species

158 DOMESTIC FOWL *Gallus* sp

Distribution: lives in a feral state on North West Is of the Capricorn Group.

RECOGNITION: 40–51cm. Plumage has reverted to the black-breasted game type of the wild species. Keeps to forested parts and apparently lives without fresh water. Nests on ground among fallen tree trunks; ten to thirteen eggs.

Introduced species

159 RING-NECKED PHEASANT *Phasianus colchicus* Linnaeus 1758

Distribution: lives wild in a number of places, notably Rottnest I, W.A., near Adelaide, King I, Bass St, southern Tasmania.

RECOGNITION: 60cm–1m, long graduated tail. *Male:* head and neck glossy dark green, white collar, red facial skin; plumage variable but mainly red and brown, mottled and scalloped on back. *Female:* smaller, dull brown, lacking green gloss on head and white collar. Terrestrial, short laboured flights ending in long glide.

Introduced species

160 PEAFOWL *Pavo cristatus* Linnaeus 1758

Distribution: lives wild on Rottnest I, W.A.

RECOGNITION: 75cm plus tail 1m. *Male:* head crested; mainly bronze-green with black scallops; long tail can be erected vertically and fanned to show large irridescent blue-green 'eyes'. Very loud raucous scream. *Female:* smaller and duller.

Family TURNICIDAE

Buttonquails

7(17) species: 6 endemic

THE BUTTONQUAILS OR BUSTARDQUAILS or hemipodes, as they are variously named, might easily be mistaken for quails of the family Phasianidae. They look very like them, in many ways behave like them, frequent similar grassy habitats and often consort with them. But they are fundamentally different and belong not only to a different family but to a different major group, which includes the cranes. One important visible difference is that buttonquails have only three toes; they lack the fourth small hind toe which is present in the true quails. They are also distinct in having the unusual characteristic of reversed male and female roles, in all but the primary sexual functions. The female is larger, more distinctly patterned, is the active partner in courtship and leaves the male to look after the eggs and bring up the family. Like the true quails they are small and plump with much reduced tail, short rounded wings and camouflage plumages, but, unlike the quails, the underparts are more or less plain buff or whitish, at most only faintly barred or blotched, except in the female of the forest-dwelling Black-breasted (button) Quail.

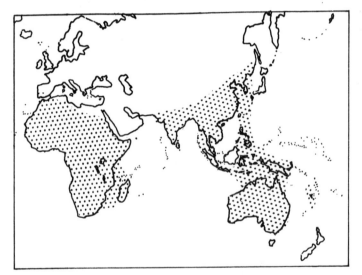

Distribution of TURNICIDAE

PLAIN WANDERER

The unique Plain Wanderer poses a problem of relationship, like a good many other Australian birds, which does not seem to have been solved to everyone's satisfaction. Current study places it closest to the Turnicidae but opinion hovers between keeping it in a family of its own or tacking it on as a subfamily of the buttonquails. The latter course is taken here for the sake of convenience and not from conviction. The Plain Wanderer has a small hind toe like the true quails, it has the reversed sexual dimorphism of the buttonquails, plumage like a bustard and head and bill rather like a plover. It lives on open, bare plains, not secretively among thick grasses; when alarmed it has an upright posture and stands on its toes on relatively long legs, all adaptations enabling it to see far and run fast. Some buttonquails, at least, assume this posture also when running.

Key to TURNICIDAE

[*Note:* Although collectively known as Buttonquails it is customary to abbreviate species names to 'quail'.]

1 Usually in dense forests......................	Black-breasted Quail	No 163
2 Usually in open forests	Painted Quail.............	No 164
3 In various kinds of open grassland	4–10	
4 Underparts whitish scalloped with black; (♀) brown breast and checked collar	Plain Wanderer	No 168
5 Breast plain buff-olive	Buff-breasted Quail........	No 165
6 Breast medium grey with pale spots	Chestnut-backed Quail.....	No 166
7 Breast cinnamon brown	8–10	
8 Breast lightly barred	Little Quail...............	No 167
9 Breast plain.................................	Red-chested Quail........	No 162
10 Breast spotted black at sides....................	Red-backed Quail........	No 161

161 RED-BACKED QUAIL *Turnix maculosa* (Temminck) 1815

Distribution: Map 32.

RECOGNITION: *cinnamon brown breast spotted with black at sides; cinnamon brown on upper back—more distinct in female.*

DESCRIPTION: 13–15cm. Sexes different. *Male:* smaller: crown blackish with central buff streak; upper back mixed grey and cinnamon brown; lower back mainly black; scapulars and shoulders buff blotched with black; face and side of neck buff speckled with black; upper breast cinnamon brown, sides spotted with black; remainder of underparts creamy white; bill brown, yellowish at base; eyes lemon-white; legs yellow. *Female:* larger; hind neck and upper back cinnamon brown and more richly brown on breast and flanks.

VARIATION: races have been described but they do not seem to be clearly defined.

HABITAT: grasslands, especially wetter kinds, old cultivations. HABITS: terrestrial; solitary or in small parties; sedentary and nomadic, perhaps migratory in southern limits (movements not well known); flight slower than most quails. BREEDING: October–July; nests on ground among grass tussocks, a scrape lined with grass, also grass stems bent and woven to form a canopy; four eggs, dull white spotted with shades of brown. VOICE: rapidly repeated 'oom'. FOOD: seeds and insects.

STATUS: not well known but apparently rare to fairly common. TAXONOMY: variable species extending to Solomon Is, New Guinea and adjacent islands, possibly also semispecies of old world superspecies.

162 RED-CHESTED QUAIL *Turnix pyrrothorax* (Gould) 1841   Pl 5

Distribution: Map 33.

RECOGNITION: *cinnamon brown breast without spots at side, no cinnamon brown on upper back.*

DESCRIPTION: 13–15cm. Sexes different. *Male:* crown and nape blackish with broad pale buff central streak; remainder of upperparts brownish-grey blotched with black and streaked with white, very few brown markings; face above and below eye buff speckled with black;

throat white; foreneck, upper breast and flanks cinnamon brown with black crescents on side of neck and side of breast; lower breast and belly white; bill blackish-brown above, pale grey below; eyes creamy-white; legs creamy-white. *Female:* face darker, especially above eye; whole underparts cinnamon brown, darker on breast; no black markings on neck or breast.

VARIATION: races have been described but they do not seem to be clearly defined.

HABITAT: various kinds of grassland. HABITS: terrestrial; solitary or in small groups, possibly family parties; sedentary and nomadic, perhaps migratory. BREEDING: October–March; nests on ground among grass, a shallow depression lined with fine dry grass and leaves and canopied over with woven grass stems; four eggs, yellowish-white spotted and blotched with shades of brown and grey. VOICE: a booming 'oom' repeated rapidly and increasing in intensity and pitch, also a gurgling 'gug' and soft whistling chirrup. FOOD: seeds and insects. STATUS: apparently rare. TAXONOMY: endemic species.

163 BLACK-BREASTED QUAIL   *Turnix melanogaster*   (Gould) 1837
Distribution: Map 34.

RECOGNITION: *male; dull brown with white edges to inner wing feathers; female; foreparts black with white spots on breast; inhabiting wet forests.*

DESCRIPTION: 15–18cm. Sexes very different. *Male:* smaller; crown and nape grey-brown edged with blackish-brown; remainder of upperparts dull brown blotched with black and with scattered white markings, especially white edges to inner wing feathers; forehead and face speckled white; throat white; foreneck and breast grey-brown blotched with white and some black; belly pale grey-brown; bill light brown; eyes white; legs pale pinkish-brown. *Female:* larger; crown, face, throat and breast black, head slightly speckled white and breast spotted white; belly dark grey-brown.

HABITAT: wet forests. HABITS: terrestrial; probably sedentary; solitary, sometimes in small parties, apparently family groups; seldom flies and then only for short distances; while sitting twists body among leaves on forest floor making saucer-shaped depression. BREEDING: December (certain), also claimed to be February–April and June–July; nests said to be simple scrape on ground in grassed areas; three to four eggs, dull white spotted and blotched with browns, greys and black. VOICE: low booming 'oom' repeated rapidly, also soft clucking. FOOD: seeds and insects.

STATUS: apparently rare but probably more common than records suggest. TAXONOMY: unique endemic species.

PAINTED QUAIL GROUP
The Painted Quail and Chestnut-backed Quail are usually listed as two species replacing each other geographically in the Cooktown area (the precise nature of the replacement is uncertain). The latter species is split into two apparently isolated populations, one at the tip of Cape York and the other in Northern Territory. It has been claimed that they may be separate species. They have distinct differences and the course is taken here of listing them as species, the Cape York population with its original name of Buff-breasted Quail. The Painted Quail has had a similar form in New Caledonia tacked on to it as a subspecies. There is justification for regarding it as a species, or semispecies in a superspecies of which the other components are the three endemic Australian species.

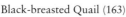

Black-breasted Quail (163)

Plain Wanderer (168)

164 PAINTED QUAIL *Turnix varia* (Latham) 1801

Distribution: Map 35.

RECOGNITION: *medium grey breast with large pale spots, purplish-grey rump, forehead and face speckled with white, thin short bill.*

DESCRIPTION: 18–20cm. Sexes slightly different, female larger and with rather more black and brown blotches on back. Centre of crown and nape purplish-grey, sides of crown blackish; remainder of upperparts mainly purplish-grey blotched with black, upper back slightly marked with cinnamon brown, back streaked with white, shoulder and inner wing blotched with white; breast and flanks medium grey, breast with large whitish spots; belly creamy white; bill grey-brown; eyes reddish-orange; legs yellow.

VARIATION: races have been described but they do not seem to be clearly defined.

HABITAT: grassy woodlands, especially rough country like lightly timbered stony hillsides.

HABITS: terrestrial; solitary or in small parties, probably family groups; sedentary and nomadic, perhaps migratory, e.g. both resident and breeding visitor in Victoria; flight low and erratic. BREEDING: September–March in south, recorded in other months in north, probably depending on rains; nests on ground, slight depression at base of tufts or tussocks of grass, lined with grass and leaves; four eggs, greenish-white spotted and blotched with brown and purple. VOICE: low drumming 'oom'. FOOD: mainly insects, also seeds.

STATUS: fairly common. TAXONOMY: endemic species, forming superspecies with Buff-breasted and Chestnut-backed Quails.

165 BUFF-BREASTED QUAIL *Turnix olivii* Robinson 1900

Distribution: Map 35.

RECOGNITION: *more or less unspotted pale buff-olive breast, very few white speckles on forehead and face, reddish-brown rump, relatively long thick bill.* (See illustrations Emu 22:1)

DESCRIPTION: 18–20cm. Sexes slightly different, female larger and less speckled on side of neck. Centre of crown and nape purplish-grey, sides of crown blackish; remainder of upperparts cinnamon brown blotched with black and streaked with white; face and throat purplish-grey; sides of neck whitish speckled with black; breast and flanks pale buff-olive; belly dull white; bill brown above, whitish below; eyes and legs yellow.

HABITAT: savanna woodlands, apparently rough ridgy country. HABITS: terrestrial; recorded in parties up to about twenty; movements unknown; flight short and low; runs with upright gait, head and neck stretched up. BREEDING: March, at least; nests on ground among rough grasses and shrubs, shallow depresssion lined with fine dry grass and thatched or domed; four eggs, whitish, blotched with black, shades of grey and reddish-brown. VOICE: deep booming 'oom' repeated, beginning low and slow and ending high and rapid, also deep humming 'gug' repeated rapidly, also (♂) 'chirp-chirp-chirp-kwaare-kwaare' and 'chu' repeated. FOOD: apparently seeds and insects.

STATUS: probably fairly common. TAXONOMY: endemic species, forming superspecies with Painted and Chestnut-backed Quails.

166 CHESTNUT-BACKED QUAIL   *Turnix castonota*   (Gould) 1839   Pl 5

Distribution: Map 35.

RECOGNITION: *medium grey breast with small whitish spots, forehead and face speckled with white, reddish-brown rump, relatively short thick bill.*

DESCRIPTION: 15–18cm. Sexes slightly different, female larger. Centre of crown and nape grey, sides blackish; remainder of upperparts walnut brown blotched with black, spotted with white on shoulders and inner wing; forehead and face speckled with white; throat and foreneck dull white with short white streaks; breast and flanks medium grey with small dull white spots; belly creamy white; bill grey-brown above, bluish-white below; eyes pale yellow; legs yellow.

HABITAT: poorly grassed localities in dry savanna woodland, like lightly timbered stony hills and sandy ridges. HABITS: terrestrial; usually recorded as gregarious, in fairly closely packed groups of up to about twenty and running or flushing together; said to be sedentary; runs upright with head and neck stretched up. BREEDING: December–March; nests on ground among grass, at base of clump or tussock, a depression lined and canopied over with grass; four eggs, dull white spotted with shades of brown. VOICE: low moaning calls when birds in a group are separated. FOOD: seeds and insects.

STATUS: common. TAXONOMY: endemic species, forming superspecies with Buff-breasted and Painted Quails.

167 LITTLE QUAIL   *Turnix velox*   (Gould) 1841

Distribution: Map 36.

RECOGNITION: *pale cinnamon brown breast lightly barred with dark brown, thin pale streak on crown of male only.*

DESCRIPTION: 13–15cm. Sexes slightly different, female larger and lacking pale central streak on crown. Crown and nape blackish with thin whitish central streak; remainder of upper-parts light reddish-brown, finely barred with black and brown and streaked with white; face above and below eye light brown; throat and belly white; breast pale cinnamon brown lightly barred with dark brown; bill pale grey; eyes yellowish-white; legs pinkish-white.

HABITAT: grasslands of various types but mainly dry lightly timbered areas and high dry downs. HABITS: terrestrial; usually in small flocks; mainly nomadic unless conditions very favourable. BREEDING: most months in some parts of range; nests on ground at base of grass tussocks, a shallow depression lined and canopied with grass; four eggs, buffy-white freckled and spotted with shades of brown and grey. VOICE: loud hooting, and squeaking call when flushed. FOOD: mainly insects, also seeds.

STATUS: fairly common. TAXONOMY: endemic species.

Genus PEDIONOMUS

(See notes page 126)

168 PLAIN WANDERER *Pedionomus torquatus* (Gould) 1840   Fig p 129
Distribution: Map 37.

RECOGNITION: *white underparts scalloped with black; (♀) black and white checked collar and cinnamon brown breast; small hind toe.*

DESCRIPTION: 15–18cm. Sexes different. *Male:* smaller; upperparts brownish-grey scalloped with white and mottled with black and buffy-white on neck and centre of wing (very like a bustard); face whitish speckled with dark brown; throat white; breast and flanks cinnamon white scalloped with black; belly buffy-white; bill yellow; eyes yellow; legs greenish-yellow. *Female:* larger; wide collar boldly checkered in black and white; large patch of cinnamon rufous on upper breast and narrow fringe of same colour on nape.

HABITAT: lightly grassed open plains. HABITS: terrestrial, sometimes temporarily landing on low snag or fence rail; usually solitary; sedentary and nomadic depending on food supply; stands and runs in upright posture with head stretched up and on long legs, sometimes up on toes; runs very fast and difficult to flush. BREEDING: variable, mostly between September and February; nests on ground, a shallow scrape; four eggs, greenish-white blotched, speckled and streaked with shades of brown and grey. VOICE: low booming 'oom'. FOOD: seeds and insects.

STATUS: rare and declining. TAXONOMY: unique endemic species.

Family GRUIDAE

Cranes

2(14) species: 1 endemic

CRANES HAVE A MORE graceful bearing than the storks to which they bear some resemblance. Unlike storks they are wholly terrestrial. They are large, standing nearly 1·5m in the case of one species, with long legs and necks and long sharply pointed bills. They have a small hind toe inserted above the level of the other three. Plumages are embellished with decorative feathers, especially about the head. A striking feature of cranes is their dancing display which is well illustrated and particularly attractive in the case of Australia's endemic species, the Brolga. For a long time the Brolga was thought to be the sole representative of the family but in recent years the Sarus Crane has been identified as a resident species in northern Queensland. It may be a recent settler or possibly has been here for a long time but has been overlooked because of its close resemblance to the Brolga.

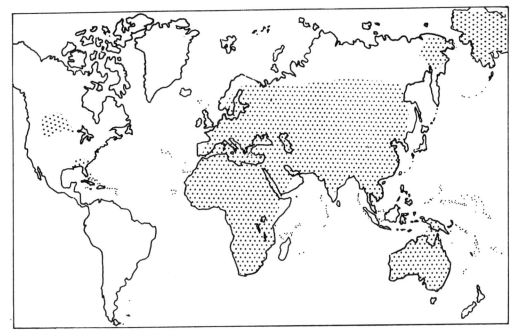

Distribution of GRUIDAE

Key to GRUIDAE

1 Face and nape red, legs dark grey .... Brolga .... No 169
2 Face, nape and upper neck red, legs mainly pinkish .... Sarus Crane ...... No 170

169 BROLGA *Grus rubicunda* (Perry) 1810   Pl 4

Distribution: Map 38.

RECOGNITION: *silvery-grey with dark tail and flight feathers, red on head (but not upper neck), dark grey legs.*

DESCRIPTION: 105–120cm, with bill 15cm; inner wing feathers extend just beyond short tail; stands 105cm on long slender legs; wingspan 2m. Sexes alike but female smaller. Silvery-grey, darker on tail, flight feathers brownish-black; head bare except for tuft of grey feathers over ear and some black hair-like feathers on black pendulous chin; bare skin of crown olive-green; bare skin of face and nape red; bill olive-green; eyes yellow; legs dark grey.

HABITAT: swampy margins of fresh and brackish waters, grasslands and cultivations. HABITS: terrestrial; gregarious, sometimes in very large flocks on suitable feeding grounds, more dispersed when breeding; sedentary except for movements between breeding and feeding grounds; graceful dancing displays; long jumping run to get airborne; flight apparently laboured with long neck and legs extended. BREEDING: October–April; nests on ground in or near moist areas, rough platform of sticks and grasses; two eggs, dull white blotched with brown. VOICE: shrill trumpeting and loud gurgling 'goolk'. FOOD: vegetable material, especially tubers of bulkuru sedge, adapts to cereal crops; also wide variety of insects.

STATUS: very common in north, uncommon to rare in south. TAXONOMY: endemic species with vagrant or introduced occurrence in southeast New Guinea.

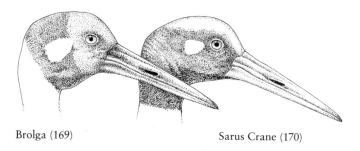

Brolga (169)   Sarus Crane (170)

170 SARUS CRANE *Grus antigone* (Linnaeus) 1758
Distribution: Map 39.

RECOGNITION: *silvery-grey with darker tail and flight feathers, bare red skin on face, nape and upper neck, legs dull pink.*

DESCRIPTION: 120cm, with bill 15cm. Sexes alike. Like Brolga but general colour darker, more brownish-grey, tip of long inner wing feathers and ear patch whiter, bare red skin of face and nape extends about 8cm on upper neck, legs dull pink.

HABITAT, etc: apparently very similar to Brolga.

STATUS: rare. TAXONOMY: species extending to southeast Asia and northern India.

Family RALLIDAE
Rails and Crakes
16(132) species: 3 endemic

Distribution: worldwide.

RAILS AND CRAKES ARE largely terrestrial and even when common in any region are often among the least well known species. Their haunts are dense ground cover like grasses and reeds in swampy places, where they keep well hidden. Some of the gallinules are more aquatic and less furtive. The Coot frequents open water. In the crakes especially, bodies are laterally compressed which enables them to move easily and silently through dense reeds and matted grasses. Some are crepuscular or nocturnal. Their most revealing and distinctive characteristic is loud harsh cries. Although difficult to flush and apparently reluctant to fly more than short distances, and then with long legs dangling, some are notable fliers and travel a long way, especially on migration. Few remote islands are without at least one representative. On the other hand a number of species have become partially or completely flightless, like the Notornis of New Zealand and the Tasmanian Native-hen. Of the sixteen Australian species, four are peculiar to the continent, or five if the rare Bush-hen of Queensland wet forests ranks as a species. They range in size from the tiny Marsh Crake, about 15cm, to the

Tasmanian Native-hen, about the size of a plump Domestic Fowl. Their typically short tails are constantly flicked. They are patterned in plain sombre colours relieved by some bright feature, like bright red bill or white under tail coverts, or the plumage is streaked, especially on the back, or barred, especially on flanks and belly. The sexes are more or less alike.

Key to RALLIDAE

Plumage plain

1	Head grey, body shades of brown	Chestnut Rail	No 175
2	General appearance blackish	4–9	
3	General appearance olive-brown	10–11	
4	Under 20cm	Spotless Crake	No 179
5	Over 30cm	6–9	
6	Forehead white..............................	Coot	
7	Forehead red................................	8–9	
8	Single white patch under tail	Swamphen	No 185
9	Two white patches under tail...................	Dusky Moorhen	No 184
10	Under 30cm, northeast Queensland	Bush-hen................	No 181
11	Over 30cm, white spots on flanks		
	Mainland, except northeast Queensland	Black-tailed Native-hen	No 182
	Tasmania	Tasmanian Native-hen	No 183

Plumage streaked, barred or mottled

1	Wings cinnamon brown, very rare	Corncrake	No 176
2	Foreparts uniformly russet	4–5	
3	Back mottled olive-brown	6–13	
4	Back black..................................	Red-necked Rail	No 173
5	Back dark brown	Malay Banded Crake	No 174
6	White streak on face	8–9	
7	No white on face	10–13	
8	Breast and belly barred black and white..........	Banded Rail	No 172
9	Underparts mainly plain white..................	White-browed Crake	No 180
10	Long thin bill, crown rufous	Lewin Water Rail	No 171
11	Short thick bill, crown not rufous	12–13	
12	Breast blackish, undertail white.................	Spotted Crake	No 178
13	Breast pale grey, undertail barred black and white ..	Marsh Crake	No 177

Genus RALLUS

A worldwide group of over a dozen species distinguished mainly by long slender bills, often coloured red. This feature is well illustrated, but with bill reddish-brown, by one of the two Australian species, the Lewin Water-rail, but less so by the Banded Rail which has a long thick bill.

171 LEWIN WATER-RAIL *Rallus pectoralis* Temminck 1831 Pl 5 Fig p 135

Distribution: Map 40.

RECOGNITION: *long thin bill, pale greyish throat and breast, barred belly and undertail, no white on face.*

DESCRIPTION: 20–23cm, slender bill 3cm. Sexes nearly alike. Upperparts broadly streaked with black on russet brown crown and nape and cinnamon brown back; dusky patch in front of eye; upper face plain russet brown; chin white; throat, lower face and breast light

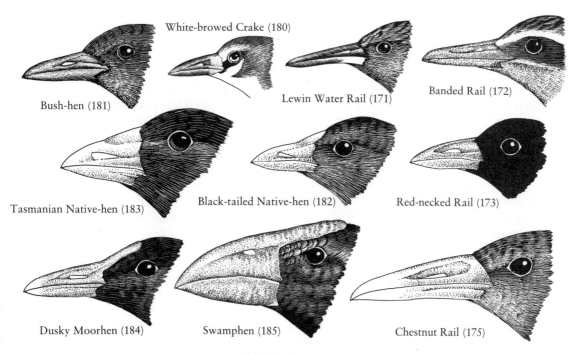

White-browed Crake (180)

Bush-hen (181)

Lewin Water Rail (171)

Banded Rail (172)

Tasmanian Native-hen (183)

Black-tailed Native-hen (182)

Red-necked Rail (173)

Dusky Moorhen (184)

Swamphen (185)

Chestnut Rail (175)

RALLIDAE BILLS

grey slightly tinged with brown (brown tinge lacking in female); shoulders, flanks, belly and undertail barred black and white; flight feathers plain black; bill reddish-brown, paler at base; eyes brown; legs pinkish-brown.

VARIATION: eastern mainland smallest (race *pectoralis*); southwest largest (race *clelandi*); Tasmania intermediate (race *brachipus*).

HABITAT: dense reedy margins of inland waters. HABITS: terrestrial and aquatic; solitary; sedentary; can swim and dive; flies reluctantly with legs dangling. BREEDING: August–December; nests among reeds and rushes, made of trampled vegetation and canopied over; four to six eggs, pale cream spotted and blotched with red and lavender-grey. VOICE: a loud metallic 'tic-tic' or 'cree-eek' repeated (♂ only?), a cat-like purr (♀?). FOOD: insects, snails, worms.

STATUS: apparently rare to uncommon. TAXONOMY: endemic races of species occurring also in New Guinea.

172 BANDED RAIL *Rallus philippensis* Linnaeus 1766   Pl 5   Fig p 135

Distribution: widely distributed mainly in coastal localities and offshore islands, less frequently inland waters.

RECOGNITION: *white streak on face, breast and belly barred black and white, brown band on breast, long thick bill.*

DESCRIPTION: 25–30cm, bill 3cm. Sexes alike. Crown to nape blackish-brown streaked with buff brown; broad white streak above eye extending to nape; hind neck and broad streak across face russet brown; upper back blackish-brown speckled with white; scapulars, lower back and tail black and tawny olive; chin white shading to grey on throat and foreneck; lower foreneck, breast and flanks barred black and white with narrow band of cinnamon buff on upper breast; centre of belly buffy-white; flight feathers blackish-brown broadly barred with white and cinnamon brown; bill brown; eyes reddish-brown; legs pinkish-brown.

VARIATION: not clearly defined; said to be darker in west (race *mellori*); smaller and darker in Cape York Peninsula (race *yorki*); remainder (race *australis*).

HABITAT: dense ground cover near water. HABITS: terrestrial; solitary but sometimes feeds in small parties; sedentary and nomadic; difficult to flush and flies low for short distance with dangling legs, runs very fast. BREEDING: September–March; nests on ground among grass, shallow scrape sometimes lined with grass and usually under tussock or some other overhanging protection; five to six eggs, dull white spotted and blotched with shades of brown and purplish-grey. VOICE: variants of three basic sounds, 'squeak', 'krik' and 'coo'. FOOD: small animals and insects, also seeds.

STATUS: common. TAXONOMY: very variable species extending to New Zealand, Fiji, Philippines and islands in east Indian Ocean.

Genus RALLINA

A group of four species distinguished by plain dark reddish-brown head and breast, and barring on the remainder of the underparts. They frequent dense forests and swamps along the margins of rivers and creeks. They range from India to southeast Asia south to New Guinea, with one species extending into coastal northeast Queensland. A vagrant of another species has been recorded from near Broome.

173 RED-NECKED RAIL *Rallina tricolor* Gray 1858   Fig p 135

Distribution: Map 41.

RECOGNITION: *head and breast plain reddish-brown, remainder of underparts barred, legs dark olive.*

DESCRIPTION: 28–30cm. Sexes alike. Head, neck and breast dark hazel brown, paler on throat and nearly white on chin; remainder of upperparts brownish-black tinged with olive on upper back; remainder of underparts blackish-brown with varying amounts of pale buff bars; wings broadly barred with white on underside, only faintly barred on upperside; bill green; eyes red; legs olive-green.

HABITAT: wet forests near water. HABITS: terrestrial; apparently solitary and sedentary; crepuscular. BREEDING: November–March; nests among thick vegetation and debris, often at base of tree or some thick clump; roughly made of leaves; four to five white eggs. VOICE: loud shrill 'kare' and short sharp 'tok' repeated many times, also melodious 'coot' rapidly repeated. FOOD: small animals and insects.

STATUS: apparently fairly common. TAXONOMY: endemic race *(robinsoni)* of species extending to New Guinea and Bismarck Archipelago.

174 MALAY BANDED CRAKE *Rallina fasciata* (Raffles) 1822

Distribution: only recorded near Broome.

RECOGNITION: like Red-necked Rail but smaller (23cm), *flanks, belly and wings barred white,* legs red, bill black.

STATUS: rare vagrant; nearest recorded normal range Moluccas.

Genus EULABEORNIS

A genus consisting only of the plain brownish and rather featureless Chestnut Rail frequenting mangroves of northern Australia and the Aru Is.

175 CHESTNUT RAIL *Eulabeornis castaneoventris* Gould 1844   Pl 5   Fig p 135

Distribution: mangroves of north coast from Broome to Normanton (doubtfully Cape York).

RECOGNITION: *grey head, olive-brown back, hazel-brown underparts; coastal mangroves.*

DESCRIPTION: 40cm with bill 5cm. Sexes alike. Head, nape and face grey; remainder of upperparts dark olive-brown; chin pinkish-white; throat and foreneck pinkish-fawn; remainder of underparts hazel; bill green, tip yellow; eyes red; legs pale greenish-yellow.

HABITAT: mangroves. HABITS: terrestrial but nesting in lower branches of mangroves; apparently solitary and sedentary; very wary and difficult to flush. BREEDING: November–February; nests in lower branches of mangroves up to about 3m, made of sticks; four eggs, pinkish-white spotted with shades of reddish-brown. VOICE: grunts and harsh screeches, sometimes separate, sometimes in sequence and repeated many times. FOOD: small aquatic animals.

STATUS: common. TAXONOMY: endemic race (or species) with one other form in Aru Is.

176 CORNCRAKE *Crex crex* (Linnaeus) 1758

Distribution: two scattered records, near Sydney and at sea off Western Australia.

RECOGNITION: General appearance like Banded Rail but paler and browner, *wings mainly plain cinnamon brown, belly barred brown and white,* no russet brown on hind neck and no brown band on breast, bill much shorter.

STATUS: rare vagrant; non-breeding migrant from palaearctic region.

Genus PORZANA

Rather more than a dozen small crakes found throughout most parts of the world. Upperparts typically shades of brown with broad pale and dark streaks, plain coloured throat and breast, usually shades of grey, and barred flanks and belly. They frequent the thick vegetation on the shallow margins of lagoons. Of the four Australian species the Spotted Crake is endemic. The White-browed Crake is sometimes put in a separate genus, *Poliolimnas.*

177 MARSH CRAKE *Porzana pusilla* (Pallas) 1776   Pl 5

Distribution: widespread, especially in south and Tasmania, but north of tropic records are few and scattered; not recorded in Northern Territory.

RECOGNITION: *pale grey throat and breast, black and white barring on undertail.*

DESCRIPTION: 15cm. Sexes alike. Crown and nape streaked brown and black; back brown and black, spotted with white on upper back and scapulars; shoulders mainly brown; face, throat and breast pale grey, nearly white on chin; flanks, belly and undertail coverts barred dark grey and dull white; bill dark brown, base green; eyes red; legs greenish-olive.

HABITAT: thick vegetation of shallow swamps. HABITS: terrestrial and aquatic, sometimes flies into low branches of bushes and trees over water; solitary; sedentary and nomadic or migratory, most birds disappear from some breeding grounds; usually very furtive in movements, flitting quickly from one tussock to another; tail constantly flicked. BREEDING:

September–February; nests in clumps or tussocks of vegetation on water or on land, or on firm ground among grass, well made of pieces of vegetation and domed over with stems bound together; four to six eggs, dark olive usually marked with darker shades. VOICE: loud harsh 'krek' (or 'crake') and a whirring 'chirr'. FOOD: small aquatic animals and insects, also vegetable matter.

STATUS: fairly common in south, uncertain elsewhere. TAXONOMY: endemic race *(palustris)* of species widespread in old world.

178 SPOTTED CRAKE   *Porzana fluminea*   Gould 1862   Pl 5

Distribution: widespread, mainly in south and Tasmania, records few and scattered north of tropic; not recorded in northern Northern Territory and Cape York Peninsula.

RECOGNITION : *blackish throat and breast, white inverted 'v' on undertail, white barring on rump.*

DESCRIPTION: 18cm. Sexes alike. Upperparts, except rump, olive-brown blotched with black and spotted with white; rump, flanks and belly barred black and white; face, throat and breast dark olive-grey, blackish at base of bill; undertail mainly white with small patch of black; bill olive-green, reddish at base, more so in male; eyes reddish-brown; legs olive-green.

VARIATION: east of Spencer Gulf longitude, darker (race *fluminea*); west of Spencer Gulf, paler grey on throat and breast (race *whitei*).

HABITAT: thick vegetation on shallow margins of fresh and brackish waters; less dependent on dense cover than other small crakes. HABITS: terrestrial and aquatic, swims well, feeds in shallow water and mud flats but near cover; sedentary and nomadic; flies readily and well but when disturbed usually seeks cover. BREEDING: August–January; nests in shallow water, in clumps of grass, bushes or reeds; a platform or shallow cup of grass often placed on bent reeds; four to six eggs, dark olive spotted with darker shades of same colour. VOICE: loud harsh 'krek' (or 'crake'), also chattering. FOOD: small aquatic animals and insects, vegetation.

STATUS: fairly common in south, uncertain elsewhere. TAXONOMY: endemic species.

179 SPOTLESS CRAKE   *Porzana tabuensis*   (Gmelin) 1789   Fig p 142

Distribution: mainly in south and Tasmania, north to Murchison River, Alice Springs and Cairns.

RECOGNITION: *blackish upperparts not marked with white, undertail mottled with white, red legs and black bill.*

DESCRIPTION: 18cm. Sexes alike. Upperparts sooty black tinged with dark umber brown on upper back and scapulars; underparts dark grey, paler on throat and nearly white on chin; under shoulders and under tail coverts brown mottled with white; bill black; eyes and eyelids red; legs red.

HABITAT: Dense timber and thickets near reedy swamps, also in drier localities, especially on coastal islands. HABITS: terrestrial; solitary; sedentary and nomadic; feeds in shallow water on margins of swamps; tail constantly flicked or held erect when running. BREEDING: September–January, some records in other months; nests among tussocks of swamp vegetation in shallow water, about 0·5m above water; a flat platform of vegetation; four to six eggs, light brown blotched with darker brown. VOICE: short sharp 'kup-kup' likened to sound of two-stroke engine (probably female), also a squeaky grunt (probably male).

FOOD: animal material, probably also vegetable.

STATUS: rare to uncommon. TAXONOMY: endemic race *(immaculata)* of species extending to Philippines and Polynesia.

180 WHITE-BROWED CRAKE *Porzana cinerea* (Vieillot) 1819   Fig p 135
Distribution: Map 42.

RECOGNITION: *white streaks on face, underparts plain white, no white marks on upperparts.*
DESCRIPTION: 18cm. Sexes alike. Crown brownish-black; remainder of upperparts mottled blackish-brown and buffy-brown, blacker on rump and tail; upper face blackish bordered by white streak below eye and with white streak from base of bill to above eye; lower face, side of neck and side of breast grey; flanks and under tail coverts cinnamon buff; centre of throat to centre of belly white; bill greenish-olive, red at base; eyes and eyering red; legs greenish-blue.
HABITAT: dense vegetation of mainly coastal swamps and mangroves. HABITS: terrestrial and aquatic, a reluctant swimmer; sometimes flies into swamp trees or climbs up branches; solitary; sedentary, perhaps nomadic and migratory (e.g. recorded as regular visitor January to June on lower Burdekin River); flicks tail. BREEDING: records between September and May, perhaps other months also; nests in swamp vegetation (including rice fields), about 0.5m above water, sometimes on floating tussocks, made of trodden down vegetation canopied over with bound stems; four eggs, dull white freckled with shades of brown. VOICE: loud chattering cry, loud sharp double 'krek', soft 'charr-r'. FOOD: small aquatic animals and insects.
STATUS: fairly common to common. TAXONOMY: race *(leucophrys),* probably endemic, of species extending to Malaysia and Polynesia. Sometimes placed in unique genus *Poliolimnas.*

Genus GALLINULA
Opinions vary on the composition of this genus. The view is accepted here that the Native-hens, *Tribonyx,* the Bush-hen, *Amaurornis* and the Swamphen, *Porphyrio,* can be included. The genus is based on the European Moorhen, plain blackish, sometimes with olive-brown tones and white on flanks and undertail, bill extended into a frontal shield. These features are repeated, in some degree, in the Australian Dusky Moorhen, a semispecies in the Moorhen superspecies, and the two Native-hens. The Bush-hen has only the beginnings of a frontal shield but it has the same general stamp of the moorhens. It may illustrate an early stock transitional between crakes and gallinules. Viewed in this way, the genus consists of about nine species of worldwide distribution.

181 BUSH-HEN *Gallinula olivacea* Meyen 1834   Pl 5   Fig p 135
Distribution: Map 43.

RECOGNITION: *plain olive-brown upperparts, cinnamon brown vent and undertail coverts.*
DESCRIPTION: 25cm. Sexes alike, except that female has only a very small frontal shield and yellower bill. Crown to back olive-brown; remainder of upperparts, including tail, russet brown; face grey-brown shading to pale smoke grey on chin and olive-grey on fore-neck and centre of breast; sides of breast and flanks grey-brown; belly, thighs and under

tail cinnamon; bill olive-green with frontal shield at base of upper mandible orange; eyes reddish-brown; legs yellowish-olive.

HABITAT: wet places with long grass and reeds among timber, along creeks or in forests. HABITS: terrestrial; solitary; sedentary; very furtive in movements. BREEDING: October–March; nests on or near ground in long grass among bushes; roughly made of grass and other vegetation bent over to form sides and roof, lined with moss; four to seven eggs, creamy white blotched and spotted with brown and lilac-grey. VOICE : a succession of loud harsh piercing notes followed by several short quieter ones. FOOD: small animals and insects, vegetation, seeds.

STATUS: rare but perhaps not as rare as records suggest. TAXONOMY: endemic race *(ruficrissa)*, perhaps distinct species, of species extending to New Guinea, Moluccas and Philippines.

182 BLACK-TAILED NATIVE-HEN *Gallinula ventralis* Gould 1836 Fig p 135

Distribution : widespread except in Cape York Peninsula; replaced by Tasmanian Native-hen in Tasmania.

RECOGNITION: *olive-brown above, large white spots on flanks, red legs (no white on black undertail).*

DESCRIPTION: 35cm. Sexes alike. Upperparts brownish-olive, darker on head and black on tail; forehead, face and throat blackish-brown; foreneck and breast blue-grey shading to black on upper flanks, which have large white spots, and black on belly and under tail; rear flanks and thighs dark grey-brown; bill above and tip pale green, below reddish; eyes yellow; legs dark red.

HABITAT: swampy margins of inland waters and adjacent plains. HABITS: terrestrial and aquatic, but sometimes far from water; gregarious; nomadic to a high degree, moving sometimes suddenly and in large numbers and long distances, especially to areas of recent heavy rainfall; also invasions of large numbers occur sporadically in various places; tail constantly flicked or carried erect. BREEDING: August–December; nests on ground or just above water in, and made with, swamp vegetation; five to seven eggs, dark green sparsely blotched and spotted with shades of brown. VOICE: harsh cackling and loud 'kak'. FOOD: vegetable matter, sometimes green vegetables from gardens.

STATUS: common to abundant. TAXONOMY: endemic species.

183 TASMANIAN NATIVE-HEN *Gallinula mortierii* Du Bus 1840 Fig p 135

Distribution: Tasmania.

RECOGNITION: *greyish-olive with russet crown, white patch on flanks, no white on undertail; large and flightless.*

DESCRIPTION: 45cm. Sexes alike. Like mainland Native-hen but upperparts more greyish-olive with russet brown on crown and nape; white patch on flanks; bill greenish-yellow; eyes bright red; legs dull yellow.

HABITAT : most kinds of inland waters, most grasslands and paddocks. HABITS : terrestrial, flightless, sometimes scrambles up sloping trunks and branches, runs at speeds recorded up to 50km per hour, sometimes dives into running water and walks along bottom for several yards against current; solitary; sedentary. BREEDING : July–October; nests near water in clumps of grass or reeds or on flat rocks, made of soft grass; seven to nine eggs, buff brown blotched and spotted with shades of brown. VOICE : loud squeaky rasp, like saw being sharpened, short grunts. FOOD : vegetable material.

STATUS: fairly common. TAXONOMY: endemic species, forming superspecies with mainland Native-hen.

184 DUSKY MOORHEN *Gallinula tenebrosa* Gould 1846   Fig p 135
Distribution: Map 44.

RECOGNITION: *uniformly blackish with two white patches on undertail and red frontal shield.*

DESCRIPTION: 35cm, legs 14cm, central toe 9cm. Sexes alike. Blackish with olive-brown tinge on back and scapulars, paler on underparts and white on vent; sides of under tail coverts white making two conspicuous white patches when tail is flicked; base of bill and frontal shield red (breeding) or greenish-yellow, tip yellow; eyes brown; legs greenish-yellow, red above 'knee'.

HABITAT: coastal and inland swamps, often in swampy places in built-up areas. HABITS: terrestrial and aquatic, runs, swims, dives, reluctant flier with laboured and heavy flight; solitary, often gregarious when not breeding; sedentary and nomadic; flicks tail. BREEDING: August–February; nests in swamp vegetation, in bushes, on ground and at base of trees, a platform made of herbage and bark; seven to nine (or more) eggs, dull white, blotched and spotted with brown. VOICE: loud and not unmusical staccato 'kurk'. FOOD: vegetable matter.

STATUS: common. TAXONOMY: endemic race *(tenebrosa)* of species extending to Borneo; replacing and probably forming a superspecies with wide-ranging G. *chloropus.*

185 SWAMPHEN *Gallinula porphyrio* (Linnaeus) 1758   Fig p 135
Distribution: Map 45.

RECOGNITION: *black with purplish sheen, one white patch under tail, thick red bill and frontal shield.*

DESCRIPTION: 45cm, legs 23cm, central toe 11·5cm. Sexes alike. Crown, nape and upper face black; lower face, neck, breast, upper belly and edge of shoulder violet-blue (see also 'variation'); remainder of upperparts brownish-black with slight gloss; lower belly and thighs dull black; under tail coverts white; bill and frontal shield red; eyes red; legs variable, usually red especially in east, sometimes brownish-red and greenish-grey.

VARIATION: over most of the range as above (race *melanotus*); in southwest, neck, breast and edge of shoulders azure blue (race *bellus*); in Tasmania, larger (race *fletcherae*).

HABITAT: inland swamps. HABITS: terrestrial, in swamp margins, rarely swims; solitary; mainly sedentary but sometimes wandering long distance; flicks tail continually; usually rather shy. BREEDING: variable, according to locality, recorded January–April, June, August–December; nests in swamp vegetation suitable for bending over and trampling down to form a platform; three to five eggs, pale buff blotched and spotted with brown and purple. VOICE: loud shriek, 'kee-ow'. FOOD: vegetable matter, frogs, molluscs.

STATUS: fairly common. TAXONOMY: endemic races of species widespread throughout old world.

Genus FULICA

A cosmopolitan group of about ten species only distantly related to the rails and put in a separate subfamily. They are distinguished, among other things, by a white frontal shield and lobed toes; plumage is black. They have some resemblance to the Dusky Moorhen, especially when on the water, but the white forehead is readily seen and it is the only rail-like bird that flocks when not breeding.

186 COOT *Fulica atra* Linnaeus 1758

Distribution: throughout.

RECOGNITION: *blackish with white forehead and no white markings on flanks or undertail.*

DESCRIPTION: 38cm. Sexes alike. Upperparts dark bluish-grey, blacker on head and neck; underparts dark grey; thin edge of white on shoulders; bill and frontal shield pale bluish-white; eyes dark red; legs blue-grey.

HABITAT: open fresh waters with swampy margins, sometimes brackish estuaries. HABITS: terrestrial and aquatic, frequently on water swimming with head jerking movement, dives; solitary breeding, gregarious at other times, sometimes in large flocks; sedentary and nomadic, possibly migratory. BREEDING: August–March; nests in swamp vegetation and stumps of swamp trees, made of herbage bent over to form platform; five to seven eggs, dull white spotted with shades of brown. VOICE: varied, but most distinctive is a loud raucous 'kwok'. FOOD: aquatic vegetation and animals.

STATUS: common. TAXONOMY: race *(australis)* extending to New Guinea of species extending throughout Europe and Asia.

Spotless Crake (179)

Family OTIDIDAE

Bustards

1(22) species: endemic

Distribution: throughout most of temperate and tropical old world, especially Africa.

BUSTARDS ARE A DISTINCT old world family with a stronghold in Africa and a shrinking range in Europe. They are large terrestrial birds of savanna habitats. A number of species have fared badly in competition with man, for their edibility encouraged hunting although many nowadays are shot more for sport than necessity. A low reproductive rate seldom provides adequate replenishment for depleted stock. The single Australian species, frequently known as Plain Turkey, has suffered badly but is still fairly plentiful in some remote areas and is, in the letter at least, protected by law. The plumage is finely vermiculated and blotched in camouflage colours and pattern; a motionless bustard can be easily overlooked even when standing quite exposed at short distance. It is robust in build with longish legs, fairly long thick neck and thick rather flattened bill. The short toes make a spoor like a miniature emu.

187 BUSTARD *Ardeotis australis* (Gray) 1829   Pl 4

Distribution: throughout but thinly scattered in the southeast and south of Perth.

RECOGNITION: *stands about 1m with thick neck, black cap and grey-brown camouflage patterned plumage.*

DESCRIPTION: 1–1.3m, stands 0.8–1m; three short toes. Sexes alike but female smaller. Forehead to crested nape black; remainder of upperparts blotched and finely vermiculated with shades of brown and black (looking dark grey-brown); face, throat, neck and upper breast finely mottled white and brown (looking grey), breast feathers elongated and partly obscuring black lower breast; shoulders black with large white spots; belly white; flight feathers grey-brown, inner feathers and outer tail feathers tipped white; bill blackish above and pale yellow below; eyes dull white; legs pale greenish-yellow.

HABITAT: open country with grass or low bushes and scattered trees. HABITS: terrestrial; solitary or in small family parties or in small flocks where fairly common; sedentary or nomadic depending on food availability; elaborate mating display with tail fanned and bent over back, wings lowered, throat puffed out and two large gular pouches inflated, accompanied by loud roar. BREEDING: variable but mainly August–December; no formed nest, eggs laid on bare ground, perhaps surrounded by some grass and twigs, usually among grass tussocks and low bushes; one to two eggs, light shades of green and brown spotted and blotched with darker shades. VOICE: low booming 'hoor' when breeding, otherwise mainly silent. FOOD: insects, especially grasshoppers, also small animals and vegetable material.

STATUS: rare to fairly common; adversely affected by man and introduced predators but efforts made to increase numbers by protection and restocking. TAXONOMY: species extending to southeast New Guinea, forming superspecies with similar bustards in India and Africa, especially the Indian Black-headed Bustard.

Family JACANIDAE

Jacanas

1(7) species

Lotusbird (188)

JACANAS OR LILYTROTTERS OR Lotusbirds, as they are variously named, are usually regarded as a specialised branch of the large 'wader' group. Their habitat is the floating vegetation of quiet inland waters where they feed and nest, and for which they are adapted by having long thin legs and very long toes. Toes are out of all proportion to relatively small bodies, but they provide a nice balance between weight and weight distribution for support on the flimsiest of plant rafts. The few grams weight of the only species found in Australia is distributed over an area of nearly 200 square cm. Young are grotesque morsels apparently all legs and toes but they can move about as soon as hatched. The floating nests sometimes get waterlogged but the eggs are protected by a layer impervious to water.

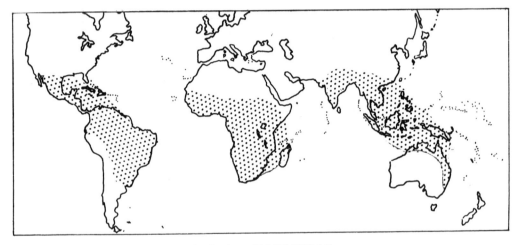

Distribution of JACANIDAE

188 LOTUSBIRD *Irediparra gallinacea* (Temm. & Laug.) 1828   Pl 5

Distribution: Map 46.

RECOGNITION: *small; black, brown and white with red comb, long thin legs and toes; walks on floating vegetation.*

DESCRIPTION: 23cm, legs 11cm, central and hind toes each 7·5cm giving footspan of 15cm. Sexes alike. Black from hind crown to upper back and joined to black breast, flanks and underwing; centre of back and shoulders drab brown; rump, tail and flight feathers black; black streak from eye to base of lower mandible; face, throat and foreneck white shading to margin of bright orange; belly and under tail coverts white; large fleshy comb on forehead and base of upper mandible crimson; base of lower mandible yellow, tip of bill black; eyes yellow; legs bluish-black.

HABITAT: still inland waters with floating vegetation. HABITS: frequents aquatic vegetation, can swim and dive; solitary or in family parties; sedentary and nomadic; flight relatively strong and direct with rapid wing beats. BREEDING: variable, recorded in most months; nests on floating vegetation, made of rushes and water weeds, loosely constructed and flat, or sometimes eggs placed on large leaf; three to four eggs, light shades of brown and yellow with an intricate pattern of closely interwoven black lines (eggs float if they fall off the nest). VOICE: loud shrill 'pee' repeated, also softer squeak. FOOD: aquatic insects and vegetation. STATUS: fairly common. TAXONOMY: endemic race *(novaehollandiae)* of species extending to New Guinea and Borneo.

Family ROSTRATULIDAE

Painted Snipe

1(2) species

PAINTED SNIPE, OF WHICH there are only two species, one in the old world and one in South America, have anatomical features which seem to relate them to the jacanas. They have only a superficial resemblance to the true snipe (family Scolopacidae). Plumage is boldly patterned and there is a central streak on the crown. Although the bill is long it is more delicate than in the snipe and is rounded at the tip. A curious but not unique feature is the reversed role of the sexes in all but the fundamentals of reproduction. The female is

Distribution of ROSTRATULIDAE

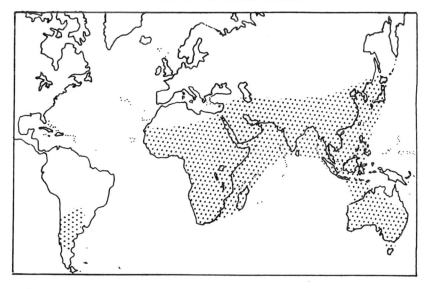

larger and more gaily coloured than the male, establishes and maintains territory and leaves the male to incubate the eggs and look after the chicks.

189 PAINTED SNIPE   *Rostratula benghalensis*   (Linnaeus) 1758   Pl 6

Distribution: widespread, apparently absent.from northern Northern Territory and Cape York Peninsula.

RECOGNITION: *long thin bill, broad whitish ring around eye, pale streak on edge of back extending as 'horse-collar' on breast; foreparts greyish in male, blackish in female; flies rather clumsily with legs dangling.*

DESCRIPTION: 25cm, with slender bill 5cm. Sexes different, female more richly coloured. *Male:* crown brownish-black finely barred with white and with broad buff central streak; pale buff eyering extending to side of nape; hind neck and upper back brownish-grey edged by broad buff streaks which extend downward to join white breast; shoulders buff-olive, lower back, wings and tail grey, all boldly spotted with white, buffy-white and cinnamon buff; base of flight feathers black; lower face, throat, foreneck and sides of breast brownish-grey speckled with white and edged with black; chin, lower breast and belly white; base of bill greyish-green shading to orange-brown tip; eyes red-brown; legs greenish-yellow. *Female:* differs mainly in having face, neck and upper breast plain blackish-brown with white eyering, patch of cinnamon rufous on hind neck, shoulders dark greenish-olive finely barred with black, white feathers concealed under scapulars.

HABITAT: shallows of inland swamps and marshes. HABITS: terrestrial, creeps with head held low and straight and tail flicked downward, furtive and quiet but not especially shy, sometimes rests on tarsus (like Emu); solitary but gregarious when not breeding; nomadic, perhaps sedentary when conditions suitable; flight slow with laboured wing beats and legs dangling. BREEDING: variable, at end of wet periods, records from October–April; nests on or near ground or at base of bush or tussock just clear of water, roughly made of twigs and grass and unlined; four eggs, creamy white intricately scrolled with black lines. VOICE: alarm, loud repeated 'kek', but mainly silent. FOOD: aquatic insects and vegetation.

STATUS: uncertain, probably fairly common. TAXONOMY: endemic race *(australis)* of species extending from southern Asia to Africa.

Painted Snipe (189)

Pied Oystercatcher (190)

Family HAEMATOPODIDAE

Oystercatchers

2(3–6) species: 1 endemic

Distribution: worldwide.

OYSTERCATCHERS ARE PLUMP BIRDS about 40–50cm in length and with pied or black plumages. It is sometimes claimed that certain black forms are melanistic phases of pied species and therefore not true species. A most distinctive feature is the long straight bill compressed laterally into a chisel shape and coloured a bright orange-red. The strong legs have slightly webbed toes. Calls are curiously similar and unmistakable, a plaintive piping 'klee-eep'. Both a pied and a black species occur in Australia, in coastal localities and in flocks of varying size. They are frequently seen probing in the soft sand near the waters edge or turning over sea-weed and stones and prising open shellfish or chiselling them off the rocks.

Key to HAEMATOPODIDAE

1 Wholly black; rocky coasts . . . . Sooty Oystercatcher . . . . No 191
2 Black and white; sandy coasts . . . . Pied Oystercatcher . . . . No 190

190 PIED OYSTERCATCHER *Haematopus ostralegus* Linnaeus 1758

Distribution: throughout in coastal localities.

RECOGNITION: *pied plumage, red bill and legs, usually on sandy shores and mud flats.*

DESCRIPTION: 45cm, with bill 7·5cm. Sexes alike. White breast and belly, white rump and upper tail coverts, white bar in wing conspicuous in flight; remainder black; bill, eyes and legs red.

HABITAT: coastal sandy beaches, mud flats and saltings. HABITS: terrestrial, feeds by wading in shallow water and probing in exposed soft mud and sand; solitary breeding and disperses when feeding but congregates in flocks at other times; does not readily mix with other shore birds except Sooty Oystercatcher; mainly sedentary, sometimes nomadic. BREEDING: variable, records August–January in south, May–September in north; nests on ground, a shallow scrape in sand; two eggs, dull white with variable amounts of dark brown spots and blotches. VOICE: loud piping 'klee-eep' and penetrating 'pee-pee'. FOOD: small animals of intertidal zone.

STATUS: fairly common. TAXONOMY: race *(longirostris)*, sometimes regarded as distinct species, extending to New Guinea and Aru Is of almost worldwide species.

191 SOOTY OYSTERCATCHER *Haematopus fuliginosus* Gould 1845

Distribution: throughout in coastal localities.

RECOGNITION: *wholly black, red bill and pink legs, usually on rocky shores.*

DESCRIPTION: 45cm, with bill 7·5cm. Sexes alike. Wholly sooty black; bill, eyes and eyelids red; legs pinkish.

VARIATION: mainly as above (race *fuliginosus*); in Gulf country and Cape York reputed to have wider area of bare skin around eye (race *ophthalmicus*).

HABITAT: preferably rocky shores. HABITS: similar to Pied. BREEDING: September–January, at least; no formed nest but eggs laid on ground among seaweed or in rocky clefts or among dense bushy growth on coral ridges or on bare sand; two eggs, pale brown to dark olive-grey spotted and blotched with darker or lighter shades of brown and grey. VOICE and FOOD: similar to Pied.

STATUS: uncommon, less common than Pied. TAXONOMY: endemic species, perhaps originating as a black mutant of the Pied Oystercatcher.

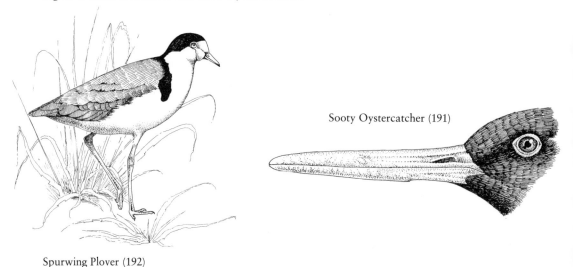

Sooty Oystercatcher (191)

Spurwing Plover (192)

Family CHARADRIIDAE
Plovers and Dotterels
17(about 56) species: 6 endemic

Distribution: worldwide.

THIS FAMILY IS PART of the vaguely defined group of 'waders' of which the next family, Scolopacidae, also forms a large section, and from which plovers and dotterels are distinguished by bills roughly shorter than the length of the head. Only some members normally wet their feet on foreshores of sand and mud, especially the non-breeding visitors, the Double-banded Dotterel from New Zealand and others from breeding grounds in the northern hemisphere. The resident plovers belong to inland wet pasture land and the unique Australian (or Inland) Dotterel—whose affinities are doubtfully established—belongs to the dry interior. They vary from about 15–35cm and have a plumpish appearance because of relatively thick head, short neck and short tail. The short bills are fairly stout, sharp pointed and thickened at the tip. On the whole plumages are more boldly patterned, in black, white, greys and browns, than in the Scolopacidae, especially in breeding dress where there is marked seasonal variation. Nests are little more than scrapes on the ground and eggs are cryptically patterned. Parents indulge in distraction displays when caring for young.

Key to CHARADRIIDAE

[Non-breeding plumages of visiting dotterels; see separate key to breeding plumages.]

1	Head with conspicuous amount of black	3–16
2	Head without conspicuous black marks...........	17–24
3	Crown wholly black	5–11
4	Crown and face with black marks................	13–16
5	Over 25cm	7–9
6	Under 20cm	10–11
7	Black crown only.............................	Masked Plover .... No 193
8	Black half collar.............................	Spurwing Plover .... No 192
9	Black breast	Banded Plover .... No 194
10	Black throat, white breast......................	Hooded Dotterel .... No 196
11	White throat, black breast	Red-kneed Dotterel....... No 195
12	Black forehead, black breast	Black-fronted Dotterel .... No 197
13	White forehead...............................	14–16
14	Underparts white.............................	Red-capped Dotterel...... No 198
15	Black ring around neck	Ringed Plover........... No 199
16	Black breast, cinnamon belly	Australian Dotterel .... No 205
17	Upperparts mainly plain grey-brown .... (Breeding plumages have brown band on foreneck or breast, except male Red-capped Dotterel.)	19–22
18	Upperparts boldly speckled .... (Breeding plumages have face and underparts black.)	23–24
19	Underparts wholly white	Red-capped Dotterel...... No 198
20	Throat and belly white, breast dusky	21–22
21	Rump whitish, contrasting with back	Double-banded Dotterel... No 200 Mongolian Dotterel ...... No 201 Large Dotterel .... No 202
22	Rump dark, uniform with back	Oriental Dotterel........ No 203 Caspian Plover........... No 204
23	Rump whitish, contrasting with back; black axillary patch	Grey Plover .... No 206
24	Rump dark, uniform with back; no axillary patch ...	Golden Plover .... No 207/8

Key to breeding plumages of dotterels which do not breed in Australia.

1	Breast brown, black collar	Double-banded Dotterel... No 200
2	Breast has broad brown band with black rear margin .	4–5
3	Narrow brown collar	6–7
4	Hind neck distinctly whitish, axillaries grey-brown uniform with underwing	Oriental Dotterel........ No 203
5	Hind neck not white, axillaries white, contrasting with dark underwing	Caspian Plover........... No 204
6	About 23cm	Large Dotterel .... No 202
7	About 18cm	Mongolian Dotterel ...... No 201

Genus VANELLUS

Currently all the 'lapwing' plovers are included in this genus, of which there are about twenty-six species. They belong mainly to the old world, especially Africa, with a few in South America. They are the largest members of the family. Among a number of features common to the group are black flight feathers and broad black subterminal band on the white tail. Wattles on the face and spurs at the angle of the wing also occur and are features of the Australian species. They have an erratic jumpy flight and are aggressive when breeding. Voices are harsh and shrill and often heard at night. Two or three species are found in Australia, depending on whether the Spurwing and Masked Plovers are considered to be races or separate species. They seem to be in a period of expansion as both have only recently settled in Western Australia and the Spurwing was first recorded in New Zealand in 1940.

SPURWING AND MASKED PLOVERS

It is difficult to decide if the Spurwing and Masked Plovers should be shown here as separate species or races of one species. For the most part they have distinct and constant differences and separate distributions, but between about Mackay and Cairns they overlap and interbreed, producing hybrid offspring. Interbreeding between populations which differ is an accepted criterion that they are races. But there are many cases where regarding them as species is more practicable. Another notable Australian example is the Black-backed and White-backed Magpies which hybridise along a narrow zone in central Victoria. This is no place to discuss the matter in detail but because in both examples the differences are quite distinct and the hybrid zone is relatively narrow, it may be less confusing to the general ornithologist if the forms are listed here as species. It is not easy to be consistent and there may be examples elsewhere in this book where the opposite view is taken.

192 SPURWING PLOVER *Vanellus novaehollandiae* Stephens 1819   Fig p 148
Distribution: Map 47.

RECOGNITION: *black crown and hind neck extending into black half collar, large yellow facial wattles, no white in wings.*

DESCRIPTION: 35cm; large facial wattles; large spur at angle of wing. Sexes alike. Crown and hind neck black and continuous with black collar which does not meet on breast; remainder of upperparts grey-brown with white rump and white tail with broad subterminal black bar; face, side of neck and underparts white; flight feathers black; face wattles, bill and eyes yellow; legs pinkish-brown.

HABITAT: moist open grasslands, swamps and estuaries. HABITS: terrestrial; dispersed and solitary when breeding, gregarious at other times, sometimes in flocks of 200 or more; sedentary with seasonal and sometimes very extensive nomadic movements, e.g. resulting in recent colonisation of Western Australia and New Zealand; wary and aggressive when breeding; flight erratic with relatively slow wingbeats. BREEDING: July–January; nests on ground, a slight depression roughly lined with a few pieces of twig and grass; four eggs, brownish-green blotched and spotted with shades of brown and grey. VOICE: harsh rasping cries variously transcribed as 'krik-krik' or 'keer-kik-ki' or 'kitta-kitta', etc, often heard at night. FOOD: small animals, insects and vegetable matter.

STATUS: common. TAXONOMY: endemic species (but recent colonist in New Zealand) or semispecies, or race of extralimital species.

193 MASKED PLOVER *Vanellus miles* (Boddaert) 1783
Distribution: Map 47.

RECOGNITION: like Spurwing Plover but differs in having *black on foreparts limited to crown and nape.*

Red-kneed Dotterel (195)

Banded (194)

Masked (193)

Spurwing (192)

'WATTLED' PLOVERS

HABITAT, etc: similar to Spurwing Plover, but BREEDING: more extended, records from September–July.

STATUS: common. TAXONOMY: endemic race *(personatus)* of species extending to New Guinea and adjacent islands, and perhaps also including Spurwing Plover.

194 BANDED PLOVER *Vanellus tricolor* (Vieillot) 1818

Distribution: Map 48.

RECOGNITION: *black crown and face joined to black breast, white streak behind eye, small red wattles at base of bill, white streak in wing visible in flight.*

DESCRIPTION: 30cm; small wattle in front of eye. Sexes alike. Crown black, lower face black continuous with black side of neck and black breast; white streak from eye to nape; remainder of upperparts grey-brown; throat, foreneck and belly white; tail white with broad black subterminal band; flight feathers black; broad white band in centre of extended wing; face wattle red; bill yellow, tip of upper mandible black; eyes yellow; legs dark red.

HABITAT: mainly various kinds of rough dry grasslands. HABITS: terrestrial; solitary breeding, gregarious at other times; sedentary and nomadic; flight erratic with quick spasmodic wingbeats; movement on ground is succession of short rapid runs and motionless standing. BREEDING: July–December or any time when conditions favourable; nests on ground, a depression with skimpy lining of twigs and grass; four eggs, greenish-olive spotted with shades of brown. VOICE: thin plaintive and rather metallic cry transcribed as 'er-chill-char' or 'a-chee-chee'. FOOD: grasshoppers, grubs and other insects, also seeds and vegetable matter.

STATUS: fairly common in Western Australia (much less common than Spurwing in eastern Australia, possibly declining). TAXONOMY: endemic species.

Genus CHARADRIUS

Members of this worldwide genus, currently about twenty-four in number, are usually known as plovers, or more particularly sand plovers, except in Australia where they are called dotterels. The only species not so named are rare and recently identified vagrants, the Ringed and Caspian Plovers. Four other species, of the ten listed for Australia, are common non-breeding visitors, three from the northern hemisphere and the Double-banded Dotterel from New Zealand. Dotterels are typically small, less than 25cm in length, with brownish-grey upperparts and white underparts. The plumage is often relieved by striking black markings on head, neck and breast. Although mainly found on sea-shores, especially pebbly beaches where their markings make them nearly invisible, they are also found on the margins of inland waters, including small pools and dams.

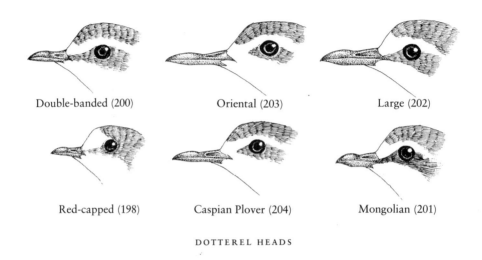

Double-banded (200)   Oriental (203)   Large (202)

Red-capped (198)   Caspian Plover (204)   Mongolian (201)

DOTTEREL HEADS

195 RED-KNEED DOTTEREL *Charadrius cinctus* (Gould) 1838   Fig p 151
Distribution: throughout.
RECOGNITION: *red bill with black tip, black head and breast, rufous on flanks.*

DESCRIPTION: 18cm. Sexes alike. Head and upper face black, continuous with black hind neck, upper back and breast; centre of back and shoulders dark grey-brown; throat and side of neck white; flanks and belly white, with patch of cinnamon rufous in centre of flank; tips of inner flight feathers white giving broad white trailing edge to extended wing and white streak on folded wing; bill deep pink, tip black; eyes dark brown; legs grey-brown, red on and above 'knee'. *Immature:* wholly grey-brown above and white below.
HABITAT: margins of coastal and inland waters. HABITS: terrestrial; solitary or in small flocks; sedentary with seasonal movements; runs swiftly in short bursts, stops and bobs head. BREEDING: October–December; nests on ground not far from water, slight depression in sand sparsely lined with dry grass, often under bushes; four eggs, brownish, speckled and finely lined with black. VOICE: a sharp 'chet-chet' usually uttered when taking flight, also soft trills. FOOD: insects.
STATUS: uncommon to fairly common. TAXONOMY: species extending to south New Guinea.

196 HOODED DOTTEREL *Charadrius cucullatus* Vieillot 1818
Distribution: Map 49.
RECOGNITION: *black head and throat, hind neck white, no black on breast.*

DESCRIPTION: 20cm. Sexes alike (statements to the contrary sometimes made). Crown, face and throat black; broad white band on nape; short black 'cape' on upper back continued on to sides of upper breast; remainder of back and shoulders brownish-grey; upper tail coverts and central tail feathers black; underparts and outer tail feathers white; inner flight feathers and centre of black outer flight feathers white, forming broad white band on extended wing; bill orange, tip black; eyes brown, eyering scarlet; legs pinkish-brown. *Immature:* lacks black; upperparts light brown with white nape; underparts white.

HABITAT: coastal beaches and estuarine mudflats, also inland salt lakes in Western Australia. HABITS: terrestrial; solitary, gregarious when not breeding, flocks usually small; sedentary; runs fast along shore, stops and bobs. BREEDING: August–January; nests on ground near shore and on open sand, unlined except for a few scattered shells; two to three eggs, pale buff-brown, spotted and blotched with blackish-brown and lavender-grey. VOICE: deep barking 'fow-fow' and short whistle. FOOD: aquatic insects and small animals.

STATUS: uncommon. TAXONOMY: endemic species.

197 BLACK-FRONTED DOTTEREL *Charadrius melanops* Vieillot 1818 Pl 6

Distribution: throughout, rarely coasts.

RECOGNITION: *black forehead band through eye, joined to black breast band and chestnut shoulder, red bill and eyering.*

DESCRIPTION: 15cm. Sexes alike. Forehead black, continuous with broad black band through eye to hind neck where it is joined to extension from black breast; white streaks over eyes meet above black forehead; crown and back dark grey-brown; scapulars dark chestnut; shoulders and inner wings grey-brown streaked with white and edged with white between shoulders and black flight feathers; throat, side of neck and belly white; upper tail coverts rufous; bill bright orange, tip black; eyes brown, eyering coral red; legs pinkish-brown.

HABITAT: margins of inland fresh waters — lakes, swamps, dams, any muddy and temporary pool, rarely brackish water. HABITS: terrestrial; solitary or in family parties; sedentary and nomadic, depending on water availability; runs rapidly and bobs, wades and sometimes swims. BREEDING: September–January; nests on ground, usually rising ground, near or well away from water, among shore debris or under bushes, or shingle near river pool, a slight depression often lined with short dry twigs; three to four eggs, pale greenish or yellowish-grey, speckled and lined with shades of dark brown and grey. VOICE: high-pitched 'pink' or 'chink', also rapid 'chip-chip-chi-chi-chi'. FOOD: insects and small animals.

STATUS: common. TAXONOMY: endemic species.

198 RED-CAPPED DOTTEREL
Charadrius ruficapillus Temminck 1822 Pl 6 Fig p 152

Distribution: throughout on coasts, rarely inland.

RECOGNITION: *white underparts, white forehead and streak above eye, (♂) reddish crown with black margin; (♀) lack of dusky breast distinguishes from similar dotterels with white foreheads.*

DESCRIPTION: 15cm. Sexes different. *Male:* centre of crown to nape and half collar cinnamon brown, with black margin in centre of crown and tip of half collar; remainder of upperparts pale grey-brown; forehead white continued as white streak over eye; black streak from base of bill through eye; side of neck and underparts white; flight feathers dark grey-brown with white at base of inner feathers forming thin white band on extended wing; central tail feathers blackish-brown, outer white; bill black; eyes dark brown; legs black. *Female*: lacks black markings and much of cinnamon brown colour, legs grey-green.

HABITAT: water margins, especially coastal where there are accumulations of broken shells, but also inland lakes and swamps. HABITS: terrestrial; solitary breeding, but sometimes in close proximity, gregarious when not breeding; sedentary; runs along shore swiftly, stops and bobs. BREEDING : July–January, also recorded March; nests on ground usually near water, among small stones or shells, or under bush, unformed; two eggs, dull greenish, spotted with dark brown and lavender-grey. VOICE: plaintive 'twink' or 'wir-wit', flute-like 'poo-eet', shrill 'kittup'. FOOD: insects, small animals, vegetable matter.

STATUS: uncommon to fairly common. TAXONOMY: near endemic species (New Guinea records uncertain, and vagrant in New Zealand); frequently listed as race of widespread *C. alexandrinus* but it seems more acceptable to regard it as a semispecies in a superspecies.

199 RINGED PLOVER* *Charadrius hiaticula* Linnaeus 1758

Distribution: few records from coasts of central New South Wales.

RECOGNITION: rather like Red-capped Dotterel with white forehead surmounted by black bar and broad black streak through eye (but crown not reddish); *white throat continuous with white hind neck* and *black bar on foreneck continued on to nape;* bill orange with black tip; legs orange.

STATUS: rare vagrant from northern hemisphere.

200 DOUBLE-BANDED DOTTEREL
Charadrius bicinctus   Jard. & Selb. 1827   Fig p 152

Distribution: southeast Queensland to Eyre Peninsula and extreme southwest.

RECOGNITION: *dusky breast, white at base of tail, dusky patch below eye not connected to base of bill, bill slender, eyes not prominent, unhurried movements.*

DESCRIPTION: 18cm. Sexes alike. *Non-breeding:* upperparts grey-brown, usually with distinct amount of white at base of tail; forehead and streak over eye whitish, often tinged with buff; dusky area below eye; underparts mostly white with dusky upper breast; flight feathers blackish with white shafts; concealed white in centre of wing becomes visible in flight; central tail feathers blackish-brown, outer white; bill black; eyes dark brown; legs grey-brown. *Breeding:* white band across black forehead; black band under eye; black bib separated by white band from chestnut breast.

HABITAT: coastal waters, occasionally inland. HABITS: gregarious, small scattered flocks near water; feeds in quiet unhurried manner, has 'rather hunched and dejected appearance whilst resting'. VOICE: repeated staccato 'pit' or 'twit', also long trill.

STATUS: common (rare in southwest); non-breeding visitor from New Zealand January–September (a few birds recorded most months but apparently not breeding.)

201 MONGOLIAN DOTTEREL *Charadrius mongolus* Pallas 1776   Fig p 152

Distribution : coasts throughout, rare inland.

RECOGNITION: *dusky breast, whitish at base of tail, dusky patch below eye joined to bill by black streak, fairly stout bill and fairly large prominent eyes.*

---

*It would be in keeping with Australian usage to substitute the name Dotterel, as in the case of three other visiting 'plovers' which have been renamed 'dotterel'.

DESCRIPTION: 18cm. Sexes alike. *Non-breeding:* upperparts brownish-grey with white on rump; forehead and streak above eye white sometimes tinged with buff; blackish patch below eye extending as black streak to base of bill; underparts white with narrow dusky band on upper breast; concealed white in centre of wing becomes visible in flight; flight feathers blackish with white shafts; tail blackish-brown edged with white; stout bill black; eyes (which are rather large and prominent) dark brown; legs grey. *Breeding:* broad white band on black forehead; face black; breast and side of neck chestnut edged with black.

HABITAT: coastal waters. HABITS: gregarious, in small flocks; alert and restless, runs fast when feeding, usually stands erect. VOICE: loud clear 'drrrit' or 'trik', also soft melodious trill.

STATUS: fairly common, rare in south; non-breeding visitor from northern hemisphere September–May, sometimes in other months, especially in north.

202 LARGE DOTTEREL *Charadrius leschenaultii* Lesson 1826   Fig pp 152/156

Distribution: coasts throughout.

RECOGNITION: *dusky breast band, white at base of tail, dark patch below eye extending to base of bill, fairly stout bill and large prominent eyes; larger than Mongolian Dotterel and looks whiter.*

DESCRIPTION: 23cm. Sexes alike. *Non-breeding:* upperparts and sides of breast grey-brown, paler on hind neck and mainly white on rump and upper tail coverts and white band in centre of wing; forehead, all around base of bill and streak above eye white; dusky patch below eye continued as dark streak to base of bill; underparts white, dusky in centre of breast; flight feathers blackish; fairly long stout bill black; large prominent eyes dark brown; legs dark grey-brown. *Breeding:* broad black band through eye; cinnamon rufous breast band; hind neck and crown reddish-pink.

HABITAT: coastal beaches, mudflats, almost any kind of open ground near sea. HABITS: solitary, small parties or flocks; wades and sometimes swims; rather less active than Mongolian but more so than Double-banded. VOICE: loud trilling notes, also quieter repeated 'treep'.

STATUS: fairly common, rare in south; non-breeding visitor from northern hemisphere, mainly October–May but also other months especially in north.

203 ORIENTAL DOTTEREL *Charadrius veredus* Gould 1848   Fig pp 152/156

Distribution: throughout, mainly inland.

RECOGNITION: *dusky breast, no white at base of tail, no white at base of inner flight feathers, axillaries not whiter than underwing, white shaft on outermost flight feather only.*

DESCRIPTION: 25cm. Sexes alike. *Non-breeding:* upperparts grey-brown, paler and more buff on neck, feathers edged with varying amounts of cinnamon and white; face pale buffy-brown with buffy-white superciliary and round base of bill whitish; breast medium buff-brown; throat and belly white; underwing, including axillaries, grey-brown; flight feathers blackish with white shaft on outer feather only; bill black; eyes brown; legs brownish-yellow. *Breeding:* breast band cinnamon rufous with black rear margin.

HABITAT: open ground, mainly inland, frequently in dry bare country far from water; solitary and gregarious, sometimes in very large flocks; active, runs swiftly, stands erect. VOICE: sharp 'klink', also softer 'chip' or 'tick'.

STATUS: fairly common to common; non-breeding visitor from northern hemisphere, about September–March. TAXONOMY: frequently regarded as subspecies of *C. asiaticus* (Caspian Plover) but good reasons have been stated for keeping as separate species.

Oriental Dotterel (203)

Large Dotterel (202)

204 CASPIAN PLOVER *Charadrius asiaticus* Pallas 1773   Fig p 152

Distribution: one record, Pine Creek, Northern Territory, 1896.

RECOGNITION: very like Oriental Dotterel and almost impossible to distinguish in the field; on close inspection, *axillaries white,* white at base of inner main flight feathers, shafts of most main flight feathers white, smaller (wing usually less than 150mm, bill usually less than 20mm).

STATUS: very rare; non-breeding visitor from northern hemisphere.

Genus PELTOHYAS

Until recently it was concluded that the unique Australian Dotterel belonged to the courser family, Glareolidae. Detailed anatomical study now suggests that its affinities lie in the present family and next to *Charadrius*. This confirms Gould's original judgement when he placed it as a close relative of the European Dotterel. In plumage colour and pattern at least, if not also in some aspects of its behaviour, it has many points of similarity with the dotterels, allowing some camouflage modifications to suit its habitat.

205 AUSTRALIAN DOTTEREL *Peltohyas australis* (Gould) 1840   Pl 6

Distribution: Map 50.

RECOGNITION: *black breast and cinnamon and chestnut belly, white forehead, black band across crown and down face.*

DESCRIPTION: 20cm. Sexes alike. Upperparts mottled blackish-brown and cinnamon buff; broad black band across crown and down face; broad black collar becomes deep V in centre of breast; forehead, front of face and throat white tinged with varying amounts of cinnamon; side of breast, flanks and underwing cinnamon brown; centre of belly chestnut; vent white; main flight feathers blackish with some concealed cinnamon brown; bill dark brown, tip black; legs pinkish-brown.

HABITAT: desert and semidesert areas, sandy or stony, bare or with low scrub or thin covering of vegetation, usually near water. HABITS: terrestrial; solitary, or small scattered parties, or moving in flocks; apparently more or less sedentary in north, with local movements depending on rains, and migratory in south; runs fast or sits close. BREEDING: August–November, also recorded April–May; no formed nest, eggs laid on ground and when bird not sitting covered with any local material, sand, seed cotton, pellets of mud, pieces of stick; three eggs, dark buffy-yellow, spotted and blotched with reddish-brown. VOICE: metallic 'quoick' and low 'kr-root'. FOOD: insects and seeds.

STATUS: fairly common. TAXONOMY: endemic species.

Genus PLUVIALIS

Three species breed in Arctic regions and migrate south in the non-breeding season, sometimes far into the southern hemisphere. They have mottled or dappled upperparts, and, in breeding plumage only, black underparts. All three are recorded as non-breeding visitors, but the European Golden Plover only very rarely.

206 GREY PLOVER *Pluvialis squatarola* (Linnaeus) 1758

Distribution: throughout, mainly in coastal areas but sometimes on inland waters.

RECOGNITION: *plump with dappled upperparts, rump and tail white contrasting with back, axillaries black, robust bill, white streak in centre of extended wing.*

DESCRIPTION: 25–28cm. Sexes alike. *Non-breeding:* upperparts dappled brownish-black and white, more white on shoulders, white at base of flight feathers giving white streak on extended wing, rump and tail white, tail with narrow black bars at tip; face, throat and breast speckled grey-brown and white, broad white band above eye; belly white; underwing pale grey with black axillaries; bill black; eyes brown; legs olive-brown. *Breeding:* underparts black; broad white stripe from above eye down side of neck.

HABITAT: seashores and estuaries, sometimes large inland lakes and swamps. HABITS: solitary, or a few birds, or small flocks, sometimes with Golden Plover. VOICE: shrill 'pee-oo-wee'.

STATUS: common; non-breeding visitor from northern hemisphere, August–April; stages of breeding plumage may be seen August–September and March–April.

Golden Plover (207)

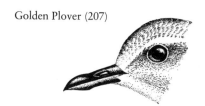

Grey Plover (206)

207 GOLDEN PLOVER (Eastern)   *Pluvialis dominica*   (Muller) 1776   Fig p 157
Distribution: throughout in coastal areas, sometimes inland swamps.

RECOGNITION: *plump with dappled upperparts, rump and tail similar to back, axillaries pale grey similar to underwing, no white in centre of extended wing.*

DESCRIPTION: 23–25cm. Sexes alike. *Non-breeding:* upperparts dappled brown, black and golden-yellow, with some white; face, throat and breast whitish, speckled with grey-brown and tinged with golden-yellow; whitish superciliary; belly dull white; underwing and axillaries pale grey; bill black; eyes brown; legs dark grey. *Breeding:* underparts black; broad white streak above eye extending along neck and side of body.

HABITAT: seashores and estuaries and adjacent grasslands, margins of inland swamps and lakes. HABITS: solitary or small flocks, larger near migration time, sometimes along with Grey Plover, fairly active and sometimes feeding further upshore than other waders, and on grassy margins. VOICE: shrill piping 'too-weet' and harsher 'queedle'.

STATUS: common; non-breeding visitor from northern hemisphere, August–April, but a few birds (non-breeding) remain; stages of breeding plumage in evidence August–September and March–April.

208 GOLDEN PLOVER (Western)   *Pluvialis apricaria*   (Linnaeus) 1758

RECOGNITION: like the eastern species but *axillaries white,* contrasting with pale grey underwing.

STATUS: rare (few records); straggler from northern hemisphere.

Family SCOLOPACIDAE

Sandpipers, etc.

31(about 70) species

Distribution: worldwide.

T HIS FAMILY IS ONE of the main sections of the vaguely defined group of 'waders', the other being the Charadriidae. All members of the Scolopacidae occurring in Australia are non-breeding visitors from the northern hemisphere. Included among these visitors, as well as the numerous sandpipers, are snipe, curlews, whimbrels, tattlers, knots, stints and godwits, Greenshank, Dunlin, Sanderling and the recently recorded Ruff. The Turnstone is tentatively included in this family but its relationships are uncertain. Current opinion places it as a subfamily of the Scolopacidae but having some affinities with the Charadriidae. The main feature which distinguishes the present family from the previous one is the length of the bill which is larger, frequently much larger, than the length of the head. Bills are modified in various ways and their shapes are useful aids to identification. Most are long, straight, and sharply pointed for probing in soft mud and sand, but several are distinctly downcurved and

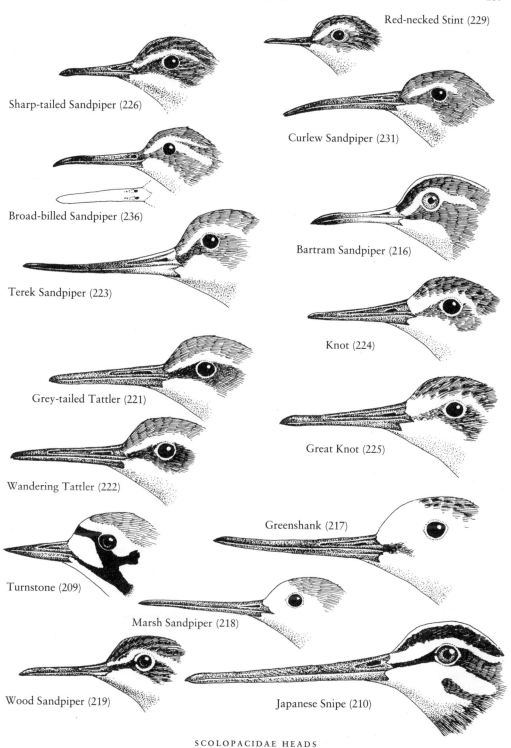

Sharp-tailed Sandpiper (226)

Red-necked Stint (229)

Curlew Sandpiper (231)

Broad-billed Sandpiper (236)

Terek Sandpiper (223)

Bartram Sandpiper (216)

Knot (224)

Grey-tailed Tattler (221)

Great Knot (225)

Wandering Tattler (222)

Turnstone (209)

Greenshank (217)

Marsh Sandpiper (218)

Wood Sandpiper (219)

Japanese Snipe (210)

SCOLOPACIDAE HEADS

others upcurved. Birds vary in size from the diminutive stints, with bodies less than 13cm, to the large curlews with bodies about 45cm, plus long downcurved bills. In Australia they are usually seen in non-breeding plumages which are mainly shades of undistinctive grey. Identification often depends on the disposition of white areas and the occurrence of dusky breasts. Assistance is frequently obtained by species collecting in mixed flocks, thus making comparisons possible. The Common Sandpiper, for example, consistently 'teeters', or see-saws, when on the ground, more so than other sandpipers. Bartram Sandpiper, which looks like a small whimbrel with a short straight bill, often perches off the ground on snags or posts. The call of the curlew is unmistakable but distinction has to be made between the voices of the two species; the rarer Western Curlew has a richer 'courli' compared with the 'kerlee' of the commoner Eastern species.

Key to SCOLOPACIDAE—Non-breeding plumages

(A) Bill distinctly downcurved: over 30cm
1 Crown boldly streaked with black; 30–45cm 3–4
2 Crown lightly streaked; 60cm 5–6
3 Rump* white; 45cm . . . . Whimbrel . . . . No 213
    *In the context of this key 'rump' includes upper
    tail coverts and base of tail.
4 Rump uniform with back; 30cm . . . . Little Whimbrel . . . . No 212
5 Rump white; rare . . . . Western Curlew . . . . No 215
6 Rump uniform with back . . . . Eastern Curlew . . . . No 214

(B) Bill slightly downcurved; under 20cm
7 Rump white . . . . Curlew Sandpiper . . . . No 230
8 Rump white at sides, dark in centre 9–10
9 Brownish, crown with dark central streak, legs olive Broad-billed Sandpiper . . . . No 235
10 Greyish, no streak on crown
    Breast dusky, legs olive . . . . Dunlin . . . . No 232
    Breast white, legs black . . . . Western Sandpiper . . . . No 233

(C) Bill upcurved
11 Rump and tail white
    Tail lightly barred, legs green . . . . Greenshank . . . . No 217
    Tip of tail boldly barred with black . . . . Bar-tailed Godwit . . . . No 238
12 No white in rump or tail . . . . Terek Sandpiper . . . . No 223

(D) Bill straight
Rump white
13 Plumage boldly variegated rufous, black and white . . Turnstone . . . . No 209
14 Tail with broad black tip . . . . Black-tailed Godwit . . . . . . No 237
15 Tail grey
    Narrow white band on rump . . . . Great Knot . . . . No 225
    Broad area of white on rump with narrow black bars Knot . . . . No 224
16 Tail white, lightly barred . . . . Marsh Sandpiper . . . . No 218
17 Tail boldly barred black and white . . . . Wood Sandpiper . . . . No 219

White at sides of rump or tail
18 Under 15cm 20–21
19 Over 18cm 22–28
20 Upperparts dark, legs yellow; rare . . . . Long-toed Stint . . . . No 230
21 Upperparts light, legs black . . . . Red-necked Stint . . . . No 229
22 Upperparts dark brownish-olive . . . . Common Sandpiper . . . . . . No 220
23 Wholly pale, wide white forehead . . . . Sanderling . . . . No 234
24 Breast pale, buff, unstreaked; rare . . . . Ruff . . . . No 239
25 Breast dusky, boldly streaked 26–28

26 Legs yellow
    Tail extends beyond folded wings; rare .... Bartram Sandpiper .... No 216
    Tail same length as folded wings .... Pectoral Sandpiper .... No 227
27 Legs greenish, tail extends well beyond folded wings . Sharp-tailed Sandpiper .... No 226
28 Legs black; rare .... Baird Sandpiper.......... No 228

No white on rump or tail

29 Face, throat and breast buffy, legs yellow; rare...... Buff-breasted Sandpiper ... No 235
30 Upperparts grey, underparts white .... Grey-tailed Tattler .... No 221
                                                            Wandering Tattler .... No 222

31 Boldly patterned black and buff, tip of tail reddish
    Tail with eighteen feathers .... Japanese Snipe.......... No 210
    Tail with twenty feathers .... Chinese .... No 211

Genus ARENARIA

The affinities of the turnstones, of which there are two species, have not been determined with certainty. It is believed that they are allied to both main wader families but closer to the Scolopacidae, of which they are currently listed as a subfamily. Turnstones are boldly variegated in black, white and reddish-brown, a conspicuous pattern which strangely camouflages the birds among the rocks, stones and seaweeds of the seashore which they normally frequent. The stumpy, chisel-shaped bill is an effective tool for probing among stones. Only one species visits Australia.

209 TURNSTONE *Arenaria interpres* (Linnaeus) 1758   Pl 6   Fig p 159
Distribution: throughout in coastal localities.

RECOGNITION: *boldly variegated in reddish-brown, black and white, orange legs.*

DESCRIPTION: 25cm, with stout bill 2·5cm. Sexes alike. *Non-breeding:* upperparts mainly dark brown mottled with cinnamon brown and black, rump and part of scapulars white; upper tail coverts black; tail white with broad black subterminal black band; throat white; breast, continuous with upper back, blackish-brown; belly white; broad white bar visible on extended wing; bill blackish; eyes brown; legs orange. *Breeding:* face patterned in black and white, the black connected to black breast; crown and neck mainly white; back and shoulders more extensively mottled in rich cinnamon brown (tortoiseshell).

HABITAT: exposed reefs and seashores, rocky or stony or littered with shells and seaweed, also adjacent dry grasslands. HABITS: active feeder, running fast and stopping to turn over stones and debris; usually in small scattered parties. VOICE: sharp 'kee-oo' and trilling 'kititit'.

STATUS: fairly common, rare in south; non-breeding visitor from northern hemisphere, September–April.

Genus GALLINAGO

Snipe (and woodcock) belie the description of 'wader' for their haunts are the dense vegetation of moist open woodlands and swampy places generally, never the margins of open water. About a dozen species are scattered over most parts of the world as residents or migrant visitors. Two species visit Australia but their relative abundance remains uncertain for they can only be distinguished by the number of feathers in their tails. Snipe are favoured game of the sportsman, not so much for their very edible qualities as for the problems associated with shooting them; they frequent country difficult and often unpleasant to negotiate, are not easily flushed and when they do rise it is suddenly from underfoot in a rapid weaving flight.

Unfortunately the now rare Ground Parrot lives in the same kind of country and has similar habits and many have fallen by mistake to the sportsman's gun.

210 JAPANESE SNIPE *Gallinago hardwickii* (Gray) 1831   Pl 6   Fig p 159
Distribution: Map 51.

RECOGNITION: *bold black and buff plumage with rufous tail, long straight bill, swift evasive flight, marshy habitats.*

DESCRIPTION: 30–33cm, with bill 7·5cm. Sexes alike. Crown black with broad central buff streak and pale buff streak above eye; remainder of upperparts boldly variegated in black and buffy-brown, forming bars on rump, broad whitish streak at sides of back; narrow black streak from bill to eye; lower face, neck and sides of breast cinnamon buff mottled with dark brown; chin, centre of breast and belly white; under shoulders and flanks boldly barred black and white; main flight feathers blackish; base of tail black, broad tip rufous brown; bill dark brown, base greenish-yellow; eyes brown; legs olive-yellow.

HABITAT: thick grassy vegetation of swamps and moist woodlands. HABITS: usually solitary or thinly scattered, but often forming small flocks, or 'wisps' when on migration; very wary and sits close when disturbed or suddenly takes flight, often with a loud sharp cry and flies swiftly and erratically to alight a short distance away and then run; reported as sometimes perching in trees. VOICE: loud harsh 'kek' or 'kresk'.

STATUS: uncommon to fairly common (readily overlooked); non-breeding visitor from northern hemisphere, August–April.

211 CHINESE SNIPE *Gallinago megala* (Swinhoe) 1861
Distribution: a few scattered records mainly in north.

RECOGNITION: like Japanese Snipe but slightly smaller; identified with certainty only in the hand by *twenty instead of eighteen tail feathers.*

STATUS: rare, but perhaps occurring more frequently than records admit; non-breeding visitor from northern hemisphere, September–March.

ASIAN DOWITCHER : see ADDENDA p. 488

Genus NUMENIUS

Curlews and whimbrels are the largest members of the family, up to 60cm in length including bills. There are eight species scattered throughout the world, breeding in the northern hemisphere and migrating to the southern. Four species come to Australia. They are a distinct group, mottled and streaked in browns and black, with long downcurved bills and characteristic cries. The two curlews listed, of which the Western species may be only of rare occurrence, have finely streaked heads, and the two whimbrels have heads broadly streaked in black and buff.

212 LITTLE WHIMBREL *Numenius minutus* Gould 1840   Pl 6
Distribution: most coastal and adjacent inland areas, probably not Tasmania.

RECOGNITION: *blackish crown with indistinct pale central streak, no white on rump, bill bicoloured, frequenting grassy areas rather than seashores.*

DESCRIPTION: 30–35cm, with slightly downcurved bill 4cm. Sexes alike. Upperparts mottled in shades of buffy-brown and blackish-brown, darkest in centre of back; crown black marked with pale buff forming an indistinct central streak; pale streak above eye and dark patch behind eye; face, neck and upper breast white, streaked with dark brown; throat and belly white; flanks and tail barred with dark brown; flight feathers black; base of bill pinkish-brown, outer half dark brown; eyes dark brown; legs olive-grey.

HABITAT: mainly inland open plains with short grass, often far from water; coastal occurrences probably birds on migration. HABITS: feeds in small scattered flocks by picking from surface or probing in softer places, but flies in close formation; squats when disturbed before taking flight when alarmed. VOICE: harsh 'tchew' and soft musical 'te-te-te'.

STATUS: generally uncommon, rare in south, but sometimes in large migrating flocks in north; non-breeding visitor from northern hemisphere, October–May. TAXONOMY: considered to be a close relative of, if not conspecific with, the rare or extinct Eskimo Curlew of Alaska.

Whimbrel (213)

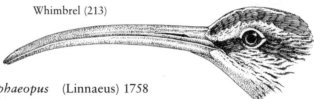

213 WHIMBREL *Numenius phaeopus* (Linnaeus) 1758

Distribution: throughout in coastal localities.

RECOGNITION: *pale grey streak in centre of crown bordered with black streaks, and whitish streak above eye, whitish rump.*

DESCRIPTION: 40–45cm, with downcurved bill 7.5cm. Sexes alike. Crown with pale grey central streak bordered with two black streaks, whitish streak above eye; back and shoulders mottled, streaked and barred light and dark grey-brown and white; rump and upper tail coverts whitish barred with grey; face and neck whitish streaked with grey-brown; chin white; breast and belly mainly whitish, streaked and barred with grey-brown; underwing boldly mottled and barred and tail barred with dark grey-brown; bill black; eyes dark brown; legs olive-grey.

HABITAT: coastal marshes, estuaries, mudflats and adjacent pastures. HABITS: often feeding on mud flats at low tide in small scattered companies, usually picking up food rather than probing for it. VOICE: calls often, a melodious shrill rippling whistle repeated frequently.

STATUS: fairly common; non-breeding visitor from northern hemisphere, July–April.

214 EASTERN CURLEW *Numenius madagascariensis* (Linnaeus) 1766

Distribution: throughout in coastal localities.

RECOGNITION: *largest wader, long downcurved bill, streaky brown plumage, no distinctive head markings, no white on rump.*

DESCRIPTION: 50–60cm, with downcurved bill 15–18cm. Sexes alike. Upperparts mottled, streaked and barred light and dark grey-brown and white (tinged with cinnamon in centre of back and upper tail coverts in breeding plumage), streaks especially on crown and lined neck; face, foreneck and underparts buffy-white streaked with grey-brown, less streaked on breast and belly; underwing boldly mottled white and blackish-brown; flight feathers blackish; tail barred blackish-brown; bill blackish-brown, pink at base; eyes brown; legs blue-grey.

HABITAT: various coastal localities. HABITS: feeds mainly by probing in soft places, especially muddy areas, sometimes rests on shallow sandy beaches until water rises up to its belly, sometimes swims; solitary or in small parties or flocks of varying size, often very large in north and near migration time. VOICE: loud ringing 'ker-lee' and several less distinctive variants.

STATUS: uncommon in southwest to common in north and east; non-breeding visitor from northern Asia, mainly mid-August to March but a few birds, probably immatures, remain during other months, even as far south as Tasmania.

215 WESTERN CURLEW   *Numenius arquata*   (Linnaeus) 1758
Distribution: recorded near Darwin.

RECOGNITION: like Eastern Curlew but *whitish on rump* and tail barred; throat and breast less heavily streaked with dark brown.

STATUS: rare vagrant from northern Europe; sight identification, once, end of March–early April in company with Eastern Curlews. (Occasional visitor in Malaysia.)

Genus BARTRAMIA
The Bartram or Upland Sandpiper, a rare vagrant in Australia, is the only species in this genus. It looks like a small Whimbrel with short straight bill and long tail.

216 BARTRAM SANDPIPER
Bartramia longicauda   (Bechstein) 1812   Pl 6   Fig p 159
Distribution: recorded near Sydney.

RECOGNITION: like Numenius species but only 30cm, with *slender straight bill 2·5cm; tail extends well beyond folded wings.* Upperparts boldly mottled with blackish-brown and buffy-brown; whitish streak above eye; breast streaked, flanks and underwing barred dark brown; *centre of rump blackish, sides white;* cinnamon brown visible in fanned tail; bill dark brown, base orange; legs chrome yellow. HABITS: frequents inland grassy plains; inclined to be solitary; sometimes perches off ground. VOICE: trilling whistle, 'tr-r-r-r-e-e-ep'.

STATUS: very rare vagrant from North America.

Genus TRINGA
This rather ill-defined group of about nine species is worldwide in distribution and consists of the typical sandpipers. They have distinctive loud, and sometimes rather plaintive, piping calls. They are usually solitary or in twos or threes. Six species are common non-breeding visitors to Australia. They vary in size from about 20cm in the Common Sandpiper to about 35cm in the long-legged Greenshank. Head bobbing and teetering (see-sawing) are common features of this group, teetering being a particularly distinctive habit of the Common Sandpiper.

217 GREENSHANK   *Tringa nebularia*   (Gunnerus) 1767   Fig p 159
Distribution: throughout.

RECOGNITION: *white rump and tail, long greenish legs, slender and slightly upturned bill.*

DESCRIPTION: 33cm, with slightly upturned bill 5cm. Sexes alike. Upperparts mainly pale brownish-grey, lighter and fairly distinctly streaked on crown and hind neck; lower back and tail white, tail slightly barred on central feathers; forehead, face and underparts white;

wings blackish, outermost flight feather with white shaft; bill black; eyes brown; legs greenish-grey.

HABITAT: seashores and margins of inland waters. HABITS: on coasts often feeds among seaweeds at edge of tide and on mud flats; sometimes swims; bobs head; flight very fast and direct with long legs extended well beyond tail. VOICE: shrill penetrating 'chew-ee'.

STATUS: fairly common; non-breeding visitor from northern hemisphere; August–April.

REDSHANK : see ADDENDA p. 488

218 MARSH SANDPIPER *Tringa stagnatilis* (Bechstein) 1803 Fig p 159

Distribution: widespread; recorded in most States.

RECOGNITION: *like Greenshank with white forehead, rump and tail, but smaller and with thin straight bill.*

DESCRIPTION: 20–23cm, with thin bill 4cm. Sexes alike. Upperparts pale brownish-grey with rump and tail white, tail barred; forehead, face and underparts white; wings blackish, outermost feather with white shaft; bill black; eyes brown; legs olive-yellow.

HABITAT: margins of various inland waters, seldom coastal. HABITS: solitary or in very small parties; very active on ground; flight graceful and very swift, weaving back and forth, legs projecting well beyond tail. VOICE: fairly loud 'tew' or 'tee-oo'.

STATUS: uncommon; non-breeding visitor from northern hemisphere; September–March.

219 WOOD SANDPIPER *Tringa glareola* Linnaeus 1758 Fig pp 159/167

Distribution: widespread; recorded in all States.

RECOGNITION: *dark back and shoulders with white speckles, white rump, white superciliary connected with white ring round eye.*

DESCRIPTION: 20cm, with thin straight bill 3cm. Sexes alike. Upperparts dark grey-brown speckled with white; rump white; tail barred white and dark brown; white streak above eye and white ring round eye; face and neck mottled dull white and grey-brown; breast grey-brown; chin and belly white; bill black; eyes brown; legs olive-green.

HABITAT: inland waters, especially where associated with swampy woodlands. HABITS: feeds in shallow waters, sometimes wading up to its belly; very active, bobs and teeters; when disturbed tends to keep close to trees and bushes, may perch off ground; solitary or groups, rarely more than five. VOICE: loud repeated 'giff' or 'chiff', also sharp whistling 'tee' or 'chee', usually in three syllables.

STATUS: uncommon; non-breeding visitor from northern hemisphere; August–April.

220 COMMON SANDPIPER *Tringa hypoleucos* Linnaeus 1758 Pl 6

Distribution: throughout.

RECOGNITION: *white at side of rump and tail, dark olive-green upperparts, dusky patch at side of breast, constant 'teetering'.*

DESCRIPTION: just under 20cm, with slender straight bill 2·5cm. Sexes alike. Upperparts dark brownish-olive with side of rump white and outer tail feathers notched white; white streak above eye and dark streak between eye and bill; face, side of neck and patch at side of breast grey-brown; remainder of underparts white; edge of shoulder white and broad white bar on extended wing; bill dark-grey, pinkish at base; eyes brown; legs pale olive-green.

HABITAT: coastal, among rocks, and inland waters, especially creeks and rivers with water running among rocks and boulders. HABITS: runs fast then stops and teeters, or flies low over water with short rapid wing-beats alternating with short glides, sometimes swims, on coasts feeds usually in rocky and stony places; solitary or in pairs. VOICE: thin piping 'twee-wee-wee'.

STATUS: fairly common in southwest to uncommon in southeast; non-breeding visitor from northern hemisphere; August–March.

GREY-TAILED AND WANDERING TATTLERS

The Grey-tailed and Wandering Tattlers are almost impossible to distinguish in the field, unless by some peculiarities of behaviour. In Australia the Grey-tailed is regarded as common and the Wandering as rare, there being only about a dozen records of the latter authenticated by specimens. It is possible that many sight records of the Grey-tailed belong to the Wandering as they may occur in mixed flocks. Identification at close quarters is possible by means of the nasal groove which in the Grey-tailed is not more than half the length of the bill and in the Wandering is about two-thirds the length. In breeding plumage the Wandering has barred underparts but in the Grey-tailed the centre of the belly and under tail coverts remain plain white.

221 GREY-TAILED TATTLER   *Tringa brevipes*   (Vieillot) 1816   Fig p 159

Distribution: throughout, mainly on coasts.

RECOGNITION : *dark streak from bill to eye and white eyebrow, white underparts, yellow legs; distinguished from Wandering Tattler by nasal groove not more than half length of bill.*
DESCRIPTION: 25cm, with straight bill 4cm. Sexes alike. *Non-breeding:* upperparts more or less plain grey-brown, sometimes with indistinct dull white barring on rump and upper tail coverts; white streak above eye and dark streak from eye to bill; face, throat and belly white; breast pale grey-brown; bill blackish, pale olive-green at base; eyes dark brown; legs yellowish. *Breeding:* face and foreneck become streaked and breast and flanks barred with dark grey-brown.
HABITAT: various coastal localities, with preference for rocky and stony shores and exposed reefs. HABITS: feeds at low tide on stony or shelly beaches or on mud-flats, quick alert jerky movements with neck outstretched, usually apart from other waders or in company with Silver Gulls. VOICE: plaintive piping 'peeep' repeated.
STATUS: fairly common in north, rare in south; non-breeding visitor from northern hemisphere; mainly August–April but a few non-breeding birds remain during other months.

222 WANDERING TATTLER   *Tringa incana*   (Gmelin) 1789   Fig p 159

Distribution : eastern and northern coasts to Northern Territory.

RECOGNITION: *like Grey-tailed Tattler and almost impossible to distinguish except by nasal groove, which is about two-thirds the length of the bill. In breeding plumage breast, flanks, belly and under tail coverts barred.*
HABITS, etc: little known and probably similar. VOICE: a monotonous rapidly repeated 'whee-wee-wee'.
STATUS: rare non-breeding visitor from North America.

Wood Sandpiper (219)

Grey-tailed Tattler (221)

223 TEREK SANDPIPER *Tringa cinerea* (Guldenstaedt) 1774 Fig p 159

Distribution: throughout in coastal localities.

RECOGNITION: *slender upcurved bill, 'high' white forehead, yellow legs, no white on rump.*

DESCRIPTION: 25cm, with slender upcurved bill 5cm. Sexes alike. Upperparts light brownish-grey, slightly paler (but not white) on rump and tail, whitish on outer tail; forehead, face and neck dull white lightly streaked with pale grey; throat, breast and belly white; edge of shoulders and main flight feathers blackish, inner flight feathers tipped with white giving a white inner trailing edge to extended wing; bill black, base dull yellow; eyes brown; legs yellow.

HABITAT: margins of coastal waters. HABITS: very active feeder, bobs and teeters; solitary or small parties. VOICE: melodious piping trill.

STATUS: uncommon, rare in south; non-breeding visitor from northern hemisphere; September–April. TAXONOMY: opinions vary on whether it should be in a genus of its own, *Xenus.*

Genus CALIDRIS

An ill-defined group of fairly small waders, apart from the two knots which are sometimes the only species included in the genus, the others being mainly in a separate genus *Erolia.* Most deserve the name wader for they customarily feed along the edge of the tide skipping about in the ebbing and flowing water. They are more gregarious than tringine species and roost in large, often mixed, flocks on sandy stretches untouched by high tide, or fly in large tight flocks.

224 KNOT *Calidris canutus* (Linnaeus) 1758 Fig p 159

Distribution: widespread in coastal localities.

RECOGNITION: *grey upperparts with white rump and thin white central bar on extended wing; smaller than Great Knot and has white on rump more extensive and slightly barred.*

DESCRIPTION: 25cm, with straight stout bill 3cm. Sexes alike. *Non-breeding:* upperparts grey scalloped with light and dark markings; rump and upper tail coverts white lightly barred with black (looking white at distance); white streak above eye and dusky band on face; lower face and underparts white with some dusky speckling on side of neck, foreneck and flanks; flight feathers blackish; thin white bar in centre of extended wing; bill dark olive-grey; eyes brown; legs olive-green. *Breeding:* crown and centre of back black with cinnamon brown blotches; face and underparts become cinnamon brown.

HABITAT: various coastal localities. HABITS: often wading in shallow sea up to its belly (hence the name Knot or Knut or Canute), much of head often submerged as bill is used in rapid probing; takes to flight in compact flocks which wheel and twist in unison with rapid wing beats. VOICE: guttural 'nut', whistling 'too-it-wit'.

STATUS: rare to uncommon, most records on eastern coasts; non-breeding visitor from northern hemisphere; September–April.

225 GREAT KNOT *Calidris tenuirostris* (Horsfield) 1821   Fig p 159
Distribution: coasts.

RECOGNITION: like Knot but larger, 30cm, and *rump more distinctly white but in a narrower band;* head fairly distinctly streaked, upperparts more boldly scalloped and breast distinctly spotted. *Breeding:* face and underparts remain white but become more heavily speckled and blotched with dark brown.

HABITAT, etc: apparently similar to Knot. VOICE: recorded as double-noted whistle.

STATUS: rare to uncommon; non-breeding visitor from northern Asia; late August–early April.

226 SHARP-TAILED SANDPIPER
Calidris acuminata (Horsfield) 1821   Pl 6   Fig p 159
Distribution: throughout.

RECOGNITION: *long pointed tail blackish in centre and extending well beyond folded wings, white at sides of rump, legs greenish.*

DESCRIPTION: 18–20cm, with straight stout bill 2·5cm. Sexes alike. *Non-breeding:* upperparts mottled and streaked in shades of light and dark grey-brown; rump and tail black in centre, white at sides; white streak above eye; face, side of neck, foreneck and breast dusky, speckled with blackish-brown (dusky breast not sharply defined from white belly); throat and belly white; most main flight feathers have white shafts; bill black; eyes dark brown; legs pale olive-green. *Breeding:* colours richer and darker; crown streaked dark rufous and black forming fairly distinct cap; face, foreneck and breast tinged cinnamon brown. (Note: Many birds show transitional colours until December; the full 'grey' non-breeding plumage may be in evidence only in December and January.)

HABITAT: coastal and inland waters, preferably brackish swamps and wet grasslands. HABITS: fairly leisurely feeder; usually in fairly large tight flocks. VOICE: sharp repeated 'whit' or 'krip' or 'chet'.

STATUS: common; non-breeding visitor from northern hemisphere; mainly August–April.

227 PECTORAL SANDPIPER *Calidris melanotos* (Vieillot) 1819
Distribution: widespread; recorded in most States.

Knot (224)

Red-necked Stint (229)

PETER SLATER

RECOGNITION: like Sharp-tailed Sandpiper but distinguished by shorter pointed *tail, about same length as folded wings; dusky breast darker and clearly defined from white chin and belly;* only outermost flight feather has white shaft; legs yellowish-green.

HABITAT: mainly inland swamps and wet grasslands, rarely seashores. HABITS: probably similar to Sharp-tailed. VOICE: reedy 'krik' or 'kreek'.

STATUS: rare, possibly more common than records indicate; non-breeding visitor from northern hemisphere; September–March.

228 BAIRD SANDPIPER   *Calidris bairdii*   (Coues) 1861

Distribution: recorded Tasmania, near Lauderdale.

RECOGNITION: like Sharp-tailed and Pectoral Sandpipers with upperparts mottled or scalloped in shades of brown and grey, blackish rump edged with white, dusky fawn breast finely streaked, white streak above eye; distinguished mainly by *relatively short black legs.* (See *Emu* 68, Pl 1.)

HABITAT: recorded from edge of salt water lagoon. HABITS: very active feeder. ˅ ICE: shrill 'kreep'.

STATUS: very rare vagrant from North America.

229 RED-NECKED STINT   *Calidris ruficollis*   (Pallas) 1776   Fig p 159

Distribution: throughout.

RECOGNITION: *very small with pale upperparts, white rump with black central streak, black legs.*

DESCRIPTION: 14cm, with straight bill 2cm. Sexes alike. *Non-breeding:* upperparts brownish-grey mottled and streaked with darker shades; rump white with black central streak; white streak above eye and dusky band on face; narrow forehead, lower face and underparts white; thin white bar in centre of extended wing; bill black; eyes brown; legs black. *Breeding:* crown and back mottled with rufous brown; white of face, throat and neck changes to rufous brown. (Note: a few birds may show transitional plumage in September, also in April when occasional birds may be in full breeding plumage.)

HABITAT: margins of coastal and inland waters. HABITS: frequently feeds on wide expanses of wet mud-flats, very active; usually in large flocks. VOICE: soft 'chit-chit'.

STATUS: common; non-breeding visitor from northern hemisphere; mainly August–April, some non-breeding birds in other months.

230 LONG-TOED STINT *Calidris subminuta* (Middendorff) 1851

Distribution: widespread; recorded in most States.

RECOGNITION: like the Red-necked Stint; distinguished by *greenish-yellow legs; also upperparts darker,* little or no white on forehead, foreneck and upper breast pale grey-brown, central toe nearly 2·5cm.

HABITAT, etc: similar to Red-necked Stint but seems to show preference for moist areas in short grasslands. VOICE: rapid high-pitched 'chee-che'.

STATUS: rare (probably occurring more frequently than records indicate) non-breeding visitor from northern hemisphere; September–March.

231 CURLEW SANDPIPER *Calidris ferruginea* (Brunnich) 1809   Fig p 159

Distribution : throughout mainly in coastal localities.

RECOGNITION: *relatively long downcurved bill, white rump.*

DESCRIPTION: 20cm, with slender downcurved bill 4cm. Sexes alike. *Non-breeding:* upperparts brownish-grey with rump white; white streak above eye and dark band through eye; face, side of neck and foreneck white speckled and lightly streaked with dark grey-brown; chin, breast and belly white; flight feathers blackish, white band in centre of extended wing; bill black; eyes dark brown; legs black. *Breeding:* upperparts mottled black, white and rufous brown; face and much of underparts rufous brown. (Note: in September and from about February there may be various amounts of rufous on head and underparts and black blotches on back.)

HABITAT: various coastal localities with salt or brackish water, rarely inland except on western salt lakes. HABITS: restless active movements when feeding; usually in flocks, sometimes very large. VOICE: clear rather musical 'chirrup'.

STATUS: common; non-breeding visitor from northern hemisphere; mainly September–April but small numbers of non-breeders remain during other months.

232 DUNLIN *Calidris alpina* (Linnaeus) 1758

Distribution: few scattered records from Cape York to Tasmania.

RECOGNITION: like Curlew Sandpiper in dimensions and general appearance; differs in having *white only at sides of rump,* bill slightly downcurved but stouter and shorter, legs shorter, breast more spotted, upperparts greyer. In breeding plumage upperparts become rufous but underparts are unchanged except for large black patch on belly.

HABITAT, etc: like Curlew Sandpiper, but in feeding has a hunched-up appearance. VOICE: short high-pitched 'treer'.

STATUS: rare vagrant (but perhaps occurring regularly) from northern hemisphere.

233 WESTERN SANDPIPER *Calidris mauri* (Cabanis) 1856

Distribution: recorded in Tasmania.

RECOGNITION: like Dunlin with slightly downcurved bill, greyish upperparts and white only at sides of rump, but smaller, 15cm; *underparts wholly white and legs black.*

HABITAT, etc: like similar species. VOICE: thin 'chee-rp'.

STATUS: rare vagrant from arctic North America.

Genus CROCETHIA

Superficially the Sanderling is very like several members of the genus *Calidris* but it is usually put in a genus of its own mainly because it does not have a small hind toe.

234 SANDERLING   *Crocethia alba*   (Pallas) 1764

Distribution: widespread in coastal localities.

RECOGNITION: *very pale appearance, wide white forehead, dark in centre of rump and white at sides.*

DESCRIPTION: 18–20cm with straight bill 2·5cm; no hind toe. Sexes alike. *Non-breeding:* upperparts very pale brownish-grey, darker in centre of rump and tail with white patch at sides of rump; black edge of shoulders and flight feathers; whitish bar in centre of wing which becomes broad white bar on extended wing; broad forehead and underparts white; bill black; eyes brown; legs black. *Breeding:* plumage becomes mainly cinnamon brown streaked and blotched with black, except on chin, lower breast and belly which remain white.

HABITAT: coastal beaches, especially sandy and where there is a gentle tide flow, sometimes mud flats. HABITS: feeds at edge of tide, characteristically running hither and thither with the moving water; has stumpy hunched-up appearance; solitary or small parties. VOICE: short shrill 'twick' or 'ket'.

STATUS: uncommon in north, rare in south; non-breeding visitor from northern hemisphere; September–March. TAXONOMY: sometimes combined with *Calidris* but absence of hind toe seems good reason for keeping in separate genus.

Genus TRYNGITES

The Buff-breasted Sandpiper, a rare vagrant in Australia, is placed in a genus of its own. It breeds in arctic North America but little is known about its migratory habits.

Sanderling (234) *breeding*

non-breeding

Broad-billed Sandpiper (236)

235 BUFF-BREASTED SANDPIPER   *Tryngites subruficollis*   (Vieillot) 1819

Distribution: few records on east coast.

RECOGNITION: size and general appearance similar to Sharp-tailed Sandpiper, 20–23cm; distinct in having *face and underparts pale buff,* no white streak above eye but thin white ring around eye; streaked brown and buff on upperparts and side of breast; only small wader with *no white in rump or tail;* inner webs of main flight feathers speckled white and dark brown; in flight upperparts uniformly dark and underwing white; *legs yellow.*

STATUS: rare vagrant from arctic North America.

Genus LIMICOLA

The Broad-billed Sandpiper, once considered very rare but now more frequently identified in Australia, is another species given the distinction of a separate genus. The bill is long and broad with outer half flattened and the tip slightly angled down.

236 BROAD-BILLED SANDPIPER
Limicola falcinellus (Pontoppidan) 1763   Fig pp 159/171

Distribution: recorded on coasts except Western Australia south of Broome.

RECOGNITION: in general appearance like Red-necked Stint but a little larger, 16·5cm, and relatively *much longer bill which is broad at tip and slightly angled down;* upperparts greyish with *dark centre of crown* emphasised by broad white streak above eye, which divides into two streaks behind eye; dusky streaked breast; *rump dark in centre and white at sides;* pale bar on shoulder and blackish at angle of shoulder.

HABITAT: coastal sandy beaches and mud flats. HABITS: characteristic up and down 'drilling' movement of head when feeding; solitary or in small parties. VOICE: sharp 'chr-r-reet'.

STATUS: uncommon non-breeding visitor from northern hemisphere.

Genus LIMOSA

Consisting of four species of godwits, two in the new world and two in the old. Both the latter occur in Australia as non-breeding visitors. They are large waders with long legs and long powerful bills, distinctly upcurved in one species.

237 BLACK-TAILED GODWIT   *Limosa limosa*   (Linnaeus) 1758

Distribution : throughout mainly in coastal localities.

RECOGNITION: *long straight bill, white rump, white tail broadly tipped with black, broad white bar on extended wing.*

DESCRIPTION: 35–40cm, with straight bill 7·5–10cm. Sexes alike. *Non-breeding:* upperparts plain grey-brown; upper tail coverts and base of tail white, terminal half of tail black; face, neck and upper breast pale grey-brown; chin, lower breast, belly and underwing white; white streak in centre of wing which becomes broad white band on extended wing; base of bill pinkish-brown, tip dark brown; eyes dark brown; legs dark brown. *Breeding:* grey-browns of head, neck and breast become cinnamon-brown; crown streaked with black and back mottled black and brown; white flanks barred with black. (Note: There seems to be few records of birds in partial or complete breeding plumage.)

HABITAT: coastal sandy beaches, mud flats and brackish marshes. HABITS: feeds rather leisurely; in small flocks of varying numbers; in flight legs extend well beyond tip of tail.

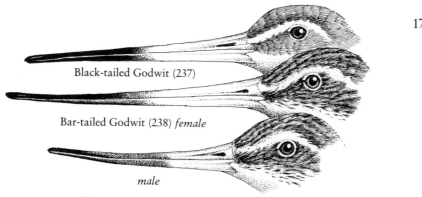

Black-tailed Godwit (237)

Bar-tailed Godwit (238) *female*

male

STATUS: fairly common in northeast, uncommon to rare elsewhere; non-breeding visitor from northern hemisphere; August–March.

238 BAR-TAILED GODWIT *Limosa lapponica* (Linnaeus) 1758

Distribution: throughout in coastal localities.

RECOGNITION: *long upcurved bill, white rump, tail barred black and white, no white streak in extended wing.*

DESCRIPTION: 35–40cm, with upcurved bill 7.5–10cm. Sexes alike, but female larger. *Non-breeding:* upperparts mottled in light and dark shades of brownish-grey, paler on neck; rump white; tail boldly barred black and white; face, foreneck and breast brownish-white; belly white with dusky bars on flanks; underwing mottled white and grey-brown; bill pale pinkish-brown, tip black; eyes brown; legs black. *Breeding:* pale areas of head and underparts become cinnamon rufous; back mottled rufous and black. (Note: birds in partial or complete breeding plumage may be seen September, February and March, especially in north.)

HABITAT: coastal sandy shores and mud flats, and adjacent marshes and pastures, seldom inland. HABITS: frequently feeds along edge of tide on wide sandy beaches; in groups of varying size; flight fast and direct with toes just reaching beyond tip of tail. VOICE: loud clear 'kew-kew' and softer 'kit-kit-kit'.

STATUS: fairly common (more common than Black-tailed); non-breeding visitor from northern hemisphere; September–March, but numbers of non-breeding birds remain during other months.

Genus PHILOMACHUS

A distinctive species in a separate genus, widespread in Europe and Asia. Its uniqueness lies mainly in the very striking breeding plumage of the male and its behaviour on the northern breeding grounds of the species.

239 RUFF (♂) & REEVE (♀) *Philomachus pugnax* (Linnaeus) 1758

Distribution: a few widely scattered records.

RECOGNITION : about size of Knot, 23–28cm; upperparts mottled brown, not grey; rump and tail dark with white patch at side of tail; *plain underparts, mainly white but slightly buffy on breast;* on close inspection slight webs between toes are distinctive; upright stance; slow deliberate walk.

STATUS: rare vagrant from northern hemisphere.

Family PHALAROPODIDAE

Phalaropes

2(3) species

Distribution: worldwide.

PHALAROPES ARE A SMALL group of aquatic 'waders'. It is thought that they might be a specialised branch of the sandpiper family; for example, they have a close resemblance to the Sanderling. A special adaptive feature is a dense undercoat of feathers on breast and belly, as in ducks, which makes them buoyant and they sit high on the water, and also carry the neck very upright. Toes are partially webbed and slightly lobed. They have the unusual characteristic of reversed male and female appearance and behaviour. Phalaropes breed in arctic and subarctic regions and disperse widely over the oceans as far as the southern hemisphere when not breeding. At this time they are almost entirely pelagic and occurrences on land are likely to be due to storms at sea. They frequent Australian seas; two have been recorded on Australian shores and the other species in New Zealand. Notes on all three are included here. Also breeding plumages of two species are illustrated but not described.

Key to PHALAROPODIDAE

[*Note:* because of close resemblance, the Sanderling is included in the key for comparison.]

1 Rump (upper tail coverts) white, no white bar on exten-
   ded wing, greyish eye patch . . . . Wilson Phalarope . . . . No 242
2 Rump with black centre and white sides, white bar on
   extended wing 3–6
3 No black eye patch, black at angle of shoulders . . . . . . Sanderling
4 Black eye patch, no black on shoulders 5–6
5 Back darker and streaked, bill long and thin (needle-like) Red-necked Phalarope . . . . No 240
6 Back paler and plain, bill short and thick (stouter look-
   ing) . . . . Grey Phalarope . . . . No 241

240 RED-NECKED PHALAROPE *Phalaropus lobatus* (Linnaeus) 1758   Pl 6

Distribution: few records on southeast coast.

RECOGNITION: 18cm. Like Sanderling in general appearance and with rump dark in centre, white at sides and white band in centre of extended wing; differs in narrower white forehead, darker grey upperparts, *black band through eye,* no black at angle of shoulders; differs from Grey Phalarope in *darker and distinctly streaked upperparts,* more slender (longer and thinner) needle-like bill, black legs.

STATUS: rare vagrant from northern hemisphere.

Unrecorded species

GREY PHALAROPE *Phalaropus fulcarius* (Linnaeus) 1758

RECOGNITION: like Red-necked Phalarope but slightly larger, 20cm, paler *upperparts* (but not as pale as Sanderling) which are *plain or only slightly streaked,* stouter bill (shorter and thicker), *yellow legs.*

STATUS: no land records but occurs as non-breeding visitor to southern seas from northern hemisphere; recorded in New Zealand.

241 WILSON PHALAROPE *Phalaropus tricolor* (Vieillot) 1819 Pl 6

Distribution: recorded on southeast coast.

RECOGNITION: differs from other two phalaropes in larger size, 23cm, *white upper tail coverts* (white patch on 'rump'), *no white bar on extended wing*, indistinct greyish (not black) bar through eye.

STATUS: rare vagrant from North America.

Red-necked Phalarope (240)

Family RECURVIROSTRIDAE

Avocets and Stilts

3(7) species: 2 endemic

Distribution: worldwide.

THE VERY DISTINCTIVE MEMBERS of this family are part of the large ill-defined group of 'waders', and are in behaviour truly wading birds. They frequent the margins of shallow waters, the avocets commonly keeping to the salt and brackish places and the stilts usually to fresh waters. All are long-legged with long necks and long sharply pointed bills. In body length the Australian species are about 38–45cm, including bills. Stilt legs are proportionately longer in relation to their bodies than any other bird except flamingoes. Toes are partially or almost completely webbed and the hind toe is rudimentary. Wings are long and pointed and tails short and square. Plumages are frequently pied but sometimes with the addition of chestnut areas, as in many other wader species especially in breeding plumage. They are gregarious and some nest in colonies. The Australian avocet is endemic, probably an early colonising offshoot from migrants of the only other old world species. One of the stilts also is endemic but sufficiently distinct to be placed in a separate genus.

Key to RECURVIROSTRIDAE

1 Bill upcurved, head reddish	Avocet..................	No 244
2 Bill straight, head white	3–4	
3 Breast chestnut.......................	Banded Stilt	No 243
4 Whole underparts white	Pied Stilt	No 242

Genus HIMANTOPUS

Members of this genus are spread widely over many countries. The current opinion is that they all belong to one species consisting of several races, although there are arguments in favour of regarding some as valid species. The endemic Australian form, the Banded Stilt, is sometimes listed as a species. It was named *leucocephalus* by Gould, hence the name White-headed Stilt which is commonly used (see page 13). In all forms the long thin bill is slightly flattened and the upper mandible is hooked at the tip. Toes are only partially webbed.

242 PIED STILT *Himantopus himantopus* (Linnaeus) 1758

Distribution: throughout.

RECOGNITION: *wholly white underparts, black patch on hind neck, no white in wings.*

DESCRIPTION: 38cm, with straight bill 6cm; folded wings extend 5cm beyond tail; legs 20cm. Sexes alike. Mainly white with black patch on hind neck, white collar and black back and wings; bill black; eyes dark red; legs pink. *Immature:* lacks black patch on hind neck, back and wings brownish, crown to hind neck grey.

HABITAT: swamps and margins of shallow coastal and inland waters. HABITS: terrestrial, feeds by wading in shallow water, usually in small flocks and sometimes in company with avocets; movements on ground graceful and dainty but in flight rather awkward looking with legs trailing behind short tail; gregarious at all seasons, though nests usually in loose colonies scattered over an area of swamp or river margin; sedentary and nomadic. BREEDING: variable but mainly August–December in south and January–March in north; nests in swamps on ground or built up in shallow water or anchored platform in deeper water, made of aquatic plants; four eggs, greyish-olive spotted, blotched and sometimes streaked with shades of dark brown and lavender-grey. VOICE: single yelping note repeated, also plaintive piping in flight. FOOD: aquatic insects, snails and small crustacea.

STATUS: fairly common, rare in Tasmania. TAXONOMY: race *(leucocephalus)* extending to Philippines of worldwide species.

Genus CLADORHYNCHUS

The endemic Banded Stilt is given generic status, perhaps on rather slender grounds; it has fully webbed toes and a chestnut breast.

243 BANDED STILT *Cladorhynchus leucocephalus* (Vieillot) 1816

Distribution: Map 52.

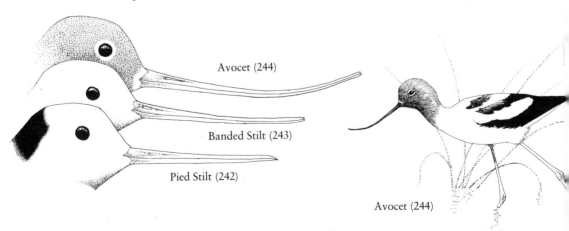

Avocet (244)

Banded Stilt (243)

Pied Stilt (242)

Avocet (244)

RECOGNITION: *chestnut breast, white back and white inner trailing edge of extended black wing.*

DESCRIPTION: 38cm, with bill nearly 7·5cm; folded wings reach tip of tail; legs 15cm; toes short and webbed. Sexes alike. Mainly white; breast chestnut; belly white with broad black central streak; wings black with broad white inner trailing edge; bill black; eyes brown; legs pink. *Immature:* no chestnut or black on underparts, wings brownish, no grey on head, back white.

HABITAT: salt and brackish estuaries and marshes, inland salt lakes. HABITS: feeds by wading in shallow water, movements very graceful; flight strong and rather less ungainly than the Pied; swims; gregarious at all seasons, sometimes in flocks of thousands; regular seasonal movements from inland breeding grounds to coasts. BREEDING: apparently between May and December, probably other times also depending on wet seasons; nests on margins and islets of inland lakes, possibly in relatively few large colonies, nests on ground on sandy spits and islets, mainly unformed; three to four eggs, fawn to white patterned with interwoven black and dark brown lines and sometimes blotches. VOICE: short yelping call and softer creeking notes (possibly Sturt's 'singular plaintive whistle'). FOOD: brine shrimps and possibly other small crustacea and insects.

STATUS: locally common. TAXONOMY: endemic species and genus.

Genus RECURVIROSTRA

As well as its unmistakable upcurved bill Avocets have webbed feet and a small hind toe. The Australian species is one of four ranging throughout the world. It is endemic but at one time it also occurred in New Zealand.

244 AVOCET *Recurvirostra novaehollandiae* Vieillot 1816   Fig p 175

Distribution: throughout, except northern Northern Territory.

RECOGNITION: *upcurved bill, chestnut head, pied body.*

DESCRIPTION: 45cm, with bill 9cm, upturned in outer half; folded wings reach tip of tail; legs 15cm, toes webbed. Sexes alike. Head and neck chestnut; body white with two broad black streaks at sides of back; wings black with inner flight feathers and centre of outer white making broad white band on extended wing; bill black; eyes reddish-brown; legs blue-grey.

HABITAT: inland waters and coastal estuaries. HABITS: terrestrial, feeds in shallow water with sweeping movement of upcurved bill or by probing or by swimming and upending; gregarious at all seasons; sedentary and nomadic, apparently some regular seasonal movements; flight rather ungainly with legs extended beyond tail. BREEDING: variable depending on suitable water conditions, but mainly August–December; nests in colonies in vegetation in or bordering shallow water, a hollow in ground roughly lined with a few pieces of vegetation; four eggs, olive spotted and blotched with dark brown and grey. VOICE: single reedy note, sharp yelp and melodious 'toot'. FOOD: small aquatic animals and insects.

STATUS: fairly common. TAXONOMY: endemic species (now extinct in New Zealand).

Family BURHINIDAE

Stone Curlews

2(9) species: 1 endemic

INCLUDED IN THE GROUP of 'waders' this small family currently consists of two genera, both of which are represented in Australia. They have an unfortunate collection of misleading common names — probably the old name 'thickknee' is most acceptable. We follow the users of the names 'Bush Curlew' and 'Beach Curlew' but the native names 'Willaroo' and 'Weeloo' would be more distinctive. These curlews are rather like the Bustard in plumage, thick legs with small feet and no hind toe, and similar short thick bills. But they are much smaller, about 50cm, have large luminescent yellow eyes and are mainly nocturnal, a habit which leads to many becoming road casualties when they get dazzled in car headlights. Normally they are rarely seen for they are very wary and lie up during daytime. When disturbed they do not readily take to the wing but run fast with head down, or squat, sometimes with head and neck stretched out on the ground, and rely for protection on their camouflage colours. Of the two Australian species one is widely distributed inland and the other is confined mainly to tropical beaches.

Key to BURHINIDAE

1 Face conspicuously patterned black and white, upperparts plain, coastal........................... Beach Curlew........... No 246
2 Face obscurely patterned, upperparts streaked, inland.. Bush Curlew .... No 245

Genera BURHINUS & ESACUS

There seem to be too few fundamental differences to justify putting the Beach Curlew in the distinct monotypic genus *Esacus*.

245 BUSH CURLEW *Burhinus magnirostris* (Latham) 1801   Pl 4

Distribution: throughout.

RECOGNITION: *white shoulder patch, streaked upperparts and breast, inland.*

DESCRIPTION: 50–56cm, with tail 18cm, extending 8–10cm beyond folded wings; bill under 5cm. Sexes alike. Upperparts brownish-grey, back blotched with black, rump streaked and tail barred brownish-black; shoulders and inner wing brownish, feathers edged with buffy-white; broad buffy-white band in centre of wing and concealed white patch in centre of black flight feathers (these two white areas make conspicuous white patches on wings in flight); forehead, streak above eye, lower face and throat white; behind eye, side of neck and breast buff with dark streaks, broader on breast; belly white; flanks and under tail coverts pinkish-buff; bill black; eyes yellow; legs olive-green.

Bush Curlew (245)

Beach Curlew (246)

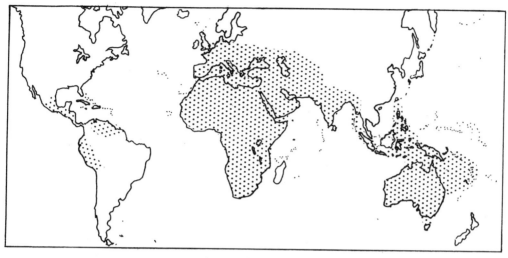

Distribution of BURHINIDAE

VARIATION: races have been described mainly on differences in size, particularly legs, but they seem to be of doubtful significance.

HABITAT: open woodlands and plains country with belts of trees, rocky wooded ranges. HABITS: terrestrial; nocturnal; solitary; sedentary; very furtive, when disturbed will usually sit close and rely on camouflage, may be easily approached—a reason for being dubbed 'stupid'. BREEDING: August–January; nests on ground, unformed depression on bare ground, often at base of small bush; two eggs, variable in colour to match ground but often brownish-grey blotched with dark brown. VOICE: loud mournful 'wee-loo' or 'ker-loo' usually uttered at night. FOOD: insects.

STATUS: fairly common, affected by introduced ground predators. TAXONOMY: species extending to south New Guinea.

246 BEACH CURLEW *Esacus magnirostris* (Vieillot) 1818   Pl 4

Distribution: mainly tropical coasts south to Point Cloates and Tweed Heads.

RECOGNITION: *plain upperparts, boldly pied facial pattern, brown shoulders.*

DESCRIPTION: 50–55cm, with bill nearly 7·5cm and tail 11cm. Sexes alike. Upperparts plain grey-brown; shoulders blackish-brown and light grey-brown separated by thin white band; inner flight feathers white and white band near tip of blackish main flight feathers; edges of crown and nape and broad band under eye black; broad streak above and behind eye and ring around eye white; throat and belly white; foreneck and breast grey-brown; tip of bill black, base yellow; eyes yellow; legs olive-yellow.

HABITAT: seashores of various kinds on mainland and islands. HABITS: terrestrial; solitary; sedentary; usually in exposed places but so well camouflaged that readily overlooked, if disturbed remains very still or moves slowly. BREEDING: (few data) records October–December; nests on open beaches, unformed; one egg, creamy white blotched and sometimes vermiculated with olive-brown. VOICE: high-pitched mournful 'wer-loo' or 'wee-loo'. FOOD: crustacea and other small animals and insects of the seashore.

STATUS: uncommon. TAXONOMY: uniform species of the Indo-Australasian region.

Family GLAREOLIDAE

Pratincoles and Coursers

2 (about 15) species: 1 endemic

PRATINCOLES AND COURSERS ARE two major divisions or subfamilies. They are clearly defined except for the unique Australian Pratincole (or Courser) which has some features of both groups and can be argued into one or the other. For present purposes it is kept with the pratincoles and coursers are not referred to in the following notes. Pratincoles, of which there are seven species ranging widely over the old world, have a number of distinctive features. They are about 20cm in length with brownish plumage and at least the base of the tail white; they have long pointed wings and usually deeply forked tails—hence the popular name 'swallow-plover'—and short arched bills; they live in flocks in plains country. Forked tail and short legs are typical of the true pratincoles but not of the Australian Pratincole which has square tail and legs of medium length. Body architecture, including short bill with wide gape, is associated with catching insects on the wing. Pratincoles, other than the odd endemic breeding species, have a pale chin and throat narrowly encircled with black. The Oriental Pratincole is a non-breeding visitor and sometimes occurs in very large flocks.

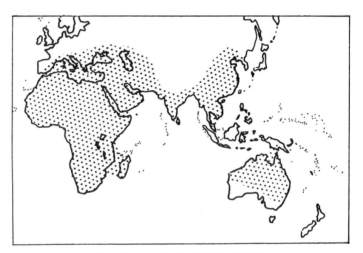

Distribution of GLAREOLIDAE

Key to GLAREOLIDAE

1 Tail forked, black throat 'necklace' .... Oriental Pratincole .... No 249
2 Tail square, no throat 'necklace' .... Australian Pratincole ..... No 248

Genus STILTIA

A separate genus for the unique Australian Pratincole which has some features similar to both pratincoles and coursers but is distinctly different from both.

247 AUSTRALIAN PRATINCOLE *Stiltia isabella* (Vieillot) 1816   Pl 6
Distribution: Map 53.

RECOGNITION: *cinnamon brown with white patch at 'rump' in flight, square tail and long pointed wings.*

DESCRIPTION: 20cm to short square tail, folded wings extending well beyond. Sexes alike. Upperparts and inner wing light cinnamon brown; lores black; throat, vent and under tail coverts white; breast pinkish-cinnamon; belly chestnut; edge of shoulder, main flight feathers and underwing black; upper tail coverts and tail white with large black patch in centre of tail; bill bright orange, tip black; eyes dark brown; legs grey-brown.

HABITAT: dry plains and other open places with sparse vegetation. HABITS: terrestrial, colours usually match ground and birds difficult to see except when running fast for short distances, or when 'bobbing', or in flight when white rump is conspicuous; feeds on ground or in flight, probable reason for curious side-slipping flight; often seen watering at stock tanks at any time of day; gregarious at all times; sedentary, nomadic and apparently migratory; young said to shelter in holes in ground. BREEDING : September–January; nests on ground often roughly defined by ring of small pebbles or sticks; two eggs, pinkish-brown spotted and blotched with dark brown and grey. VOICE : plaintive whistle, 'tu-whee'. FOOD : insects. STATUS: common. TAXONOMY: monotypic species, endemic breeding (doubtfully breeding in southern New Guinea), non-breeding visitor to New Guinea, Borneo and adjacent areas.

Genus GLAREOLA

A group of about three very similar species with deeply forked tails, short legs and long pointed wings giving a wingspan of about two feet.

248 ORIENTAL PRATINCOLE *Glareola pratincola* (Linnaeus) 1766

Distribution: scattered records throughout except southwest and Tasmania.

RECOGNITION: *forked tail and long pointed wings, like large swallow in flight; mainly dark with pale throat encircled with black.*

DESCRIPTION: 20cm to tip of forked tail, folded wings extend beyond. Sexes alike. Upperparts and breast olive-brown; chin and throat pale buff speckled with black and encircled by narrow black band; belly and under tail coverts pale pinkish-buff; flight feathers black; underwing black with broad chestnut band; tail white at base, blackish at tip; bill black; eyes dark brown; legs black.

HABITAT: dry plains with short vegetation. HABITS: terrestrial, feeds on ground and in flight; flocks often mix with similar dry country species, Australian Pratincole and Australian Dotterel. VOICE: loud 'cherr' or 'chet'. FOOD: insects.

STATUS: fairly common in northwest, rare vagrant elsewhere; non-breeding visitor from northern Asia; mainly November and December. TAXONOMY: considered to belong to race *maldivarum,* sometimes listed as species.

Oriental Pratincole (248)

Family STERCORARIIDAE

Skuas

4(4) species

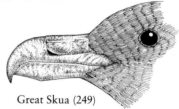

Great Skua (249)

[*Note:* currently the skuas are considered to be closely related to the gull group and each is given subfamily status in the family Laridae. But for convenience here they are listed as a separate family.]

Distribution: circumpolar and oceanwide.

MEMBERS OF THIS SMALL family of piratical sea-birds are regular visitors to Australian waters in their non-breeding seasons. One species belongs to the antarctic and the other three range from the arctic across tropical oceans to the southern hemisphere. They vary in size from about 35–60cm with wingspans of 1–1.5m, or about the size of a Silver Gull to a Pacific Gull. They are gull-like in general appearance as well as size, including bill shape, but they are dark plumaged; all except the Great Skua have light and dark phases, the light forms having mainly white underparts. A distinctive feature, in adults only, is the extension of the central pair of tail feathers, from very short in the Great Skua to very long in the Long-tailed Skua. Bases of the flight feathers are white, sometimes extensively, forming conspicuous white patches or bands on blackish underwings. The piratical habits of skuas are centred on harassing other well-fed birds until they disgorge their food, the victim presumably lightening its load to escape from its tormentor. Skuas also have scavenging and predatory habits.

Key to STERCORARIIDAE

[*Note:* immatures do not have extended tail feathers.]

Central tail feathers:

1 Very slightly extended—conspicuous white flash on under-
   wing... Great Skua .... No 249
2 Moderately extended—
   feather tips blunt; conspicuous white flash on underwing .. Pomarine Skua...... No 251
   feathers sharply pointed; little or no white on underwing .. Arctic Skua......... No 250
3 Greatly extended and very thin—
   little or no white on underwing .... Long-tailed Skua .... No 252

---

249 GREAT SKUA *Stercorarius skua* (Brunnich) 1764   Pl 7

Distribution: southern coasts north to Geraldton and Fraser Island.

RECOGNITION: *short fan-shaped tail with very little extension to central tail feathers; conspicuous amount of white on underwing.*

DESCRIPTION: 60cm; wingspan 2.5m; tail rounded with very little extension to central feathers. Sexes alike. Dark grey-brown, sometimes blotched with buff, paler on underparts; base of flight feathers white making large white patch on underside of extended wing; bill black; eyes dark brown; legs black.

HABITAT: usually pelagic but sometimes inshore, in harbours and sheltered bays. HABITS: sometimes scavenging in wake of ships or around ships at anchor, and bold enough to be hand fed; solitary or in flocks.

STATUS: fairly common; non-breeding visitor from antarctic; April–November. TAXONOMY: most records are of race *lonnbergi*; race *maccormicki* (sometimes regarded as species) recorded infrequently.

250 ARCTIC SKUA *Stercorarius parasiticus* (Linnaeus) 1758

Distribution: throughout in coastal and offshore waters.

RECOGNITION: *fairly long squarish tail with central feathers distinctly extended and sharply pointed; little or no white on underwing.*

DESCRIPTION: 40cm; wingspan 1m; central tail feathers extend 10cm. Sexes alike. Upperparts blackish-brown; underparts variable, either blackish-brown, paler than upperparts or mainly white or intermediate with dusky breast band, when white usually with distinct pale collar tinged with yellow; very little white at base of flight feathers; bill dark grey; eyes brown; legs black.

STATUS: fairly common in east, rare in west; non-breeding visitor from northern hemisphere; September–April.

251 POMARINE SKUA *Stercorarius pomarinus* (Temminck) 1815 Pl 7

Distribution: southern coasts from mid-New South Wales to southwest Western Australia.

RECOGNITION: like Arctic Skua but larger, 50cm with wingspan 1·25m; *extended central tail feathers broad and twisted at tip; conspicuous white band in centre of underwing;* upper tail coverts white or barred black and white; bill olive-grey; eyes brown; legs black.

STATUS: fairly common (less common than Arctic) in east, rare in west; non-breeding visitor from northern hemisphere; September–April.

252 LONG-TAILED SKUA *Stercorarius longicaudus* Vieillot 1809

Distribution: few records from southeast.

RECOGNITION: *black cap, white collar and underparts, long thin central tail feathers.*

DESCRIPTION: 35cm, plus narrow central tail feathers extended 25cm. Sexes alike. Forehead to nape black; white collar continuous with white breast and throat; back and belly light brownish-grey; flight feathers black usually with white bases forming conspicuous white band on underwing (there is also a rare dark phase—wholly dark brown); bill black; eyes dark brown; legs blue or bluish-grey.

STATUS: rare vagrant from northern hemisphere.

Family LARIDAE
Gulls, Noddies, Terns
24(about 80) species: 1 endemic

Distribution: worldwide.

THERE ARE TWO MAIN sections of this large family, the gulls and terns; noddies are a small group which link the two but seem closer to the terns. All are gregarious; exceedingly noisy breeding colonies, called 'gulleries' and 'terneries', are well known features of some coasts and islands. They are aquatic, usually frequenting sea shores, but sometimes inland waters, like the Whiskered Tern in Australia. Some gulls appear to be spreading inland, apparently enticed by pickings from human settlement, offal and refuse, and insect life exposed by the plough. All are web-footed though terns rarely swim. Gulls are stoutly built and usually large—few are as dainty as the Silver Gull. They are white with grey or black backs and shoulders, pointed wings, square tails, large bills with upper mandible sharply curved at the tip, and red or yellow legs. They have a relatively slow and steady wingbeat and frequently soar and glide. Most terns are much smaller than gulls and more slender in appearance, often with deeply forked tails and rapid erratic flight, like swallows— hence the name 'sea-swallow'. A typical feature is a conspicuous amount of black about the head, often in the form of a cap. Bills are slender and pointed. They hunt by hovering over their prey, like the Kestrel, and the splashes of diving terns may be seen as they plummet into the shallow waters of some sheltered bay. In contrast, noddies are mainly dark, in outward appearance at least like melanistic forms of the more usual white terns, and with a white cap taking the place of a black one. They are mainly tropical.

Key to LARIDAE

White with black or pale grey back and wings, rounded tails, thick hooked bills; immatures of black-backed species are wholly sooty brown. Parents feed young by swallowing food and then regurgitating beside chicks . . . . Gulls

Black, or blackish with pale head, or wholly white, slender pointed bills, tail wedge-shaped or barely forked. Parents feed young by swallowing food and then regurgitating directly into chick gullet . . . . Noddies

Grey or black above and white below (rarely black) with black cap or black nape, slender pointed bills, tail moderately or deeply forked. Parents feed young by carrying food to them in their bills . . . . Terns

GULLS

1 Back grey, 38cm	Silver Gull	No 253
2 Back black, 60cm (immatures wholly sooty brown)	3–4	
3 Black band in white tail	Pacific Gull	No 254
4 Tail wholly white	Kelp Gull	No 255

NODDIES

1 White except for black eyering	White Noddy	No 260
2 Dark grey with pale grey head	Grey Noddy	No 259
3 Blackish with whitish forehead	4–7	
4 Tail wedge-shaped	Common Noddy	No 256
5 Tail square or slightly forked	6–7	

TERNS

Small, 25cm

1 Forehead white, crown to nape black.............	5–6
2 Forehead to nape black.......................	Whiskered Tern (breeding) No 272
3 Forehead to crown white, nape black or mottled black	7–9
4 Whole head black (rare)	10–11
5 Lores black, east and north coasts	Little Tern .... No 275
6 Lores white, south and west coasts	Fairy Tern .... No 276
7 Upperparts uniformly pale grey.................	Whiskered Tern *(non-breeding)*......... No 272
8 Upperparts medium grey with white rump and collar	White-winged Black Tern *(non-breeding)*......... No 273
9 Upperparts dark grey with white collar	Black Tern *(non-breeding)*.. No 274
10 Breast, belly and under shoulders black	White-winged Black Tern .. No 273
11 Breast and belly black	Black Tern *(breeding)*...... No 274

Large, 30–60cm

12 Back black or blackish	14–15
13 Back grey	16–29
14 White of forehead extends over eye	Bridled Tern............. No 271
15 White of forehead just reaches eye	Sooty Tern .... No 270
16 Black on head confined to nape and streak through eye	Black-naped Tern .... No 266
17 Black cap crested on nape, bill yellowish.......	19–20
18 Black cap without crest, bill not yellow........	21–29
19 Forehead white.............................	Crested Tern .... No 263
20 Forehead black.............................	Lesser Crested Tern .... No 264
21 Tail deeply forked, external feathers extended into long streamers	23–27
22 Tail shallow forked	28–29
23 Forehead white.............................	White-fronted Tern........ No 269 Common Tern *(non-breeding)*......... No 267
24 Forehead black.............................	25–27
25 Tail grey, bill black	Roseate Tern............. No 265
26 Tail white, bill red and black...................	Common Tern *(breeding)*.. No 267
27 Tail white, bill red	Arctic Tern.............. No 268
28 Large (60cm), bill red	Caspian Tern............. No 262
29 Medium (38cm), bill black	Gull-billed Tern.......... No 261

Alternative key to LARIDAE
GULLS

Silvery-grey: small and common	Silver Gull .... No 253
Black-backed: large with white head and underparts; uncommon	{Pacific Gull.............. No 254 {Kelp Gull .... No 255

NODDIES

Black: white forehead; wedge- or shallow-forked tails; tropical offshore and pelagic waters .... (black-backed terns have white underparts).	{Common Noddy .... No 256 {Lesser Noddy............ No 257 {White-backed Noddy ...... No 258
Small: grey or white; no black on head; very rare	{Grey Noddy .... No 259 {White Noddy .... No 260

TERNS

Large: heavy black pointed bill; shallow forked tail;
usually inland . . . . Gull-billed Tern . . . . No 261

Crested: (crest not very distinct in Caspian); large ⌠Caspian Tern . . . . No 262
shallow forked tails; usually coastal . . . . ⟨Crested Tern . . . . No 263
⌡Lesser Crested Tern . . . . No 264

Swallow-tailed: tips of deeply forked tails ending in ⌠Roseate Tern . . . . No 265
streamers; large—(a) *white-backed:* usually coastal; (a)⎮Black-naped Tern . . . . No 266
two common and mainly in north, one fairly com- ⟨Common Tern . . . . No 267
mon in south, two rare. (b) *black-backed:* under- ⎮Arctic Tern . . . . No 268
parts white (black-backed noddies have black ⌡White-fronted Tern . . . . No 269
underparts); tropical offshore and pelagic waters . . (b)⌠Sooty Tern . . . . No 270
⌡Bridled Tern . . . . No 271

Marsh terns: small; shallow forked tails; often some ⌠Whiskered Tern . . . . No 272
black on body; inland or coastal; one very rare . . . . . . ⟨White-winged Black Tern . . No 273
⌡Black Tern . . . . No 274

Least terns: small; black only on head; shallow forked ⌠Little Tern . . . . No 275
tails; coastal . . . . ⌡Fairy Tern . . . . No 276

Genus LARUS

A large and varied cosmopolitan group of some forty species often popularly known as seagulls. They are mainly coastal species many of which readily adapt to human environments. They are large and stoutly built—the Silver Gull of Australia being possibly one of the smallest and daintiest—with long pointed wings, more or less square tails, large bills hooked at the tip and webbed feet.

253 SILVER GULL *Larus novaehollandiae* Stephens 1826   Pl 7

Distribution: throughout, mainly coastal but sometimes inland.

RECOGNITION: *small, white with grey back.*

DESCRIPTION: 38cm. Sexes alike. Mainly white with centre of back, shoulders and inner wing pale grey; broad tip of wing black edged with white and subterminal white patches on longest feathers, often referred to as 'windows'; bill and legs bright scarlet; eyes white.

VARIATION: races have been described mainly on amount of white in black wingtip; in south (race *novaehollandiae*); in north (race *forsteri*); in Tasmania (race *gunni*).

HABITAT: coastal and inland waters. HABITS: terrestrial and aquatic; gregarious at all seasons; sedentary and nomadic, many dispersing from breeding grounds sometimes with regular seasonal movements, especially between inland breeding grounds and coasts; flight light and graceful. BREEDING: variable, but usually in one of two periods or sometimes in both, September–December and March–June; nests in colonies on ground, preferably or of necessity on small islands or anything surrounded by water, roughly made of any available material or on bare ground or among rocks; two to three eggs, brownish-olive blotched with brown and black (but variable). VOICE: loud harsh 'kwarr'. FOOD: omnivorous.

STATUS: very common in south, less common in north. TAXONOMY: species extending to south New Guinea, New Caledonia, New Zealand and Chatham I.

254 PACIFIC GULL *Larus pacificus* Latham 1801   Pl 7

Distribution: southern coasts north to Point Cloates in the west and mid-New South Wales in the east.

RECOGNITION: *large, white with black back and wings and black band in tail; large bill distinguishes immatures.*

DESCRIPTION: 60cm, bill 6cm and very thick; wingspan 2·5m. Sexes alike. White with black back and upper wings, except for broad white trailing edge and narrow white inner leading edge of wing; tail has narrow subterminal black band; bill yellow, tip red; eyes creamy-white, ring around eye yellow; legs yellow. *Immature:* uniformly mottled brown; bill, eyes and legs shades of brown.

HABITAT: coastal waters and offshore islands. HABITS: terrestrial and aquatic, feeds on surface of sea, also by diving, sometimes by dropping hardshelled prey on rocks; loosely gregarious; sedentary and nomadic, especially immatures. BREEDING: August–November; nests in loose colonies on coastal islands, on ground on sandy beaches and rocky headlands, nest well made of various grasses; two to three eggs, grey-brown, blotched with dark brown. VOICE: sharp 'ow-ow' varying to louder and harsher 'yow-woo' or 'yao' or 'kiaw'. FOOD: omnivorous.

STATUS: fairly common. TAXONOMY: endemic species.

Kelp Gull (255)

Pacific Gull (254)

255 KELP GULL *Larus dominicanus* Lichtenstein 1823

Distribution: southeast coast north to south Queensland and west to extreme southwest.

RECOGNITION: like Pacific Gull but slightly smaller, *lacks black band in white tail,* more distinct white leading edge to wing and white 'windows' at tip, much thinner yellow bill which has patch of red near tip of lower mandible. *Immature:* like Pacific Gull but bill much thinner.

HABITAT, etc : apparently much the same as Pacific Gull ; recorded breeding November–February. VOICE : hoarse 'gor-ah', also wailing 'waaaah' and 'wo-wo'.

STATUS: rare resident perhaps colonist from New Zealand. TAXONOMY: species extending widely throughout antarctic and subantarctic.

Genus ANOUS

Tern-like in general appearance but mainly black with tails slightly forked or wedge-shaped. Bills are slender and pointed, and bills and legs are usually black. There are about seven species, widespread mainly in tropical and subtropical seas, of which three breed on offshore Australian islands. At non-breeding times they are pelagic. The genera *Proselsterna* and *Gygis* are included as they do not seem to be distinct.

256 COMMON NODDY *Anous stolidus* (Linnaeus) 1758   Pl 7

Distribution: tropical seas, rarely further south than Abrolhos Is and Capricorn Group.

RECOGNITION: *sooty black with whitish forehead and pale grey crown, wedge-shaped tail.* (*Note:* large 'black' terns are white below with deeply forked tails.)

DESCRIPTION: 38cm, with bill 4cm; folded wings extend to tip of long wedge-shaped tail. Sexes alike. Sooty brown with near white forehead shading to pale grey crown and sharply demarcated from black face; white sickle-shaped marks above and below eye; wings and tail black; bill black; eyes dark brown; legs brownish-black.

HABITAT: offshore waters and islands. HABITS: pelagic, nesting and roosting on islands; dives to take food from surface, swims and sometimes rests on water; gregarious, sometimes in enormous dusky 'clouds'; sedentary, usually dispersing only short distances from roosting and breeding grounds; flight steady and strong but not as graceful as terns. BREEDING: variable, in most months, but sometimes in two periods, September–November and March–May; nests in colonies, on ground or in low shrubs, unformed or roughly made of any available material; one egg, dull white, blotched with shades of brown, red or purple. VOICE: loud 'kraa', also repeated 'kuk' and 'kree-aw'. FOOD: fish and squid.

STATUS: abundant in nesting areas. TAXONOMY: race, *(pileatus)* extending to Indian and western Pacific Oceans, of circumtropical species.

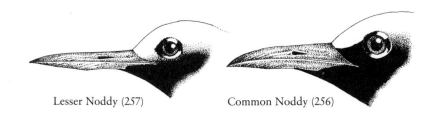

Lesser Noddy (257)   Common Noddy (256)

257 LESSER NODDY *Anous tenuirostris* (Temminck) 1823

Distribution: Abrolhos Is and adjacent seas.

RECOGNITION: like Common Noddy but smaller, 28–30cm, bill relatively longer and more slender, *tail square or very slightly forked, white of forehead and crown shades to blackish lower face.* Also like White-capped Noddy, which occurs only in northeastern seas.

HABITAT: offshore islands. HABITS: frequents offshore and inshore waters and comes to land to roost at night; feeds by diving to surface; gregarious, in 'immense' numbers; sedentary, seldom far from breeding grounds; flight fast and rather fluttery. BREEDING: August–December, or longer; nests in trees, especially mangroves, made of seaweed bound with excrement; one egg, dull white blotched with brown or purple. VOICE: loud rattling call, also croaking and purring. FOOD: fish and squid.

STATUS: abundant locally. TAXONOMY: species with one other breeding colony on Seychelles Is.

258 WHITE-CAPPED NODDY *Anous minutus* Boie 1844

Distribution: islands of Coral Sea and tropical Queensland coast.

RECOGNITION: like Lesser Noddy in size and general appearance and with *tail square or slightly forked,* but face pattern like Common Noddy with *white forehead and crown sharply demarcated from black face.*

HABITAT: coastal and offshore islands. HABITS: picks up food by diving to surface, usually feeds closer inshore than other noddies, returns to land to roost at night; gregarious at all seasons; sedentary. BREEDING: August–January; nests in trees and bushes, made of sticks, grasses and leaves cemented with excreta; one egg, pale grey blotched with purplish-red. VOICE: crackling 'krikrikrik', a harsh staccato rattle and sharp 'care'. FOOD: fish and squid. STATUS: abundant. TAXONOMY: variable species extending throughout much of Pacific. (Sometimes regarded as same species as Lesser Noddy.)

259 GREY NODDY *Anous caeruleus* (Bennett) 1840

Distribution: eastern seas.

RECOGNITION: *30cm; tail forked. Pale bluish-grey (smoke grey), darker on back and white on centre of underwing; black ring around eye; bill, eyes and legs black, webs yellow.*

STATUS: rare vagrant; very few records.

260 WHITE NODDY *Anous albus* (Sparrman) 1786

Distribution: eastern seas.

RECOGNITION: *33cm; tail forked. Mainly white with narrow black ring around eye; bill black, base blue; eyes brown; legs black.*

HABITS: light airy flight, constantly rising and dipping and catching food on surface.

STATUS: rare vagrant; very few records.

Genus STERNA

Terns have a graceful appearance, like swallows but large and white. They are associated with coastal and inland waters where they may be seen fluttering and hovering before plummeting down to seize prey. Distinctive features are black caps, sometimes extended into crests on the nape, and forked tails, slightly forked in the marsh terns and deeply forked in most others. Plumage is mainly white but some species have large areas of black on the body, especially in breeding plumage. There are nearly forty species of which sixteen are recorded in Australia. This large group can be subdivided into smaller sections, like marsh terns and crested terns, but the conclusion is that they are all closely related and should be kept in one genus.

261 GULL-BILLED TERN *Sterna nilotica* Gmelin 1789

Distribution: throughout.

RECOGNITION: *large, black cap from forehead to nape, shallow forked tail, black bill, often inland.*

DESCRIPTION: 40cm, with thick bill nearly 5cm; folded wings extend beyond forked tail. Sexes alike. *Breeding:* forehead, crown and nape black; remainder of upperparts very pale grey; underparts white; flight feathers darker grey becoming very dark at tip; bill black; eyes dark brown; legs black. *Non-breeding:* forehead to nape mottled black and white with large black patch behind eye.

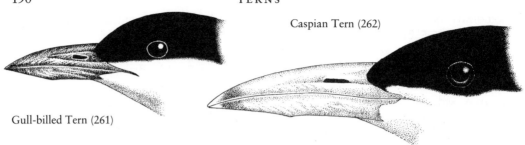

Caspian Tern (262)

Gull-billed Tern (261)

HABITAT: coastal and inland waters. HABITS: feeds by hawking over water and descending in shallow glides to seize food with bill held vertical (the smaller Whiskered Tern in similar situations descends rapidly); gregarious at all seasons; sedentary and nomadic, movements between inland breeding areas and coastal non-breeding. BREEDING: September–March; nests on ground, a rough scrape sometimes with twigs and soil; two to three eggs, brown to green, blotched with brown and black. VOICE: harsh 'kuh-wuk' and 'che-ah'. FOOD: fish and various small animals and insects.

STATUS: fairly common in north, less common in south, rare in Tasmania. TAXONOMY: endemic race *(macrotarsa)* of worldwide species.

262 CASPIAN TERN   *Sterna caspia*   Pallas 1770   Pl 7

Distribution: throughout in coastal waters, sometimes inland.

RECOGNITION: *very large; black cap from forehead to nape, shallow forked tail, red bill; mainly coastal.*

DESCRIPTION: 60cm, with bill 7·5cm; wingspan about 2·5m; folded wings extend beyond forked tail; nape slightly crested. Sexes alike. *Breeding:* forehead to nape and to below eye black; remainder of upperparts pale grey, whiter on tail and darker on wings, especially near tip; underparts white; bill bright red; eyes dark brown; legs black. *Non-breeding:* forehead to crown mottled black and white, blacker on face.

HABITAT: coastal waters, sometimes permanent inland waters, especially when not breeding. HABITS: on feeding flights head held down and tail fanned, hovers and then dives under water; solitary and gregarious; mainly sedentary with local movements. BREEDING: September–December, other times also in north; nests on ground on sandy or stony shores, a scrape roughly defined with sticks and food debris; one to two eggs, pale grey-brown, sparsely blotched with darker brown. VOICE: harsh scream. FOOD: mainly fish.

STATUS: fairly common. TAXONOMY: southern breeding form (race *strenua*) extending to New Zealand of species ranging widely in northern hemisphere.

263 CRESTED TERN   *Sterna bergii*   Lichtenstein 1823   Pl 7

Distribution: throughout in coastal localities.

RECOGNITION: *forehead white, crown to nape black with nape feathers extended into crest, greenish-yellow bill.*

DESCRIPTION: 45cm, with bill 6cm; wingspan over 1m; nape feathers extended into erectile crest. Sexes alike. *Breeding:* forehead white; crown to nape black; hind neck white; remainder of upperparts medium grey with trailing edge of wing white; underparts white;

bill lemon-yellow, tinged with green at base; eyes brown; legs dark brown. *Non-breeding:* crown mottled black and white, but crest remains black.

HABITAT: coasts, sometimes inland waters near coast. HABITS: on feeding flights head held down and tail fanned, dives into water; gregarious at all seasons; north and south dispersal movements from breeding grounds. BREEDING: September–December in east and south, March–June in north, both periods in west; nests in colonies on sandy beaches and rocky headlands, unformed; eggs laid on grass, bare sand or shingle; one egg, variable, often pale buff blotched with brown and black. VOICE: harsh 'krow' and 'korr'. FOOD: mainly fish.

STATUS: common. TAXONOMY: race *(cristata)* extending to Malaysia of species widespread on islands and coasts of Indian Ocean.

264 LESSER CRESTED TERN *Sterna bengalensis* Lesson 1831

Distribution: northern coasts south to Point Cloates and Moreton Bay.

RECOGNITION: very similar to Crested Tern but smaller, 38cm, *little or no white on forehead, bill orange-yellow.*

HABITAT, etc : like Crested Tern ; nests on rubble banks ; probably sedentary.

STATUS: uncommon, but perhaps frequently overlooked because of resemblance to Crested Tern. TAXONOMY: species extending to southern Asia and Mediterranean.

265 ROSEATE TERN *Sterna dougallii* Montagu 1813   Fig p 192

Distribution: northern coasts rarely further south than Abrolhos Is and Capricorn Is.

RECOGNITION: *black from forehead to nape, tail grey, white tail streamers extend beyond folded wings.*

DESCRIPTION: 38cm, with bill 4cm and deeply forked tail 18cm, not including greatly extended outer tail feathers. Sexes alike. *Breeding:* forehead to crown and to below eye black; upper-parts, including tail, pale grey, white on hind neck and trailing edge of wing, blackish on leading edge of wing; underparts white with pale rose tint on breast; bill black or red but usually red with black tip; eyes dark brown; legs red. *Non-breeding:* forehead mottled black and white, bill black.

HABITAT: coastal and sometimes offshore waters. HABITS: usually feeds near nesting and roosting grounds, dives from a height; gregarious at all seasons; probably sedentary; flight light and buoyant. BREEDING: September–December, also February–May in west; nests mainly on offshore islands, on ground in shingly places and often under shrubs, roughly made of grass stems and stones; two eggs, variable, often greenish-grey blotched with brown. VOICE: harsh guttural 'aaark' and two-syllable whistle. FOOD: fish.

STATUS: fairly common. TAXONOMY: endemic race *(gracilis)* of species widely distributed throughout old world and to eastern North America.

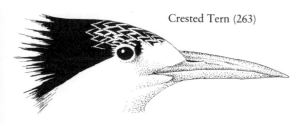

Crested Tern (263)

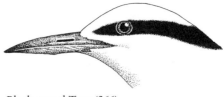

Black-naped Tern (266)

266 BLACK-NAPED TERN   *Sterna sumatrana*   Raffles 1822   Fig p 191

Distribution: northeastern coasts.

RECOGNITION: like Roseate Tern but smaller, 30cm, and clearly distinguished by *white forehead and crown, black nape continuous with thin black streak through eye;* bill and legs black.

HABITAT: coral pools and lagoons. HABITS: feeds by diving and skimming or catching prey while hovering over surface; gregarious at all seasons; apparently sedentary. BREEDING: September–January; nests on ground among shingle, a scrape; two eggs, creamy-white blotched with shades of brown and grey. VOICE: short sharp 'tsii-chee-chi-chip' and 'chit-chit-chit-rer'. FOOD: fish.

STATUS: fairly common. TAXONOMY: race *(sumatrana)* in southwest Pacific of species extending to western Indian Ocean.

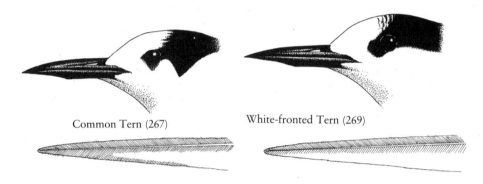

Common Tern (267)   White-fronted Tern (269)

HEAD AND TIP OF SECOND WING FEATHER
(non-breeding)

267 COMMON TERN   *Sterna hirundo*   Linnaeus 1758

Distribution: mainly east coast (race *longipennis*), scattered records elsewhere.

RECOGNITION: *Non-breeding:* very like non-breeding White-fronted Tern except for *streaky black and white crown and less black in front of eye.* Breeding: like Roseate Tern in having forehead to nape black but distinguished by *white rump and tail and streamers shorter than folded wings;* distinguished from Arctic Tern by white wedge on inner web of second main flight feather and *bill black* (race *longipennis*) or *red with black tip.*

STATUS: fairly common non-breeding visitor from northern hemisphere; July–March.

268 ARCTIC TERN   *Sterna paradisea*   Pontoppidan 1763

Distribution: scattered coastal records.

RECOGNITION: like Common Tern but sides of tail grey, *bill red,* no white wedge on inner web of second main flight feather; when seen together underparts darker grey, bill and legs shorter.

STATUS: rare vagrant from northern hemisphere.

269 WHITE-FRONTED TERN   *Sterna striata*   Gmelin 1789   Pl 7

Distribution: southeast coasts to eastern South Australia and south Queensland.

RECOGNITION: *white forehead, black bill, tail streamers extend beyond folded wings.*

DESCRIPTION: 40cm, with bill 4cm; tail deeply forked and outer feathers extended into streamers. Sexes alike. *Breeding:* forehead white; crown to nape black; hind neck and trailing edge of wing white; remainder of upperparts pale grey; underparts white with rosy tinge; bill black; eyes dark brown; legs reddish-brown. *Non-breeding:* black crown mottled with white, very like non-breeding Common Tern but distinct black patch in front of eye, rusty tinge on throat and breast.

Roseate Tern (265)

HABITAT: coastal waters. HABITS: feed on surface prey taken at low level, sometimes sits on water. VOICE: sharp whistling 'tsit-tsit'.

STATUS: uncommon, but sometimes in large flocks, especially after storms; non-breeding visitor from New Zealand; mainly between February and September.

270 SOOTY TERN *Sterna fuscata* Linnaeus 1756

Distribution: northern coasts, south to Abrolhos Is and Capricorn Group, rarely to north New South Wales.

RECOGNITION: *black above and white below ('black' noddies are black below), white of forehead reaches to just above eye.*

DESCRIPTION: 45cm, with bill 4cm; tail deeply forked and with streamers from outer feathers. Sexes alike. Upperparts to below eye black except for white forehead reaching to just above eye; leading edge of wing and tail streamers white; underparts white; bill black; eyes brown; legs black.

HABITAT: pelagic and Barrier Reef islands, rarely near mainland. HABITS: feeds on surface prey, sometimes at night, rarely lands on water; gregarious at all seasons; mainly sedentary, adults disperse only short distance from breeding grounds but juveniles wander long distances until mature. BREEDING: variable, September–November in south, March–November in north; nests on ground, a rough scrape sometimes under shade of bush; one egg, dull white blotched with dark purple or purplish-brown. VOICE: loud 'wideawake' call, also various barking sounds and loud screams. FOOD: mainly squid.

STATUS: common to abundant. TAXONOMY: race *(serrator)* extending to New Guinea and New Caledonia of circumtropical species.

Bridled Tern (271)   Sooty Tern (270)

271 BRIDLED TERN *Sterna anaethetus* Scopoli 1786   Fig p 193

Distribution: western, northern and Queensland coasts.

RECOGNITION: like Sooty Tern but slightly smaller, 40cm, *white of forehead narrower and extends over and beyond eye,* black crown slightly contrasts with remainder of dark brownish-grey upperparts; bill and legs black.

HABITAT, etc: similar to Sooty, but roosts regularly on land at night. VOICE: a barking staccato 'wep-wep' or 'wup-wup', also various grating sounds.

STATUS: common. TAXONOMY: race *(anaethetus)* extending to southern India and Japan of circumtropical species.

272 WHISKERED TERN *Sterna hybrida* Pallas 1811   Pl 7

Distribution: throughout.

RECOGNITION: *small, shallow forked tail, rump grey like back, underparts blackish (breeding) or white (non-breeding); inland.*

DESCRIPTION: 25cm, with bill just over 2·5cm; folded wings extend beyond shallow forked tail. Sexes alike. *Breeding:* forehead to nape black; remainder of upperparts pale grey, darker on wingtips; face and throat white; breast and belly dark grey; underwing and under tail coverts white; bill red; eyes brown; legs red. *Non-breeding:* forehead and crown mainly white; face and nape mottled black and white; underparts white:

HABITAT: inland waters. HABITS: feeds on water or on land, hawks slowly over water taking food from surface or by partly submerging; feeds also on ploughed land; gregarious at all seasons; sedentary, nomadic and possibly migratory, apparently regular seasonal movements from and to southern localities. BREEDING: September–December, possibly also at other times, especially in north; nests in colonies on water, anchored to vegetation or floating, made of water vegetation or twigs; three eggs, variable, grey to green, blotched with dark brown. VOICE: reedy staccato 'kitt' or 'ki-itt'. FOOD: various small animals and insects.

STATUS: fairly common. TAXONOMY: race *(fluviatilis)* extending to New Guinea and Moluccas of species widespread in old world.

273 WHITE-WINGED BLACK TERN *Sterna leucoptera* Temminck 1815

Distribution: throughout mainly in coastal districts.

RECOGNITION: *non-breeding:* like Whiskered Tern but distinguished by *white rump contrasting with dark grey back and pale grey tail,* black patches in front of and behind eye; slightly smaller and bill relatively smaller. *Breeding:* body above and below black; under shoulders black; upper shoulders white.

HABITAT: coastal waters. HABITS: recorded that does not break surface of water when feeding as does Whiskered Tern.

STATUS: fairly common; non-breeding visitor from temperate Europe and Asia; September to March.

274 BLACK TERN *Sterna nigra* Linnaeus 1758

Distribution: very few records, no specimens collected.

RECOGNITION: like White-winged Black Tern but distinguished (non-breeding) by *grey rump uniform with back and tail,* dark grey shoulders, and (breeding) by grey shoulders uniform with wings and back and underwings uniformly pale grey.

STATUS: rare vagrant from northern hemisphere.

275 LITTLE TERN *Sterna albifrons* Pallas 1764

Distribution : east and north coasts from east Tasmania to Broome, rarely south coast to Spencer Gulf.

RECOGNITION: *small, like Fairy Tern but black band through eye extends to base of bill, white of forehead extends over and beyond eye, black tip to yellow bill.*

DESCRIPTION: 25cm, with bill 3cm; folded wings reach tip of shallow forked tail. Sexes alike. *Breeding:* forehead white, extending above and just beyond eye; crown and nape black, extending through eye to base of bill; back and wings pale grey, black on outer flight feathers; tail white; bill yellow, tip black; eyes brown; legs yellow. *Non-breeding:* crown whitish, only nape and streak through eye black, but black does not reach bill (difficult to distinguish from Fairy Tern except by pattern of black on outer flight feathers).

HABITAT: coastal waters. HABITS: feeds by diving in shallow waters; gregarious at all seasons, sometimes in huge flocks; sedentary with dispersal, nomadic and migratory movements. BREEDING: variable, August–December in north, January–March in south; nests in colonies, on ground, a scrape sometimes edged with stones or shells; two eggs, pale fawn grey, blotched with brown. VOICE: harsh shrieking 'kree-ik' and chattering 'kirri-kirri'. FOOD: fish.

STATUS : common. TAXONOMY : race *(sinensis)* extending through south and east Asia to Manchuria, of cosmopolitan species.

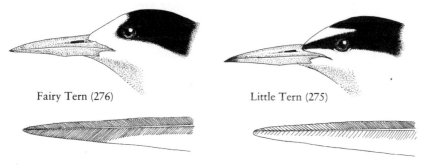

Fairy Tern (276)   Little Tern (275)

HEAD AND TIP OF OUTER WING FEATHER

276 FAIRY TERN *Sterna nereis* (Gould) 1842   Pl 7

Distribution: south and west coasts from Wilson's Promontory and Tasmania to Broome.

RECOGNITION: similar to Little Tern, distinguished *(breeding)* by *black on face not reaching base of bill*—or lores white, white of forehead just reaches eye, bill brighter orange-yellow without black tip, less black on outer flight feathers; and *(non-breeding)* almost impossible to distinguish except by black on outer flight feathers.

HABITAT, etc: similar to Little Tern; apparently more sedentary.

STATUS: common. TAXONOMY: endemic race *(nereis)* of species extending to New Zealand and New Caledonia.

Family COLUMBIDAE

Pigeons and Doves

26(289) species: 14 endemic: 3 introduced

Distribution: worldwide.

THE NAMES PIGEON AND dove are interchangeable; they do not refer to distinct groups. Although members of this large and successful family vary greatly in size, form and colour they are unmistakable to anyone first acquainted with the Domestic Pigeon, or any other representative. But features which distinguish them are not easily itemised. Bills are usually rather delicate with nostrils opening, as in parrots, in a large soft basal cere; legs are short, plumages are often in soft pastel colours, but equally often in vivid pigments and iridescent sheens; they have a rapid noisy flight when taking off; they have soft cooing voices and elegant mating displays; they have an appealing gentleness. Much of their success is due to their adaptability, as illustrated for instance by the domestication of the Rock Pigeon and the readiness with which many accept the human environment. They have adapted to all kinds of habitat from rain forest, probably their original home, to treeless deserts, wherever fruits, berries and seeds are available. A staple diet of hard desert seeds requires a regular intake of water and characteristic features of dry country species is the rhythm of their drinking habits and the amount they can consume at a time. Times of drinking are usually geared to just before or after sunrise or sunset, possibly times when they are least vulnerable to predators; they arrive in great flocks, also a protective measure, and drink deeply with heads nearly immersed, not by sipping as many birds do. Then they disperse widely and for long distances to feeding and breeding areas. In Australia the bronzewing group is peculiar to the continent and provides most of the endemic species. They have been particularly successful in finding unoccupied niches; for example the pheasant family is poorly represented, in comparison with many other countries, and a place which might have been occupied by some game bird is taken by the plumed pigeons, which seem to look and behave very like partridges elsewhere.

Key to COLUMBIDAE

Larger than Domestic Pigeon: over 33cm

1 Reddish-brown, long broad tail . . . . Brown Pigeon . . . . No 281
2 Greyish, brown tufted crest, tail black with broad white
   band. . . . . Topknot Pigeon. . . . . No 302
3 Dark grey, white forehead, 'necklace' and belly . . . . . . Wonga Pigeon . . . . No 296
4 Pale head, purple breast, yellow belly . . . . Wompoo Pigeon . . . . No 298
5 Head and neck white. 6–8

6 Back and underparts white. . . . . Torres Strait Pigeon . . . . . No 301
7 Back black, underparts white ♂(Foreparts grey brown♀) White-headed Pigeon . . . . No 277
8 Back and breast-band black . . . . Banded Pigeon. . . . . No 297

Domestic Pigeon: 33cm

9 Variable, usually green and purple sheen on neck, two
   black bands on wing, rump and patch on underwing
   white . . . . Domestic Pigeon . . . . No 278

Smaller than Domestic Pigeon: under 33cm

10 Very small, shoulders speckled white . . . . Diamond Dove . . . . No 295

Genus COLUMBA

This cosmopolitan group of 'typical' pigeons consists of some fifty or so species, only one of which is represented in Australia, apart from the introduced Domestic Pigeon. The White-headed Pigeon of eastern rain forests, although quite distinct in appearance, is related to a number of other forms in the southwest Pacific area in which there is well marked sexual dimorphism.

277 WHITE-HEADED PIGEON *Columba leucomela* Temminck 1821

Distribution: Map 54.

RECOGNITION: *white head and underparts, black back, wings and tail (male); brown foreparts with white throat (female).*

DESCRIPTION: 38–41cm. Sexes different. *Male:* head and neck white; back, wings and tail black with purple and green iridescence; underparts dull creamy-white; bill reddish, cere and tip white or pale yellow; eyes orange; legs brownish-pink. *Female:* differs in having foreparts, including upper breast, grey-brown with pink iridescence; throat white.

HABITAT: forests and woodlands, rarely open country. HABITS: mainly arboreal but sometimes feeds on ground; solitary or in small flocks; apparently sedentary, perhaps partly nomadic.

BREEDING: July–December; nests in trees, usually at low levels, roughly made of twigs; one white egg. VOICE: low-pitched 'oom' and 'oo-ooo'. FOOD: fruits, berries, seeds. STATUS: fairly common. TAXONOMY: endemic species.

Introduced species

278 DOMESTIC PIGEON   *Columba livia*   Gmelin 1789

Distribution: various urban localities, especially in coastal districts.

RECOGNITION: 33cm. Sexes alike. Variable, usually blue-grey with *green and purple sheen on neck,* two black bars near centre of wing, *white rump and white on underwing;* but under domestication colours and patterns have greatly altered.

HABITAT: usually around homesteads unless established in a feral state. BREEDING: nests in holes and caves or similar situations around homestead buildings, as under eaves, rafters in outhouses, under bridges, etc; two white eggs.

STATUS: common and likely to increase and extend range.

Genus STREPTOPELIA

The name turtledove originally belonged to members of this group, of which there are about seventeen species in tropical and warmer temperate parts of the old world. The two species now in Australia have been introduced; the nearest natural occurrence of the genus is in Timor. They are relatively small with long graduated tails and some striking 'badge' in the neck area, sometimes a black half collar, or in the present instance, patches of checked colours.

Introduced species

279 SPOTTED DOVE   *Streptopelia chinensis*   (Scopoli) 1786

Distribution: various urban localities mainly in coastal districts.

RECOGNITION: *bluish-grey head, checked patch of black, white and buff on hind neck.*

DESCRIPTION: 28cm, with long graduated tail. Sexes alike. Head bluish-grey with slight pink tinge; large patch on hind neck checked black, white and buff; remainder of upperparts grey-brown, edge of shoulder bluish and tail tipped white; chin white; throat and breast purplish-pink; belly buffish-grey; bill black; eyes orange, bare skin around eye purplish; legs pink.

HABITAT: trees and woods in urban and cultivated areas. HABITS: often feeding on ground in city parks and gardens; solitary or in small parties. BREEDING: variable; nests in bushes or on buildings, roughly made of sticks; two white eggs. VOICE: soft cooing, some variant of 'coo-croo-oo' and 'cuk-a-crrroo, cuk-cuk'. FOOD : seeds.

STATUS: common and apparently increasing.

Introduced species

280 SENEGAL TURTLEDOVE   *Streptopelia senegalensis*   (Linnaeus) 1766

Distribution: urban localities, to date mainly in southwest Western Australia.

RECOGNITION: *pinkish-purple head, checked patch of black and reddish brown on foreneck, bluish shoulder and rump.*

DESCRIPTION: 25cm, with long graduated tail. Sexes nearly alike, female less reddish-brown. Head, neck and breast reddish-purple, patch on foreneck checked black and reddish-brown; back reddish-brown; shoulders and rump blue-grey; belly creamy-white; centre tail grey-brown, outer dark grey tipped white.

HABITAT: urban parks and gardens, cultivation in drier areas. HABITS: feeds on ground. BREEDING: variable; nests in bushes or in and around buildings, roughly made of sticks; two white eggs. VOICE: variants of soft bubbling 'coo-coo'. FOOD: seeds.

STATUS: fairly common and apparently increasing.

Genus MACROPYGIA

A group of eight large forest species of the Indo-Australian region are distinguished by brown plumage, large graduated tails and more or less barred appearance. They are widely known as cuckoo doves. The name of the single endemic Australian species has been simplified from Large Brown Cuckoo Dove to Brown Pigeon.

281 BROWN PIGEON *Macropygia phasianella* (Temminck) 1821 Pl 8
Distribution: Map 55.

RECOGNITION: *large, uniformly reddish-brown, long broad graduated tail, eastern rain forests.*

DESCRIPTION: 40cm, with broad graduated tail 20cm. Sexes slightly different, female lacks glossy colours on hind neck and pink tinge on upper breast. Upperparts russet brown, hind neck with pink and green iridescence; upper breast pinkish-brown, throat, lower breast and belly cinnamon brown; bill black; eyes, an outer circle of deep crimson and inner circle of blue; legs red.

HABITAT: rain forests. HABITS: largely arboreal, keeping to lower forest layers, sometimes on ground in clearings, tail sometimes used as support when clambering among branches; solitary or small parties of five or six; apparently sedentary. BREEDING: October–January, perhaps also at other times; nests in lower branches of trees up to about 7m, made of twigs and leaves, sometimes quite bulky; one egg, pale creamy-white. VOICE: loud 'whoop-a-whoop' or 'woork', frequently repeated and often followed by succession of short 'coos'. FOOD: fruits and berries.

STATUS: common. TAXONOMY: endemic but barely distinct race *(phasianella)* of species extending to Sumatra and Philippines.

Genus CHALCOPHAPS

Emerald doves or green-winged pigeons, of which there are two species in the Indo-Australian region, are closely related to the larger group of bronzewing pigeons. They are plump with relatively short rounded tails, glossy green shoulders and two broad bands of colour on the lower back. They feed mainly on the ground in forests and woodlands. Only one species occurs in Australia.

282 GREEN-WINGED PIGEON *Chalcophaps indica* (Linnaeus) 1758 Pl 8
Distribution: Map 56.

RECOGNITION: *glossy green back and shoulders, dark rump with two pale bars.*

DESCRIPTION: 25–28cm. Sexes slightly different, female lacks vinaceous tints. Head and underparts vinaceous brown shading to purplish on nape and centre of upper back and lighter on throat and belly; back and inner shoulders iridescent bronzy green; rump blackish-brown with two broad pale grey bars; edge of shoulder white; under shoulder dark cinnamon; flight feathers black with concealed cinnamon; centre of tail blackish-brown, sides blue-grey with dark subterminal band and white tip; bill reddish-orange; eyes dark brown; legs pinkish-red.

HABITAT: forests. HABITS: arboreal and terrestrial, lives in trees, feeds mainly on ground; solitary or in small parties; movements not established. BREEDING: mainly August–February, possibly other times; nests in bushes and fairly low in trees, well made of sticks and twigs; two eggs, pale cream or buff. VOICE: loud 'coo' repeated monotonously. FOOD: berries and seeds, perhaps insects.

STATUS: fairly common. TAXONOMY: race *(chrysochlora)* extending to Timor, New Guinea and New Caledonia, of species ranging to southeast Asia and India.

BRONZEWING PIGEONS

There is a group of ten pigeons peculiar to Australia which merits separate comment. They are the bronzewings, so named from the patch of iridescent colour present in their wings; it is conspicuous in some, like the Common and Brush Bronzewings, but obscured and insignificant in the two rock pigeons. On present understanding these species are arranged in three genera, *Phaps, Ocyphaps* and *Petrophassa* although, as usual, opinions on this matter vary. It is possible that these pigeons originated and diverged from some immigrant which had common ancestry with the extralimital emerald doves, *Chalcophaps*. Most have striking facial patterns, as in the Flock and Squatter Pigeons, but odd ones again are the curious rock pigeons of the Kimberley area and Arnhemland; this suggests that if glossy wings and bold facial patterns are ancient features then the rock pigeons have diverged most, probably in response to environments where such features are a hindrance to survival. All are mainly ground feeders, a habit present in the forest emerald dove stock, which would be an advantage in adapting to Australia's desert conditions. The plumed pigeons are entirely terrestrial.

Genus PHAPS

Two species of plump appearance, streaked face pattern and a conspicuous amount of iridescence in the wings. The widespread Common Bronzewing is a dry country species and the Brush Bronzewing, of more restricted distribution, is a bird of woodland habitats.

283 COMMON BRONZEWING *Phaps chalcoptera* (Latham) 1790   Pl 8

Distribution: throughout except Cape York Peninsula.

RECOGNITION: *white streak across face, iridescent blotches on shoulder, white throat and pink or buffish breast.*

DESCRIPTION: 30cm. Sexes slightly different. *Male:* forehead creamy-white; centre of crown and sides of nape to behind eye purplish-brown; remainder of upperparts drab brown, feathers edged with pale buff or rufous; broad black bar from eye to bill; long white streak below eye; face blue-grey; throat white; upper breast pinkish-buff, paler on lower breast and belly; shoulders blue-grey with large spots and patches of iridescent bronze and green forming broken bars; under shoulders cinnamon; flight feathers and centre of tail blackish brown, sides of tail blue-grey with broad blackish subterminal bar; bill purplish-black; eyes reddish-brown; legs purplish-pink. *Female:* differs mainly in dull grey forehead, centre of crown and sides of nape reddish-brown, breast grey-buff.

VARIATION: very slight but races sometimes recognised—in southeast darker and larger (race *chalcoptera*); centre and southwest slightly redder (race *murchisoni*); northwest smaller and paler (race *consobrina*).

HABITAT: dry woodlands and open country with scattered shrubs and trees. HABITS: largely terrestrial but often nesting in trees and bushes; solitary, but sometimes forms flocks when not breeding, congregates in large numbers to drink before sunrise and after sunset, alights at some distance and walks to water; sedentary or partly nomadic; flight low, swift and direct. BREEDING: variable, but mainly August–November; nests in trees or bushes on horizontal forks, or on ground, a rough platform of sticks; two white eggs. VOICE: deep low-pitched 'oom-oom'. FOOD: berries, seeds, cultivated grains.

STATUS: common. TAXONOMY: endemic species.

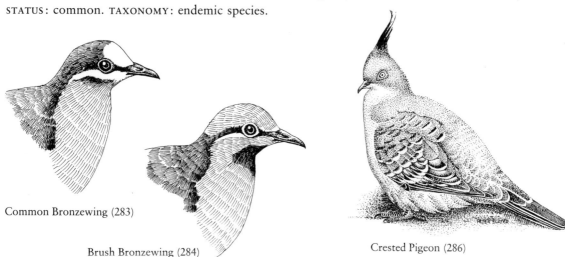

Common Bronzewing (283)

Brush Bronzewing (284)

Crested Pigeon (286)

284 BRUSH BRONZEWING *Phaps elegans* (Temminck) 1810   Pl 8
Distribution: Map 57.

RECOGNITION: *dark brown and white streaks across face, iridescent blotches on shoulders, dark brown throat, blue-grey or greyish breast.*

DESCRIPTION: 28cm. Sexes slightly different. *Male:* forehead light russet brown, sometimes greyish; crown and nape blue-grey; hind neck dark chestnut continuous with streak through eye to bill and bordered below on face with white; remainder of upperparts and shoulders brown, with two wide broken bars of iridescent bronze, blue and green in centre of wing; throat chestnut; lower face, side of neck and underparts pale blue-grey sometimes tinged with pale chestnut; outer tail blue-grey with blackish subterminal band; bill black; eyes dark brown; legs pinkish. *Female:* lacks much of chestnut except on throat and streak through eye; forehead and crown dark grey.

HABITAT: low cover in woodlands, bushy heaths, especially coastal but sometimes far inland.

HABITS: mainly terrestrial; solitary and sedentary; flight low and direct and of short duration, drinks about sunset. BREEDING: variable, but mainly October–January; nests on or close to ground, sometimes under grass tufts, a rough platform of twigs; two white eggs. VOICE: loud 'coo' or 'oop' repeated. FOOD: berries and seeds, possibly some insects. STATUS: fairly common, possibly decreasing. TAXONOMY: endemic species.

285 FLOCK PIGEON *Phaps histrionica* (Gould) 1841   Pl 8

Distribution: Map 57.

RECOGNITION: *black head with white forehead and white 'horseshoe' behind eye (male), back brown.*

DESCRIPTION: 28cm. Sexes different. *Male:* head black with white forehead and white half circle behind eye; foreneck white; back dark buff; breast and belly blue-grey; edge of shoulders white; patch of iridescent blue and green in centre of wing; most flight feathers tipped white; outer tail feathers blue-grey with black subterminal bar and white tips; bill and eyes blackish; legs purplish-grey. *Female:* lacks black and white head markings, face and throat dull black, iridescent colours and white on wing tips much reduced, breast dark buff like back.

HABITAT: open country. HABITS: terrestrial; mainly solitary breeding and gregarious at other times, sometimes congregating in very large flocks (said to be great fluctuations in numbers but this might be local); nomadic; drinks at sunset—claimed to be precisely during period of sun's disappearance. BREEDING: variable, but apparently in some places fairly regular in relation to regular seeding of grasses; nests on ground, usually under any available shelter, like grass tussocks, a shallow scrape; two eggs, creamy-white. VOICE: soft double 'coo', apparently only at breeding times. FOOD: mainly grass seeds. STATUS: uncertain. TAXONOMY: endemic species.

Genus OCYPHAPS

The Crested Pigeon, a slim long-tailed species, is a distinct member of the bronzewing group which, it is deduced, has returned to mainly arboreal habits from a terrestrial ancestry. Its slender erect crest is similar to that of the plumed pigeons.

286 CRESTED PIGEON *Ocyphaps lophotes* (Temminck) 1822   Fig p 201

Distribution: Map 58.

RECOGNITION: *greyish with white tipped black tail, thin erect black crest, barred shoulders.*

DESCRIPTION: 30cm, with tail 15cm; thin erect black crest 5–7.5cm. Sexes alike. Head pale blue-grey; sides of neck pale pinkish-bronze; back and rump pale buff-olive; shoulders barred black and buff; partly concealed patch in wing; centre iridescent purple and green; centre of tail drab with slight greenish sheen, remainder black tipped white; under shoulders tipped white; bill black, grey at base; eyes reddish-orange, bare skin around eye red; legs pinkish-red.

HABITAT: woodlands and open country with bushes and trees, and open water at no great distance. HABITS: feeds on ground but never far from trees to which it flies when disturbed and to roost and nest; solitary breeding but often congregating in flocks when feeding or drinking, just after sunrise and less frequently before sunset, in flocks when not breeding; sedentary and nomadic; wing beats of flocks in flight make strange metallic sound. BREEDING: most months but especially September–February; nests in bushes and trees, usually below 3m, a flimsy platform of sticks on forks or on creepers or mistletoe; two white eggs. VOICE: variants of soft 'oo-oo'. FOOD: seeds.

STATUS: very common. TAXONOMY: endemic species.

Genus PETROPHASSA

Each of the three pairs of species which make up this group are frequently listed as separate genera, *Petrophassa*, *Lophophaps* and *Geophaps*, but although they look quite different recent studies indicate that they are basically alike. The two units in each pair are very similar and replace each other geographically. It is doubtful if they come in contact and if they do whether they interbreed. There might easily be a hybrid zone in the case of the plumed pigeons. Although similar each form is distinct and it is evident that speciation has advanced far enough for them to be regarded as separate species, or semispecies in superspecies.

287 PLUMED PIGEON *Petrophassa plumifera* (Gould) 1842   Pl 8
Distribution: Map 59.

RECOGNITION: *small (20cm), cinnamon brown with long thin erect crest, white belly; always on ground.*

DESCRIPTION: 20cm; thin erect crest 5cm. Sexes alike. Forehead blue-grey; crown dark cinnamon, crest pale buff; remainder of upperparts fawn; black stripe above and below eye; throat white; foreneck black; breast cinnamon with white and black bars on lower breast; belly white; shoulders barred black and buff; small patch of iridescent purple in centre of wing; flight feathers dark cinnamon; outer tail feathers have broad black tip; bill dark brown; eyes yellow, bare skin around eye bright red; legs purplish-black.

VARIATION: in north smaller and duller (race *plumifera*); in centre larger and more brightly coloured (race *leucogaster*).

HABITAT: dry areas, especially with stony hills and rocky outcrops. HABITS: terrestrial, runs rapidly, flies with few rapid wingbeats then glides low over ground for short distance, sometimes perches on prominent rock; solitary except when in family parties; sedentary.
BREEDING: January–September, but probably most months depending on suitable conditions; nests on ground, often under tufts of grass or shelter of large stones, a shallow scrape lined with short pieces of grass; two white eggs. VOICE: variants of low musical 'coo-ooorr' or 'ooorr-oo'. FOOD: seeds.

STATUS: probably common. TAXONOMY: endemic species, or forming superspecies or species with Red-plumed Pigeon.

288 RED-PLUMED PIGEON *Petrophassa ferruginea* (Gould) 1865
Distribution: Map 59.

RECOGNITION: like Plumed Pigeon but *whole underparts cinnamon brown* with irregular black band on breast; smaller and more richly coloured.

HABITAT, etc: similar to Plumed Pigeon.

289 SQUATTER PIGEON *Petrophassa scripta* (Temminck) 1821
Distribution: Map 60.

RECOGNITION: *black and white patterned face, forehead and crown brown, white patch at side of breast; usually on ground.*

DESCRIPTION: 28cm. Sexes alike. Upperparts dark brown; face patterned black and white; throat white; breast dark brown with white patch at sides; belly blue-grey; vent buffish; patch of iridescent green and purple on inner wing; flight feathers brown with buff tips; outer tail feathers black; bill black; eyes brown, bare skin around eye bluish-white to reddish-orange; legs purplish-red.

HABITAT: various kinds of open woodland country. HABITS: mainly terrestrial but sometimes flies into trees, especially when disturbed, sometimes erects crown feathers; gregarious; sedentary. BREEDING: variable, recorded most months; nests on ground in short grass, a shallow depression lined with grass and leaves; two eggs, creamy-white. VOICE: loud 'coo-coo' repeated. FOOD: seeds.

STATUS: fairly common but believed to be decreasing. TAXONOMY: endemic species, forming superspecies with Partridge Pigeon.

290 PARTRIDGE PIGEON   *Petrophassa smithii*   (Jard. & Selb.) 1830
Distribution: Map 60.

RECOGNITION: like Squatter Pigeon with drab brown upperparts and white throat, but slightly smaller, 25cm, and has *distinct face pattern*; upper breast has inconspicuous *patch of blue-grey with black scallops;* lower breast pinkish-brown; belly brown and buff; flanks white; bill black; eyes whitish, bare skin around eye bright red; legs reddish-purple.

HABITAT, etc: similar to Squatter Pigeon.

STATUS: common. TAXONOMY: endemic species, forming superspecies with Squatter Pigeon.

291 WHITE-QUILLED ROCK PIGEON   *Petrophassa albipennis*   Gould 1840
Distribution: Map 61.

RECOGNITION: *dark brown with large white patch on open wing; on ground in rocky hills.*

DESCRIPTION: 30cm, long broad tail, short rounded wings. Sexes alike except that male slightly redder and female greyer. Blackish-brown, feathers of foreparts with opalescent grey centres and throat checked white and dark brown; base of flight feathers white making conspicuous white patch on extended wing; usually small concealed iridescent spots in centre of wing; bill blackish-brown; eyes brown; legs black.

VARIATION: Kimberleys generally, much white in wing (race *albipennis*); Victoria River area, very little white in wing (race *boothi*).

HABITAT: sandstone cliffs. HABITS: terrestrial, frequenting rocks and stones; solitary or in family parties; probably sedentary; short flutter and glide flight with loud 'frrip-frrip' of wings audible for long distance. BREEDING: various months, records April–September; nests on or among rocks on ground, a rough platform of sticks or a scrape lined with grass; two eggs, creamy-white. VOICE: loud 'coo-carook' and soft cooing notes. FOOD: seeds.

STATUS: fairly common to common. TAXONOMY: endemic species forming superspecies with Chestnut-quilled Rock Pigeon.

292 CHESTNUT-QUILLED ROCK PIGEON
Petrophassa rufipennis   Collett 1898
Distribution: Map 61.

Partridge Pigeon (290)

Squatter Pigeon (289)

Chestnut-quilled Rock Pigeon (292)

RECOGNITION: like White-quilled Rock Pigeon in general appearance, differs in having *concealed wing patch chestnut*, foreparts speckled pearly-white, throat and thin streaks above and below eye white, patch of black between eye and bill.

HABITAT: tumbled rocks in sandstone ridges. HABITS, etc: apparently similar to White-quilled species; in small flocks when not breeding.

STATUS: fairly common to common. TAXONOMY: endemic species forming superspecies with White-quilled Rock Pigeon.

Genus GEOPELIA

Three species all occurring in Australia, but only the tiny Diamond Dove is endemic. They have a superficial resemblance to the turtledoves (*Streptopelia*) with slender build and long graduated tails, but their affinities seem to be with the bronzewings, like the Crested Pigeon for instance, and like it also, they live in trees but feed mainly on the ground.

293 BAR-SHOULDERED DOVE *Geopelia humeralis* (Temminck) 1821   Pl 8

Distribution: Map 62.

RECOGNITION: *pale bluish-grey head, barred nape and shoulders, plain foreneck and breast.*

DESCRIPTION: 28cm, with graduated tail 15cm. Sexes alike. Head and upper breast blue-grey; throat white; hind neck and upper back cinnamon or 'coppery'; remainder of upperparts brown; upperparts from nape barred and scalloped with black; lower breast pinkish-white; belly white; concealed patch of chestnut in wing; tail greyish-chestnut, outer feathers tipped white; bill and bare skin around eye blue-grey; eyes greenish-yellow; legs dark red.

VARIATION: throughout most of range as above (race *humeralis*); in extreme west, paler above and pinker below (race *headlandi*).

HABITAT: well wooded localities near water, also mangroves. HABITS: probably mainly terrestrial except when nesting; solitary or in scattered flocks; sedentary. BREEDING: variable, recorded most months; nests in trees and shrubs, usually below about 3m, roughly made of twigs and lined with rootlets; two white eggs. VOICE: loud 'coo coo-oo' and softer 'coo-ooh'. FOOD: mainly seeds.

STATUS: very common. TAXONOMY: endemic races of species extending to southern New Guinea.

294 PEACEFUL DOVE *Geopelia striata* (Linnaeus) 1766
Distribution: Map 63.

RECOGNITION: *small and greyish with long pointed tail, dark bars on foreneck and upper breast as well as on most of upperparts.*

DESCRIPTION: 23cm, with graduated tail 10cm. Sexes alike. Forehead and face blue-grey; crown grey-brown; throat white; neck, mantle and upper breast barred dark brown and pale blue-grey; remainder of upperparts and shoulders grey-brown barred and scalloped with black; lower breast pinkish-white; belly white; under shoulders chestnut; outer tail feathers black broadly tipped white; bill grey-brown or grey-blue; eyes bluish-white, bare skin around eye grey-blue; legs purplish-pink.

VARIATION: east, and south of tropic, darker and greyer (race *tranquilla*); northwest, browner and redder (race *clelandi*); north, smaller and intermediate in colour (race *placida*).

HABITAT: woodlands and savannas. HABITS: lives in trees and bushes but feeds mostly on ground; mainly solitary but sometimes in small flocks when feeding and watering; sedentary and nomadic. BREEDING: variable, but mainly November–February in south; nests in trees and bushes near ground or up to about 3m, a rough platform of twigs; two white eggs. VOICE: various cooing and clucking sounds, like 'croodle clu-clu-clu' and 'coo-luc'. FOOD: seeds and some insects.

STATUS: common, especially in north. TAXONOMY: variable species extending to Malaysia.

295 DIAMOND DOVE *Geopelia cuneata* (Latham) 1801
Distribution: Map 64.

RECOGNITION: *small and greyish with long pointed tail, speckled white on shoulders, often in small flocks.*

DESCRIPTION: 20cm, with graduated tail 10cm. Sexes alike but female has slightly browner foreparts. Head, breast and flanks pale blue-grey shading on upperparts to buffy-brown and on underparts to white; shoulders slate-grey speckled with white; under shoulders blue-grey; flight feathers chestnut; tail blackish-brown broadly tipped and edged with white; bill blue-grey, tip black; eyes and bare skin around eye red; legs pinkish-red.

HABITAT: various kinds of savanna country. HABITS: lives in trees and bushes but feeds mostly on ground; mainly gregarious but flocks are small; sedentary and partly nomadic; flight fast and direct and often well above trees. BREEDING: variable, in most months; nests

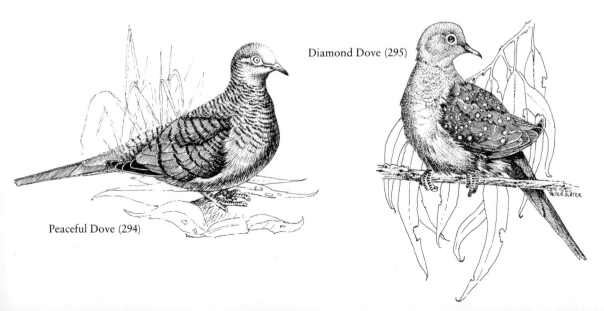

Diamond Dove (295)

Peaceful Dove (294)

on forks low down in trees and bushes or on ground, a frail platform of twigs; two white eggs. VOICE: mournful 'coo-coo' repeated, and harsher 'cor-coo', often at night when breeding. FOOD: mainly seeds.

STATUS: very common, especially in south. TAXONOMY: endemic species.

Genus LEUCOSARCIA

A one-species genus peculiar to Australia. Current opinion holds that the Wonga Pigeon has affinities with the bronzewings, that it is a forest species which may have recently evolved from them or is the present representative of an ancient stock from which the bronzewings originated. Although frequenting forests it spends much of its time on the ground.

296 WONGA PIGEON *Leucosarcia melanoleuca* (Latham) 1801   Fig p 208
Distribution: Map 65.

RECOGNITION: *dark grey; white forehead, white 'necklace', white belly and flanks with large black spots on flanks.*

DESCRIPTION: 38–40cm. Sexes alike. Forehead, face and throat white; black streak between eye and bill; upperparts and breast dark bluish-grey, breast with white 'necklace' joined in middle to white belly; flanks white spotted with black; vent and under tail coverts brownish-white; wings dark brown; bill black; eyes brown, bare skin around eye red; legs reddish-brown.

HABITAT: rain forests. HABITS: lives in trees but feeds mostly on ground; solitary but sometimes feeds in small parties; sedentary. BREEDING: October–January, but some records at other times; nests in trees fairly high up, a rough structure of twigs; two white eggs. VOICE: loud 'coo-coo' monotonously repeated, also 'wonk-a' repeated. FOOD: mainly seeds.

STATUS: fairly common. TAXONOMY: endemic species and genus.

Genus PTILINOPUS

This is a group of about fifty fruit pigeons belonging exclusively to tropical Australasia. As their collective name indicates, their principal diet is fruits and berries. They live in trees, in forests and well-wooded habitats, including mangroves. They are brightly coloured (except the group of banded pigeons) often in patterns of vivid hues, especially on the head, a feature which have earned them scientific superlatives as 'superbus' and 'magnificus'. There are four species in Australia all of which are connected as species or semispecies with external populations. They seem to be (geologically) recent colonists which have established footholds in coastal forests and woodlands of the north and northeast.

297 BANDED PIGEON *Ptilinopus alligator* Collett 1896   Fig p 208
Distribution: Map 66.

RECOGNITION: *white head, neck and breast separated from grey belly by broad black band.*

DESCRIPTION: 33–36cm, with tail 15cm. Sexes alike. Head, neck and upper breast creamy-white; back and wings black mottled grey; rump and upper tail coverts pale grey; broad black band on lower breast; belly pale grey; tail black with broad pale grey tip; bill grey-green, tip yellow; eyes red; legs red.

Wonga Pigeon (296)

Banded Pigeon (297)

HABITAT: wooded rocky ridges. HABITS: (largely unknown) arboreal and probably sedentary, observed in small parties, probably families. BREEDING: recorded September; nests in trees close to cliffs, extremely scanty platform of twigs; one white egg. VOICE: deep booming recorded. FOOD: known to eat wild figs.

STATUS: not known. TAXONOMY: endemic species or semispecies with similar forms in Timor and parts of Indonesia.

298 WOMPOO PIGEON *Ptilinopus magnificus* (Temminck) 1821   Pl 8

Distribution: Map 66.

RECOGNITION: *pale head, purple breast, yellow belly; rain forests.*

DESCRIPTION: 38–50cm, with tail 15–23cm. Sexes alike. Head and neck pale dove grey; upperparts peacock green, slightly yellow on mantle; foreneck and breast dark purple; belly and under shoulders bright yellow; irregular band of bright yellow in centre of wings; flight feathers dark green; bill red, tip yellow; eyes reddish-orange; legs green.

VARIATION: becomes progressively smaller from south to north (and continued into New Guinea), stages often indicated by three races (*magnificus*, *keri* and *assimilis*).

HABITAT: rain forests. HABITS: arboreal, rarely on ground; solitary or in small parties; apparently sedentary. BREEDING: August–February; nests in trees usually high up, a substantial structure of twigs and tendrils; one white egg. VOICE: loud and deep 'wom-poo'. FOOD: fruits and berries, especially figs.

STATUS: common. TAXONOMY: endemic races of species extending to New Guinea.

299 PURPLE-CROWNED PIGEON *Ptilinopus superbus* (Temminck) 1810   Pl 8

Distribution: Map 67.

RECOGNITION: *upperparts mainly bright green, white belly and flanks with green blotches on flanks.*

DESCRIPTION: 23cm. Sexes different. *Male:* forehead and crown dark purple (petunia violet); face green; nape and mantle terracotta; remainder of upperparts mainly brownish-green spotted with black; throat and foreneck pale ash-grey; upper breast pale violet-grey speckled with dark violet; lower breast a band of purplish-black (plum); belly and flanks creamy-white, flanks blotched with green; patch of purplish-black on edge of shoulders; feathers on inner shoulders tipped with bright yellow; flight feathers black; centre of tail greenish, sides blackish with white tip; bill dull green; eyes greenish-yellow; legs red. *Female:* upperparts mainly bluish-green; hind crown bluish-black; throat violet-white; breast violet-grey tinged with green; belly yellowish-white.

HABITAT: forests and mangroves. HABITS: arboreal; solitary but often flocks when feeding; nomadic, perhaps migratory. BREEDING: September–February; nests in trees and bushes, a rough platform of twigs; one white egg. VOICE: low booming 'oom'. FOOD: fruits and berries.

STATUS: common. TAXONOMY: variable species extending to New Guinea and Celebes.

300 RED-CROWNED PIGEON *Ptilinopus regina* Swainson 1825   Pl 8

Distribution: Map 68.

RECOGNITION: *mainly greenish upperparts, purplish patch on breast, yellow belly and yellow tipped tail.*

DESCRIPTION: 23cm. Sexes alike, but some colours less brilliant in female. Crown purplish-red with golden-yellow border; face and hind neck grey-green; remainder of upperparts dull green, tail with yellow tip; feathers of inner shoulders tipped yellow; throat and side of neck ash-grey and green and having a hackled appearance; centre of lower breast purplish-red; belly and under tail coverts reddish-orange; under tail grey; bill dark green; eyes reddish-orange; legs dark grey-green.

VARIATION: east coast, crown purplish-red and general colours darker (race *regina*); Northern Territory, crown and central patch on breast pink (race *ewingi*).

HABITAT: forests and woodlands including mangroves. HABITS: arboreal; often gregarious when feeding, clambers among the branches like a parrot; nomadic and possibly migratory. BREEDING: October–February; nests in trees and bushes usually high up, a sparse platform of twigs; one white egg. VOICE: continuous 'coo-coo-coo' increasing in speed and becoming softer. FOOD: fruits and berries.

STATUS: common. TAXONOMY: variable species extending to east Indonesian islands.

Genus DUCULA

Another large group of fruit pigeons, sometimes called imperial pigeons. Although there are about thirty-five species in the Papuan region, only one has reached Australia and it has only a slender hold in the north and northeast. It has not established a permanent residence for it 'commutes' as a breeding visitor across Torres Strait—hence the popular name. The alternative name Nutmeg Pigeon is also given to several relatives which share its liking for this food.

301 TORRES STRAIT PIGEON *Ducula spilorrhoa* (Gray) 1858

Distribution: Map 69.

RECOGNITION: *white with wide black tips to wings and tail.*

DESCRIPTION: 38cm. Sexes alike. Mainly white; flight feathers and tip of tail black, black spots around vent and on thighs; bill grey, tip yellow; eyes dark brown, bare skin around eye blue-grey; legs blue-grey.

HABITAT: dense woodlands and mangroves on coasts and coastal islands. HABITS: arboreal; gregarious, breeding in large flocks on coastal islands and commuting daily to feeding grounds on mainland, flies high to mainland and low over water on return flight, very noisy on breeding grounds; migratory, breeding visitor September–April. BREEDING: October–January; nests in trees at any height, rarely on ground, a flat platform of twigs and branches, unusually substantial for a pigeon; one white egg. VOICE: variants of deep 'coo-hoo' repeated at brief intervals. FOOD: fruits and berries, especially nutmeg.

STATUS: common locally, at least, but has suffered much from persecution. TAXONOMY: belongs to one of a group of three species forming a superspecies.

Genus LOPHOLAIMUS

The Topknot Pigeon is isolated in a genus of its own because of its curious features and obscure origins. It may be a relic of a once widespread group, perhaps an early branch of the bronzewings. It has a peculiar double crest, feathers on the cere and a large laterally compressed bill. Plumage is mainly grey with black and white markings.

302 TOPKNOT PIGEON   *Lopholaimus antarcticus*   (Shaw) 1749

Distribution: Map 70.

RECOGNITION: *large and greyish, white bar on black tail, black flight feathers, large tufted crest.*

DESCRIPTION: 45cm; crest 7·5cm. Sexes alike. Forehead feathers extended and grey, crown feathers extended into brown and black crest; remainder of upperparts dark grey, paler on back and feathers hackled; underparts pale grey; flight feathers black; base of tail grey, remainder black with broad white central bar; bill grey-green, tip reddish (thick and laterally compressed); eyes orange; legs reddish-purple.

HABITAT: forests and woodlands. HABITS: arboreal, usually keeps to forest canopy; apparently solitary breeding but gregarious at other times, sometimes in very large flocks (hence alternative name, Flock Pigeon); sedentary and nomadic; perhaps migratory. BREEDING: October–January; nests high up in trees, a rough platform of strong twigs; one white egg. VOICE: low guttural 'quook-quook' and 'wir-hig-a'. FOOD: fruits and berries.

STATUS: fairly common. TAXONOMY: endemic species and genus.

Topknot Pigeon (302)

Family PSITTACIDAE

Lorikeets, Cockatoos, Parrots

55(315) species: 48 endemic

MEMBERS OF THE PARROT family are very distinctive regardless of size or colour. Bills are short and deep and the upper mandible is curved and sharply pointed; it is hinged at the base and can be elevated. At the base of the bill there is a fleshy cere in which the nostrils are placed. Short curved bills and short necks give parrots in flight a blunt-headed appearance. Legs are short and the feet have two toes pointing forward and two backward (zygodactylous).

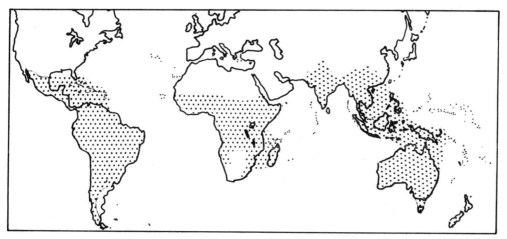

Distribution of PSITTACIDAE

Feet and bills have unusual versatility as feet can be used to hold food and convey it to the mouth and bills often act as third limbs enabling parrots to show great agility when clambering among branches. In spite of the similarity of bills to those of hawks and eagles, parrots are not flesh eaters. They are mainly vegetarian, apart from a few which take grubs and insects—but even the most specialised vegetable feeders include a quota of insects in their diet, especially when feeding young. Seeds of every description are the main source of food, from grass seeds to seeds of fruits and the kernels of hard nuts. Honey also is important, so much so that certain species, especially the lorikeets, have brush-tipped tongues for lapping up nectar. Most parrots are gregarious and have harsh shrill voices. They nest in holes, usually in trees but sometimes in banks and termite mounds (ant-beds), and among rocks and ground vegetation when trees are scarce or not available. There is seldom any well formed nest, just a few chips of wood or wood dust. Eggs are relatively small and invariably white. Parrots are a successful group and nowhere is this more evident than in Australia where they have adapted to all kinds of environment, from rain forests to arid interior, wet heaths and rocky coasts, and in the process have evolved many unique forms. Out of fifty-five species listed here no less than forty-eight are endemic; groups such as the rosellas and ringnecks and the numerous 'grass parrots' are peculiar to Australia, as is the little Budgerigar which has become a domestic cage bird all over the world. Most parrots readily accept captivity and semi-domestication, and their aptitude for vocal mimicry, as well as other attributes, endears them as pets and conveys the impression that they are more intelligent than perhaps they really are.

Key to PSITTACIDAE

[Additional keys under genera in italics]

1 Grey above, rose-pink below	Galah	No 318
2 Mainly white or pale pink	*Cacatua*	Nos 319–322
3 Black, long crest, Cape York	Palm Cockatoo	No 312
4 Black with red or white in tail	*Calyptorhynchus*	Nos 313–316
5 Dark grey, head red (♂)	Gang-gang Cockatoo	No 317
6 Wispy head crest, face and shoulders white	Cockatiel	No 311
7 Red or yellow collar		
Underwing red	*Trichoglossus*	Nos 303–305
Underwing not red	*Barnardius*	Nos 347–348
8 Foreparts red		
Face blue	Crimson Rosella	No 340
Rump purple (♂)	King Parrot	No 330
Belly blue, Cape York (♀)	Red-sided Parrot	No 324
9 Face mask red		
Shoulder and underwing red; southeast	Swift Parrot	No 357
Underwing blue and black; Cape York (♂)	Red-cheeked Parrot	No 325
10 Face mask yellow	Budgerigar	No 323
11 Crown red		
Underwing black	Varied Lorikeet	No 306
Face yellow	Red-capped Parrot	No 349
12 Face with red patch, short tail	*Glossopsitta*	Nos 307–309
13 Head and wing with red and blue, very small	Fig Parrot	No 310
14 Forehead blue or with blue bar	*Neophema*	Nos 331–337
15 Foreparts green		
Flanks and underwing red (♂)	Red-sided Parrot	No 324
Shoulders red	Red-winged Parrot	No 329
Belly red, rump blue (♀)	King Parrot	No 330
Boldly speckled with black	*Pezoporus*	Nos 338–339
16 Shoulders with patch of red, yellow or chestnut, tail black broadly edged and tipped with bluish-white	*Psephotus*	Nos 350–356
17 Back broadly scalloped or marbled with black	*Platycercus*	Nos 340–346
18 Bill red, tail very long and thin	*Polytelis*	Nos 326–328

Genus TRICHOGLOSSUS

The greater part of this small genus of lorikeets consists of numerous forms scattered over many islands from Bali to New Caledonia. Although clearly they are variants originating from a common stock it is difficult to say which are races and which, if any, are species. A usual practice is to regard them as races but it seems that some may have evolved beyond that and should at least be accepted as semispecies. This is so in the case of the Australian Rainbow and Red-collared Lorikeets. They have distinct features and exist as separate populations, or if they do meet there is no evidence that they hybridise. For present purposes, therefore, it seems suitable to treat them as separate species. The Rainbow and Scaly-breasted Lorikeets are common in eastern coastal districts where they frequently consort in the same nectar bearing trees and bushes. They fly rapidly, as if propelled by some explosive force, and screech noisily. All have long graduated tails and reddish bills.

Key to TRICHOGLOSSUS

1 Head and body green	....	Scaly-breasted Lorikeet	.... No 305
2 Head violet-blue	....	3–4	
3 Collar green; east of Carpentaria	....	Rainbow Lorikeet	.... No 303
4 Collar red; west of Carpentaria	....	Red-collared Lorikeet	...... No 304

303 RAINBOW LORIKEET *Trichoglossus moluccanus* (Gmelin) 1788   Pl 9
Distribution: Map 71.

RECOGNITION: *dark blue head and belly, reddish-orange breast, pale green collar.*

DESCRIPTION: 25–30cm, with tail 13–15cm. Sexes alike. Head dark violet-blue; collar pale greenish-yellow; remainder of upperparts dark green; breast yellow splashed with red, extending as broken band to mantle; belly blue-black; vent and under tail green and yellow; under shoulders red; concealed yellow in wing; bill reddish-orange; eyes pale orange; legs grey.

VARIATION: south of tropic, larger (race *moluccanus*); north of tropic, smaller (race *septentrionalis*).

HABITAT: forests and woodlands, city parks and suburban trees, sometimes mangroves and mallee. HABITS: arboreal; gregarious; nomadic; usually in fairly large noisy flocks, often mixed with other lorikeets; flight swift and direct. BREEDING: variable, but mainly September–January; nests in holes in trees usually high up, unlined; two white eggs. VOICE: shrill screeches. FOOD: mainly honey, also flowers and fruits, sometimes insects.

STATUS: common. TAXONOMY: endemic species or semispecies forming superspecies with Red-collared Lorikeet and other extralimital forms.

304 RED-COLLARED LORIKEET *Trichoglossus rubritorquis* Vig. & Horsf. 1827
Distribution: Map 71.

RECOGNITION: like Rainbow Lorikeet, but *collar red, mantle blue-black contrasting with green back, belly greenish-black.*

HABITS, etc: apparently similar in most respects to Rainbow Lorikeet.

305 SCALY-BREASTED LORIKEET *Trichoglossus chlorolepidotus* (Kuhl) 1820
Distribution: Map 72.

RECOGNITION: *mainly dark green with red underwings and yellow scaly or scallop markings on breast.*

DESCRIPTION: 20cm. Sexes alike. Mainly green with head slightly bluish; underparts and mantle scalloped with yellow; underwing red; wing has concealed patch of pink; bill red; eyes pink; legs light grey.

VARIATION: South of mid-Queensland, larger (race *chlorolepidotus*); Cape York, smaller (race *neglectus*). Rare xanthochroic (yellow) variants have been recorded.

HABITAT: coastal woodlands and open forests, city parks and suburban trees. HABITS: arboreal, gregarious; nomadic; often in noisy flocks with other lorikeets, especially the Rainbow; swift direct flight. BREEDING: variable, but less frequently in March and April; nests in deep holes in trees, usually high up, unlined; two white eggs. VOICE: a loud screech. FOOD: mainly honey, also flowers, leaves and seeds, sometimes insects.

STATUS: common. TAXONOMY: endemic species closely related to similar widespread extra-limital species.

Genus PSITTEUTELES

Some authorities would put this genus in *Trichoglossus*; it also has affinities with *Glossopsitta*. In its present composition it consists of several species, only one of which occurs in Australia, where it is endemic. The Varied Lorikeet is readily distinguished from other honey-eating parrots by its bright red cap. It is often found in large flocks gorging on the honey of flowering gums, or flying high from one feeding ground to another.

306 VARIED LORIKEET *Psitteuteles versicolor* (Lear) 1831   Pl 9

Distribution: Map 73.

RECOGNITION: *mainly green with red cap and black underwings.*

DESCRIPTION: 18–20cm. Sexes alike. Forehead and crown dark red; remainder of body mainly green finely streaked with pale green above and yellow below; patch of yellow behind eye; face, throat and collar tinged with blue; underwing black; bill dark cinnamon red; eyes buff-brown, bare skin around eye and cere bluish-white; legs grey.

HABITAT: forests and woodlands. HABITS: arboreal; gregarious; nomadic; usually keeps to tree canopies and flies high, in compact flocks, between feeding grounds; flight swift and direct. BREEDING: variable but mainly April–December; nests in holes in trees fairly high up, a bed of wood chips or green leaves; two to four white eggs. VOICE: piercing scream. FOOD: mainly honey, also flowers and seeds.

STATUS: common. TAXONOMY: endemic uniform species of genus extending to Indonesia and the Philippines.

Genus GLOSSOPSITTA

Three lorikeets found only in Australia have short pointed tails and patches of red on the face.

Key to GLOSSOPSITTA

1 Crown green, throat red	Little Lorikeet	No 308
2 Crown blue, throat green	Musk Lorikeet	No 307
3 Crown violet-black, throat blue-green	Purple-crowned Lorikeet	No 309

307 MUSK LORIKEET *Glossopsitta concinna* (Shaw) 1791   Pl 9

Distribution: Map 73.

RECOGNITION: *mainly green with broad red band from forehead through eye, yellow underwing.*

DESCRIPTION: 23cm. Sexes alike, but crown less blue in female. Forehead through eye to side of neck red; crown blue; mantle brown; side of breast golden-yellow; under shoulder greenish-yellow; remainder of plumage green; bill grey-brown, tip reddish-orange; eyes orange; legs grey-brown.

HABITAT: open forests and woodlands. HABITS: arboreal; gregarious; nomadic; southern populations at least partly migratory with movement north about January to April; usually keeps to tree canopies and flies high in noisy, compact flocks; often mixed with other lorikeets when feeding; flight swift and direct. BREEDING: August–January; nests in holes in trees, usually high up and near water; two white eggs. VOICE: shrill screech. FOOD: mainly honey but also flowers and fruits and sometimes insects.

STATUS: common. TAXONOMY: endemic species and genus.

308 LITTLE LORIKEET *Glossopsitta pusilla* (Shaw) 1790

Distribution: Map 74.

RECOGNITION: *Mainly green with red mask, black bill, yellowish patch on underwing.*

DESCRIPTION: 15–18cm. Sexes alike. Forehead to throat red, forming a 'mask'; upper back golden-brown; under shoulders yellowish; remainder of plumage shades of green slightly streaked with lighter green, especially on face; bill black; eyes brownish-orange; legs grey-brown.

HABITAT: open forests and woodlands. HABITS: arboreal, gregarious and nomadic; usually in small flocks of ten to twenty birds high in tree canopies or flying high between feeding grounds; flight swift and direct. BREEDING: mainly August–January in south but often earlier in north; nests in holes in trees usually high up and near water; three to five white eggs. VOICE: shrill screech and loud 'jeet-jeet'. FOOD: mainly honey but also flowers and fruits.

STATUS: common. TAXONOMY: endemic species and genus.

309 PURPLE-CROWNED LORIKEET

Glossopsitta porphyrocephala (Dietrichsen) 1837   Pl 9

Distribution: Map 75.

RECOGNITION: *greenish above and bluish below with red underwing, purple crown.*

DESCRIPTION: 15–18cm. Sexes alike. Forehead and ear coverts reddish-orange; crown dark violet; nape light green; remainder of upperparts shades of green with tinge of brown on mantle; breast and belly blue-grey; edge of shoulders bright blue; under shoulders and flanks red; bill black; eyes dark brown; legs pinkish-grey.

HABITAT: open forests, woodlands, savannas and mallee. HABITS: arboreal; gregarious; nomadic; in small parties or flocks in tree canopies or flying high between feeding grounds; flight swift and direct. BREEDING: August–December; nests in holes in trees usually near water and cometimes many pairs in a small area; four to six white eggs. VOICE: shrill sharp 'zit-zit' especially uttered in flight. FOOD: mainly honey, also flowers and fruits.

STATUS: common. TAXONOMY: endemic species and genus.

Genus PSITTACULIROSTRIS

A group generally known as fig parrots and currently consisting of five species. They belong to the rain forests of northeast Australia and New Guinea. Features are distinctive but relationships are obscure. They have relatively short tails and very variable brightly coloured plumages. The Australian variants are in widely separated groups, have distinctive characteristics and are undoubtedly species in the making.

310 FIG PARROT *Psittaculirostris diopthalma* (Homb. & Jacq.) 1841   Pl 9

Distribution: Map 75.

RECOGNITION: *very small with short tail, mainly green with red and blue on head and wings, yellow flanks.*

DESCRIPTION: 13–18cm. Sexes nearly alike or different, the differences being in amount of red and blue on head (see 'variation'). Upperparts dark green; underparts pale green; flanks yellow; inner wing tipped with red, outer wing black, edged with blue; bill grey, tip dark; eyes dark brown; legs grey-green.

VARIATION: Iron Range area of Cape York—*male:* forehead, face and ear coverts red edged with pale violet; patch above eye blue; *female:* forehead and area round eye blue; face below eye brown edged with pale violet (race *marshalli*). Cooktown to Tully area—*male:* forehead, lower face and ear coverts red, edged with pale violet below; lores blue; *female:* similar but red on face replaced with blue and pale brown (race *macleayana*). Mary River, Queensland, to Macleay River, N.S.W.—*male:* forehead mixed blue and dull red; upper face red tipped with green; lower face and ear coverts red or reddish-yellow edged with violet; *female:* similar to male but most of red on face tipped with green (race *coxeni*).

HABITAT: rain forests and adjacent woodlands. HABITS: arboreal; gregarious, in small flocks in forest canopy, running mouse-like along branches or flying above tree-tops; less noisy than most similar small parrots; flight swift and direct. BREEDING: period unknown; nests in holes in branches; two white eggs. VOICE: feeble screech or 'yyit-yyit', uttered mainly in flight. FOOD: fruits, especially figs, also honey, flowers and seeds.

STATUS: uncertain, reported common in some localities. TAXONOMY: endemic races (or semispecies) of species widespread in New Guinea and adjacent islands.

Genus NYMPHICUS

The relationships of the Cockatiel seem rather obscure and it is placed in a genus of its own. Present opinion is that it has some affinity with the cockatoos. It is endemic. The Cockatiel is slender in build with long pointed tail and wings and a rapid erratic flight. At rest the whitish head and grey wispy crest are distinctive.

311 COCKATIEL *Nymphicus hollandicus* (Kerr) 1792

Distribution: widespread in dry country, not Tasmania.

RECOGNITION: *slim and grey with long pointed tail, whitish head and wispy crest, large white shoulder patches.*

DESCRIPTION: 25–28cm, with pointed tail 15cm; crest 5cm. Sexes different. *Male:* forehead, base of crest and face pale lemon-yellow; ear patch reddish-orange; large white patch on shoulders; remainder of plumage dark grey to brownish-grey; bill grey; eyes brown; legs grey. *Female:* forehead and face brown; rump and tail barred and mottled with lemon-yellow.

HABITAT: open woodlands and wooded savannas. HABITS: arboreal but feeds mainly on ground; gregarious, usually in flocks of up to ten but sometimes more; nomadic, migratory in southern part of range; flight swift and erratic. BREEDING: variable, often depending on rains; nests in holes in trees usually near water, a bed of wood dust; four to seven white

Cockatiel (311)

Palm Cockatoo (312)

eggs. VOICE: melodious warble uttered in flight. FOOD: mainly seeds, but also fruits and berries.

STATUS: common. TAXONOMY: endemic species and genus.

Genus PROBOSCIGER

Although it has affinities with other black cockatoos, the large Palm Cockatoo is placed in a genus of its own. It belongs to New Guinea with a bridge-head population in the extreme tip of Cape York. The erectile crest frequently found in cockatoos is long and straggly, the bill is very large and sharply pointed and the face below the eye is bare; unlike other black cockatoos it does not have a band of colour in the tail. It feeds largely on the seeds of pandanus palm.

312 PALM COCKATOO *Probosciger aterrimus* (Gmelin) 1788

Distribution: Map 76.

RECOGNITION: *large and black with very long crest, tail wholly black; tip of Cape York only.*

DESCRIPTION: 60cm, with broad tail 30cm; crest 15cm. Sexes alike, but female has smaller bill and face patch. Entirely black except for large red patch of bare skin below eye; bill black; eyes brown; legs black.

HABITAT: forests and adjacent woodlands. HABITS: arboreal, usually in canopies of tall trees; solitary or in pairs or small parties; apparently sedentary; flight slow and laboured with frequent glides. BREEDING: August–January; nests in deep holes in trees high up, a bed of chopped twigs; one white egg. VOICE: a loud harsh shriek and various whistling notes. FOOD: seeds of the pandanus palm mainly, but also other seeds and fruits as well as leaves and flowers.

STATUS: common. TAXONOMY: race *(aterrimus)* extending to New Guinea of Papuan species.

Genus CALYPTORHYNCHUS

A group of four species peculiar to Australia. They are large cockatoos distinguished by black plumage with a wide band of contrasting colour in their broad tails. The White-tailed and Yellow-tailed species are western and eastern forms recently diverged from a common stock and might be regarded as races, although here treated as species. In the southeast the

Yellow-tailed, Red-tailed and Glossy can be found in close association and taking the same kind of food, but they do not flock together in the way that most feeding lorikeets do. Both the Glossy and Red-tailed have a broad band of red in the tail but the Glossy is a smaller bird, lacks a distinct crest and is, in fact, less glossy on the head than is the Red-tailed.

Key to CALYPTORHYNCHUS

1 Tail band white .... White-tailed Cockatoo ..... No 313
2 Tail band yellow .... Yellow-tailed Cockatoo .... No 314
3 Tail band red 4–5

4 Head distinctly crested .... Red-tailed Cockatoo....... No 316
5 Head not distinctly crested..................... Glossy Cockatoo.......... No 315

313 WHITE-TAILED COCKATOO *Calyptorhynchus baudinii* Lear 1832

Distribution: Map 76.

RECOGNITION: *large and black with wide white band in centre of long broad tail.*

DESCRIPTION: 51–56cm, with tail about half. Sexes slightly different. *Male:* mainly brownish-black; tail has wide central band of white; patch over ear dull white; bill brownish; eyes reddish-brown, bare skin round eye pink; legs grey-brown. *Female:* bare skin round eye dark grey; bill whitish.

VARIATION: forested southwest, bill narrow (race *baudinii*); inland areas, bill shorter and thicker (race *latirostris*).

HABITAT: heavily timbered areas to mallee and sandplain country. HABITS: arboreal; gregarious; nomadic, with evidence of regular seasonal movements in some areas. BREEDING: August–January, immediately after rainfall peak; nests in holes in large trees, usually high up and especially in salmon gum and wandoo; one to two white eggs, but only one chick reared. VOICE: loud wailing cries, higher pitched than Red-tailed. FOOD: tree seeds, honey, fruits (raids orchards) and grubs.

STATUS: fairly common. TAXONOMY: endemic species or semispecies, perhaps conspecific with Yellow-tailed Cockatoo.

314 YELLOW-TAILED COCKATOO *Calyptorhynchus funereus* (Shaw) 1794

Distribution: Map 76.

RECOGNITION: *large and black with wide yellow band in centre of long broad tail.*

DESCRIPTION: 60–65cm, with tail about half. Sexes alike, but female has yellow tail band more densely speckled with brown. Brownish-black, rather lighter on belly; tail has wide central band of pale yellow speckled with dark brown; patch over ear pale yellow; bill dark grey; eye reddish-brown, bare skin around eye pinkish-brown; legs grey-brown.

HABITAT: timbered areas from rain forest to dry woodlands and adjacent open country. HABITS: arboreal, rarely on ground; in pairs or family parties (often three) or small flocks; nomadic, possibly with some regular seasonal movements; flight seems laboured and erratic, broad tail usually fanned on alighting and displaying wide yellow band. BREEDING: variable, mainly April–July in north and September–January in south; nests in holes in trees usually high up, a platform of wood chips and dust; two white eggs. VOICE: a loud harsh 'kee-ow' uttered in flight. FOOD: timber boring larvae, obtained by stripping bark, sometimes seeds, honey and fruits.

STATUS: fairly common. TAXONOMY: endemic species or semispecies, perhaps conspecific with White-tailed Cockatoo.

315 GLOSSY COCKATOO *Calyptorhynchus lathami* (Temm) 1807
Distribution: Map 77.

RECOGNITION: *large and black with wide red band (barred black in female) in centre of long broad tail; no distinct crest.*

DESCRIPTION: 46–50cm, with broad tail about half. Sexes slightly different. *Male:* blackish-brown, browner on head and underparts; tail has wide central band of bright red; bill grey; eyes dark brown; legs grey. *Female:* red or reddish-yellow tail band wider and barred with black; sometimes irregular patches of yellow in head area, especially throat and sides of neck.

HABITAT: forests and woodlands with casuarina trees. HABITS: arboreal; in pairs or family parties (perhaps flocking if in sufficient numbers); nomadic. BREEDING: March–August; nests in holes in trees (usually dead) high up; one white egg. VOICE: soft double caw, rendered as 'tarr-red', also feeble whining calls. FOOD: mainly tree seeds like casuarina and forest oak.

STATUS: rare and apparently dwindling. TAXONOMY: endemic species.

316 RED-TAILED COCKATOO *Calyptorhynchus banksii* (Lathem) 1790
Distribution: throughout, in scattered populations.

RECOGNITION: *large and black with wide red band in centre of long broad tail, head distinctly crested.*

DESCRIPTION: 60cm, with tail about half; head distinctly crested. Sexes different. *Male:* glossy black; wide red band in centre of tail; bill grey; eyes dark brown; legs grey. *Female* and immature: blackish-brown; head and shoulder speckled with lemon-yellow; underparts barred white, yellow and red; tail barred bright red with some yellow, barring in middle broad and forming distinct red patch.

HABITAT: forests and woodlands. HABITS: arboreal, sometimes feeds on ground in sparsely wooded areas; gregarious, usually in small flocks or family parties, sometimes very large flocks; nomadic, sometimes flying high in noisy bands. BREEDING: April–October; nests in holes in trees usually high up and near water; one white egg. VOICE: loud grating 'kree' or 'kurr'. FOOD: mainly tree seeds, like casuarina, also fruits, honey, insects.

STATUS: common, in north, apparently declining in south. TAXONOMY: endemic species.

Genus CALLOCEPHALON
The Gang-gang Cockatoo of restricted range in mountain forests of the extreme southeast has a number of distinctive features which qualify it for separation in a genus of its own. It has a peculiar wispy crest curled forward. The sexes are different, the male having a bright red head.

317 GANG-GANG COCKATOO *Callocephalon fimbriatum* (Grant) 1803 Pl 10
Distribution: Map 78.

RECOGNITION: *dark grey, male has bright red head.*

DESCRIPTION: 30–33cm; short wispy crest curled forward. Sexes different. *Male:* head bright red; remainder dark brownish-grey lightly scalloped and barred with white; bill grey-brown; eyes dark brown; legs grey. *Female*: head grey-brown; underparts slightly barred with red, especially on belly.

HABITAT: mountain forests, especially densely wooded gullies, and adjacent lowland woodlands. HABITS: arboreal; gregarious; nomadic, with fairly definite seasonal altitudinal movements; flight relatively slow and appearing rather laboured. BREEDING: October–January; nests in holes in trees, high up and usually near water; two white eggs. VOICE: loud creaking note ending abruptly. FOOD: mainly tree seeds, also various fruits and insects.

STATUS: common in parts of limited range. TAXONOMY: endemic species and genus.

Genus EOLOPHUS

The Galah is sometimes included with the white cockatoos but it also seems to have some affinity with the Gang-gang and current opinion leans in favour of keeping it in a separate genus.

318 GALAH *Eolophus roseicapilla* (Vieillot) 1817   Pl 10

Distribution: throughout.

RECOGNITION: *grey with deep pink underparts—a flock will be silver-grey then suddenly change to pink as the birds wheel in unison.*

DESCRIPTION: 35cm; short crest. Sexes alike. Crown white tinged with red; remainder of upperparts silver-grey, but almost white on rump and centre of wings and tail; lower face, collar and underparts rose-pink; under shoulders red; vent grey; bill bluish-white; eyes dark brown (red in female), bare skin around eye red or white; legs dark grey.

VARIATION: east and north, darker and ring around eye red (race *roseicapilla*); west, paler, especially on crown, and ring around eye white (race *assimilis*).

HABITAT: various kinds of open wooded country and adjacent plains. HABITS: arboreal but usually feeds on ground; gregarious; mainly sedentary but with some nomadic movements, especially on periphery of distribution; flight strong with rather slow wing beats and movements sometimes erratic. BREEDING: variable, in most months somewhere; nests in holes in trees, holes often well bitten round entrance, a bed of broken green leaves; two to five white eggs. VOICE: high-pitched metallic tinkle and loud harsh screams. FOOD: seeds and bulbous roots, also cereals.

STATUS: very common and thriving; rare in southern and eastern coastal areas and in Tasmania. TAXONOMY: endemic species and genus.

Genus CACATUA

The white cockatoos—a genus consisting of nearly a dozen species ranging from the Celebes and Philippines to New Guinea, with four in Australia, two of which are endemic. Long erectile crests are typically associated with white cockatoos, but they are short in the corellas. In appearance they are plump, about 30cm in length with relatively short tails. The sexes are alike, or nearly so. Some are accomplished mimics and readily imitate human speech. In Australia they mainly frequent dry country and commonly associate in noisy flocks, sometimes very large.

319 SULPHUR-CRESTED COCKATOO *Cacatua galerita* (Latham) 1790

Distribution: Map 79.

RECOGNITION: *white with long yellow crest.*

DESCRIPTION: 40–43cm; crest 7·5–13cm. Sexes alike. White with sulphur yellow crest, a tinge of same colour on underwings and undertail, and on face behind eye; bill black; eyes dark brown to reddish-brown, redder in female; legs black.

VARIATION: in east, fairly distinct amount of yellow behind the eye and rather smaller bill (race *galerita*); in northwest, little or no yellow behind eye and bill stouter (race *fitzroyi*).

HABITAT: forests, woodlands and scattered heavy timber in open country, especially near water. HABITS: arboreal, but often feeding on ground; gregarious, with a well-organised sentinel warning system; sedentary, with some seasonal altitudinal movements in mountainous country; beat and glide flight. BREEDING: variable, in most months except February–April, usually May–August in north and August–January in south; nests in holes in trees high up, sometimes in cliff holes; two white eggs. VOICE: loud harsh squawk. FOOD: seeds of various kinds, including grain, bulbous roots and sometimes insects.

STATUS: common in many areas but uncommon to rare (declining) in others; although profiting by cultivation does not seem to tolerate human settlement. TAXONOMY: endemic races of species extending to New Guinea and adjacent islands.

320 MAJOR MITCHELL *Cacatua leadbeateri* (Vigors) 1831

Distribution: Map 78.

RECOGNITION: *pinkish-white, underwing vivid pink, broad red and yellow band in white crest.*

DESCRIPTION: 38–41cm; crest 10cm. Sexes alike. Shades of pale salmon-pink with vent and under tail coverts white; some red on forehead, crest mainly red with yellow centre and white tip; bill grey-brown; eyes dark brown to pale reddish-brown, redder in female; legs dark grey.

HABITAT: patches of timber in arid areas. HABITS: arboreal, but often feeding on ground; gregarious, but because of rarity flocks are small, or may be in pairs or in company with other cockatoos; mainly sedentary but nomadic in adverse conditions; flight a beat and glide, usually fairly low and for short distances. BREEDING: August–December; nests in holes in trees, a bed of chips of wood and bark; two to four white eggs. VOICE: loud wailing call (almost musical) and harsh screech. FOOD: various seeds and roots, also cereal crops.

STATUS: uncommon to rare and apparently declining, perhaps from natural causes rather than human interference. TAXONOMY: endemic species.

THE CORELLAS

There are two corellas. They look very alike except for bill shape and other minor differences and they seem to have separate distributions. Some authorities believe they interbreed where they come in contact in Western Australia and conclude they are races of a single species. We agree with those who regard them as separate species, the Long-billed, old and declining, and the Little, vigorous and thriving and rapidly extending its range.

321 LITTLE CORELLA *Cacatua sanguinea* Gould 1842

Distribution: Map 80. [*Note:* limits are only approximate as range is extending.]

RECOGNITION: *white, without distinct crest; bill stumpy and rounded.*

DESCRIPTION: 35–38cm; crown feathers can be erected but do not form distinct crest. Sexes alike. White with some flecks of red between eyes and bill, and patches of sulphur yellow on underwing and undertail; bill grey-brown; eyes dark brown, bare skin around eye blue-grey; legs grey.

HABITAT: well timbered localities, especially woodlands along watercourses in dry areas, sometimes mangroves and trees in city suburbs. HABITS: arboreal but frequently feeding on ground; gregarious, sometimes in very large noisy flocks; nomadic, sometimes appearing sporadically in places well outside known range; beat and glide flight on rather erratic course. BREEDING: variable, in most months but restricted periods claimed for some areas; nests in holes in trees, sometimes in cliffs and reported in old broken termite mounds, a bed of wood dust without green leaves; three to four white eggs. VOICE: loud harsh screech. FOOD: various seeds, including grain, also fruits, roots and insects.

STATUS: abundant and benefiting from most land uses. TAXONOMY: species extending to south-east New Guinea; one extralimital race on Tenimber Islands.

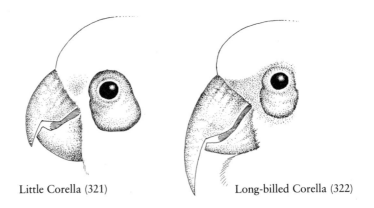

Little Corella (321)   Long-billed Corella (322)

322 LONG-BILLED CORELLA *Cacatua tenuirostris* (Gould) 1840

Distribution: Map 80.

RECOGNITION: *white, without distinct crest; bill long and nearly straight; restricted distribution.*

DESCRIPTION: 38cm. Sexes alike. White; forehead to eyes scarlet; varying amounts of scarlet on throat and breast and base of nape feathers; bill grey-brown; eyes dark brown, bare skin around eye blue-grey; legs grey.

VARIATION: eastern section, distinct amount of red on throat and breast and base of nape feathers (race *tenuirostris*); western section, little or no red on throat, breast and nape (race *pastinator*).

HABITAT: woodlands of various kinds and adjacent grasslands, usually near water. HABITS: arboreal but feeds mainly on ground; gregarious, size of flocks depending on numbers available, often very few; nomadic; beat and glide flight which is rather erratic. BREEDING: August–November; nests in holes in trees high up and near water; two to three white eggs. VOICE: loud harsh screech. FOOD: various seeds and bulbs, including grain; apparently a more frequent digger than the Little Corella.

STATUS: uncommon to rare and apparently declining, perhaps largely due to natural causes. TAXONOMY: endemic species.

Genus MELOPSITTACUS

The affinities of the abundant, nearly ubiquitous and peculiarly Australian Budgerigar are not clear. Possibly its adaptations for survival in arid environments has obscured its origins. In general appearance it is something like a miniature neophema dressed in green and gold but some authorities find connections with the Ground Parrot. It survives in almost universal bondage as a domestic pet.

323 BUDGERIGAR *Melopsittacus undulatus* (Shaw) 1805

Distribution: widespread; rare or absent from Cape York, east of Dividing Range and extreme southwest, but extending there in periods of drought; not Tasmania.

RECOGNITION: *small, long pointed tail, green with bright yellow mask and black barred back; in flocks.*

DESCRIPTION: 18cm, with tail 10cm. Sexes alike. Forehead and throat yellow, throat with black dots and separated from face by narrow bar of violet-blue; face, hind crown, nape and shoulders greenish-yellow closely barred with dark drab brown; remainder of body green; wing and tail feathers blackish-brown; bill greyish-yellow, base and cere blue in male, brownish in breeding female; eyes yellow; legs pinkish-grey.

HABITAT: wooded savannas. HABITS: arboreal but often feeds on ground; gregarious at all seasons, sometimes forming enormous flocks; nomadic. BREEDING: variable, often depending on rains, otherwise August–January in south and June–September in north; nests in holes in trees, logs and fence posts, a bed of wood dust; four to six white eggs. VOICE: chirrup and loud harsh screech. FOOD: seeds of low growing plants and grass, sometimes cereals.

STATUS: abundant. TAXONOMY: endemic species and genus.

Genus ECLECTUS

A genus extending from Sumba through New Guinea to the Solomon Is and across Torres St to Cape York where the only representative is the Red-sided Parrot. Although it has distinct features it is currently regarded as a race of a wider ranging species. Members of the genus have extreme sexual dimorphism with the unusual feature of the female being the more brightly coloured partner. They are plump forest birds with short square tails and cere covered with feathers.

324 RED-SIDED PARROT *Eclectus roratus* (Muller) 1776

Distribution: Map 81.

RECOGNITION: *male green with large patch of red on flanks and under shoulders; female mainly red with belly and under shoulders blue.*

DESCRIPTION: 33cm. Sexes different. *Male:* mainly green, shiny and lustrous; flanks and under shoulders crimson; remainder of underwing black and tip of upperwing purplish-black; centre of upper tail green; sides black tipped with pale yellow; undertail black; upper mandible reddish-orange, tip pale yellow, lower mandible black; eyes orange; legs dark grey. *Female:* head to mantle and breast crimson; edge of mantle, belly and under shoulders blue (ultramarine); lower back dark reddish-brown; under flight feathers black; bill black; eyes yellow; legs dark olive-green.

HABITAT: rain forests and adjacent timber. HABITS: arboreal; gregarious, apparently even breeding communally; sedentary, sometimes flying high over forests to feeding and roosting places; flight strong and direct with relatively slow wing beats. BREEDING: probably September–November; nests in holes in trees, preferably deciduous, at edge of forest or clearing and near water; two white eggs. VOICE: loud harsh 'krraark', also plaintive wailing and melodious whistling notes. FOOD: fruits, seeds and honey.

STATUS: common. TAXONOMY: endemic form (race *macgillivrayi*) of variable and mainly extralimital species.

Genus GEOFFROYUS

The three very similar species which comprise this genus extend from the Sunda Is through New Guinea to the Solomon Is and Cape York. They are medium sized with relatively short tails and marked sexual dimorphism, the male being the brighter coloured partner. The species which has colonised the tip of Cape York is the wide-ranging Red-cheeked Parrot whose many variants are considered to belong to a single species. Cape York and Aru Is birds are racially the same.

325 RED-CHEEKED PARROT *Geoffroyus geoffroyi* (Bechstein) 1811   Pl 10

Distribution: Map 83.

RECOGNITION: *mainly green with blue and black underwings; male has scarlet face and throat and blue crown; female has head mainly brown; forests at tip of Cape York.*

DESCRIPTION: 23cm. Sexes different. *Male:* forehead, face and throat scarlet; crown and nape violet-blue; remainder of upperparts grass green with small patch of russet on inner shoulders; underparts paler green; flight feathers black edged with green; under flight feathers black; under shoulders and upper flanks blue; upper mandible scarlet, lower brown; eyes creamy-white; legs dark-olive. *Female:* whole head and bill dark brown.

HABITAT: rain forests. HABITS: arboreal; gregarious; sedentary, with local feeding movements; flight swift and direct with short rapid wing beats. BREEDING: possibly August–December; nests in holes in trees high up (so far as known); three white eggs. VOICE: loud harsh notes in two or three syllables, uttered in flight. FOOD: seeds and fruits.

STATUS: common. TAXONOMY: either endemic form (race *maclennani*) or belonging to the Aru Is form (race *aruensis*) of variable extralimital species.

Genus POLYTELIS

Three distinct species, all now uncommon if not rare, make up this peculiarly Australian group. They are graceful birds with coral or rose-red bills, long narrow tails and long pointed wings. Shape of wings and tails may be associated with swift flight. They are adapted to open country and more terrestrial than the rosellas and ringnecks, and take refuge in speedy flight rather than tree cover.

Key to POLYTELIS

1 Shoulders and rump yellow . . . . Regent Parrot . . . . No 327
2 Shoulders and rump dark green . . . . Superb Parrot . . . . No 326
3 Shoulders green, rump blue . . . . Alexandra Parrot . . . . No 328

326 SUPERB PARROT *Polytelis swainsonii* (Desmarest) 1826   Pl 10

Distribution: Map 81.

RECOGNITION: *slim and pale green (hence alternative name 'Green Leek') with long thin blackish tail; male bright yellow on forehead and throat, and red on foreneck.*

DESCRIPTION: 35–40cm, with narrow tail 20–25cm. Sexes different. *Male:* mainly glossy green with tinge of blue on outer wing feathers; forehead and throat yellow and gorget of red on foreneck; underside of flight feathers and undertail black; bill coral-red; eyes dark yellow; legs brown. *Female:* shades of green with some flecks of red round vent and pink on inner margins of tail feathers.

HABITAT: wooded watercourses and well watered savannas. HABITS: arboreal but often feeding on ground; gregarious, in small flocks at all seasons; sedentary with some nomadic movements; flight swift and direct. BREEDING: September–December; nests in holes in trees high up, often in horizontal branches over water; four to six white eggs. VOICE: a 'prolonged warble ending abruptly' uttered in flight and a 'gentle twitter'. FOOD: seeds mainly, including fruit seeds, also honey and flowers.

STATUS: fairly stable small population in restricted area. TAXONOMY: endemic species of endemic genus.

327 REGENT PARROT *Polytelis anthopeplus* (Lear) 1831

Distribution: Map 81.

RECOGNITION: *slim with long thin tail; male bright yellow with dark green back and flash of red in wings; female dull green with patch of bright yellow on shoulders.*

DESCRIPTION: 38cm, with narrow tail 20–23cm. Sexes different. *Male:* mainly yellow with tinge of olive-green on crown and nape; upper back dark olive-yellow; partly concealed red bar between yellow shoulder and blue-black flight feathers; tail blue-black; bill coral-red; eyes dull yellow; legs olive. *Female:* mainly dull olive-green, darker above and yellower on belly; patch of bright greenish-yellow on shoulder; some red in centre of wing; tail feathers edged with pinkish-red.

HABITAT: heavy timber, especially along water courses, and patches of partly cleared forests. HABITS: arboreal, perches with body parallel to branch, often feeds on ground; gregarious, but flocks small because of rarity; apparently nomadic, especially in west; flight swift and direct. BREEDING: August–January, occasionally later; nests deep in holes in trees, often trunks of gums near water, a bed of wood dust; four white eggs. VOICE: a rather harsh and high-pitched warble. FOOD: mainly seeds, including fruit seeds and grain, also flowers and leaves.

STATUS: uncommon to rare in east, perhaps declining naturally; fairly common in west and apparently thriving. TAXONOMY: endemic species of endemic genus.

328 ALEXANDRA PARROT *Polytelis alexandrae* Gould 1863

Distribution: Map 81.

RECOGNITION: *slim with long thin tail; violet rump, greenish-yellow shoulders, rose-pink throat.*

DESCRIPTION: 38–46cm, with narrow pointed tail 23–30cm, shorter in female. Sexes slightly different. *Male:* crown and face sky-blue; back greenish-olive; rump violet; throat rose-pink; breast and belly pale olive-green; shoulders pale greenish-yellow; flight and tail feathers greenish-brown, inner webs of tail feathers rose-red; bill rose-red; eyes yellow; legs grey. *Female:* blue of head and violet of rump duller and greyer.

HABITAT: arid country with porcupine grass and scattered trees. HABITS: arboreal but frequently feeds on ground and often far from water; gregarious at all seasons; nomadic, occurring sporadically in various places often at intervals of many years; flight irregular and undulating, close to ground for short distances and swift and straight when high up and travelling far. BREEDING: September–January; nests in holes in trees, sometimes in colonies; four to six white eggs. VOICE: loud harsh warble and 'soft twitter'—but mainly silent. FOOD: seeds mainly, especially porcupine grass (but diet little known).

STATUS: apparently uncommon to rare. TAXONOMY: endemic species of endemic genus.

Genus APROSMICTUS

Two species, one on Timor and Wetar and the other in southern New Guinea and northeast Australia, make up this genus. They are plump with long broad tails and mainly green with striking patches of red and black. There is marked sexual dimorphism. They live almost exclusively in forest and woodland canopies, taking to the wing only reluctantly and then in rather slow and laboured flight.

329 RED-WINGED PARROT *Aprosmictus erythropterus* (Gmelin) 1788   Pl 10

Distribution: Map 82.

RECOGNITION: *plump with square tail; male green with red shoulders.*

DESCRIPTION: 30cm, with broad tail about half. Sexes different. *Male:* head bright green, sometimes with bluish tinge on crown; back black; rump blue (ultramarine); upper tail coverts bright green; underparts including under shoulders and flanks, bright green; shoulders bright scarlet; under flight feathers and undertail black; bill reddish; eyes orange; legs grey. *Female:* mainly bright apple-green, a small area of red on shoulders and dull blue on rump.

VARIATION: in east, and south of about Townsville, rather larger and duller with wash of blue on crown (race *erythropterus*); in north, smaller and brighter (race *coccinopterus*).

HABITAT: open forests and woodlands and well timbered places along rivers and creeks, also mangroves. HABITS: arboreal, rarely on ground; gregarious, families or small flocks; sedentary with peripheral nomadic movements. BREEDING: variable, in most months in some parts of range, but mainly August–February; nests in holes in trees usually high up and near water;

three to five white eggs. VOICE: loud metallic double note, like 'chink-chink', uttered in flight, also a loud screech. FOOD: seeds mainly, including fruit seeds, also honey and insects.

STATUS: common. TAXONOMY: species doubtfully subdivided into races, extending more or less unchanged across Torres St to southern New Guinea.

Genus ALISTERUS

The endemic King Parrot and two related species in New Guinea and associated western islands are sometimes included in the same genus as the Red-winged Parrot, but current opinion seems to favour their separation. In the King Parrot the sexes are different and the male has a very striking pattern of red, black and green. It is a forest canopy species.

330 KING PARROT *Alisterus scapularis* (Lichtenstein) 1818
Distribution: Map 83.

RECOGNITION: *male: red head and underparts, purple rump (Crimson Rosella similar but has blue on face and throat and no purple on rump); female: mainly green.*

DESCRIPTION: 40–45cm, with graduated tail about half. Sexes different. *Male:* head and underparts bright scarlet; collar and rump dark violet-blue; mantle and upper wings dark green with pale green scapulars; underwing dusky; tail black tinged with violet; upper mandible red, tip black, lower mandible black; eyes yellow; legs grey. *Female:* mainly dark green with red only on lower belly, bluish on rump; bill blackish.

VARIATION: south of tropic, rather larger (race *scapularis*); north of tropic, rather smaller and richer in colour (race *minor*).

HABITAT: forests. HABITS: arboreal, rarely on ground; gregarious, families or small flocks; nomadic, but apparently also some regular seasonal movements; relatively inactive with rather slow movements, but quite strong in flight. BREEDING: September–January; nests in holes in trees, openings high up but nests often near ground level; three to six white eggs. VOICE: shrill double note and high-pitched shriek. FOOD: seeds mainly, including fruit seeds, also honey and insects.

STATUS: common, but affected by destruction of heavy timber. TAXONOMY: endemic species.

Genus NEOPHEMA

Seven species are included in this distinct and uniform group which has close affinities with *Psephotus*. They are peculiar to Australia and are distributed mainly south of the tropic. They are successful colonisers of dry habitats; if it is assumed that the ancestral parrots were forest birds then the neophemas may be the present end product of adaptation away from the forest environment. They live in open country, including rocky coasts and coastal islands, and although spending most of their time on the ground they still require timber for nesting, a log or fence post suffices for all except the Rock Parrot which nests under rocks and stones. They run with great speed and fly rapidly, sometimes for long distances, especially when going to water. The seven species are much alike in general build and colour pattern; long pointed tails account for more than half the total length of 23cm; the colours are mainly greens and yellows with some quite distinctive feature in each, except the Bourke Parrot which is blue-grey and rose-pink, one reason why it is sometimes placed in a separate genus.

Key to NEOPHEMA

1 Mainly blue-grey and rose-pink................. Bourke Parrot .... No 331
2 Mainly green and yellow....................... 3–12

3 Breast red .... (♂) Scarlet-breasted Parrot ..... No 337
4 Breast green or greenish-yellow 5–12

5 Face and forehead turquoise .... Turquoise Parrot.......... No 336
6 Face and forehead yellowish, blue bar on forehead   7–12

7 Lores bright yellow 9–10
8 Lores green or greenish-yellow 11–12

9 Shoulder mainly violet-blue .... Blue-winged Parrot .... No 333
10 Shoulder mainly green........................ Elegant Parrot .... No 332

11 Mainly olive-green, west of Adelaide .... Rock Parrot .... No 335
12 Mainly emerald-green, east of Adelaide .... Orange-bellied Parrot...... No 334

331 BOURKE PARROT *Neophema bourkii* (Gould) 1841
Distribution: Map 84.

RECOGNITION: *blue-grey and rose-pink, small and usually on ground.*

DESCRIPTION: 20–23cm, with tail 13cm. Sexes alike but female slightly duller. Upperparts dark grey-brown; forehead tinged with blue; shoulder feathers edged with creamy-white; underparts shading from pinkish-brown on throat to reddish-pink on belly; flanks and under tail coverts pale blue; tail blackish-brown, outer feathers broadly tipped with white; bill dark grey; eyes dark brown; legs grey.

HABITAT: sparsely wooded savannas, especially clumps of mulga. HABITS: arboreal but often on ground; gregarious, sometimes in flocks of up to one hundred; sedentary and nomadic, apparently a local population may remain in one area for several years and then move to another; goes to water after dark and early dawn, sometimes later in the morning; flight swift, low and direct. BREEDING: variable, sometimes depending on rains, but mainly August– December; nests in low holes in small trees; four to five white eggs. VOICE: a soft musical 'chu-wee' in flight, also a warbling whistle. FOOD: seeds mainly, also green shoots.

STATUS: common. TAXONOMY: endemic species.

ELEGANT AND BLUE-WINGED PARROTS

Elegant and Blue-winged Parrots are very alike. Although usually regarded as two species they could be geographical variants of one. Their distinctive features appear to intergrade where the two forms meet and identification can be difficult; the Elegant is generally more yellow, has a smaller amount of violet-blue on the shoulder, and the forehead bar usually extends beyond the eye.

332 ELEGANT PARROT *Neophema elegans* (Gould) 1837   Pl 9
Distribution: Map 85.

RECOGNITION: *greenish-yellow with blue markings and bright yellow patch on face. Distinguished from Blue-winged Parrot by narrow edge of blue on shoulders and forehead bar usually extending beyond eye.*

DESCRIPTION: 20–23cm, with tail 10–13cm. Sexes alike but female duller. Upperparts yellowish-green, shading to paler on neck and breast; bar on forehead deep violet-blue bordered above with pale blue, usually extending beyond eye; lores and base of bill bright yellow; belly yellow, sometimes slightly orange in centre; under tail coverts and outer tail feathers yellow, central feathers bluish-green tipped with yellow; edge of shoulder violet-blue bordered with pale blue, remainder of shoulder yellowish-green; flight feathers black, outer feathers edged with violet-blue; bill grey-brown; eyes dark brown; legs grey.

HABITAT: forest clearings, woodlands and various kinds of open country, including coastal dunes with some timber. HABITS: largely terrestrial but nesting in trees; gregarious, flocks of ten to twenty or more; sedentary, but nomadic in dry marginal areas, flight swift, low and erratic, or high and direct. BREEDING: August–November; nests in holes in trees, often high up; four to five white eggs. VOICE: a sharp 'zit-zit' uttered in flight. FOOD: seeds, mainly of ground vegetation.

STATUS: fairly common to common. TAXONOMY: endemic species, perhaps conspecific with Blue-winged Parrot.

333 BLUE-WINGED PARROT *Neophema chrysostomus* (Kuhl) 1820 Pl 9
Distribution: Map 85.

RECOGNITION: like Elegant Parrot but upperparts greener, less yellow, shading to golden on crown; *violet-blue edge of shoulder much wider; forehead bar barely or just reaching eye.*

HABITAT, etc: more or less similar to Elegant Parrot except—HABITS: migratory, apparently regular seasonal movements, especially between Tasmania and mainland. BREEDING: October–January; nests usually high up in trees.

STATUS: common. TAXONOMY: endemic species, perhaps conspecific with Elegant Parrot.

ORANGE-BELLIED AND ROCK PARROTS

The Orange-bellied and Rock Parrots are very alike and replace each other along the south coast. They might be no more than geographical variants of a single species but it is usual to accept them as species. It seems likely that they originated from a stock in the neophema group which became adapted to rough and often treeless coastal habitats and mainly terrestrial habits. A common feature which distinguishes them from other members of the genus is the absence of bright yellow on the facial area which makes the forehead bar much less conspicuous.

334 ORANGE-BELLIED PARROT *Neophema chrysogaster* (Latham) 1790 Pl 9
Distribution: Map 84.

RECOGNITION: like other neophemas in general description. Differs in having *upperparts emerald-green; narrow ring of bright yellow around eye;* face yellowish-green uniform with neck and breast and making forehead bar less conspicuous; *orange patch in centre of yellow belly.*

HABITAT: coastal and island rough grasslands, sand dunes and tidal flats. HABITS: mainly terrestrial but nests in trees, possibly also on ground; usually solitary, perhaps because of small numbers; probably migratory and travelling at night; flight low erratic flutter-and-glide ending in sudden drop to ground. BREEDING: at least November and December; nests in holes in trees, perhaps also on ground; four to six white eggs. VOICE: soft tinkling and distinctive loud chittering alarm. FOOD: seeds of ground vegetation.

STATUS: rare, perhaps less so on certain islands. TAXONOMY: endemic species, closely related to Rock Parrot.

335 ROCK PARROT *Neophema petrophila* (Gould) 1840   Pl 9
Distribution: Map 84.

RECOGNITION: like Orange-bellied Parrot but more robust appearance; *upperparts dark brownish-olive; facial markings around eye and base of bill pale blue;* forehead bar not conspicuous; inner wing pale blue with very little violet-blue; *no orange on yellow belly.*

HABITAT: rocky areas and sand dunes on coasts and coastal islands. HABITS: terrestrial; gregarious; small parties and sometimes large flocks; sedentary, except for movements between islands and mainland, probably connected with feeding; flight erratic flutter-and-glide, like Orange-bellied. BREEDING: August–October; nests on ground in crevices among rocks, or sheltered by slabs; four to five white eggs. VOICE: a sharp 'tsit-tseet'. FOOD: seeds of ground vegetation.

STATUS: Common. TAXONOMY: endemic species, closely related to Orange-bellied Parrot.

TURQUOISE AND SCARLET-BREASTED PARROTS

Turquoise and Scarlet-breasted Parrots make a complementary pair of eastern and western species. They are very alike and must have stemmed from a once widespread common stock. They are now separated by much of western New South Wales, although the Turquoise seems to be increasing and spreading westward. Records of the Scarlet-breasted in the range of the Turquoise seem to be based on sight misidentifications. The principal common feature is an extensive area of blue on forehead and face, at a distance seeming like a black mask; also there is greater sexual dimorphism than in other neophema species, the females being much duller than the males.

336 TURQUOISE PARROT *Neophema pulchella* (Shaw) 1792   Pl 9
Distribution: Map 86.

RECOGNITION: like other neophemas in general description but upperparts emerald-green; *forehead and face turquoise-blue, appearing like black mask at a distance* and obscuring violet-blue forehead bar; edge of shoulder turquoise-blue, centre reddish-chestnut; *breast and belly yellow,* occasionally some red in centre of belly. *Female:* less blue on head, but distinct amount on lower face; lores buff; no chestnut on wing.

HABITAT: savanna woodlands and well wooded localities, especially sheltered valleys among rocky hills, with adjacent grassy areas. HABITS: arboreal but often feeds on ground; solitary or gregarious, sometimes quite large flocks; sedentary with perhaps some local seasonal movements; flight swift erratic flutter. BREEDING: August–December; nests in holes in trees, fallen timber or fence posts; four to five white eggs. VOICE: soft whistle in two syllables. FOOD: seeds of ground vegetation, especially grasses.

STATUS: fairly common. TAXONOMY: endemic species, closely related to Scarlet-breasted Parrot.

337 SCARLET-BREASTED PARROT *Neophema splendida* (Gould) 1840   Pl 9
Distribution: Map 86.

RECOGNITION: like Turquoise Parrot but *turquoise-blue of head extends to nape and neck;*

no forehead bar; *breast red;* throat violet-blue. *Female:* blue on head duller, breast green. HABITAT: open dry country preferably with clumps of trees and shrubs. HABITS: mainly terrestrial but apparently requires trees or shrubs for nesting; gregarious when numbers adequate, but usually in pairs; probably sedentary when conditions favourable, otherwise nomadic; flight erratic flutter. BREEDING: probably between August and January but variable depending on rains; nests in holes, in bushes and trees so far as known; three to five white eggs. VOICE: soft twitter. FOOD: seeds of ground vegetation.

STATUS: apparently rare, but perhaps more numerous than records indicate. TAXONOMY: endemic species, closely related to Turquoise Parrot.

Genus PEZOPORUS

The two species of this endemic genus (sometimes in separate genera) are generally described as primitive although in fact it could be argued, on the grounds that parrots were originally forest birds, that they have advanced a long way in adapting to an entirely terrestrial habitat —a process, unfortunately, which has left them ill-equipped to cope with introduced ground predators. It is thought that nearest relatives may be the declining New Zealand Kakapo, to which they bear at least a superficial resemblance in terrestrial habits and grass-green plumage with black markings, and the vigorous and successful Budgerigar.

338 GROUND PARROT *Pezoporus wallicus*   (Kerr) 1792

Distribution: Map 87.

RECOGNITION: *grass-green, densely blotched and barred with black and yellow; on ground in wet coastal heaths.*

DESCRIPTION: 33–36cm, with long pointed tail 20cm. Sexes alike. Upperparts dark grass-green densely marked with black, which forms streaks on crown, and some yellow; narrow red bar on forehead; throat and breast light green with few markings; lower breast and belly greenish-yellow barred with black; yellow ring around eye; yellow bar on wing, more distinct on underwing; centre of tail green barred with yellow, sides yellow barred with black; bill bluish-brown; eyes dull brown; legs pinkish-brown.

Ground Parrot (338)

VARIATION: eastern mainland, lighter with greener underparts (race *wallicus*); Tasmania, darker green (race *leachi*); west, underparts yellower (race *flaviventris*).

HABITAT: margins of swampy coastal heaths and rough waste land. HABITS: terrestrial; in isolated colonies but not truly gregarious unless flocking during nomadic movements; apparently sedentary with some nomadism, possibly flying at night; mainly crepuscular or nocturnal; flight swift and erratic, usually of short duration but sometimes for long distances before pitching to ground. BREEDING: September–December; nests in or at base of tussocks or low bushes, a hollow scratched in sand and filled with dry leaves and twigs, lined with grass and partly domed with stalks of fern; three to four dull white eggs. VOICE: a high-pitched musical 'tee' or 'tsit' repeated several times at varying pitches. FOOD: seeds and tender grass shoots. STATUS: rare, adversely affected by land settlement, by changes to habitat and by introduced ground predators. TAXONOMY: endemic species, closely related to Night Parrot.

339 NIGHT PARROT *Pezoporus occidentalis* (Gould) 1861

Distribution: Map 87. [NOTE: range shown on map covers area in which species has been recorded; little is known about its present occurrence.]

RECOGNITION: like Ground Parrot but *tail much shorter,* about 10cm, plumage lighter green, more yellowish; belly uniformly yellow; *no red on forehead.*

HABITAT: arid country with porcupine grass and samphire bushes. HABITS: terrestrial; probably solitary except when flocking to water or moving to new feeding grounds; apparently sedentary or perhaps nomadic in relation to rains and seeding of porcupine grass; nocturnal, remains concealed under tussocks during day; flight low and direct for short distances, ending in glide. BREEDING: season unknown; nests near base of porcupine grass tussocks, possibly also in limestone caves, a rough platform of sticks; white eggs, probably four. VOICE: 'sweet, low, two-tone whistle', 'low, drawn-out mournful whistle' when flying to and from water, frog-like 'croaking alarm note'. FOOD: seeds of ground vegetation, especially porcupine grass.

STATUS: rare, perhaps extinct. TAXONOMY: endemic species, closely related to Ground Parrot.

Genus PLATYCERCUS

Rosellas are a relatively large group of similar and very successful parrots peculiar to Australia. They are 25–38cm in length, about half being tail, and are distinguished by the scalloped or marbled pattern of the back. Wings are short and rounded and flight is undulating and not very strong. They are mainly ground feeders, often along road margins, but rarely venture far from trees to which they fly when not feeding or when disturbed. Seven species are listed here but opinions vary on whether some forms are species or races, especially *elegans, flaveolus* and *caledonicus.* These three are confined to the southeast corner and are distinguished by having a patch of violet on the face. The remainder form a group of very similar species which more or less replace each other round the greater part of the periphery of the continent. Incidentally, the name Rosella is derived from Rosehill, now a western suburb of Sydney, a district where early colonists named a common bird there the 'Rose-hill Parakeet', which became 'Rose-hiller' and eventually 'Rosella'—a fortunate evolution of a distinctive name for an Australian bird.

Key to PLATYCERCUS

VIOLET-FACED ROSELLAS

A group of rosellas have violet on the lower part of the face and edge of the shoulders. Although varying considerably in basic plumage colour they are clearly related and are sometimes regarded as variants of one species. But distinct differences are associated with separate distributions and for practical purposes it seems most suitable to recognise three species, as follows.

CRIMSON ROSELLA .... *Platycercus elegans*
    Ground colour crimson,   *elegans*
    back darker.. *fleurieuensis*
                                 nigrescens
    Ground colour reddish-orange,   *adelaidae*
    back paler .... *subadelaidae*
YELLOW ROSELLA .... *Platycercus flaveolus*
    Ground colour yellow, red on forehead
GREEN ROSELLA .... *Platycercus caledonicus*
    Ground colour yellow, back blackish-green; Tasmania

340 CRIMSON ROSELLA *Platycercus elegans* (Gmelin) 1788

Distribution: Map 88.

RECOGNITION: *red head and underparts, mottled back and violet patch on face (male King Parrot similar but has purple rump and lacks violet on face).*

DESCRIPTION: 33–36cm, with broad tail 18–20cm. Sexes alike. Head and body deep crimson or reddish-orange, on upper back heavily mottled with black or grey; face and throat violet; edge of shoulders violet; inner shoulders and flight feathers black; tail varying from deep violet basally to pale violet at outer tip; bill pinkish-brown; eyes dark brown; legs grey-brown.

VARIATION: coastal areas of southeast and isolated population in Cairns area, head and body mainly crimson (races *elegans*, *fleurieuensis* and *nigrescens*); Adelaide to Flinders Range, head and body mainly reddish-orange (races *adelaidae* and *subadelaidae*).

HABITAT: forests of various kinds and well wooded localities at all altitudes. HABITS: arboreal, sometimes feeds on ground; gregarious, mainly when not breeding; sedentary with some nomadic movements at periphery of range; flight undulating and relatively slow. BREEDING: September–February; nests in holes in trees at varying heights; five white eggs. VOICE: shrill whistle in three syllables, loud harsh screech and softer musical notes. FOOD: various seeds, including fruit seeds, also flowers, honey and insects.

STATUS: common. TAXONOMY: endemic species, doubtfully separable from similar adjacent forms.

341 YELLOW ROSELLA   *Platycercus flaveolus*   Gould 1837
Distribution: Map 88.

RECOGNITION: like Crimson Rosella in general appearance but has *ground colour of head and body yellow* instead of red, except for a *small patch of red on forehead.*

HABITAT, etc: similar to the Crimson Rosella but rather more sedentary and more confined to heavy timber; breeding August–January; four to five white eggs.

STATUS: fairly common in restricted area. TAXONOMY: endemic and probably distinct species, doubtfully hybridising with Crimson Rosella.

342 GREEN ROSELLA   *Platycercus caledonicus*   (Gmelin) 1788
Distribution: Map 88.

RECOGNITION: like Yellow Rosella in general appearance but yellows are duller and *back is blackish-green* faintly scalloped with yellow and lightly washed with yellow on rump.

HABITAT, etc: similar to Crimson and Yellow Rosellas.

STATUS: common. TAXONOMY: endemic species peculiar to Tasmania and closely related to mainland species.

FOUR REGIONAL ROSELLAS

Four rosellas, Western, Eastern, Pale-headed and Northern, are distributed round the periphery of the continent, except in the west between Geraldton and Broome. Only the Eastern and Pale-headed come in contact, in the eastern border between Queensland and New South Wales, where they intermingle slightly and show some evidence of interbreeding. It seems that these four rosellas have derived from a recent common stock and illustrate stages in speciation following isolation due to various factors. All have distinct features and are treated here as species.

343 WESTERN ROSELLA   *Platycercus icterotis*   (Kuhl) 1820   Pl 10
Distribution: Map 89.

RECOGNITION: *red head and underparts, lower face yellow, extreme southwest.*

DESCRIPTION: 25–28cm. Sexes different. *Male:* head and underparts red, brighter on head but duller and tinged with yellow on underparts; cheeks yellow; back black, feathers broadly edged with dark green; shoulders above and below dark violet; central tail feathers dark green, outer bluish-white; bill bluish-brown; eyes dark brown; legs grey-brown. *Female:* forehead red; crown green; underparts dull red, tinged with yellow on breast and green on belly.

VARIATION: an ill-defined variant in drier areas has back feathers dark grey edged with mottled red and buff, and very little green in centre of tail (race *xanthogenys*).

HABITAT: open forests and woodlands. HABITS: arboreal but feeds mainly on ground, often at roadsides; largely solitary except for family parties; sedentary with some local seasonal movements; flight of short duration, light and swift. BREEDING: August–December; nests in holes in trees; three to seven white eggs. VOICE: a soft and rather musical 'chink-chink'.

FOOD: various seeds, usually obtained on ground; also berries and fruits, sometimes from orchards.

STATUS: common; declared a pest in certain fruit growing areas. TAXONOMY: endemic species, possibly forming superspecies with three other peripheral rosellas.

344 EASTERN ROSELLA *Platycercus eximius* (Shaw) 1792
Distribution: Map 89.

RECOGNITION: *red head and white throat, yellow rump and belly, mottled back.*

DESCRIPTION: 28–30cm. Sexes alike, but colours duller in female. Head to upper breast bright red except for white throat; back black and yellow; rump greenish-yellow; lower breast yellow shading to greenish-yellow on belly; edge of shoulder violet; remainder of wing black; central tail feathers dark green, outer bluish-white; bill bluish-white; eyes dark brown; legs grey-brown.

VARIATION: margins of back feathers lemon-yellow (race *eximius*) except in north where they are golden-yellow (race *ceciliae*); in Tasmania more red on breast and more white on throat (race *diemenensis*).

HABITAT: woodlands. HABITS: arboreal, but often feeds on ground; solitary breeding, at other times single or in small flocks; sedentary; swift undulating flight. BREEDING: September–January; nests in holes—in trees, fallen timber, fence posts, old burrows—a bed of chipped rotten wood; four to nine white eggs. VOICE: shrill screech and rather musical whistle, often in three syllables, also bell-like 'ping'. FOOD: seeds of various kinds, including berries, also honey.

STATUS: very common and thriving, benefiting from the thinning out of heavy timber. TAXONOMY: endemic species, closely related to Pale-headed Rosella, with which it interbreeds in a narrow zone.

345 PALE-HEADED ROSELLA *Platycercus adscitus* (Latham) 1790
Distribution: Map 89.

RECOGNITION: *yellow head (sometimes almost white), violet breast and belly, red under tail coverts.*

DESCRIPTION: 30cm. Sexes alike. Head shades of pale yellow; throat white; back black, feathers edged with bright yellow; rump pale greenish-blue; breast and belly violet; under tail coverts red; edge of shoulders and centre of wing violet; remainder of wing black; central tail feathers greenish-violet above, black below, outer deep violet tipped with pale violet; bill bluish-white; eyes dark brown or yellowish-brown; legs grey.

VARIATION: north of about Cairns, patch of pale violet on lower face (race *adscitus*); south of Cairns, lower part of face white (race *palliceps*).

HABITAT, etc: more or less similar to Eastern Rosella, except that breeding season varies, September–January in south, February–June in north; eggs are fewer, three to five.

STATUS, etc: similar to Eastern Rosella; where they overlap they interbreed but hybrids restricted to a narrow zone.

346 NORTHERN ROSELLA *Platycercus venustus* (Kuhl) 1820   Pl 10
Distribution: Map 89.

RECOGNITION: *black cap and yellow body colour, red under tail coverts.*

DESCRIPTION: 28cm. Sexes alike. Upper part of head black; lower face white edged with violet below; back mainly black, some feathers broadly edged with pale yellow; rump and under-parts pale yellow with some black scallops on foreneck and upper breast; under tail coverts red; shoulders violet; flight feathers black, basally edged with violet; central tail feathers blue-green, outer violet above, black below and tipped with violet-white; bill blue-grey; eyes dark brown; legs blue-black.

HABITAT: woodlands. HABITS: arboreal, often feeds on ground; solitary and gregarious, in very small flocks; sedentary; flight swift and undulating, low over ground. BREEDING: June–August; nests in holes in trees; two to four white eggs. VOICE: high pitched double whistle. FOOD: seeds of various kinds, also fruits, berries and flowers.

STATUS: uncommon to rare and apparently decreasing, possibly from natural causes. TAXONOMY: endemic species closely related to three other peripheral rosella species.

Genus BARNARDIUS

Ringnecks are distinguished by a narrow yellow partial collar and by certain osteological features. The wings are short and rounded and the long broad tails are graduated. Ringnecks are widely distributed south of the tropic, frequent open dry country with scattered trees and often feed on the ground. The group consists of two sections, east and west of a line from Spencer Gulf through Lake Torrens, Lake Eyre and the Simpson Desert. Segregation is not complete for hybrid features are found in populations in the Flinders Ranges. It is a matter of opinion if the sections are to be regarded as races or species. As they have distinct features except where they hybridise it seems more practical in the present context to list them as species. The hybrid population is added as a race of the eastern section. Signs of speciation are also evident in both sections, in fact some maintain that the Cloncurry Parrot, here listed as a race of *Barnardius barnardi,* can be recognised as a separate species *Barnardius macgillivrayi.*

Key to BARNARDIUS

1 Crown and neck black .... Western Ringneck ..... No 347
2 Crown greenish-yellow, nape olive-green .... Eastern Ringneck ..... No 348

347 WESTERN RINGNECK *Barnardius zonarius* (Shaw) 1805

Distribution: Map 90.

RECOGNITION: *yellow collar and belly, blackish head.*

DESCRIPTION: 35–40cm, graduated tail about half. Sexes alike. Upperparts of head blackish-brown; lower part of face and throat dark violet-blue; collar bright yellow; remainder of upperparts and breast shades of dark green; shoulders shades of light green; centre of wing dark violet-blue; tip of wings black; belly yellow; vent and under tail coverts greenish-yellow; tail greenish, outer feathers broadly tipped with pale violet-blue; bill bluish-white; eyes brown; legs grey.

VARIATION: in extreme southwest larger, narrow red band on forehead, upperparts yellowish-green and yellow on belly diffuse (race *semitorquatus*): in most other areas, little or no red on forehead, upperparts bluish-green and yellow of belly clearly defined (race *zonarius*); in northern populations, greens and yellows generally brighter (race *occidentalis*).

HABITAT: timbered country, from coastal forest to inland sparse woodlands. HABITS: arboreal but often feeds on ground; gregarious; sedentary, with some nomadic movements in dry areas; flight swift and undulating and generally low over ground. BREEDING: August–February in south but variable in dry inland; nests in holes in trees; five to six white eggs. VOICE: a high pitched whistle in two or three syllables, latter has given rise to alternative name of 'twenty-eight parrot' and seems to be used only by birds in southwest. FOOD: various seeds, including cereals, seed capsules, fruits, berries and grubs.

STATUS: common to abundant, declared a pest in some fruit growing areas. TAXONOMY: endemic species closely related to Eastern Ringneck.

348 EASTERN RINGNECK *Barnardius barnardi* (Vig. & Horsf.) 1827
Distribution: Map 90.

RECOGNITION: *red forehead (except in extreme north), yellow patch on underparts, greenish-yellow crown, blue-green back, yellow collar (not as conspicuous as in western species).*

DESCRIPTION: 33–36cm, with broad graduated tail 18cm. Sexes alike. Crown pale green to yellowish-green; forehead usually red; nape dull olive-green; lower face green tinged with varying amounts of blue; collar bright yellow; back shades of blue-green and olive-green; rump and underparts light green with patch of yellow, sometimes tinged with red, between breast and belly; shoulders yellow and olive-yellow; flight feathers black edged with violet-blue; centre of tail green, sides violet-blue broadly tipped with bluish-white; bill bluish-white; eyes brown; legs grey.

VARIATION: over greater part of range forehead red, yellow patch on belly tinged with red (race *barnardi*); in Flinders Range a hybrid population has features intermediate with western species (race *whitei*); in Cloncurry area no red on forehead, colours lighter and brighter and yellow patch on belly broad (race *macgillivrayi*—sometimes regarded as distinct species).

HABITAT: woodlands, especially mallee and mulga, and wooded savannas; northern race in rocky timbered hills with porcupine grass. HABITS: arboreal, often feeds on ground; in pairs or small flocks; sedentary; flight undulating and low over ground. BREEDING: August–May; nests in holes in trees, a bed of wood dust; four to six white eggs. VOICE: high pitched whistle and sharp repeated 'chink'. FOOD: seeds of various kinds, fruits, berries and flowers.

STATUS: common but adversely affected by land settlement and probably declining. TAXONOMY: endemic species closely related to Western Ringneck.

Genus PURPUREICEPHALUS

The Red-capped Parrot, native to the forests of the extreme southwest, is the only member of this genus. Some authorities think it is a close relative of a species in New Caledonia and a relict form of a once widespread group. The Australian species, although mainly a forest bird, frequently feeds on the ground. The bill is adapted for opening hard fruits; wings are short and rounded. A distinctive feature is a large patch of yellow on the side of the face and neck, and a patch of the same colour on the rump.

349 RED-CAPPED PARROT *Purpureicephalus spurius* (Kuhl) 1820
Distribution: Map 91.

RECOGNITION: *dark red cap, pale greenish-yellow face and rump, violet breast.*

DESCRIPTION: 35cm, with broad graduated tail 20cm. Sexes slightly different, female duller with brownish tinge on red crown and blue breast. Forehead to nape dark red; back blue-green; rump pale greenish-yellow; face and throat greenish-yellow; breast, belly and under shoulders violet; vent and under tail coverts dark red; shoulders blue-green edged with violet; flight feathers black edged basally with violet-black; central tail feathers greenish above, black below, outer shading from dark violet to violet-white at tips; bill blue-brown; eyes brown; legs grey-brown.

HABITAT: mainly forests and various heavily timbered woodlands. HABITS: arboreal but sometimes feeds on ground; in pairs or family parties; sedentary; flight rapid and with little undulation. BREEDING: August–December; nests in holes in trees high up; four to seven white eggs. VOICE: harsh grating 'shrek' often repeated. FOOD: various seeds, especially of marri gum (bill specially adapted to extract seeds), also wild and cultivated fruits and flowers.

STATUS: common, but persecuted because of damage to orchards. TAXONOMY: endemic species and genus.

Red-capped Parrot (349)

Genus PSEPHOTUS

Another peculiarly Australian group of parrots with long, broad graduated tails, like the rosellas and ringnecks, but smaller in build. Their principal distinguishing features are plain instead of mottled backs, face patch absent, or poorly defined, and marked differences between the sexes, except in the Blue-bonnet. For the most part they are less dependent on trees, live in more open country and spend much of their time on the ground. They seem to illustrate a stage of emancipation from an arboreal to a terrestrial existence, a process essential to the survival of many forms in the Australian environment. This is illustrated particularly in the case of the now nearly extinct Golden-shouldered Parrot which has adapted to the use of termite mounds (ant-beds) for nesting instead of trees. Most of the species are very colourful and suffer from persecution by cage bird enthusiasts.

Key to PSEPHOTUS

1 Forehead, face and crown green	Red-rumped Parrot	No 352
2 Forehead red, face blue-green, crown black	Paradise Parrot	No 354
3 Forehead and crown black, face blue-green	Hooded Parrot	No 356
4 Forehead and face blue, crown brown	6–7	
5 Forehead yellow, face blue green	8–9	
6 Shoulder patch reddish-pink	Naretha Parrot	No 351
7 Shoulder patch golden or chestnut	Blue-bonnet	No 350
8 Crown blue-green	Mulga Parrot	No 353
9 Crown black	Golden-shouldered Parrot	No 355

350 BLUE-BONNET *Psephotus haematogaster* (Gould) 1837   Pl 10
Distribution: Map 91.

RECOGNITION: *bright blue face mask (not 'bonnet'), golden-yellow on shoulders with yellow belly, or chestnut on shoulders with mainly red belly (depending on locality).*

DESCRIPTION: 28–30cm, with tail 18cm. Sexes alike. Face mask violet-blue; upperparts drab brown, sometimes with wash of golden-yellow on upper tail coverts; breast mottled drab brown and creamy-buff; belly and under tail coverts pale yellow blotched with varying amounts of blood red; edge of shoulder above and below blue; centre of shoulder and inner wing golden-yellow or reddish-chestnut; base of flight feathers deep violet-blue, tip black; centre of tail drab brown, remainder violet-blue above and black below with broad tip of creamy-white; bill bluish-white; eyes brown; legs grey-brown.

VARIATION: southeast, red only in centre of yellow belly, centre of shoulders golden-yellow (race *haematogaster*); northeast, most of belly and under tail coverts red, centre of shoulders reddish-chestnut (race *haematorrhous*); in west—Lake Eyre region—plumage much paler (race *pallescens*).

HABITAT: open country with scattered trees providing nest holes. HABITS: frequently on ground or in low bushes but trees also required, however small; gregarious; sedentary with nomadic tendencies in drought periods; flight erratic and undulating low over ground. BREEDING: mainly July–December but can be variable depending on rains; nests in holes in trees, sometimes near ground in small trees; four to seven white eggs. VOICE: harsh repeated 'chuck', also high pitched whistling 'cheerie'. FOOD: seeds, blossoms, fruits and honey.

STATUS: common. TAXONOMY: endemic species of which Naretha Parrot is recent offshoot race or species.

NARETHA PARROT

Many authorities regard the Naretha Parrot as a race of the Blue-bonnet. There is little doubt that they are branches of the same stock but the Naretha has certain distinct features, an isolated range (so far as is known), and its name is retained in common usage. For these reasons and because it is not well known, it can be listed as a species, thus attracting more attention.

351 NARETHA PARROT *Psephotus narethae* White 1921
Distribution: Map 91.

RECOGNITION: similar to Blue-bonnet but smaller, 25–28cm, forehead and upper face ultramarine-blue, lower face violet-blue, crown and nape light brown mottled with creamy-buff, rump and upper tail coverts golden-yellow, sometimes extending onto back, belly plain yellow, *patch of reddish pink on shoulders.*

HABITAT: semidesert areas with scattering of casuarinas, especially sheoak which provides nest holes. HABITS, etc: probably similar to Blue Bonnet. VOICE: soft flute like 'cloote-cloote', and noisy chatter.

352 RED-RUMPED PARROT *Psephotus haematonotus* (Gould) 1837
Distribution: Map 92.

RECOGNITION: *green foreparts of male, with red rump and yellow patch on belly; female lacks red on rump and is browner.*

DESCRIPTION: 25cm, with tail 15cm. Sexes different. *Male:* whole head and breast pale blue-green; back olive-green; rump red; centre of belly yellow; vent and under tail coverts white; inner wing pale blue-green with a patch of yellow on shoulders; flight feathers violet-blue tipped with black; upper tail coverts and centre of tail green, sides blue-green broadly tipped with creamy-white; bill blue-grey, eyes brown; legs grey. *Female:* foreparts olive-brown, blotched with creamy-white on face and breast; rump green; very little yellow in centre of belly.

HABITAT: open woodlands and dry country with scattered timber, even where open water is very scarce. HABITS: arboreal but usually feeds on ground; gregarious, usually flocks of ten to twenty, but sometimes much larger where species common; sedentary; flight strong and direct, low flutter and glide or high and steady. BREEDING: August–December mainly, but in some areas variable depending on rains; nests in holes in trees, stumps and fence posts; four to seven white eggs. VOICE: shrill whistle in flight, also melodious warble. FOOD: seeds mainly.

STATUS: common. TAXONOMY: endemic species.

MULGA PARROT GROUP

It seems that a group of adjacent species distributed round the continent, except in the north-west, belong to a recent common stock. All are basically similar in colour pattern although colours in the pattern differ. They are the Mulga, which is common and widespread south of the tropic, the Paradise, now probably extinct but at one time common in southeast Queensland, the Golden-shouldered in Cape York, perhaps heading for the same fate, and the Hooded in the northern part of Northern Territory. Some regard the last two as races of one species but they have distinct differences and are widely separated and it is more practical to list them here as species. Evidence of close affinity between Mulga and Paradise is found in hybrid specimens. Among a number of similarities the Paradise, Golden-shouldered and Hooded share the same habit of using holes in termite mounds as nesting sites, hence the name 'ant-hill parrots'; but this is not necessarily proof of common origin for the habit is not unique to these parrots.

353 **MULGA PARROT** *Psephotus varius* Clark 1910   Pl 10

Distribution: Map 93.

RECOGNITION: *blue-green head with yellow forehead, yellow patch on shoulder and reddish-orange belly; female has mainly brownish shades.*

DESCRIPTION: 28–30cm, with tail 18cm. Sexes different. *Male:* forehead orange-yellow; crown, face and breast blue-green; patch of reddish-brown on nape; back olive-green; rump barred blue-green, greenish-yellow and black; belly varying amounts of lemon-yellow and reddish-orange; centre of wing pale emerald-green and violet-blue, tips black; under shoulders violet-blue; upper tail coverts greenish-yellow with centre patch of reddish-brown; centre of tail blue-green above, black below, sides pale blue-green and violet broadly tipped with violet-white; bill blue-grey with black tip; eyes brown; legs grey. *Female:* forehead dull yellow; head and upperparts olive-brown; brown patches on nape, centre of shoulders and centre of upper tail coverts; throat and breast grey-brown; belly greenish-yellow.

HABITAT: dry to arid savannas with scanty timber of various kinds. HABITS: arboreal but feeds mainly on ground; solitary, pairs or family parties—not in flocks except sometimes fortuitously when feeding; sedentary, but nomadic in drought conditions; flight swift and undulating and close to ground. BREEDING: variable but mainly July–December; nests in holes in trees, a bed of wood dust; four to six white eggs. VOICE: a loud whistling 'jeep', repeated. FOOD: various seeds and other vegetable material, also grubs.

STATUS: common. TAXONOMY: endemic species.

354 PARADISE PARROT *Psephotus pulcherrimus* (Gould) 1845 Pl 10

Distribution: Map 93. [*Note:* the area shown is where the species is known to have occurred; currently there do not appear to be any certain records.]

RECOGNITION: *black crown with red forehead and blue-green face; female mainly brown and grey.*

DESCRIPTION: 28–30cm, with tail 18cm. Sexes different. *Male:* forehead red; crown to nape sooty black; face, side of neck and breast blue-green; throat and foreneck bright green; back grey-brown; rump blue-green; shoulders and belly red; flight feathers black tinged with violet-blue; centre of tail olive-blue and dull violet above, black below, sides light violet-blue broadly tipped with creamy-white; bill blue-grey; eyes brown; legs grey-brown. *Female:* red patch on shoulder much smaller; face, throat and breast brownish-yellow; belly pale blue with small central patch of dull red.

HABITAT: woodlands with termite mounds, especially along valleys. HABITS: arboreal but feeds mainly on ground; in pairs or family parties, probably not flocking; probably sedentary; flight swift, undulating and low. BREEDING: period uncertain; nests in holes, in termite mounds, banks and trees; four to five white eggs. VOICE: soft sharp plaintive pipe. FOOD: seeds, mainly grasses.

STATUS: rare, probably extinct. TAXONOMY: endemic species.

355 GOLDEN-SHOULDERED PARROT *Psephotus chrysopterygius* Gould 1857

Distribution: Map 93.

RECOGNITION: *black crown with yellow forehead and blue-green face, yellow shoulder patch; female mainly shades of brown and no yellow on shoulders.*

DESCRIPTION: 25cm, with tail 15cm. Sexes different. *Male:* forehead yellow; crown to nape sooty black; back grey-brown; face, throat, breast, flanks and rump blue-green; belly and under tail coverts white blotched with red; shoulders yellow; flight feathers blackish-brown; centre of tail blue-green above, black below, sides pale blue-green with dull white tips; bill blue-grey; eyes brown; legs grey-brown. *Female:* forehead pale buff; head and body above and below mainly pale greenish-brown, darker on crown and nape; no yellow on shoulders and only a few red blotches on white belly; rump blue-green.

HABITAT: open wooded flats with termite mounds. HABITS: arboreal but feeds mainly on ground; gregarious, in small parties, probably families; sedentary; flight swift with slight undulations. BREEDING: April–September; nests in holes excavated in termite mounds, unlined; four to six white eggs. (Nests are kept clean by larvae of a moth which eats nestling excreta; the moth is found only in such nests and its breeding cycle is geared to parrots—a unique example of symbiosis). VOICE: soft musical whistle, 'joee-joee'. FOOD: mainly grass seeds.

STATUS: apparently rare, but perhaps locally common. TAXONOMY: endemic species perhaps conspecific with Hooded Parrot.

356 HOODED PARROT *Psephotus dissimilis* Collett 1898
Distribution: Map 93.

RECOGNITION: like Golden-shouldered but *forehead sooty black,* uniform with crown and nape, and not yellow; belly blue-green like rest of underparts, only under tail coverts coloured red and white.

HABITAT, etc: mainly similar to Golden-shouldered, except—BREEDING: May–January; five eggs, usually two broods. VOICE: high-pitched, harsh or sharp and rather metallic.

STATUS: uncommon; locally plentiful only around Pine Creek. TAXONOMY: endemic species perhaps conspecific with Golden-shouldered Parrot.

Genus LATHAMUS
The relationships of the endemic Swift Parrot are obscure. It has certain resemblances to the lorikeets, like brush tongue and honeyeating habits but such features are regarded as superficial. Basically it seems to have most affinity with the platycercus-psephotus group, either an offshoot from a primitive common source or recently adapted.

357 SWIFT PARROT *Lathamus discolor* (White) 1790   Pl 9
Distribution: Map 94.

RECOGNITION: *greenish, long thin tail red at base on underside, red on face and throat; voice soft metallic 'clink'.*

DESCRIPTION: 25cm, with sharp-pointed tail 13cm. Sexes alike but female has duller colours. Upperparts dark green; underparts yellowish-green, sometimes splashed with red; forehead, throat and foreneck red; lores yellow, crown, face and edge of wing purplish-blue; shoulders and underwing red; flight feathers black edged with yellow; base of undertail red; bill pinkish-brown; eyes reddish-brown; legs grey-brown.

HABITAT: forests and woodlands, sometimes city parks and suburban trees. HABITS: arboreal, but also frequents low vegetation in open country; gregarious, even when breeding, and sometimes migrating in large flocks; migratory between Tasmanian breeding area (August–April) and mainland (March–September), occurrence in mainland localities sometimes regular and sometimes sporadic and irruptive. BREEDING: October–January; nests in holes in trees at about 7–20m; four to five eggs. VOICE: rapid metallic 'clink' uttered in flight. FOOD: mainly honey, but also insects, especially scale insects, berries and seeds.

STATUS: common. TAXONOMY: endemic species and genus.

Family CUCULIDAE
Cuckoos and Coucals
12(127) species: 3 endemic

Distribution: worldwide.

TWO MAIN SUBDIVISIONS OF this family are represented in Australia, the parasitic cuckoos, and the coucals which build nests and rear young in the orthodox way. There are twelve parasitic cuckoos out of nearly fifty widespread throughout the old world. In appearance they are typically long and slender with long and often graduated tails, short legs with zygodactylous toes (outer toe reversible so that it grips behind instead of in front), bills fairly stout and slightly downcurved, plumages mainly greys and browns, frequently with barred underparts, like some birds of prey, and immature plumages sometimes resembling those of the species they parasitise. They are largely insectivorous with a notable liking for hairy caterpillars. They are mainly solitary and often migratory, frequently travelling great distances and posing problems to behaviourists who wonder how young cuckoos find the migration routes traversed by their parents some weeks in advance. But their most notorious feature is the curious habit of making use of other species to rear their offspring. They have, with varying degrees of success, transferred all domestic duties to foster parents at the cost of the fosterer's own eggs and nestlings. The parasitic cuckoos are not the only birds which have discovered this curious evolutionary avenue (incidentally with its potential dead end as survival depends on the continued existence of the species they persecute) nor are all members of the cuckoo family parasitic. The coucals are not. This large section of some twenty-seven old world species is represented in Australia only by the Pheasant Coucal. Coucals have the slender shape of the cuckoos, but with larger tails which give them a heavy and clumsy appearance; they are reluctant fliers. Bills are thick and rather like those of megapodes or domestic fowls. They live mainly in dense ground vegetation and thickets and have a characteristic deep resonant whooping call, which is rather disconcerting when heard for the first time at close quarters.

Key to CUCULIDAE

Large: 40–60cm

1 Wholly black .... (♂)   Koel..................... No 367
   or head mainly black, back brown-spotted white (♀)

2 Mainly black with brown wings *or* upperparts cinnamon brown, streaked white ....   Pheasant Coucal .... No 369

3 Whitish head and underparts, black band near tip of tail ....   Channelbill Cuckoo .... No 368

Medium: 23–30cm

4 Belly boldly barred black ....   Oriental Cuckoo .... No 359

5 Belly plain   6–10

6 Underparts pale grey ....   Pallid Cuckoo .... No 358

7 Underparts rich rufous ....   Chestnut-breasted Cuckoo.. No 362

8 Underparts cinnamon buff   9–10

358 PALLID CUCKOO *Cuculus pallidus* (Latham) 1801   Fig p 249

Distribution: throughout.

RECOGNITION: *slim and grey, long broad tail, plain underparts.*

DESCRIPTION: 30cm, with broad tail 15cm. Sexes different. *Male:* upperparts dark grey with small white patches on nape and near angle of shoulder; forehead, throat and breast pale grey shading to white on vent and under tail coverts; flight and tail feathers dark brownish-grey, inner web of flight feathers barred white, tail feathers notched and barred white; bill black; eyes brown, eyelid bright yellow; legs olive. *Female:* streaked and blotched with cinnamon brown on nape, back and shoulders. *Immature:* mainly brown variously mottled and blotched with white and black.

HABITAT: various kinds of woodland. HABITS: sits in exposed situations and swoops to ground to feed; solitary but usually gathers in flocks before migrating; movements not well known and apparently rather complex; present in numbers in different areas at different times, e.g. in southwest May–November; in southeast September–January; in Northern Territory, September-March in north and January–September in south; in flight might easily be mistaken for a hawk. BREEDING: variable, see under 'movements' above; eggs variable but often pinkish and lightly spotted. VOICE: a succession of rapid notes beginning low and ending high (♂), harsh 'kyeer' (♀). FOOD: grasshoppers and beetles.

STATUS: fairly common. TAXONOMY: endemic species.

359 ORIENTAL CUCKOO *Cuculus saturatus* Blyth 1843   Fig p 243

Distribution: Map 95.

RECOGNITION: like Pallid Cuckoo but sexes alike; *breast and belly buffy-white boldly barred dark brown;* dark grey upperparts have bluish tinge; face and throat pale grey; no white spot on nape. (There is an uncommon profusely barred brown adult phase.) *Immature:* upperparts boldly barred dark brown and cinnamon brown; underparts white barred dark brown.

HABITAT: forests and woodlands. HABITS: mainly in trees but sometimes feeds on ground, often perches on limbs close to trunk; solitary or in small scattered parties; migratory; swift gliding flight and readily mistaken for a hawk. VOICE: harsh 'gaak-gaak-gak-ak-ak-ak'. FOOD: caterpillars, cicadas and other insects.

STATUS: uncommon; non-breeding visitor from northern Asia; November–April.

Genus CACOMANTIS

A group of five species belonging to the Oriental and Australasian regions of which three occur in Australia, none being endemic. They are about 23-30cm in length with only tails barred or notched with white. Underparts are sometimes richly coloured.

360 FANTAILED CUCKOO *Cacomantis pyrrophanus* (Vieillot) 1817   Pl 11
Distribution: Map 96.
RECOGNITION; *plain dark blue-grey above and pale brown below, bright yellow eyering.*
DESCRIPTION: 25cm, with broad tail 15cm. Sexes alike. Upperparts dark bluish-grey with brownish wings; white patch near angle of shoulder; chin pale grey; throat, breast and belly shades of cinnamon brown; under tail coverts cinnamon; tail purplish-black notched and barred with white; broad white streak on underside of flight feathers; bill black, base brownish; eyes brown; legs olive-brown, soles of feet bright yellow. *Immature:* upperparts dark olive-brown scalloped with rufous; underparts mottled olive-brown and pale grey and tinged with buff.
HABITAT: forests and woodlands. HABITS: mainly arboreal but often feeds on ground, frequently perches on exposed boughs; solitary; sedentary, nomadic and migratory, movements apparently rather complex, numbers increasing and decreasing in different areas at different times but usually some birds remaining; fans and tilts tail on alighting. BREEDING: variable but mainly August–December in south, recorded other times elsewhere; usually parasitises species with domed nest like those of scrub wrens and heath wrens, eggs usually placed by means of bill, perhaps foot; eggs dull white finely speckled and blotched with shades of brown and purple. VOICE: soft rapid trill in descending scale, also single whistle. FOOD: caterpillars and other insects.
STATUS: common. TAXONOMY: endemic breeding race *(prionurus)* extending to Aru Is of species ranging to New Guinea and New Caledonia.

361 BRUSH CUCKOO *Cacomantis variolosus* (Vig. & Horsf.) 1826
Distribution: Map 97.
RECOGNITION: *pale bluish-grey head, brownish back, light brown below, grey eyering.*
DESCRIPTION: 23cm, with tail 11cm. Sexes alike. Head and hind neck pale bluish-grey; remainder of upperparts grey-brown with slight bronze-green sheen; white patch near angle of wing; underparts pale shades of cinnamon brown; broad streak of buffy-white on under side of flight feathers; tail dark grey-brown notched with white; bill black, base olive; eyes chestnut, eyering grey; legs greyish-olive. *Immature:* upperparts barred and streaked dark brown and cinnamon brown; underparts white barred with blackish-brown.
VARIATION: southern birds darker (race *variolosus*); northern birds paler (race *dumetorum*).
HABITAT: wet forests and mangroves. HABITS: arboreal but sometimes feeds on ground; solitary; sedentary and migratory, in south present September–March. BREEDING: variable, recorded most months but mainly September–December in south; usually parasitises birds with open nests, frequently Leaden and Satin Flycatchers; egg dull white lightly spotted with brown. VOICE: series of mournful whistling notes on a descending scale. FOOD: caterpillars and other insects.
STATUS: fairly common. TAXONOMY: endemic breeding races, migrating to New Guinea, of species ranging to Malaysia and Solomon Is.

362 CHESTNUT-BREASTED CUCKOO *Cacomantis castaneiventris* (Gould) 1867
Distribution: Map 98.

RECOGNITION: *bluish-black above, rich rufous below, bright yellow legs.*

DESCRIPTION: 23cm, with broad tail 11cm. Sexes alike. Face and upperparts very dark glossy blue-grey; underparts cinnamon rufous; whitish patch near angle of shoulders; broad white streak on underwing; tail tipped and sparsely notched with white; bill black, base of lower mandible yellow-brown, eyes yellow-brown, eyelids red (♂) yellow (♀); legs bright yellow. *Immature:* not barred; upperparts plain sepia; underparts mottled cinnamon brown and brownish-grey, whitish on lower belly.

HABITAT: rain forests. HABITS: little known except that it keeps to rain forests. BREEDING: little known. VOICE: trilling call. FOOD: insects.

STATUS: not known. TAXONOMY: endemic race *(castaneiventris)* of Papuan species.

Genus CHRYSOCOCCYX

Current opinion places all glossy cuckoos in this one genus, including the Australian Black-eared Cuckoo which is not glossy but similar in most other respects; it is sometimes listed in a separate genus *Misocalius*. There are about twelve species, four in Australia, the number depending on which forms are accepted as species. They range widely over the southern parts of the old world. They are small, under 18cm, with varying amounts of iridescent bronze and green on the upperparts and, in the Indo-Australian group, boldly barred on the underparts. Migratory habits are variable, some species or races of species travelling long distances and others being more or less sedentary.

363 LITTLE BRONZE CUCKOO *Chrysococcyx malayanus* (Raffles) 1822
Distribution: Map 99.

RECOGNITION: *upperparts uniform glossy bronze-green, male has bright red eye and eyering.*

DESCRIPTION: 15cm, with broad tail about half. Sexes alike except for eye colour. Upperparts glossy bronze-green, extending to below eye and slightly darker on crown, white eyebrow; underparts white boldly barred glossy bronze-green; base of flight feathers fawn making broad band on underwing; tail feathers have varying amounts of cinnamon rufous, outermost pair with large spots partly black and partly white, others tipped black and white; bill black; eyes and eyering bright red (♂), brown (♀); legs bluish-black.

VARIATION: east of Normanton, some *rufous on all tail feathers,* also on edges of wing and tail coverts and tinge on breast (race *russatus*); west of Normanton, rufous only on base of three tail feathers next to outermost (race *minutillus*).

HABITAT: forests and mangroves. HABITS: arboreal; solitary; sedentary or partly migratory (some records of non-breeding visitors to extralimital northern islands). BREEDING: October–March; hosts mainly *Gerygone* warblers; eggs plain olive-green or olive-brown. VOICE: rapid high-pitched trill. FOOD: insects, especially caterpillars.

STATUS: common. TAXONOMY: endemic race *(minutillus)* and extralimital race *(russatus)* extending to New Guinea of species ranging to Borneo and Malaysia. (Some authorities regard these forms as species.)

364 GOLDEN BRONZE CUCKOO *Chrysococcyx lucidus* (Gmelin) 1788   Pl 11
Distribution: Map 100.

RECOGNITION: *purple-bronze crown and hind neck contrasting with bronze-green back and shoulders, barred face; unbroken bars on belly.*

DESCRIPTION: 18cm, with broad tail about half. Sexes alike. Crown and hind neck purple-bronze; remainder of upperparts mottled glossy green and bronze; forehead, face and underparts white boldly barred glossy bronze-green; outermost tail feather mainly black with large white spots and tinged with rufous, tip white, much rufous on next to outermost tail feather; bill black; eyes pale fawn; legs dark grey.

VARIATION: resident breeding form as described (race *plagosus*); migrant from New Zealand, greenish sheen on crown and hind neck, pure white spots and bars on outermost tail feather, little or no rufous on next to outermost feather (race *lucidus*).

HABITAT: forests and woodlands. HABITS: arboreal; solitary but sometimes in small scattered flocks of about ten birds; migratory, moves north after breeding, some birds reaching Sumba Is, New Guinea and Solomon Is. BREEDING: August–December; hosts mainly *Gerygone* and *Rhipidura* species; eggs plain olive-green or olive-bronze. VOICE: high pitched repeated 'fwee' or 'pee' ending in drawn out 'pee-er'. FOOD: caterpillars and other insects.

STATUS: *plagosus*—common; breeds in south, non-breeding visitor and passage migrant elsewhere. *lucidus*—rare; non-breeding visitor and passage migrant from New Zealand on east coast; between February and September. TAXONOMY: races of species widely distributed in Papuan region.

365 HORSFIELD BRONZE CUCKOO
Chrysococcyx basalis (Horsfield) 1821   Pl 11
Distribution: throughout.

RECOGNITION: *throat streaked (not barred), broad whitish streak above eye extending to side of neck; broken bars on belly.*

DESCRIPTION: 18cm, with broad tail nearly half. Sexes alike. Forehead to hind neck dark fawn brown with slight bronze sheen; remainder of upperparts glossy bronze-green; broad whitish streak above eye extending to side of neck and dark streak through eye; remainder of face and underparts pale buff streaked on throat and barred on breast and flanks with bronze, bars usually incomplete in centre of belly; broad pale cinnamon streak on underwing; outermost tail feather barred black and white, remainder dark rufous at base, except central pair; bill black; eyes greenish-yellow; legs dark blue-grey.

HABITAT: various kinds of savanna. HABITS: arboreal, often sits on bare branch or twig high up in bush or tree; solitary; largely migratory, especially southern breeding populations most of which leave for north in March and return south in September; movements in relation to breeding in northern populations are not clearly defined. BREEDING: August–February; hosts usually *Malurus* species, but also *Acanthiza* and *Petroica*, and many others occasionally; eggs pinkish-white, evenly speckled reddish-brown (not zoned as in *Malurus* host). VOICE: high-pitched leisurely 'pee-er' or 'sphew' repeated in descending scale. FOOD: caterpillars and other insects, berries also recorded.

STATUS: common. TAXONOMY: endemic breeding species migrating to Malaysia and Borneo.

366 BLACK-EARED CUCKOO *Chrysococcyx osculans* (Gould) 1847   Pl 11
Distribution: throughout except southeast coastal districts, Tasmania and extreme southwest.

RECOGNITION: *plain greyish above and whitish below with black patch behind eye and white eyebrow.*

DESCRIPTION: 18cm, with broad tail about half. Sexes alike. Upperparts brownish-grey, greyer on forehead and crown and much paler on rump; broad white streak above eye and large black patch behind eye; throat to breast and underwing pale cinnamon-buff; chin and belly white; tail blackish tipped white, inner web of outer feather barred dull white; bill black; eyes dark brown; legs bluish-black.

HABITAT: drier kinds of woodland, including mallee and mulga. HABITS: arboreal; solitary or in small scattered parties; largely migratory, most southern populations at least move north, but elsewhere movement pattern in relation to breeding not clear. BREEDING: August–December, in south at least, but records in other months in north; hosts mainly Speckled Warbler and Redthroat; eggs dark blood red. VOICE: plaintive whistle 'peer' repeated or 'pee-o-wit-pee-o-weer'. FOOD: caterpillars and beetles.

STATUS: uncommon. TAXONOMY: endemic breeding species with some migration to Aru Is, Moluccas, etc.

Genus EUDYNAMYS

A large group of forms ranging from India to New Zealand are considered to belong to a single species, the Koel, but there is not much information about some, especially their breeding ranges, and it may be that there are several valid species. The two Australian races are sometimes listed as a separate species. The Koel is sexually dimorphic; it is large with a long broad tail, boldly barred in the female; the call is very distinctive.

367 KOEL *Eudynamys scolopacea* Linnaeus 1758   Pl 24
Distribution: Map 101.

RECOGNITION: *male glossy black with bright red eyes; female mainly brown with white speckles above and long broad tail with bold white bars.*

DESCRIPTION: 40cm, with broad tail 20cm; fairly thick bill. Sexes different. *Male:* glossy blue-black; bill olive-green; eyes red; legs bluish-olive. *Female:* forehead to nape and face glossy blue-black, sometimes streaked with rufous; remainder of upperparts bronze-brown boldly spotted with white; streak below eye and underparts pale cinnamon-buff with thin broken bars of bronze-brown; tail brown, boldly barred with white.

VARIATION: east of Normanton, female has crown and lower face streaked with buff (race *cyanocephalus*); west of Normanton, no buff on crown or face (race *subcyanocephalus*).

HABITAT: forests and thick woodlands, often timbered areas of city suburbs. HABITS: arboreal; solitary; migratory. BREEDING: November–February; hosts mainly friarbirds and other large honeyeaters; eggs pinkish-red spotted and streaked with purplish-red. VOICE: loud harsh 'koo-eel' and 'wurra-wurra'. FOOD: mainly fruit, also some insects.

STATUS: common; breeding visitor, September–April, migrating to islands north of Australia. TAXONOMY: races of very variable species extending to India, China and New Zealand.

Genus SCYTHROPS

The Channelbill has some features which suggest fairly close affinity with the Koel, but it has others, like massive channelled bill, which are unique and it is segregated in a genus of its

Pallid Cuckoo (358)

Pheasant Coucal (369)

Channelbill Cuckoo (368)

Koel (367) *male*

CUCULIDAE HEADS

own. It does not have a very extensive range, only to about the Celebes and New Guinea and associated islands.

368 CHANNELBILL CUCKOO *Scythrops novaehollandiae* Latham 1790

Distribution: Map 102.

RECOGNITION: *whitish head and massive pale bill, long broad tail with black subterminal band.*

DESCRIPTION: 60cm, with broad tail 25cm; massive bill 6cm with deep groove in upper mandible. Sexes alike. Head and neck ash grey; remainder of upperparts olive-grey boldly scalloped with blackish-brown; remainder of underparts whitish with some dark bars on flanks; tail has broad subterminal black band and broad white tip, remainder grey with inner webs on under side toothed black and white; bill pale grey-brown; eyes and bare skin around eye bright scarlet; legs bluish-grey.

HABITAT: forests and woodlands. HABITS: arboreal, usually keeps high up in tree canopies; solitary but sometimes gregarious when not breeding, often in flocks of up to fifty or so; migratory, arrives about time of northern 'wet' and popularly called 'rain bird' or 'storm bird'. BREEDING: October–January; hosts mainly currawongs, also crows and magpies; eggs pinkish-buff blotched with reddish-brown, usually a close match with those of host species. VOICE: loud raucous 'ee-awk ee-awk ca-ca-ca'. FOOD: fruit, berries, insects.

STATUS: fairly common; breeding visitor, September–March, migrating to islands north of mainland. TAXONOMY: species ranging to New Guinea, Celebes, etc.

Genus CENTROPUS

The only genus in a main subdivision of the cuckoo family. It consists of some twenty-seven species widely distributed throughout Africa, India, Malaysia and Australasia, only one of which reaches Australia. Coucals are distinguished by their non-parasitic habits; they build nests and rear their own young. All are very similar in appearance; they are up to about 60cm in length, the larger part of which is a broad tail which seems to be an encumbrance when the bird is off the ground. They flutter clumsily on short flights or when scrambling among bushes, but keep mainly to the ground in dense vegetation. Wings are short and rounded and bills short and thick.

369 PHEASANT COUCAL *Centropus phasiainus* (Latham) 1801   Fig p 249
Distribution: Map 103.

RECOGNITION: *very long broad tail, black body and brown wings, or wholly brown; on ground or in shrubbery.*

DESCRIPTION: 60cm, of which broad tail is more than half; shafts of feathers are thick and stiff making plumage hard and spiky. Sexes alike. *Breeding:* head and body black; wings mainly buff, mottled with brown on outer webs and deep pinkish-brown barred with black on inner webs; shafts of shoulder feathers whitish; tail mainly black, barred with speckled grey; bill black; eyes red; legs bluish-black. *Non-breeding:* crown to upper back dark cinnamon brown, streaked with white shafts; face and side of neck streaked white and brown; underparts mainly pale buff shading to blackish on belly; tail barred and speckled with buff and brown; bill pale brownish; eyes dark brown; legs dark blue-grey. (Note: plumage is variable because transitions from one phase to the other are very gradual.) HABITAT: various kinds of thicket vegetation in damp localities. HABITS: mainly terrestrial, seldom flies except when forced to, flight very laboured flutter and glide, sometimes scrambles about in bushes and lower parts of trees, or stands on low snags and fence posts; solitary; sedentary. BREEDING: variable, but mainly between August and February; nests on or near ground in tufts of grass, made of short pieces of rush and lined with fresh leaves, grass pulled over to form a hood; four eggs, dull white. VOICE: a run of loud deep booming notes consisting of 'hoop' or 'whoop' and 'hoo' varying in speed and pitch, higher in male and lower in female. FOOD: insects and small animals.

STATUS: common. TAXONOMY: species extending to New Guinea.

OWLS

OWLS ARE A LARGE and distinct group of raptors which, with a few exceptions, hunt prey at night. Soft plumages, especially in the barn owls, make wingbeats silent—hence poetic references to "ghostly flight". Eyes are large to make maximum use of dim light during nocturnal movements, and these and their associated large optic lobes give rise to heads of unusual size. Eyes are directed forward, as in man, a feature which together with the daylight habit of immobile silent staring gives an appearance popularly associated with deep thinking and wisdom. More importantly, forward vision deprives owls of the all round vision which most birds have, but this is compensated by a flexible neck which permits the head to be swivelled so that birds may face over their backs. The large eyes are set in feather discs which form 'masks' or 'ruffs' of variable distinctness and sometimes give the face a flattened appearance. Bills are short and deeply hooked and partly concealed in facial feathers. Nostrils open in a soft cere at the base of the bill. The outer toe is reversible (zygodactylous) although it is usually placed sideways rather than behind. Claws are large and powerful, and tails are short. Plumages are mostly in camouflage colours and patterns, a useful protective adaptation, for owls are notoriously prone to persecution by other, and often much smaller birds; a screaming mob of Noisy Miners baiting a Boobook Owl is a common disturbance in some city suburbs. There is a wide range of sizes, the endemic Powerful Owl of Australia being one of the largest at about 60cm in length. Nests are in holes in trees, often borrowed from other species, or in holes among rocks. Eggs are invariably white. Owls are usually divided into two families, a small group, of one genus, the barn owls, and a large group of all the others. Some authorities claim that there is little basic difference to separate the two families but at least they are easily distinguished by outward appearance.

Key to OWL FAMILIES

1 Eye discs nearly meet on forehead .... TYTONIDAE .... Page 251
2 Eye discs separated by broad forehead .... STRIGIDAE .... Page 253

Barn Owl (370)

Boobook Owl (374)

Family TYTONIDAE

Barn Owls

4(10) species

Distribution: worldwide.

THE FEW SPECIES OF this family belong to one genus of which the Barn Owl proper, *Tyto alba,* in numerous racial forms, is found over much of the world. Greatest divergence into species occurs in the Australasian region. A feature of all owls is the feathers around the eye which radiate out in rough semblance of a disc. In the barn owls the discs are most clearly defined; they have dark margins which meet on the chin and come close together on the forehead, the two sections thus forming a heart-shaped mask over the whole face. Other features are long legs and a soft silky plumage which is neither barred nor streaked on the body.

Key to TYTONIDAE

1 Blackish-brown, wings and tail not barred .... Sooty Owl .... No 372
2 Some light cinnamon in plumage, wings and tail barred 3-6

3 Back not extensively vermiculated, tarsus at least 8cm .... Grass Owl .... No 373
4 Back extensively vermiculated, tarsus about 5cm 5-6

5 Tarsus feathered .... Masked Owl ...... No 371
6 Tarsus almost bare .... Barn Owl .... No 370

370 BARN OWL *Tyto alba* (Scopoli) 1769 Fig p 251

Distribution: throughout.

RECOGNITION: *tarsus nearly bare, usually much cinnamon on upperparts, back extensively vermiculated.*

DESCRIPTION: 33–36cm. Sexes alike. Face mask silky white circled by narrow band in shades of dark brown; dark brown patch in front of eye; upperparts mottled light cinnamon brown and grey with much black vermiculation and light and dark grey speckling (sometimes the brown pigment is partly or almost entirely absent and plumage is nearly pure grey); wings and tail barred with blackish-brown; underparts silky white sparsely spotted with dark grey; bill dull white; eyes black; toes pale grey.

HABITAT: most kinds, but least common in heavily timbered areas. HABITS: arboreal and terrestrial; solitary, probably sedentary; nocturnal: roosts in daytime in concealed places, holes in trees, among rocks and caves or in buildings; erratic fluttering flight low over ground. BREEDING: April–October; nests in deep hollows, in trees, among rocks, in caves, a bed of wood dust or other debris; three to six white eggs. VOICE; loud harsh screech, but calls infrequently. FOOD: small animals.

STATUS: common. TAXONOMY: race *(delicatula)*, extending to Solomon Is, of nearly world-wide variable species.

371 MASKED OWL *Tyto novaehollandiae* (Stephens) 1826

Distribution: Map 104.

RECOGNITION: *very like Barn Owl but larger and tarsus feathered, also plumage very variable.*

DESCRIPTION: 38–40cm. Sexes alike, but female distinctly larger. Plumage variable; face mask white to brownish-grey edged with dark brown; upperparts generally shades of brown and grey speckled with rather diffuse pale grey spots; wings and tail barred; underparts varying from near silky white with few dark spots to cinnamon brown with numerous brown and pale grey spots; bill white; eyes brown; toes dull white.

VARIATION: does not seem to be clearly defined geographically; about five races are currently recognised, some being darker, as in Tasmania (race *castanops*) and other paler, as in the north (race *kimberli*).

HABITAT: mainly forests and savanna woodlands. HABITS: arboreal, but sometimes among rocks and in caves; solitary; sedentary; nocturnal, roosts in daytime in concealed places. BREEDING: apparently variable, mostly between March and October; nests in holes; usually two white eggs. VOICE: loud unpleasant squawk or screech, like Barn Owl but lower pitched. FOOD: small animals and insects, especially grasshoppers.

STATUS: apparently uncommon. TAXONOMY: variable species extending to New Guinea and some adjacent islands.

372 SOOTY OWL *Tyto tenebricosa* (Gould) 1845

Distribution: Map 105.

RECOGNITION: *No bars on wings or tail, dark brownish-grey; restricted to some eastern forests.*

DESCRIPTION: 33–40cm. Sexes alike. Face mask pale grey-brown with blackish margin, blackish around eyes; upperparts dark brownish-grey speckled with white and pale grey;

underparts mottled in shades of brownish-grey and buff and diffusely speckled with pale grey; bill pale brown; eyes dark brown; toes brown.

VARIATION: southern population larger and darker with small white spots (race *tenebricosa*); northern population smaller, paler and with larger white spots (race *multipunctata*).

HABITAT: forests. HABITS: not well known; arboreal and apparently solitary and sedentary; nocturnal, roosts in daytime in hollows and dense vegetation. BREEDING: variable, January–September; nests in holes; three white eggs. VOICE: loud whistling screech. FOOD: small animals and insects.

STATUS: rare. TAXONOMY: endemic races of species extending to New Guinea.

373 GRASS OWL *Tyto longimembris* (Jerdon) 1839 Pl 11

Distribution: scattered records throughout.

RECOGNITION: *very like Barn Owl but upperparts mottled blackish-brown, tarsus at least 8cm and almost bare.*

DESCRIPTION: 33–36cm. Sexes alike. Face mask whitish with dusky patch in front of eye and blackish margin; upper parts mottled sepia, or dark brown, and cinnamon brown with scattered whitish spots and very little vermiculation; wings and tail barred, tail conspicuously whitish or pinkish-cinnamon with narrow dark brown bars; underparts cinnamon white speckled with dark grey; bill buffy-yellow; eyes blue-black; legs and toes yellowish-brown.

HABITAT: grasslands. HABITS: terrestrial; solitary, but some records of several birds in one small area (probably depending on food supply); apparently sedentary; nocturnal, roosts during daytime in grass clumps. BREEDING: few data, but at least May to July; nests on ground under grass tussocks, lined with grass; four white eggs. VOICE: no record. FOOD: small animals.

STATUS: apparently rare, but probably commoner than scattered records show. TAXONOMY: race *(longimembris)* extending to India of variable species sometimes united with African grass owls.

Family STRIGIDAE

Owls

4(120) species: 1 endemic

Distribution: worldwide.

THE FOUR SPECIES OF this large family which occur in Australia belong to the same genus, *Ninox,* a group of sixteen species ranging from India to Japan and New Zealand. Owls of this family are readily distinguished from the barn owls by the pattern of the face. The feather discs round each eye are smaller and widely separated on the forehead. They do not form a large mask or ruff covering the whole face; faces are more hawk-like in appearance. In the Australian species the body plumage is boldly barred or streaked or marked with chevrons, as in the Powerful Owl.

Key to STRIGIDAE

374 BOOBOOK OWL *Ninox novaeseelandiae* (Gmelin) 1788   Pl 11   Fig p 251

Distribution: throughout.

RECOGNITION: *boldly streaked underparts, like Barking Owl, but little more than 30cm in length, area round eye very dark and upperparts usually in shades of warm brown.*

DESCRIPTION: 30–35cm. Sexes alike. Area around eye blackish-brown; upperparts shades of brown, from dark chestnut to light brown, sometimes plain or mottled with white spots of varying distinctness, especially on shoulders; throat whitish; breast and belly streaked with shades of brown and dull white, whitish streaks or large dots, especially on thighs; bill blue-grey, brownish on upperside; eyes greenish-yellow; toes whitish.

VARIATION: seven variants are currently listed of which the three main ones are: east, medium brown with poorly defined white spots (race *boobook*); centre and north, paler with large white spots (race *ocellata*); far west, dark with more rufous underparts (race *rufigaster*).

HABITAT: woodlands of various kinds, or wherever there are trees suitable for nesting and roosting. HABITS: arboreal but takes food from ground; solitary; sedentary; nocturnal. BREEDING: September–November; nests in holes or hollows in trees, a platform of wood dust or shredded bark; two to three white eggs. VOICE: short and rapidly repeated 'mopoke', also a quieter 'por' repeated in rapid succession, and a sharp 'whow-whow'. FOOD: small animals and insects.

STATUS: common. TAXONOMY: very variable species extending to Timor and southern New Guinea.

375 BARKING OWL *Ninox connivens* (Latham) 1801

Distribution: Map 106.

RECOGNITION: *boldly streaked underparts, like Boobook Owl, but nearly 45cm; area around eye pale and upperparts in shades of grey-brown.*

DESCRIPTION: 40–45cm. Sexes alike. Area around eye pale grey-brown; upperparts shades of grey-brown blotched and spotted with white mainly on shoulders and sometimes on collar; throat buffy-white; breast and belly streaked grey-brown and buffy-white; bill blackish; eyes yellow; toes yellow.

VARIATION: southeast and extreme southwest, dark grey-brown (race *connivens*); northwest, rather browner (race *occidentalis*); Cape York, rather smaller and darker (race *peninsularis*).

HABITAT: forests and woodlands, especially riverine forests with nearby grassland and savanna woodland. HABITS: arboreal but takes food on ground, also hawks for insects around tree tops; solitary; sedentary; nocturnal, roosts in daytime in tree foliage. BREEDING: August–October; nests in trees, usually large open hollows and often in tea-trees, lined with finely chopped wood; two to three white eggs. VOICE: loud double 'wuk-wuk', like barking, also loud raucous scream. FOOD: small animals and insects.

STATUS: common. TAXONOMY: variable species extending to New Guinea and Moluccas.

376 RUFOUS OWL *Ninox rufa* (Gould) 1846
Distribution: Map 107.

RECOGNITION: *barred all over, area around eye dark.*

DESCRIPTION: 43–50cm. Sexes alike but male larger. Area around eye dusky; upperparts dark brown, paler on collar and darker on shoulders, with numerous thin bars of buffy-white; underparts barred buffy-white and dull brown, paler on belly; bill pinkish-brown; eyes yellow; toes yellow.

VARIATION: three isolated populations slightly different: northern larger (race *rufa*); north-eastern smaller (race *marginata*); central coastal Queensland darkest (race *queenslandica*).

HABITAT: wet forests. HABITS: little known. BREEDING: recorded July; nests in holes in trees; two to three white eggs. VOICE: said to be like Powerful Owl. FOOD: small animals and insects.

STATUS: rare to uncommon. TAXONOMY: endemic races of species extending to New Guinea and Aru Is.

377 POWERFUL OWL *Ninox strenua* (Gould) 1838
Distribution: Map 107.

RECOGNITION: *large, underparts boldly marked with chevrons.*

DESCRIPTION: 60cm; wingspan 1·25m. Sexes alike. Crown brown streaked with white; remainder of upperparts dark brown boldly barred with pale grey; underparts buffy-white boldly marked with dark buff-brown chevrons; bill blackish-brown; eyes yellow; toes grey.

HABITAT: forests, especially deep forest gullies. HABITS: arboreal but takes ground prey; solitary; sedentary; nocturnal, roosts during daytime in tree hollows or among dense foliage. BREEDING: May–September; nests in hollow limbs or spouts of large forest trees, a bed of wood dust; two to three white eggs. VOICE: loud deep and slowly uttered 'woo-hoo' or 'wouf-wouf', also 'loud and rather terrifying scream ending in low moan'. FOOD: various medium-sized animals and birds.

STATUS: rare to uncommon. TAXONOMY: endemic species.

Tawny Frogmouth (378)

Family PODARGIDAE
Frogmouths
3(12) species: 1 endemic

FROGMOUTHS ARE WELL NAMED for they have very wide flat bills and an enormous gape, giving a head of grotesque appearance for a bird. In other ways they look like large nightjars to which they are closely related at family level. They have similar soft plumages in varied colours and patterns, mottled greys, browns and buffs. They are special-

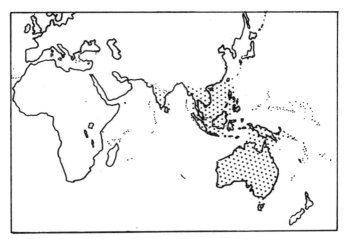

Distribution of PODARGIDAE

ists in camouflage, in behaviour as well as colour. An alarmed frogmouth in daylight freezes in an attitude and position which gives it a close resemblance to part of a tree; sometimes on a dead bough the extended head is easily mistaken for a broken end. Such behaviour is associated, whether as cause or effect is not readily determined, with lethargic habits; they are nocturnal in their movements and then only take short laboured flights to pick up sitting prey. Contrary to popular statements they do not fly with gaping mouths to scoop up insects, as nightjars do. They feed on various small and mainly ground-frequenting animals and insects. Nests are flimsy structures of sticks placed in tree forks, and eggs are white. The family consists of two ill-defined genera only one of which, *Podargus,* occurs in Australia and all three species are present.

Key to PODARGIDAE

Frogmouths are very alike and it is difficult to make a field key to identification which has any real significance. Distribution is a useful guide, but of course species might easily occur outside their present known ranges. The endemic and very variable Tawny Frogmouth ranges widely through-out the whole continent; it is well over 30cm in length and has bright orange-yellow eyes. The Papuan Frogmouth is recorded only from Cape York Peninsula north of about the Flinders River; it is much larger and has bright red eyes. The Marbled Frogmouth has only been recorded at the tip of Cape York; it is similar to the Tawny in having orange eyes but is just over 30cm in length and the plumage is marbled rather than streaked.

378 TAWNY FROGMOUTH *Podargus strigoides* (Latham) 1801   Fig p 255

Distribution: throughout.

RECOGNITION: *looks like part of a broken limb on a bare bough, sits rigid with large head in line with body and sometimes pointing vertical, camouflage patterns in greys and browns usually much streaked, bright orange-yellow eyes.*

DESCRIPTION: 38–40cm; tail rather less than half; tuft of bristle-like feathers at base of bill. Sexes alike. Entire plumage various shades of browns and greys, sometimes almost entirely grey or tawny, generally paler on underparts; liberally marked with black, usually in form of streaks, and marbled with pale patches, especially on shoulders and underparts and often on edges of flight feathers; tail usually barred but not very distinctly; bill dark brown; eyes bright orange-yellow; legs olive-brown.

VARIATION: about six to eight races are currently listed (many more have been described); some are still held to be separate species but they are only doubtfully definable; much variation seems to be associated with colour changes suitable to different environments and size seems to vary independently of colour.

HABITAT: various kinds of woodland or wherever there are a few large trees, doubtfully in rain forest. HABITS: arboreal but often feeds on ground, also may roost on ground, especially when feeding young; solitary; sedentary; nocturnal. BREEDING: August–February; nests in tree forks, broken stumps, on masses of parasitic growth in shady places, a loose structure of small sticks and twigs; two to three white eggs. VOICE: rapidly repeated 'oom'. FOOD: small animals and insects.

STATUS: common. TAXONOMY: very variable endemic species.

379 PAPUAN FROGMOUTH *Podargus papuensis* Quoy & Gaim. 1830   Pl 11
Distribution: Map 108.

RECOGNITION: like Tawny Frogmouth but much larger, 48–56cm, with tail rather more than half; plumage very variable, from pale grey to rufous and very dark, usually more *spotted or marbled with white* and less streaked than the Tawny; *eyes red;* bill greenish-yellow; legs grey.

VARIATION: several colour variants have been described as races but they do not seem to have any geographical significance.

HABITAT: forests and thick woodlands. HABITS: similar to Tawny. BREEDING: October–January; nests in tree forks; one white egg. VOICE: series of 'ooms' repeated for long periods, also rapid succession of 'hoos'. FOOD: apparently mainly insects.

STATUS: probably fairly common. TAXONOMY: species extending to western Papuan islands.

380 MARBLED FROGMOUTH *Podargus ocellatus* Quoy & Gaim. 1830
Distribution: Map 108.

RECOGNITION: like Tawny Frogmouth but *smaller, 33–38cm,* with tail rather less than half; plumage variable but mainly shades of grey-brown and red-brown (the latter said to be usually females) marbled with off-white and with *white spots on shoulders* more conspicuous than in other species; bill pinkish-brown; *eyes orange;* legs yellowish-olive.

HABITAT: forests. HABITS: apparently similar to Tawny Frogmouth. BREEDING: few data, August–October at least; nests on horizontal bough, made of sticks; one white egg. VOICE: no data. FOOD: insects, perhaps small animals.

STATUS: uncertain, recorded at one time as fairly common. TAXONOMY: endemic race (*marmoratus*) of species extending to western Papuan islands and Solomon Is.

Family AEGOTHELIDAE

Owlet Nightjars

1(8) species

THE SMALL GROUP OF owlet nightjars are closely related to the frogmouths and true nightjars but differ sufficiently from both in anatomical and other features to be placed in a separate family. There is only one genus. Owlet nightjars have the same kind of very variable camouflage plumage as their related families. Bills are small, as in nightjars, and partly obscured by forehead feathers. A distinctive habit is using tree hollows for roosting and nesting. They are nocturnal and usually hunt insect prey on the wing. When perched they sit like owls but could not be mistaken for a small owl because of their long barred tails. Possibly because of their resemblance to owls they are readily mobbed by other birds.

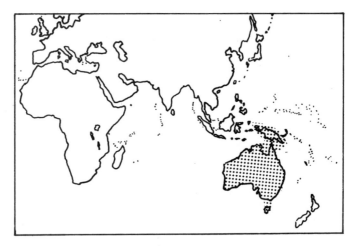

Distribution of AEGOTHELIDAE

381 OWLET NIGHTJAR *Aegotheles cristatus* (White) 1790   Pl 11

Distribution: throughout.

RECOGNITION: *like small owl but with long barred tail; may be seen sitting at mouth of tree hole, from which it may emerge when tree is tapped.*

DESCRIPTION: 23cm, with broad square tail nearly 13cm. Sexes alike. Shades of grey and brown, sometimes very dark or very pale but always with pattern of dark markings on face and crown and narrow dark collar on hind neck; often patches of brown above and behind eye; back and shoulders finely barred; chin and throat white; breast and belly dark, grey or brown, and mottled or finely barred; tail broad with wide bars; bill blackish, pale at base; eyes brown; legs pink.

VARIATION: three races are currently listed but they do not seem to be clearly defined.

HABITAT: forests, including mangroves, and woodlands of various kinds. HABITS: arboreal, usually feeds by catching insects in flight, but sometimes on ground (may be seen on ground in car headlights); solitary; sedentary; nocturnal, roosts in daytime in tree holes, may be seen sitting at entrance or may emerge when tree is tapped. BREEDING: July–December; nests in holes in trees, a bed of gum leaves; three to four white eggs. VOICE: various shrill harsh notes, like 'yeer-yeer'. FOOD: insects.

STATUS: fairly common. TAXONOMY: species extending to southern New Guinea.

Family CAPRIMULGIDAE
Nightjars
3(67) species: 1 endemic

Distribution: nearly worldwide.

THERE ARE TWO MAIN subdivisions of this large family, one in the new world and one in both new and old. They have the same kind of soft and very variable camouflage plumage as frogmouths and owlet nightjars, shades of browns and greys, blotched and vermiculated, spotted and barred. In the nightjars patterns are often relieved with patches of white on throat and neck, and on wings and tips of tail feathers. Tails are long and barred; wings are pointed, as in most birds which catch their food in the air, for it gives greater control when changing direction. Heads are flat and wide with large eyes, an adaptation associated with nocturnal habits; bills are small and weak for they have little function except to provide a rigid margin to a wide gape whose insect-catching capacity is increased by a fringe of long bristles, except in the genus *Eurostopodus*. Nightjars are mainly terrestrial but when they alight in trees they sit or crouch parallel with boughs. Usually they nest and roost on the ground where they merge perfectly with their surroundings. A nightjar even when disturbed and alighting again at no great distance is a difficult object to locate. They are most often seen in car headlights.

Key to CAPRIMULGIDAE

1 Outer tail feathers broadly tipped with white or pale buff . . . . White-tailed Nightjar . . . . . . No 384
2 No white or buff in tail 3–4
3 Broad white bar on wing . . . . Spotted Nightjar . . . . No 382
4 Little or no white on wing . . . . White-throated Nightjar . . . . No 383

Genus EUROSTOPODUS
A group of about ten species in the Indo-Australian region distinguished principally by the absence of bristles at the edge of the mouth.

382 SPOTTED NIGHTJAR *Eurostopodus guttatus* (Vig. & Horsf.) 1826   Pl 11
Distribution: throughout except Tasmania and heavily timbered areas.

RECOGNITION: *broad white bar on wing, plumage light grey marked with black and pale cinnamon brown.*

DESCRIPTION: 30cm, with tail 15–18cm. Sexes alike. Crown mottled light grey and boldly marked with black and cinnamon brown in centre; hind neck brown; remainder of upperparts mottled light brownish-grey, boldly streaked with black and light brown on upper back and scapulars, and spotted and marked with same colours elsewhere; face, throat and breast mottled brown and black with broad white band across throat, and black on lower breast forming bars which extend on to cinnamon brown belly; flight feathers mainly black with broad white central band; tail barred; bill blackish-brown; eyes grey; legs pale grey.

VARIATION: ill-defined, but races recognised are: as described (race *guttatus*); northwest, darker (race *harterti*); Groote Eylandt, buff parts richer in tone (race *gilberti*).

HABITAT: various kinds of dry woodland especially where there is much ground litter. HABITS: mainly terrestrial but sometimes alights or roosts on low boughs or snags; solitary; sedentary and possibly migratory; nocturnal, roosts in daytime under trees or bushes; noiseless erratic flight. BREEDING: variable, mainly April–October in south, October–December in north; nests on ground usually under some kind of shelter like bush or tussock, unformed; one egg, usually greenish-yellow spotted and blotched with shades of dark brown. VOICE: gobbling sound. FOOD: insects.

STATUS: common. TAXONOMY: endemic species, probably migrating to New Guinea and Aru Is.

383 WHITE-THROATED NIGHTJAR
Eurostopodus mystacalis   (Temm. & Laug.) 1826

Distribution: Map 109.

RECOGNITION: *large white patch at side of throat, plumage mainly blackish, only few white spots on wing.*

DESCRIPTION: 35cm, with tail 15–18cm. Sexes alike. Mainly blackish mottled with brownish-grey, especially on shoulders, inner wing and central tail feathers; hind neck indistinctly rufous; throat and breast blackish with large white patches on sides of throat, sometimes joined in centre; belly dark greyish-brown barred with black; wings black spotted with brown and a few small white spots; undertail faintly barred with dark brown; bill black; eyes dark reddish-brown; legs pinkish-brown.

HABITAT: heavily timbered parts especially where there are stony ridges with shrubs and ground litter. HABITS: terrestrial; solitary; migratory, but movements not well known; light noiseless erratic flight. BREEDING: October–February; nests on ground among litter, unformed; one egg, dark cream spotted and blotched with purplish-brown. VOICE: loud 'kook' repeated with increasing speed and ascending scale about a dozen times. FOOD: insects.

STATUS: apparently uncommon. TAXONOMY: endemic breeding race *(mystacalis)*, migrant to New Guinea, of species extending to Solomon Is.

Genus CAPRIMULGUS

This is the main group of nightjars and although it consists of nearly forty species only one has reached Australia. It is distinguished from the previous genus by the presence of a row of long bristles at the edge of the mouth.

384 WHITE-TAILED NIGHTJAR *Caprimulgus macrurus* Horsfield 1821
Distribution: Map 110.

RECOGNITION: *broad white, or pale buff tips to outer tail feathers, 'chop-chop' call.*

DESCRIPTION: 25cm, with tail 12–15cm. Sexes alike. General appearance like Spotted Nightjar with white throat and white patch in wings; differs in having broad white tips to outer tail feathers and dull white band on breast; also fewer light brown markings on upperparts, none on crown and no black and brown streaks on scapulars; brown of belly duller and greyer; bill blackish; eyes and legs dark brown.

HABITAT: various kinds of wet timbered localities. HABITS: mainly terrestrial; solitary; sedentary; nocturnal. BREEDING: August–November; nests on ground, unformed; two eggs, pinkish-cream with cloudy marks of bluish-grey. VOICE: loud sonorous 'chop' repeated, often in groups of three 'like someone tapping the end of a log with a hammer'. FOOD: insects.

STATUS: common. TAXONOMY: race *(yorki)* extending to New Guinea and other islands, of very variable species ranging to India and Philippine Is.

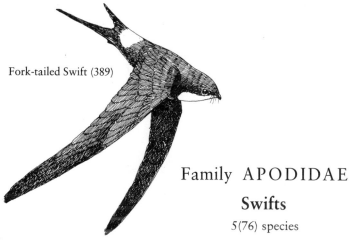

Fork-tailed Swift (389)

Family APODIDAE

Swifts

5(76) species

Distribution: worldwide.

SWIFTS ARE OFTEN POPULARLY grouped with swallows but they are not closely related. Similarity of general appearance is superficial and largely due to the habit they share of catching insect prey on the wing. Swifts can be distinguished from swallows by their longer and narrower wings which have a bowed or sickle-shaped appearance in flight, and they move much faster. Swifts are adapted for long periods of effortless gliding, speedy flight and rapid changes in direction, to catch insects which are scooped into wide gaping mouths. They are so completely conditioned to life in the air that they can perform most functions, even copulating and 'roosting', while flying; some species can remain in the air all night. Even in nesting there is a move away from terrestrial ties for cave swiftlets of the genus *Collocalia* use saliva mostly, rather than vegetable material, in nest construction; the Edible-nest Swiftlet builds nests entirely of saliva—hence their use as human food. In plumage colour swifts are mainly black, sometimes glossed, or sooty brown, often relieved with patches of white, especially on throat, rump or belly. Tails are of varying lengths and shapes, and in certain species, when used as extra support when birds cling to vertical surfaces, strengthened with stiffened shafts which may extend as spines beyond the tip of the tail. Legs are short and weak and serve only to carry the clawed toes used for clinging. The family is poorly represented in Australia. Only the Grey Swiftlet is resident, in northeast Queensland.

Key to APODIDAE

1 Throat dark, under 13cm	3–6	
2 Throat white, over 15cm	7–8	
3 Rump whitish	Grey Swiftlet	No 385
4 Rump uniform with back	5–6	
5 Belly smoke grey	Uniform Swiftlet	No 386
6 Belly white	Glossy Swiftlet	No 387
7 Rump white, tail forked	Fork-tailed Swift	No 389
8 Vent white, tail square	Spine-tailed Swift	No 388

Genus COLLOCALIA

The swiftlets belong to this genus. It consists of a group of about sixteen species of small swifts which range widely throughout southeast Asia and the islands of the Indian and Pacific Oceans. They nest in caves and some have developed the ability to find their way about in dark recesses by means of echolocation: they utter rattling or clicking sounds whose wave reflections from surfaces are translated into distance, in the manner that light waves are analysed by eyes. Swiftlets are also noted for the amount of saliva used in nest construction. Nearly all species include some vegetable material but a few, notably the Edible-nest Swiftlet, make nests entirely of saliva. Swiftlets are not well known largely because specific identification, even in the hand, is very difficult.

Grey Swiftlet (385)

Spine-tailed Swift (388)

385 GREY SWIFTLET   *Collocalia spodiopygia*   (Peale) 1848   Pl 12

Distribution: Map 111.

RECOGNITION: *small with whitish rump (martins have white rumps but are also whitish below and have broad wings).*

DESCRIPTION: 11·5cm; folded wings extend 2·5cm beyond slightly forked tail. Sexes alike. Upperparts brownish-black, blacker and slightly glossed on wings and tail; rump pale grey (whitish at distance) with fine dark streaks; underparts brownish-grey; eyes dark brown; feet blackish.

HABITAT: near suitable nesting caves where flying insects are plentiful, like forest clearings and river gorges. HABITS: in the air except when roosting and nesting in caves; gregarious, usually in small flocks; sedentary; flight swift and erratic; in dark caves utter sounds whose echoes enable them to find their way about. BREEDING: September–February; nests in colonies in caves, bracket shaped and attached to walls and roofs, made of saliva mixed with vegetable material; one white egg. VOICE: utters rattling and clicking sounds in dark caves. FOOD: flying insects. (Note: nests in caves at Chillagoe, north Queensland, differ in shape and arrangement from those at Tully; the two populations may be different races or species.) STATUS: fairly common. TAXONOMY: endemic race *(terraereginae)* of very variable species extending to Fiji and Tonga.

386 UNIFORM SWIFTLET *Collocalia vanikorensis* (Quoy & Gaim.) 1830
Distribution: tip of Cape York.

RECOGNITION: like Grey Swiftlet but *lacks whitish on rump;* in the hand concealed white will be found at base of back feathers.

HABITAT, etc: probably similar to Grey Swiftlet but few Australian data.

STATUS: uncertain; probably non-breeding visitor from New Guinea.

387 GLOSSY SWIFTLET *Collocalia esculenta* (Linnaeus) 1758
Distribution: Cape York to near Mackay.

RECOGNITION: like Grey Swiftlet but smaller, 9cm. *belly white and upperparts glossed bluish-green.*

HABITAT, etc: probably similar to Grey Swiftlet. BREEDING: apparently not breeding in Australia but if it does is unlikely to use dark caves because it is not known to utter echo-location sounds.

STATUS: uncertain; probably non-breeding visitor from New Guinea.

Genus CHAETURA

A group of about twenty species nearly worldwide in distribution. It includes, in the present context, *Hirundapus,* a genus sometimes used for the Spine-tailed Swift, the only species occurring in Australia. It is a non-breeding visitor from the northern hemisphere.

388 SPINE-TAILED SWIFT *Chaetura caudacuta* (Latham) 1801
Distribution: Map 112.

RECOGNITION: *Large with white under tail coverts, short square tail.*

DESCRIPTION: 20cm; folded wings extend 5cm beyond tail; tail short and square with stiff shafts extending as short spines. Sexes alike. Upperparts brownish-black slightly glossed with bluish-green, except for large pale grey brown area in centre of back; patch of white on trailing edge of inner wing; breast and belly brownish black; rear flanks and under tail coverts white.

HABITAT: variable, depending on supply of flying insects and weather conditions. HABITS: usually seen in loose flocks flying at various heights, frequent changes in wing beat. VOICE: apparently silent.

STATUS: common; non-breeding visitor from northern hemisphere; mainly September–April, but a few remain during other months, especially in the north, and without breeding.

Genus APUS

A group of about ten old world species most of which have forked tails, like the only species which occurs in Australia, as a non-breeding visitor from the northern hemisphere; mostly associated with northern low pressure systems or tropical cyclones.

389 FORK-TAILED SWIFT *Apus pacificus* (Latham) 1801   Fig p 261

Distribution: throughout.

RECOGNITION: *large with white rump and long forked tail.*

DESCRIPTION: 18cm, folded wings extend 5cm beyond tip of forked tail; wingspan 40cm. Sexes alike. Upperparts black except for white rump; throat white; remainder of underparts black scalloped with pale grey.

HABITAT: variable, wherever food and weather conditions suitable. HABITS: usually in scattered flocks wheeling at great speed and at various heights.

STATUS: common; non-breeding visitor from northern hemisphere; mainly October–April, but a few remain during other months, especially in the north and without breeding.

Family ALCEDINIDAE
Kingfishers
10(87) species: 2 endemic

Distribution: worldwide

ALTHOUGH KINGFISHERS HAVE MANY variable features they are very uniform in general appearance and behaviour; there are unmistakable similarities, for example, between such extreme forms as the Kookaburra and the Azure Kingfisher. Distinctive features are the shape of the large bill, large head and short neck and legs, the characteristic upright stance on some snag, bough or telegraph wire, and the fixed or 'frozen' attitude, released only when the bird swoops to catch some fish or insect. Only a few, like the Azure Kingfisher, find their food, which may be any small form of aquatic life, including fish, in fresh or salt water; but given the opportunity almost any of the forest or woodland species will dive for fish in man-made environments. Most feed on insects, which they catch on the wing or on the ground, and may live far from water, like the Forest Kingfisher. Kingfishers well deserve their regal description for nearly all are garbed in rich metallic purples, blues and reds. Even the relatively dull Kookaburra has its patches of bright 'kingfisher' colour. The inactivity of kingfishers, which do not clamber about among the branches as many birds do, is reflected in their relatively weak legs and feet; legs are short and some toes are fused together (syndactylous), and occasionally a toe is missing. Wings are short and rounded, a shape unsuited for long sustained flight. Tails are variable, sometimes very short as in the two *Ceyx* species, or very long as in the White-tailed Kingfisher.

Key to ALCEDINIDAE

Genus CEYX

About eleven species distinguished mainly by having only three toes, but sometimes absorbed in the much larger genus *Alcedo*. The two Australian species are very alike except for size and colour of underparts. They have relatively long bills, stumpy tails and feed in water, one along watercourses and the other in mangroves.

390 AZURE KINGFISHER *Ceyx azureus* (Latham) 1801   Pl 12   Fig p 266
Distribution: Map 113.

RECOGNITION: *rufous below and wholly violet-blue above, stumpy tail.*

DESCRIPTION: 18cm, with bill 5cm. Sexes alike. Face and upperparts, side of breast and sometimes flanks shiny violet-blue, rather more cobalt on rump; buffy-white patch in front of eye; cinnamon white streak on side of neck; throat cinnamon white; breast and belly shades of cinnamon rufous; wings dull blackish; bill black, sometimes tipped with cream or red; eyes dark brown; legs red.

VARIATION: south, larger and colours duller (race *azurea*); north, smaller and colours richer —west of Normanton darker underparts and violet-blue flanks (race *pulchra*) and east of Normanton lighter underparts (race *mixta*).

HABITAT: inland waters, coastal creeks and estuaries, including mangroves. HABITS: feeds by diving into water from low perch or from edge of water, bobs when perched; solitary; sedentary; flight rapid and direct low over water. BREEDING: variable, mainly October–December in south, December–April in north; nests in banks or upturned roots of fallen trees, near water, chamber at end of about 15cm tunnel; five white eggs. VOICE: shrill 'pee' repeated, often uttered in flight. FOOD: fish and other aquatic animals, and insects.

STATUS: fairly common. TAXONOMY: endemic races of species extending to New Guinea and some adjacent islands.

391 LITTLE KINGFISHER *Ceyx pusillus* Temminck 1836
Distribution: Map 114.

RECOGNITION: *very like Azure Kingfisher but much smaller and underparts wholly white.*

DESCRIPTION: 11cm, with bill 3cm; tail very short. Sexes alike. Face, upperparts and side of breast shiny violet-blue; white spot in front of eye and white fleck on side of neck; underparts white, sometimes flecked with black on breast; flanks black; flight feathers black; bill black; eyes dark brown; legs blackish-brown.

VARIATION: Cape York, slight tinge of green on forehead (race *halli*); Northern Territory, rather bluer, less violet, on upperparts (race *ramsayi*).

HABITAT: mangroves, estuaries and lower reaches of rivers. HABITS: dives into water from low perch, bobs head when perched; solitary; sedentary; flies very fast and low over water; (rather shy and elusive and not well known). BREEDING: apparently about November–February; nests in banks, chamber at end of short tunnel; five white eggs. VOICE: shrill 'peep' repeated. FOOD: fish and other aquatic animals.

STATUS: uncommon, but perhaps not so uncommon as records suggest. TAXONOMY: Endemic races of variable species extending to Moluccas and Solomon Is.

Genus DACELO

Four species of 'giant' kingfishers ranging throughout western Papuan islands and southern New Guinea with two species occurring in Australia. The well-known Kookaburra or Laughing Jackass, widely famed for its raucous 'laughter', is endemic; it has been introduced to Tasmania and the southwest. Plumages are relatively dull but with patches of bright colour and bills are large and wide with upper and lower mandibles of different colours. They feed on the ground.

392 KOOKABURRA *Dacelo gigas* (Boddaert) 1783

Distribution: Map 115.

RECOGNITION: *large, rump and patch on shoulder dull blue, broad white band above eye.*

DESCRIPTION: 38–40cm, with thick bill 5·5cm. Sexes alike. Head mainly white with slightly streaked blackish-brown patch in centre of crown and broad band on face and narrow band on hind neck; centre of back and wings brownish-black boldly mottled with dull blue on shoulders; concealed white in centre of wing; rump mottled brown and dull blue; tail cinnamon rufous barred with black and broadly tipped with white on outer feathers; underparts white; bill black above, creamy white below; eyes brown; legs greenish-grey.

VARIATION: there seems to be an appreciable reduction in size from south to north: south of tropic, larger (race *novaeguineae*); north of tropic, smaller (race *minor*).

Kookaburra (392)

Azure Kingfisher (390)

HABITAT: dry forests and savanna woodlands. HABITS: arboreal but often feeds on ground prey and sometimes nests in holes in ground; solitary except that families of up to five may remain together until next breeding season; sedentary; flight rather heavy and not long sustained; when hunting sits in rigid attitude with bill pointing down then suddenly swoops; sometimes mobbed by small birds. BREEDING: September–January, sometimes up to April or May; nests in hollows, in trees at varying heights or in termite mounds or holes in banks or in buildings; three white eggs. VOICE: raucous 'laughter'. FOOD: insects and small animals, domestic food scraps.

STATUS: very common. TAXONOMY: endemic species.

393 BLUE-WINGED KOOKABURRA *Dacelo leachii* Vig. & Horsf. 1826 Pl 12

Distribution: Map 116.

RECOGNITION: *crown streaked, rump and patch on shoulders bright blue.*

DESCRIPTION: 35–38cm. Sexes differ in tail pattern. *Male:* crown and face streaked white and black; hind neck, breast and belly creamy-buff; throat white; back brownish-black; rump and shoulders bright blue (methyl blue); centre of wing and most of tail dark violet-blue; flight feathers black with concealed white patch in centre; outer tail feathers barred dark blue and white, tipped with white; bill brownish-black above, whitish below; eyes buffy-white; legs dull olive-green. *Female:* tail cinnamon rufous barred with dark blue.

VARIATION: throughout most of range from Brisbane to Derby as above (race *leachii*); Melville Is and adjacent mainland, generally darker, browner on upperparts and buffier on breast (race *cervina*); tip of Cape York, smaller and not quite so dark (race *kempi*); mid-Western Australia, generally paler, near white on head (race *cliftoni*).

HABITAT: open forests and savanna woodlands. HABITS: similar to Kookaburra. BREEDING: September–January; nests in holes in trees and termite nests and mounds; three white eggs. VOICE: harsh scream, quite unlike raucous laughter of Kookaburra. FOOD: insects and small animals, also known to take fish.

STATUS: common. TAXONOMY: endemic races of species extending to southeast New Guinea.

Genus HALCYON

A group widely distributed in the old world. Many of its forty or so species are not very different island forms which might be regarded as races or at most semispecies. They are of medium size in the kingfisher range, the five Australian species are 18–25cm, with moderate lengths of bills and tails. They live in woodlands and forests, including mangroves and feed largely on terrestrial or aquatic insects. Some authorities include the Yellow-billed Kingfisher in this group while others keep it in a separate genus *Syma*.

394 FOREST KINGFISHER *Halcyon macleayii* Jard. & Selb. 1830

Distribution: Map 117.

RECOGNITION: *violet-blue crown, pale blue rump, male has white collar.*

DESCRIPTION: 20cm, with bill 3cm. Sexes different. *Male:* large white spot in front of eye; forehead and face behind eye black shading to deep violet-purple on crown and nape; broad white collar continuous with white underparts, flanks tinged with pale cinnamon; back greenish-blue; rump pale blue; upper tail and shoulders deep violet-blue; flight feathers black with concealed white patch in centre; bill black, whitish at base of lower mandible; eyes dark brown; legs black. *Female:* incomplete white collar.

VARIATION: west of Normanton, back bluer and white wing patch larger (race *macleayii*); east of Normanton, back greener and white wing patch smaller (race *incincta*).

HABITAT: savanna woodland, open forests, wooded swamps, mangroves. HABITS: arboreal but may feed on ground; solitary or family parties; sedentary, mainly north of tropic, breeding visitor south of tropic between September and March, though some remain during other months, and non-breeding visitor to New Guinea, April–September. BREEDING: September–January; nests in tree holes and tree termite nests, unlined; five white eggs. VOICE: loud harsh 't-reek' repeated slowly. FOOD: insects and small animals.

STATUS: common in north, uncommon to rare in south. TAXONOMY: endemic races of species extending to eastern New Guinea and adjacent islands.

395 RED-BACKED KINGFISHER *Halcyon pyrrhopygia* Gould 1840 Pl 12

Distribution: throughout except Tasmania.

RECOGNITION: *Cinnamon rufous rump, blue-green crown streaked with white.*

DESCRIPTION: 20–23cm, with bill 4cm. Sexes slightly different. *Male:* forehead to nape dull blue-green streaked with white and edged with white above eye; broad black band from base of bill through eye to hind neck; white collar continuous with white underparts; upper back greenish-blue; lower back and rump cinnamon rufous; tail bluish-green; wings mainly violet-blue with webs of inner flight feathers black and underwing white; bill black, base of lower mandible pinkish-white; eyes brownish; legs dark olive-brown. *Female:* crown greenish-black, back and wings dull green rather than blue and violet.

HABITAT: dry woodlands and wooded savannas, especially along (frequently dry) rivers and creeks. HABITS: arboreal and terrestrial, usually nesting in ground; solitary; mainly sedentary in north and migratory in south where it is breeding visitor between September and March. BREEDING: August–December, sometimes on to February; nests in holes excavated in vertical banks and termite mounds; three to five white eggs. VOICE: mournful descending whistle 'ter-lp', or single squeaking 'ki'. FOOD: insects and small animals.

STATUS: fairly common, rare in coastal districts. TAXONOMY: endemic species.

396 SACRED KINGFISHER *Halcyon sancta* Vig. & Horsf. 1827 Pl 12

Distribution: throughout.

RECOGNITION: *crown plain greenish, rump bluish-green like back, rufous tinge on white underparts.*

DESCRIPTION: 20cm, with bill 3cm. Sexes alike. Forehead and crown uniformly greenish; pale buff spot in front of eye and patch on nape; broad black band through eye to nape; broad white collar continuous with white underparts, including underwing, tinged with varying shades of cinnamon rufous; back and rump dull bluish-green; shoulders and tail violet-blue; flight feathers black; bill black, pinkish-white at base of lower mandible; eyes dark brown; legs grey-brown.

VARIATION: informed opinion leans to the conclusion that variation in the colour of the underparts is not related to distribution and no races are accepted; the greatest tendency to near white seems to be in southern areas (therefore it is unlikely that this species will be confused with the Mangrove Kingfisher where the two are in close proximity).

Mangrove
Kingfisher (397)

White-tailed Kingfisher (399)

HABITAT: forests and woodlands, sometimes mangroves. HABITS: arboreal but feeds mainly on ground or in water; solitary; migratory, also dispersal movements in northern 'wet', perhaps some populations sedentary. BREEDING: October–January; nests in holes, in trees at various heights, termite nests and mounds, and banks; five white eggs. VOICE: loud four syllabled 'ki-ki-ki-ki' repeated at intervals. FOOD: terrestrial and aquatic insects and small animals.

STATUS: common, less so in Tasmania; breeding visitor in south September to March, resident in north, non-breeding migrant to New Guinea. TAXONOMY: variable species ranging widely from Sumatra to New Zealand.

397 MANGROVE KINGFISHER *Halcyon chloris* (Boddaert) 1783

Distribution: northern coasts from Carnarvon to north New South Wales.

RECOGNITION: *like Sacred Kingfisher but larger, 23–25cm, white patch in front of eye smaller, back and rump bluish-green, white areas not tinged with rufous, confined to seashore habitats, has distinctive double note.*

HABITAT: mangroves and adjacent timber. HABITS: similar to Sacred Kingfisher. BREEDING: September–January; nests in holes, in trees and termite nests; three white eggs. VOICE: double-noted 'kik-kik' or 'ke-kik' repeated several times. FOOD: small animals and insects of littoral zone.

STATUS: fairly common; breeding visitor September to March, migrating to New Guinea and other islands, but a few remain during other months. TAXONOMY: race *(sordidus)* of species or superspecies ranging widely throughout southwest Pacific islands to India and Africa.

398 YELLOW-BILLED KINGFISHER *Halcyon torotoro* (Lesson) 1827

Distribution: extreme tip of Cape York.

RECOGNITION: *yellow bill and brown head, female has black patch on crown.*

DESCRIPTION: 18cm, with serrated bill 3cm. Sexes slightly different. *Male:* head, neck and breast cinnamon brown, paler on breast, with black ring around eye and black band at side of neck; upper back black; shoulders and inner wings greenish-olive; rump and tail greenish-blue; throat and centre of belly whitish; bill yellow, tip of upper mandible brown; eyes dark brown; legs yellow. *Female:* large patch of black in centre of crown, black bands at side of neck sometimes joined to form half collar.

HABITAT: margins of rain forest. HABITS: hunts from stances on low boughs; solitary; apparently sedentary. BREEDING: November–January; nests in holes excavated in tree termite nests; three white eggs. VOICE: loud clear trilling whistle, usually preceded by a series of staccato notes. FOOD: insects and small animals.

STATUS: uncertain. TAXONOMY: endemic race *(flavirostris)* of species extending to New Guinea and associated islands.

Genus TANYSIPTERA

The eight species which comprise this group are sometimes known as paradise kingfishers. The central tail feathers are extended into long narrow streamers, sometimes wide at the tip. They belong to forests of the New Guinea area and one species has bridged Torres Strait, but only temporarily as a breeding visitor.

399 WHITE-TAILED KINGFISHER
Tanysiptera sylvia   Gould 1850   Pl 12   Fig p 269

Distribution: northeast Cape York south to about Gladstone.

RECOGNITION: *white rump and long white tail streamers.*

DESCRIPTION: 20cm, plus two central tail feathers extended up to 18cm. Sexes alike, except that female has tail streamers shorter and edged with blue for most of length. Crown and shoulders shiny violet-blue; broad jet black streak through eye; upper back black with patch in centre usually white but sometimes tinged with cinnamon (doubtfully female); lower back, rump and central tail feathers white; underparts cinnamon brown; wing and outer tail feathers dull black edged with violet-blue; bill reddish-orange; eyes black; legs red.

HABITAT: lowland rain forest. HABITS: keeps to dense parts of forest but readily seen and easily identified when it flits across clearings and gullies; solitary; migratory. BREEDING: October–January; nests excavated in 'live' termite nests on ground or low in trees, but occasionally fairly high (termites accept intrusion and seal off sides of tunnel, and apparently also seal off entrance when birds leave); three white eggs. VOICE: loud trill or grasshopper-like chirrup. FOOD: insects and small animals.

STATUS: faily common; breeding visitor from New Guinea, October to April. TAXONOMY: endemic breeding race *(sylvia)* of variable species extending to New Guinea and Bismarck Archipelago.

COMMON PARADISE KINGFISHER   *Tanysiptera galatea:* this New Guinea species has been recorded in Australian territory at Darnley I, 76km southeast of Daru.

Family MEROPIDAE
Bee-eaters
1(24) species: endemic   Rainbowbird (400)

BEE-EATERS ARE CHARACTERISTIC in appearance and behaviour. Plumages are predominantly green decorated with bright patches of reds, yellows and blues—hence the name Rainbowbird. A broad black band across the face forms a line continuous with the long slightly decurved and sharply pointed bill. Wings are long and pointed and tails fairly long, usually with the central pair of feathers narrow and extended at the tip. Legs are short and toes slender with forward toes fused together. The single Australian species is about 20cm in length, distinctly larger than the swallows and martins which share the same habit of hawking insects on the wing. Bee-eaters, like many flycatchers, dart out from perches on boughs, snags or telegraph wires, or hawk around for long periods more in the manner of swallows. Although essentially arboreal they nest in long tunnels excavated in the ground.

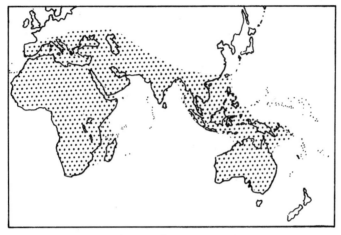

Distribution of MEROPIDAE

400 RAINBOWBIRD   *Merops ornatus*   Latham 1801   Pl 12

Distribution: throughout except Tasmania.

RECOGNITION: *mainly apple green with yellow throat, black tail and orange underwing.*

DESCRIPTION: 20cm, with sharply pointed decurved bill 4cm, plus narrow tips of central tail feathers extended 2·5cm. Sexes alike. Forehead and crown, upper back and shoulders apple green; nape cinnamon buff; rump light blue; broad black band through eye edged with light blue below; throat yellowish with black patch on foreneck; breast greenish shading to bluish-green on belly and pale blue on under tail coverts; flight feathers mainly brown tipped with black; underwing orange-yellow; tail mainly black, central feathers tinged with greenish-blue; bill black; eyes red; legs grey.

HABITAT: open timbered country, especially river and creek courses with banks suitable for nests. HABITS: arboreal but nests in ground; hunts insects on wing by hawking or darting from stance on bough or post, often telegraph wire; gregarious, sometimes in large flocks when migrating, but often solitary when breeding; migratory, especially in south but possibly sedentary in some northern habitats; swift erratic flight when hunting insects.

BREEDING: August–February; nests in tunnels excavated in banks or flat ground, often paddocks, unlined chamber; four to five white eggs. VOICE: whirring 'pirr' repeated and frequently uttered in flight. FOOD: insects, usually bees and wasps.

STATUS: common; breeding visitor in south, resident and passage migrant in north, non-breeding in region from Sunda Is to Solomon Is. TAXONOMY: endemic breeding species, except for small resident population in southeast New Guinea.

Family CORACIIDAE

Rollers

1(17) species

ROLLERS GET THEIR NAME from the habit of rolling or tumbling in display flight. They are fairly large, the single Australian species being about 30cm, with relatively large head, short neck and short wide bill. Tails are long and frequently forked, sometimes with outermost pair of feathers greatly extended. Plumage colours are predominantly bright blues and violets sometimes toned down with browns. Legs are short and weak. They are usually solitary and hunt insects on the wing from high exposed perches. They nest in holes and eggs are white. Notes are harsh.

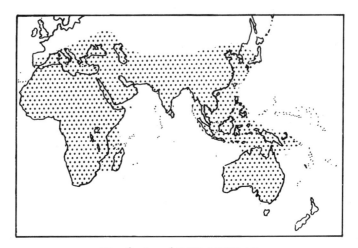

Distribution of CORACIIDAE

401 DOLLARBIRD *Eurystomus orientalis* (Linnaeus) 1766   Pl 11

Distribution: Map 118.

RECOGNITION: *fairly large, perched high on bare branch, short red bill, in flight 'dollar-size' whitish patch on wing.*

DESCRIPTION: 30cm. Sexes alike. Head and neck dark grey-brown shading to bluish-olive on back; throat deep violet streaked with pale blue; breast, belly and shoulders greenish-olive; flight feathers black edged basally with deep violet and with partly concealed patch of pale blue which becomes large 'dollar' spot on extended underwing; bill, legs and ring around eye red; eyes brown.

HABITAT: woodlands. HABITS: arboreal, frequently perched on high bare or dead bough, swooping out to fly around high up and then alight on another perch; solitary; migratory; flight consists of slow flaps and wide banking glides. BREEDING: October–January; nests in holes in dead trees usually high up, unlined; four white eggs. VOICE: rough harsh 'kak' repeated, usually uttered in flight. FOOD: mainly flying insects.

STATUS: fairly common: breeding visitor September to April, non-breeding in New Guinea and adjacent islands. TAXONOMY: endemic race *(pacificus)* of variable species ranging to India, China and Solomon Is.

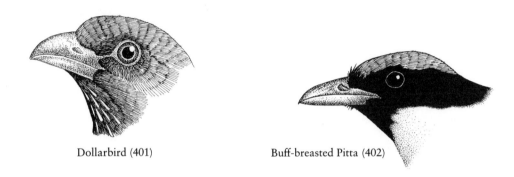

Dollarbird (401)   Buff-breasted Pitta (402)

Family PITTIDAE

Pittas

4(23) species: 1 endemic

PITTAS HAVE A DISTINCTIVE and very uniform appearance. Their general similarity has usually kept them in a single genus, *Pitta*. Relatively short wings and tails emphasise plump build; legs and feet are large and strong; bills are stout; the Australian species vary in size from 15–25cm. Greatest variation is found in plumage colours and patterns, which are remarkably bright, as in the Black-breasted or Rainbow Pitta, Australia's endemic species. Rich browns and greens are enhanced with reds and blues, and patches of black and white.

Distribution of PITTIDAE

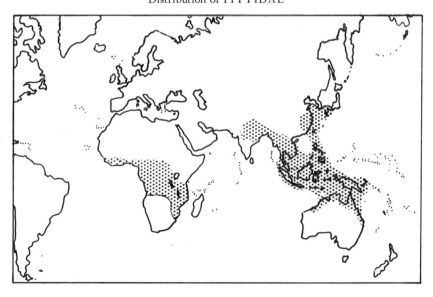

Pittas belong to wet forests where they live mainly on the ground, feeding on insects and grubs in turned over litter, but they may climb high into tree tops to sing. Voices are loud and distinctive and often the easiest means of identification, for the birds are shy and in spite of their rich colours are not readily seen, unless exposed in forest clearings and tracks. Nests are on or near the ground, well made and domed, with a side entrance; eggs are glossy.

Key to PITTIDAE

1 Underparts black .... Black-breasted Pitta .... : . No 404
2 Breast blue, belly red .... Blue-breasted Pitta ...... No 405
3 Breast buff....................................... 4–5
4 Throat black..................................... Buff-breasted Pitta ...... No 402
5 Throat white; rare............................... Blue-winged Pitta .... No 403

402 BUFF-BREASTED PITTA *Pitta versicolor* Swainson 1825   Pl 12   Fig p 273
Distribution: Map 119.

RECOGNITION: *buff breast and black throat.*

DESCRIPTION: 20–25cm. Sexes alike. Forehead to crown dark brown (burnt sienna) with black streaks in centre of crown; face, throat and hind neck blackish, edged with buff; back and inner wing olive-green, sometimes flecked with black; shoulders and tip of rump feathers pale shiny blue (beryl); breast and flanks deep buff; centre of belly black; vent and under tail coverts deep pink; flight feathers black with concealed white central bar; tail black with dark green tip; bill black; eyes dark brown; legs pinkish-brown.

VARIATION: races have been described but they do not seem to be clearly defined; northern birds may be slightly smaller.

HABITAT: rain forests. HABITS: terrestrial but sometimes in trees to roost or sing; very shy and elusive especially when breeding; solitary; movements not well known, recorded as sedentary in some areas and migratory in others. BREEDING: October–January; nests on or near ground, at base of trees or among rocks or fallen timber or low crotches of trees, made of twigs and moss and lined with leaves and grass or fibres, domed, with side entrance often with an approach platform of rotten wood or animal dung; four eggs, creamy-white finely or densely marked with shades of brown and grey, both kinds in one clutch. VOICE: resonant three-note whistle, the last higher pitched, sometimes translated as 'want a watch'; also sharp 'keow'. FOOD: insects.

STATUS: fairly common. TAXONOMY: endemic race *(versicolor)*, perhaps non-breeding migrant to New Guinea, of variable species extending to Malaysia; species forms a super-species with others throughout India and Africa.

403 BLUE-WINGED PITTA *Pitta moluccensis* (Muller) 1776
Distribution: Map 119.

RECOGNITION: like Buff-breasted Pitta but differs in having *white throat*, purplish-blue on shoulders and rump, white patch on wing very large and extending to tip of some of inner feathers, brown of crown much paler.

STATUS: rare vagrant from Malaysia.

404 BLACK-BREASTED PITTA *Pitta iris* Gould 1842   Pl 12
Distribution: Map 119.

RECOGNITION: *black head and underparts.*

DESCRIPTION: 15–18cm. Sexes alike. Head, neck and underparts mainly black with light reddish-brown streak on side of crown; vent and under tail coverts scarlet; back and inner wing olive-green; shoulders and tip of rump shiny light blue; main flight feathers black with concealed white central spot; tail black with olive-green tip; bill black; eyes dark brown; legs pinkish-brown.

HABITAT: rain and bamboo forests and mangroves. HABITS: (not well known) mainly terrestrial, sometimes in trees; solitary; sedentary. BREEDING: December–March; nests on ground, loosely made of twigs, strips of bamboo leaves and other vegetation, lined with grass; four eggs, dull white with scattered blackish markings. VOICE: loud clear whistle sometimes translated as 'want-a-whip'. FOOD: Insects and other small invertebrates.

STATUS: uncommon. TAXONOMY: endemic species.

405 BLUE-BREASTED PITTA *Pitta erythrogaster* (Temminck) 1823

Distribution: Map 120.

RECOGNITION: *bright blue breast band and scarlet belly.*

DESCRIPTION: 18cm. Sexes alike. Forehead and crown blackish-brown; hind neck red-brown; back dark blue-green shading to purplish-blue on shoulders and centre of wing, and on rump and tail; face and chin purplish-blue; throat to breast black with broad light blue band on breast; belly deep scarlet; flight feathers black with concealed white central patch; bill black; eyes dark brown; legs dark blue-grey.

HABITAT: forests and thick woodlands, especially stony situations with dense low cover. HABITS: (not well known) terrestrial, but often climbs to top of tall trees to call; solitary; sedentary, but claimed to migrate to New Guinea. BREEDING: October–January; nests on ground in dense cover, made of twigs and leaves and lined with fibre; three to four eggs, pale buff lightly spotted and blotched with purplish-grey. VOICE: mournful double whistle (in New Guinea described as rasping 'karaa'). FOOD: insects and snails, which are extracted by smashing shells on rocks.

STATUS: uncommon. TAXONOMY: race *(macklotii)*, also in New Guinea, of species extending to Celebes and Philippines.

Family MENURIDAE

Lyrebirds

Endemic family of 2 species

LYREBIRDS ARE ONLY FOUND in Australia. They are a unique group with obscure relationships; their closest affinity, on the basis of certain anatomical features, is judged to be with another unique Australian family, the scrub-birds. Lyrebirds have long been noted for the curious lyre-like appearance of the tail feathers of the male, but it is only in recent years that it was recorded how they are used in graceful dances, performed on specially prepared mounds or scrapes on the forest floor. These displays are usually accompanied by a rich variety of loud clear notes, many mimicking the voices of other birds and animals. Lyrebirds are about 30cm in length with tails twice as long; body plumage is in dull brown and grey; bills have the conical shape found in domestic fowls; legs and toes are large and strong and used for moving litter and mould, by a grasping action, in search of grubs and other insects; eyes are large; wings short and rounded and used mainly for gliding. Although largely terrestrial, lyrebirds jump into trees to roost and their domed nests are often located up to a metre off the ground.

Key to MENURIDAE

1 Upperparts dark grey-brown, under tail coverts grey ..   Superb Lyrebird.......... No 406
2 Upperparts dark rufous brown, under tail coverts
   chestnut..................................   Albert Lyrebird .... No 407

406 SUPERB LYREBIRD   *Menura superba*   Davies 1800   Pl 4

Distribution: Map 121.

RECOGNITION: *dark grey-brown with long tail, lyre-shaped in male, under tail coverts grey.*

DESCRIPTION: 80–95cm, with lyre-shaped tail of male 55–60cm, female 45–50cm; crown slightly crested; legs and toes large; bare skin of face bluish-black. Sexes alike except for tails. Upperparts dark grey-brown, darker on crown and face, paler on rump and more rufous on wings and upper tail coverts; underparts pale grey-brown with varying amounts of rufous brown on throat and foreneck; male tail has central feathers very filamentous, blackish above and silver-grey below, outer pair gracefully curved into lyre-shape, blackish-brown above and grey or white below with rufous notches on inner webs; female tail graduated and coloured as body; bill black; eyes blackish-brown; legs black.

VARIATION: over most of range inner web of lyre feathers white and diffusely notched with rufous (race *superba*); small area in northern limit of range, on New South Wales and Queensland border, generally paler and greyer with inner webs of lyre feathers grey and clearly notched with rufous (race *edwardi*).

HABITAT: mountain forests, especially dense fern gullies *(superba)*; among granite outcrops in open timbered country with much ground litter *(edwardi)*. HABITS: mainly terrestrial but roosts and sometimes nests in trees; obtains food by turning over leaves and mould by scratching and grasping action of feet (sometimes accompanied by Yellow Robin); makes small clearings and mounds on which male bird struts and displays by erecting and spreading

Superb Lyrebird (406) *female*

tail until it hangs over body like a shimmering white curtain; solitary but often communal when not breeding; sedentary; wings used to aid jumping into trees or up among rocks, flight a jump and glide, or glide from some elevated perch. BREEDING: June–September; nests on ground (rarely *edwardi*) at tree butts or among logs and stones, or in thick vine canopies or among rocks in cliffs or high ledges; a platform of sticks and moss, sometimes surrounded with leaves and strips of bark and untidily domed with grass and fibre, with side entrance, and lined with feathers when egg is laid; one egg, grey or purplish-brown, spotted and streaked with dark brown and blue-grey. VOICE: wide variety of sounds uttered by both sexes, some loud clear and musical and others harsher, like sharp 'kerwist' (alarm) and repeated 'choo' or 'nap'; also notes mimicking voices of many birds and animals. FOOD: grubs, worms, insects.

STATUS: fairly common. TAXONOMY: endemic species of endemic family.

407 ALBERT LYREBIRD *Menura alberti* Gould 1850 Pl 4

Distribution: Map 121.

RECOGNITION: like Superb Lyrebird in main features but more rufous on back and upper tail coverts and tinged with rusty brown on underparts; most distinctive features are *chestnut under tail coverts,* visible when tail is erected in display, and *absence of lyre-shaped outer tail feathers.*

HABITAT: mountain forests with rocks and cliffs. HABITS, etc: generally similar to Superb Lyrebird but males usually display from fallen logs, not from specially cleared areas and mounds; nests on rock ledges and stumps, rarely on ground.

STATUS: fairly common in small areas. TAXONOMY: endemic species of endemic family.

Family ATRICHORNITHIDAE
Scrub-birds
Endemic family of 2 species

SCRUB-BIRDS ARE UNIQUE in form and peculiar to Australia. On anatomical grounds they are considered to be closest in affinity to the lyrebirds. The genealogy of both is obscure; they may represent a primitive avian stock which has survived in isolation. The Noisy Scrub-bird of the extreme southwest was thought to be extinct for a long time and its rediscovery in recent years stirred interest and emotions far beyond Australia. Apparently it retains only a tenuous hold in one small area and recent studies suggest that it is most exacting in the conditions suitable to its survival. Scrub-birds are about 15–23cm in length of which broad graduated tails are nearly half. Plumages are nondescript dull dark browns with some lighter patches. Wings are short and rounded and birds are reluctant to fly but not flightless. They keep on or near the ground in dense vegetation where they run about like small mammals, burrowing among leaves and searching in hollow logs for food. In common with some other dull coloured and furtive species their most remarkable characteristic is their voice, which is rich and varied in tone and possesses a ventriloquial quality disconcerting to anyone trying to locate the source of sound. They are also accomplished mimics of other birds' voices.

Key to ATRICHORNITHIDAE

408 RUFOUS SCRUB-BIRD   *Atrichornis rufescens*   (Ramsay) 1866   Pl 12

Distribution: Map 122.

RECOGNITION: *rufous brown with whitish throat, long broad tail; on forest floor in thick undergrowth; loud clear voice.*

DESCRIPTION: 16cm, with broad graduated tail 7.5cm; legs and toes large; short rounded wings; plumage has silky sheen. Sexes slightly different, female lacks dark breast patch. Upperparts rufous brown, more rufous on wings and tail, back and shoulders scalloped with blackish-brown and upper tail coverts and tail narrowly barred with same colour; face and side of neck rufous indistinctly barred with dark brown; throat whitish, whiter on chin and sides; remainder of underparts rufous with blackish patch on breast; bill dark pinkish-brown; eyes dark brown; legs reddish-brown.

VARIATION: New South Wales population, lighter above and bill shorter (race *rufescens*); Queensland population (McPherson Range), darker above and bill longer (race *jacksoni*). HABITAT: mountain forests with dense tangled undergrowth. HABITS: terrestrial, creeps rat-like on forest floor among leaves and vegetation or runs at great speed with head and tail erect, rarely flies; very elusive; solitary; sedentary. BREEDING: September–November; nests on or close to ground, in tufts of grass or other vegetation, dome-shaped with side entrance, loosely made of dry leaves and grass and lined with paste of wood pulp; two eggs, light pinkish-buff blotched with shades of brown. VOICE: loud clear notes, resonant and ventriloquial, sometimes melodious whistle, sometimes repeated 'chip' or 'chit', sometimes mimic of other bird voices; female utters softer 'tick' and high-pitched squeal. FOOD: insects and seeds.

STATUS: uncommon. TAXONOMY: endemic species of endemic family.

409 NOISY SCRUB-BIRD   *Atrichornis clamosus*   (Gould) 1844   Pl 12

Distribution: Map 122.

RECOGNITION: *blackish-brown with broad white streak at side of chin, short rounded wings; on or near ground in dense scrub; loud clear voice.*

DESCRIPTION: 23cm, with broad graduated tail 10cm; large legs and toes; short rounded wings; plumage has silky sheen. Sexes nearly alike, female lacks black on upper breast. Upperparts dark rufous brown (umber) narrowly and obscurely scalloped with black on crown and back and with bars on rump, wings and tail; face, side of throat and flanks greyish-brown; chin and sides of throat white, forming inverted 'V'; centre of throat to upper breast black; lower breast white; belly and under tail coverts rufous; bill pinkish-brown, darker above and paler below; eyes dark brown; legs pinkish-brown.

HABITAT: dense vegetation of coastal scrub and hill gullies. HABITS: terrestrial, or near ground in bushes and low banksias, especially when calling, head and tail held erect when calling, scurries with swift rat-like appearance; solitary; sedentary. BREEDING: recorded June; nests on ground, made of dried rushes, thicker at base, domed with side entrance and with 'plaster' lining; one egg, dull white spotted and blotched with pale brown. VOICE: loud, clear piercing 'cheap' or 'chip' repeated rapidly; rich vibrant song, frequently in mimic of other bird voices. FOOD: insects and seeds.

STATUS: rare, to date population estimated as less than 500. TAXONOMY: endemic species of endemic family.

Family ALAUDIDAE
Larks
2(75) species: 1 introduced

Distribution: widely distributed in the old world but only one species in the new.

AFRICA HAS THE LARGEST number of lark species and may be their ancestral home. They are spread out in diminishing numbers throughout Europe and Asia to Malaysia. Only one has reached Australia and still retains connection at species level with populations in India and Africa. The family is absent from the southwest Pacific area. Larks belong to grassy habitats of various kinds, from semi-deserts to wooded savannas. They are essentially ground birds, often exposed in open places with little cover for protection from predation, and therefore camouflage colours and patterns are important. Plumages are in shades of brown, often closely matching soil colour, streaked and blotched with blackish tones, and sometimes relieved with patches of richer colours, usually on the underparts or in concealed places. In the genus *Mirafra*, to which the sole Australian representative the Bushlark belongs, there is a reddish patch at the base of the flight feathers, visible only when the wing is extended. The skylark of Europe is an introduced and now well established colonist. Larks are especially noted for their voices, whose pleasing qualities have inspired poets. Songs are uttered in soaring flights which are distinctive for each species. Lark habitats are shared by species of other families and as camouflage is equally important to them they all look very alike. Larks can always be distinguished with certainty by close examination of the rear side of the tarsus, which consists of a number of scutes or scales instead of a single one. Aids to field identification are given in the following key.

Key to LARK-LIKE SPECIES

[Birds with streaked and mottled brown plumages frequenting mostly dry grasslands.]

1 Tail with white edges 3–6
2 Tail without white edges 7–8

3 Wing with reddish-brown patch .... Bushlark .... No 410
4 Wing lacks reddish-brown 5–6

410 BUSHLARK *Mirafra javanica* Horsfield 1821   Pl 13

Distribution: Map 123.

RECOGNITION: *white-edged tail, reddish-brown patch in wing, distinct pale eyebrow, squat appearance with short thick bill.*

DESCRIPTION: 13cm. Sexes alike. Colours variable but pattern fairly constant—dark above and light below, distinct pale eyebrow, black speckled breast, outer pair of tail feathers mainly white; feathers of upperparts have black or dark grey centres and margins of different widths whose colour varies from buffy-white to rich cinnamon brown; corresponding colour of underparts is a shade lighter than marginal colour of feathers on upperparts, varying from near white to light cinnamon brown, but in latter case chin is usually whitish; breast speckled with black; in all variants wings have cinnamon rufous patch at base of main flight feathers, visible in extended wing, and shoulder feathers edged with same colour; bill dark pinkish-brown, paler below; eyes grey-brown; legs pinkish-yellow.

VARIATION: very variable in general colour and many races have been described of which about a dozen are currently listed (see Mayr and McEvey, *Emu*, 60:155–192). There is some evidence of a broad general pattern in which populations (1) east of Adelaide and south of Atherton Tableland have upperparts mainly black or blackish-brown; (2) central area from Flinders Range to Gulf of Carpentaria upperparts mainly shades of greyish-brown; (3) northwest upperparts mainly shades of cinnamon rufous. But in detail extreme variants may occur within a range of 150km or so. This complicated situation is not easily summarised under racial names. The important point is that the basic pattern is constant but general colour may conform with general soil colour.

HABITAT: grasslands, especially open areas with short grass, paddocks and pasturelands, some evidence that denser grasses preferred when not breeding. HABITS: terrestrial but sometimes sings from low perches; solitary but with social tendencies when not breeding; sedentary; flight slow with rapid wingbeats, erratic with fairly definite flight display pattern when singing, tendency to flutter briefly above grass before dropping to ground. BREEDING: September–April, commencement in north depending on onset of rains; nests on ground at base of tussocks, made of grass and fine rootlets, open or partly or completely domed with side entrance; two to three eggs, dull white spotted with dark grey and brown. VOICE: wide range of melodious notes, including mimicry of other bird songs, uttered for long periods during soaring flight and by day and night, also sings from low perches. FOOD: insects and seeds.

STATUS: common and benefiting from use of land for pasture and grain. TAXONOMY: endemic race *(horsfieldi)* of species extending to India and Africa.

Introduced species

411 SKYLARK *Alauda arvensis* Linnaeus 1758

Distribution: Various localities in southeast, especially round Adelaide, Melbourne and Sydney, also Tasmania.

RECOGNITION: *like Bushlark but larger, lacks rufous in wing, bill more slender; streaked throat and shorter legs distinguishes from Pipit.*

DESCRIPTION: 18cm. Sexes alike. Upperparts mottled with blackish-brown feather centres and pale cinnamon buff to cinnamon brown margins; fairly distinct buff eyebrow; throat whitish, breast and flanks dull brown, belly whitish, and all except centre of belly speckled blackish-brown, densest on breast; white on outer pair of tail feathers and outer web of second pair; bill blackish-brown, lighter below; eyes brown; legs pale pinkish-brown.

HABITAT: grasslands. HABITS: terrestrial; solitary; sedentary; flight with rapid wingbeats, erratic and soaring. BREEDING: September–January; nests on ground, cup-shaped depression among grass; four to five eggs, dull white spotted with dark brown. VOICE: melodious long-sustained song uttered in flight or from ground or perch. FOOD: insects and seeds.

STATUS: introduced and well established.

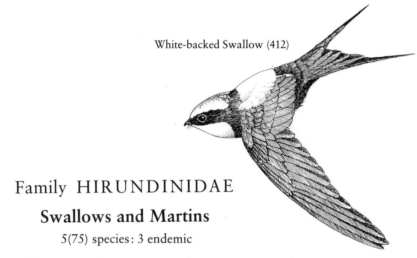

White-backed Swallow (412)

Family HIRUNDINIDAE

Swallows and Martins

5(75) species: 3 endemic

THE NAMES 'SWALLOW' AND 'martin' are more or less synonymous; the Tree Martin for example is equally well known as Tree Swallow, but 'martin' is often preferred for species with shallow forked tails and sometimes white rumps. Swallows and martins have a general likeness to swifts (family Apodidae) and woodswallows (family Artamidae) but they are not closely related to either. They appear similar because they have the same habit of catching insects on the wing during long periods of flight. Swallows are not as completely adapted as swifts to aerial habits. They are less streamlined, having relatively short, broad and straight wings, also they perch frequently in exposed places, as on branches and telegraph wires. (Swifts have long thin bowed wings, giving a pick-axe appearance and rarely alight at other than nest and roosting places; woodswallows have a bat-wing appearance and a flutter-and-glide flight.) Swallows are small, the Australian species are less than 18cm, even including long forked tails. They have small feet and slender bills with wide gape. Plumages are mainly black above and white below with reddish patches. They are mostly gregarious, flying in loose flocks and nesting and roosting communally. They are sometimes sedentary but with nomadic tendencies which in some species, and populations of the same species, take the form of a distinct migration pattern. An alternative to movement in search of food is regulation of metabolic activity to match local resources (which can be very variable in the case of airborne insects), a device known to be used by certain swifts. The extreme of reduced metabolism is a torpid condition, called hibernation when extended over a long period. This state was not known in birds, or dismissed as mythological, until recently discovered in an American nightjar and the Australian White-backed Swallow. It may occur in other species.

Key to HIRUNDINIDAE

1 Tail deeply forked, rump black .... Swallows
2 Tail nearly square, rump white .... Martins

Swallows

3 Upper back and crown white.................... White-backed Swallow..... No 412
4 Upperparts black 5–6
5 Throat light rufous .... Welcome Swallow......... No 413
6 Throat dark rufous with black margin............. Barn Swallow............. No 414

Martins

7 Forehead to nape rufous....................... Fairy Martin .... No 416
8 Forehead rufous, crown to nape black .... Tree Martin .... No 415

Genus CHERAMOECA

A single species. The endemic White-backed Swallow is considered to have characteristics which separate it as a distinct species. It is unique also in having the ability to become torpid in cold conditions thus conserving energy when food supply is scarce.

412 WHITE-BACKED SWALLOW

Cheramoeca leucosternum (Gould) 1841   Fig p 281

Distribution: Map 124.

RECOGNITION: *white upper back, crown and throat, otherwise black with deeply forked tail.*

DESCRIPTION: 15cm, with deeply forked tail just over 7·5cm. Sexes alike. Head to upper back, breast and under shoulders mainly white, centre of crown dark grey, black between bill and eye continued as dark grey band across face and on hind neck; remainder of plumage glossy blue-black; bill black; eyes dull brown; legs grey-brown.

HABITAT: open country with sandy banks suitable for nesting tunnels, as along creek and river courses.

HABITS: terrestrial with aerial feeding; solitary or more usually in small parties, which sometimes roost together in one nest tunnel; sedentary, perhaps migratory in south but records of disappearance when not breeding may be accounted for by birds remaining torpid in nest tunnels; flight erratic and swooping with rapid wing beats. BREEDING: August– December; nests in ground, in tunnels excavated in soft sand banks, about 60cm deep and ending in chamber with bed of bark chips, leaves, grasses and rootlets; four to five white eggs. VOICE: single 'check' uttered in flight which in parties of flying birds sounds like harsh twittering. FOOD: flying insects.

STATUS: common. TAXONOMY: endemic species of endemic genus.

Genus HIRUNDO

A group of about a dozen species almost worldwide in occurrence. In Australia the endemic Welcome Swallow forms a superspecies with the Pacific Swallow, and the Barn Swallow is a rare non-breeding migrant from the northern hemisphere. Both are distinguished by rufous on forehead and throat.

413 WELCOME SWALLOW *Hirundo neoxena* Gould 1843 Pl 13

Distribution: Map 125.

RECOGNITION: *deeply forked tail, black above and dull white below with light reddish throat, no black on breast.*

DESCRIPTION: 15cm, with deeply forked tail rather more than half. Sexes alike. Forehead, throat and upper breast russet brown; crown and back glossy blue-black; wings and tail dull black, tail has inconspicuous subterminal white band; lower breast and belly dull white; bill black; eyes dark brown; legs black.

VARIATION: races currently listed are not well defined; west side of continent, rather larger (race *carteri*); east side, rather smaller (race *neoxena*); north of Rockhampton, rather less white in tail (race *parsoni*).

HABITAT: most kinds except forest and desert. HABITS: aerial feeder; sometimes loosely communal when breeding, gregarious when not breeding, often in large flocks; partly sedentary, but mainly sedentary in west; largely migratory in east where it is mostly a breeding visitor in extreme south and non-breeding visitor in extreme north; there are indications that disappearance from some breeding localities may be partly accounted for by birds lying up in holes in a torpid condition (hibernation). BREEDING: August–April; nests half-cup-shaped attached to vertical surfaces in hollows or places with overhanging protection in trees, caves and buildings; made of various materials bound with mud and lined with feathers, grass and hair; three to four eggs, white variously speckled and blotched with brown and lavender-grey. VOICE: single 'seet' uttered in flight, which in flocks becomes high-pitched twittering. FOOD: flying insects.

STATUS: common. TAXONOMY: endemic species forming superspecies with Pacific Swallow.

414 BARN SWALLOW *Hirundo rustica* Linnaeus 1758 Pl 13

Distribution: northern localities from Derby to Innisfail.

RECOGNITION: very like Welcome Swallow and not easily distinguished from it; differs in forehead and throat being dark rufous rather than light reddish-brown and in having a *black band on foreneck* and *silvery-white breast and belly.*

STATUS: rare vagrant; non-breeding visitor from northern hemisphere, September–March.

TAXONOMY: specimens belong to eastern Asiatic race (*gutturalis*).

Genus PETROCHELIDON

This genus is sometimes included with *Hirundo*. There is little to distinguish it. As constituted at present it consists of ten species scattered throughout most of the world. The two Australian species have nearly square tails and white rumps. Both are endemic except that the Tree Martin extends into New Guinea and beyond in the non-breeding season.

415 TREE MARTIN *Petrochelidon nigricans* (Vieillot) 1817

Distribution: throughout.

RECOGNITION: *black above with dull white rump, reddish forehead (not crown) and shallow forked tail.*

DESCRIPTION: 13cm; shallow forked tail. Sexes alike. Narrow brown forehead; crown and back glossy blue-black; rump and upper tail coverts dull white with black shaft streaks; underparts mainly dull white, greyer on breast with some black shaft streaks, especially on throat, light brownish on flanks and under shoulders; wings and tail dull black; bill black; eyes dark brown; legs blackish.

VARIATION: east, rather larger (race *nigricans*); west and northwest, rather smaller (race *neglecta*).

HABITAT: open woodlands, especially with large spreading trees, sometimes town buildings. HABITS: aerial feeder; solitary or gregarious, depending on availability of nest sites, usually gregarious when not breeding, sometimes roosting in large flocks; sedentary and migratory, mainly breeding visitor in south, non-breeding in north, less defined in west with long drawn out passage movements; flight rapid and darting. BREEDING: August–January; nests in holes in trees, cliffs or buildings, entered by narrow openings, which may be reduced with mud plaster, made of grass and lined with leaves; four eggs, white spotted with light brown and mauve. VOICE: high-pitched twitter. FOOD: flying insects.

STATUS: very common. TAXONOMY: endemic races migrating to New Guinea and other islands of species extending to Timor and Sunda Is.

416 FAIRY MARTIN *Petrochelidon ariel* (Gould) 1843

Distribution: throughout.

RECOGNITION: *black above with clear white rump and brown head, shallow forked tail.*

DESCRIPTION: 12cm; shallow forked tail. Sexes alike. Forehead to nape dark rufous brown with black shaft streaks; face dark grey-brown; upper back shiny blue-black lightly streaked with white; rump and upper tail coverts dull white; underparts mainly white, throat greyish and streaked with black, flanks and under shoulders tinged with brown; wings and tail dull black; bill black; eyes dark brown; legs black.

HABITAT: various kinds of open country near water. HABITS: aerial feeder; gregarious at all times even when nest building; sedentary, nomadic and migratory, breeding visitor in extreme south and non-breeding in extreme north. BREEDING: August–January; nests in clusters attached to almost any vertical or overhung surface near moist mud, roughly pear-shaped with short downbent entrance tunnel at top, made of mud and lined with fine grass and feathers; four to five eggs, white, often lightly speckled with reddish-brown. VOICE: high-pitched weak twitter. FOOD: flying insects.

STATUS: common, except in far north where it is uncommon. TAXONOMY: endemic species; vagrant to southeast New Guinea.

Tree Martin (415)

Family MOTACILLIDAE
Pipits and Wagtails
4(48) species

Distribution: worldwide

IT IS CURIOUS THAT this large and ubiquitous family is poorly represented in Australia, where conditions seem to be favourable for the settlement and adaptive development of open country terrestrial species. The principal and common representative is the resident (Richard's) Pipit—as there is only one pipit species the qualification is not used—with several wagtails as rare visitors. Pipits and wagtails are mainly terrestrial; they are of slim build with slender pointed bills and long tails, especially long and constantly wagged or bobbed up and down in the wagtails (not to be confused with the lateral tail swinging movement of Willie Wagtail). Some are gregarious except when breeding, but form only loose flocks. Pipits have a streaked brown plumage, a camouflage pattern similar to that of other species frequenting short grass paddocks and similar places (see key page 279) and wagtails have a patched plumage consisting mostly of combinations of black, white and yellow.

Key to MOTACILLIDAE

1 Underparts buffy-white, upperparts streaked .... Pipit.................... No 417
2 Underparts yellow 3–5

3 Whole head yellow .... Yellow-headed Wagtail .... No 419
4 Crown blue-grey, back and rump olive-green .... Blue-headed Wagtail....... No 418
5 Crown and back grey, rump yellow .... Grey Wagtail .... No 420

Genus ANTHUS

Most pipits belong to this group which consists of about thirty-four species worldwide in distribution. They have dull brown plumages streaked with blackish-brown, rarely with any brighter colours. Bills are slender and legs and toes long, sometimes equipped with spur-like claws.

417 PIPIT *Anthus novaeseelandiae* (Gmelin) 1789

Distribution: throughout.

RECOGNITION: *brown with blackish streaks, slender bill, tail edged with white, no rufous in wing.*

DESCRIPTION: 16cm. Sexes alike. Feathers of upperparts have blackish centres and buff to cinnamon brown margins, making a streaked and mottled appearance; light buff eyebrow; throat white edged with broken blackish streak; breast light cinnamon buff with blackish-brown streaks; belly light buff; tail edged with white (white extends to half inner web of second pair of feathers—in Bushlark and Skylark on outer web only); bill blackish-brown above and at tip, below brownish-white; eyes dark brown; legs light pinkish-brown.

VARIATION: numerous variants have been named of which five are currently listed. They are based mainly on slight differences in colour and pattern which do not seem to be satisfactorily related to seasonal changes and camouflage coloration.

HABITAT: open areas, preferably with scanty vegetation. HABITS: terrestrial, sometimes perches on low snags or fences, rarely higher; usually solitary when breeding but sometimes nests grouped in close proximity, congregates in loose flocks when not breeding; sedentary and nomadic; rapid undulating flight with frequent direction changes and of short duration, drops straight to ground, runs rapidly in short bursts. BREEDING: August–April; nests on ground in or under tussocks, a depression scantily or well lined with grass, fibres and sometimes feathers; three eggs, spotted with shades of brown and grey. VOICE: plaintive sharp chirp, short trilling song of limited range. FOOD: seeds and insects.

STATUS: very common, less common in north. TAXONOMY: variable species ranging throughout most of the old world.

Genus MOTACILLA

There are ten species in this genus, consisting of all but one of the wagtails, and they occur widely throughout the old world. Several north temperate forms migrate to the southern hemisphere as non-breeding visitors and three of these are rare vagrants in Australia. Although basically similar to pipits their plumages are in plain colours and tails are larger and more frequently wagged.

418 BLUE-HEADED WAGTAIL *Motacilla flava* Linnaeus 1758

[*Note:* an Asiatic form of the European Yellow Wagtail is distinguished by a blue-grey crown and is frequently named Blue-headed Wagtail. It is this form which has been identified in Australia and it seems reasonable to use its more descriptive name.]

Distribution: scattered records in north from near Rockhampton to near Derby.

RECOGNITION: 15cm, of which tail is half. Sexes alike. Crown blue-grey; remainder of upperparts olive-green; white eyebrow; underparts bright yellow; wings and tail black, latter with white edges.

HABITS: usually on ground near water; tail constantly bobbed. VOICE: repeated 'weet'.

STATUS: rare vagrant, from northern hemisphere. TAXONOMY: specimens identified as probably Siberia/Alaska race *(tschutschensis)*.

419 YELLOW-HEADED WAGTAIL *Motacilla citreola* Pallas 1776

Distribution: recorded near Sydney, doubtfully near Port Hedland.

RECOGNITION: like Blue-headed Wagtail but *whole head* as well as underparts *bright yellow; nape black;* back and wings dark grey, *shoulders with two white bars;* tail blackish with white edges.

HABITS: like Blue-headed Wagtail; flight undulating and jerky. VOICE: shrill 'chip' uttered in flight.

STATUS: rare vagrant, from northern Asia (nearest recorded regular occurrence apparently Burma).

420 GREY WAGTAIL *Motacilla cinerea* (Tunstall) 1771

Distribution: recorded near Innisfail.

RECOGNITION: like Blue-headed Wagtail but *crown and back grey; rump bright yellow;* throat and eyebrow white; breast and belly pale yellow; flight feathers black with white bar; tail black with white edges.

HABITS, etc: like Blue-headed Wagtail.

STATUS: rare vagrant, from northern hemisphere (recorded frequently in New Guinea).

Family CAMPEPHAGIDAE
Cuckoo-shrikes and Trillers
7(70) species: 1 endemic

AS WELL AS CUCKOO-SHRIKES and trillers there are the distinctive minevets of east Asia which are not represented in Australia. The cuckoo-shrikes, belonging mostly to the large genus *Coracina*, do not have a close affinity with cuckoos or shrikes. They have a superficial resemblance to the *Cuculus* cuckoos; they are roughly similar in size, about 25–35cm, are typically bluish or brownish-grey, have long bodies and long tails and sometimes barring on the underparts. Casual observation could easily place many in the cuckoo family, but cuckoo-shrikes do not have barred tails, and cuckoos do not refold or shuffle their wings after settling as do most *Coracina* species. The nearest resemblance to shrikes is in their notched and slightly hooked bills but they are not used for the same eating habits. The trillers, genus *Lalage*, are smaller, the two Australian species about 18–20cm, and are superficially unlike the cuckoo-shrikes; the sexes are different, the males being partly black and white, and wings are sharply pointed. Both generic and common names refer to their superb voices. Apart from the unique Australian Ground Cuckoo-shrike, members of the family are largely arboreal.

Distribution of CAMPEPHAGIDAE

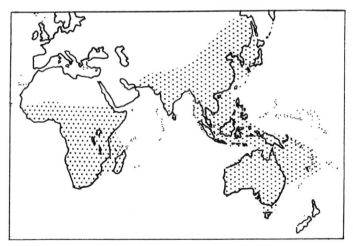

Key to CAMPEPHAGIDAE

1 Mainly pied, under 20cm..................... 4–5
2 Mainly grey, over 25cm 6–12
3 Mainly brownish 13–14

4 Eyebrow white, vent brown.................... Pied Triller................ No 427
5 Shoulder white, vent white..................(♂) White-winged Triller .... No 426

6 Rump white with black bars .... Ground Cuckoo-shrike ...... No 421
7 Rump grey like back........................ 8–12

8 Belly barred black and white .... Barred Cuckoo-shrike........ No 424
9 Underparts dark grey.....................(♂) Cicadabird .... No 425
10 Belly white............................... 11–12

11 Throat black
    Crown pale grey......................... Black-faced Cuckoo-shrike.... No 422
    Crown black or mottled black .... Little Cuckoo-shrike .... No 423
12 Throat grey, black on face
    Black round and behind eye .... Black-faced Cuckoo-shrike... No 422
    Black only in front of eye .... Little Cuckoo-shrike .... No 423

13 Underparts barred, over 25cm.............(♀) Cicadabird .... No 425
14 Underparts plain buffy-white, under 18cm....(♀) White-winged Triller .... No 426

Genus PTEROPODOCYS

John Gould regarded the endemic Ground Cuckoo-shrike to be generically distinct from related species, mainly because of its longer legs and tail and narrow bill. These might be adaptive features associated with its terrestrial habits and it has been suggested, but not widely accepted, that the species should be included in *Coracina*.

421 GROUND CUCKOO-SHRIKE *Pteropodocys maxima* (Ruppell) 1839   Pl 13

Distribution: Map 126.

RECOGNITION: *long black forked tail, white rump with black bars; usually on ground in open country.*

DESCRIPTION: 36cm, with forked tail 20cm. Sexes alike. Crown and back pale grey; face and throat slightly darker grey; rump, breast and belly white narrowly barred with black; wings black, underwing white and barred on under-shoulder; tail mainly black, but white at edge and central feathers tipped white; bill and legs blackish; eyes buffy-white.

HABITAT: wooded savannas. HABITS: mainly terrestrial, feeds on ground but flies into trees when disturbed or to roost and nest, stands erect on branch and shuffles wings, when walking moves head back and fore like a pigeon, runs fast, flight undulating, slow and fluttery; solitary or in family parties which keep together most of year; sedentary and nomadic; very shy. BREEDING: August–December in south, November–March in north; nests fairly low in trees, on horizontal forks, loosely and scantily made of twigs, rootlets and grasses, interwoven with cobwebs, fur or wool; two to three eggs, olive-green sometimes spotted with brown. VOICE: rippling 'chee-er-chee-er' and piping 'queel'. FOOD: insects.

STATUS: fairly common. TAXONOMY: endemic species and genus.

Genus CORACINA

This is the largest section of the family, consisting of about forty species of which four occur in Australia; they appear to be relatively recent colonists and none is endemic. Plumages are

PLATE 1   Albatrosses Shearwaters Petrels

Red-tailed
Tropicbird

Fleshy-footed
Shearwater

Little
Shearwater

Cape Petrel

Short-tailed
Shearwater

Shoemaker

Wedge-tailed
Shearwater

Gannet

White-capped
Albatross

Black-browed
Albatross

Lesser Frigatebird
(male)

PLATE 2   Herons Ducks

Grass
Whistleduck

Water
Whistleduck

Straw-necked Ibis

Green Pygmy Goose
(male)

Green Pygmy Goose
(female)

White-necked Heron

White-faced Heron

Crested Grebe

Little Bittern

Grey Teal

Chestnut Teal (m

Chestnut Teal (female)

PETER SLATER

PLATE 3 Hawks Eagles Falcons

Kestrel

Little Falcon

Collared
Sparrowhawk

Crested Hawk

Brahminy Kite

Whistling
Kite

Little Eagle

Black-breasted
Buzzard

Spotted Harrier

Swamp
Harrier

PLATE 4   Megapodes Lyrebirds Brolga

Beach
Curlew

Bush
Curlew

Brush Turkey

Brolga

Bustard

Albert
Lyrebird
(male)

Mallee Fowl

Scrub Fowl

Superb Lyrebird
(male)

PLATE 5   Quails Crakes

Chestnut-backed Quail

Brown Quail

(male)
King Quail
(female)

Marsh Crake

Red-chested Quail
(female)

Lotusbird

Spotted Crake

Bush-hen

Chestnut Rail

Lewin Water Rail

Banded Rail

PETER SLATER

PLATE 6   Sandpipers Dotterels Snipe

Australian Dotterel

Red-capped
Dotterel (male)

Black-fronted
Dotterel

Australian Pratincole

Bartram
Sandpiper

Wilson
Phalarope

Common Sandpiper

Red-necked Phalarope

Little Whimbrel

Turnstone
(non-breeding)

Sharp-tailed Sandpiper

Painted
Snipe

Japanese Snipe

PETER SLATER

PLATE 7 Skuas Gulls Terns

Whiskered Tern

Fairy Tern

White-fronted Tern

Silver Gull

Common Noddy

Caspian Tern

Crested Tern

Great Skua

Pomarine Skua

Pacific Gull

PLATE 8 Pigeons Doves

Green-winged
Pigeon

Wompoo Pigeon

Red-crowned Pigeon

Purple-crowned
Pigeon

Brown Pigeon

Bar-shouldered
Dove

Flock Pigeon

Plumed Pigeon

Brush Bronzewing

Common
Bronzewing

PETER SLATER

PLATE 9   Small Parrots

Purple-crowned Lorikeet

Swift Parrot

Varied Lorikeet

Musk Lorikeet

Rainbow Lorikeet

Fig Parrot
(race *macleayana*)
(male)

Scarlet-
breasted
Parrot

Rock
Parrot

Elegant
Parrot

Blue-
winged
Parrot

Orange-
bellied
Parrot

Turquoise
Parrot

PETER SLATER

PLATE 10   Large Parrots

Blue-bonnet

Mulga
Parrot
(male)

Superb
Parrot
(male)

Paradise
Parrot
(male)

Northern
Rosella

Red-winged Parrot (male)

Western
Rosella (male)

Galah

Gang-gang
Cockatoo
(male)

Red-cheeked
Parrot (male)

PLATE 11   Cuckoos Owls Nightjar

Papuan Frogmouth

Dollarbird

Boobook Owl

Fantailed Cuckoo

Owlet Nightjar

Golden Bronze Cuckoo

Horsfield Bronze Cuckoo

Black-eared Cuckoo

Spotted Nightjar

Grass Owl

PLATE 12 Kingfishers Pittas Scrub-birds

Azure Kingfisher

Blue-winged Kookaburra (male)

White-tailed Kingfisher

Sacred Kingfisher

Red-backed Kingfisher (male)

Grey Swiftlet

Rainbowbird

Noisy Scrub-bird

Buff-breasted Pitta

Black-breasted Pitta

Rufous Scrub-bird

PLATE 13 Larks Logrunners Quail-thrush

Welcome
Swallow

Barn
Swallow

Southern
Logrunner (female)

Western Whipbird

Chestnut-crowned Babbler

Southern Scrub Robin

Rufous Songlark

Bushlark

Cinnamon
Quail-thrush
(male)

Ground Cuckoo-shrike

PLATE 14 Fairy Wrens Emuwrens Grasswrens

Variegated Wren
(male)

(female)

(male)

Banded Wren

White-winged Wren
(male)

Lilac-crowned Wren
(male)

Southern Emuwren
(male)

Red-backed Wren
(male)

Grey Grasswren
(male)

Striated Grasswren
(male)

(female)

(male)

Black
Grasswren

Thick-billed Grasswren
(male)

PLATE 15 Warblers Thornbills Scrubwrens

White-throated Warbler

White-tailed Warbler

Yellow-rumped Thornbill

Little Grassbird

Striated Thornbill

Yellow-throated Scrubwren (male)

Pilotbird

Spinifexbird

Rock Warbler

Eastern Bristlebird

Chestnut-rumped Heathwren

Peter Slater

PLATE 16   Flycatchers Robins

Buff-sided Robin

Lemon-breasted
Flycatcher

Yellow
Flycatcher

Pale-yellow
Robin (race *nana*)

Eastern Yellow Robin
(race *viridior*)

Redcapped Robin
(male)

Rose Robin (male)

Scarlet Robin
(male)

Flame Robin
(male)

Pink Robin
(male)

PETER SLATER

PLATE 17   Flycatchers Chats Whistlers

Pearly-winged Flycatcher

(male)

(female)

Shining Flycatcher

Boat-billed Flycatcher (male)
(race *secundus*)

Golden Whistler
(male)

Gilbert Whistler
(male)

Orange Chat (male)

Crimson Chat (male)

Rufous Fantail

Crested Bellbird
(male)

Western Thrush

PLATE 18   Treecreepers Pardalotes Silvereyes

Yellow Silvereye

Western Silvereye

Yellow-breasted
Sunbird (male)

Black-capped
Sittella (female)

(male)

Yellow-rumped Pardalote

Mistletoebird

Fortyspotted Pardalote

Striated
Pardalote

(female)

Brown Treecreeper

Rufous
Treecreeper

PETER SLATER

Red-browed
Treecreeper (male)

PLATE 19   Small Honeyeaters

Banded
Honeyeater

Mallee
Honeyeater

Grey
Honeyeater

Red-throated
Honeyeater

Purple-gaped
Honeyeater

Yellow-fronted
Honeyeater

White-plumed
Honeyeater

Pale-yellow
Honeyeater

Red-headed
Honeyeater

Western
Spinebill

Tawny-crowned
Honeyeater

Scarlet
Honeyeater

Golden-backed
Honeyeater

PLATE 20   Large Honeyeaters

Bell Miner

Varied Honeyeater

Yellow-tufted
Honeyeater

Helmeted
Honeyeater

White-eyed
Honeyeater

Lewin Honeyeater

Mottled
Honeyeater

Little
Wattlebird

Blue-faced
Honeyeater

Regent Honeyeater

PLATE 21   Finches

Blue-faced Finch

Pictorella Finch

Chestnut-breasted Finch

Plum-headed Finch (male)

Masked Finch

Gouldian Finch

Painted Finch (male)

Star Finch

Beautiful Firetail

Crimson Finch (male)

Red-browed Finch

PLATE 22   Orioles Bowerbirds

Green
Catbird

Yellow
Figbird

(male)

Yellow
Oriole

(female)

Satin Bowerbird
(female)

Paradise
Riflebird
(female)

Stagemaker

Spotted Bowerbird

(female)

(male)

Regent Bowerbird

Apostlebird

PLATE 23 Large Pied Birds

Mudlark
(male)

White-winged
Chough

White-backed
Magpie

Grey
Butcherbird

Black-throated
Butcherbird

Pied
Currawong

Black-backed
Magpie

PLATE 24   Large Black Birds

Satin Bowerbird
(male)

Magnificent Riflebird (male)

Shining
Starling

Koel (male)

Manucode

Black Butcherbird

Spangled
Drongo

mainly shades of pearly-grey (they are sometimes called greybirds) with some black about the head and sometimes black bars. They have an elongated shape of about 25–35cm. They are typically woodland species except for the forest Cicadabird, which is sometimes put in a genus of its own, *Edolisoma*.

422 BLACK-FACED CUCKOO-SHRIKE *Coracina novaehollandiae* (Gmelin) 1789

Distribution: throughout.

RECOGNITION: *pearly-grey with black on face and throat; subadult has only black band from bill to behind eye.*

DESCRIPTION: 33cm, with broad rounded tail 15cm. Sexes alike. Forehead, face and throat black; upperparts grey; breast dark grey; belly and under-shoulders white; main flight feathers black edged with white; terminal half of tail black tipped with white; bill and legs black; eyes dark brown. *Immature and subadult:* black only on face, a broad black band from bill to behind eye; throat and breast mottled grey and white.

VARIATION: not clearly defined: in Tasmania, bill rather smaller (race *novaehollandiae*); on mainland, bill rather larger (race *melanops*); mid-Western Australia, generally paler (race *subpallida*).

HABITAT: most timbered areas other than wet forests, sometimes wooded suburbs and orchards. HABITS: arboreal, rarely on ground, feeds in tree canopies, sometimes takes flying insects; solitary or family parties or small flocks, occasionally large flocks in far north; sedentary, especially in north, nomadic and migratory, especially in southeast, apparently not in Western Australia; flight direct and undulating, on alighting wings are refolded or shuffled, an action exaggerated in mating display when wings are alternately raised high in fairly quick succession. BREEDING: August–February; nests in trees on fairly high tree forks, a shallow cup made of twigs and bark resembling branch and bound with cobwebs; two to three eggs, variable but often shades of olive spotted with brown and dull red. VOICE: soft churring. FOOD: insects, fruit and seeds.

STATUS: common. TAXONOMY: endemic breeding races, some migrating to New Guinea and other islands, of variable species extending to northern India.

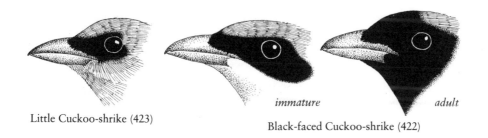

Little Cuckoo-shrike (423)

immature   *adult*

Black-faced Cuckoo-shrike (422)

423 LITTLE CUCKOO-SHRIKE *Coracina papuensis* (Gmelin) 1788

[*Note: C. robusta* now considered to be race of this species but the established name 'Little' is retained.]

Distribution: Map 127.

RECOGNITION: *in usual white-throated phase, black on face only in front of eye; in uncommon black-faced phase, crown often mottled and breast barred with black.*

DESCRIPTION: 28cm. Sexes alike, but male has small white patch on rear upper margin of eye. *Usual plumage:* forehead and from base of bill to front margin of eye black; upperparts pale blue-grey; underparts white, sometimes pale grey on breast; main flight feathers black edged with white; bill and legs black; eyes brown. *Uncommon plumage:* whole face, throat and most of crown black, breast barred with black—or various intermediate stages (occurring only in southern race, *robusta*, and at one time considered to be immature plumage of species of that name).

VARIATION: west of Normanton palest, little or no grey on breast (race *hypoleuca*); north of about Townsville, slightly darker and distinctly greyish on breast (race *stalkeri*); south of Townsville darkest, darker grey on breast which is sometimes barred with black and sometimes whole head with varying amounts of black (race *robusta*).

HABITAT: well timbered areas, including mangroves. HABITS: arboreal, keeps to tree canopies and leafy branches; solitary or in small parties; sedentary, especially in north, nomadic; undulating flight with wings alternately flapped and closed. BREEDING: August–March; nests in trees on high horizontal forks of small branches, made of twigs and grass bound with cobwebs; two to three eggs, shades of olive spotted with dark reddish-brown. VOICE: loud 'keer-serk' often uttered on wing, also shrill 'kissik' or 'quissik' repeated. FOOD: insects from tree foliage or taken on wing, also fruit.

STATUS: common in north, rare in south. TAXONOMY: races, some endemic, of species extending to New Guinea, Moluccas and Solomon Is.

424 BARRED CUCKOO-SHRIKE   *Coracina lineata*   (Swainson) 1825   Fig p 292
Distribution: Map 128.

RECOGNITION: *breast and belly barred black and white, black between bill and eye, pale yellow eyes.*

DESCRIPTION: 28cm. Sexes alike. Band from forehead to eye black; upperparts, throat and foreneck blue-grey; breast, belly and under-shoulders barred black and white; flight feathers black; tail black, grey at base; bill and legs black; eyes pale yellow.

HABITAT: rain forests. HABITS: arboreal, keeps to high open canopies; solitary but in small flocks when not breeding, sometimes roosting in large flocks; sedentary and nomadic, possibly migratory in south. BREEDING: October–January; nests in trees, in forks of high branches, made of fine twigs bound with cobwebs; two eggs, dull white or with greenish tinge, spotted with browns and greys. VOICE: weak or soft 'chirp'. FOOD: insects and fruit.

STATUS: fairly common, rare in south. TAXONOMY: endemic race *(lineata)* of species extending to New Guinea and Solomon Is.

425 CICADABIRD   *Coracina tenuirostris*   (Jardine) 1831
Distribution: Map 129.

RECOGNITION: *male, mainly dark blue-grey with white patch on underwing; female, brownish with barred underparts.*

DESCRIPTION: 25cm. Sexes very different. *Male:* mainly dark bluish-grey; black band from bill to behind eye; flight feathers black edged with grey; large white patch in centre of underwing; outer tail feathers black edged with grey; bill and legs black; eyes dark brown. *Female*: upperparts grey-brown; wing feathers edged with light brown; brownish eyebrow; black between bill and eye, remainder of face mottled black and buffy-white; underparts buff-brown barred with black; under-shoulders cinnamon brown; under tail coverts pale buff; bill blackish-brown.

VARIATION: general tendency for larger size and less black on face in south, smaller and more black in north: races currently listed; east (race *tenuirostris*, also sometimes *obscurus* in Cape York); northwest (race *melvillensis*).

HABITAT: forests of various kinds and mangroves; well timbered mountain ridges in south. HABITS: arboreal, usually in high canopies; solitary or small parties; migratory, breeding visitor throughout, about August–April, but possibly some at other times in far north, males recorded as departing before females and immatures. BREEDING: October–February; nests in tree canopies, on slender forked branches, a small shallow cup made of fine twigs, pieces of bark and lichen bound with cobweb; one egg, pale green, spotted and blotched with reddish-brown and grey. VOICE: loud prolonged buzz, rather like Cicada stridulation, also sharp whistling 'tcheep'. FOOD: insects gathered mainly from tree foliage.

STATUS: uncommon, mainly breeding visitor migrating to New Guinea. TAXONOMY: species ranging from Celebes to Solomon Is.

Genus LALAGE

This group of nine Australasian and Polynesian species seems more akin to *Campephaga* (of Africa) than *Coracina* but shows some affinity with both. Of the two Australian species one is sedentary and the other a breeding visitor. They are relatively small, under 20cm, and there is a fairly marked sexual dimorphism; males are largely black and white and females brown. They are particularly noted for musical trilling songs.

426 WHITE-WINGED TRILLER *Lalage sueurii* (Vieillot) 1818

Distribution: throughout.

RECOGNITION: *male, white patch on shoulders, no white eyebrow; female and non-breeding male, plain buffy-white underparts; like Pied Honeyeater (No 616) but has short bill and white throat.* [*Note*: most Australian males are unique both in this species and in the family as a whole in having distinct breeding and non-breeding plumages. About January to February there is a complete post-breeding moult into plumage similar to, but not identical with, the female; between July and November—depending on region—there is a partial moult into breeding plumage.]

DESCRIPTION: 18cm. Sexes different. *Male, breeding*: upperparts shiny black with grey rump; wing black with mainly white shoulder and inner flight feathers edged with white; tail black, outer feathers tipped with white. *Male, non-breeding*: crown and back brownish; breast and flanks tinged with buff; otherwise as breeding including bill and legs black; eyes dark brown. *Female*: differs from non-breeding male in having rump less grey; wings and tail blackish-brown with buff edges; underparts plain buffy-white; bill blackish-brown, pale at base.

HABITAT: lightly timbered areas, including suburban parks and gardens. HABITS: arboreal, but feeds mostly on ground; solitary and gregarious, sometimes nesting in close communities; possibly sedentary and nomadic but also distinct north–south migration, breeding visitor roughly south of tropic, mainly non-breeding visitor in north (also in New Guinea), in between apparently sedentary but local breeders may move north and be replaced by others which have bred further south; flight steady and direct. BREEDING: September–February; nests in trees and saplings at moderate heights, in forks or on bare limbs, small frail cup made of twigs and grass and camouflaged with bark attached with cobwebs; two to three eggs, green blotched and streaked with reddish-brown and blue-grey. VOICE: melodious prolonged trill or warble. FOOD: insects, mainly obtained on ground.

STATUS: fairly common to common. TAXONOMY: endemic race *(tricolor)* of species with one other race in Timor, east Java and south Celebes.

427 PIED TRILLER   *Lalage leucomela*   (Vig. & Horsf.) 1826

Distribution: Map 130.

RECOGNITION: *male: white eyebrow, two white bars on shoulder; female: barred underparts (also some bars on male of race rufiventris).*

DESCRIPTION: 19cm. Sexes different. *Male:* upperparts shiny black with grey on rump; white eyebrow, two white bars on shoulders, white edges to central feathers forming streak on wing, white tips to outer tail feathers; lower face and throat dull white; breast and flanks pale grey; centre of belly and under tail coverts light cinnamon brown; underwing mainly white; bill black; eyes dark brown; legs dark grey. *Female:* dark areas of upperparts dull brownish-black; throat to breast and flanks light brownish-grey barred with black; remainder as in male.

VARIATION: east as far north as Cooktown, as above (race *leucomela*); north of Cooktown, male has breast and flanks near white, paler and less cinnamon on belly (race *yorki*); Northern Territory, male nearly like eastern female with barring on throat to breast and flanks, less grey on rump (race *rufiventris*).

HABITAT: wet forests and mangroves, especially edges, and adjacent open forests, usually near coast. HABITS: arboreal, often in outer foliage of trees at various heights moving slowly and unobtrusively; solitary; sedentary. BREEDING: August–February; nests on branches and tree forks, a shallow cup roughly made of a few twigs bound with cobwebs and decorated with bark; one egg, pale green spotted and blotched with reddish-brown and grey. VOICE: trilling song, less varied than White-winged Triller. FOOD: fruit and insects.

STATUS: common. TAXONOMY: endemic races of species extending to New Guinea and adjacent islands.

Pied Triller
(427) *male*

Barred Cuckoo-shrike (424)

Introduced family

Family PYCNONOTIDAE
Bulbuls
1(109) species: introduced

BULBULS BELONG TO THE old world and they are mainly tropical in distribution. They are relatively small, about 15–30cm, with plumages in plain colours, often dark about the head which is sometimes crested, and usually with some contrasting patch of bright colour, like red or yellow at the vent. They live in trees and bushes, many readily adapting to suburban parks and gardens. They are gregarious and rather noisy but have quite pleasant songs. By far the largest genus is *Pycnonotus,* which includes the Red-whiskered Bulbul introduced to Australia from China.

428 RED-WHISKERED BULBUL *Pycnonotus jocosus* (Linnaeus) 1758

Distribution: vicinity of Sydney, Melbourne and Adelaide.

RECOGNITION: *black crown with crest, red patch on face, red patch under tail.*

DESCRIPTION: 20cm; head crested. Sexes alike. Forehead to nape, side of neck and side of breast black; remainder of upperparts greyish-brown; patch under and behind eye scarlet; cheeks white, separated by black bar from white throat and foreneck; remainder of underparts dull white, greyer on flanks; under tail coverts scarlet; outer tail feathers tipped with white; bill and legs black; eyes brown.

HABITAT: suburban parks and gardens, extending to adjacent woodlands. HABITS: arboreal and gregarious; flight low and not vigorous. BREEDING: September–February; nests in bushes and low trees, made of small twigs, leaves and strips of bark; three eggs, white spotted and blotched with reddish-brown. VOICE: harsh shrill whistle and low chatter, also pleasant song. FOOD: berries and insects.

STATUS: well established and common.

MUSCICAPID ASSEMBLAGE

THE FOLLOWING GROUPS ARE listed here as families, Turdidae, Maluridae, Sylviidae, Muscicapidae, Monarchidae, Pachycephalidae, Ephthianuridae. In the opinion of many taxonomists they are subfamilies of one large family, which takes its name from the oldest genus, *Muscicapa.* It is not from disagreement with this conclusion that subfamilies are here elevated to family rank but for convenience. In any case these groups, subfamilies or families, are mostly of uncertain composition and not easy to define in terms of common characteristics. It is particularly difficult to know where to place some of the numerous Australian endemic species, such as the fairy wrens, emuwrens and grasswrens.

Family TURDIDAE
Thrushes
5(about 300) species: 1 endemic, 2 introduced

Distribution: worldwide.

THE COMPOSITION AND CHARACTERISTICS of this family are not clearly defined. As understood at present it has few representatives in the Australasian region, and some of these are doubtfully included. The three Australian species, occurring naturally, belong to two quite different groups. The only species resembling the true thrushes is the Ground Thrush, which has obvious similarities with the introduced Song Thrush, belonging to the typical genus *Turdus*. It is the southern extension of an east Asian species, with numerous relatives elsewhere in the old world, and this pattern suggests that it is a comparatively recent colonist. Included in the family, but with little conviction, are the two scrub robins. They are thought by some to be primitive thrushes, and by others to belong to the babbler family, perhaps having affinity with *Cinclosoma*. It is certain at least that they have been in Australia a long time, and indeed might have evolved there from some ancient, perhaps thrush-like stock. Little can be said regarding the characteristics of the family except that bills are fairly slender; that in most species the juveniles have spotted plumages; that they are mainly terrestrial, feeding among ground litter of forests and woodlands, and usually nesting on or near the ground.

Key to TURDIDAE

1 Plain black or brown......................... Blackbird .... No 432
2 Drab brown, darker above, lighter below 3–6

3 Scalloped with black above and below .... Ground Thrush .... No 431
4 Spotted with black on breast................... Song Thrush................ No 433
5 Face white with black vertical band............. Northern Scrub Robin........ No 430
6 Face grey brown with white eyering............. Southern Scrub Robin........ No 429

Genus DRYMODES

There are two species of scrub robins, one in the south and endemic, the other in the north with connections in New Guinea. In Australia both have discontinuous distributions suggesting shrinkage of once widespread populations. Affinity with the true thrushes is sometimes questioned.

429 SOUTHERN SCRUB ROBIN *Drymodes brunneopygia* Gould 1840 Pl 13

Distribution: Map 131.

RECOGNITION: *drab brown with rufous rump, white eyering, two white bars on shoulders; on ground in open scrub.*

DESCRIPTION: 19–20cm, with tail about half. Sexes alike but female distinctly smaller. Upperparts dark grey-brown (dark drab) shading to dark cinnamon rufous on rump and upper tail coverts; face light drab with dull white lores and eyering; breast and flanks light drab; chin and centre of belly whitish; vent and under tail coverts light cinnamon; wings blackish-brown with two white bars on shoulders and concealed white bar on flight feathers; tail blackish-brown edged with dark rufous and tipped with white; bill and legs black; eyes dark brown.

VARIATION: eastern populations darker (race *brunneopygia*); western populations paler (race *pallida*).

HABITAT: mallee and scrubby sandplain. HABITS: terrestrial, often in vicinity of low bushes and keeping well hidden, hops about on ground with tail partially cocked, seldom flies into bushes; solitary; sedentary. BREEDING: July–October in west, September–January in east; nests on or near ground in open patches of grass or under bushes, a shallow cup made of stout twigs, usually with others scattered nearby, lined with rootlets and grass; one egg, dull white to greenish-grey, spotted and blotched with brown and black. VOICE: loud sharp 'chip-per-pree-e', also piercing 'pee-ee-e'. FOOD: insects.

STATUS: rather uncommon. TAXONOMY: endemic species.

430 NORTHERN SCRUB ROBIN *Drymodes superciliaris* Gould 1850

Distribution: Map 131.

RECOGNITION: *reddish-brown back, white face with vertical black band; on ground in forests.*

DESCRIPTION: 19–20cm, with tail about half. Sexes alike but female distinctly smaller. Crown dark brown shading to cinnamon brown on back and dark cinnamon rufous on upper tail coverts and outer tail feathers; underparts white tinged with pinkish-buff, or dark cinnamon buff, on breast and flanks; face whitish with broad black vertical band; wings black with two pale buff bars on shoulders, white edges to central flight feathers and broad concealed white bar; outer tail feathers tipped with white; bill black; eyes brown; legs pinkish-brown.

VARIATION: Cape York, generally lighter with breast and flanks pinkish-buff (race *superciliaris*); Roper River area, generally darker with breast and flanks cinnamon buff (race *colcloughi*).

HABITAT: open parts of forests, especially edges. HABITS: terrestrial, walks or runs on ground with body horizontal, turns over leaves and other debris in search of food; solitary; sedentary. BREEDING: October–January; nests on ground close to trees, made of small sticks and lined with fibres and surrounded with dead leaves; two eggs, greyish, spotted and blotched with dark reddish-brown. VOICE: thin sharp whistle. FOOD: small animal life of ground litter, especially snails.

STATUS: common locally in Cape York; uncertain in Northern Territory—occurrence not well authenticated. TAXONOMY: endemic races of species extending to New Guinea and Aru Is.

Northern Scrub Robin (430)

Ground Thrush (431)

Genus ZOOTHERA

As currently determined, a group of about thirty species ranging throughout the old world and North America. The only representative in Australia is the Ground Thrush, sometimes called Scaled Ground Thrush because it is scalloped with black over most of its drab brown plumage. The Australian populations are a southern extension of a variable species found over much of Asia and India to Indonesia and New Guinea. Although (geologically) recent immigrants they have been isolated from the main stock for so long some would have it that they should be regarded as one or more separate species, or possibly semispecies of a super-species.

431 GROUND THRUSH　*Zoothera dauma*　(Latham) 1790　　　　　　Fig p 295

Distribution: Map 132.

RECOGNITION: *bronze-brown above and white below with overall black scallops or scaly markings; on or near forest floors.*

DESCRIPTION: 25–28cm. Sexes alike. Upperparts light bronze-brown; face and underparts white; most feathers have rounded black tips giving a scaly or scalloped appearance, densest on breast and sometimes absent from throat and centre of belly; fairly distinct black streaks from base of bill to below eye and on edge of throat; underwing black and white; tail sometimes has white on inner web of outer pair of feathers; bill black; eyes dark brown; legs dark grey.

VARIATION: four races are listed, based mainly on depth of colour of upperparts and bill size: Tasmania (race *macrorhyncha*); southeast mainland (race *lunulata*); northern New South Wales and southern Queensland (race *heinei*); Atherton tableland, larger bill (race *cuneata*).

HABITAT: forests and dense thickets, especially damp gullies. HABITS: mainly terrestrial, usually on or within about 3–5m from ground, and may be heard before being seen on ground turning over litter; relies on camouflage for protection and is relatively easily approached; solitary; sedentary. BREEDING: July–December, early in south, late in north; nests below about 4m in low forks, on stumps or in dense bushes, made of leaves and grass and finished on outside with green moss; two to three eggs, light green, spotted and blotched with reddish-brown. VOICE: rather silent, but has flute-like whistle and low melodious warble uttered usually at dusk or dawn. FOOD: insects and other small invertebrates.

STATUS: fairly common, uncommon in far north. TAXONOMY: endemic races (or semispecies) of widespread species.

Introduced species

432 BLACKBIRD　*Turdus merula*　Linnaeus 1758

Distribution: Victoria and Tasmania and vicinity of Adelaide, Sydney and Canberra.

RECOGNITION: 25cm. Sexes different. *Male:* black; bill and eyering bright yellow. *Female:* brown, paler below and slightly mottled.

HABITS: mainly on ground or low in bushes and trees, but sings high up in trees. BREEDING: September–January; nests in low vegetation, especially bushes, made of grass and bound, but not lined, with mud; four eggs, greenish-blue spotted with reddish-brown. VOICE: harsh alarm note and melodious warbling (richer and more varied than Song Thrush). FOOD: insects and fruit.

STATUS: common and thriving.

Introduced species

433 SONG THRUSH   *Turdus philomelos*   Brehm 1831

Distribution: mainly vicinity of Melbourne.

RECOGNITION: 23cm. Sexes alike. Upperparts plain brown; breast and flanks buff-yellow spotted with blackish-brown; belly white.

HABITS: mainly on ground or low in vegetation, but sings high up in trees. BREEDING: September–January; nests in bushes, made of grass and mud and lined with mud; four eggs, rich blue spotted with black. VOICE: loud, clear melodious song (rather more repetitive than Blackbird). FOOD: mainly insects.

STATUS: fairly common.

Family TIMALIIDAE
Babblers
13(about 280) species: 11 endemic

Distribution: throughout much of old world except for genus of one species in western North America.

THE TRUE BABBLERS ARE quite distinctive; once seen and heard babblers are not readily mistaken, except perhaps—in Australia only—for the Apostlebird (see Grallinidae) for both are highly sociable, keeping in small compact parties which maintain a constant noisy chatter, either on the ground or in bushes and other low vegetation; indeed similarity in behaviour has led to confusion for the Grey-crowned Babbler is also known as Apostlebird. But babblers have slender bills which are fairly long and downcurved; they have a whitish streak or band above the eye and white tipped tails; they build twig nests. The true babblers which live in chattering companies are represented in Australia by members of the near endemic genus *Pomatostomus*. The problem is to know what other groups bear close enough relationship to be included in the same family. Australia has a number of distinctive and endemic, or nearly endemic, genera which some taxonomists believe have such affinity. They are *Cinclosoma,* quail-thrushes, *Psophodes,* whipbirds, and *Orthonyx,* logrunners. Except for *Orthonyx,* which is sometimes placed in a separate family, they have long and broad graduated tails which are mainly black with white tips, and all are wholly or mainly terrestrial; they have short rounded wings and are relatively poor fliers.

Key to TIMALIIDAE

[Additional keys under genera]

1 Tail plain, broad and spiky; plumage dark above and white below (♀ with rufous throat); in rain forests and mostly on ground .... *Orthonyx* ..... Nos 434–435
2 Tail long, broad and graduated, mainly black and tipped with white 3–6
3 Head crested, white at side of throat .... *Psophodes* .... Nos 443–445
4 Whitish streak or band above eye 5–6

5 Mainly grey-brown or blackish-brown; fairly long decurved
  bill; always in small noisy parties, in woodlands and on or
  near ground .... *Pomatostomus* . Nos 439–442
6 Mainly chestnut or cinnamon brown; solitary; always on
  ground.. *Cinclosoma* ... Nos 436–438

Genus ORTHONYX

A small group known as logrunners or spinetails, the latter because tail shafts are hard and
bare at the tip. The group consists of one endemic Australian species and a population which
is linked specifically with others in New Guinea—perhaps it would be better to regard these
very isolated populations as semispecies. Logrunners belong to rain forest floors where they
turn over leaves or scratch among mould using strong feet to scatter debris or lift it aside, in
the manner of lyrebirds. They fly into trees but rarely very high. They are brownish with
white throat and breast, except females which have a rufous throat.

Key to ORTHONYX

1 Back mottled; east coast south of tropic.......... Southern Logrunner .... No 434
2 Back plain; Cooktown-Ingham area............. Northern Logrunner........ No 435

434 SOUTHERN LOGRUNNER *Orthonyx temminckii* Ranzini 1822   Pl 13
Distribution: Map 133.

RECOGNITION: *very dark mottled back, white below except for brown throat of female; on
forest floors.*

DESCRIPTION: 18–20cm, without tail spines. Sexes different. *Male:* crown and nape rufous
grey, feathers edged with black; back boldly mottled rufous grey and black; rump and upper
tail coverts dark rufous brown; face from above eye and side of neck grey; black patch at side
of throat; chin to belly white; flanks and under tail coverts grey tinged with rufous; shoulders
black with two grey bars; flight feathers blackish-brown; tail blackish-brown with stiff
shafts extending as bare spines; bill blackish; eyes dark brown; legs black. *Female:* smaller;
chin and throat cinnamon brown.

HABITAT: rain forests. HABITS: terrestrial but sometimes flies into trees when disturbed or to
roost; frequents dank open places with soft humus to scratch for grubs and similar food,
spreads and presses tail on ground for support while using large strong feet to shift leaves
and mould; short wings make whirring sound on brief flights; solitary; sedentary. BREEDING:
March–October; nests on ground, on slope or against rock or tree trunk, a rough platform
of sticks partly hooded over with interwoven twigs and leaves and often covered with moss;
two white eggs. VOICE: loud, short, sharp and resonant 'be-kweek be-kweek-kweek-kweek',
uttered mostly at dawn and dusk, also soft 'tweet' when feeding. FOOD: grubs and other
invertebrates in leaf mould.

STATUS: locally common. TAXONOMY: endemic race, or semispecies, of species found also in
New Guinea.

435 NORTHERN LOGRUNNER *Orthonyx spaldingi* Ramsay 1868
Distribution: Map 133.

RECOGNITION: *plain blackish back, white below except for rufous throat of female; on
forest floors.*

DESCRIPTION: 25–27cm. Sexes different. *Male:* head, face and side of neck jet black; back and flanks black tinged with rufous olive; throat, breast and belly white; wings and tail brownish-black, hard shafts of tail feathers extended as bare spines; bill black; eyes brownish-black; legs black. *Female:* smaller; throat and upper breast cinnamon rufous; head less jet black and back tinged with rufous brown.

HABITAT: rain forests, especially at high altitudes. HABITS: similar to southern species, but sometimes in small parties. BREEDING: May–November; nests similar to southern species but sometimes located off ground up to 4m in suitable places, as on elk-horn ferns; one white egg. VOICE: loud resonant 'chow-chilla' (hence alternative common name) often followed by 'chow-chow-chowy chook-chook', mostly uttered about dawn, also softer clucking sounds. FOOD: insects, grubs and other small invertebrates.

STATUS: locally common. TAXONOMY: endemic species.

Genus CINCLOSOMA

The distinctive species which form this group have the imprecise name quail-thrush, instead of the original 'ground-thrush' (now reserved for another species) and the later 'ground-bird'. Connection with the true thrushes is probably rather remote and the quail-like characteristic is the noisy whirring of short wings in flight. The generic name adopted as a vernacular would be a unique alternative. Apart from one close relative in a small area in southeast New Guinea quail-thrushes are a truly Australian group consisting of about three or four species. They are terrestrial and live in desert country and dry woodlands. Plumages have camouflage patterns, hence striking differences in obviously related forms, and colours are mostly various shades of brown, with black shoulders marked with white and black tails tipped with white.

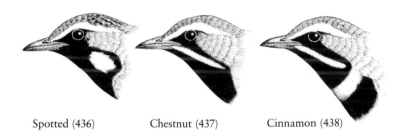

Spotted (436)　　　　Chestnut (437)　　　　Cinnamon (438)

MALE QUAIL-THRUSHES

Key to CINCLOSOMA

1	Chin and throat black		3–5 (males)
2	Chin and throat not black....................		6–8 (females)
3	Side of neck white ....(♂)	Spotted Quail-thrush	No 436
4	Foreneck light chestnut, breast black ....(♂)	Cinnamon-Quail-thrush......	No 438
5	Foreneck and breast black ....(♂)	Chestnut Quail-thrush	No 437
6	Side of neck chestnut ....(♀)	Spotted Quail-thrush	No 436
7	Side of throat cream, breast grey-brown ......(♀)	Cinnamon Quail-thrush......	No 438
8	Side of throat white, breast grey.............(♀)	Chestnut Quail-thrush	No 437

436 SPOTTED QUAIL-THRUSH *Cinclosoma punctatum* (Shaw) 1795 Fig p 299
Distribution: Map 134.

RECOGNITION: *black shoulders with white spots and black tail with white tip, patch at side of neck white in male chestnut in female; on ground in dry scrubby hills.*

DESCRIPTION: 27–30cm. Sexes different. *Male:* upperparts olive-brown blotched with black; inner wing streaked with black and chestnut; shoulders black spotted with white; broad streak above eye white to light buff; lower half of face, throat and foreneck black; large white patch on side of neck; upper breast grey, separated by black band from white lower breast and belly; flanks and under tail coverts light chestnut heavily blotched with black; tail (except central feathers) black broadly tipped with white; bill black; eyes light brown; legs pinkish-brown. *Female:* distinctly smaller; patch on side of neck chestnut; throat and foreneck whitish; no black band on breast; less black on shoulders.

HABITAT: dry forests and woodlands, especially stony and scrubby hillsides. HABITS: terrestrial, rarely flies into trees; solitary; sedentary; keeps well hidden, runs fast, takes flight with noisy whirring wings and flies low for short distance. BREEDING: August–February; nests on ground, in depression, well hidden under tussocks, stones or fallen logs, loosely made of bark strips and grass and often with platform of leaves at entrance; two to three eggs, dull white, spotted and blotched with reddish-brown and pale grey. VOICE: thin piping whistle. FOOD: seeds and insects.

STATUS: uncommon to fairly common; much affected by land settlement. TAXONOMY: endemic species.

437 CHESTNUT QUAIL-THRUSH
     Cinclosoma castanotum Gould 1840   Fig p 299

[*Note:* the variants included here as races of this species although showing some marked differences have certain basic similarities and they appear to replace each other geographically. They are at least species in the making but there does not seem to be a definite yardstick to decide if any qualify for recognition as full species. The nearest to that status may be *alisteri*, which is sometimes listed as Nullarbor Quail-thrush.]

Distribution: Map 135.

RECOGNITION: *black shoulders speckled with white, black tail tipped with white, male has chin to breast black, female has buffy patch at side of throat; terrestrial.*

DESCRIPTION: 20–23cm. Sexes different. *Male:* upperparts (see variation); whitish streak above eye; black streak from base of bill to eye and side of neck; lower face and side of throat white; chin, centre of throat and breast black; belly white, sometimes blotched with black at edge of flank; shoulders black speckled with white; tail black (except central feathers) tipped with white; bill black; eyes reddish-brown; legs grey-brown. *Female:* centre of throat grey speckled with white; side of throat and streak above eye white; foreneck and breast grey; shoulders mainly dark brown speckled with white.

VARIATION: southeast South Australia to southwest New South Wales and northwest Victoria, also extreme southwest Western Australia—upperparts, flanks and sides of breast grey-brown (drab), except for varying amounts of light or dark chestnut on rump, usually less pronounced in female (races *castanotum, mayri, morgani* and *dundasi*); central and northwest South Australia, southwest Northern Territory and west central Western Australia—head, nape and upper tail drab brown, back and rump dark cinnamon to chestnut (race *clarum*); Nullarbor Plain—whole upperparts dark cinnamon, smaller (race *alisteri*).

HABITAT: various kinds of dry woodlands and heaths, especially where stony. HABITS: terrestrial, but occasionally perches in bushes to sing, skulks under or behind bushes, runs very fast, flies low with distinct whirring of wings for short distances; solitary; sedentary. BREEDING: May–October; nests on ground in thick scrub and under shelter of bush, a shallow depression with strips of bark and lined with leaves; two to three eggs, creamy-white, sometimes with greenish or bluish tinge, spotted and blotched with shades of brown and grey. VOICE: thin piercing whistle, also harsh alarm note and feeble song. FOOD: seeds. STATUS: fairly common. TAXONOMY: endemic species.

438 CINNAMON QUAIL-THRUSH

Cinclosoma cinnamomeum   Gould 1846   Pl 13   Fig p 299

Distribution: Map 136.

RECOGNITION: *like desert forms of Chestnut Quail-thrush but male has light chestnut foreneck separating black throat from black breast, female has side of throat cream.*

DESCRIPTION: 20cm. Sexes different. *Male:* upperparts and flanks shades of cinnamon brown, greyish tinge on crown and nape; broad buffy-white stripe above eye; chin and throat black with white patch at side of throat; upper breast black; lower breast and belly mainly white or white with cinnamon margins and blotched with varying amounts of black; shoulders black speckled with white; tail (except central feathers) black broadly tipped with white; bill black; eyes dark brown; legs dark grey. *Female:* head fawn or grey-brown more or less contrasting with cinnamon back; throat and foreneck cream to buff; shoulder blackish-brown speckled with white.

VARIATION: central area, much paler (race *cinnamomeum*); eastern and western populations, much darker (races, east *castaneothorax*; west, *marginatum*—some authorities regard one or both as separate species).

HABITAT: semidesert scrub in mainly sandy localities. HABITS: terrestrial but sometimes perches just off ground in low scrub, skulks among bushes, uses holes and burrows to escape hawks and heat, feeds mostly at dawn and dusk; solitary but sometimes family parties form loose flocks; apparently sedentary; flight low with noisy whirring wings. BREEDING: variable, recorded most months; nests on ground, in shallow depression in or under bush or close to fallen branch, lined with twigs and pieces of bark; two to three eggs, light buff spotted with shades of dark brown and grey. VOICE: thin high-pitched whistle—seems to be of longer duration than the note of the Chestnut species. FOOD: mainly seeds, also insects. STATUS: fairly common. TAXONOMY: endemic species

Genus POMATOSTOMUS

Four species which represent the true babblers in Australia. Except for a small population of the Grey-crowned Babbler in southern New Guinea they are endemic. Babblers are dark brownish-grey with conspicuous broad white eyebrows and black tails with broad white tips; they are about 18–25cm in length. But their most distinctive characteristic (which they share with the Apostlebird) is that they do everything together in small groups, to the accompaniment of much noisy chattering, even to going through the various stages of the breeding cycle, normally the function of a single pair.

Key to POMATOSTOMUS

1	Crown chestnut, white wing bars*	Chestnut-crowned Babbler....	No 440
2	Crown grey, no white wing bars	3–6	
3	Crown pale grey.........................	Grey-crowned Babbler	No 439
4	Crown dark grey	5–6	
5	White throat sharply separated from black breast..	Hall Babbler...............	No 442
6	White throat shading to black belly	White-browed Babbler	No 441

* Usually not visible in flight.

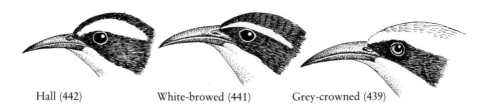

Hall (442)   White-browed (441)   Grey-crowned (439)

BABBLERS

439 GREY-CROWNED BABBLER

Pomatostomus temporalis   (Vig. & Horsf.) 1827

Distribution: Map 137.

RECOGNITION: *crown appearing white but has narrow grey streak in centre, patch of cinnamon brown on underwing and on upperside of extended wing.*

DESCRIPTION: 23–26cm, fairly long thin decurved bill. Sexes alike. Centre of crown to nape grey; remainder of crown to above eye, and sometimes forehead, white; back and wings dark brownish-grey, cinnamon brown patch visible in centre of extended wing; rump and tail black, tail broadly tipped with white; throat white shading in varying proportions to cinnamon rufous in centre of belly; flanks brownish-black; vent and under tail coverts black; bill black; eyes pale lemon to dark brown; legs black.

VARIATION: east of Flinders and Diamantina Rivers, grey crown streak broad and extending to bill, more white and less cinnamon on breast (race *temporalis*, which has south to north clinal variation from larger and darker to smaller and paler); west of Flinders and Diamantina Rivers, grey streak on crown narrow and not extending to bill, less white and more cinnamon on breast (race *rubeculus;* section in extreme west doubtfully separable by even narrower grey crown streak and blacker upperparts—race *nigrescens*).

HABITAT: woodlands of various kinds. HABITS: frequents bushes and trees fairly low down and feeds mainly on ground, turning over bark and stones, runs and hops and bounces, flight laboured and for short distances; gregarious, in noisy chattering groups of about five to twelve which keep in close company, communally build nests and feed young and roost together in 'dummy' nests; sedentary. BREEDING: July–February; often breeds in communal groups, consisting of a mated pair assisted by immature birds; nests in saplings and trees, usually in topmost branches or at end of long limbs (often several nests in one tree), dome shaped with spout-like top entrance, loosely made of interwoven twigs and rootlets, lined with grass and bark with fur or wool; two to three eggs, shades of brown vermiculated with dark brown. VOICE: short squeaking and mewling, also churring. FOOD: insects and seeds.

STATUS: common. TAXONOMY: races of species extending to southern New Guinea.

440 CHESTNUT-CROWNED BABBLER

Pomatostomus ruficeps (Hartlaub) 1852 Pl 13

Distribution: Map 137.

RECOGNITION: *two white shoulder bars and dark chestnut crown.*

DESCRIPTION: 22cm; fairly long thin decurved bill. Sexes alike. Crown dark chestnut (umber) edged with narrow white streak above eye extending from bill to nape; broad blackish streak through eye; upperparts dark grey lightly tinged with brown and scalloped with pale grey; wings brownish-black with two broad white bars on shoulders; throat to centre of belly white; flanks dark grey tinged with brown; axillary feathers tipped with cinnamon brown; vent and under tail coverts black tipped with white; tail black broadly tipped with white; bill blackish, base of lower mandible bluish-white; eyes brown; legs dark-grey.

HABITAT: timber patches along creeks and in saltbush country. HABITS: mainly similar to other babblers, but more elusive and difficult to approach; recorded as forming 'playgrounds' where birds run in follow-my-leader fashion under bushes so frequently as to form clear circular tracks. BREEDING: July–December; nests similar to other babblers but bulkier than White-browed in the same areas and apparently located higher up; four to five eggs, shades of brown with blackish-brown vermiculations. VOICE: harsh rapid 'tchat-a-tchat'. FOOD: insects and seeds.

STATUS: fairly common; overlapping with White-browed but apparently not with Grey-crowned. TAXONOMY: endemic species.

441 WHITE-BROWED BABBLER

Pomatostomus superciliosus (Vig. & Horsf.) 1827

Distribution: Map 138.

RECOGNITION: *white throat shading into dull white breast and blackish belly, thin white eyebrow, no brown in wings.*

DESCRIPTION: 20cm; fairly long thin decurved bill. Sexes alike. Upperparts dark grey with slight brownish tinge; thin white eyebrow extending from bill to nape, edged with black; blackish-brown band through eye; throat and foreneck white shading to dull white breast and grey flanks and belly; tail blackish broadly tipped with white; bill black, dull white at base of lower mandible; eyes reddish-brown; legs dark grey.

VARIATION: over most of range, as above (race *superciliosus*); Gascoyne area, Western Australia, smaller (race *gwendolinae*).

HABITAT: dry woodlands and semideserts with scattered stunted trees and bushes. HABITS: very similar to other babblers. BREEDING: July–December; nests similar to other babblers but usually fairly low and larger than nest of Hall Babbler; three to four eggs, shades of brown with dark brown vermiculations. VOICE: various loud clear whistles, reedy 'chur-r-r-r', loud 'chuck-chuck-chuck'. FOOD: insects and seeds.

STATUS: fairly common. TAXONOMY: endemic species.

442 HALL BABBLER *Pomatostomus halli* Cowles 1964

Distribution: Map 138.

RECOGNITION: *like White-browed Babbler but white throat and foreneck sharply separated from black breast and belly, broad white eyebrow.*

DESCRIPTION: 18cm; long thin decurved bill. Sexes alike. Upperparts blackish with brown tinge on crown and nape; broad white eyebrow; broad black streak through eye; throat and foreneck white; breast and belly sooty-black; tail black with broad white tip; bill black, whitish at base of lower mandible; eyes reddish-brown; legs black.

HABITAT: fairly well wooded localities. HABITS: similar to other babblers. BREEDING: period not known; nests similar to other babblers but smaller. VOICE: not recorded. FOOD: insects and seeds.

STATUS: not known. TAXONOMY: endemic species.

Genus PSOPHODES

An endemic genus consisting of two whipbirds and the Wedgebill, the latter sometimes put in a separate genus *Sphenostoma*. They are about 20–28cm with long broad graduated tails thinly tipped with white, and small but distinct crests. They live on or near the ground in dense vegetation of bushes and thickets and can run with speed. They have loud and distinctive voices of which the explosive whip-crack of the Eastern Whipbird is one of the most arresting sounds of eastern forests.

Key to PSOPHODES

1 White streak on wing, no white at side of throat.... Wedgebill .... No 445
2 White at side of throat, no white streak in wing.... 3–4

3 Large white patch on side of throat............. Eastern Whipbird............ No 443
4 Narrow white band on side of throat........... Western Whipbird........... No 444

443 EASTERN WHIPBIRD *Psophodes olivaceus* Latham 1801
Distribution: Map 139.

RECOGNITION: *appearing blackish with large white patch at side of throat and long graduated tail tipped white or light brown; loud whip-crack note (Rufous Whistler has somewhat similar note but not so loud, clear or emphatic).*

DESCRIPTION: 25–28cm, with broad graduated tail 13–15cm; crest 2·5cm. Sexes alike. Head and crest black shading to very dark olive-brown (medal bronze) on remainder of upperparts; side of neck and throat white; centre of throat black mottled with white; breast black shading to dark grey on belly and olive-brown on flanks; centre of breast and belly mottled with white; tail tipped with dull white or light brown; bill black; eyes and legs dark olive-brown.

Hall Babbler (442)

Wedgebill (445)

VARIATION: north to Rockhampton, tip of tail dull white and tinge of grey on olive-brown flanks (race *olivaceus*); Townsville to Cooktown, tip of tail light brown and little or no grey on flanks (race *lateralis*).

HABITAT: dense thickets in or near wet forests. HABITS: on or near ground, feeds among leaves and other ground debris, hops and runs swiftly, clambers among bushes, occasionally flies direct with rapid wingbeats for short distance; solitary or in small parties; sedentary. BREEDING: July–December; nests near ground in thick undergrowth, loosely made of twigs and rootlets; two eggs, greenish or bluish-white with reddish-brown squiggles. VOICE: male utters loud chuckling sounds and various whistles often ending in explosive whip-crack, sometimes followed immediately by whistle and chuckle from female. FOOD: insects.

STATUS: common. TAXONOMY: endemic species.

444 WESTERN WHIPBIRD *Psophodes nigrogularis* Gould 1844   Pl 13
Distribution: Map 139.

RECOGNITION: *broad black patch on throat and foreneck with white outer margin, tail with black subterminal bar and white tip; on or near ground in low dense scrub.*

DESCRIPTION: 23cm, with graduated tail about half; crest nearly 2·5cm. Sexes alike. Upperparts dark greenish-olive; throat and foreneck black with white streak at outer margin; remainder of underparts greyish-olive, sometimes white in centre of breast and belly; tail with broad black subterminal bar and whitish tip; bill blackish-brown; eyes red; legs slate black.

VARIATION: western populations, white streak at side of throat has black margins, no white in centre of underparts (race *nigrogularis*); eastern populations, white at side of throat without black margins, white in centre of breast and belly (races *leucogaster* and *pondalowiensis*).

HABITAT: low dense thickets, mainly now on coastal sandhills but perhaps also in mallee scrub. HABITS: mostly on or near ground, hops and runs fast, sometimes with tail erect, rarely perches low in trees, flies infrequently but flight fast and direct with rapid wingbeats and of short duration; solitary or in small parties; sedentary. BREEDING: July–November; nests near ground in thick vegetation, a shallow cup made of twigs, bark strips and grass; two eggs, pale blue lightly spotted with black and reddish-brown. VOICE: loud harsh grating sounds (not easily described but distinctive when once heard), songs variously translated such as 'happy birthday to you' (eastern birds) and 'it's for teacher' by male followed immediately by 'pick it up' by female (western birds). FOOD: insects.

STATUS: fairly common in very restricted areas. TAXONOMY: endemic species.

445 WEDGEBILL *Psophodes cristatus* (Gould) 1838
Distribution: Map 139.

RECOGNITION: *drab brown with short crest, white bar on wing, broad white tip to graduated tail; on or near ground in semidesert country.*

DESCRIPTION: 20cm, with broad tail about half; crest 2·5cm. Sexes alike. Upperparts drab brown, shading to darker on rump and darkest on tip of crest, flight feathers and tail; throat dull white; remainder of underparts very pale drab; white streak on wing and broad white tip to tail; bill blackish-brown; eyes reddish-brown; legs dark grey.

VARIATION: populations east and west of the Lakes Eyre and Torrens region are said to differ in voice, habitat and behaviour; names are *cristatus* (east) and *occidentalis* (west).

HABITAT: mulga, low scrub and arid tree savanna. HABITS: on or near ground, runs fast, flies low often with tail fanned, perches low in bushes, especially when singing; solitary or in small flocks; sedentary. BREEDING: variable depending on rains but mainly July–December; nests low down in thick scrubby bushes, bunches of mistletoe or clumps of porcupine grass, shallow cup roughly made of sticks and twigs and lined with grass and rootlets; two to three eggs, greenish or bluish with spots and squiggles of black and greyish-purple. VOICE: harsh squeaky notes like ungreased wheel, also loud clear bell-like song translated as 'did you get drunk' and 'sweet Kitty Lintoff', repeated monotonously. FOOD: insects.

STATUS: fairly common. TAXONOMY: endemic species.

Blue Wren (446) *male*

Family MALURIDAE

Fairy-wrens, Emuwrens, Grasswrens

24(total not known) species: all endemic

Distribution: Australia plus uncertain extralimital range.

THE FAMILY TAKES ITS name from the fairy-wrens, genus *Malurus*. As stated previously (page 293) most taxonomists regard the fairy-wrens and species associated with them (sometimes listed as totalling about eighty) as a subfamily of a much larger family assemblage. But for convenience here they are referred to as a family. The composition of this subfamily or family is not defined with certainty. It need only be stated here that current opinion places in close relationship to the fairy-wrens two other distinct Australian endemic groups, the grasswrens, *Amytornis,* and the emuwrens, *Stipiturus.* The name 'wren' is borrowed from a European bird of that name (sometimes known in Britain as 'Jenny Wren') because the Australian species have similar characteristics without being closely related; like their name-sake they are small shy birds which skulk in low vegetation and have the habit of cocking their long tails over their backs. Additional information on each 'wren' group is given under genera.

Key to MALURIDAE

1 Tail feathers have open webs . . . .   *Stipiturus* . . . Nos 459–461
2 Tail feathers have closed webs.   3–4
3 Males boldly patterned in bright colours; under 15cm; in
   tangled undergrowth. . . . .   *Malurus* . . . . Nos 446–458
4 Plumage streaked in shades of brown; over 15cm; mainly
   terrestrial. . . . .   *Amytornis* . . Nos 462–469

Genus MALURUS

The fairy-wrens belong to Australia, except for one species in New Guinea. The number of species is uncertain. What is clear is that there are five groups of distinctly different forms, on the basis of male colour pattern in breeding plumage; other plumages are nondescript browns with few distinctive features. Three groups are each considered to be single species, the White-winged, Red-backed and Lilac-crowned Wrens (the custom is followed of abbreviating 'fairy-wren' to 'wren'). They do not have prominent and erectile ear covets like the remaining two groups each of which consists of a number of forms which replace each other geographically. They are divided into species more or less arbitrarily either because of isolation or on the evidence of overlapping without interbreeding. One is distinguished by its chestnut shoulders and is referred to here as the 'chestnut' group and another consists of variants of the common Blue Wren and is referred to as the 'blue' group. Breeding males of these five groups are readily distinguished. It is more difficult to distinguish species in each of the 'chestnut' and 'blue' groups, but only where they meet or overlap in range, otherwise identification can be made by location. As well as colourful male plumages and long cocked tails these diminutive wrens live socially in small groups, mainly of one family, and frequent various kinds of shrubby vegetation. These groups have strong territorial attachments and are more or less sedentary.

Key to MALURUS: 'Coloured' Males

[It should be noted that as 'coloured' birds are breeding males they are much fewer in number than 'brown' birds, which consist of non-breeding males (sometimes also breeding), females and immatures of both sexes; at certain times there may not be any 'coloured' males in a particular group. Also when disturbed they seem to keep more in cover and are less frequently seen.]

1 Crown black, back red...................... Red-backed Wren .... No 457
2 Crown mauve with black centre............... Lilac-crowned Wren .... No 458
3 Crown shades of blue 4–19

4 Shoulders white............................ White-winged Wren......... No 456
5 Shoulders chestnut......................... 7–15 ('chestnut' group)
6 Shoulders blackish or brown .... 16–19 ('blue' group)

7 Crown bright blue (methyl or cobalt) 9–10
8 Crown purplish or violet-blue 11–15

9 Upper back light blue, lower back black; extreme
    east.................................... Variegated Wren........... No 450
10 Upper back black, lower back light blue; extreme
    southwest .... Red-winged Wren.......... No 453

11 Throat and breast purplish-black .... Blue-breasted Wren......... No 452
12 Throat and breast pure black................. 13–15

13 Flanks white.............................. Purple-backed Wren........ No 451
14 Flanks buff............................... Lovely Wren............... No 454
15 Flanks violet .... Lavender-flanked Wren ...... No 455

16 Back and rump violet-blue................... Banded Wren .... No 449
17 Back bluish, rump black 18–19

18 Belly white............................... Blue Wren................. No 446
19 Belly bluish
    Purplish sheen on blue back .... Black-backed Wren......... No 447
    No purplish sheen on back................. Turquoise Wren .... No 448

Key to MALURUS: 'Brown' Females

[Note: birds in 'brown' plumage include non-breeding males. They are usually distinguished by black (instead of brown) bills and they lack the facial features of the females referred to in the key.]

1 No russet on face .... White-winged Wren......... No 456
2 Russet patch below and behind eye............. Lilac-crowned Wren .... No 458

'BLUE' GROUP

446 BLUE WREN   *Malurus cyaneus*   (Latham) 1783   Fig p 306

Distribution: Map 140.

RECOGNITION: *blackish or grey-brown shoulders distinguish this and related species from other wrens; white (not blue) belly separates Blue from adjacent Black-backed Wren. Females have rather shorter and less coloured tails and rather less rufous around eye than chestnut-shouldered wrens.*

DESCRIPTION: 13cm, with graduated tail 6cm. Sexes very different when male in breeding plumage but at other times nearly alike. *Male breeding:* forehead and crown, erectile cheek feathers and mantle shiny blue with slight purple tinge (methyl or salvia blue); jet black from gape through eye to broad collar on hind neck; shoulders, lower back and rump black; throat to upper breast black with slight purple sheen, ending in narrow jet black band on breast; lower breast and belly drab white, breast sometimes slightly tinged with blue; flight feathers grey-brown; tail black with dull purple sheen; bill black; eyes dark brown; legs brown. *Male non-breeding:* upperparts grey brown (drab or fawn); underparts dull white; tail as in breeding plumage. *Female:* similar to non-breeding male but has russet-brown on face from base of bill to around eye; brown bill; drab brown tail with little or no purplish sheen.

VARIATION: based mainly on lighter and darker shades: Tasmania, darkest and most richly coloured (race *cyaneus*); north of Sydney, palest (race *cyanochlamys*); intermediate, King and Flinders Is (race *elizabethae*) and mainland south of Sydney (race *australis*).

HABITAT: bushes and other low tangled vegetation in various kinds of woodland and savanna, also parks and gardens. HABITS: on or near ground, hopping and flitting energetically with cocked tail, foraging among dense vegetation or on the ground, or flying fast and direct between bushes; in small family parties which keep close together and follow one another from bush to bush; sedentary, each group maintaining a territory. BREEDING: July–February, sometimes other months; nests near ground in tussocks and bushes, dome-shaped with side entrance, made of grass, rootlets and bark fibre, bound with cobwebs and lined with fine grass, hair, wool or feathers; three to four eggs, pale pink, finely spotted with reddish-brown. VOICE: a succession of short high notes which become faster and end in a loud trill, also constant peeping or 'pripping' while feeding. FOOD: insects.

STATUS: fairly common. TAXONOMY: endemic species or semispecies.

447 BLACK-BACKED WREN   *Malurus melanotus*   Gould 1841

Distribution: Map 140.

RECOGNITION: *male breeding:* like Blue Wren but blue areas are violet, especially *throat violet-blue* (not black), *belly violet-blue* (not white), *upper tail coverts blackish*, some central wing feathers edged with varying amounts of blue-green; differs from Turquoise Wren in having *forehead and crown violet-blue* (not cerulean blue). *Male non-breeding:* also has some

blue-green on wing as well as tail. *Female:* like Blue Wren but tail has distinct purplish sheen.
HABITAT: woodland and savanna with dense shrubs and bushes, tussock grassland. HABITS: similar to Blue Wren but frequently in pairs rather than parties. BREEDING: September–December; nests in grass tussocks and low in bushes, similar to Blue Wren; three to four eggs, pinkish-white finely spotted with reddish-brown. VOICE: similar to Blue Wren. FOOD: insects. STATUS: fairly common. TAXONOMY: endemic species or semispecies.

448 TURQUOISE WREN *Malurus callainus* Gould 1867
Distribution: Map 140.

RECOGNITION: *male breeding:* like Black-backed Wren but *forehead and crown, mantle, upper tail coverts and belly shiny cerulean blue* (not violet-blue), edges of wing feathers and tail also have this colour; differs from Banded Wren in having *lower back black* (not violet-blue). *Male non-breeding:* vivid blue on wings and tail distinctive. *Female:* distinguished from overlapping Variegated Wren by smaller rufous face patch.
HABITAT: arid shrub woodland and tussock grassland. HABITS: like Black-backed Wren but apparently perches and sings higher in trees, observed to move cocked tail from side to side; probably less sedentary than related species. BREEDING: variable, but mainly November–April; otherwise similar to Black-backed and Banded Wrens; three to four eggs, dull white finely speckled with reddish-brown. VOICE: long trilling 'trreeree', lower pitched and less sibilant than overlapping White-winged Wren. FOOD: insects.
STATUS: fairly common. TAXONOMY: endemic species or semispecies (sometimes regarded as race of Banded Wren, as birds in extreme west of range are transitional, in lacking black bar on lower back).

449 BANDED WREN *Malurus splendens* (Quoy & Gaim.) 1830   Pl 14
Distribution: Map 140.

RECOGNITION: like Turquoise Wren but *lower back violet-blue* (not black)—concealed bases of some feathers black; mainly violet-blue above and below except for black collar and black breast band; wings bright greenish-blue. Female paler than Red-winged Wren.
VARIATION: extreme southwest darker (race *splendens*); dry interior paler (race *riordiani*).
HABITAT: forests, woodlands and savanna with dense shrubs. HABITS: similar to Turquoise Wren, including side to side movement of cocked tail, sings from fairly high and exposed situations; mostly in small parties at all times with much communal behaviour, including feeding of young, usually keeps well in cover especially if disturbed. BREEDING: September–January; nests similar to Turquoise Wren; three to four eggs, white spotted with reddish-brown. VOICE: short reeling warble, also regular short 'scrip' or 'tip'. FOOD: insects.
STATUS: common, but not so well adapted to human settlement as Blue Wren. TAXONOMY: endemic species or semispecies (sometimes regarded as conspecific with Turquoise Wren).

'CHESTNUT' GROUP

450 VARIEGATED WREN *Malurus lamberti* Vig. & Horsf. 1827   Pl 14
Distribution: Map 141.

RECOGNITION: *chestnut shoulders distinguish this and similar species from other wrens; bright blue (not purplish-blue) crown and back and buff (not white) flanks separate Varie-*

gated from adjacent Purple-backed Wren. Females have longer and darker coloured tails and rather more rufous around eye than 'blue' wren group.

DESCRIPTION: 14cm, with graduated tail 7·5cm. Sexes very different when male in breeding plumage but at other times very similar. *Male breeding:* forehead and crown and upper back shiny methyl blue; erectile face feathers shiny cerulean blue; lower face, throat and breast, hind neck and lower back velvet black; belly white; flanks and under tail coverts buff; shoulders dark reddish-brown (chestnut); flight feathers blackish-brown; tail dull blue-green, sometimes with white tip; bill black; eyes dark brown; legs brown. *Male non-breeding:* upperparts drab to fawn brown; underparts buffy-white, palest on throat and belly and slightly cinnamon on side of breast and flanks; dull white on face between eye and bill. *Female:* similar to non-breeding male except for rufous brown on face from bill to around eye and bill reddish-brown.

HABITAT: thickets and brushwood wherever they occur, heathland and mangroves. HABITS: on or near ground; usually in small parties moving through bushes and calling quietly, males more elusive; sedentary, parties seldom seem to move far from large bush. BREEDING: mainly July–January; nests on or near ground among grass and flower stems, but sometimes up to 3m, especially in mistletoe clumps or suspended from tea-tree foliage, dome-shaped with side entrance, made of shredded bark and grass bound with cobweb and lined with fur or hair; three to four eggs, pinkish-white speckled with reddish-brown. VOICE: soft high-pitched trilling or chirping 'tsrreee' or 'tsi-tsi-tsi' and similar variants. FOOD: insects.

STATUS: fairly common, apparently not so well adapted to human settlement as 'blue' wrens. TAXONOMY: endemic species or semispecies (sometimes regarded as conspecific with Purple-backed Wren).

451 PURPLE-BACKED WREN   *Malurus assimilis*   North 1901
Distribution: Map 141.

RECOGNITION: like Variegated Wren but *hind crown and upper back shiny violet-blue* (not methyl blue); erectile *face feathers shiny cobalt blue* (darker than methyl blue); *flanks mainly white* (not buff); black breast sometimes has narrow purplish margins; differs from Blue-breasted and Red-winged Wrens by pure black (not purplish-black) throat and breast.

VARIATION: this wide ranging species is sometimes divided into an ill-defined eastern race (*assimilis*) and western race (*mastersi*); on Bernier I, more violet on crown and forehead (race *bernieri*).

HABITAT: dense vegetation of various kinds from mangroves and coastal dune thickets to arid saltbush and tussock grass. HABITS, etc: similar to Variegated Wren; breeding September–January.

STATUS: fairly common. TAXONOMY: endemic species or semispecies (sometimes regarded as race of Variegated Wren with which there is some evidence of interbreeding; overlaps with Blue-breasted Wren and occupies same habitats but apparently the two species keep separate).

452 BLUE-BREASTED WREN   *Malurus pulcherrimus*   Gould 1844
Distribution: Map 141.

RECOGNITION: like Purple-backed Wren with which it partly overlaps but *black throat and breast have deep violet sheen;* crown more violet-blue and erectile face feathers tinged with violet; differs from adjacent Red-winged Wren by *violet-blue* (not blue-green) *crown and mantle*.

HABITAT: similar to Purple-backed Wren but where they overlap perhaps keeping to denser thickets. HABITS, etc: similar to Purple-backed Wren.

STATUS: fairly common. TAXONOMY: endemic species or semispecies.

453 RED-WINGED WREN *Malurus elegans* Gould 1837
Distribution: Map 141.

RECOGNITION: like adjacent Blue-breasted Wren but distinguished by *blue-green or cobalt* (not purplish) *crown and mantle;* lower back light silvery-blue; rather less purplish sheen on black throat and breast. Female reddish-brown facial patch does not extend around eye as in female Blue-breasted Wren; darker than female Banded Wren and wings show slight reddish tinge.

HABITAT: swampy thickets. HABITS, etc: similar to Blue-breasted Wren; breeding October–November.

STATUS: becoming uncommon, mainly due to loss of habitat. TAXONOMY: endemic species or semispecies. (Overlaps with Blue-breasted Wren in east of range but occupies different habitat.)

454 LOVELY WREN *Malurus amabilis* Gould 1850
Distribution: Map 141.

RECOGNITION: like adjacent Purple-backed Wren but differs mainly in *non-breeding male and female being partly brightly coloured. Male breeding: flanks buff* (not white), outer edge of outer tail feathers white and broad white tips to all feathers, sometimes slight violet tinge to margin of black breast. *Male non-breeding:* upperparts and face like breeding male except for buffy-white from bill to around eye, underparts buffy-white. *Female:* upperparts and face more or less uniform dull blue-grey, buffy-white patch around eye to bill, bill brown.

HABITAT: dense thicket vegetation of forest and woodland, and borders of creeks and mangroves. HABITS, etc: similar to Purple-backed Wren, breeding August–December.

STATUS: fairly common. TAXONOMY: endemic species or semispecies; closest affinity with Lavender-flanked Wren.

455 LAVENDER-FLANKED WREN *Malurus dulcis* Mathews 1908
Distribution: Map 141.

RECOGNITION: like Lovely Wren but *breeding male* differs in having a *patch of violet on flank* adjacent to black breast, remainder of flank white (not pale buff); less white in tail; *female* as in Lovely Wren but apparently in Kimberley area face patch rufous rather than buffy-white.

HABITAT: low dense vegetation including porcupine grass on sandstone ridges. HABITS, etc: apparently similar to other 'chestnut' wrens.

STATUS: apparently fairly common. TAXONOMY: endemic species or semispecies; sometimes regarded as conspecific with the Lovely Wren; there may be some close connection with the Purple-backed Wren in south Kimberley; also Kimberley population may be distinct from Arnhemland population.

OTHER WRENS

456 WHITE-WINGED WREN *Malurus leucopterus* Dumont 1824   Pl 14
Distribution: Map 142.

RECOGNITION: *white shoulders and wholly blue or blackish body.*

DESCRIPTION: 11·5cm, with tail 6·5cm. Sexes very different. *Male:* whole body and tail glossy blue (cornflower, cobalt or phenyl) or glossy black with tinge of purplish-blue; shoulders and scapulars white; flight feathers dull blackish-brown; bill black; eyes dark brown; legs grey-brown. *Female:* upperparts light fawn to drab brown; underparts white with buff tinge on flanks; tail dull blue-grey; bill pinkish-brown.

VARIATION: coastal islands of central Western Australia, body blackish (race *leucopterus*); throughout continental range, body cobalt (race *leuconotus*; name originally given to a bird which had white on upper back, and called 'White-backed Superb Warbler' by Gould, latterly 'White-backed Wren'. Birds with varying amounts of white on upper back occur in the Lakes Torrens–Frome area; it seems to be an unstable feature—perhaps due to excessive wearing of black tips exposing white bases of feathers—and current opinion is that it does not indicate a valid species or race).

HABITAT: low bushes and tussock grasses of various kinds in arid, often treeless country. HABITS: on or near ground, said to make use of holes in ground as refuge from hawks and heat, when disturbed becomes very furtive; usually in small parties flitting from bush to bush one after another; sedentary and nomadic. BREEDING: variable depending on conditions, but mainly July–December; nests similar to other wrens; three to four eggs, white finely spotted with dull red. VOICE: like 'tsree' of overlapping Purple-backed Wren but higher pitched, also 'see' and 'sit' repeated and trilling 'trwee'. FOOD: insects.

STATUS: fairly common to common. TAXONOMY: endemic species.

457 RED-BACKED WREN *Malurus melanocephalus* (Latham) 1801   Pl 14
Distribution: Map 143.

RECOGNITION: *black with red back and brown wings.*

DESCRIPTION: 11·5cm, with graduated tail 6cm. Sexes very different when male in breeding plumage, otherwise nearly alike (males sometimes breed in 'brown' plumage). *Male breeding:* back red (varying from scarlet to crimson); remainder of body and tail velvety blue-black; wings grey-brown; legs yellowish-brown. *Male non-breeding:* upperparts grey-brown (tawny ochraceous); underparts white with tinge of cinnamon buff on flanks. *Female:* similar to non-breeding male but face has large yellowish patch below eye; bill brown.

VARIATION: south of Townsville, back scarlet (race *melanocephalus*); north of Cairns and west to Derby, back crimson (race *cruentatus*); Townsville to Cairns, intermediate (race *pyrrhonotus*).

HABITAT: coarse grasses of various kinds, especially with scattered low bushes and in both moist and dry areas. HABITS: on or near ground; apparently solitary when breeding but in small parties at other times; sedentary. BREEDING: recorded most months, but mainly August–January; nests and eggs similar to other wrens but perhaps nests more often in grass tussocks. VOICE: soft twitter. FOOD: insects.

STATUS: fairly common to common. TAXONOMY: endemic species.

458 LILAC-CROWNED WREN   *Malurus coronatus*   Gould 1857   Pl 14
Distribution: Map 144.

RECOGNITION: *male has mauve crown with black central spot; female has reddish-brown patch below eye; both have bright blue tails.*

DESCRIPTION: 15cm, with graduated tail 7·5cm. Sexes different. *Male breeding:* crown mauve with black centre; face and nape black; back and wings cinnamon tawny; throat and fore-neck white shading to light buff on belly and flanks; tail methyl blue with white tip, and white outer edge to outer feathers; bill black; eyes brown; legs pinkish-brown. *Male non-breeding:* lacks mauve and black on head except for some black on face which is separated from crown by thin white streak, sometimes tinged with mauve. *Female:* similar except that face below eye has patch of umber-brown, area around eye to bill white, forehead blackish-brown sometimes tinged with blue.

VARIATION: western populations, upperparts paler and female lacks blue tinge on forehead (race *coronatus*); eastern populations, upperparts darker and female has tinge of blue on forehead and small black spot in front of eye (race *caeruleus*).

HABITAT: vegetation along water margins, coarse grass, shrubs, pandanus palm, low man-groves. HABITS: on or near ground in thick vegetation, keeps low down among bush and tree roots when feeding; very elusive; recorded in small parties; apparently sedentary and very local. BREEDING: January–June; nests similar to other wrens but entrance may have extended short platform; three eggs, pale pink spotted and blotched with darker pink. VOICE: shrill high pitched 'cheepa' repeated, also low twitter. FOOD: insects.

STATUS: fairly common locally. TAXONOMY: endemic species.

Genus STIPITURUS

The emuwrens. In contrast to their namesake emuwrens are among the smallest of birds. The name connection originates from the open filamentous structure of the tail feathers, which resemble Emu feathers to an extraordinary degree. Upperparts are shades of brown streaked with black and males have bright blue throats. The remarkable appearance of emuwrens and their presence in early settled areas gave rise to a wealth of references in early history. They are exclusively Australian and range widely in various kinds of dense tangled undergrowth in moist and very arid localities. They live closely confined, creeping about like mice, seldom flying and then only for short distances. They can be difficult to locate especially when disturbed. Basically there is only one emuwren but isolation in diverse habitats has given rise to some small but distinct differences and three forms are recognisable. It could be claimed that they are races rather than species but a compromise is to regard them as semispecies in a superspecies. As habitats and distributions are distinct species can be identified by these characteristics.

Key to STIPITURUS

1 Swamps and wet heathland of extreme southwest and
   southeast . . . .   Southern Emuwren . . . . No 459
2 Arid porcupine grass areas of centre and west . . . . . .   Rufous Emuwren . . . . No 460
3 Mallee of lower Murray . . . .   Mallee Emuwren . . . . No 461

459 SOUTHERN EMUWREN   *Stipiturus malachurus*   (Shaw) 1798   Pl 14
Distribution: Map 145.

RECOGNITION: *long cocked filamentous tail, blue throat of male; near ground in dense vegetation; distribution.*

DESCRIPTION: nearly 8cm, plus filamentous tail 13cm. Sexes different. *Male:* upperparts shades of cinnamon brown broadly streaked with blackish-brown; streak above eye, throat and foreneck light violet-blue (ultramarine); face, side of body and edge of wing feathers cinnamon brown, face finely streaked with white; centre of breast and belly dull white; bill blackish-brown; eyes dark reddish-brown; legs light brown. *Female:* similar to male but blue areas replaced by cinnamon brown.

VARIATION: slight differences in amount and richness of cinnamon brown and width of black streaks has resulted in the description of about five races, of which *littleri* in Tasmania and *westernensis* in southwest are possibly valid.

HABITAT: swampy heathland and, especially in west, low scrub on arid sandhills. HABITS: hops and feeds on ground and creeps about well concealed in low vegetation, tail usually cocked; furtive and reluctant to fly and then only for very short distance; usually solitary but sometimes in fairly large concentrations, or in small flocks; sedentary. BREEDING: August–December; nests near ground in grass tussocks and low bushes, well concealed, domed with wide side entrance and shallow cup, loosely made of grass and fine rootlets and lined with moss; three eggs, pinkish-white speckled and blotched with reddish-brown. VOICE: faint version of malurid chirp and twitter. FOOD: insects.

STATUS: fairly common locally; suffers from destruction of habitat but sometimes occupies secondary growth in cleared forest. TAXONOMY: endemic species or semispecies.

460 RUFOUS EMUWREN *Stipiturus ruficeps* Campbell 1899

Distribution: Map 145.

RECOGNITION: like Southern Emuwren but smaller, tail *shorter and less filamentous;* forehead and crown tawny, plain or indistinctly streaked; upperparts browner and less streaked; *violet-blue of throat and foreneck brighter and extending over most of face;* breast and belly of male and whole underparts of female light cinnamon buff.

HABITAT: porcupine grass and other low dense vegetation, especially on stony ridges and sandhills. HABITS, etc: similar to Southern Emuwren, breeding more often determined by rains, nests in clumps of porcupine grass often lined with vegetable down, two eggs.

STATUS: fairly common. TAXONOMY: endemic species or superspecies.

461 MALLEE EMUWREN *Stipiturus mallee* Campbell 1908

Distribution: Map 145.

RECOGNITION: intermediate in general appearance between Southern and Rufous Emuwrens; smaller than Southern Emuwren, including tail, which is less filamentous, but bill longer; browner on forehead and crown; dark streaks on upperparts narrower and browner; paler cinnamon rufous on sides of breast and flanks, and no cinnamon rufous on wings; male has rather *more violet-blue on face, which extends above and behind eye.*

HABITAT: Porcupine grass in mallee. HABITS, etc: similar to other species; three eggs.

STATUS: probably fairly common but extremely furtive. TAXONOMY: endemic species or semispecies.

Genus AMYTORNIS

Grasswrens belong to arid places. Although much has been written on their features and relationships they are probably less well known than any other group of similar size and distribution. Their haunts are remote and they are extremely furtive in their habits. The Grey Grasswren was discovered only a few years ago, the Eyrean Grasswren although found in 1874 was not recorded again until 1961, the Black Grasswren of the Kimberley area was rediscovered after a lapse of nearly sixty years. In general appearance grasswrens are similar to the fairy-wrens, small with long cocked tail and rapid jerky movements. But their brown plumages are streaked with white and sometimes patched with black. They live in the arid and forbidding fastnesses of porcupine and cane grass country and among tumbled mazes of broken rocks, where they find refuge in holes and crevices. They are reluctant to fly but bounce and scuttle at speed over the ground. They appear to be largely inactive during the day and mostly silent. The eight species currently recognised seem to belong to two main groups, perhaps superspecies, headed respectively by the widely distributed Thick-billed and Striated Grasswrens, with the Grey Grasswren of rather uncertain connections.

Key to AMYTORNIS

1 Upperparts grey-brown, black patch at side of throat	Grey Grasswren	No 469
2 Upperparts mainly black.	5–6	
3 Upperparts rufous brown	7–8	
4 Upperparts cinnamon brown.	9–12	
5 Throat dark; Kimberley.	Black Grasswren	No 468
6 Throat white; Arnhemland.	White-throated Grasswren. .	No 467
7 Throat white.	Striated Grasswren	No 465
8 Throat and breast white.	Dorothy Grasswren.	No 466
9 Underparts white.	Eyrean Grasswren.	No 464
10 Underparts cinnamon brown.	11-12	
11 Bill thin and pointed.	Thin-billed Grasswren.	No 463
12 Bill thick and blunt	Thick-billed Grasswren.	No 462

462 THICK-BILLED GRASSWREN *Amytornis textilis* (Dumont) 1824   Pl 14

Distribution: Map 146.

RECOGNITION: *cinnamon brown, paler below, overall paler than Thin-billed species with thicker and shorter bill; female has russet on flanks; frequents salt-bush plains.*

DESCRIPTION: 15–18cm, with tail about half; bill relatively short and deep. Sexes slightly different, female has patch of rufous on flanks. Upperparts, face and side of neck cinnamon brown with white or whitish streaks; underparts pale greyish-buff with whitish streaks on throat, breast and flanks, and whitish area in centre of belly; rather indistinct rufous lores and black moustache; underwing has patch of pale pinkish-brown; tail dark brown; bill mainly blackish; eyes brown; legs dark grey-brown.

VARIATION: Western Australia and western South Australia, darker above and below with white streaks more conspicuous (race *textilis*); northern South Australia, southern Northern Territory and New South Wales, paler above and below with streaks less conspicuous, chin usually whitish and unstreaked (race *modestus*); Eyre Peninsula, intermediate (race *myall*).

HABITAT: flats with saltbush and similar shrubs, flood debris along watercourses. HABITS: on or near ground, very furtive and difficult to observe, scurries at speed, often with tail cocked, between bushes, rarely flies; apparently solitary or in family parties; sedentary.

BREEDING: rain dependent; nests in bushes or river debris, near ground and well concealed, open or partly domed, loosely made of dry grass and lined with soft grass; two to three eggs, pinkish-white speckled and blotched with shades of brown. VOICE: high-pitched squeak and twitter. FOOD: insects, seeds and fruits.

STATUS: uncertain, probably fairly common. TAXONOMY: endemic species, perhaps closely related to Thin-billed and Eyrean Grasswrens.

463 THIN-BILLED GRASSWREN   *Amytornis purnelli*   (Mathews) 1914
Distribution: Map 146.

RECOGNITION: like Thick-billed species but *bill more pointed, longer and more slender;* overall darker cinnamon brown, blackish on crown and slightly rufous on rump.

VARIATION: central area, flanks greyish-brown (race *purnelli*); Mt. Isa area, flanks of male only pale grey (race *ballarae*).

HABITAT: rocky hillsides with porcupine grass. HABITS: similar to Thick-billed but distinctly less furtive, flits and scurries among rocks and takes refuge in holes and crevices; apparently breeding later where the two species overlap.

STATUS: probably fairly common. TAXONOMY: endemic species, perhaps closely related to Thick-billed Grasswren.

464 EYREAN GRASSWREN   *Amytornis goyderi*   (Gould) 1875
Distribution: Map 146.

RECOGNITION: *cinnamon brown above, mainly white below; very restricted range.*

DESCRIPTION: 14cm, with graduated tail rather more than half; bill thick and blunt. (Female not known). Face and upperparts light brown, greyish-brown on crown, cinnamon on nape and back, rufous on rump, streaked with white at least as far as lower back; indistinct black moustache; underparts white; flanks cinnamon; wings and tail drab brown, tail feathers tipped with buff and edged with cinnamon; bill light grey-brown; legs dark brown.

HABITAT: dense cane grass in sandhill country, on lower Macuba River north of Lake Eyre. HABITS: on or near ground, very furtive and keeps well hidden, scurries and flutters between tussock clumps with wings slightly extended and tail partly fanned; probably solitary and sedentary. BREEDING: season unknown; nests in cane grass and blue bush, near ground, made of interwoven grass leaves and stems and lined with vegetable down, partly domed with side entrance; two eggs, pinkish cream with irregular spots and blotches of orange and purplish brown. VOICE: faint high-pitched 'swi-it'. FOOD: not recorded.

STATUS: apparently very rare. TAXONOMY: endemic species, probably having close affinity with Thick-billed Grasswren.

465 STRIATED GRASSWREN   *Amytornis striatus*   (Gould) 1839   Pl 14
Distribution: Map 147.

RECOGNITION: *rufous brown streaked upperparts, white throat, black moustache.*

DESCRIPTION: 15–18cm, with graduated tail about half. Sexes slightly different, female has rufous patch on flank. Face and upperparts shades of cinnamon rufous, streaked with white edged with varying amounts of black, blackest on forehead and face; rufous eyebrow and black moustache; throat white to creamy white; upper breast dusky-buff with varying amounts of white streaking; lower breast and belly creamy-buff to cinnamon buff; wings

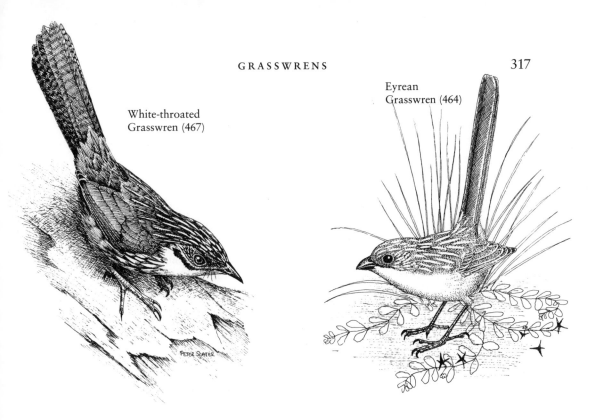

White-throated
Grasswren (467)

Eyrean
Grasswren (464)

blackish-brown with rufous patch in centre and on underwing; tail blackish-brown; bill blackish; eyes brown; legs blue-grey.

VARIATION: not clearly defined but apparently in southeast, upperparts duller and less rufous and belly whiter (race *striatus*); remainder, including Queensland, upperparts richer rufous and belly darker (race *whitei*).

HABITAT: desert plains, mallee and hilly areas with porcupine grass. HABITS: similar to Thick-billed. BREEDING: apparently variable; nests in grass clumps, usually in crown, domed and made of grass lined with vegetable down; three eggs, white speckled with shades of red, brown and grey. VOICE: loud musical 'tu-tu' and pleasant rippling song, also plaintive high-pitched 'peep'. FOOD: insects, probably seeds.

STATUS: apparently uncommon but possibly fairly common. TAXONOMY: endemic species.

466 DOROTHY GRASSWREN *Amytornis dorotheae* Mathews 1914

Distribution: Map 147.

RECOGNITION: [Comparisons are usually made with White-throated Grasswren but the three specimens known to date are much more like Striated Grasswren.] Like Striated Grasswren but *white of throat extends to breast and centre of belly*, indistinct broad white streaks on flanks, blacker on crown and face. (Female not known.)

HABITAT: sandstone ranges with porcupine grass on lower McArthur River. HABITS and BREEDING: similar to Striated Grasswren but lives among rocks and breeding season not known. VOICE: known to utter short 'chirp'. FOOD: not recorded.

STATUS: not known but apparently rare. TAXONOMY: endemic species but could be regarded as race or semispecies of Striated Grasswren.

467 WHITE-THROATED GRASSWREN
Amytornis woodwardi   Hartert 1905   Fig p 317
Distribution: Map 147.

RECOGNITION: *black upperparts, chestnut rump, belly chestnut (♂) or cinnamon (♀), white throat; restricted distribution.*

DESCRIPTION: 20cm, with graduated tail about half. Sexes slightly different, female has belly chestnut. Head, face, side of neck and back black streaked with white; rump chestnut; upper tail coverts black and chestnut with some white streaks; wings and tail black; black moustache; throat and foreneck white, extending as broad white streaks on black breast; belly chestnut; bill black; eyes brown; legs dark brown.

HABITAT: small gullies with porcupine grass at edge of bare sandstone plateaus. HABITS: in low vegetation, runs at speed with head and tail lowered, hides in crevices; solitary or in small parties. BREEDING: December–March; nests in clumps of porcupine grass, well above ground, domed with side entrance, made of dry grass and leaves; two eggs, white lightly spotted and blotched with reddish-brown and purplish-grey. VOICE: shary 't-r-r-r-t' or 'pit-pit-pit', loud varied song of notes and trills. FOOD: insects and seeds.

STATUS: apparently fairly common in restricted area. TAXONOMY: endemic species; probably closest affinity to Striated Grasswren.

468 BLACK GRASSWREN *Amytornis housei*   (Milligan) 1902   Pl 14
Distribution: Map 147.

RECOGNITION: *mainly black with chestnut rump; female has light chestnut underparts.*

DESCRIPTION: 20cm, with graduated tail about half. Sexes different. *Male:* head, upper back and underparts black streaked with white except on belly; lower back chestnut; rump and upper tail coverts black and chestnut; tail black; bill black; eyes dark brown; legs brownish-black. *Female:* similar except breast and belly light chestnut.

HABITAT: rocky gorges with porcupine grass. HABITS: similar to other rock frequenting species. BREEDING: not known. VOICE: call recorded as 'similar to malurids but harsher and more continuous' and alarm note as 'loud ticking interspersed with grating sounds and accompanied by tail flicking'. FOOD: insects and seeds.

STATUS: not known; probably fairly common in restricted area. TAXONOMY: endemic species; probably related to Striated Grasswren.

469 GREY GRASSWREN *Amytornis barbatus*   Faval. & McEvey 1968   Pl 14
Distribution: Map 147.

RECOGNITION: *light grey-brown upperparts, mainly white below with black patch at side of throat; restricted range.*

DESCRIPTION: 18cm, with graduated tail distinctly more than half. Sexes alike. Upperparts light grey-brown with broad white streaks edged with black, especially on forehead and crown; face white with black band through eye; black patch at side of throat; underparts white lightly streaked and speckled with black on breast; wings blackish, inner feathers edged with pale brown and rufous patch at base of outer flight feathers; tail black broadly edged with pale brown and dull white; bill black; eyes reddish-brown; legs black.

HABITAT: cane grass and clumps of dwarf lignum in swamp plains. HABITS: in low vegetation, runs at speed but apparently prefers to flit between grass clumps and bushes, flight swift and direct low over ground, perches on tops of bushes. BREEDING: at least July; nests in cane grass clumps and lignum bushes, from very low up to 1m, well concealed and partly domed, loosely made of grass, lined with fine grass and other soft materials; two eggs, white or pinkish-white finely speckled with shades of dark brown. VOICE: 'double-syllabled and high-pitched' and uttered as 'prolonged twittering', also triple 'tsit-tsit-tsit' often uttered while perched on dead stick. FOOD: seeds and insects.

STATUS: not known. TAXONOMY: endemic species; perhaps with closest relationship to Striated Grasswren.

Mangrove Warbler (487)

Family SYLVIIDAE
Warblers
52(about 360) species: 43 endemic

Distribution: worldwide except in far north and in south of South America.

THE WARBLERS ARE AN ill-defined family, or subfamily, except in the restricted sense of the genus *Sylvia* and its near relatives. Opinions differ widely on what other groups should be included and how they should be listed in relation to each other. The problem is particularly apparent in the case of numerous unique groups of small Australian birds which would seem to qualify for admission. It is hard to say how many of the forty-three endemic species of the fifty-two listed here have truly sprung from the same ancestral stock as the modern sylviids, or how many have grown to resemble the true warblers because they live in much the same way. There is a possible link from *Phylloscopus* to *Gerygone* and *Acanthiza*, and perhaps through *Acrocephalus* but other connections might be hard to find. The species included here and their arrangement reflect the opinions of a number of specialists but are not conclusive. The main characteristics of warblers are that they have thin pointed bills for picking up insects; that they are small, mostly less than 15cm; that they have plumages in subdued tones, mainly shades of brown, rarely relieved by bright colours except on the rumps of some thornbills; that they have mostly domed nests and melodious voices. It is not a very useful exercise to try to provide a key to identification but the following may be of some assistance.

Key to SYLVIIDAE
[Additional keys are provided when generic names are given.]
1 Mainly dark reddish-brown; on forest floors
    Hawkesbury Sandstone area .... Rock Warbler .... No 520
    Rain forest of extreme southeast .... Pilotbird .... No 521

Weebill (490)   Little Thornbill (491)

TWO SIMILAR WARBLERS (SEE KEY ABOVE)

Genus ACROCEPHALUS

The reed warblers, of which about twenty species are currently recognised, range widely throughout the old world, wherever there are dense reeds or grass in moist places. They are a numerous and successful group but are furtive and nondescript. Plumages are in shades of plain dull brown above and buff below with few distinctive features, but most species can be identified by their voices. There are several whose identity as species is not clear and this is so in the case of the reed warbler found commonly throughout Australia. Sometimes it is claimed to be a species, or a race of one of two widespread species. A solution seems to be to regard it as a semispecies of whatever superspecies is decided upon and by so doing retain its original scientific name.

470 REED WARBLER *Acrocephalus australis* (Gould) 1838
Distribution: throughout.

RECOGNITION: *plain dark brown upperparts with buffy-white eyebrow; loud clear notes; in dense reedy vegetation.*

DESCRIPTION: 16–17cm. Sexes alike. Upperparts buffy-brown (walnut), darker on head; buffy-white eyebrow; underparts buffy-white, whiter on throat and centre of belly, more cinnamon buff on side of breast and flanks; bill and legs blackish-brown; eyes grey-brown.

VARIATION: three variants doubtfully distinguishable: southeast, as described (race *australis*); west, darker (race *gouldi*); Cape York, paler with more rufous flanks (race *cervinus*).

HABITAT: thick vegetation in wet places, sometimes remotely isolated clumps of reeds and rushes, also mangroves. HABITS: usually keeps well concealed in vegetation, sometimes sings from exposed places; solitary, but populations may be fairly dense; movements not well known but apparently vary from migratory in south to nomadic and sedentary in north.

BREEDING: September–February; nests in thick vegetation at various heights, bound to upright stems, deep cup narrow at rim, made of interwoven strips of reed and rush and sometimes lined with grass; three to four eggs, dull white to pale buff spotted and blotched with brown and grey. VOICE: loud rich melodious song transcribed as 'twitchee-twitchee-twitchee-quarty-quarty-quarty', also loud sharp 'chat'. FOOD: insects.

STATUS: common. TAXONOMY: species or semispecies extending to Solomon Is.

[GREAT REED WARBLER *Acrocephalus arundinaceus*
This species is sometimes included in the Australian list on the evidence of one specimen obtained on Melville I in 1912 and determined to be a migrant from the northern hemisphere; its identification has been questioned. There is no feature by which non-breeding birds can easily be distinguished; wings are said to be rather longer, over 80mm, as against less than 80mm in the Reed Warbler. More exact information is required.]

Genus CISTICOLA

A group of about forty species, sometimes known as fantail warblers or grass warblers, although nowadays the generic name is often more suitably adopted for common use. Their stronghold is Africa. Only two species are found north of the Sahara. One extends into southern Europe and Asia, the other belongs to regions east of India. Both are found in Australia. They are very small, less than 10cm with relatively short tails, have streaky brown plumages and frequent moist grasslands over which they sometimes flutter like butterflies. The two species are very alike but have distinct nests and eggs and different voices.

Key to CISTICOLA

[*Note:* non-breeding plumages are very difficult to distinguish, even at close quarters or in the hand.]

1 Crown cinnamon rufous ('golden')............. Golden Cisticola (breeding).... No 471
2 Crown dark brown, slightly streaked........... Streaked Cisticola (breeding).. No 472
3 Crown distinctly streaked..................... 4–5

Females and non-breeding males

4 Nape and rump with little or no streaking........ Golden Cisticola .... No 471
5 Nape and rump streaked .... Streaked Cisticola .... No 472

471 GOLDEN CISTICOLA *Cisticola exilis* (Vig. & Horsf.) 1827

Distribution: Map 148.

RECOGNITION: *very small, brown streaked, associated with moist grasslands; distinguished from much rarer Streaked Cisticola by 'golden' crown when breeding and by distinctive 'zzzit-plik' call.*

DESCRIPTION: 10cm. Sexes different. *Male breeding:* back and wings broadly streaked blackish-brown and shades of cinnamon buff; crown and rump plain cinnamon rufous (the 'golden' crown is spread out and made conspicuous in breeding display); centre of under-parts white; face, side of neck and flanks pale cinnamon rufous; tail blackish-brown; feathers narrowly edged and tipped with cinnamon rufous; bill blackish-brown above, paler below; eyes brownish (olive to golden); legs pale pinkish-brown. *Male non-breeding and female:* upperparts broadly streaked except for fairly distinct cinnamon rufous band on hind neck and narrow band on rump; tail longer.

VARIATION: east and south, streaks wider and blacker (race *exilis*); north of Atherton Table-land, streaks narrower and tinged with brown (race *diminuta*); Gulf of Carpentaria west-ward, dark streaks much narrower and plumage generally paler (race *alexandrae*) except Arnhemland where cinnamon rufous colours duller (race *lineocapilla*).

HABITAT: thick grass and other vegetation generally in and around low-lying moist areas.
HABITS: creeps among tangled herbage, sometimes feeds on ground, perches on top of grass tussocks or low bushes to sing, flies with erratic butterfly movement low over grassland ending with sudden dive; solitary but populations can be quite dense; sedentary. BREEDING: September–April; nests bound into low dense vegetation, ball-shaped with high side entrance, made of grasses and leaves sewn with cobwebs and vegetable down; three to four eggs, glossy sky-blue spotted and blotched with reddish-brown. VOICE: repetitive low grating 'zzzit' followed by loud explosive bell-like 'plik'. FOOD: insects.
STATUS: common. TAXONOMY: species extending to central India and southern China.

472 STREAKED CISTICOLA *Cisticola juncidis* (Rafinesque) 1810

Distribution: Map 149.

RECOGNITION: like Golden Cisticola but differs by—*breeding: head and nape dark fawn brown, slightly streaked; rump more cinnamon rufous; more distinct buffy-white streak over eye and tail broadly tipped with dull white. Non-breeding:* rather more heavily streaked, especially on nape and rump. Distinctive loud metallic note, 'lik-lik'.

VARIATION: Queensland populations assigned to endemic race *(normani)*; Northern Territory populations given racial status *(leanyeri)* but doubtfully distinguished from Burma-Java race.

HABITAT: grassy margins of coastal flood plains. HABITS: more or less similar to Golden Cisticola. BREEDING: December–April; nests in low grass, made of dry grass lined with rootlets and vegetable down, contained in an inverted pear-shaped structure formed by grass stems pulled together and bound with cobwebs, open at the top; three to four eggs, dull pale blue finely speckled with pale brown. VOICE: loud metallic 'lik-lik' usually uttered in display flight in breeding season, each double note synchronised with undulation; also single 'lik' repeated rapidly. FOOD: insects.
STATUS: fairly common in restricted habitats. TAXONOMY: species extending to southern Asia, southern Europe and throughout Africa.

Genus MEGALURUS

The grassbirds, grass warblers, canegrass warblers or marsh warblers, as they are variously named, consist of five species distributed in eastern parts of the old world. Two occur in Australia, one as an extension of a New Guinea species and the other an endemic species in the south. As their names suggest they live in swamps, places wetter than those favoured by the cisticolas, which they resemble in having brown streaked bodies. But they are larger and darker with long graduated tails and a white streak through the eye.

Key to MEGALURUS

1 Crown brown streaked black; 14cm .... Little Grassbird .... No 473
2 Crown plain rufous; 18cm .... Tawny Grassbird........... No 474

473 LITTLE GRASSBIRD *Megalurus gramineus* (Gould) 1845 Pl 15

Distribution: Map 150.

RECOGNITION: *brown with black streaked upperparts, long graduated tail; in swamp grasses; distinguished from Tawny Grassbird by streaked crown and smaller size.*

DESCRIPTION: 14cm, with graduated tail 6cm. Sexes alike. Upperparts cinnamon brown to cinnamon rufous broadly streaked with brownish-black, more uniformly rufous on forehead and rump; broad white stripe through eye; underparts whitish, whitest and sometimes speckled with brown on throat and foreneck, and light buff on flanks; wings mainly grey-brown with black inner feathers broadly edged with white; bill pinkish-brown, paler below; eyes pale brown; legs brown.

VARIATION: Tasmania, underparts darker (race *gramineus*); east mainland, paler with little or no dark marks on foreneck (race *goulburni*); southwest, overall darker with distinct dark striations on foreneck (race *thomasi*).

HABITAT: grass and bush vegetation on coastal and inland swamps. HABITS: very furtive, usually keeps low in vegetation where it creeps about, seldom flies and then only for short distances, but presence on temporary swamps indicates that long flights are undertaken; solitary, though sometimes quite large populations in small area; usually sedentary on permanent swamps. BREEDING: variable, but mainly August–January; nests low down in thick vegetation, sometimes over water, cup-shaped, made of grasses lined with feathers and often with feathers protruding above rim of nest to form a rough canopy; three to four eggs, white sometimes tinged with pink and speckled with red. VOICE: plaintive high-pitched 'pee-pee' repeated, sometimes uttered at night. FOOD: insects and small aquatic animals.

STATUS: fairly common to common. TAXONOMY: endemic species, rarely in southeast New Guinea.

474 TAWNY GRASSBIRD *Megalurus timoriensis* Wallace 1863

Distribution: Map 151.

RECOGNITION: similar to Little Grassbird but *larger, 19cm, forehead and crown plain rufous, rather more rufous on nape, no white margins to inner wing feathers and no streaks on whitish underparts; distinctive voice.*

HABITAT: as for Little Grassbird but also wet heaths and thick grass and low bushes in drier areas, like forest clearings and hillsides. HABITS: generally keeps well in cover but more in evidence when breeding, perches high up in grass tops or in bushes and performs distinctive display song-flight; solitary; sedentary with some indication of nomadic or seasonal movements. BREEDING: August–April; nests in dense cover, deep cup made of grasses and lined with finer material; three eggs, pale pink freckled with shades of brown and grey. VOICE: rich and varied song uttered in display flight, also loud chirping 'tsi-lik'. FOOD: insects. STATUS: uncommon. TAXONOMY: endemic race *(alisteri)* of species extending to Philippine Is.

Genus CINCLORHAMPHUS

The two songlarks which comprise this genus belong to Australia. Their relationships are uncertain. Brown streaked plumage and open country habitat deceptively suggest affinity with the Pipit or Bushlark, but they are readily distinguished in the field by lack of white margin to the tail, relatively thin bills and, in the large male Brown Songlark, by its mainly black underparts. The sexes are distinctly different in size. Current opinion places the songlarks closest in affinity with the grassbirds and Spinifexbird. (See key page 279.)

Key to CINCLORHAMPHUS

1 Upper tail coverts rufous .... Rufous Songlark ...... No 475
2 Upper tail coverts not rufous; male has black underparts.. Brown Songlark....... No 476

475 RUFOUS SONGLARK *Cinclorhamphus mathewsi* Iredale 1911   Pl 13

Distribution: throughout except Cape York Peninsula north of Normanton-Townsville and Tasmania.

RECOGNITION: *streaky brown upperparts with rufous rump, lacks white margin of tail typical of Pipit and Bushlark.*

DESCRIPTION: 15–18cm. Sexes alike but male larger. Upperparts blackish-brown with feathers margined in various widths and shades of grey-brown to cinnamon brown, giving a broadly streaked appearance; upper tail coverts plain dark cinnamon brown; tail uniformly blackish-brown, thinly edged with pale buff; indistinct dull white streak above eye and dusky patch in front of eye; underparts vinaceous buff, whiter on throat, duskier on breast and darker buff on vent and under tail coverts; foreneck and upper breast sometimes spotted with dark brown—apparently a feature of immatures; bill black; eyes brown; legs grey.

HABITAT: various kinds of savanna, especially with large ring-barked trees. HABITS: feeds mainly on ground but readily flies into trees, especially high bare limbs, and sings there, or sings on the wing, flies low over ground between tussocks and bushes; solitary; largely migratory, breeding visitor in south, September–March, but varying numbers may remain; apparently non-breeding visitor in far north and probably sedentary and nomadic in intermediate areas. BREEDING: September–February; nests on ground well hidden among grass and other vegetation, a hollow lined with dried grass and sometimes hair; three to four eggs, shades of pale red spotted with dark red. VOICE: musical trill often followed by sharp 'witchy-weedle', in flight repeated whip-like 'wit-cher'. FOOD: insects and seeds. STATUS: common. TAXONOMY: endemic species and genus.

476 BROWN SONGLARK *Cinclorhamphus cruralis* (Vig. & Horsf.) 1827

Distribution: throughout except Tasmania, rare in extreme north.

RECOGNITION: *brown streaked upperparts, male large with black underparts, female has blackish patch in centre of belly, no white margin to tail; distinctive song flight.*

DESCRIPTION: 18–25cm, male large. Sexes different. *Male:* upperparts shades of grey-brown to cinnamon brown broadly streaked with blackish-brown; indistinct dull white streak above eye and dusky patch in front of eye; underparts mainly brownish-black, but in fresh plumage speckled white on throat and foreneck, and pale band across breast; flanks and vent buff; tail blackish-brown thinly edged with pale buff; bill black; eyes brown; legs pinkish-brown. *Female:* similar but upperparts slightly paler; underparts mainly light buff, whiter on throat and blackish-brown patch in centre of belly; bill pinkish-brown.

Brown Songlark (476) *male*

HABITAT: grasslands and dry scrub, also lightly timbered areas. HABITS: mainly terrestrial, sometimes on low perches, with tail cocked, rarely in trees except to call or sing, soaring song-flight with long glides. BREEDING: variable but mainly between August and April; nests on ground under tussocks, cup-shaped hollow lined with grass and softer material; three to four eggs, shades of pink speckled with red. VOICE: rather harsh grating 'pitch-a-paddle' uttered in flight or from high perch. FOOD: insects and seeds. STATUS: common. TAXONOMY: endemic species and genus.

Genus EREMIORNIS

The Spinifexbird is one of a number of lone species with uncertain relationships. Superficially it is like a reed warbler (but in the arid porcupine grass) for it is plain brown above and dull white below, and employs the same art of furtive concealment, but there the resemblance apparently ceases. It seems to have more features in common with the squirrel warblers (*Schoenicola*) of Africa and India. A distinctive feature of the Spinifexbird is the unusual length of the tail coverts, the upper covering at least two-thirds of the broad graduated tail.

477 SPINIFEXBIRD *Eremiornis carteri* North 1900   Pl 15
Distribution: Map 152.

RECOGNITION: *dull rufous brown above and whitish below, long graduated tail with buffy-white tip; in porcupine grass.*

DESCRIPTION: 15cm; upper tail coverts extend about two-thirds length of broad graduated tail. Sexes alike. Upperparts cinnamon brown shading to rufous on forehead; dull white streak above eye; underparts buffy-white shading to pinkish-buff on side of breast and flanks, dull white on throat and cinnamon buff on under tail coverts; tail dark brown broadly tipped with light buff; bill black above, blue-grey below; eyes light brown; legs dark grey.

VARIATION: Cloncurry area, said to be smaller and less reddish on upperparts (race *queens-landicus*).

HABITAT: porcupine grass, usually interspersed with shrubs, or mainly dense low bushes. HABITS: skulks among vegetation, apparently not very active, sometimes on ground, hopping with broad clumsy-looking tail partly cocked or flying with tail drooping, sings from top of vegetation; apparently solitary and sedentary. BREEDING: August–November; nests near ground in grass tussocks and other vegetation, deep cup well made of shredded grass and lined with fine material; two eggs, pale pink finely speckled with shades of brown and lilac. VOICE: short melodious warble, short sharp 'tik' or grating 'chuk'. FOOD: insects. STATUS: uncommon. TAXONOMY: endemic species and genus.

Genus DASYORNIS

The endemic and unique bristlebirds are placed here, but without conviction that they have close affinity with the preceding grass warblers. Among typical features are strong rictal bristles, a slightly 'lacquered' plumage with a silvery sheen, and domed nests; some notes however are songlark in character. On the taxonomic tree they are out on a twig of their own but possibly on the sylviid branch. Like the scrub-birds they have shrunk from what must have been large and widespread populations to small relict groups in heaths and coastal scrubs on opposite sides of the continent. Two distinct groups have representatives on each side, one is usually regarded as consisting of two species and the other of two races.

Key to DASYORNIS

1 Crown rufous; east and west .... Rufous Bristlebird.......... No 480
2 Crown brown
    Eastern localities .... Eastern Bristlebird.......... No 478
    Western localities.......................... Western Bristlebird.......... No 479

478 EASTERN BRISTLEBIRD *Dasyornis brachypterus* (Latham) 1801   Pl 15

Distribution: Map 153.

RECOGNITION: *dark brown upperparts with cinnamon brown in centre of wing and base of tail, strong rictal bristles—visible at very close quarters; occurs near ground in dense heathy scrub.* (Rufous Scrub-bird occurs in same area in northern New South Wales; it has the same general appearance and habits but frequents thick ground vegetation in rain forest and voice is different—but it is an accomplished mimic.)

DESCRIPTION: 21–22cm, with broad graduated tail about half; plumage has silvery sheen and is slightly hard, as if lacquered. Sexes alike. Upperparts dark grey-brown (snuff brown) with cinnamon brown on centre of wing and base of tail; inconspicuous light buff streak above eye; throat and foreneck very pale grey-brown, browner on breast which is lightly scalloped with dark brown; centre of belly pale grey-brown; flanks dark brown; bill dark brown, paler below; eyes reddish-brown; legs grey-brown.

HABITAT: dense heathlands of coasts and mountains. HABITS: on or near ground in dense vegetation, scratches among ground litter, runs fast with tail partly cocked and sometimes fanned, flies reluctantly; solitary and sedentary. BREEDING: August–December; nests near ground in thick vegetation, domed with side entrance, made of coarse grass, rough externally and compactly lined with finer materials; two eggs, shades of light brown spotted with darker brown and bluish-grey. VOICE: clear musical notes transcribed as 'it-wooa-weet-eip' and variations, also sharp 'zeip' or 'tzink' and low 'tuck'. FOOD: insects and seeds. STATUS: rare and in restricted areas. TAXONOMY: endemic species and genus.

479 WESTERN BRISTLEBIRD   *Dasyornis longirostris*   (Gould) 1840
Distribution: Map 153.

RECOGNITION: similar to Eastern Bristlebird, differs in being *smaller, 18cm,* but with *bill longer; blacker in centre of crown;* upperparts vaguely spotted with grey.

HABITAT, etc: similar to eastern species; frequents dense low scrub, call notes transcribed as 'chip-pee-tee-peetle-pet', also shrill whistle and metallic 'tink'.

STATUS: rare, known only from one small area east of Albany, but in historic times ranged north to Perth. TAXONOMY: endemic species and genus.

480 RUFOUS BRISTLEBIRD   *Dasyornis broadbenti*   (McCoy) 1867
Distribution: Map 153.

RECOGNITION: *dark brown with rufous crown, whitish on chin and centre of belly, rictal bristles visible at very close quarters; near ground in dense coastal thickets.*

DESCRIPTION: 23–25cm, broad graduated tail about half; plumage has slightly hard feel and silvery sheen, as if lacquered. Crown and face behind eye cinnamon brown to cinnamon rufous; remainder of upperparts dark grey-brown (snuff brown), but rather more cinnamon brown in centre of wing and base of tail; indistinct greyish streak above eye; tip of chin and centre of belly pale grey to brownish-grey; breast grey scalloped with dark brown; flanks dark brown; bill and legs dark brown; eyes reddish-brown.

VARIATION: Victoria, crown cinnamon brown, chin and belly brownish-grey (race *broadbenti*); Coorong, S.A., crown cinnamon rufous, chin and centre of belly pale grey (race *whitei*); Western Australia (Cape Naturaliste to Cape Mentelle), smaller and crown richer rufous (race *litoralis*).

HABITAT: dense scrub and thickets near coast. HABITS, etc: apparently very similar to other bristlebirds. VOICE: loud penetrating 'cheep-cheep-chew-chew-ee-e', also sharp 'tweek'. FOOD: insects and seeds.

STATUS: rare (west), locally common (east), adversely affected by human activities. TAXONOMY: endemic species and genus.

Genus GERYGONE

A group of small warblers, sometimes called fairy warblers (it is reasonably suggested that the name 'gerygone' should be adopted as the common name). They belong to the Australasian region and may be an offshoot of the phylloscopids or leaf warblers of other parts of the old world, which they resemble and largely replace. There are about eighteen species of which nine occur in Australia, five with connecting populations in New Guinea. They are found mainly in the high rainfall areas of the north and east—being replaced in drier habitats by the related thornbills. The gerygonids have few distinctive features other than some white on tail, forehead and eyebrow; they live mostly among foliage; they are solitary or in loosely attached small flocks; they have melodious and varied songs. The close similarity of many forms confused taxonomists acquainted only with skin specimens but field ornithologists found differences in voice and behaviour which leave little doubt as to the main divisions. It is said—perhaps not always on first hand knowledge—that nests of several species are built close to those of wasps and hornets but whether this is intentional or accidental would be worth investigating.

TYPICAL ACANTHIZID AND GERYGONID

Brown Thornbill (493)

Large-billed Warbler (485)

Key to GERYGONE

1 Breast and belly yellow	3–6	
2 Breast and belly white	7–13	
3 Throat sooty brown (♂)	Black-throated Warbler	No 482
4 Throat white or tinged yellow	5–6	
5 Upperparts brownish	White-throated Warbler	No 481
6 Upperparts greenish		
White at tip of tail	Fairy Warbler	No 483
No white at tip of tail (♀)	Black-throated Warbler	No 482
7 Base of tail white	White-tailed Warbler	No 488
8 Base of tail not white	9–13	
9 Back greenish, crown brown	Green-backed Warbler	No 484
10 Back and crown greenish-brown, no white on face	Large-billed Warbler	No 485
11 Back and crown brownish, white on face	12–13	
12 Buff eyebrow, white forehead	Dusky Warbler	No 486
13 White eyebrow		
White forehead	Brown Warbler	No 489
No white on forehead	Mangrove Warbler	No 487

481 WHITE-THROATED WARBLER *Gerygone olivacea* (Gould) 1838   Pl 15
Distribution: Map 154.

RECOGNITION: *clearly defined white throat contrasting with yellow breast and belly, brownish upperparts.*

DESCRIPTION: 11cm. Sexes alike. Upperparts shades of grey-brown, sometimes with tinge of golden-brown on rump; throat white; breast and belly bright yellow (rarely has black band on breast); wings brownish with pale edges to feathers; tail blackish-brown, white at base and with white spots near tip of most feathers; bill black; eyes bright red; legs black.

VARIATION: not well defined: east, slightly larger and darker (race *olivacea*); north, slightly smaller and paler (races *flavigasta* and *rogersi*).

HABITAT: open forests and woodlands, big trees along watercourses. HABITS: arboreal, lives among tree foliage usually high up, where it forages and flits very actively, sometimes catches insects on wing; solitary or in scattered groups; partly migratory, mainly breeding visitor in extreme south and non-breeding visitor in extreme north. BREEDING: August–January; nests high up in tree foliage suspended from twigs, sometimes near hornets nests; oval with long 'tail' and domed with hooded entrance near top, made of bark strips and fibres interwoven with cobwebs and lined with feathers or plant down; two to three eggs, white or tinged with pink and speckled with dull red. VOICE: rather wistful sweet descending trill sometimes described as 'a cascade of liquid notes'. FOOD: insects.

STATUS: common. TAXONOMY: near endemic species—only one small external population in the vicinity of Port Moresby, southeast New Guinea.

482 BLACK-THROATED WARBLER *Gerygone palpebrosa* Wallace 1865
Distribution: Map 155.

RECOGNITION: *dull greenish upperparts, male has sooty black throat and female has white throat.*

DESCRIPTION: 10cm. Sexes different. *Male:* upperparts olive-green; white patch on forehead in front of eye; face and throat blackish-brown with white moustache streak; breast and belly yellow; wings and tail brown (no white in tail); bill and legs blackish; eyes reddish-orange. *Female:* throat white.

VARIATION: Cape York, face and throat sooty black (race *personata*); north of Johnstone River (near Tully) to Cooktown, face and throat dusky brown (race *johnstoni*).

HABITAT: mangroves, low dense vegetation by creeks, and forest margins and clearings. HABITS, etc: similar to White-throated Warbler, but apparently sedentary; nests spherical with 'tail', breeding October–January. VOICE: pretty undulating warble and soft twitter. FOOD: insects.

STATUS: common. TAXONOMY: races of species widespread in New Guinea.

483 FAIRY WARBLER *Gerygone flavida* Ramsay 1877
Distribution: Map 155.

RECOGNITION: *dull greenish upperparts, very pale yellow throat with black spot at tip of chin, white at tip of tail.*

DESCRIPTION: 10cm. Sexes slightly different. *Male:* upperparts dull greenish; face dull brown; tip of chin black; throat very pale yellow or dull white; white moustache; dusky eyering; breast and belly yellow; wings and tail brown, tail with white spots at tip; bill and legs black; eyes reddish-brown. *Female:* lacks white moustache and eyering paler.

HABITAT, etc: more or less similar to Black-throated Warbler, dense substage vegetation in or near rain forest and mangroves, but possibly where two species in close proximity keeps to high tree foliage. VOICE: bright melodious song, sometimes transcribed as a cheerful 'tit-e-tit-yu', also an animated chatter. FOOD: insects and seeds.

STATUS: uncertain, probably fairly common. TAXONOMY: endemic species, possibly an offshoot from the Black-throated Warbler.

484 GREEN-BACKED WARBLER *Gerygone chloronota* Gould 1842

Distribution: Map 155.

RECOGNITION: *greenish back, brown head, no white on face.*

DESCRIPTION: 9cm. Sexes alike. Crown, face and nape grey-brown; remainder of upperparts olive-green; underparts white with flanks and vent olive-yellow; flight and tail feathers brown; bill grey-green above, white below; eyes reddish-brown; legs dark grey.

HABITAT: mangroves and other wet coastal vegetation. HABITS: little recorded except that it creeps about in dense vegetation. BREEDING: December–February; nests more or less similar to other gerygone species; two to three eggs, white speckled with reddish-brown. VOICE: not well described. FOOD: insects.

STATUS: common (although not well known). TAXONOMY: endemic race *(chloronota)* of species widespread in New Guinea.

485 LARGE-BILLED WARBLER *Gerygone magnirostris* Gould 1842   Fig p 328

Distribution: Map 156.

RECOGNITION: *greenish-brown upperparts, only white marking on head is thin eyering; mainly in mangroves.*

DESCRIPTION: 11–12cm. Sexes alike. Face and upperparts brownish-olive; thin white eyering; underparts buffy-white; tail has broad blackish subterminal bar (no white spots at tip); bill black; eyes reddish-brown; legs dark grey.

HABITAT: mangroves and other wet coastal thickets and adjacent forests. HABITS: arboreal, an active acrobat of foliage; apparently mainly solitary and sedentary. BREEDING: September–April; nests suspended among foliage at varying heights but often low over water and near hornet nests, a large untidy collection of grasses, bark and fibres bound with cobweb and with a ragged 'tail', looking like debris left by receding floods, low hooded side entrance and egg cavity lined with feathers; two to three eggs, white or tinged with pink speckled with reddish-brown. VOICE: varied musical song in double and triple notes, also soft chatter. FOOD: insects, especially leaf scale.

STATUS: mostly common. TAXONOMY: endemic race of species extending throughout New Guinea and adjacent islands.

486 DUSKY WARBLER *Gerygone tenebrosa* (Hall) 1901

Distribution: Map 156.

RECOGNITION: *dull white forehead, pale buff streak over white eye; in mangroves east of Wyndham.*

DESCRIPTION: 11–12cm. Sexes alike. Face and upperparts light rufous brown, greyer on head and more rufous on rump; narrow dull white forehead continued as pale buff streak over eye; underparts white tinged with buff, darker buff on flanks; grey-brown tail has indistinct dark subterminal band; bill and legs black; eyes white.

HABITAT: mangroves, coastal and river swamps. HABITS: not well known, lives among foliage of trees and bushes, apparently solitary and sedentary. BREEDING: probably October–January; nests suspended from twigs and branches, domed with hooded side entrance near top, made of bark strips bound with cobwebs; two eggs, white speckled with reddish-brown. VOICE: said to resemble notes of White-tailed Warbler. FOOD: insects.

STATUS: not known, probably fairly common. TAXONOMY: endemic species; previously considered to be race of Large-billed Warbler.

487 MANGROVE WARBLER *Gerygone levigaster* Gould 1842 Fig p 319
Distribution: Map 157.

RECOGNITION: *white spots at tip of tail, white eyebrow; in mangroves; difficult to distinguish from Brown Warbler except by habitat and voice.*

DESCRIPTION: 10cm. Sexes alike. Face and upperparts grey-brown; white streak over eye and dusky spot in front of eye; underparts dull white, lightest on throat and under tail coverts; tail has broad diffuse subterminal blackish band and white spots at tip; bill and legs black; eyes reddish. *Immature:* areas white in adult are yellowish.

VARIATION: north coast, upperparts greyer (race *levigaster*); east coast south of Mackay, upperparts browner (race *cantator*).

HABITAT: mangroves and margins of rivers and creeks. HABITS, etc: similar to other gerygonids with oval shaped nests; breeding August–February. VOICE: melodious, varied and sustained, described as 'cascade of melody' and quite distinctive. FOOD: insects.

STATUS: common. TAXONOMY: endemic species.

488 WHITE-TAILED WARBLER *Gerygone fusca* (Gould) 1838 Pl 15
Distribution: Map 157.

RECOGNITION: *white underparts, tail has white on outer base and white spots at tip. Grey Honeyeater (665) very similar and may be in same flock, but does not have white eyebrow or white base of tail.*

DESCRIPTION: nearly 10cm. Sexes alike. Upperparts shades of olive-brown; underparts dull white tinged with grey on throat and breast; indistinct dull white eyebrow, thin white eyering and dusky spot in front of eye; outer half of tail blackish with large white spots at tip, basal half white; bill and legs black; eyes reddish-brown.

VARIATION: west, upperparts darkest (race *fusca*); central area, palest (race *musgravi*); east, intermediate (race *exsul*).

HABITAT: canopy foliage of dry forests and various woodlands, suburban parks. HABITS, etc: similar to other gerygonids with oval shaped nests; breeding September–January. VOICE: thin clear warble of varied notes, also soft 'peu-peu' uttered spasmodically while foraging. FOOD: insects.

STATUS: common. TAXONOMY: endemic species.

489 BROWN WARBLER *Gerygone mouki* Mathews 1912
Distribution: Map 158.

RECOGNITION: *white spots at tip of tail, white eyebrow, violet-grey face; mainly mountain rain forests, rarely mangroves; difficult to distinguish from Mangrove Warbler except by habitat and voice.*

DESCRIPTION: 9cm. Sexes alike. Upperparts varying from dark greyish-olive to buffy-brown, darker on head and lighter on rump; underparts white tinged with varying amounts of light buff; face violet-grey; narrow dull white forehead, white streak over eye and blackish spot in front of eye; tail has broad diffuse subterminal black band and creamy white spots at tip; bill black; eyes reddish-brown; legs black, soles of feet buff.

VARIATION: about Cooktown to Bowen, upperparts greyish-olive (races *mouki* and *amalia*); about Brisbane to Sydney, upperparts buffy-brown (race *richmondi*).

HABITAT: rain forests, especially mountain, rarely mangroves. HABITS, etc: similar to other gerygonids with oval shaped nests; breeding September–February. VOICE: clear thin melodious warble, sometimes transcribed as 'what-is-it' or 'which-is-it', in ascending scale and constantly repeated. FOOD: insects.

STATUS: common. TAXONOMY: endemic species; sometimes linked specifically with New Zealand *G. igata*; sometimes the two main Australian isolates are regarded as separate species, *G. mouki* and *G. richmondi*.

Genus SMICRORNIS

The endemic and widespread Weebill is put in a genus of its own. Although in some ways similar to both gerygonids and acanthizids, it does not readily fit into either group. Currently it is believed to lie somewhere between the two probably with closer affinity to *Acanthiza*. Its diminutive size, short bill and yellowish tinged plumage are distinctive features.

490 WEEBILL   *Smicrornis Brevirostris*   Gould 1838   Fig p 320
Distribution: throughout except Tasmania.

RECOGNITION: *very short bill, light buff eyebrow, yellow underparts (sometimes whitish on throat but not clearly defined white patch as in White-throated Warbler).*

DESCRIPTION: 8–9cm. Sexes alike. Upperparts shades of light to dark yellowish-olive, rather more grey-brown on crown and brighter on rump; eyebrow light buff; underparts buffy-yellow to yellow, lighter or near white on throat and richer on belly and flanks; wings and tail blackish-brown, tail with dull white spots near tip; bill brown, paler below; eyes light yellow; legs brown.

VARIATION: seven variants currently named but the general trend is: south, upperparts mainly dark olive-brown; centre, upperparts pale brownish-olive; north, upperparts bright yellowish-olive.

HABITAT: dry forests to semi-deserts, wherever there is plentiful leafy cover. HABITS: arboreal, among foliage actively foraging, flitting, hovering; solitary or in small parties of up to twenty, sometimes in company with other warblers; apparently sedentary and nomadic. BREEDING: most months in some part of range; nests in trees among twigs, a cup frequently domed with side entrance (without hood), made of leaves and buds and similar materials, lined with feathers; two to three eggs, light buff to pinkish-brown faintly speckled with brown. VOICE: short high-pitched warble transcribed as 'wee-eet-wit-it' or 'pee-pee-pwee-weep', also throaty 'tchik' or 'tiz'. FOOD: insects.

STATUS: common. TAXONOMY: endemic species; the yellow northern form used to be regarded as a separate species, *S. flavescens*, Yellow Weebill—the brown southern one being Brown Weebill.

Genus ACANTHIZA

A group originally called tits because of superficial similarities with the European titmice but now better known as thornbills. There are about twelve species endemic to Australia and one in New Guinea. This is an interesting, perhaps questionable linkage, because the acanthizids largely replace the gerygonids south of the tropic and in areas which get roughly less than thirty inches of rainfall. They are very similar in size and habits to the warblers but have more distinctive features, like brightly contrasting rump colours (except in the Little and Western Thornbills) and streaked or scalloped forehead, face or throat; they are more inclined to congregate in flocks and keep in close company.

Key to ACANTHIZA

1 Throat and breast blotched with black, white
   under tail coverts; Tasmania .... Tasmanian Thornbill .... No 495
2 Throat and breast streaked with black 4–5
3 Throat and breast not blotched or streaked 6–9

4 Forehead streaked white; back olive-green ... Striated Thornbill .... No 492
5 Forehead scalloped white; back brownish
   Widespread mainly south of tropic.......... Brown Thornbill .... No 493
                                             Broad-tailed Thornbill .... No 494
   Mainly Atherton Tableland................ Mountain Thornbill .... No 496

6 Rump yellow, forehead black spotted white .... Yellow-rumped Thornbill ...... No 501
7 Rump buff, forehead scalloped buff
   Frequenting samphire flats .... Samphire Thornbill............ No 499
   Frequenting open woodlands............... Buff-rumped Thornbill .... No 500
8 Rump tawny
   Forehead streaked black................... Slate-backed Thornbill........ No 497
   Forehead scalloped white .... Chestnut-rumped Thornbill..... No 502
9 Rump like back
   Face brown streaked white................ Little Thornbill .... No 491
   Face plain .... Western Thornbill............. No 498

491 LITTLE THORNBILL *Acanthiza nana* Vig. & Horsf. 1827 Fig p 320
Distribution: Map 159.

RECOGNITION: *streaked face, yellow underparts, rump same colour as back; like Weebill but lacks pale eyebrow, and rather less yellow.*

DESCRIPTION: 9cm. Sexes alike. Upperparts shades of dark olive-green to buff-olive; ear coverts streaked dark brown and buffy-white; underparts shades of bright olive-yellow to pale buff-yellow, shading to buff or honey yellow on throat; tail brown with broad black subterminal band; bill and legs black; eyes dark brown.

VARIATION: west of Dividing Range, generally paler and less richly coloured (race *modesta*); east of Range, colours richer, lighter in north (race *flava*), darker in south (races *nana* and *mathewsi*).

HABITAT: dry forests and woodlands, including brigalow scrub and some mallee. HABITS: arboreal, restlessly hops and flits among foliage; gregarious, usually in small wandering flocks; sedentary. BREEDING: August–December; nests suspended from outer twigs, pear-shaped, domed with side entrance, made of interwoven dry grasses and fibres, sometimes decorated with moss and often lined with feathers; two to four eggs, dull white blotched and spotted with reddish-brown and lilac. VOICE: constant 'tzit-tzit' while moving about, rather harsher than Striated Thornbill. FOOD: insects.

STATUS: common. TAXONOMY: endemic species.

492 STRIATED THORNBILL *Acanthiza lineata* Gould 1838 Pl 15
Distribution: Map 160.

RECOGNITION: *white streaks on forehead and dark streaks on throat and breast; head and throat look slightly paler than body.*

DESCRIPTION: 9cm. Sexes alike. Head and face brownish-olive with thin white streaks on forehead; remainder of upperparts shades of dull olive-green; throat and breast pale buff-olive with varying amounts of diffuse dark streaking; belly yellowish-buff; under tail coverts cinnamon buff; tail dark brown with broad subterminal black bar; bill dark brown; eyes brownish-grey; legs dark grey.

VARIATION: New South Wales, generally paler (race *lineata*); Victoria and Kangaroo I, generally darker (race *chandleri*); Mt Lofty Ranges, upperparts greener and flanks yellower (race *clelendi*); Queensland, apparently less streaked on throat and breast (race *alberti*).

HABITAT: dry forests and woodlands, usually in denser timber than Little Thornbill but often occur together. HABITS: arboreal, actively forages among foliage and on bark; gregarious, usually in small flocks; sedentary. BREEDING: July–December; nests similar to Little Thornbill; three eggs, pale pink or cream spotted and speckled with reddish-brown. VOICE: constant 'zit-zit', softer than Little Thornbill. FOOD: insects.

STATUS: fairly common. TAXONOMY: endemic species.

493 BROWN THORNBILL   *Acanthiza pusilla*   White 1790   Fig p 328

Distribution: Map 161.

RECOGNITION: *pale 'scales' on rufous forehead, streaked throat and breast, cinnamon rufous rump, half cocked tail; distinguished from Tasmanian Thornbill by buff under tail coverts.*

DESCRIPTION: 10cm. Sexes alike. Forehead rufous brown with pale edges to feathers; upperparts shades of olive-brown with upper tail coverts and base of tail cinnamon rufous; tail dull brown with subterminal black bar of varying width and pale, sometimes whitish, tip; throat and breast white streaked with black; belly white; flanks, vent and under tail coverts shades of pale olive; bill black; eyes reddish-brown; legs black.

VARIATION: southern Queensland, paler with less distinct streaks on breast (race *bunya*); coastal New South Wales, darker with more distinct streaks (race *pusilla*); Victoria, more brownish than olive on back (race *maculata*); Tasmania, bill distinctly longer (race *diemenensis*).

HABITAT: lower layers of forests and dense woodlands. HABITS: in low foliage up to about 4 or 5m, actively foraging, carries tail half cocked; often more solitary than other thornbills but gregarious when not breeding; sedentary. BREEDING: July–December; nests in twiggy branches in low bushes, sometimes in bracken and ferns, pear-shaped with hooded side entrance, made of grass and bark and lined with feathers, sometimes decorated with cocoons and blossom; three eggs, dull white speckled with reddish-brown. VOICE: short warble 'which-whichy-woo', also churring chatter and sharp 'tzit-tzit'. FOOD: insects and vegetable matter.

STATUS: common. TAXONOMY: endemic species forming superspecies with Broad-tailed Thornbill.

494 BROAD-TAILED THORNBILL   *Acanthiza apicalis*   Gould 1847

[*Note:* current opinion is in favour of splitting *pusilla* into two species. On the features of specimens the many variants have long been divided into two main sections one of which is headed by *apicalis*. In the field it is maintained that the two sections are readily distinguished by several characteristics.]

Distribution: Map 161.

RECOGNITION: very like the Brown Thornbill, but *forehead browner* (less rufous) and *scales whiter;* upperparts tinged with citrine (less olive); *upper tail coverts and base of tail reddish-brown* or tawny; flanks and under tail coverts cinnamon buff; black tail band wider and white tip more distinct; *carries tail fully cocked.* (See *Emu,* 25: 229.)

VARIATION: inland New South Wales, 'rump' richer rufous (race *albiventris*); South Australia and central Western Australia, variably pale and grey (race *whitlocki*); extreme southwest, generally darker (race *apicalis*); extreme southwest coast, forehead more rufous (race *leeuwinensis*).

HABITAT: undergrowth in mulga, short mallee, dry low scrub; race *leeuwinensis,* damp coastal thickets. HABITS, etc: similar to Brown Thornbill except for more pronounced and regular tail cocking, rarely gregarious; voice said to be stronger and more penetrating.

STATUS: common. TAXONOMY: endemic species or semispecies forming superspecies with Brown Thornbill.

495 TASMANIAN THORNBILL *Acanthiza ewingi* Gould 1844

Distribution: Tasmania including King and Flinders Is.

RECOGNITION: like Brown Thornbill, but *forehead tawny-brown lightly dappled with dark brown* (without pale 'scales'); face, *throat and breast* dappled light and dark grey (not streaked); belly and flanks buffy-white; *under tail coverts white;* centre of wing cinnamon brown with black margins.

HABITAT, etc: similar to Brown Thornbill, but possibly keeping to denser forests, mostly solitary and sedentary, except for local movements, nests generally less untidy looking, has distinctive song only in breeding season.

STATUS: common. TAXONOMY: endemic species, probably an earlier colonist of Brown Thornbill stock.

496 MOUNTAIN THORNBILL *Acanthiza katherina* De Vis 1905

Distribution: Map 161.

RECOGNITION: like Brown Thornbill, but *forehead buff-olive with very indistinct pale 'scales';* upperparts olive-green with upper tail coverts dull rufous; *throat dull white with indistinct dark streaks;* breast pale yellow shading to greenish-yellow on belly and flanks; *eyes creamy-white or pale yellow.* (See *Emu,* 25: 229.)

HABITAT: mountain forest. HABITS: not known except that frequents forest canopy. BREEDING, etc: not known.

STATUS: not known. TAXONOMY: endemic species, perhaps forming a link between *A. pusilla* and *A. murina* of New Guinea.

497 SLATE-BACKED THORNBILL *Acanthiza robustirostris* Milligan 1903

Distribution: Map 162.

RECOGNITION: *grey appearance with dark streaks on pale grey forehead, unstreaked breast, pinkish cinnamon 'rump'.*

DESCRIPTION: 9cm. Sexes alike. Forehead pale grey with blackish streaks; crown bluish-grey; back grey-brown (drab); underparts whitish, with greyish-buff tinge on throat and foreneck and cinnamon tinge on breast and belly; upper tail coverts and base of tail pinkish-cinnamon; remainder of tail blackish with dull white tip; bill black; eyes reddish-brown; legs black.

HABITAT: mulga and low bushes, especially where fairly dense. HABITS: keeps to trees and bushes, rarely on ground (unlike Chestnut-tailed in same area); gregarious when not breeding. BREEDING: variable, depending on rains but mainly July–October; nests and eggs similar to Brown Thornbill. VOICE: low sibilant 'seep' or 'see-e' and harsh 'tchrit', also soft trisyllabic warble. FOOD: insects.

STATUS: common. TAXONOMY: endemic species.

498 WESTERN THORNBILL *Acanthiza inornata* Gould 1840
Distribution: Map 163.

RECOGNITION: *uniformly brownish above and pale buff below, whitish eyes, no conspicuous markings.*

DESCRIPTION: 10cm. Sexes alike. Upperparts dark olive-brown, forehead and face dappled with light brown; underparts pale buff; tail brown with indistinct subterminal black band; bill blackish-brown; eyes pale grey or creamy-white; legs grey-brown.

VARIATION: northern populations, slightly greyer above and whiter below (race *inornata*); southern, slightly browner above and buffier below (race *mastersi*).

HABITAT: undergrowth in dry forests and open woodlands. HABITS: usually in low foliage, sometimes forages on ground, mainly quiet and unobtrusive; gregarious and sedentary. BREEDING: September–December; nests in holes in trees or behind loose bark or deep in thick foliage; nest construction and eggs similar to Brown Thornbill. VOICE: soft twittering and notes imitating other species, but mostly silent. FOOD: insects.

STATUS: common. TAXONOMY: endemic species, forming superspecies with Samphire and Buff-rumped Thornbills.

499 SAMPHIRE THORNBILL *Acanthiza iredalei* Mathews 1911
Distribution: Map 163.

RECOGNITION: *creamy-buff rump and whitish 'scales' on forehead; very like nearly adjacent Buff-rumped Thornbill but lacks pinkish-cinnamon at base of tail.*

DESCRIPTION: 9cm. Sexes alike. Upperparts pale to dark olive with whitish 'scales' on forehead and speckles on face; rump and upper tail coverts creamy-buff; throat and foreneck cream with greyish 'scales', shading to creamy-buff on belly; tail blackish-brown at base shading to black subterminally and dull white at tip; bill black; eyes pale cream; legs black.

VARIATION: throughout most of range, pale olive (race *iredalei*); east of Spencer Gulf, slightly darker (race *hedleyi*); samphire flats north of Adelaide, much darker (race *rosinae*).

HABITAT: semideserts with saltbush and samphire and similar vegetation. HABITS: on or near ground in low vegetation, follow each other in loose order from bush to bush, but frequently feeding on ground; sedentary. BREEDING: July–November; nests in low bushes, construction and eggs similar to Brown Thornbill. VOICE: tinkling twitter like 'tsit-tsit-tsit' and more musical 'seu-seu' or 'teow-teow'. FOOD: insects.

STATUS: fairly common, possibly common. TAXONOMY: endemic species, forming super-species with Western and Buff-rumped Thornbills.

500 BUFF-RUMPED THORNBILL Acanthiza reguloides Vig. & Horsf. 1827
Distribution: Map 163.

RECOGNITION: very like Samphire Thornbill in having whitish 'scales' on forehead, greyish speckles or 'scales' on throat, buffy-yellow rump and whitish eye, but differs in having *basal half of tail pinkish-cinnamon.*

VARIATION: throughout most of range, rump buffy-yellow (race *reguloides*); near Adelaide, rump brownish-yellow (race *australis*); Atherton Tableland, underparts bright yellow (race *squamata*).

HABITAT: various kinds of lightly timbered country. HABITS: arboreal and terrestrial, feeds from ground to tree tops, among foliage and on bark; in small parties; sedentary. BREEDING: August–December; nests in any kind of recess up to about 3m, holes in trees and fence posts, behind loose bark or cracks in trunk; construction and eggs like Brown Thornbill. VOICE: tinkling or jingling notes. FOOD: insects.

STATUS: common. TAXONOMY: endemic species, forming superspecies with Western and Samphire Thornbills; the population of the Atherton rain forests might be a separate species, *Acanthiza squamata* Varied Thornbill.

501 YELLOW-RUMPED THORNBILL
Acanthiza chrysorrhoa (Quoy & Gaim.) 1870   Pl 15
Distribution: Map 164.

RECOGNITION: *bright yellow rump, whitish base of tail, black forehead with white spots, black streak through eye.*

DESCRIPTION: 10cm. Sexes alike. Forehead black with large white spots; crown and nape greyish to brownish-grey; back buff to yellowish-olive or grey-brown; rump and upper tail coverts bright yellow; face whitish with thin black streak through eye and white streak above eye; underparts vary from mainly white to yellowish or rufous buff with darker breast and flanks; base of tail whitish edged with pale yellow shading to fairly distinct subterminal black band and white or pale yellow tip; bill black; eyes brown; legs black.

VARIATION: New South Wales and south Queensland, back olive-buff and underparts mainly yellowish-buff (race *chrysorrhoa*); northwest Queensland, back yellowish-olive and under-parts mainly yellowish-white (race *normantoni*); Victoria and Tasmania, darker (race *sandlandi*); interior, paler (races *ferdinandi* east interior, *alexanderi* west interior); extreme southwest, back grey-brown and underparts rufous buff (race *multi*).

HABITAT: open woodlands and various kinds of savanna. HABITS: arboreal and terrestrial, frequently feeds on ground, also in bushes and tree foliage; after breeding forms small loose-knit flocks; sedentary except for wandering flock movements. BREEDING: June–December; breeds communally; untidy nests suspended in low foliage, consisting of hooded brood chamber with low overhung entrance and surmounted by one or more open cups of uncertain function, made of various grasses and fibres and lined with feathers; three eggs, white or pinkish lightly speckled with reddish-brown. VOICE: melodious trill in descending scale, high-pitched tinkling twitter, harsh 'tschaik'. FOOD: insects and some vegetable material like seeds.

STATUS: very common. TAXONOMY: endemic species.

502 CHESTNUT-RUMPED THORNBILL   *Acanthiza uropygialis*   Gould 1838

Distribution: Map 165.

RECOGNITION: *reddish-brown rump and white 'scaled' forehead, white underparts and white eye; mostly on ground.*

DESCRIPTION: 9cm. Sexes alike. Forehead reddish-brown with white 'scales'; crown and back drab brown; rump and upper tail coverts reddish-brown or tawny; face speckled white; underparts white tinged with grey on throat and foreneck, slightly tinged with buff on remainder; tail has blackish terminal half tipped with dull white; bill slaty black; eyes white; legs black.

VARIATION: southern populations and most of central, darker (race *uropygialis*); remainder, paler (race *augusta*).

HABITAT: dry savanna and woodland like mulga and mallee. HABITS: terrestrial and arboreal, feeds mostly on ground, also in bushes and low tree foliage, seldom high up; gregarious when not breeding, forming small restless flocks; sedentary. BREEDING: July–December; nests in various recesses, holes in trees, cavities in dead trunks, stumps and posts, construction and eggs similar to Brown Thornbill. VOICE: short melodious song, various soft clear calls like 'seee, tit-tit-tit, seee' and 'se-sese-se' and harsh 'tseu'. FOOD: insects and apparently seeds.

STATUS: common. TAXONOMY: endemic species.

Genus APHELOCEPHALA

A group of at least three species which have some resemblance to the thornbills both in appearance and habits but which are sufficiently distinct to be kept apart from them. The face pattern is a striking and unmistakable feature. It consists of a broad and nearly vertical white face band, which does not reach the centre of the forehead, emphasised by the dark remainder of the face. Two species have either a band or a bar on the breast. They belong to the arid interior where they usually feed on the gound and fly into bushes and low foliage.

Key to APHELOCEPHALA

1 Back brown, no markings on breast............	Southern Whiteface............	No 503
2 Back chestnut, band or bar on breast..........	3–4	
3 Breast with black bar......................	Banded Whiteface............	No 504
4 Breast with chestnut band..................	Chestnut-breasted Whiteface....	No 505

503 SOUTHERN WHITEFACE   *Aphelocephala leucopsis*   (Gould) 1840

Distribution: Map 166.

RECOGNITION: *dumpy appearance; near vertical division of white front part of face and forehead from blackish remainder; drab brown back, no bar or band on breast.*

DESCRIPTION: 10cm. Sexes alike. Upperparts dark grey-brown shading to blackish-brown on crown and hind part of face vertically in front of eye, sharply defined by sooty-black line from white forehead and face, vertical dark streak in centre of forehead; underparts creamy white with varying amounts of brown on flanks; tail blackish-brown tipped with white; bill black; eyes whitish; legs black.

VARIATION: south and east of Lake Eyre, flanks slightly tinged with brown (race *leucopsis*); centre, flanks fawn (race *whitei*); Western Australia, flanks cinnamon rufous (race *castaneiventris*).

HABITAT: woodland and savanna to arid scrub. HABITS: arboreal and terrestrial, feeds mostly on ground but readily takes to trees although adapted to treeless low bush; turns over ground litter in search of food, apparently independent of open water; gregarious, in small loose flocks; sedentary. BREEDING: variable, but mainly July–December, sometimes up to March; nests almost anywhere, including holes in trees and ground, bushes and tree forks, dome-shaped, large and untidy, made of various materials and lined with feathers or fur; two to five eggs, whitish or shades of pale brown or grey, sometimes speckled or blotched with shades of brown or red. VOICE: tinkling twitter or long trill of bell-like notes, also low soft 'tik-tik-tik'. FOOD: mainly seeds, sometimes insects.

STATUS: common. TAXONOMY: endemic species of small endemic genus; there are indications of speciation in the three races listed.

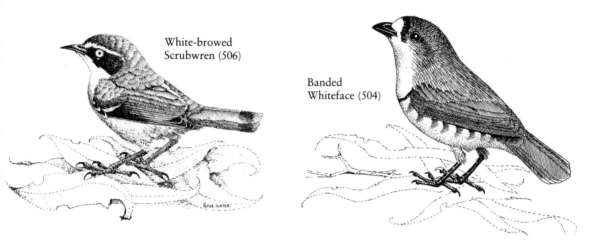

White-browed
Scrubwren (506)

Banded
Whiteface (504)

504 BANDED WHITEFACE *Aphelocephala nigricincta* (North) 1855
Distribution: Map 167.

RECOGNITION: like Southern Whiteface in general appearance and pattern, including white eyes, but *upperparts cinnamon brown, more rufous on rump* and shading to grey-brown on crown, whitish *underparts have narrow black breast* band, flanks blotched with rufous.

HABITAT: saltbush and porcupine grass areas usually with patches of mulga—generally rather barer places than where Southern Whiteface found but the two do occur together. HABITS: mainly similar to Southern Whiteface, usually on ground where progression is by hops, or in bushes, but trees also seem important; gregarious and possibly sedentary. BREEDING: apparently associated with rains, said to build nests before rains but to delay breeding; nests in bushes—never in holes like Southern Whiteface—or mulga trees, domed with long tunnel entrance, roughly made of twigs and lined with feathers, sometimes including part of tunnel; two to four eggs, like Southern Whiteface, but said to be paler with blotches more diffuse. VOICE: tinkling trill or twitter, like Southern Whiteface but more musical and clearly distinguishable, also liquid 'pee-pee-pee'. FOOD: mainly seeds but also insects.

STATUS: uncertain. TAXONOMY: endemic species of small endemic genus; possibly has close relationship with Chestnut-breasted Whiteface.

505 CHESTNUT-BREASTED WHITEFACE
Aphelocephala pectoralis (Gould) 1871

Distribution: Map 167.

RECOGNITION: very like Banded Whiteface except for *broad breast band of cinnamon brown and greyer crown.*

HABITAT: gibber plains with scattered bushes and mulga; said to occur along with Banded Whiteface between Oodnadatta and Everard Range. HABITS: apparently similar to Banded Whiteface, hopping and picking up seeds and flying into bushes. BREEDING: not known. VOICE: described as weak titter or chatter. FOOD: seeds and insects.

STATUS: uncertain. TAXONOMY: endemic species of endemic genus; possibly has close relationship with Banded Whiteface.

Genus SERICORNIS

The relationships of the scrubwrens has presented problems to taxonomists since Gould named the genus in 1838 and admitted 'the members require to be closely investigated'. The pattern of affinities may be getting clearer but there is still much research to be done. The only distinctive feature mentioned by Gould is a soft silky plumage impervious to wet. The limits of the genus are extended here to include the Scrubtit of Tasmania, *Acanthornis,* and the heathwrens, *Hylacola,* in all about seventeen species of which six occur only in New Guinea and one bridges Torres Strait. The Fernwren, *Oreoscopus,* might also belong but it and several other species of doubtful connections are kept in separate genera. Members included are slightly larger than warblers and thornbills, less plump in appearance, dull browns in plumage colour sometimes with yellowish underparts but with few distinctive features, except sometimes a white eyebrow or white bar on the shoulder or some speckling on the breast. Mostly they frequent thick undergrowth, often in forest habitats and other moist places. Secretive habits are associated with loud clear voices.

Key to SERICORNIS, CALAMANTHUS AND CHTHONICOLA

1 Face and shoulders without markings	Large-billed Scrubwren.........	No 510
	Atherton Scrubwren	No 511
2 Face and shoulders with markings...........	3–13	
3 Throat and eyebrow yellow, face black........	Yellow-throated Scrubwren.....	No 512
4 Throat white, eyebrow buff, white spot on shoulder; Tasmania....................	Brown Scrubwren	No 508
5 Throat and eyebrow white..................	6–13	
6 Breast spotted.........................	Spotted Scrubwren	No 507
7 Breast streaked........................	9–10	
8 Breast plain..........................	11–13	
9 Back plain		
White spot on shoulder	Shy Heathwren	No 515
No white spot on shoulder...............	Chestnut-rumped Heathwren....	No 514
10 Back streaked or blotched		
Crown streaked dark brown on buff-olive ..	Striated Fieldwren.............	No 518
Crown speckled white on dark brown	Speckled Warbler.............	No 519
11 White eyering and lores; Tasmania	Scrubtit....................	No 513
12 White streak below eye	White-browed Scrubwren	No 506
13 White or buff spot at side of forehead	Little Scrubwren	No 509

Speckled Warbler (519)   Striated Fieldwren (518)

HEAD PATTERNS (SEE KEY OPPOSITE)

WHITE-BROWED GROUP

A group of basically similar forms, Spotted, Brown and White-browed Scrubwrens, extends in southern coastal regions from Shark Bay in Western Australia to the Atherton Tableland, and in Tasmania. There is little doubt that they belong to the same stock. The group is rather variable and at one time or another about twenty forms have been named as species or races. The present tendency is to regard them as a superspecies divisible into two or three semi-species. The isolated Tasmanian section is an obvious choice for separation but the eastern and western mainland sections intergrade or hybridise in the Adelaide region, and to the purist this is proof that they are the same species. Away from the narrow hybrid zone the two sections have recognisable differences and the course taken here is to regard them as separate species.

506 WHITE-BROWED SCRUBWREN

Sericornis frontalis (Vig. & Horsf.) 1827   Fig p 339

Distribution: Map 168.

RECOGNITION: *white throat and eyebrow, white line below eye, breast plain (but may show spots in zone of contact with Spotted Scrubwren).*

DESCRIPTION: 11cm. Sexes slightly different. *Male:* upperparts shades of dark tawny-olive, darker and greyer on head and more tawny on rump and upper tail coverts; forehead, lores and face blackish with white eyebrow and white spot below eye; throat white variably speckled and streaked; breast and belly light buffy-yellow; flanks buff-olive; shoulders blackish with broken white bar; tail dark brown with subterminal black band of variable distinctiveness and with or without white tip; bill blackish-brown, paler below; eyes dark brown or pale buff. *Female:* face and lores grey-brown, no streaks on throat.

VARIATION: south of Queensland throat mostly streaked, indistinct black tail band and pale tip, eyes brown (race *frontalis*); Queensland, throat plain, distinct black tail band and white tip, eyes pale buff (race *laevigaster*).

HABITAT: dense bushy vegetation and tangled undergrowth in various situations along coastal belt. HABITS: on or near ground moving by short hops, lively and usually keeping well hidden; solitary or in small groups; sedentary. BREEDING: July–January; nests close to ground, domed with side entrance, made of leaves and fibres and lined with soft material; three eggs, pale blue or purplish spotted with dark brown. VOICE: loud chattering rattle. FOOD: insects and other small animals, also seeds.

STATUS: common. TAXONOMY: endemic species or semispecies forming superspecies with Spotted and Brown Scrubwrens.

507 SPOTTED SCRUBWREN *Sericornis maculatus*   Gould 1847
Distribution: Map 168.

RECOGNITION: very like White-browed Scrubwren but *breast spotted with black,* upperparts more greyish-brown, *breast and belly white or lemon-buff,* more white flecks on shoulders.

VARIATION: extreme southwest (Dongara to Bremer Bay), breast and belly lemon-buff (race *maculatus*); remainder, breast and belly white, northern populations paler (race *balstoni*), eastern populations darker (race *mellori*).

HABITAT, etc: similar to White-browed species, but sometimes in more open and drier thickets and undergrowth and higher up. VOICE: clear musical 'tse-tseu-ee' or 'tsree-ee' ascending in scale, also harsher 'zit-zit' or 'tchit-tchit'.

STATUS: common. TAXONOMY: endemic species or semispecies.

508 BROWN SCRUBWREN *Sericornis humilis*   Gould 1838
Distribution: Map 168.

RECOGNITION: very like White-browed Scrubwren but larger, 14cm, upperparts dark cinnamon brown, *indistinct buff or near white eyebrow, white spot at edge of shoulder;* Tasmania only. These features also distinguish it from the Scrubtit of Tasmania.

VARIATION: like other members of this superspecies there is some variation especially in populations isolated on Bass Strait islands. It is claimed both that they show characters intermediate with the White-browed and that the two species occur together without interbreeding.

HABITAT, etc: similar to White-browed. VOICE: apparently less musical than other species and described as like squeak of rusty wheel; also has 'zit-zit' or 'chip-chip' call.

STATUS: common. TAXONOMY: endemic species or semispecies.

509 LITTLE SCRUBWREN *Sericornis beccarii*   Salvadori 1874
Distribution: Map 168.

RECOGNITION: *white throat, white or buff eyebrow and spot at side of forehead, plain breast; tip of Cape York.*

DESCRIPTION: 11cm. Sexes alike or slightly different. *Male:* upperparts shades of brown, more cinnamon on crown and more rufous on rump and upper tail coverts; spot at side of forehead white or buff; lores and face blackish-brown with short thin eyebrow and lower eyelid white or buff; underparts mainly pale yellow, white on throat with faint dark streaks and greyish-buff on flanks; bill pinkish-brown, paler below; eyes orange-red; legs pale pinkish-brown. *Female:* blackish areas of face replaced by brown, sometimes lacks facial spots and streaks.

VARIATION: north of Lockhardt and Archer Rivers, upperparts olive-brown, spots and streaks on face white (race *minimus*); south, upperparts cinnamon brown, spots and streaks buff (or absent) and pattern diffuse (race *dubius*).

HABITAT, etc: (very little information available, even on New Guinea races). In forest undergrowth, on or near ground fossicking among ground litter or in low foliage, seen in small parties mixed with other species; nests and eggs so far recorded similar to White-browed.
VOICE: described as fine sweet song. FOOD: insects.

STATUS: common (but not well known). TAXONOMY: races of variable and widespread New Guinea species; the race *dubius* may be an earlier colonist than *minimus* and may be a separate species, or nearly so.

510 LARGE-BILLED SCRUBWREN *Sericornis magnirostris* Gould 1838
Distribution: Map 169.

RECOGNITION: *face and shoulders without distinct markings, relatively large black bill; mainly arboreal.*

DESCRIPTION: 12–13cm. Sexes alike. Upperparts dark buff-olive sometimes becoming browner on crown and more tawny on rump; forehead and face light buff; underparts shades of light buff-olive, more buff on throat and under tail coverts; bill black; eyes dark reddish-brown; legs light yellowish-brown.

VARIATION: throughout most of range, back more olive and contrasting with crown and rump, underparts lighter buff-olive (race *magnirostris*); about Tully to Cooktown, darker and duller (race *viridior*).

HABITAT: forest substage and undergrowth. HABITS: mainly arboreal but in middle and lower forest levels, rarely on ground, actively feeds by working up tree trunks and branches and lianas and among foliage; solitary or in small parties, probably families; sedentary. BREEDING: July–January; nests in trees and bushes and among palm fronds, domed with side entrance, made of leaves and fibres (frequently appropriate materials from nests of Yellow-throated Scrubwren and often also occupy their nests); three to four eggs, dull white or light grey-brown with dark spots and lines. VOICE: soft musical twitter and harsh chatter, but apparently mainly silent. FOOD: insects.

STATUS: fairly common. TAXONOMY: endemic species.

511 ATHERTON SCRUBWREN *Sericornis keri* Mathews 1920
Distribution: Map 169.

RECOGNITION: superficially like the Large-billed Scrubwren especially in the lack of distinct facial markings, but differs in having *forehead and face darker*, more olive-brown, like crown and back; *bill shorter* and legs and feet longer. HABITAT and HABITS: like Large-billed Scrubwren but probably less arboreal and more often in ground vegetation. BREEDING: nest and eggs recorded November, on 'open bank at side of road, well concealed by grasses and slender ferns', side entrance near top, made of leaves and fibres and lined with feathers; two eggs, colour as in Large-billed Scrubwren. FOOD: beetles and small molluscs.

512 YELLOW-THROATED SCRUBWREN
Sericornis lathami (Stephens) 1817   Pl 15
Distribution: Map 170.

RECOGNITION: *black face between yellow throat and long eyebrow streak extending to side of neck; on or close to forest floor.*

DESCRIPTION: 14cm. Sexes nearly alike, female duller with olive-brown face patch. Upperparts olive-brown, darker on crown and slightly rufous on tail; broad eyebrow stripe from bill to nape lemon-yellow, sometimes white near bill; throat lemon-yellow; breast and flanks buff-olive sometimes tinged with yellow; belly white; bill black; eyes light brown; legs pinkish-brown.

VARIATION: southern population, as described (race *lathami*); Cooktown to Tully, slightly darker (race *cairnsi*).

HABITAT: rain forest. HABITS: mainly terrestrial, on or near ground in low substage, hops on forest floor, sometimes in company with Logrunners, to pick up insects disturbed by them; solitary or in family groups; sedentary. BREEDING: August–March; nests suspended from low branches and vines, usually below 3m, a large domed untidy mass of twigs and leaves sometimes decorated with moss, lined with feathers; two to three eggs, shades of brown, more glossy than those of other scrubwrens. VOICE: varied, and accomplished mimic; mostly clear melodious whistling song and harsh 'pit-pit-pit'. FOOD: insects and seeds. STATUS: fairly common. TAXONOMY: endemic species.

513 SCRUBTIT   *Sericornis magnus*   (Gould) 1855

Distribution: Map 170.

RECOGNITION: *white eyering as well as white lores and eyebrow; white flecks on shoulder, Tasmania.*

DESCRIPTION: 10cm. Sexes alike. Upperparts dark cinnamon brown; face dark greyish with dull white lores, white eyebrow and white eyering; throat white; breast and belly pale lemon-yellow; white flecks on shoulders; tail with broad subterminal black band and white edges to inner feathers; bill blackish-brown; eyes dark brown; legs pinkish-brown.

HABITAT: forest undergrowth and dense vegetation on moorland creeks and swamps. HABITS: mainly in thick vegetation up to about 5m, sometimes forages at low levels on tree trunks or perches on low branches; solitary and sedentary. BREEDING: September–January; nests near ground or suspended in bushes and ferns below about 3m, domed with side entrance, made of bark strips and rootlets and lined with soft material; three to four eggs, pearly-white, blotched with reddish-brown. VOICE: various whistling notes, 'to-wee-to' or 'to-wee-to-wee'; closely similar to Brown Scrubwren and Brown Thornbill in same area. FOOD: insects. STATUS: fairly common. TAXONOMY: endemic species, sometimes kept in separate genus, *Acanthornis*.

> [CHARLEVILLE HEATHWREN   *Sericornis tyrannulus*   De Vis 1905
> Based on a specimen collected near Charleville but now lost. Efforts to find similar birds in the Charleville area have proved unsuccessful. Some think that the specimen was wrongly localised and possibly belonged to New Guinea, but it does not fit any species known there. The description might fit a *Sericornis* or a *Hylacola*—included here with *Sericornis*—but neither have been recorded near Charleville. A heathwren would be the more likely to occur so far from the coast.]

514 CHESTNUT-RUMPED HEATHWREN
Sericornis pyrrhopygia   (Vig. & Horsf.) 1827   Pl 15

Distribution: Map 171.

RECOGNITION: *boldly streaked breast, white eyebrow, rufous 'rump', cocked tail.*

DESCRIPTION: 12cm. Sexes alike. Upperparts shading from grey-brown on forehead and crown to brown on back and cinnamon brown on rump; upper and under tail coverts rufous; white eyebrow; face, throat and breast dull white streaked with blackish-brown; belly light buff; tail dark brown with blackish-brown broad subterminal band and dull white tip; bill blackish-brown; eyes light brown; legs light brown.

HABITAT: woodland thickets, low scrub and open heath. HABITS: mainly terrestrial, on or near ground, actively hopping with tail erect, or in low bushes, more inclined to flit from bush to bush than Shy Heathwren; solitary or in small parties; sedentary. BREEDING: June–November; nests on ground in shallow depression or near ground in bush or grass clump, domed with side entrance; made of dried grass and bark strips woven into a felted mass and lined with feathers; three to four eggs, pinkish brown lightly blotched and capped with dark brown. VOICE: wide range of loud musical notes, also an accomplished mimic. FOOD: insects.

STATUS: fairly common. TAXONOMY: endemic species closely related to Shy Heathwren.

515 SHY HEATHWREN *Sericornis cauta* Gould 1842
Distribution: Map 171.

RECOGNITION: very like Chestnut-rumped Heathwren but slightly smaller, has distinct *white patch on edge of shoulder,* darker (chestnut) upper tail coverts, *bolder streaks on breast;* white underparts lack yellow tinge.

HABITAT: bushes and similar low vegetation mainly in mallee country (where the two species overlap they are said to occupy different habitats). HABITS, etc: similar to Chestnut-rumped but said to be more on ground and less frequently flitting between bushes; eggs dark pinkish brown with nearly black cap. VOICE: melodious 'chee-chee-chick-a-dee'.

STATUS: fairly common. TAXONOMY: endemic species closely related to Chestnut-rumped Heathwren.

Genus OREOSCOPUS

Originally thought to be and described as a *Sericornis,* the Fernwren was later placed in this genus; there may be reasonable grounds for returning it. The Fernwren is similar in general appearance and habits to the scrubwrens but has a black patch on the breast and larger bill. It may be a relict form of the original scrubwren stock which was probably widespread in the Australian wet period.

Fernwren (516)

516 FERNWREN *Oreoscopus gutturalis* (De Vis) 1889
Distribution: Map 172.

RECOGNITION: *dark bronze-brown with white chin, long bill and black patch on breast; rain forest floor.*

DESCRIPTION: 14cm, with bill 2cm. Sexes alike, but possibly eyebrow speckled white in male and continuous white in female. Upperparts dark bronze-brown, blacker on crown and lighter on rump, and slightly 'scaled' with white on forehead; face dark grey-brown; white eyebrow; chin and broad malar streak white; black patch on throat and foreneck; remainder of underparts grey-brown; bill black; eyes dark brown; legs light pinkish-brown. HABITAT: rain forest undergrowth. HABITS: (not well known) mainly terrestrial, lives on forest floor, hops, bows head and elevates tail; apparently solitary and sedentary. BREEDING: August–February; nests on ground, recorded in cavities in banks, domed with slightly overhung side entrance, made of rootlets, twigs, leaves and moss and lined with fur; two eggs, white sometimes faintly speckled with brown. VOICE: said to be mainly silent but harsh scolding recorded consisting of 'rapid staccato notes in descending scale'. FOOD: apparently insects.

STATUS: not known. TAXONOMY: endemic species and genus perhaps closely related to *Sericornis*.

Genus PYRRHOLAEMUS

Gould found the Redthroat a bird of 'singular form' and gave it generic rank. Later it was transferred to *Sericornis* but is now back in *Pyrrholaemus*. It may be that the Redthroat is a branch of the wet forest scrubwren stock which has adapted to drier conditions. They have many characteristics in common.

517 REDTHROAT   *Pyrrholaemus brunneus*   Gould 1840
Distribution: Map 172.

RECOGNITION: *drab brown with white-tipped tail and white lores, male has brown throat; like thornbill without contrasting rump.*

DESCRIPTION: 12cm. Sexes slightly different, female lacks brown throat. Upperparts olive-brown to grey-brown with some white flecks or 'scales' on forehead; throat tawny cinnamon; breast pale grey-brown; belly white; flanks and under tail coverts cinnamon buff; tail blackish-brown, outer feathers broadly tipped with white; bill and legs blackish-brown; eyes shades of brown with whitish outer ring. HABITAT: saltbush and similar semi-arid scrub. HABITS: on or near ground actively foraging near or at base of bushes, or feeding in bushes or in low branches, hops rapidly or flies low with dipping flight; solitary or in small parties; sedentary. BREEDING: August–December; nests near ground, domed with side entrance, made of grass and bark and lined with feathers; three to four eggs, brown shaded darker at thick end. VOICE: very vocal; has wide range of musical warbling notes and is an accomplished mimic; also a harsh chatter and softer 'tchick-ick'. FOOD: mainly insects but also seeds.

STATUS: probably fairly common. TAXONOMY: endemic species and genus possibly related to the scrubwrens.

Genus CALAMANTHUS

The fieldwrens also have a number of characteristics in common with the *Sericornis* group. They may be further out on the divergent branch representing the heathwrens. Their wide distribution and integrated variability suggests that they are comparatively recent terrestrial colonists of mainly arid habitats.

[*Note:* fieldwrens are rather variable. Some twenty forms have been described as species or subspecies. Current opinion is divided between recognising one species or two, the other being the Rufous Fieldwren, *C. campestris*. Only one is accepted here as the course adopted is to regard as species such forms as are clearly distinguishable over most of their ranges, with perhaps a limited hybrid zone. The fieldwrens do not seem to fit into this pattern. There is gradual change in several features and certain identification of separate named species may not be possible over a wide area.]

518 STRIATED FIELDWREN

Calamanthus fuliginosus (Vig. & Horsf.) 1827   Fig p 341

Distribution: Map 173.

RECOGNITION: (see key to *Sericornis,* page 340) *Streaked above and below, crown with dark streaks on buff-olive; cocked tail; in timbered country.*

DESCRIPTION: 12cm. Sexes alike. Very variable; all variants streaked blackish-brown above and below and tail with subterminal black band and pale tip; principal variants are (1) ground colour of upperparts dark olive-buff, sometimes greenish, with little or no rufous on forehead and upper tail coverts; eyebrow creamy-buff or whitish; underparts shades of buff, sometimes near white on throat and tinged with cinnamon on flanks and under tail coverts; tip of tail greyish; (2) ground colour of upperparts light olive tawny with forehead and upper tail coverts cinnamon rufous; eyebrow white; underparts pale buff to white; tip of tail dull white; (3) intermediates—bill dark grey-brown to pinkish-brown; eyes brown to golden-brown; legs pinkish-brown.

VARIATION: about fifteen races currently listed; variant (1) in southeast, including Tasmania, (race *fuliginosus*), and southwest (race *montanellus*); others (mainly race *campestris* with *isabellinus* in centre and west).

HABITAT: open treeless country from moist heaths to bushy scrub and desolate gibber plains with little cover. HABITS: mainly terrestrial, forages on ground or skulks or creeps mouse-like or hops at speed with tail cocked, or in bushes or tussocks, sometimes on exposed perch to sing; solitary and sedentary. BREEDING: variable, depending on rains in arid regions, recorded July–April; nests on ground or low in bush or tussock, domed with side entrance, loosely made of grasses and lined with soft materials; three to four eggs, brownish blotched or shaded with darker brown. VOICE: loud musical 'whirr-whirr-chick-chick-whirr-ree-ree'. FOOD: insects.

STATUS: common. TAXONOMY: endemic species and genus, possibly a derivative of *Sericornis*.

Genus CHTHONICOLA

The Speckled Warbler is one of the few Australian species originally put in the genus *Sylvia* on which the family is based. It has also been in *Calamanthus* and is said to have affinities with both *Pyrrholaemus* and *Acanthiza*. Possibly it is best to retain it in this separate genus. It may illustrate an intermediate stage in adaptation from forest to arid habitats.

519 SPECKLED WARBLER

Chthonicola sagittata (Latham) 1801   Fig p 341

Distribution: Map 174.

RECOGNITION: (see key to *Sericornis* page 340). *Streaked above and below, crown speckled white on dark umber; on ground in timbered country.*

DESCRIPTION: 11–12cm. Sexes alike. Forehead and crown blackish-brown speckled or streaked with white and edged with cinnamon rufous; white lores and eyebrow; back grey-brown densely blotched with blackish-brown; rump and upper tail coverts plain fawn; tail black broadly tipped with white; face and underparts white blotched with black, blotches sometimes forming broad arrows or streaks on breast; vent and under tail coverts light cinnamon brown; bill dark grey-brown; eyes brown; legs bluish-grey.

HABITAT: woodlands with low scrub at various altitudes. HABITS: mainly terrestrial, actively hops and flits over ground or flies into bushes or low branches, especially when disturbed; solitary or in small scattered parties; sedentary, perhaps nomadic or migratory in south. BREEDING: September–January or later; nests on ground in slight depression under bush or tussock, made of grass and bark and surrounding vegetation gathered over to form a hood, side entrance at ground level, sometimes also a cup-shaped 'dummy' nest near entrance; three eggs, dark reddish-brown; favourite host of Black-eared Cuckoo. VOICE: subdued musical chatter. FOOD: insects and seeds.

STATUS: fairly common. TAXONOMY: endemic species and genus.

Genus ORIGMA

A genus for the unique Rock Warbler, a terrestrial inhabitant of the Hawkesbury Sandstone area around Sydney. Its origins and affinities are uncertain. It was first placed in *Sylvia* and taxonomists nowadays can do no better than to keep it in the warbler family.

520 ROCK WARBLER *Origma solitaria* (Lewin) 1808   Pl 15

Distribution: Map 174.

RECOGNITION: *plain dark brown with white throat; on ground and rocks near water in Sydney area.*

DESCRIPTION: 14cm. Sexes alike. Upperparts blackish-brown, more cinnamon brown on forehead and face; throat white speckled with black; remainder of underparts rich cinnamon brown; tail sooty-black; bill and legs blackish-brown; eyes reddish-brown.

HABITAT: ravines and rocky gullies with open water in the Hawkesbury Sandstone. HABITS: mainly terrestrial, rarely in bushes and trees, hops rapidly over ground and rocks or flits low over ground from rock to rock, moves in jerky manner on vertical rocks, frequently near water; solitary and sedentary. BREEDING: August–December; nests suspended from overhanging rocks and roofs of caves, attached by cobwebs, globular with side entrance, made of fibres, grass and moss and lined with soft materials; three white eggs. VOICE: shrill melancholy call like 'good-bye', repeated high-pitched short note, and rasping note. FOOD: mainly insects but also some vegetable material.

STATUS: fairly common. TAXONOMY: endemic species and genus with uncertain affinities.

Genus PYCNOPTILUS

The unique Pilotbird is placed in this genus. It has a general resemblance in appearance and biology to the Rock Warbler and also in some respects to the Yellow-throated Scrubwren. On the evidence of a single specimen of unknown origin Gould placed it near the Bristlebirds and made an inspired deduction regarding its habits. It lives in the same dense forest under-growth as the lyrebird and its name derives from their being found together, but perhaps more by accident than design.

521 PILOTBIRD *Pycnoptilus floccosus*   Gould 1850   Pl 15

Distribution: Map 175.

RECOGNITION: *uniformly dark brown with whitish belly; on ground in dense forests.*

DESCRIPTION: 16–17cm. Sexes alike. Mainly blackish-brown with forehead, ring round eye, throat and breast cinnamon buff, breast scalloped with sepia, centre of belly whitish, under tail coverts cinnamon rufous; bill and legs blackish-brown; eyes red.

HABITAT: forest floors, moist places with leaf mould. HABITS: terrestrial, turns over debris with its feet, flicks tail, said to accompany lyrebirds but both species fossick in the same manner and same places; solitary and sedentary. BREEDING: August–January; nests on or near ground among litter or base of some clump of vegetation, sometimes or perhaps usually on slope of bank, domed with side entrance, loosely made of bark strips and other material and lined with feathers; two eggs, dark purplish-brown unmarked or diffusely blotched with black. VOICE: various musical phrases, like 'what-a-whit-ee-tou' or 'tui-whit' or one sometimes transcribed as 'guinea-a-week'. FOOD: insects.

STATUS: uncommon and perhaps declining. TAXONOMY: endemic species and genus of uncertain affinity.

Brown
Flycatcher (522)

Family MUSCICAPIDAE

Flycatchers

23(about 320) species: 13 endemic

FLYCATCHERS ARE NOT EASILY defined solely on fly-catching habits for many birds—including some hawks—take insects on the wing and several groups are highly specialised for that purpose. As in the case of warblers it is difficult to find the limits of the family or subfamily on the basis of close affinity with the typical genus *Muscicapa*. Some taxonomists would have it that no Australian species qualify for inclusion while others spread their nets widely. It is easily seen for example, by those who know both, that the Brown Flycatcher or Jacky Winter resembles in outward appearance and behaviour the Spotted Flycatcher of Europe but whether it is because they share the same ancestor or the same habits is not easily decided. It may be, therefore, that some of the species are included here on the basis of common behaviour rather than affinity. Perhaps it could be said that muscicapids are small insect-eating birds showing various stages in learning to take their prey on the wing but on the whole not really efficient or well adapted for it. There is a tendency to have wide gapes, achieved by flattening the base of the bill, and mouths edged with stiff bristles to extend the catching area. Most Australian species are distinctly patterned and some have brilliant patches of colour, especially reds and yellows. They are mainly small, plus or minus 15cm, sometimes with long tails which are fanned and wagged from side to side.

Key to MUSCICAPIDAE

[Additional keys are found where genera have more than one species.]

1 Shades of red on breast (mainly males) . . . . *Petroica* . . . . Nos 526–532
2 Belly and sometimes breast yellow . . . . { *Microeca* . . . . Nos 522–525
  { *Eopsaltria* . . . . Nos 537–541
3 Brownish or olive-brown above, white below . . . . { *Microeca* . . . . Nos 522–525
  { Grey-headed Robin . . . . No 534
  { *Poecilodryas* . . . . Nos 535–536
4 Black or dark grey above, white below
  Tail fanning habit . . . . *Rhipidura* . . . . Nos 542–545
  { *Petroica* . . . . Nos 526–532
  Others . . . . { Mangrove Robin . . . . No 533
  { *Eopsaltria* . . . . Nos 537–541
5 More or less wholly dark grey-brown: Tasmania . . *Petroica* . . . . Nos 526–532
6 Forehead and rump rufous . . . . *Rhipidura* . . . . Nos 542–545

Genus MICROECA

Probably nearest in affinity to the genus *Muscicapa*, this group of six or seven species belongs to Australia and New Guinea. There are four in Australia all of which are similar in poise and behaviour to the common Brown Flycatcher or Jacky Winter, but two in the far north have yellow underparts. Typically they perch upright on low perches and dart out to take insects on the wing or on the ground.

Key to MICROECA

1 Brown above, white below 3–5
2 Green above, yellow below 5–6

3 Tail has white outer margin . . . . Brown Flycatcher . . . . No 522
4 Tail wholly brownish . . . . Brown-tailed Flycatcher . . . . . . No 524

5 Head grey . . . . Yellow Flycatcher . . . . No 525
6 Head greenish like back . . . . Lemon-breasted Flycatcher . . . . No 523

522 BROWN FLYCATCHER *Microeca leucophaea* (Latham) 1801   Fig p 349
Distribution: Map 176.

RECOGNITION: *grey-brown above, white below, blackish tail with broad white margins contrasting with back; often perched on low bare branches or snags.*

DESCRIPTION: 12–13cm. Sexes alike. Upperparts shades of grey-brown, blackish on wing tips and centre of tail; outer tail feathers mainly white; shoulder and inner flight feathers tipped with white; face streaked white and eyebrow dull white; underparts white or creamy with breast grey or light buff; bill blackish-brown; eyes dark brown; legs black.

VARIATION: coastal southeast from Adelaide to central Queensland, darkest (race *leucophaea*); north, paler (race *pallida*); centre, palest (race *barcoo*); south and west from Victorian mallee, basal half of outer tail feathers black—not white (race *assimilis*).

HABITAT: open timbered country including town parks and domestic gardens. HABITS:

mainly arboreal, usually perches on bare branches at various heights but often fairly low, darts out to catch flying insects or sometimes takes them on the ground or on trunks, frequently swings tail from side to side; solitary and sedentary. BREEDING: August–December; nests in trees in horizontal forks usually fairly high, shallow saucer made of grass and hair and decorated with bark; two eggs, pale bluish-green blotched and spotted with brown and grey. VOICE: variants of prolonged musical 'peter-peter' or 'pretty-pretty'. FOOD: insects. STATUS: very common. TAXONOMY: near endemic species (small population of distinct race at Port Moresby in New Guinea).

523 LEMON-BREASTED FLYCATCHER *Microeca flavigaster* Gould 1842 Pl 16
Distribution: Map 177.

RECOGNITION: *mainly uniform yellowish-olive above and yellow below; general appearance and behaviour like Brown Flycatcher.*

DESCRIPTION: 11–12cm. Sexes alike. Upperparts yellowish-olive, slightly yellower on rump; margins of inner flight feathers pale buffy-yellow; underparts yellow, near white on throat and dusky on side of breast and flanks; tail blackish-brown, tips of outer feathers pale buff; bill blackish-brown; eyes dark brown; legs dark grey.

VARIATION: Northern Territory and Cape York populations have been separated on degree of whiteness of throat and tone of yellow (races *flavigaster* and *terraereginae*) but the distinction is not clear.

HABITAT: mangrove and forest and adjacent woodland. HABITS: similar to Brown Flycatcher. BREEDING: September–January; nests similar to Brown Flycatcher but smaller—less than 5cm across; one egg, pale blue spotted with dark red. VOICE: whistling musical phrase of about seven notes, similar to Brown Flycatcher but rather more varied. FOOD: insects. STATUS: common. TAXONOMY: species extending to southern New Guinea.

524 KIMBERLEY FLYCATCHER *Microeca tormenti* Mathews 1916
Distribution: vicinity of Derby, Kimberley area.

RECOGNITION: like Lemon-breasted Flycatcher but upperparts less yellow and underparts mainly white.

HABITAT etc: similar to Lemon-breasted Flycatcher.

[Note. The form *tormenti* was regarded as a race of the species *Microeca brunneicauda* but *brunneicauda* was shown to be a misidentification and the name became obsolete. Consequently *tormenti* could be attached to the species *M. flavigaster*, which it resembles closely, or be regarded as a species in its own right. Official recognition has been given to the latter with the common name Kimberley Flycatcher.]

525 YELLOW FLYCATCHER *Microeca griseoceps* De Vis 1893 Pl 16
Distribution: tip of Cape York, perhaps Atherton Tableland.

RECOGNITION: like Lemon-breasted Flycatcher but *crown and nape grey;* very like Pale-yellow Robin but smaller, and bill has *upper mandible black, lower maize yellow;* the White-faced Robin in same area has much white on face.

HABITAT: forests. HABITS, etc: little is known with certainty; it seems preferable not to repeat information questionably attributed to this species. Remarks on New Guinea population are: 'A rather uncommon bird of the forest substage and taller second growth where it sits up rather straight and quietly. Its song is a fine trill with changes in volume.'*

STATUS: unknown. TAXONOMY: extension of nominate race of uncommon New Guinea species.

Genus PETROICA

Most Australian muscicapids, as understood here, are called 'robin' although the original Robin Redbreast belongs to the thrush family. Only some have red breasts and they belong to this genus of twelve species, seven of which are endemic. It is the males which are red breasted and, less distinctly, the female Scarlet Robin. This feature is also found in the Mistletoebird belonging to a different family, Dicaeidae (included here for identification purposes). The sexes are different in most members of the group, the exception being the dull coloured Dusky Robin of Tasmania. Both sexes have a white or red mark on the forehead and or white or pale buff streaks or patches on the wing, sometimes on the tail; these features are not present in the Mistletoebird which is further distinguished by a black streak in the centre of the white belly.

Key to PETROICA (Males only)

1	Black and white (whole head and neck black)....	Hooded Robin..............	No 531
2	Dark grey-brown, white on wings; Tasmania....	Dusky Robin	No 532
3	Black and white with red breast................	4–12	
4	Forehead with large red patch	Red-capped Robin	No 528
5	Forehead with white patch or spot.............	7–12	
[6	Forehead black; black streak on white belly......	Mistletoebird	No 595]
7	Wing with broad white streak	9–10	
8	No white on wing...........................	11–12	
9	Throat black...............................	Scarlet Robin	No 526
10	Throat red.................................	Flame Robin...............	No 527
11	Tail with white on outer feathers	Rose Robin................	No 529
12	Tail wholly black...........................	Pink Robin................	No 530

526 SCARLET ROBIN *Petroica multicolor* (Gmelin) 1789   Pl 16

Distribution: Map 178.

RECOGNITION: *large white patch on forehead, broad white streak on wing; very like Flame Robin but throat black; female has tinge of red on breast.*

DESCRIPTION: 12–13cm. Sexes very different. *Male:* breast scarlet; large white patch on forehead; white streak on wing; belly and margin of tail white; remainder black; bill and legs black; eyes dark brown. *Female:* breast tinged with red; small white spot on forehead; buffy-white streak and bar on wing; belly and margin of tail white; remainder grey brown.

VARIATION: only recognised in females: eastern populations, paler (race *boodang*); western, darker on back and throat (race *campbelli*).

HABITAT: dry forests and woodlands, parks and gardens. HABITS: arboreal and terrestrial, forages actively among foliage of trees and bushes and on the ground; solitary or in family groups; sedentary with local nomadic movements, apparently to more open habitats when

---

Handbook of New Guinea Birds, Rand and Gilliard, 1967.

not breeding. BREEDING: July–December; nests in trees usually below about 5m, in vertical forks or horizontal boughs or tree hollows, cup-shaped, well made of bark strips and grass bound with cobwebs and lined with soft material; three eggs, greyish or greenish-white, blotched and spotted with pale brown. VOICE: trilling notes. FOOD: insects.

STATUS: fairly common. TAXONOMY: endemic races of species extending to Samoa and Fiji; possibly forming superspecies with Red-capped Robin.

527 FLAME ROBIN *Petroica phoenicia* Gould 1837 Pl 16
Distribution: Map 179.

RECOGNITION: *small white patch on forehead, broad white streak on wing; very like Scarlet Robin but throat red.*

DESCRIPTION: 13–14cm. Sexes very different. *Male:* throat (not chin) to middle of belly flame red or reddish-orange; small white spot on forehead; vent and part of outermost tail feather white; broad white longitudinal streak on wing; remainder dark grey, blacker on tail and wing tips; bill, eyes and legs blackish. *Female:* upperparts brown (dark fawn) with indistinct pale buff spot on forehead and pale buff bars on wing; underparts pale buff, whiter on belly and sometimes with tinge of reddish-orange on throat and breast.

HABITAT: mainly dry forests and woodlands when breeding and open country when not breeding. HABITS: arboreal and terrestrial, feeds mostly on or near ground, restlessly flitting from place to place, or perhaps exposed on bushes or posts; solitary or in fairly large flocks when not breeding, sometimes flocks of one sex; sedentary or partially nomadic or migratory, moving to and from Tasmania, between high and low country, and heavy timber to open country. BREEDING: September–January; nest sites variable, tree forks at various heights or tree clefts, or almost any kind of hollow, even among upturned roots and banks; made of grass and bark strips bound with cobwebs and lined with soft material; three eggs, pale bluish or greenish speckled with reddish-brown. VOICE: thin piping trill. FOOD: insects.

STATUS: very common in Tasmania, less common on mainland. TAXONOMY: endemic species.

528 RED-CAPPED ROBIN *Petroica goodenovii* (Vig. & Horsf.) 1827 Pl 16
Distribution: widespread except Tasmania, Cape York and heavy rainfall areas.

RECOGNITION: *red patch on forehead of male; female has tinge of rusty brown.*

DESCRIPTION: 11–12cm. Sexes very different. *Male:* forehead and breast scarlet; belly, broad streak on wing and edge of tail white; remainder black; bill and legs black; eyes dark brown. *Female:* upperparts grey-brown with rusty tinge on forehead and darker tail; underparts and edge of tail dull white; small white patch in centre of wing.

HABITAT: varied; edge of rain forest to semi-arid desert with scattered trees. HABITS: arboreal and terrestrial, usually low in trees or in bushes or on ground, actively flits about frequently cocking tail or sits on bare branches or tops of bushes; solitary or in family parties; sedentary or partly nomadic, particularly in drought, and migratory, especially in south. BREEDING: variable, but mainly July–December; nests in tree forks usually low down, well made cup of fine grass and rootlets bound with moss and cobwebs and lined with soft material; two to three eggs, pale green spotted with reddish-brown and dark grey. VOICE: melodious trill 'tick-it-ter-ri-ri-ri' and harsh sharp 'tchet-tchet'. FOOD: insects, only sometimes caught in flight.

STATUS: common. TAXONOMY: endemic species; possibly forming superspecies with Scarlet Robin.

529 ROSE ROBIN *Petroica rosea* Gould 1839   Pl 16
Distribution: Map 180.

RECOGNITION: *both sexes have white at edge of tail and small white spot on forehead, male has no white on wing.*

DESCRIPTION: 12cm. Sexes very different. *Male:* breast rose red; white spot on forehead; belly and outer tail feathers white; remainder dark grey; bill black; eyes dark brown; legs dark brown, soles orange-yellow. *Female:* upperparts grey-brown with two pale buff bars on wing and small spot on forehead; underparts pale grey brown, darker on breast and sometimes with tinge of red, whiter on belly and outer tail feathers.

HABITAT: forests, mainly wet forests when breeding and open forests at other times. HABITS: arboreal, darts out to take insects on wing often with tail fanned, returns to various perches and flicks and droops wings; mostly solitary; sedentary but also has nomadic or dispersal movements or regular seasonal movements between high and low ground and from rain forest to dry forest. BREEDING: September–December; nests in high tree forks, cup-shaped, made of various fibres and moss bound with cobweb, decorated with lichen and lined with soft material; two to three eggs, pale bluish or greenish speckled with purplish-brown. VOICE: high-pitched 'tick-a-tick-a-tick-pee-pee', also harsher churring. FOOD: insects. STATUS: common. TAXONOMY: endemic species.

530 PINK ROBIN *Petroica rodinogaster* (Drapiez) 1819   Pl 16
Distribution: Map 181.

RECOGNITION: *both sexes lack white in tail, male usually has white spot on forehead but no white on wing.*

DESCRIPTION: 12cm. Sexes very different. *Male:* breast and belly pink; vent and under tail coverts white and usually small white spot on forehead; remainder of plumage very dark grey; bill black; eyes dark brown; legs blackish-brown, soles orange. *Female:* upperparts dark brown with two buffish-brown bars or spots on wing, sometimes pale buff spot on forehead; underparts pale pinkish-brown, greyer on breast.

HABITAT: wet forest substage, sometimes dry forest. HABITS: on or near ground, feeds on ground or in flight, or sits quietly on some low perch, rarely in open, flicks wings; solitary; sedentary and nomadic or with regular seasonal movements, probably altitudinal and from denser to more open forests. BREEDING: September–December; nests in low vegetation usually under 5m, cup-shaped, made of fibres bound with cobweb and draped with lichens, lined with soft materials; three to four eggs, pale green spotted with shades of brown and grey. VOICE: slight warble, also 'tick-tick', like snapping twig. FOOD: insects. STATUS: common in Tasmania, uncommon on mainland. TAXONOMY: endemic species.

531 HOODED ROBIN *Petroica cucullata* (Latham) 1801
Distribution: widespread except Tasmania and north of about Rockhampton–Normanton (old record from Rockingham Bay does not seem to have been confirmed).

RECOGNITION: *Male black and white with wholly black head and neck, both sexes have white streak on wing and base of tail.*

DESCRIPTION: 14–17cm. Sexes different, including female smaller. *Male:* black and white; white on breast, belly, basal half of tail, edge of mantle, streak on wing and concealed bar in wing; remainder black; bill and legs black; eyes dark brown. *Female:* grey-brown where male is black, except for grey throat and foreneck.

Hooded Robin (531) *male*

VARIATION: much of wide coastal belt south of tropic, larger and more white in tail (race *cucullata*); interior and north, smaller and less white in tail (race *picata*).

HABITAT: open forest to arid tree savanna. HABITS: arboreal and terrestrial, actively flits about between low perches on trees or fallen timber and ground, feeds in flight and stationary; solitary or family groups; sedentary or nomadic or perhaps has regular seasonal movements, especially in south. BREEDING: September–December; nests in tree forks or clefts or hollows, usually below about 5m, cup-shaped, made of grasses and fibres bound with cobweb and lined with soft material; two eggs, sometimes differently coloured, shades of pale blue, green or brown, slightly shaded with dark reddish-brown. VOICE: long twittering trill or chatter; usually fairly quiet. FOOD: insects.

STATUS: common. TAXONOMY: endemic species.

532 DUSKY ROBIN *Petroica vittata* (Quoy & Gaim.) 1830

Distribution: Tasmania and Bass St islands.

RECOGNITION: *dull brown with white in centre of wing, edge of shoulder and edge of tail; often on low perches in clearings and around homesteads.*

DESCRIPTION: 16–17cm. Sexes alike. Upperparts dark brown (sepia), white in centre of wing continuous with concealed white bar, white at edge of shoulders and at outer edge and tip of tail; underparts dull white slightly grey-brown on breast; bill, legs and eyes brownish-black.

VARIATION: mostly as above (race *vittata*); King I, apparently more olive above and browner below (race *kingi*).

HABITAT: relatively open places in forests and woodlands especially with fallen timber and other forest debris. HABITS: arboreal and terrestrial, perches on low branches or stumps or snags, darting out to catch insects on wing or on ground; practices injury-feigning behaviour to protect young; solitary and sedentary. BREEDING: July–December; nests low in trees or in bushes or old tree stumps, cup-shaped, made of grass and bark and lined with fine material; three eggs, bluish or olive-green shaded with brown. VOICE: loud 'choo-wee, choo-we-er', also more subdued notes. FOOD: insects.

STATUS: common, adapted to settled areas but subject to predation. TAXONOMY: endemic species; sometimes regarded as isolated variant of Hooded Robin and both put in separate genus, *Melanodryas*.

Genus PENEOENANTHE

There is a separate genus for the Mangrove Robin whose relationships are uncertain. Possibly it is a variant of some widespread generalised form which has adapted to a mangrove habitat. It has some features in common with the Hooded Robin, like white wing streak and white base of tail.

533 MANGROVE ROBIN *Peneoenanthe pulverulenta* (Bonaparte) 1851

Distribution: north coast from Exmouth Gulf to Rockingham Bay.

RECOGNITION: *dark grey above and white below, basal half of tail white; in mangroves.*

DESCRIPTION: 16cm. Sexes alike. Upperparts dark grey with brownish tinge on crown, brownish-grey wings with concealed white band, and dusky streak through eye; underparts white, sometimes greyish on breast; tail blackish-brown with basal half white except on central pair of feathers; bill black; eyes dark reddish-brown; legs black.

VARIATION: ill-defined changes in shades of grey from palest in west (race *cinereiceps*); intermediate in centre (race *alligator*); darkest in east (race *leucura*).

HABITAT: mangroves. HABITS: arboreal and terrestrial, feeds among low branches and on ground, sits motionless on low perches and darts to ground, flicks tail; solitary or in family groups; sedentary. BREEDING: September–January; nests in mangroves usually in forks up to about 5m, cup-shaped, made of bark strips bound with cobwebs, decorated with pieces of bark and lichen and lined with fine fibres; two eggs, shades of green spotted with reddish-brown and lilac-grey. VOICE: musical and varied song; short clear whistle. FOOD: insects.

STATUS: Uncertain, probably fairly common. TAXONOMY: species extending to New Guinea; sometimes put in genus *Poecilodryas*.

Genus HETEROMYIAS

A genus of two species or semispecies, one in the forests of the Atherton Tableland and the other in New Guinea. They are very similar and seem recently evolved from the same stock forming a more or less continuous population when rain forests were more widespread. Their other connections are not certain but possibly they have some close affinity with *Poecilodryas*.

534 GREY-HEADED ROBIN *Heteromyias cinereifrons* (Ramsay) 1875

Distribution: Map 181.

RECOGNITION: *brownish above with grey head and whitish below, white in centre of wing; on or near ground in rain forest.* (See *Emu*, 33: 157.)

DESCRIPTION: 17cm. Sexes alike. Forehead to nape grey-brown, more ashy-grey above eye; back olive-brown shading to more cinnamon brown on rump and upper tail coverts; black patch in front of eye and black behind eye shading to brownish eye coverts; white of throat extending to patch below eye and nearly complete white eyering; breast pale grey; belly white; flanks and vent cinnamon brown; wing blackish-brown with white bar in centre; bill blackish-brown; eyes dark brown; legs pinkish-brown.

HABITAT: rain forest. HABITS: arboreal and terrestrial, on or near ground, darts back and forth between low perches and ground, readily seen about margin of forest roads or flitting low across tracks, flicks tail; solitary; sedentary. BREEDING: September–January; nests low down in forks or horizontal branches of bushes or small palms or lawyer vines, cup-shaped, roughly made of fibres and twigs decorated with moss and lichen; one egg, shades of pale buff or green spotted with dark brown-grey. VOICE: single loud whistle followed by several lower notes. FOOD: insects.

STATUS: fairly common. TAXONOMY: endemic species, closely related to similar species in New Guinea.

Genus POECILODRYAS

A group of six species, to which is sometimes added *Peneoenanthe*—the Mangrove Robin; there are no clear guiding lines to either course. The Mangrove Robin has a white-banded tail and lacks white markings on face and wings; the two species of *Poecilodryas* in Australia have boldly marked white patterns on face and wings and white tip only to the tail. They are very alike and have separate distributions, neatly illustrating a superspecies.

Key to POECILODRYAS

1 Flanks and under tail coverts white; east of Normanton   White-browed Robin .... No 535
2 Flanks and under tail coverts buff; west of Burketown..   Buff-sided Robin .... No 536

535 WHITE-BROWED ROBIN   *Poecilodryas superciliosa*   (Gould) 1847
Distribution: Map 182.

RECOGNITION: *olive-brown above and white below, white eyebrow and white band in centre of wing.*

DESCRIPTION: 15cm. Sexes alike. Upperparts olive-brown, darker on crown and face; underparts white, breast tinged with grey; broad white eyebrow; wings blackish-brown with white shoulder edge and large white patch in centre which becomes broad white bar on extended wing; tail blackish-brown broadly tipped with white except on central feather; bill black; eyes brown; legs blackish-brown.

HABITAT: forests, especially wet, doubtfully mangroves. HABITS: arboreal and terrestrial, feeds among low dense vegetation, on trunks and on ground, cocks tail and droops wings; solitary and sedentary. BREEDING: October–January; nests in trees on horizontal forks, cup-shaped, loosely made of leaves and fibres bound with cobweb; two eggs, greenish and spotted with reddish and purplish-brown. VOICE: loud clear whistle and harsh chatter. FOOD: insects.

STATUS: fairly common. TAXONOMY: endemic species or semispecies, forming superspecies with Buff-sided Robin.

536 BUFF-SIDED ROBIN   *Poecilodryas cerviniventris*   (Gould) 1857   Pl 16
Distribution: Map 182.

RECOGNITION: like White-browed Robin but *flanks and under tail coverts orange-buff, crown and face patch sooty-black,* breast distinctly grey.

HABITAT, etc: similar to White-browed Robin, perhaps more often in mangroves but information scanty and sometimes contradictory; breeding November–March.

STATUS: fairly common. TAXONOMY: endemic species or semispecies, forming superspecies with White-browed Robin.

Genus EOPSALTRIA

A group of what might be described as 'robin yellowbellies'. Included are two species frequently listed in a separate genus *Tregellasia*. In all there are four to six species depending on which forms of the Yellow Robin are to be accepted as species. Only one species has connections in New Guinea. With one exception they have yellow on the underparts and sometimes on the rump. The exception is the White-breasted Robin of coastal scrub in the extreme southwest, but it is believed to have evolved from a 'yellow' stock. A near neighbour and relative, the Yellow Robin of the west, seems to be on the way to losing yellow pigment also for the breast is grey, whereas its counterpart in the east has most of the underparts yellow. It is the Yellow Robin which poses the species problem. One part is resolved here by listing the grey-breasted form west of Spencer Gulf as an outlier of the South Western Australia species. The more difficult part is whether the eastern section consists of one or two species. Most southern birds have a dull olive-yellow rump, most northern birds have a bright yellow rump. How these two variants sort themselves out on the ground is far from clear. Some say they are separated in the New England highlands by a narrow overlap zone, others say that either colour may be found anywhere. Until the situation is clarified it is proposed to list only one species. The reader can help by noting the occurrence of olive-yellow or bright yellow rumps.

Key to EOPSALTRIA

1 Underparts white . . . . White-breasted Robin . . . . No 539
2 Breast grey, belly yellow . . . . Western Yellow Robin . . . . No 538
3 Breast and belly yellow 4–7

4 Back grey, rump yellow . . . . Eastern Yellow Robin . . . . No 537
5 Back and rump greenish-olive, white face marks . . 6–7

6 Lores buffy-white; south of Cooktown . . . . Pale-yellow Robin . . . . No 540
7 Face mainly white; north of Cooktown . . . . White-faced Robin . . . . No 541

537 EASTERN YELLOW ROBIN *Eopsaltria australis* (White) 1790   Pl 16

Distribution: Map 183.

RECOGNITION: *bright yellow underparts, yellow rump contrasting with grey back; low down in thick vegetation, sometimes clinging sideways to trunks.*

DESCRIPTION: 13–14cm. Sexes alike. Upperparts dark ash-grey, sometimes tinged with olive, lighter on forehead and face, with rump and upper tail coverts olive-yellow to bright yellow; underparts mainly bright yellow, sometimes tinged with olive, especially on flanks; chin and part of throat white; wings grey-brown with concealed whitish bars, under shoulders mottled white, sometimes showing white at edge of shoulders; tail grey-brown narrowly tipped with dull white; bill black; eyes dark brown; legs blackish-brown.

VARIATION: some variants seem fairly distinct, as in Victoria where yellows are more olive (race *viridior*), and in coastal districts from Clarence River to Cooktown where yellows are brighter (race *chrysorrhoa*—sometimes listed as species); remainder ill-defined (race *australis* in New South Wales, *coomooboolaroo* in east central Queensland, *magnirostris* with doubtfully larger bill consisting of the northern isolated section of *chrysorrhoa*).

HABITAT: mainly dry forest and woodland, town parks and suburban gardens. HABITS: arboreal and terrestrial, on or near ground in fairly thick vegetation, sits on low branches or snags, flits from perch to perch or to ground, frequently alights sideways on lower parts of tree trunks; solitary; sedentary or nomadic or perhaps seasonal altitudinal movements. BREEDING: July–January; nests in trees and bushes at varying heights but usually fairly low, in various situations, cup-shaped, made of grass and bark strips bound with cobwebs, often decorated with pieces of bark and lichen, lined with fibres and leaves; two to three eggs, shades of green speckled with dark reddish-brown. VOICE: monotonous piping 'joee-joee' and harsh 'chit-chit'. FOOD: insects.

STATUS: common. TAXONOMY: endemic species; forms superspecies with Western Yellow Robin.

538 WESTERN YELLOW ROBIN *Eopsaltria griseogularis* Gould 1838
Distribution: Map 183.

RECOGNITION: very like Eastern Yellow Robin but *breast grey and chin to foreneck white*.

VARIATION: southwest of line from just south of Shark Bay through Merredin and Norseman, rump mainly bright yellow (race *griseogularis*); remainder, including Eyre Peninsula, rump olive-yellow (race *rosinae*).

HABITAT, etc: similar to eastern species; breeding August–October, usually two eggs.

STATUS: common. TAXONOMY: endemic species; forms superspecies with Eastern Yellow Robin.

539 WHITE-BREASTED ROBIN
  Eopsaltria georgiana (Quoy & Gaim.) 1830   Fig p 361
Distribution: Map 183.

RECOGNITION: *blackish above and white below with white-tipped tail; dense coastal scrub of extreme southwest*.

DESCRIPTION: 13–14cm. Sexes alike. Upperparts dark bluish-grey, paler above eye; lores and band behind eye blackish; underparts white with greyish tinge on breast; under shoulders blotched white sometimes showing as white edge to shoulder; concealed whitish bar on wing; tail blackish tipped white except on central feathers; bill black; eyes dark brown; legs blackish-brown.

HABITAT: dense coastal scrub, gully thickets in Darling Range, homestead gardens near close cover. HABITS: similar to Yellow Robin including clinging sideways to tree trunks; apparently also some local or regular seasonal movements. BREEDING: September–December; nests similar to Yellow Robins and usually placed near ground, unlined; two eggs, variable, even in one clutch, light shades of olive, brown and blue, very faintly marked. VOICE: whistling 'wee-oh' also harsh 'whit-whit-churr'. FOOD: insects.

STATUS: fairly common. TAXONOMY: endemic species; possibly early derivative of Yellow Robin stock.

540 PALE-YELLOW ROBIN *Eopsaltria capito* Gould 1851 Pl 16

Distribution: Map 184.

RECOGNITION: *greenish-olive above and yellow below with whitish lores and throat; for differences from Yellow Flycatcher see next species.*

DESCRIPTION: 12–14cm; tail relatively short and wing long. Sexes alike. Upperparts greenish-olive, more brownish-olive on crown and greyer on face; lores and thin ring round eye white, feathers sometimes tipped light rufous; throat and foreneck white; remainder of underparts yellow, almost olive on sides of breast and flanks; wings and tail brownish-olive, under wing has indistinct patch of creamy-brown; bill black; eyes reddish-brown; legs pinkish-brown.

VARIATION: southern population, white lores and eyering and slightly larger (race *capito*); northern population, lores and eyering tinged with pale rufous and slightly smaller (race *nana*).

HABITAT: rain forest. HABITS: similar to other yellow robins but possibly taking insects more often on the wing, seems to be associated particularly with lawyer vine; sedentary. BREEDING: August–January; nests in forks of saplings but most frequently in lawyer vines; two eggs, shades of green blotched and spotted with shades of dark brown. VOICE: low twitter and churring. FOOD: insects.

STATUS: fairly common. TAXONOMY: endemic species.

541 WHITE-FACED ROBIN *Eopsaltria leucops* (Salvad.) 1876

Distribution: Map 184.

RECOGNITION: *greenish-yellow above and yellow below with throat and most of face white.* (Yellow Flycatcher in same area has bill black above and yellow below, is smaller and lacks distinct face markings.)

DESCRIPTION: 14cm. Sexes alike. Narrow centre of forehead, crown and nape to side of neck blackish; remainder of upperparts greenish-olive; side of forehead, lores and ring round eye white, continuous with white throat; underparts yellow, almost olive on side of breast and flanks; slight creamy white patch on underwing; bill black; eyes reddish-brown or brown; legs dull yellow.

HABITAT, etc: similar to Pale-yellow Robin; voice noted as musical song and harsh 'chee-chee'.

STATUS: apparently fairly common. TAXONOMY: endemic race *(albigularis)* of variable species widespread in New Guinea.

Genus RHIPIDURA

A group of about twelve fantail flycatchers widely distributed in the Australasian region. Their position in the flycatcher assemblage is far from clear. They are a distinctive group and sometimes are given subfamily or family rank. There are four species in Australia, none of which is endemic. Except for the Rufous Fantail they are mainly black or grey and white, have relatively long tails which are regularly spread like a fan and wagged from side to side. When perched the body is more or less horizontal, tails are slightly raised and wings slightly drooped. They flit restlessly from perch to perch and flutter as they catch insects in flight.

White-breasted
Robin (539)

Grey Fantail (542)

Key to RHIPIDURA

1 Forehead and rump reddish-brown.............. Rufous Fantail.............. No 544
2 Upperparts black .... Willie Wagtail .... No 545
3 Upperparts grey-brown....................... 4–5
4 Shoulder with white bars .... Grey Fantail................ No 542
5 Shoulder without white....................... Northern Fantail .... No 543

542 GREY FANTAIL *Rhipidura fuliginosa* (Sparrman) 1787

Distribution: Map 185.

RECOGNITION: *dark grey above and buffy below; two white streaks on face and two on shoulders; frequent tail fanning.*

DESCRIPTION: 15cm, with tail 9 cm; bill flattened and very small, about 5mm. Sexes alike. Upperparts shades of grey-brown; two white or creamy white streaks on face and two thin white bars on shoulder; throat and foreneck white or creamy white fringed with sooty-black 'bib'; lower breast and belly cinnamon buff; under tail coverts white; tail black shading to white at edges and tip, shafts white except on central pair; bill black; eyes dark brown; legs black.

VARIATION: two main divisions: (1) roughly east of Queensland/Northern Territory border to Spencer Gulf, sharply contrasting white and dark face pattern; Tasmania and adjacent mainland, darker (race *albiscapa*); remainder lighter, (race *alisteri*). (2) West of above, face pattern more diffuse: southwest, darker (race *preissi*); northwest, lighter (race *phasiana*); apparently isolated population in centre, much more white in tail (race *albicauda*).

HABITAT: forests and woodlands, mangroves, city parks and gardens. HABITS: arboreal, mostly below 6–8m, restlessly flits from perch to perch snapping insects in flight, fans and swings tail; solitary; sedentary, nomadic and apparently migratory, seasonal arrivals and departures in various localities. BREEDING: September–January; nests in trees and bushes at varying heights between about 1–8m, on slender branches, cup-shaped and like inverted pear, often with long tail of bark from bottom, made of bark fibres bound with cobwebs and lined with fine grass; two to three eggs, pale buff speckled with shades of brown and grey. VOICE: high-pitched musical twitter ending on high note. FOOD: insects, usually taken in flight.

STATUS: common. TAXONOMY: species extending to New Zealand; vagrant south New Guinea.

543 NORTHERN FANTAIL *Rhipidura rufiventris* (Vieillot) 1818
Distribution: Map 186.

RECOGNITION: like Grey Fantail but has *no distinct white bars on shoulder*, only *one white streak on face,* above eye, and no white shafts to tail feathers; 'bib' grey-brown (not sooty-black), bill nearly twice as long, 10mm.

HABITAT: variable; mainly open forest, sometimes wet forest and mangroves. HABITS: similar to Grey Fantail but less active, more inclined to sit and hunt from perches (like Brown Flycatcher) and to take food on ground, also fans tail less frequently; movements apparently not well known. BREEDING: July–February; nests and eggs similar to Grey Fantail. VOICE: musical phrase of tinkling notes, also repeated 'chuk'. FOOD: insects.

STATUS: common. TAXONOMY: species extending to Solomon Is and Moluccas.

544 RUFOUS FANTAIL *Rhipidura rufifrons* (Latham) 1801   Pl 17
Distribution: Map 187.

RECOGNITION: *tail-fanning flycatcher with rufous forehead and rump.*

DESCRIPTION: 15cm, with tail 9cm; bill slightly flattened. Sexes alike. Forehead to above eye reddish-brown; crown and back dusky-brown shading to reddish-brown on rump, upper tail coverts and base of tail; remainder of tail blackish-brown with broad white tip; lores and face below eye blackish with white half ring on under side of eye; throat white; foreneck black shading to black and white breast and creamy white centre of belly; flanks and under tail coverts cinnamon; bill black; eyes dark brown; legs blackish-brown.

VARIATION: east of Normanton, basal half of tail reddish-brown and tip pearly-grey (race *rufifrons*); west of Normanton, less reddish-brown in tail and tip white (race *dryas*).

HABITAT: mainly wet forests and mangroves when breeding, also more open timber at other times. HABITS: similar to the Grey Fantail but apparently feeds more often on ground; movements not well known but there seems to be a certain amount of regular, but incomplete, altitudinal and latitudinal migration. BREEDING: November–February; nests and eggs similar to Grey Fantail. VOICE: noted as monotonous 'chunk-chunk'.

STATUS: fairly common. TAXONOMY: endemic races, one apparently partial migrant to New Guinea, of species extending to Solomon Is, Micronesia and Lesser Sunda Is.

545 WILLIE WAGTAIL *Rhipidura leucophrys* (Latham) 1801
Distribution: throughout; doubtfully Tasmania.

RECOGNITION: *black above with white eyebrow, white below with black throat (Restless Flycatcher has white throat and no eyebrow); fans and swings long tail.*

Willie Wagtail (545)

DESCRIPTION: 20cm, with tail 10–12cm. Sexes alike. Whole head, including throat and neck, and upperparts slightly glossy black; white eyebrow and sometimes white flecks on throat and foreneck and white edge to shoulder; breast and belly white; flight feathers sooty-black; bill black; eyes dark brown; legs black.

HABITAT: varied, from edge of rain forest to edge of desert, including parks and gardens. HABITS: arboreal and terrestrial, frequently feeds on ground as well as in flight, sometimes feeds around stock, using their backs as perches, active and aggressive, fans and constantly swings tail; solitary; sedentary and nomadic, especially where there are wet seasons, possibly some regular seasonal movements. BREEDING: June–February; nests in trees on horizontal branches at varying heights, but also in almost any situation above ground, made of grass or bark strips or fibre tightly felted with cobwebs; four eggs, pale cream spotted with brown. VOICE: short musical song sometimes transcribed as 'sweet-pretty-creature', also harsh two-syllabled rattle. FOOD: insects.

STATUS: very common and well adapted to human environment. TAXONOMY: endemic race (*leucophys*) of species extending to New Guinea, Moluccas and Solomon Is.

Family MONARCHIDAE
Flycatchers
12(total uncertain) species: 5 endemic

Distribution: old world, mainly tropics and subtropics.

THE GROUPS INCLUDED IN this family are sometimes listed in the songbird hierarchy as a section of a muscicapid subfamily, on a par with fantail flycatchers and whistlers. Some taxonomists claim that they should have subfamily or family rank. The characteristics and limits of the family are not easily defined on present knowledge. *Myiagra* seems to have some connections with Rhipidura, among other things in plumage pattern and tail-swinging behaviour, also some features in common with the paradise flycatchers of the Oriental and Ethiopian regions. All have well developed bristles fringing the mouth and bills basally depressed to varying degrees. In *Monarcha* the anterior part of the bill is deep and strong while in the Boatbill or Boat-billed Flycatcher the whole bill is extremely flattened and wide. The affinities of this last named curious species are very uncertain and it is included here because there does not seem to be any other suitable place for it. The family consists mainly of rain forest species and most take insects on the wing but not as a regular habit.

Key to MONARCHIDAE
[Additional keys are provided when genera are named.]
1 Wholly black.............................(♂) Shining Flycatcher........... No 549
2 Black and brown above, white below.........(♀) Shining Flycatcher........... No 549
3 Wholly black above, white below .... Restless Flycatcher........... No 550

4 Black above with white on face and shoulders, white
  below....................................... White-eared Flycatcher....... No 554
5 Black or dark grey above, white below with black*
  (♂) or brown (♀) throat.................... *Myiagra* (Part)......... Nos 546–550
  *Like Willie Wagtail but without white eyebrow.
6 Blackish (♂) or greenish (♀) above, yellow below
  with white throat......................... Boat-billed Flycatcher........ No 557
7 Pied with white ruff collar and rump .... *Arses* .... Nos 555–556
8 Grey with black 'mask' and brown breast or belly.. *Monarcha* (Part) .... Nos 551–554

Genus MYIAGRA

A group of about six species of which five occur in Australia, two being endemic, counting the Satin Flycatcher which is a non-breeding visitor to New Guinea. The genus includes the Restless Flycatcher, at one time in *Seisura* and the Shining Flycatcher, previously in *Piezorhynchus*. One characteristic of all except the Broad-billed Flycatcher is that the sexes have different plumages. The males of three Australian species have a plumage pattern similar to the Willie Wagtail but they lack Willie's white eyebrow and they live in mainly wetter habitats. All have distinctly flattened bills.

Key to MYIAGRA

1 Wholly black ....(♂) Shining Flycatcher........... No 549
2 Upperparts black and brown, underparts white (♀) Shining Flycatcher........... No 549
3 Upperparts glossy black, throat black, belly white
  (♂) .... Satin Flycatcher............. No 547
4 Upperparts black, underparts white........... Restless Flycatcher .... No 550
5 Upperparts shades of dull bluish 6–10
6 Throat black............................(♂) Leaden Flycatcher .... No 546
7 Throat brown............................. 8–10
8 Throat and breast brown
  Upperparts greenish-blue................... Broad-billed Flycatcher...... No 548
  Upperparts greyish-blue................ (♀) Leaden Flycatcher .... No 546
9 Throat only brown .... (♀) Satin Flycatcher .... No 547
10 Upperparts greenish-blue .... Broad-billed Flycatcher...... No 548

546 LEADEN FLYCATCHER *Myiagra rubecula* (Latham) 1801

Distribution: Map 188.

RECOGNITION: like Satin Flycatcher but mainly *dull blue-grey on upperparts, male has blackish throat and upper breast and female brown throat and breast; vibrates tail on alighting.*

DESCRIPTION: 15cm; crown slightly crested; bill flattened. Sexes different. *Male:* upperparts dull bluish-grey shading to slightly glossed blue-green on head, throat and upper breast; lower breast, belly and underwing white; wings blackish; bill blue-grey; eyes blackish-brown; legs black. *Female:* upperparts paler and lack greenish gloss; throat to breast cinnamon buff; wings and tail, brownish, sometimes white edge and tip.

VARIATION: east of Carpentaria, bill broader—south of tropic, lores blue-grey (race *rubecula*); north of tropic, lores jet black (race *yorki*); west of Carpentaria, bill narrower and lores jet black (race *concinna*).

HABITAT: forests, mangroves and adjacent woodlands. HABITS: arboreal, feeds among leaves and branches and darts out to catch insects in flight, on alighting frequently quivers tail, often with crest raised; sometimes sings from high perches; solitary; mainly sedentary

Restless Flycatcher (550)

Leaden Flycatcher (546) *male*

in tropics, or at least present all year in most known habitats, but breeding visitor in south—September–March in Sydney area—some migrants reach southern New Guinea. BREEDING: October–January; nests in trees at various heights, often on dead branches under green foliage, cup-shaped, made of bark strips bound with cobwebs, decorated with lichen and lined with rootlets; three eggs, pale cream and spotted with dark brown and lilac-grey. VOICE: whistling buzz, like 'zhee-zhee' or 'too-whee', also short harsh or rasping notes. FOOD: insects.

STATUS: common in north, uncommon to rare in south of range. TAXONOMY: species extending to New Guinea.

547 SATIN FLYCATCHER *Myiagra cyanoleuca* (Vieillot) 1818
Distribution: Map 189.

RECOGNITION: very like Leaden Flycatcher but male has *glossy black head and upperparts,* black of throat extends to breast; female has *upperparts more brownish-blue* and brown of throat does not extend to upper breast.

HABITAT, etc: similar to the Leaden Flycatcher but apparently more confined to upland and mountain forests and feeds high in trees; breeding visitor in south, especially Tasmania, September–March, and passage migrant along Dividing Range as far as New Guinea.

STATUS: common in Tasmania but records elsewhere scanty, perhaps because of similarity to Leaden Flycatcher. TAXONOMY: endemic breeding species partly migrating to New Guinea.

548 BROAD-BILLED FLYCATCHER *Myiagra ruficollis* (Vieillot) 1818
Distribution: north coast from Derby to Cooktown.

RECOGNITION: almost identical with female Leaden and Satin Flycatchers; sexes are alike and have cinnamon buff throat and breast; *upperparts more greenish-blue* and look slightly paler at a distance; tail has narrow white margins and tip; flattened bill very broad; more confined to mangroves.

HABITAT: mangroves and similar wet coastal thickets. HABITS, etc: similar to Leaden Flycatcher, hunts among low vegetation, perches frequently, shakes tail; solitary and apparently sedentary; nests often low over water, two eggs.

STATUS: apparently uncommon. TAXONOMY: race *(mimikae)* extending to New Guinea of species extending also to Aru Is and Timor.

549 SHINING FLYCATCHER *Myiagra alecto* (Temm. & Laug.) 1827 Pl 17

Distribution: Map 190.

RECOGNITION: *male wholly black, female mainly chestnut with black head and white underparts; in mangroves and other swamps.*

DESCRIPTION: 18cm; head slightly crested. Sexes very different. *Male:* black with purplish-green gloss; bill dark blue-grey; eyes reddish-brown; legs black. *Female:* head and neck like male; remainder of upperparts chestnut brown; underparts white.

VARIATION: Derby area, female has crown grey-brown with slight sheen, male has belly sooty-black and bill longer (race *tormenti*); North Kimberley to Carpentaria, female has crown glossy black and back darker brown, male is intermediate (race *nitida*); east of Carpentaria, female as previous but back paler, male has belly glossy black and bill shorter (race *wardelli*).

HABITAT: mangroves and similar swamp vegetation on coasts and along rivers. HABITS: arboreal but near and sometimes feeding on ground in dense vegetation, or perches erect and darts out to catch insects in flight; solitary; movements uncertain but possibly sedentary.

BREEDING: November–March; nests usually fairly low in forks of bushes and saplings in open shaded places, construction and eggs similar to Leaden Flycatcher but clutch of two. VOICE: fairly lengthy soft whistle, also harsh 'creek'. FOOD: insects.

STATUS: fairly common. TAXONOMY: variable species extending to Moluccas, New Guinea and various other islands; has been allocated to various genera *Piezorhynchus, Seisura, Monarcha.*

550 RESTLESS FLYCATCHER *Myiagra inquieta* (Latham) 1801 Fig p 365

Distribution: Map 191.

RECOGNITION: *black above and white below (similar-looking Willie Wagtail has black throat); hovers briefly when feeding.*

DESCRIPTION: 18–20cm, with tail about half; short crest. Sexes alike except female slightly less glossy and has faint tinge of brown on throat. Face and upperparts glossy blue-black; tail wholly black; underparts white; under shoulders black and underwings whitish; bill and legs black; eyes dark brown.

VARIATION: southwest, largest and dullest (race *westralensis*); north of tropic, smallest and brightest (race *nana*); elsewhere, intermediate (race *inquieta*).

HABITAT: open forests and woodlands. HABITS: arboreal but sometimes drops to ground for insects, often perches on bare branches, darts constantly from one perch to another taking insects in flight, frequently hovers briefly when feeding, sometimes at tops of swamp reeds and paddock grass, hovers with wings half spread and crest erect; solitary; sedentary and possibly nomadic. BREEDING: August–February; nests in trees usually fairly high and far out on horizontal branches, made of bark strips and grass bound with cobweb, decorated with lichens and lined with soft material; four eggs, white or pale buff spotted with purplish-brown. VOICE: musical 'tuwhee tu-whee' and harsh rasping, described as scissors-grinding sound. FOOD: insects.

STATUS: uncommon, sometimes fairly common locally. TAXONOMY: near endemic species.

Genus MONARCHA

The generic and sometimes colloquial name 'monarch' for the typical members of this genus might be adopted with advantage as the common name. They are only infrequent 'fly-catchers' although they have broad based, but long and deep, bills and bristle-edged mouths. There are about ten species, four in Australia, but various authorities have different ideas about which species should be included. Of the four listed here three are distinctively patterned in grey and rufous with black 'mask' and the fourth is pied.

White-eared Flycatcher (554)   Spectacled Flycatcher (553)   Pearly-winged Flycatcher (551)

Key to MONARCHA

1 Upperparts black with white patches on face, under-
  parts white .... White-eared Flycatcher....... No 554
2 Upperparts grey with black mask, rufous on under
  parts.................................... 3–6
3 Breast rufous............................. Spectacled Flycatcher .... No 553
4 Belly rufous.............................. 5–6
5 Back pale grey, tail black .... Black-winged Flycatcher...... No 552
6 Back and tail dark grey .... Pearly-winged Flycatcher..... No 551

551 PEARLY-WINGED FLYCATCHER

Monarcha melanopsis   (Vieillot) 1818   Pl 17
Distribution: Map 192.

RECOGNITION: *grey with rufous belly, black mask emphasised by very pale face; greyish wings and tail distinguish from very rare Black-winged Flycatcher.*

DESCRIPTION: 18cm. Sexes alike. Forehead and throat black, forming a 'mask'; face, including area in front of eye, very pale grey (looking white at distance); thin black ring round eye; upperparts, side of neck and breast slate grey; belly, under shoulders and under tail coverts rufous; wings and tail grey-brown; bill and legs blue-grey; eyes dark brown.

VARIATION: south of about Townsville, slightly darker and larger (race *melanopsis*); north, slightly paler and smaller (race *pallida*).

HABITAT: mainly forests, sometimes woodland. HABITS: arboreal, feeds among branches and foliage about mid-forest layer, relatively inactive and slow moving, sometimes picks insects from leaves while briefly hovering, rarely takes insects in flight; solitary; apparently sedentary north of tropic with local nomadic movements, as from forest to woodland, migratory south of tropic, breeding visitor September–March, some migrants reach New Guinea. BREEDING: October–January; nests in trees especially along creeks and gullies, in forks in thick foliage fairly high, cup-shaped, made of moss and fibres bound with cobweb and lined with fine material; two eggs, white spotted with red. VOICE: rich whistling phrase, or parts of it, sometimes transcribed as 'why-you-which-ye-e-ou', also various harsher grinding notes. FOOD: insects.

STATUS: fairly common, uncommon in south. TAXONOMY: possibly endemic species partly migrating to New Guinea; it does not seem to be established with certainty if there is a breeding population in New Guinea.

552 BLACK-WINGED FLYCATCHER   *Monarcha frater*   Sclater 1874

Distribution: mainly tip of Cape York, but may occur as far south as Atherton Tableland.

RECOGNITION: nearly identical with Pearly-winged Flycatcher, differs in having *wing and tail feathers blackish, black face mask extending close to the eye,* upperparts paler, ashy or pearly-grey.

HABITS, etc: apparently similar to Pearly-winged but there are few observations on the species either in Australia or New Guinea.

STATUS: uncertain, possibly breeding visitor only. TAXONOMY: race *(periopthalmicus)* of variable species widespread in New Guinea. It is still uncertain if Pearly-winged and Black-winged Flycatchers are races of one species, the former breeding in Australia and the latter in New Guinea with an outpost in Cape York, the two intermingling in the non-breeding season. Current views, based on various factors, lean to the conclusion that they are separate species morphologically very alike but reproductively isolated (sibling species). It would be helpful to know if the two breed in the same habitat at Cape York.

553 SPECTACLED FLYCATCHER
Monarcha trivirgata   (Temminck) 1829   Fig p 367

Distribution: Map 193.

RECOGNITION: *something like Pearly-winged Flycatcher but breast and side of neck rufous, tip of tail white.*

DESCRIPTION: 15cm. Sexes alike. Black 'mask' covering forehead, throat and broad band through eye; upperparts dark blue-grey; sides of throat and neck, breast and flanks cinnamon rufous shading to near white on belly; flight feathers dusky edged with grey; tail black broadly tipped with white except in centre; bill and legs dark blue-grey; eyes dark brown.

VARIATION: over most of range, as above (race *gouldi*); tip of Cape York, flanks and belly white (race *albiventris*).

HABITAT: wet forests and mangroves and adjacent woodland. HABITS: arboreal but sometimes feeds on ground, usually in dense low vegetation moving rapidly and quietly, but also at high levels; solitary; sedentary in north and breeding visitor in south, about September–February. BREEDING: October–January; nests in saplings and bushes, in forks usually fairly low, cup-shaped, made of bark strips bound with cobweb and lined with fine material; two eggs, creamy white spotted with shades of reddish-brown. VOICE: repeated 'pree-eet pree-eet', also rasping chatter and harsh growl or croak. FOOD: insects.

STATUS: fairly common, rare in south. TAXONOMY: endemic races of species extending to Timor, Moluccas and New Guinea.

554 WHITE-EARED FLYCATCHER *Monarcha leucotis* Gould 1850 Fig p 367
Distribution: Map 194.

RECOGNITION: *black above and white below, white patches on face and bars on wing; rather like Grey Fantail but blacker, has white rump and does not fan tail.*

DESCRIPTION: 14cm. Sexes alike. Face and upperparts black with white patches in front of, above and behind eye and on side of nape, two white bars on shoulders, white upper tail coverts and broad white tips to outer tail feathers; throat white (feathers extended) and nearly enclosed by narrow black ring; belly and under shoulders white; breast and flanks grey; bill bluish-black, pale bluish-grey at base; eyes dark brown; legs black. HABITAT: wet forests and mangroves. HABITS: arboreal, feeds mostly on wing, hovering and fluttering around foliage of tree canopies at various heights; solitary but sometimes in company with other species of similar feeding habits; sedentary, but probably breeding visitor in south. BREEDING: October–January; nests in trees and bushes, in forks under about 5m, inverted cone shape, made of bark and moss bound with cobweb and lined with fine fibres; two eggs, whitish spotted with reddish-brown. VOICE: plaintive song phrase in three syllables rising on the first and falling on the last, also harsh buzzing 'chrrk-chrrk-chrrk' often followed by flute-like whistle. FOOD: insects. STATUS: fairly common in north, rare in south. TAXONOMY: endemic species or semispecies (or race) forming superspecies (or species) with similar forms in Moluccas.

Genus ARSES

Two very similar species both of which occur in northern Queensland, one being endemic. They are basically like monarchs but the broad white frill-like collar and fleshy eyerims have placed them in a separate genus. They belong to rain forests where they sometimes behave like treecreepers by climbing up trunks in search of insects. Toes and claws are well developed.

Key to ARSES

1 Black band on breast........................ Pied Flycatcher............. No 555
2 No band on breast......................... Frill-necked Flycatcher....... No 556

555 PIED FLYCATCHER *Arses kaupi* Gould 1851
Distribution: Map 195.

RECOGNITION: *black above with white collar and rump, white below with black breast band.*

DESCRIPTION: 15cm. Sexes slightly different. *Male:* black with slight bluish gloss on head and face, upper back, wings, tail and breast; throat and foreneck white continuous with broad white collar of lengthened feathers; lower back and belly white; sometimes a small black spot at tip of chin; bill blue-grey; eyes dark brown, slightly enlarged bare skin round eye pale blue; legs dark grey-blue. *Female:* white collar narrower and separated from white throat by extension of black from side of face, white of both collar and throat slightly speckled with black. HABITAT: rain forest and adjacent open forest. HABITS: arboreal, very active, flits from branch to branch catching insects in flight or feeds among foliage or flutters and climbs up tree trunks and boughs like treecreeper, erects white frill-like collar and fans tail; solitary and sedentary. BREEDING: October–January; nests in trees and bushes up to about 10m, suspended on thin branches or lianas, cup-shaped, an open weave of twigs and tendrils bound with cobweb and lightly decorated with lichen; two eggs, pale pink speckled with shades of brown and grey. VOICE: soft 'chrr-chrr' and harsh grating. FOOD: insects. STATUS: fairly common. TAXONOMY: endemic species closely related to Frill-necked Flycatcher.

Frill-necked Flycatcher (556)

Pied Flycatcher (555)

female   *male*

556 FRILL-NECKED FLYCATCHER   *Arses lorealis*   De Vis 1895
Distribution: Map 195.

RECOGNITION: very like Pied Flycatcher, but *male lacks black breast band,* has apex of chin black and fleshy eyerim bright blue; *female has white lores* continued as narrow streak to forehead, no black on chin and sometimes a tinge of rusty brown on breast.

HABITAT, etc: similar to Pied Flycatcher.

STATUS: apparently fairly common. TAXONOMY: endemic species or semispecies (or race) forming superspecies (or species) with several forms in New Guinea and adjacent islands.

Genus MACHAERIRHYNCHUS

John Gould named this genus for two rather curious species. He described them as 'very singular and distinct forms among the smaller flycatchers with bills laterally developed to a greater extent than in any other bird of their size'. Their relationship to *Monarcha* is uncertain and they are placed in this family without any conviction that they belong to it. They have fly-catching habits and rain forest habitats. Only one species extends from New Guinea into Cape York.

557 BOAT-BILLED FLYCATCHER
        Machaerirhynchus flaviventer   Gould 1851   Pl 17
Distribution: Map 196.

RECOGNITION: *dark above, yellow below, long yellow eyebrow, broad flat bill; rain forests.*
DESCRIPTION: 12cm; very broad flat bill. Sexes slightly different. *Male:* upperparts dull black with varying amounts of dark olive on back; broad yellow streak from forehead over eye to side of nape; throat and underwing white; remainder of underparts bright yellow; wing black with two white bars on shoulder and thin edge of white or yellow on

most feathers; tail black thinly edged and broadly tipped with white; bill black; eyes blackish-brown; legs dark blue-grey. *Female*: upperparts yellowish-olive with dark areas brownish-black, underparts have more white and less yellow.

VARIATION: Cape York, male has back more olive and wing feathers edged with yellow (race *flaviventer*); Cooktown-Cardwell area, males blacker on back and wing feathers edged with white (race *secundus*).

HABITAT: rain forest. HABITS: arboreal, feeds among foliage of bushes and trees at various heights, actively moves from branch to branch sometimes making short sallies to catch insects in flight; solitary and sedentary. BREEDING: October–March; nests in trees usually fairly high and in forks of slender branches, shallow cup, made of bark strips bound with cobweb, decorated with lichen and lined with fine tendrils; two eggs, pearly-white lightly spotted with shades of red and purple. VOICE: melodious trill of several varied notes and soft twittering 'tizzz-tizzz' while feeding. FOOD: insects.

STATUS: fairly common. TAXONOMY: endemic races of species extending to New Guinea.

Family PACHYCEPHALIDAE

Whistlers, Thrushes

20(about 50) species: 15 endemic

Distribution: Australasian and southeast Oriental regions.

THE 'THICKHEADS' AND THEIR associates bear little resemblance to the true flycatchers but taxonomists find connecting links and they are placed as a subfamily (elevated here to family) at the perimeter of the muscicapid assemblage. They are robust in build with relatively thick heads. Bills are well developed, sometimes thick and laterally compressed rather than flattened, and more or less distinctly hooked, hence the reason for the common name 'shrike-thrush' for certain species. Bristles at the edge of the mouth are not much in evidence. Most are nondescript in appearance, dull grey-browns with few distinctive features, apart from exceptions like the bright yellows of the male Golden Whistler and the shriketits, and the boldly patterned and crested head of the shriketits and Crested Bellbird. As is mostly the case, drab plumages are offset by attractive voices, in this case by some of the best songsters to be found anywhere. Unlike some of the more volatile flycatchers, the fantails for example, these birds are relatively inactive and slow moving, possibly because instead of catching insects in flight they live mainly on caterpillars and grubs, sometimes obtained by stripping bark.

Key to PACHYCEPHALIDAE

[Additional keys provided when genera are named.]

1 White bands on black crested head . . . . *Falcunculus* . . . . Nos 574–576
2 White 'mask' on black crested head . . . . Crested Bellbird . . . . No 577

3 Small (14cm) plain above and below, or large (16–
   20cm) with clearly defined throat patch either
   brown or white or white circled with black
   (mostly ♂)................................. *Pachycephala* .... Nos 558–566
4 Large (18–24cm), bills large, head without clearly
   defined head pattern other than diffuse whitish or
   buffish lores.............................. *Colluricincla* .... Nos 567–573

Genus PACHYCEPHALA

A group of about thirty species of wide distribution within the family area. Nine are here listed for Australia with six endemic, that is accepting that the Golden Whistler variants consist of a number of semispecies. They were originally named and are still sometimes called 'thickheads' but are now better known in Australia as 'whistlers'. They are distinguished both by relatively thick heads and loud clear whistling notes. They are robust in build, relatively inactive and sedentary. In most species the sexes are different and some males have striking plumage patterns. Several species and females are drab and featureless and the following key may not be of much help in identifying them.

Key to PACHYCEPHALA

1 About 14cm; northern coasts
   Belly whitish; Arnhemland.................. Brown Whistler .... No 565
   Belly pale yellowish; Cape York.............. Grey Whistler............... No 566
2 Over 16cm; widely distributed................ 3–17
3 Throat white circled with black................ 9–11
4 Throat cinnamon brown...................... 12–13
5 Throat whitish speckled dark grey.............. Olive Whistler.............. No 562
6 Throat whitish streaked dark grey.............. 14–15
7 Throat brownish speckled dark grey............ 16–17
8 Throat and breast dark grey................(♀) Gilbert Whistler............. No 563
                                        (♀) Red-lored Whistler .... No 564
9 Belly white ....(♂) White-bellied Whistler........ No 559
10 Belly cinnamon buff ....(♂) Rufous Whistler............. No 558
11 Belly yellow.............................(♂) Golden Whistler............. No 560
                                        (♂) Mangrove Golden Whistler.... No 561
12 Yellow on wing..........................(♂) Red-lored Whistler .... No 564
13 No yellow on wing........................(♂) Gilbert Whistler............. No 563
14 Throat distinctly streaked.................(♀) Rufous Whistler............. No 558
15 Throat lightly streaked ....(♀) White-bellied Whistler........ No 559
16 Tail black ....(♀) Mangrove Golden Whistler.... No 561
17 Tail greenish-yellow ....(♀) Golden Whistler............. No 560

558 RUFOUS WHISTLER *Pachycephala rufiventris* (Latham) 1801   Fig p 374
Distribution: throughout except Tasmania.

RECOGNITION: *male dark grey above with black band on face continued round white throat, breast and belly cinnamon brown; female lacks face pattern and has dark streaks on breast.*

DESCRIPTION: 16cm. Sexes different. *Male:* upperparts dark olive-grey; black lores and band on face continued to encircle white throat; breast and belly shades of cinnamon brown (nearly white in Cape York and white in New Guinea); wing and tail feathers blackish-

brown; bill black; eyes reddish-brown; legs dark grey-brown.
(Note: males may begin breeding in immature streaked plumage similar to female.) Female: lacks black feature; throat white, breast and belly pale buff; lower face, throat, breast, flanks and sometimes belly heavily streaked with blackish-brown; bill blackish-brown.

VARIATION: although six races are currently listed for Australia the species seems remarkably uniform throughout its range; at most there appears to be a general tendency for peripheral populations to be richer toned and darker and for those in the interior to be slightly paler. HABITAT: most kinds of timbered areas, including mangroves but mainly dry forests and woodlands, sometimes parks and gardens. HABITS: arboreal, moves about over all kinds of bush and tree vegetation at various heights feeding among foliage and bark, sings from perches usually fairly high and on bare branches or boughs; solitary; mainly sedentary but nomadic and migratory in southeast. BREEDING: September–March; nests in tree forks or on parasitic growths up to about 7m, cup-shaped, loosely made of woven grass and fibres and lined with fine rootlets; two to three eggs, olive blotched with dark brown. VOICE: clear melodious phrase followed by trill, also rapid 'pee-pee-pee, joey-joey-joey' followed by sharp 'e-chong' (a whip-crack similar to Whipbird's but softer and less explosive). FOOD: insects and berries.

STATUS: common. TAXONOMY: species extending to New Guinea and Moluccas.

559 WHITE-BELLIED* WHISTLER Pachycephala lanioides Gould 1840

Distribution: mangroves from Carnarvon to Burketown.

RECOGNITION: *male has black head and breast, white throat and belly; female brown with boldly streaked underparts.*

DESCRIPTION: 18–20cm. Sexes different. *Male:* black of head and neck joined to black upper breast, black edged with dark chestnut forming distinct hind collar; back and edges of shoulder feathers dark grey; throat and belly white; wings and tail black; bill black; eyes reddish-brown; legs dark grey. *Female:* upperparts brownish-grey; underparts pale buff, whiter on throat and greyer on breast, all with dark streaks.

VARIATION: apparently most evident in females. Current named forms are: Carnarvon area, female upperparts darker and browner (race *carnarvoni*); Port Hedland area, underparts paler and more heavily streaked (race *bulleri*); mainly Kimberley coasts, underparts less streaked (race *lanioides*); remaining coasts, more olive-grey with less streaked underparts and both sexes smaller (race *fretorum*).

HABITAT: mangroves, mostly along creeks. HABITS: arboreal but sometimes feeds on ground, flits about in mangroves usually fairly low or perches on low branches over water, stands with upright pose, almost bittern-like when disturbed; solitary and apparently sedentary. BREEDING: November–January; nests in mangrove forks, flimsy open cup; two eggs, light olive marked with dark reddish-brown. VOICE: richer than Rufous Whistler; loud clear musical phrase, also whistling 'per-weet' with second syllable louder, and soft whistling 'twit' repeated regularly. FOOD: insects and small animals from mangrove mud.

STATUS: uncertain, probably fairly common locally. TAXONOMY: endemic species.

---

*A descriptive name proposed by Vernacular Names Committee, 1898; the current name 'White-breasted' seems a prudish misnomer.

GOLDEN WHISTLERS

The Golden Whistler is currently listed as a member of a group of about seventy-three subspecies extending from Java to New Caledonia, of which twelve are in Australia. Some taxonomists claim that this vast assemblage consists of a number of near species or semispecies and that the group is a superspecies. Two such species-in-the-making or semispecies are recognised in Australia, one keeping mostly to the northern mangroves and the other to the heavily wooded habitats of the east and south. They are in close proximity from about Mackay to Cairns but apparently do not interbreed. Although very alike they have distinguishing features as well as separate habitats. The opinion is that they can be listed as species— one having the original name *P. pectoralis*, Golden Whistler, and the other *P. melanura* with the suggested name Mangrove Golden Whistler. If this conclusion is accepted, as it is tentatively here, then these are endemic species.

560 GOLDEN WHISTLER *Pachycephala pectoralis* (Latham) 1801   Pl 17
Distribution: Map 197.

RECOGNITION: *male has black head, white throat bordered with black, and yellow breast and belly; female is in shades of grey-brown above and buffy below.*

DESCRIPTION: 16cm. Sexes very different. *Male:* black head joined to black band round white throat; bright yellow collar joined to yellow breast and belly; back olive-yellow; wings black edged on inner feathers with greyish-yellow and on shoulders with bright yellow; tail black with varying amounts of grey at base or wholly grey; bill and legs black; eyes dark brown. *Female:* (more variable than male). Upperparts olive-grey to olive-brown, yellower in north where head also greyer and under tail coverts yellow; throat and breast greyish, slightly mottled on throat; belly cinnamon buff to cinnamon white.

VARIATION: north of northern New South Wales, male has tail almost wholly black and female has yellow under tail coverts (races *ashbyi* and *queenslandica*); Tasmania, male tail wholly grey and female belly and undertail coverts near white (race *glaucura*); south and southwest, male tail has grey base, and female belly and under tail coverts cinnamon buff (races *fuliginosa* and *occidentalis*).

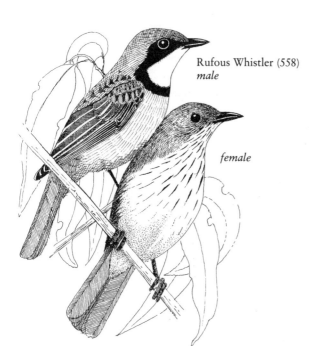

Rufous Whistler (558)
male

female

Olive Whistler (562)

HABITAT: forests and woodlands, fairly dense timber especially when breeding. HABITS: arboreal, feeds among foliage and branches at various heights, relatively inactive, frequently perches; solitary; mostly sedentary but there are some local nomadic movements. BREEDING: September–January; nests in forks of small trees and bushes usually below about 6–7m, shallow cup well made of grass and bark and leaves and lined with fine grass; two eggs, pale yellowish-buff spotted with dark reddish-brown and grey. VOICE: melodious phrase of loud clear whistling notes, also a call with a mild whip-like ending 'wi-wi-wi-*wit*', and a soft plaintive 'seeep'. FOOD: insects, sometimes berries.

STATUS: common. TAXONOMY: endemic species (see note above).

561 MANGROVE GOLDEN WHISTLER *Pachycephala melanura* Gould 1842
Distribution: Map 197.

RECOGNITION: very like Golden Whistler but *slightly smaller with more rounded* (less pointed) *wings* and *confined to mangroves* and similar dense coastal vegetation; male has more grey (less yellow) on margins of inner wing feathers and base of tail is greenish-yellow (not grey or black); bill longer and thinner; where species are in close proximity in north Queensland female has yellow (not buffy) belly and black (not brownish-yellow) tail.

VARIATION: (not well known). Eastern section, male has black tail and female much yellow on belly (race *violetae* or *spinicauda*); western section, male has greenish-yellow base of tail and female much less yellow on belly (races *melanura* and *bynoei*).

HABITAT: mangroves and similar coast vegetation. HABITS, etc: apparently more or less similar to Golden Whistler.

STATUS: uncommon. TAXONOMY: endemic species (see above).

562 OLIVE WHISTLER *Pachycephala olivacea* Vig. & Horsf. 1827
Distribution: Map 198.

RECOGNITION: *olive-brown with white throat and brown belly; male has grey head and breast.*

DESCRIPTION: 18–20cm. Sexes different. *Male:* crown and side of neck dark grey joined to light grey breast; remainder of upperparts olive-brown, slightly cinnamon on rump; throat and foreneck white speckled with grey; belly and flanks cinnamon buff; bill and legs blackish-brown; eyes dark brown. *Female:* crown olive-brown like back, side of neck and breast brown like belly.

VARIATION: over most of range, crown dark grey (race *olivacea*); extreme north, crown paler, more bluish-grey and thin margin of yellow on tail feathers (race *macphersonianus*).

HABITAT: forests and thickets, especially mountain forest north of Sydney, almost exclusively isolated patches of beech *(Nothophagus)*. HABITS: terrestrial and arboreal, spends much of time on ground among dense vegatation; solitary and sedentary. BREEDING: September–January; nests in bush and sapling forks, especially in dense grassy thickets, usually fairly low, cup-shaped, rather loosely made of grass and twigs lined with soft material; two to three eggs, pale buff spotted with shades of brown and grey. VOICE: loud clear melodious song, other notes transcribed as 'I'll whit you', call note 'your cranky' and slow drawn out 'peee-pooo'. FOOD: insects and berries.

STATUS: common in south, uncommon in north. TAXONOMY: endemic species.

563 GILBERT WHISTLER *Pachycephala inornata* Gould 1841   Pl 17
Distribution: Map 198.

RECOGNITION: *grey with cinnamon throat and buff belly; black in front of eye distinguishes from rare Red-lored Whistler; female greyish rather like the Grey Thrush but has shorter bill and legs.*

DESCRIPTION: 18–20cm. Sexes different. *Male:* upperparts brownish-grey, darker on head; face in front of eye black; throat and foreneck dark cinnamon; breast and flanks pale grey; belly and under tail coverts buffy-white; bill and legs black; eyes reddish-brown. *Female:* whole underparts light greyish-buff, darker on breast; bill and legs dark olive-grey; eyes dull brown.

VARIATION: east of about Eucla, generally paler (race *inornata*); west of Eucla, generally darker and richer in colour (race *gilbertii*).

HABITAT: dry woodlands like mallee. HABITS: terrestrial and arboreal, on or near ground, feeds mainly on ground or among low bushes hopping quietly from branch to branch; solitary; sedentary. BREEDING: August–January; nests in forks in dense bushes and low trees, usually below about 3m, deep cup roughly made of interwoven twigs and bark strips and sometimes wool, lined with fine bark and rootlets; two to three eggs, white to light buff spotted with shades of brown. VOICE: musical whistle, 'er-whit-er-whit' or 'er-with', a loud 'pooo-eee' and harsher rapidly repeated 'chook' or 'chut' or 'chop'. FOOD: insects, berries and seeds.

STATUS: fairly common, less so in west. TAXONOMY: endemic species; relationship with sibling Red-lored Whistler not clear.

564 RED-LORED WHISTLER *Pachycephala rufogularis* Gould 1841
Distribution: Map 198.

RECOGNITION: very like Gilbert Whistler, but slightly larger, sexes alike (except that browns rather paler in female), *area in front of eye as well as throat cinnamon brown,* browner on belly and all brown areas less richly coloured.

HABITAT: whipstick mallee and porcupine grass. HABITS: similar to Gilbert Whistler. BREEDING: September–December; nests in shady parts of porcupine grass clumps and bushes, more compact and neat, especially at rim, than Gilbert Whistler, made of bark, leaves and rootlets usually with some green vegetation woven in; two eggs, similar to Gilbert Whistler. VOICE: similar to but distinct from Gilbert, loud clear whistle followed by sound like breath drawn in through partly closed lips. FOOD: insects and berries.

STATUS: fairly common, locally. TAXONOMY: endemic species; relationship with sibling Gilbert Whistler uncertain.

565 BROWN WHISTLER *Pachycephala simplex* Gould 1843
Distribution: Map 199.

RECOGNITION: *pale grey-brown above and dull white below.*

DESCRIPTION: 14cm. Sexes alike. Face and upperparts grey-brown; underparts whitish tinged with vinaceous buff on breast which has faint dark streaks; bill and legs black; eyes light brown.

HABITAT: mangroves and monsoon forest. HABITS: arboreal but sometimes feeds on ground, usually in substage vegetation flitting from branch to branch quietly feeding; solitary; sedentary. BREEDING: December–February; nests in forks of trees and bushes low down, cup-shaped, made of rough grasses and lined with softer material; two eggs, pale buff spotted with dark brown. VOICE: rich, varied and melodious. FOOD: insects.

STATUS: common. TAXONOMY: endemic race *(simplex)* of species extending to New Guinea. *Note:* current opinion has reverted to an earlier conception that the races listed under this species consist of two species, *P. simplex* and *P. griseiceps,* belonging mainly to New Guinea but each represented in Australia, the Brown Whistler and Grey Whistler.

566 GREY WHISTLER *Pachycephala griseiceps* Gray 1858
Distribution: Map 199.

RECOGNITION: like the Brown Whistler in general appearance, differs in having *back tinged with greenish-olive* making a contrast with dark grey-brown crown and face; throat white to pale pinkish-buff, breast darker vinaceous buff with faint dark streaks, *belly pale lemon yellow;* bill brown; eyes brown; legs bluish-grey.

HABITAT: mainly rain forest. HABITS, etc: similar to Brown Whistler but possibly more often in high foliage. VOICE: melodious whistling phrase.

STATUS: common. TAXONOMY: endemic race *(peninsulae)* of species extending to Aru Is and New Guinea. (See under previous species.)

Genus COLLURICINCLA

It was thought that the species first named in this genus had close affinity with both shrikes and thrushes, hence the rather cumbersome and misleading compound name 'shrike-thrush' by which it and other members are sometimes known. In some contexts the 'thrush' part is dropped but here the practice is followed of omitting the 'shrike' part. Most members of the genus resemble some of the non-spotted thrushes in size and general appearance, especially plump build; also in relatively dull plumages and superb voices. The genus is mainly Australian with the widespread Grey Thrush extending into New Guinea (as species or superspecies) and the Rufous Thrush widespread in New Guinea extending into Queensland. The latter species is considered to be a link between *Pachycephala* and *Colluricincla* and is sometimes put in a separate genus. The Grey Thrush is here regarded as a superspecies consisting in Australia of three separately named semispecies.

Key to COLLURICINCLA

1 Head and rump grey, back brown	Grey Thrush................	No 567
2 Upperparts uniform slate-grey.................	4–5	
3 Upperparts uniform grey-brown to olive-brown ..	6–11	
4 Underparts whitish...........................	Western Thrush	No 569
5 Underparts cinnamon buff.....................	Stripe-breasted Thrush	No 572
6 Underparts whitish...........................	Brown Thrush	No 568
7 Underparts with some cinnamon buff...........	8–9	
8 Coastal Queensland..........................	Rufous Thrush..............	No 570
9 Northern Territory and Western Australia		
Habitat sandstone cliffs.....................	Sandstone Thrush	No 573
Habitat mangroves and swamps	Little Thrush...............	No 571

GREY THRUSH SUPERSPECIES

The following three forms are geographical variants of the same stock. They are sometimes listed as races of one species but they have fairly distinctive features which remain constant over most of their ranges. Also there is little evidence of interbreeding except possibly at fairly narrow contact zones. If they are not quite true species they seem to be well on the way to becoming so. They could be regarded at least as semispecies which gives them claim to separate species names.

567 GREY THRUSH *Colluricincla harmonica*   Latham 1801
Distribution: Map 200.

RECOGNITION: *grey head and rump contrasting with brown back, pale grey below.*

DESCRIPTION: 23cm. Sexes slightly different. *Male:* upperparts mostly dark grey with dark brown back; lores white, sometimes extending above eye; underparts pale grey, darker on breast and indistinct dark streaks on throat and breast; bill black; eyes brown; legs dark grey. *Female:* slight tinge of brown on grey upperparts, white lores less distinct, streaks on breast more distinct, bill blackish-brown.

VARIATION: New South Wales and Victoria, darker (race *harmonica*); Queensland, paler (race *oblita*); southwest Queensland and northeast South Australia, much paler (race *anda*); Tasmania, bill larger (race *strigata*).

HABITAT: forests and woodlands including suburban parks. HABITS: arboreal and terrestrial, feeds mostly on ground, when in trees usually keeps fairly low; solitary; sedentary. BREEDING: July–December; nests in various sites, on ground or rock ledges, in dense bush, tree forks and hollows, old nests of other species; bowl shaped, made of bark strips and grass loosely or compactly bound and lined with rootlets; three eggs, pearly-white or cream lightly spotted with olive-brown and grey. VOICE: wide range of loud clear melodious phrases, frequent call a ringing whistle 'whit, whit-whit', almost like the Rufous Whistler but louder. FOOD: insects and small animals.

STATUS: common. TAXONOMY: endemic species or semispecies of superspecies with one form in New Guinea.

568 BROWN THRUSH *Colluricincla brunnea*   Gould 1840
Distribution: Map 200.

RECOGNITION: very like Grey Thrush, differs (as well as in distribution) by *uniform dull grey-brown upperparts, underparts paler shade of same dull colour,* lores either indistinct and grey or conspicuous and white and continued over eye in male; *female has distinct cinnamon brown eyebrow,* cinnamon buff on under tail coverts and cinnamon brown in centre of wing.

VARIATION: west of Gulf, slightly browner on upperparts and greyer on face (race *brunnea*); east of Gulf, slightly greyer on upperparts and whiter on face with distinct white eyebrow (race *superciliosa*).

HABITAT: forests and woodlands with low thickets, especially along waterways. HABITS: similar to Grey Thrush. BREEDING: October–February; nests and eggs similar to Grey Thrush. VOICE and FOOD: as for Grey Thrush.

STATUS: fairly common. TAXONOMY: endemic species or semispecies.

569 WESTERN THRUSH   *Colluricincla rufiventris*   Gould 1840   Pl 17

Distribution: Map 200.

RECOGNITION: very like Grey Thrush, differs (as well as in distribution) by *uniform grey upperparts only slightly tinged with olive;* throat and breast grey shading to pale buff on belly and deeper buff or cinnamon buff on vent and under tail coverts; females, as in other species of this group, have more distinct dark streaks on throat and breast, a slightly more rufous tinge, and central wing feathers edged with brown.

VARIATION: coastal areas of southwest, darker (race *rufiventris*); dry inland areas, paler (race *serventyi*).

HABITAT: similar to previous species, well timbered localities, thickets and dense vegetation along creeks. HABITS, BREEDING, etc: similar to Grey Thrush, but nests said to be neater in build and eggs smaller.

STATUS: common. TAXONOMY: endemic species or semispecies.

570 RUFOUS THRUSH   *Colluricincla megarhyncha*   Quoy & Gaim. 1830

Distribution: Map 201.

RECOGNITION: *olive-brown above, pinkish-cinnamon below with whitish throat, pale bill; rain forests of northeast.*

DESCRIPTION: 18cm. Sexes alike. Upperparts olive-brown, outer wing feathers sometimes distinctly edged with dark cinnamon brown; throat near white or light cinnamon buff; remainder of underparts, including under wing and under tail coverts pinkish-cinnamon; faint dark streaks on throat and breast; bill light brown; eyes grey-brown; legs purplish-grey.

VARIATION: south of about Cooktown, slightly larger and richer in colour (race *gouldii*); north and west of Cooktown, slightly smaller and greyer (race *normani*).

HABITAT: forest, swamp-woodland and mangroves. HABITS: arboreal, usually feeds in low thick vegetation and on ground; solitary; sedentary. BREEDING: September–February; nests in tree forks and dense vegetation below about 4m, cup-shaped, made of interwoven leaves and tendrils bound with cobweb and lined with fine rootlets; two to three eggs, white or tinged with pink and spotted with reddish-brown and grey. VOICE: various short melodious phrases in clear whistling notes, like 'tu-whee, wot-wot', also harsh rasping whistle rather like a sneeze. FOOD: insects.

STATUS: common. TAXONOMY: races of variable species widespread from Celebes to islands east of New Guinea; sometimes assigned to a separate genus *Myiolestes* linking *Pachycephala* with *Colluricincla*.

Rufous Thrush (570)

571 LITTLE THRUSH *Colluricincla parvula* Gould 1845

Distribution: Map 201.

RECOGNITION: *brown above, white throat and buff breast; mangroves and wet thickets of Northern Territory.*

DESCRIPTION: 18cm. Sexes alike. Upperparts buff-brown; face and throat dull white; breast, flanks and underwing cinnamon buff, throat and breast faintly streaked; centre of belly dull white; bill blackish-brown; eyes reddish-brown; legs bluish-grey.

HABITAT: mangroves and similar swampy thickets. HABITS: on or near ground in dense thickets feeding among vegetation or in litter, has been observed to 'ant' apparently with millipedes; solitary; sedentary. BREEDING: period uncertain, recorded November–January; nests not well known but recorded in dense bush in low tree hollows, cup-shaped and made of bark and twigs; two eggs, white tinged with pink and spotted with reddish-brown and grey. VOICE: few data, but said to be loud and melodious like related species. FOOD: insects. STATUS: probably common. TAXONOMY: endemic species; possibly a derivative of the Rufous Thrush.

572 STRIPE-BREASTED THRUSH *Colluricincla boweri* Ramsay 1885

Distribution: Map 202.

RECOGNITION: *blue-grey above, pinkish-brown below with whitish throat, black bill; mountain forests of Atherton area.*

DESCRIPTION: 19–20cm. Sexes alike. Upperparts dark blue-grey barely tinged with brown; face in front of eye greyish, shading to throat tinged with pinkish-brown which becomes dark pinkish-cinnamon on remainder of underparts, including underwing and under tail coverts; throat and breast streaked with dark grey; bill black; eyes dark chestnut brown; legs dark slate grey.

HABITAT: mountain rain forest. HABITS: arboreal, perches or feeds among foliage at various heights, sometimes in tree tops, but mostly in low dense vegetation, or on ground; solitary; sedentary. BREEDING: October–December; nests and eggs similar to other thrushes, usually placed in dense vegetation below about 10m. VOICE: little information, said to be melodious as in other thrushes. FOOD: insects.

STATUS: apparently common. TAXONOMY: endemic species; may have close affinity with Sandstone Thrush.

573 SANDSTONE THRUSH *Colluricincla woodwardi* Hartert 1905

Distribution: Map 202.

RECOGNITION: *dark brown above, light brown below with pale throat; associated with sandstone cliffs.*

DESCRIPTION: 24cm. Sexes alike. Upperparts dark brown (sepia) with slight tinge of grey on head; face in front of eye and throat buffy-white shading to pinkish-cinnamon on remainder of underparts, including under wing and under tail coverts, throat and breast lightly streaked; bill blackish-brown; eyes reddish-brown; legs dark brown.

HABITAT: cliffs and tumbled boulders in sandstone ranges. HABITS: terrestrial, lives on cliffs and among boulders, searches for food in cracks and crannies, perches on topmost pinnacles of rocks; solitary; sedentary. BREEDING: period unknown, recorded December; nests in rock crevices and on ledges, cup-shaped, apparently made of porcupine grass; two to three eggs, white spotted with brown and grey. VOICE: recorded as melodious song and loud clear rather metallic 'pwink'. FOOD: insects.

STATUS: uncertain; possibly common locally. TAXONOMY: endemic species; may have close affinity with Bower Thrush.

Genus FALCUNCULUS

The very distinctive and endemic Shriketit is placed in a genus of its own. Some taxonomists find it sufficiently unique to place it in a separate family along with several other species, but most seem to agree that its affinities lie with the whistlers and thrushes. There is only a superficial resemblance to the true shrikes (not in Australia) in the hooked tip of the large laterally compressed bill, and to the tits (of Europe) in the black and white head pattern and yellow underparts. The alternative name Barktit might be more suitable as these birds frequently cling to tree trunks and strip bark in search of insects and grubs. The Shriketit seems to be on the decline for its once widespread population has shrunk to three main isolated groups, and one of these now seems to consist of a few isolated communities. Each of the main groups has distinctive features and the usual problem arises about whether they are races or species. They are sometimes listed as species and that course is taken here by regarding the three groups as semispecies of a superspecies.

Eastern Shriketit (574)

male   female

574 EASTERN SHRIKETIT *Falcunculus frontatus* (Latham) 1801
Distribution: Map 203.

RECOGNITION: *black crested head with two broad white bands, facial pair usually meet on forehead, belly as well as breast yellow, wing and tail feathers edged with grey.*

DESCRIPTION: 17–19cm. Bill deep, laterally compressed and slightly hooked; crown feathers extended into short crest. Sexes slightly different. *Male:* head, throat and foreneck black with two broad white bands above eye and below eye extending to lores, which usually meet in centre of forehead; back greenish-yellow (citrine); breast, belly and under tail coverts yellow; wings and tail black with grey edges to feathers; outer margin of tail white; bill black; eyes red; legs grey. *Female:* throat and foreneck yellow.

HABITAT: dry forests and woodlands. HABITS: arboreal, feeds on tree trunks, sometimes tearing bark to get insects and grubs, and among foliage of trees and bushes; solitary or in small parties, probably families; sedentary with some nomadic movements. BREEDING: August–January; nests in slender forks of high branches of trees and saplings, deep cup made of bark strips tightly woven and felted with cobweb, decorated with moss and lichen and lined with fine grass; male snips off twigs above nest; two to three eggs, white blotched and speckled with dark brown, olive and grey. VOICE: chatter or chuckle sometimes written as 'knock-at-the-door-whack', also long single whistle. FOOD: insects of various kinds; it has been noted that only selected parts of some insects are eaten.

STATUS: fairly common. TAXONOMY: endemic species or semispecies of endemic genus.

575 NORTHERN SHRIKETIT *Falcunculus whitei* Campbell 1910

Distribution: Map 203.

RECOGNITION: very like Eastern Shriketit, differs in *smaller size,* 14–16cm; green of back more yellow, *wing and tail feathers edged with yellow.*

HABITAT, etc: recorded in dry stringy bark ridges on McArthur River; very little else is known of this species but probably similar to Eastern Shriketit.

STATUS: uncertain; only records seem to be from three widely separated localities. TAXONOMY: endemic species or semispecies of endemic genus.

576 WESTERN SHRIKETIT *Falcunculus leucogaster* Gould 1838

Distribution: Map 203.

RECOGNITION: like Eastern Shriketit, differs in being slightly smaller, 15–17cm, in having *belly white, not yellow,* wing and tail feathers edged with greenish-yellow, white sides of forehead separated by black centre, more yellow in green upperparts.

HABITAT, etc: similar to eastern species; voice recorded as soft, clear 'ko' or 'koo' or 'too-ee, too-ee'.

STATUS: fairly common. TAXONOMY: endemic species or semispecies of endemic genus.

Genus OREOICA

The Crested Bellbird was originally placed with *Falcunculus,* and may be a dry country variant of a stock common to both, but it has long been in a genus of its own. It has features which also suggest relationship with the thrushes and whistlers. The bill is large but not distinctly hooked and the head is crested. The sexes are different, especially in head features. The species is mainly a ground feeder. It has a wide range of notes some of which are bell-like and ventriloquial which makes it difficult to locate a bird by its voice.

577 CRESTED BELLBIRD *Oreoica gutturalis* (Vig. & Horsf.) 1827   Pl 17

Distribution: Map 204.

RECOGNITION: *brown above with short crest; male has large white face 'mask', black crest and bib and bright orange eye; often on ground.*

DESCRIPTION: 20cm; short crest. Sexes different. *Male:* black crest connected by thin black line surrounding white forehead and white chin to black foreneck and upper breast; remainder of head and face smoke-grey; remainder of upperparts mainly buff-brown but more cinnamon on rump and edges of wing feathers; lower breast and belly buffy-white; flanks and under tail coverts light cinnamon buff; bill black; eyes orange; legs dark grey. *Female:* crest only black; face, foreneck and breast buff-brown like back; chin creamy-white; bill dark brown; eyes reddish-brown.

VARIATION: throughout most of range, darker (race *gutturalis*); northern limits west of gulf, paler (race *pallescens*).

HABITAT: dry woodlands to arid scrub with scattered trees. HABITS: arboreal and terrestrial, feeds mostly on ground, hops rapidly, flies low between bushes or into low branches of trees; before eggs hatch hairy caterpillars, known as bush worms, are paralysed and stored around nest as food for young; solitary or in small parties, probably families; sedentary and nomadic, perhaps with some regular seasonal movements. BREEDING: variable but mostly between August and March; nests in various places below about 2m, in forks of dead brush, hollow stumps, etc, deep cup made of fine sticks and twigs or bark and lined with fine bark and fibres; two to four eggs, white or tinged with blue lightly blotched with dark brown and grey, sometimes black. VOICE: varied and ventriloquial and transcribed in many ways; typical phrase is 'tip-tip-tip-tip, top-o-the-wattle' commencing in low soft tones with head horizontal and ending louder with head thrown back, then repeated apparently from a different source; also duet calls, male says 'tik-tik-tik' and female responds with bell-like 'tonk-tonk'. FOOD: insects.

STATUS: common and apparently extending range. TAXONOMY: endemic species.

Family EPHTHIANURIDAE

Chats

Endemic family of 5 species

TAXONOMISTS ARE PUZZLED TO know where the chats fit into the avian tree. The general view is that they lie somewhere in the muscicapid assemblage, perhaps on the warbler branch. But many who have studied them are not satisfied with this conclusion and put them, temporarily, at the margin on a main limb of at least subfamily rank, here raised to family. Observers for many years have noted some behavioural similarities with the pipits, especially in the Desert Chat, but this is superficial. Other characteristics with deeper significance suggest affinity with some section of the honeyeater family (a family possibly of very mixed origin). Whatever their relationships the chats illustrate stages in adaptation to arid conditions, the unique climate of the interior where the very scanty rainfall is unpredictable as to time and place. At one extreme the Yellow Chat lives in isolated sedentary groups in marshy habitats on the lower reaches of rivers, and at the other the Crimson Chat is a desert nomad with variable breeding seasons. In *Ephthianura* the sexes differ, the males mostly having bright colours. The Desert Chat differs in this and other characteristics and is put in a separate genus.

Key to EPHTHIANURIDAE

1 Crown, rump and breast crimson (♂); rump only crimson (♀)   Crimson Chat . . . . . . No 579
2 Underparts white with black breast band . . . .   White-fronted Chat. . No 578
3 Underparts mainly yellow.   4–8

4 Rump not yellow . . . .   Desert Chat . . . . No 582
5 Rump yellow   6–8

6 Chin black. . . . . (♂)   Orange Chat . . . . No 580
7 Breast with black band . . . . (♂)   Yellow Chat. . . . . No 581
8 No black on underparts . . . . (♀)   Orange Chat . . . . No 580
                                                                          (♀)   Yellow Chat. . . . . No 581

Genus EPHTHIANURA

Four of the five Australian chats, all of which are small with relatively short tails. Sexes differ, males being mostly in brilliant colours. They live in open places, often wet or dry bush wasteland, and feed mostly on the ground where they walk or run with great speed or readily perch in exposed places. They are gregarious, except possibly the rare Yellow Chat, and sometimes wander in large flocks.

578 WHITE-FRONTED CHAT   *Ephthianura albifrons*   (Jard. & Selby) 1828

Distribution: Map 205.

RECOGNITION: *white underparts with black band on breast, male has large white 'mask'; usually in wastelands.*

DESCRIPTION: 11–12cm. Sexes different. *Male:* large white 'front' covering forepart of head from mid-crown, and face to upper breast; nape and side of neck black joined to broad black breast band on otherwise white underparts; back grey lightly mottled with dark grey; wings brownish-black; upper tail black with broad white tips to inner webs of all except central pair of feathers; bill black; eyes pinkish-white; legs dark grey. *Female:* upperparts uniform grey-brown (dull fawn); underparts buffy-white with narrow dull black band on breast.

HABITAT: low bushes in various 'waste' places, salt flats, heaths, blue-bush plains. HABITS: mainly terrestrial, on or near ground in low bushes, often on open ground, runs actively in short bursts, perches on tops of low bushes and tussocks; solitary breeder, but usually in loose communal association; sedentary and nomadic, some movements possibly qualify as migratory. BREEDING: July–January; nests in low bushes and tussocks, cup-shaped, made of fine grass and fibres and lined with vegetable down; three to four eggs, white spotted with reddish-brown. VOICE: metallic 'tin-tac' or 'tang' (like Zebra Finch). FOOD: insects, sometimes seeds.

STATUS: common. TAXONOMY: endemic species and genus.

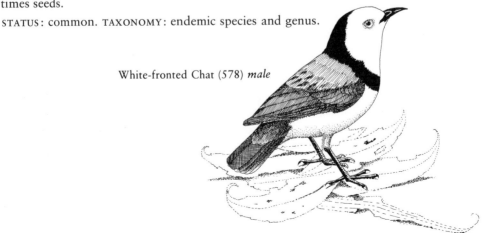

White-fronted Chat (578) *male*

579 CRIMSON CHAT *Ephthianura tricolor* Gould 1841 Pl 17
Distribution: Map 206.

RECOGNITION: *crimson rump of both sexes, male has crimson crown and breast; in savanna woodlands; sometimes in large nomadic flocks.*

DESCRIPTION: 10–11cm. Sexes different. *Male:* crown, rump and breast crimson; belly and flanks mottled crimson and white; throat white; face, side of neck and back mottled blackish-brown and grey-brown; wings blackish-brown, feathers broadly edged with white; tail blackish-brown broadly tipped with white; bill black; eyes white or pale cream; legs dark grey. *Female:* rump, tail and wings similar to male; head brown shading to grey-brown with dark mottling on back; underparts white with varying amounts of pinkish-buff on breast and flanks.

(*Note:* it is stated that males lose much of their bright plumage after breeding but there does not seem to be any certain information on this point.)

HABITAT: low bushes in grass plains and tree savanna. HABITS: mainly terrestrial, on or near ground in bushes or grass tussocks or low in trees, feeds mostly on ground, walks or runs at speed or flits restlessly; male has display flight with wings V-shaped and crimson crown feathers erect; observed to fix large insects in tree forks and tear them apart as butcherbirds do; inserts bill in flower corollas for insects, or perhaps honey (has brush-tipped tongue like most honeyeaters); mostly community breeder and gregarious at other times; partly sedentary but also has general north–south movement in nomadic flocks which may settle in different areas in different seasons to breed. BREEDING: variable, largely dependent on rains but periods fairly definite in certain areas; nests in bushes and tussocks, cup-shaped, made of grass and twigs and lined with finer material; three to four eggs, pinkish-white speckled with reddish-purple. VOICE: melodious whistle 'wheee-wheee-wheee', ringing 'cheng-cheng-cheng-cheng', rather harsh 'tsch-tch-tch', high-pitched 'seee-ee'. FOOD: insects.

STATUS: common. TAXONOMY: endemic species and genus.

580 ORANGE CHAT *Ephthianura aurifrons* Gould 1838 Pl 17
Distribution: Map 207.

RECOGNITION: *yellow rump of both sexes, male has black chin and yellow crown; female very like Desert Chat but distinguished by yellow rump and by perching on bushes.*

DESCRIPTION: 11–12cm. Sexes different. *Male:* head, rump and underparts bright reddish-orange except for black lower face and throat; back yellow to yellowish-fawn densely mottled with blackish-brown; wings and tail blackish, tail thinly edged and tipped with white; bill black; eyes reddish-brown; legs dark grey. *Female:* fawn upperparts and yellow underparts; very like Desert Chat but has yellow rump and buffy-white (not yellow) throat.

HABITAT: samphire and saltbush and similar vegetation, especially on margins of inland salt lakes. HABITS and BREEDING: mostly similar to Crimson Chat with probably more restricted breeding period, August–February, and less nomadic, but movements not well known. VOICE: single drawn out cheep, also husky chirping 'tang' or 'teng'. FOOD: insects.

STATUS: fairly common. TAXONOMY: endemic species and genus; perhaps a derivative of a once more widespread Yellow Chat.

581 YELLOW CHAT *Ephthianura crocea* Cast. & Ramsay 1877
Distribution: Map 207.

RECOGNITION: very like Orange Chat but *yellow areas lemon-coloured;* also has separate distribution; *male has yellow throat and black breast band.*

VARIATION: there are slight differences between the isolated populations; they are regarded as races.

HABITAT: Marshy swamps and saltbush lagoons on lower reaches of large rivers, sometimes in trees. HABITS: not well known; arboreal or among low shrubs near water margins, reported to feed among tree foliage near Derby, rarely on ground, very furtive; apparently solitary; sedentary. BREEDING: November–January, at least; nests near ground among thick vegetation, construction and eggs similar to other chats. VOICE: no details.

STATUS: recorded common in Northern Territory, apparently rare elsewhere. TAXONOMY: endemic species and genus; remnants of once widespread stock from which Orange Chat may have evolved.

Genus ASHBYIA

The Desert or Gibber Chat is usually kept in a genus separate from the other chats, principally because the sexes are alike. Its discoverer and others since have noted that in some ways it behaves like a pipit—it seems like a yellow-bellied pipit with a much shortened tail—but this is not thought to indicate affinity. It is curious that Sturt did not record it for the centre of its distribution lies in the stony desert named after him. Its curious fluttering flight and the patch of bright yellow as it appears when standing upright on a mound readily attract attention. As in the case of some other species living in shelterless environments, it takes refuge in holes in the ground.

582 DESERT CHAT *Ashbyia lovensis* (Ashby) 1911
Distribution: Map 208.

RECOGNITION: *fawn above and yellow below; like female Orange Chat but lacks yellow rump and it never perches; in stony deserts.*

DESCRIPTION: 12cm. Sexes alike. Upperparts shade of fawn slightly mottled with blackish-brown; face and underparts bright lemon-yellow, sometimes with varying amounts of pale fawn on breast and flanks; wings and tail blackish-brown, tail edged and tipped with buffy-white; bill black; eyes pale cream; legs grey.

HABITAT: arid and often stony plains. HABITS: terrestrial, walks or runs at speed, wags tail like pipit, perches upright on stones or small humps (not on bushes) when bright yellow underparts become conspicuous, rises with lark-like flutter, climbs fairly high then dives rapidly and glides low over ground; apparently solitary and sedentary. BREEDING: May–October recorded, but possibly any time when conditions suitable; nests on ground in small depressions or sheltered between large stones (doubtfully in holes although noted to use holes as refuges), nests made of dried vegetation and lined with fine materials; two to four eggs (most in favourable seasons), pale cream lightly blotched brown. VOICE: little information but repeated 'whit' has been noted. FOOD: insects and seeds.

STATUS: apparently fairly common. TAXONOMY: endemic species and genus.

Family NEOSITTIDAE

Sittellas

5(7) species: all endemic.

THE SITTELLAS ARE SOMETIMES included in the wide-ranging nuthatch family, Sittidae, but current opinion favours the view that they evolved independently. Members of both families find most of their food on tree bark and have developed the ability to move in any direction on trunks and boughs—unlike the two separate groups of treecreepers which can only move upwards. Sittellas seem to defy gravity as they run in quick jerky bursts up and down trunks and over and under boughs picking insects from cracks and crevices in the bark. They are small, about 10–12cm, and in flight display a broad band of colour in the wing, mostly pale cinnamon but white in northern forms. They are widely distributed wherever there are groups of trees, except in wet forests. They are often seen wandering in small restless parties which usually keep to the high foliage. The sittellas vary a good deal in appearance throughout their range, but no two variants are found together and the problem arises whether to classify them as races or species. Much depends on whether the major distinct variants interbreed at zones of contact and views on this point differ; it is accepted here that they do. Each variant is clearly distinguishable, except in hybrid zones, and the practical course is taken of listing them as species and regarding them as semispecies (species in the making) of a superspecies.

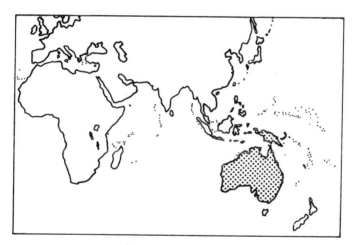

Distribution of NEOSITTIDAE

Key to NEOSITTIDAE

1 White patch in wing	3–4	
2 Cinnamon patch in wing	5–7	
3 Underparts plain white	White-winged Sittella	No 587
4 Underparts white streaked black	Striated Sittella	No 585
5 Crown black	Black-capped Sittella	No 586
6 Crown brown	Orange-winged Sittella	No 583
7 Whole head white	White-headed Sittella	No 584

583 ORANGE-WINGED SITTELLA   *Neositta chrysoptera*   (Latham) 1801

Distribution: Map 209.

RECOGNITION: *small (12cm), streaked grey and black with white rump and white-tipped tail, pale brown patch in open wing, plain brown crown.*

DESCRIPTION: 10–12cm. Sexes slightly different. *Male:* crown and face dusky brown, contrasting with back streaked grey and black; rump white; tail black tipped with white; concealed patch in wing pale cinnamon brown; underparts white lightly streaked with dusky brown; under tail coverts barred black and white; bill blackish-brown with patch of yellow at base; eyes pale orange, eyelids pale yellow; legs pale yellow. *Female:* differs in having throat dusky white speckled with grey-brown.

HABITAT: open forests and well wooded areas. HABITS: arboreal, usually high up in trees moving actively in any direction, working over trunks and boughs and constantly flitting from place to place; gregarious, in small parties; sedentary but with nomadic movements in small area. BREEDING: August–January; nests in forks in dead branches, usually high up, made of fibre and bark and closely matching branch—sometimes looks like broken end of branch; three eggs, variable but often bluish-white speckled and blotched with black and dark reddish-brown. VOICE: thin 'tzir, zit-zit, tzir, zit-zat-zat'. FOOD: insects, mainly obtained from bark.

STATUS: fairly common. TAXONOMY: endemic species or semispecies; hybridises with Black-capped Sittella in west and White-headed Sittella in north.

584 WHITE-HEADED SITTELLA   *Neositta leucocephala*   Gould 1838

Distribution: Map 209.

RECOGNITION: like Orange-winged Sittella but *whole head white* or near white and underparts more heavily streaked with black. Female differs from male in having dusky instead of white throat.

HABITAT, etc: similar to Orange-winged Sittella; mostly in forests, gregarious at all seasons, in small parties; nomadic within a restricted area.

STATUS: fairly common. TAXONOMY: endemic species or semispecies; hybridises with Orange-winged and Striated Sittellas.

585 STRIATED SITTELLA   *Neositta striata*   Gould 1869

Distribution: Map 209.

RECOGNITION: like Orange-winged Sittella but has *white (not pale brown) concealed wing patch, black crown,* and *white underparts heavily streaked with black;* bill varies from mainly black with yellow base in south to mainly yellow with black tip in north; *male* has face streaked black and white, *female* has black face and throat as well as crown.

HABITAT, etc: similar to Orange-winged Sittella; voice recorded as 'tweety-tweet' or 'tweet-tic-tweet', repeated frequently.

STATUS: fairly common. TAXONOMY: endemic species or semispecies; hybridises with White-headed Sittella but apparently not with White-winged Sittella.

586 BLACK-CAPPED SITTELLA   *Neositta pileata*   Gould 1838   Pl 18

Distribution: Map 209.

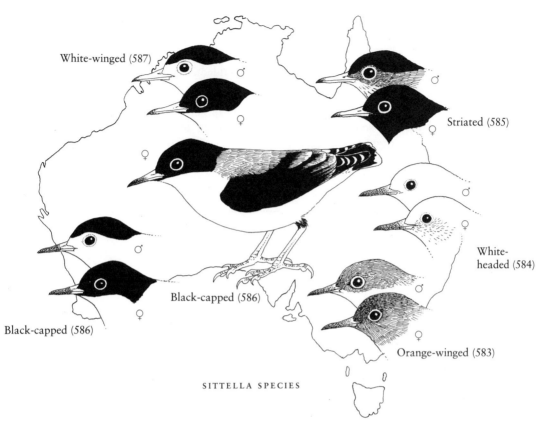

White-winged (587)

Striated (585)

White-headed (584)

Black-capped (586)

Black-capped (586)

Orange-winged (583)

SITTELLA SPECIES

RECOGNITION: like Orange-winged Sittella but slightly larger, *crown black, back less streaked, underparts plain white; male* has face white, *female* has face black.

HABITAT, etc: similar to Orange-winged Sittella, but drier kinds of forest and woodland, like mulga and trees along creeks; voice recorded as short 'trit-trit' and high-pitched 'psee-psee' in flight.

STATUS: fairly common. TAXONOMY: endemic species or semispecies; hybridises with Orange-winged Sittella and White-winged Sittella between about 20°–24° S in Northern Territory.

587 WHITE-WINGED SITTELLA *Neositta leucoptera* Gould 1839

Distribution: Map 209.

RECOGNITION: like Black-capped Sittella but slightly smaller, *concealed patch in wing white* (not brown), *back more heavily streaked, bill mainly yellow with black tip.*

HABITAT, etc: similar to Black-capped Sittella; voice described as soft twittering 'twit-twit, eert-it eert-it', also thin double whistle.

STATUS: fairly common. TAXONOMY: endemic species or semispecies; hybridises with Black-capped Sittella between about 20°–24° S in Northern Territory, but apparently not with Striated Sittella.

Family CLIMACTERIDAE

Treecreepers

7(8) species: all endemic.

IT IS DOUBTFUL IF the members of this family have affinity with either the treecreepers of the northern hemisphere (family Certhiidae) or the nuthatches (family Sittidae) with each of which they are sometimes combined. Until such doubts are resolved the best course seems to be to keep them as a separate family. Treecreepers are sometimes popularly known as woodpeckers but Australia is one of the few countries in the world where the woodpecker family (Picidae) is not represented. The feeding behaviour of the Australian treecreepers is

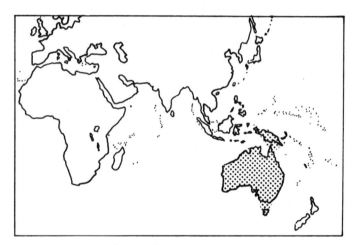

Distribution of CLIMACTERIDAE

similar to that of their European counterpart. They are adapted to climb up tree trunks and boughs (unlike the smaller sittellas which can move in any direction). They climb spirally in short hops, and when probing in the bark for insects frequently use tails for extra support. Bills are long and thin and decurved. They flit to the base of another tree, or to the ground where they also feed. In flight a broad pale band in the wing becomes visible. Their habits confine them to timbered country, from wet coastal forests to patches of mulga and creekside trees in the dry interior. They are about 12–18cm in length with camouflage plumage patterns. Seven species are listed here but the number varies according to which forms are regarded as species. The family provides classical illustrations of the process of species formation. One form occurs in New Guinea. It seems to have closest affinity with the White-throated Treecreeper and is often linked to it racially, but the view taken here is that it is a separate species or semispecies.

Key to CLIMACTERIDAE

1 Crown black, back sepia, eyebrow chestnut; south-
   east forests............................... Red-browed Treecreeper...... No 592
2 Upperparts uniformly black or cinnamon black;
   mainly north of tropic..................... 4–5

BROWN TREECREEPER GROUP

The Brown, Black, Black-tailed and Rufous Treecreepers, as recognised here, replace each other round Australia. Probably they evolved from a stock of uniform appearance widespread in the forests of the Tertiary period. The subsequent dessication and disappearance of forests during the vicissitudes of the Pleistocene Ice Ages except from isolated peripheral pockets allowed the sections of this forest-dependent and sedentary species to acquire different features. The later amelioration of climate, with extension of woodland coverage brought the isolated groups closer together again, perhaps sometimes in contact. This process, if interpreted correctly, illustrates several stages in the formation of species and gives taxonomists a problem in deciding which are truly species.

588 BROWN TREECREEPER *Climacteris picumnus* Temm. & Laug. 1824 Pl 18
Distribution: Map 210.

RECOGNITION: *light grey-brown above, greyer on face and neck; the White-browed Treecreeper is similar but darker, especially on head, and has distinct white eyebrow.*

DESCRIPTION: 15cm. Sexes slightly different. *Male:* upperparts light grey-brown, darker on crown but paler on face and neck; indistinct pale buff eyebrow; throat creamy-white; small black patch on foreneck; upper breast pale buff-brown; lower breast and belly pale buff-brown with creamy white streaks edged with black; under tail coverts barred black and creamy white; tail dark grey-brown with broad black band in centre; concealed pale buff patch on centre of wing; bill black; eyes dark brown; legs dark grey. *Female:* differs in having patch on foreneck chestnut.

HABITAT: forests and woodlands. HABITS: arboreal, but sometimes feeds on ground; usually feeds by clinging to tree trunks and boughs and spiraling upward in jerky movements and picking insects from bark, flits from one tree to base of another, flight short flutter and glide when pale wing patch becomes visible; solitary and sedentary. BREEDING: mostly between June and January; nests usually low down in trees, stumps and fence posts, rarely in banks, cup-shaped, made of grasses and hair or fur and lined with feathers; three to four eggs, pinkish-white densely spotted with shades of dark red. VOICE: loud sharp 'pink-pink'.
FOOD: insects.

STATUS: common. TAXONOMY: endemic species or semispecies, forming superspecies with Black, Black-tailed and Rufous Treecreepers.

589 BLACK TREECREEPER *Climacteris melanota* Gould 1847

Distribution: Map 210.

RECOGNITION: very like Brown Treecreeper but *upperparts sooty black,* more *conspicuous creamy white eyebrow and throat, no black band in tail* (tail wholly black).

HABITAT, etc: similar to Brown Treecreeper; said to build nest fairly high up, above about 3m, to use bark in its construction and to include pieces of charcoal; two to three eggs.

STATUS: apparently common. TAXONOMY: endemic species or semispecies; frequently regarded as race of Brown Treecreeper, or forming superspecies with it.

590 BLACK-TAILED TREECREEPER *Climacteris melanura* Gould 1843

Distribution: Map 210.

RECOGNITION: *blackish above, throat streaked (male) or white (female);* like Black Treecreeper but *lacks white eyebrow and distributions different.*

DESCRIPTION: 15–18cm. Sexes slightly different. *Male:* upperparts blackish; throat and foreneck streaked black and white; breast and belly shades of dark brown; under tail coverts black tipped or barred with white; large concealed patch of pale cinnamon in wing; bill and legs black; eyes dark brown. *Female:* differs in having throat white and foreneck streaked white and dark brown.

VARIATION: Burketown to Broome, upperparts sooty black, breast and belly greyish-chestnut (race *melanura*); De Grey River to Murchison River, upperparts cinnamon black, breast and belly dark cinnamon brown (race *wellsi*).

HABITAT: open forests and woodlands. HABITS: similar to Brown Treecreeper, but noted that tail not pressed against tree trunk. BREEDING: August–January; nests similar to Brown; two to three eggs. VOICE: loud piping whistle, also metallic 'chick' or 'chink' or 'ting'. FOOD: insects, especially ants.

STATUS: fairly common. TAXONOMY: endemic species or semispecies; race *wellsi* frequently regarded as separate species, Allied Treecreeper; forms superspecies (see Brown Treecreeper).

591 RUFOUS TREECREEPER *Climacteris rufa* Gould 1841   Pl 18

Distribution: Map 210.

RECOGNITION: *reddish-brown above and below.*

DESCRIPTION: 15cm. Sexes slightly different. *Male:* upperparts rufous grey-brown, darker on crown and more cinnamon on rump; face, including eyebrow, and underparts cinnamon rufous, paler on throat and belly, greyer on breast which is streaked with black and buffy-white; broad black band in tail; concealed pale cinnamon patch in wing; bill brown; eyes reddish-brown; legs blackish-brown. *Female:* differs only in having upper breast streaked chestnut and buffy-white.

VARIATION: minor, two named races doubtfully valid.

HABITAT: forests to open woodland and mallee. HABITS and BREEDING: similar to Brown Treecreeper. VOICE: single 'tsit' or 'tweet' repeated slowly, also shrill 'tsoo-tsoo'.

STATUS: fairly common, especially in arid habitats. TAXONOMY: endemic species or semispecies; forms superspecies (see Brown Treecreeper).

592 RED-BROWED TREECREEPER *Climacteris erythrops* Gould 1841 Pl 18
Distribution: Map 211.

RECOGNITION: *reddish eyebrow, black crown contrasting with sepia back, white throat.*

DESCRIPTION: 15cm. Sexes slightly different. *Male:* crown and neck sooty black; back blackish-brown (sepia); rump and tail grey, tail with broad black central band; chestnut eyebrow and streak below eye; throat white; upper breast grey; lower breast and belly grey with broad white streaks edged with black; under tail coverts barred black and buffish-white; concealed pale buff band in wing; bill and legs black; eyes brown. *Female:* differs in having upper breast chestnut streaked with white.

HABITAT: mostly forest and dense woodland especially in hilly and mountainous country. HABITS: similar to other treecreepers, flight described as rapid and undulating, recorded as sometimes in small flocks of about six in number. BREEDING: August–January; nests similar to other species but usually high up, over about 5–6m; two eggs, pinkish-white speckled with reddish-brown. VOICE: tremulous or rippling notes, also high-pitched and harsh—quite distinct from other species in same area. FOOD: insects.

STATUS: fairly common. TAXONOMY: endemic species, possibly forming superspecies with White-browed Treecreeper.

593 WHITE-BROWED TREECREEPER *Climacteris affinis* Blyth 1864
Distribution: Map 211.

RECOGNITION: *dark grey-brown above with white eyebrow; like Brown Treecreeper but darker on head and neck and greyer on rump and tail (eastern race).*

DESCRIPTION: 14cm. Sexes slightly different. *Male:* crown and face dark grey with white eyebrow; back dark grey-brown; rump and tail grey-brown or grey, tail with broad black central band; throat white; upper breast grey; lower breast and belly grey boldly streaked with white edged with black; under tail coverts barred black and buffy-white; pale brown patch in centre of wing; bill and legs black; eyes brown. *Female:* differs in having small patch of light chestnut on upper breast and tinge of chestnut above eyebrow.

VARIATION: east of Spencer Gulf and Simpson Desert, rump and tail grey (race *affinis*); west, rump and tail grey-brown like back (race *superciliosus*).

Black Treecreeper (589)

White-throated Treecreeper (594)

HABITAT: mulga and mallee, patches of woodland in open country. HABITS and BREEDING: similar to Brown Treecreeper; two to three eggs. VOICE: loud staccato call, soft piping 'seep-seep', low tremulous notes.

STATUS: fairly common. TAXONOMY: endemic species, possibly forming superspecies with Red-browed Treecreeper.

594 WHITE-THROATED TREECREEPER
Climacteris leucophaea (Latham) 1801   Fig p 393

Distribution: Map 212.

RECOGNITION: *dark olive-brown above (no differentiated eyebrow); female has small brown patch on side of neck.*

DESCRIPTION: 12–15cm. Sexes slightly different. *Male:* crown blackish-brown sometimes with pale scaly marks on forehead; back dark olive-brown; tail dark grey-brown with broad black band; throat varying from white to pale buff-brown; upper breast buff-brown or grey-brown; lower breast and belly light or dark buff blotched with blackish-brown; flanks streaked with pale buff edged with black; concealed patch of cinnamon in wing; bill, eyes and legs blackish-brown. *Female:* differs in having small patch of cinnamon on side of neck.

VARIATION: throughout most of range, colours medium (race *leucophaea*); extreme south-west of range, sometimes restricted to Mt Lofty, Adelaide, generally paler, near white below (race *grisescens*); Atherton Tableland, small and much darker, near black above and dark grey-fawn below (race *minor*).

HABITAT: forests and dense woodlands. HABITS: similar to other treecreepers but apparently seldom on ground. BREEDING: similar to other species, nests usually fairly high up; two to three eggs, pale cream lightly speckled dark brown (different to eggs of other treecreepers). VOICE: loud piercing whistle, also succession of loud staccato notes.

STATUS: fairly common. TAXONOMY: endemic species. (*Note:* this forest species has close relatives in New Guinea which are differentiated into local races. All are sometimes regarded as one species and sometimes as separate species on each continent. Of the Australian populations the form *minor* is sometimes listed as a distinct species, and the race *grisescens* is doubtfully valid.)

Family DICAEIDAE
Flowerpeckers
9(58) species: 8 endemic

FLOWERPECKERS ARE CONSIDERED TO be nearest in relationship to the sunbirds, an affinity not readily apparent in the outward appearance and behaviour of the Australian representatives. This consists of a small group of pardalotes or diamond-birds, an endemic genus, and the Mistletoebird, a member of a large genus widespread throughout the range of the family. Flowerpeckers are small with short square tails and bills of varying shape. The Australian species are under 10cm in length.

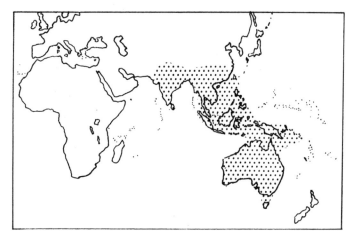

Distribution of DICAEIDAE

Key to DICAEIDAE

1 Upperparts black, breast red..............(♂)   Mistletoebird .... No 595
   (Like a robin, see *Petroica* key, page 352)
2 Plumage brownish with white spots   4–6
3 Plumage brownish with white streaks, red or yellow
   'flash' in wing   7–10
4 Wings only spotted; Tasmania ....   Fortyspotted Pardalote .... No 598
5 Wings and crown spotted
   Rump reddish...........................   Spotted Pardalote .... No 596
   Rump yellow...........................   Yellow-rumped Pardalote .... No 597
6 Crown only spotted.......................   Red-browed Pardalote .... No 599
7 Crown plain black, red wing flash ....   Black-headed Pardalote ...... No 603
8 Crown streaked   9–10
9 Wing flash yellow..........................   Yellow-tipped Pardalote...... No 600
10 Wing flash red
   White wing streak narrow ....   Red-tipped Pardalote .... No 601
   White wing streak broad...................   Striated Pardalote........... No 602

Genus DICAEUM

There are some thirty-six species in this genus but only one, the Mistletoebird, has reached Australia; it has external racial connections. Members of the genus are mostly berry feeders, the Australian representative, as its name suggests, favouring those of the mistletoe, except when feeding young on insects. It is highly nomadic when not breeding and may be found wherever mistletoe is in fruit. It is like one of the red-breasted robins but has no spot on the forehead and has a black streak on the white belly; also it may often be seen with a berry in its bill looking like a lump of bubble-gum. Wings are relatively long and pointed.

595 MISTLETOEBIRD *Dicaeum hirundinaceum* (Shaw & Nodder) 1792   Pl 18

Distribution: throughout, except Tasmania.

RECOGNITION: *male has wholly black upperparts, red throat and breast, black streak in centre of white belly. (Scarlet Robin has red forehead and black throat.)*

DESCRIPTION: 10cm. Sexes very different. *Male:* upperparts, including face, wings and tail, glossy blue-black; throat, breast and under tail coverts scarlet; belly creamy-white with broad black central streak; bill blackish-brown; eyes dark brown; legs black. *Female:* upperparts dark brownish-grey, sometimes with faint gloss; underparts creamy-white blotched with grey on breast and flanks; under tail coverts pale red.

HABITAT: forests and woodlands, most kinds of tree associations. HABITS: arboreal, feeds in tree foliage especially where there are clumps of mistletoe with ripe berries; solitary and nomadic, possibly with some regular migratory pattern. BREEDING: variable, but mainly between September and March; nests in trees at various heights, suspended from outer branches, inverted cone-shaped with side slit opening near top, made of cobwebs and plant down woven to felt-like consistency; three white eggs. VOICE: among numerous transcriptions are: high-pitched 'tic' or 'chirp', often uttered in flight; soft 'twit-twee'; harsh 'krik-krik'. FOOD: berries, especially of mistletoe species, also insects when feeding young.

STATUS: fairly common. TAXONOMY: species extending to Aru Is and Indonesia.

Genus PARDALOTUS

The pardalotes are only found in Australia. They are considered to be an aberrant offshoot of the flowerpeckers, possibly a group which evolved along specialised lines from an early colonist. All are under 10cm in length. They feed on insects among foliage, sometimes taking them from flower corollas and getting smeared with honey. By their size and behaviour they could be mistaken for warblers or thornbills but they have thick blunt bills, plumages with bright markings and loud sharp notes which are repeated rather monotonously. Pardalotes are divided into two main sections, one having white spots and the other white streaks on the wings and usually on the crown. (The spots are white tips and the streaks white edges to the feathers.) The white streaked group also have a red or yellow 'flash' on the wing and yellow lores. The Red-lored Pardalote is considered to be intermediate with white spotted crown and red lores. Of the spotted group the Spotted and Yellow-rumped Pardalotes are little more than geographical variants of each other. The Fortyspotted, only in Tasmania, is thought to be an early colonist. Of the streaked group, the Red-tipped is believed to be a hybrid of the Yellow-tipped and Striated which has become stabilised and breeds true. The Striated and Black-headed interbreed in a narrow overlap zone and are sometimes listed as one species. All nest in holes, in the ground or in trees.

596 SPOTTED PARDALOTE

Pardalotus punctatus (Shaw and Nodder) 1792   Fig p 398

Distribution: Map 213.

RECOGNITION: *large white spots (yellow in female) on black crown, wings and tail; reddish rump distinguishes from Yellow-rumped Pardalote.*

DESCRIPTION: 9cm. Sexes slightly different. *Male:* crown and wings black spotted with white; white eyebrow; back cinnamon brown and dark grey; rump dark cinnamon rufous; upper tail coverts dark crimson; tail black broadly tipped with white; face and sides of neck finely streaked light and dark grey; throat and under tail coverts orange-yellow; breast and belly cinnamon brown; bill black; eyes dark brown; legs dark grey. *Female:* differs in having spots pale yellow, throat and under tail coverts buff.

HABITAT: forests and woodlands. HABITS: arboreal and terrestrial, actively feeds among outer foliage of trees and shrubs, clinging in any position; solitary or in small flocks, often with other species; sedentary but apparently with some regular seasonal movements in Western Australia. BREEDING: August–December; nests in holes in banks or sometimes upturned tree roots, in chamber at end of horizontal or slightly upward-sloping tunnel, globular and made of grass and bark strips; four white eggs. VOICE: monotonously repeated 'pee-too', second part slightly lower in pitch than the first. FOOD: insects.

STATUS: common. TAXONOMY: endemic species, closely related to Yellow-rumped Pardalote.

597 YELLOW-RUMPED PARDALOTE
Pardalotus xanthopygus McCoy 1867   Pl 18

Distribution: Map 213.

RECOGNITION: like Spotted Pardalote with *upper tail coverts crimson, but rump lemon-yellow;* throat and under tail coverts also lemon-yellow; breast and belly creamy-white.

HABITAT: mainly dry woodlands like mallee. HABITS, etc: similar to Spotted Pardalote, noted as feeding on ground; nests recorded in tunnels in flat or sloping ground, not necessarily banks. VOICE: loud resonant 'teung' and 'teung-teung', recorded that double note uttered by one bird in response to single note uttered by another.

STATUS: common. TAXONOMY: endemic species, closely related to Spotted Pardalote.

598 FORTYSPOTTED PARDALOTE   *Pardalotus quadragintus*   Gould 1838   Pl 18

Distribution: Tasmania and Flinders I, Bass Strait.

RECOGNITION: *white spots on wing and tip of tail only, crown olive green like back.*

DESCRIPTION: 9cm; bill slightly hooked. Sexes alike. Upperparts dull olive green, darker on crown and slightly tinged with yellow on rump; wings black with large white spots (roughly forty in number); tail dark grey with white tip; face and chin dull yellowish; throat and breast blotched light and dark grey; belly greyish, white in centre tinged with yellow, more distinctly yellow on under tail coverts; bill brownish-black; eyes dark brown; legs brown.

HABITAT: forests. HABITS: similar to other species, keeps mostly to forest canopy. BREEDING: August–December; nests in tree hollows and sometimes burrows, cup-shaped, made of grass; three to four white eggs. VOICE: clear high-pitched double note, the second syllable slightly lower than first. FOOD: insects.

STATUS: uncommon. TAXONOMY: endemic species; considered to be a primitive form of Spotted Pardalote stock.

599 RED-BROWED PARDALOTE   *Pardalotus rubricatus*   Gould 1838

Distribution: Map 213.

RECOGNITION: *white spots on black crown and tail but not on wing, scarlet and buff eyebrow, yellow rump.*

DESCRIPTION: 9cm. Sexes alike. Crown black with large white spots; lores scarlet continued

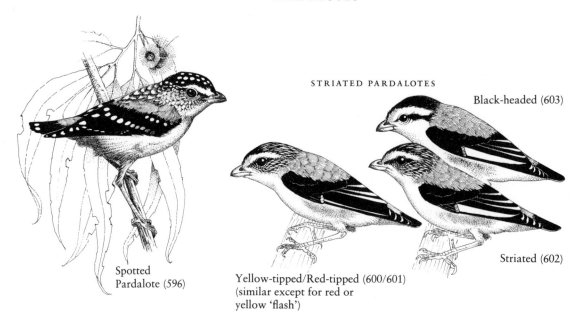

STRIATED PARDALOTES

Black-headed (603)

Striated (602)

Spotted
Pardalote (596)

Yellow-tipped/Red-tipped (600/601)
(similar except for red or
yellow 'flash')

as pale cinnamon brown eyebrow; back shades of greyish-brown to olive-brown; rump and upper tail coverts yellow; face and side of neck pale grey-brown; underparts buff-white with patch of bright yellow on upper breast and yellow under tail coverts; wing blackish-brown with large central area of golden-yellow; base of tail grey-brown, remainder black with narrow white tip; bill black above, pearly-grey below; eyes pale yellow; legs grey-brown.

VARIATION: southern part of range, upperparts greyish-brown (race *rubricatus*); northern part, except Normanton to Cape York, upperparts slightly darker and more brownish (race *parryi*); Normanton area, upperparts darker and with slight scaly pattern (race *carpentariae*); Cape York, upperparts darker olive-brown (race *yorki*).

HABITAT: trees along watercourses, also bushes and shrubs, especially in winter. HABITS: similar to Spotted Pardalote. BREEDING: mainly between June and February; nests similar to Spotted Pardalote; two to three white eggs. VOICE: repetitive phrase 'tweet, tweet-tweet-tweet-tweet' first syllable long and four short and fast; or 'pwer, pwe-ti-ti-tit' immediately answered by 'dee-dee-dee-di-di-di', three long and three short. FOOD: insects.

STATUS: common. TAXONOMY: endemic species; possibly intermediate between, or early hybrid of spotted and streaked groups.

600 YELLOW-TIPPED PARDALOTE *Pardalotus striatus* (Gmelin) 1789
Distribution: Map 214.
RECOGNITION: *white streaks on black crown, yellow lores and yellow wing 'flash'.*
DESCRIPTION: 10cm. Sexes alike. Crown black with white streaks; lores lemon-yellow continued as broad white eyebrow; back brownish-grey, browner on rump; face finely streaked black and white; throat yellow; sides of neck and breast pale grey-brown; centre of breast and belly very pale yellow; flanks buff-brown; wings black with central yellow spot and thin white streak and inner feathers edged with cinnamon brown; tail black tipped with white; bill black; eyes olive-brown; legs brown.

HABITAT: dry forest and woodland. HABITS: similar to Spotted Pardalote, actively forages in tree foliage, usually high up, sometimes in small flocks and in company with other species. BREEDING: August–December; nests in tree hollows, occasionally in holes in banks, shape variable, made of grass and tree bark and often feathers; four white eggs. VOICE: sharp persistent 'pick-it-up', or 'willyeu' or 'sleep baby'. FOOD: insects.

STATUS: common. TAXONOMY: endemic species; apparently interbreeds with Striated Pardalote.

601 RED-TIPPED PARDALOTE *Pardalotus ornatus* Temm. & Laug. 1826
Distribution: Map 215.

RECOGNITION: identical with Yellow-tipped Pardalote in most respects, including narrow white wing streak; differs in having *red wing 'flash'*.

HABITAT, etc: similar to Yellow-tipped; voice recorded as persistent 'wit-e-chu'.

STATUS: apparently common. TAXONOMY: endemic species; considered to be a species which has evolved from a cross between the Yellow-tipped and Striated Pardalotes.

602 STRIATED PARDALOTE *Pardalotus substriatus* Mathews 1912   Pl 18
Distribution: Map 216.

RECOGNITION: identical with Yellow-tipped Pardalote in most respects; differs in having *red wing 'flash' and broad white wing streak;* inner wing feathers broadly edged with white.

HABITAT, etc: similar to Yellow-tipped Pardalote, but frequents woodlands in more arid country; voice described as persistent 'wit-e-cheu' and in Western Australia as 'witta-witta' and 'be-quik' or 'pick-wick'.

STATUS: common. TAXONOMY: endemic species; interbreeds with Yellow-tipped and Black-headed Pardalotes.

603 BLACK-HEADED PARDALOTE *Pardalotus melanocephalus* Gould 1838
Distribution: Map 216.

RECOGNITION: like Striated Pardalote in many respects, including red wing 'flash' and broad white streak in wing; differs in having *crown and face black without white streaks, lores orange-yellow, rump cinnamon brown or yellow.*

VARIATION: south of broad band southwest from Cooktown to Ingham, rump cinnamon brown (race *melanocephalus*); north and west of band, rump bright yellow (race *uropygialis*).

HABITAT and HABITS: similar to other pardalotes. BREEDING: May–December; nests mostly in holes in banks, construction and eggs similar to other species. VOICE: loud sharp 'chip, chip-chip' and softer 'figaro' repeated monotonously.

STATUS: common. TAXONOMY: endemic species; *uropygialis* is sometimes regarded as a species; the two are connected by a relatively narrow zone of intergradation. This species also hybridises with the Striated Pardalote.

Family NECTARINIIDAE

Sunbirds

1(116) species

SUNBIRDS ARE CONSIDERED TO have fairly close affinity with the flowerpeckers. Their main stronghold is in Africa and numbers of species decrease towards the east. Only one has reached Australia, apparently as a recent colonist to the northeast Queensland coast where it seems to be creeping southward. Sunbirds, for the most part, are quite distinctive. They are relatively small, the 12cm of the Yellow-breasted Sunbird is about average; they have long thin decurved bills, sometimes serrated near the tip; they have tubular tongues, an adaptation for sucking honey. Insects as well as nectar are extracted from flower corollas, sometimes while birds hover briefly but more often while clinging to foliage. Sexes are different in plumage, males being brightly coloured, usually with some iridescent areas.

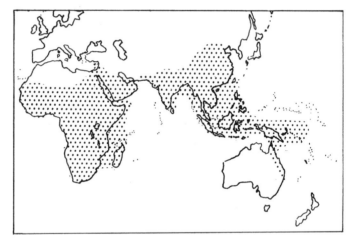

Distribution of NECTARINIIDAE

604 YELLOW-BREASTED SUNBIRD *Nectarinia jugularis* (Linnaeus) 1766 Pl 18
Distribution: Map 217

RECOGNITION: *bright yellow underparts, dark iridescent throat of male, long thin decurved bill; hovering and darting movements.* (Several small honeyeaters have thin decurved bills and Black Honeyeater at least hovers briefly and darts in flight—but none has yellow on underparts or iridescent throat.)

DESCRIPTION: 12cm, with slender decurved bill 2cm. Sexes different. *Male:* upperparts olive-yellow; chin to upper breast black with purple iridescence and edged with yellow on chin and throat; eyebrow yellowish; breast and belly bright orange-yellow; wings blackish-brown; tail black, outer feathers tipped with white; bill black; eyes dark brown; legs black. *Female:* whole underparts bright yellow.

HABITAT: mangroves, edge of rain forest. HABITS: arboreal, probes in flowers for honey and insects, darts from place to place, sometimes catches insects in flight, hovers briefly beside flowers or clings to foliage; solitary and sedentary. BREEDING: most months but mainly August–March; nests suspended from twigs of bushes and low trees, sometimes any convenient place in homestead buildings; hooded, with long 'tail' and side entrance near top; made of various fine fibres and bark bound with cobweb and lined with vegetable down; two to three eggs, greenish-grey mottled with dark reddish-brown. VOICE: shrill 'tsee-tsee-tsee-tss-ss-ss'. FOOD: insects and honey.

STATUS: common. TAXONOMY: race (*frenata*) extending to New Guinea of species ranging from Andaman Is to Bismarck Archipelago.

Family ZOSTEROPIDAE

Silvereyes

4(app 80) species: 2 endemic

Eastern Silvereye (605)

K̲NOWN ALSO AS WHITE-EYES and more frequently now by adopted generic name zosterops. The relationships of this distinct group are uncertain but in a number of respects they are like the sunbirds and flowerpeckers, and especially some honeyeaters with which they were at one time combined. The most conspicuous feature is a ring of white feathers round the eye. Plumages are otherwise undistinctive and in shades of dull green and yellow with areas of grey and white. They are relatively small, mostly less than 12cm, with thin bills slightly decurved and sharply pointed. Most species are in the genus *Zosterops* of which four occur in Australia. They are distributed round the periphery of the continent and

Distribution of ZOSTEROPIDAE

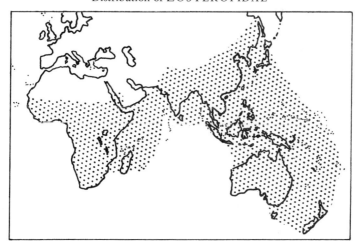

more or less replace each other. They live among trees and bushes but often feed on the ground. They have brush-tipped tongues with which they extract honey and fruit juice, but also feed on insects.

Key to ZOSTEROPIDAE

1 Back grey, crown and rump greenish .... Eastern Silvereye .... No 605
2 Whole upperparts dark green .... Western Silvereye............ No 606
3 Whole upperparts greenish-yellow 4–5

4 Underparts yellow .... Yellow Silvereye .... No 607
5 Throat yellow, breast and belly white............ Pale Silvereye .... No 608

605 EASTERN SILVEREYE   *Zosterops lateralis*   (Latham) 1801   Fig p 401
Distribution: Map 218.

RECOGNITION: *white eyering, grey back.*

DESCRIPTION: 12cm. Sexes alike. Crown and face olive-green; broad white ring round eye; lores blackish; back dark grey; rump and upper tail coverts green; throat lemon-yellow, sometimes grey in centre; breast and belly pale grey, shading to buff or brown on flanks; under tail coverts yellow; shoulders greenish-yellow; wings and tail blackish edged with greenish-yellow; bill blackish, pale at base; eyes shades of brown; legs grey-brown.

VARIATION: Tasmania (and non-breeding visitor on mainland from Adelaide to Brisbane), throat grey in centre and flanks brown (race *lateralis*); west of central Victoria, similar but flanks buff (race *halmaturina*); east of central Victoria and north to Mackay, whole throat yellow (race *familiaris*); north of Mackay, similar but under tail coverts dark yellow (race *ramsayi*); Capricorn Is, like *lateralis* but much larger (race *chlorocephala*).

HABITAT: various kinds of tree and bush associations. HABITS: arboreal, usually low down in trees and bushes, feeds among foliage while clinging like a thornbill; sometimes feeds on ground moving in short hops, occasionally in open country; solitary but gregarious when not breeding, sometimes in large flocks; movements not well known but apparently sedentary and nomadic with extensive north–south migration in eastern populations, especially Tasmania. BREEDING: September–February; nests in bushes and low trees, attached by rim, cup-shaped; lightly made of vegetable and animal fibres bound and decorated with cobweb; two to three eggs, pale blue. VOICE: warbling song of varied notes, high-pitched plaintive 'cheeu' and shorter 'chew'. FOOD: fruit and seeds, honey and insects.

STATUS: common. TAXONOMY: species extending to New Zealand and islands east to Fiji; the Western Silvereye is sometimes included.

606 WESTERN SILVEREYE   *Zosterops gouldi*   Bonaparte 1850   Pl 18
Distribution: Map 218.

RECOGNITION: like Eastern Silvereye but *whole upperparts dark olive-green; throat wholly yellow;* breast and belly pale grey; flanks pale buff.

HABITAT, etc: similar in most respects to Eastern Silvereye; breeding August–December in south, June–September in north.

STATUS: common. TAXONOMY: endemic species (or race of Eastern Silvereye).

607 YELLOW SILVEREYE   *Zosterops lutea*   Gould 1843   Pl 18
Distribution: Map 218.

RECOGNITION: like Eastern Silvereye but slightly smaller, 10cm; *upperparts pale olive-yellow;* base of forehead and *underparts bright lemon-yellow.* Mostly associated with mangroves.

VARIATION: east of Wyndham, colours brighter (race *lutea*); west of Wyndham, colours duller—upperparts slightly greyer (race *balstoni*).

HABITAT: mangroves, but wanders into adjoining country when not breeding. HABITS, etc: similar to Eastern Silvereye, recorded in small parties in mangroves and large flocks when wandering in coastal scrub; breeding October–March.

STATUS: common. TAXONOMY: endemic species.

608 PALE SILVEREYE *Zosterops chloris* Bonaparte 1850

Distribution: Map 218 (mainland records not verified).

RECOGNITION: like Yellow Silvereye with upperparts light olive-yellow, edge of forehead, throat and under tail coverts bright lemon-yellow; but *breast and belly pale greyish, darker on flanks and centre of belly white.*

HABITAT, etc: similar to other species; voice apparently not described.

STATUS: common. TAXONOMY: race (*albiventris*) occurring in southwest Coral Sea and Torres Strait, the most easterly population of species extending west to Indonesian islands.

Family MELIPHAGIDAE

Honeyeaters

70(170) species: 54 endemic

HONEYEATERS ARE AS NUMEROUS among Australian birds and as typical of the continent as eucalypts are of its plants, with the interesting connection that flowering gums provide an abundance of nectar at all seasons for the successful development of honey-eating species, and by assisting pollination the birds contribute to the success of the eucalypts. The brush tongue, which is the principal feature linking members of the family, is associated with the habit of eating honey, and also fruits or fruit juices—the Painted Honeyeater is a notable consumer of mistletoe berries. There is also similarity in bill shape (a more useful guide in the field). Bills are variants of the same basic decurved and sharply pointed pattern, very long in the spinebills, fairly short in the miners and decorated with 'knobs' in the friar-birds. But these features are not unique to honeyeaters and some taxonomists take the view that the family has not stemmed from a single source, as can be reasonably assumed in the case of many families, but that it consists of offshoots from various groups which acquired honey-eating habits and associated characteristics. The family as recognised at present consists of groups so diverse that they have earned separate names, like friarbirds, miners, wattlebirds and spinebills. There is greater range in size than is usually found in song-bird families. Some are as small as warblers, like the Grey Honeyeater at 10cm, or larger than magpies, like the Yellow Wattlebird at nearly 50cm. Plumage colours are mostly dull greens and browns but are often relieved by distinctively shaped patches of white or yellow on faces and necks, particularly useful in identifying members of the large and rather nondescript meliphagid group. But a few are quite colourful like the Scarlet Honeyeater. Honeyeaters belong to timbered habitats of various kinds. None is truly terrestrial or even takes to the ground for any length of time, except for the Singing Honeyeater in Western Australia. Most live in forests and woodlands and only a few, like the Singing Honeyeater, are adapted to arid country.

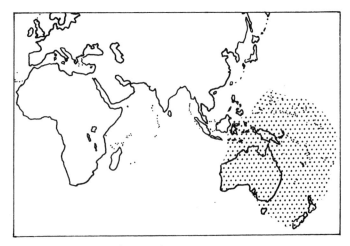

Distribution of MELIPHAGIDAE

Key to MELIPHAGIDAE

[*Note:* it is not difficult to decide if a bird is quite small or quite large, say less than 15cm or over 23cm. These two groups account for 28 and 16 species respectively. The remaining 26 are intermediate. They lie mainly in the size range 15–20cm, like the common and widespread Lewin and Singing Honeyeaters. On the whole this intermediate group is more likely to be confused with the small group, except perhaps the Regent Honeyeater (21–22cm) a distinctive black and yellow bird rather like a small rosella parrot but with a wholly black head. Additional keys are provided under general.]

Small: under 15cm
[*Note:* the word 'Honeyeater' is omitted.]

1 Bill relatively long
　　Head and throat black. . . . . Black . . . . No 615
　　Throat brown with black and white bibs . . . . *Acanthorhynchus* . . Nos 669–670
2 Head and rump red . . . . *Myzomela* (part) . . . Nos 613–614
3 Crown black, back greenish-yellow . . . . *Melithreptus* . . . . . . Nos 641–647
4 Shoulders with white spots, back blotched brown and
　　black . . . . Brush-throated. . . . . No 611
5 Dull brown with black bars on white breast. . . . . Bar-breasted. . . . . No 660
6 Black above, white below
　　Black breast band. . . . . Banded . . . . No 668
　　Wing with bright yellow patch . . . . Painted . . . . No 666
7 Greyish above, whitish below. Grey. . . . . No 665
8 Wholly dark greyish-brown . . . . Dusky . . . . No 612

9 Dull greenish-olive above, yellowish below.......... Green-backed........... No 609
10 Yellowish-olive above, yellow on face with black and
    yellow markings............................ *Meliphaga**........ Nos 617–640
11 Dull brownish above, mainly white below 12–15
12 Throat and breast pale grey-brown .... Brown.................. No 610
13 Throat brown, breast white .... Red-throated .... No 664
14 Throat white, breast dark brown .... Rufous-banded......... No 663
15 Throat white, breast pale brown.................... Brown-backed .... No 661

    * Four similar species, *fusca, flavescens, plumula* and *chrysops*, and the grey-headed *keart-landi*. The Graceful Honeyeater also fits here but it is a small edition of the Lewins and is included with them in the medium group.

Large: over 23cm

1 Face bare, purplish, bluish or blackish
    Crown black, back green....................... Blue-faced.............. No 648
    Crown brown or grey, back grey-brown .... *Philemon.*......... Nos 649–654
2 Brownish-grey above, whitish below, some black or
    yellow on head, bill yellow..................... *Manorina**........ Nos 671–674

    * Except Bell Miner (18cm) which is readily distinguished by bell-like notes, yellow bill and legs and all green plumage.

3 Upperparts brownish-grey, mottled or streaked 4–5
4 Streaked white on head and neck, no white at tip of tail Striped .... No 662
5 Upperparts mottled or streaked, tail tipped white,
    sometimes wattles on face .... *Anthochaera* ...... Nos 675–678

Medium: 15–23cm

1 Black and yellow, whole head and neck black, much
    yellow on wing and outer tail................... Regent................. No 667
2 Pied: white on breast and belly, rump and base of tail,
    broad streak on wing, remainder black........... Pied .... No 616
3 Several white streaks and patches on side of head,
    sometimes boldly streaked black and white, some-
    times bright yellow patch on wing............... *Phylidonyris*....... Nos 655–659
4 General colour greenish or grey-brown, often with
    conspicuous amounts of yellow, especially at edges
    of flight feathers; sometimes streaks on breast; head
    and neck often patterned in combinations of black,
    yellow and white .... *Meliphaga* .... Nos 617–640
    (Except White-gaped Honeyeater which is dull grey-
    brown without yellow and has white edge to mouth.)

Brush-throated
Honeyeater (611)

Genus GLYCICHAERA

One species belonging to New Guinea and apparently only represented in Australia by a population in the Claudie River area of Cape York. It is small and a rather nondescript olive and greenish-yellow, rather like a silvereye *(Zosterops)* but without white eyering. The feathers of the lower back are long and fluffy.

609 GREEN-BACKED HONEYEATER *Glycichaera fallax* Salvadori 1878

Distribution: Map 219.

RECOGNITION: *olive-green above, yellowish below; like silvereye but no white eyering; restricted distribution.*

DESCRIPTION: 12cm. Sexes alike. Face and upperparts light olive-green, darker on head; throat dull white; breast greyish-yellow; belly yellow; wings and tail grey-brown; bill pinkish-brown, darker above and paler below; eyes brown; legs blue-grey.

HABITAT: forest canopies. HABITS: little known except that it frequents canopies of high trees. BREEDING: not known. VOICE: not known. FOOD: insects recorded.

STATUS: not known. TAXONOMY: race *(claudi)* of New Guinea species; sometimes regarded as distinct species.

Genus LICHMERA

Two rather nondescript small species, one with New Guinea connections. The endemic species in Cape York may be an earlier colonist; it has inconspicuous yellow ear tufts and white spots on the shoulders.

Key to LICHMERA

[*Note:* the word 'Honeyeater' is omitted.]
1 Head and back blackish, white spots on shoulders . . . . Brush-throated. . . . No 611
2 Head and back greenish-olive, no white on shoulders . . . . Brown . . . . No 610

610 BROWN HONEYEATER *Lichmera indistincta* (Vig. & Horsf.) 1827

Distribution: Map 219.

RECOGNITION: *dull brown tinged with olive above and buff below, slight flash of yellow behind eye.*

DESCRIPTION: 12–15cm. Sexes alike. Upperparts dull olive-brown, greyer on head and blackish on face; black patch below and behind eye speckled white and tipped with yellow; throat and breast grey-brown shading to creamy-buff belly with yellow tinge; wings and tail dark grey edged with yellow; bill black, gape yellow; eyes reddish-brown; legs grey.

VARIATION: west of Barkly Tableland and Simpson Desert, larger (race *indistincta*); east, smaller (race *ocularis*); Melville I. birds also said to be distinct.

HABITAT: varied: mangrove, forest, woodland, thickets, suburban parks and gardens. HABITS: arboreal, feeds among flowering trees and shrubs, very active and restless, sometimes catches insects on wing; solitary or in parties or flocks; sedentary and nomadic. BREEDING: June–January; nests suspended in foliage of bushes and low trees, cup-shaped, compactly made of shredded bark and grasses bound with cobweb and lined with vegetable down; two white eggs lightly spotted with reddish-brown. VOICE: loud penetrating chirruping whistle, like Reed Warbler but less musical, also high-pitched buzzing 'zeet-zeet-zeet' frequently repeated. FOOD: honey and insects.

STATUS: common. TAXONOMY: endemic races of species extending to Aru Is and Indonesia.

611 BRUSH-THROATED HONEYEATER
Lichmera cockerelli (Gould) 1869   Fig p 405

Distribution: Map 219.

RECOGNITION: *blackish head and back, yellow ear-tufts, white spots on shoulders.*

DESCRIPTION: 14cm. Sexes alike. Upperparts mottled sooty-black and olive-brown, shading to dark grey on crown and forehead; face blackish finely speckled with pale grey; yellow ear-tufts and thin yellow streak at edge of throat; underparts mainly whitish, on throat and breast fan-shaped streaks of white on grey ground (edges of feathers on throat and foreneck hair-like); wings dark brown with row of white spots on shoulders and wash of yellow on flight feathers; tail dark brown edged with yellow; bill black; eyes reddish-brown; legs dark blue-grey.

HABITAT: tea-tree swamps and riverside thickets. HABITS: not well known: apparently in low vegetation and very active; possibly nomadic (recorded as plentiful in one area and then disappearing). BREEDING: January–May; nests low in bushes and small trees, suspended by rims in forks, cup-shaped, sparsely made of fibres bound with cobweb and lined with fine grass; two eggs, pinkish with dark spots. VOICE: noted as similar to Brown Honeyeater. FOOD: honey and insects.

STATUS: recorded as locally fairly common. TAXONOMY: endemic species.

Genus MYZOMELA

Only three of this group of about twenty-two species have reached Australia where they cling to the northern and eastern seaboards. It seems they have not been established long enough to become separated as species from similar populations in New Guinea. One is a non-descript dusky brown and the other two are among the most colourful members of the family. They replace each other in distribution and are divergent forms of the same stock which may have arrived as colonists from different sources or at different times.

Key to MYZOMELA

[*Note:* the word 'Honeyeater' is omitted.]

1 Upperparts red and black 3–4
2 Upperparts grey-brown 5–6
3 Head, throat and breast red . . . . (♂) Scarlet . . . . No 614
4 Head and throat only red . . . . (♂) Red-headed . . . . No 613
5 Underparts fawn brown, 14cm . . . . Dusky . . . . No 612
6 Belly whitish, 10cm . . . . (♀) Red-headed . . . . No 613
                                                              (♀) Scarlet . . . . No 614

612 DUSKY HONEYEATER *Myzomela obscura* Gould 1843

Distribution: Map 220.

RECOGNITION: *uniformly dark without distinctive markings—looks blackish at distance, like a very dark Brown Honeyeater.*

DESCRIPTION: 13–14cm. Sexes alike, but female smaller. Face, throat and upperparts dark grey-brown (dark drab), blackest in head area; underparts fawn-brown, paler on belly; bill black; eyes olive-brown; legs dark grey, soles creamy-yellow.

VARIATION: two races *(harterti* and *munna)* described respectively as darker and paler do not seem to be distinguishable.

HABITAT: mangrove and other swamps, forests and adjacent woodland. HABITS: arboreal, feeds at various heights among foliage, active and unobtrusive; solitary or in small parties; sedentary and nomadic. BREEDING: September–December; nests suspended in foliage of bushes and low trees, cup-shaped, made of fibres and grasses; two eggs, whitish freckled with shades of reddish-brown. VOICE: sharp 'chirp-chrip-chirp', also harsher notes. FOOD: honey and insects.

STATUS: fairly common. TAXONOMY: species extending to southern New Guinea, Aru Is and Moluccas.

613 RED-HEADED HONEYEATER *Myzomela erthrocephala* Gould 1840 Pl 19

Distribution: Map 221.

RECOGNITION: *small, about 10cm, male has crimson head sharply defined from dark back and breast; mainly mangroves.*

DESCRIPTION: 10–11cm. Sexes very different. *Male:* whole head crimson sharply defined from back and breast; lores black; rump crimson; remainder of upperparts and breast sooty-brown, shading to pale grey-brown on belly; bill black; eyes dark brown; legs dark grey, soles buff-yellow. *Female:* tinge of crimson on forehead and throat; upperparts grey-brown; underparts dull white.

VARIATION: races have been described but they are not well defined.

HABITAT: mangrove and similar coastal vegetation. HABITS: arboreal, frequently among low foliage, very active; solitary or in feeding parties; apparently sedentary. BREEDING: October–January; nests in trees, usually fairly low, suspended in foliage, cup-shaped, made of bark strips and fibres and lined with grass; two white eggs speckled with reddish-brown. VOICE: thin 'chirp' and harsh whistle. FOOD: honey and insects.

STATUS: fairly common. TAXONOMY: species extending to Lesser Sunda Is and southern New Guinea, closely related to Scarlet Honeyeater.

614 SCARLET HONEYEATER *Myzomela sanguinolenta* (Latham) 1801 Pl 19

Distribution: Map 221.

RECOGNITION: like Red-headed Honeyeater but *crimson on head of male extends to breast* and shades to pale creamy-grey belly, *back blotched red and black;* female rather more olive-brown with at most a tinge of red at base of bill.

HABITAT: mangrove, coastal forest and savanna woodland, at high altitudes in northern limits. HABITS: arboreal, actively feeds among foliage, usually high up; solitary but in flocks when feeding; sedentary and nomadic, especially in south, possibly migratory. BREEDING: similar to Red-headed Honeyeater. VOICE: tinkling bell-like 'clink-clink-clink'. FOOD: honey and insects.

STATUS: fairly common to common. TAXONOMY: race *(sanguinolenta)* of species extending from Celebes to New Caledonia; closely related to Red-headed Honeyeater.

Genus CERTHIONYX

Two black and white species of doubtful affinity are kept together in this genus; both are endemic and belong to the arid interior. Some taxonomists claim that the Black Honeyeater should be in *Myzomela* or in a genus of its own. Its identification as a honeyeater has been questioned. It could easily be mistaken for a sunbird by its hovering and darting flight.

Key to CERTHIONYX

1 Upperparts wholly black; 12cm................ Black Honeyeater .... No 615
2 Upperparts black and white; 18cm .... Pied Honeyeater .... No 616

615 BLACK HONEYEATER *Certhionyx niger* (Gould) 1838   Fig p 410

Distribution: Map 222.

RECOGNITION: *black head and upperparts, white belly, long bill, darting flight; like Yellow-breasted Sunbird but without yellow belly.*

DESCRIPTION: 12cm, relatively long pointed wings, and long bill. Sexes different. *Male:* sooty-black except for white belly, flanks and side of breast; bill, eyes and legs black. *Female:* upperparts buff-brown with most feathers, except on head, edged with pale buff; pale buff eyebrow; throat and breast pale grey-brown; belly dull white; bill and legs blackish-brown; eyes dark brown.

HABITAT: arid shrub savanna, sometimes up to forest fringe. HABITS: frequents creekside thickets and low bushes, even in arid stony places; very active, darts and hovers beside flowers; solitary but in flocks when not breeding; highly nomadic, disappears from locality for several years and then reappears; also tendency to north–south migration pattern.
BREEDING: variable but most records September–December (period for any pair very short); nests in bushes and low branches, shallow cup, loosely made of grass and twigs bound with cobweb; two eggs, buff-yellow speckled with reddish-brown and blue-grey. VOICE: faint plaintive 'peeee'. FOOD: honey and insects.

STATUS: uncertain; apparently fairly common. TAXONOMY: endemic species of uncertain affinity.

616 PIED HONEYEATER *Certhionyx variegatus* Lesson 1830   Fig p 410

Distribution: Map 223.

RECOGNITION: *black with white rump, shoulders and belly; relatively long bill; like White-winged Triller but has long bill and black throat.*

DESCRIPTION: 17cm. Sexes different. *Male:* head, throat and back black; rump, breast and belly white; wings black with broad white streak; tail white with central black streak and broad black tip; bill and legs blue-grey; eyes dark brown, bare skin below eye bright sky-blue. *Female:* upperparts grey-brown mottled with pale buff on shoulders; throat and breast pale grey-brown with short brown streaks; belly white.

HABITAT: arid bush savanna. HABITS: frequents bushes and thickets, rather secretive but active in flight, has distinctive aerial display, flies vertically, turns over and tumbles down with tail fanned; solitary or in small parties; highly nomadic with little evidence of migration pattern.
BREEDING: variable in period July–March depending on rains but mainly September–December; nests in forks of bushes and low trees, up to about 5m, cup-shaped, well made of

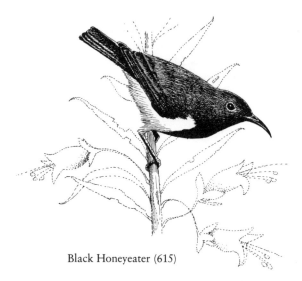

Black Honeyeater (615)

Pied Honeyeater (616) *display flight*

grass bound with cobweb; two to three eggs, white or pale buff spotted and blotched with dark brown and grey.

VOICE: piercing whistle, 'te-titee-tee-tee' uttered during display flight. FOOD: honey and insects.

STATUS: fairly common. TAXONOMY: endemic species.

Genus MELIPHAGA

This is one of the largest and most common groups of Australian birds. There are twenty-four out of thirty-six species of which twenty are endemic. One or several species occur in almost any kind of country from rain forest (Lewin Honeyeater) to arid heathland (White-eared Honeyeater) and straggling vegetation of inland deserts (Singing and Grey-headed Honeyeaters). Many species are common but several are rare, like the White-lined and Helmeted Honeyeaters. Members of this genus are medium-sized, about 15 to 20cm, and most are characterised by greenish-olive upperparts and whitish, sometimes streaked, underparts. Many have distinctive patches of bright yellow on chin and throat and especially as ear-tufts; an exception is the White-eared Honeyeater with white ear-tufts and black throat. The White-gaped Honeyeater is uniformly dull olive-grey except for an indistinct white edge to the mouth.

Key to MELIPHAGA

[*Note:* the word 'Honeyeater' is omitted.]
Crown more or less uniform with back

1 Plumage mostly yellow .... Yellow.............. No 620
2 White gape, no face or neck markings .... White-gaped.......... No 637
3 White streak below eyes
  Nape speckled white; Cape York .... Tawny-breasted....... No 638
  Nape not white; Arnhemland..................... White-lined .... No 621
4 Yellow streak on face, black ear coverts: tropical rain
  forest .... Mountain .... No 640

5 Yellow streak on face, ends in white tuft, black streaks
 above and below .... Yellow-faced .... No 630
 ⎧ Lewin .... No 617
6 Yellow streak below eye, large yellow ear coverts (see text) ⎨ Lesser Lewin......... No 618
 ⎩ Graceful .... No 619
7 Broad black band on face, yellow patch below.......... 10–12
8 Face plain, grey or black ear coverts tipped yellow or white 13–15
9 Dusky lores, dusky ear coverts tipped yellow........... 16–17

10 Throat buffy-white .... Singing .... No 622
11 Throat yellow................................... Mangrove........... No 623
12 Underparts yellow .... Varied .... No 624

13 Ear coverts grey tipped yellow...................... Fuscous............. No 625
14 Ear coverts black tipped yellow..................... Pale-yellow .... No 626
15 Ear coverts black tipped white...................... White-plumed .... No 627

16 Underparts clearly streaked .... Mallee.............. No 628
17 Underparts faintly streaked........................ Yellow-fronted....... No 629

Crown distinctly contrasting with back
18 Crown black, back mottled black and white .... Mottled............. No 639
19 Crown grey, back olive or green 21–24
20 Crown yellowish, face black 25–26

21 Broad black band through eye ends in yellow tuft ...... Purple-gaped .... No 631
22 Face black, dark grey ear coverts, yellow patch on neck.. Grey-headed......... No 632
23 Large white ear coverts, black throat................. White-eared .... No 633
24 Grey ear coverts tipped yellow, yellow throat; Tasmania Yellow-throated ...... No 634

25 Back dark olive, tail not tipped white................ Yellow-tufted........ No 635
26 Back blackish, tail broadly tipped white .... Helmeted .... No 636

617 LEWIN HONEYEATER *Meliphaga lewinii* (Swainson) 1808 Pl 20
Distribution: Map 224.

RECOGNITION: *dark olive green above, light yellowish-olive below, bright yellow ear-tufts; loud musical staccato notes; like Lesser Lewin and Graceful but looks darker than Lesser Lewin, mouth streak whiter and ear-tufts square in appearance; usually in heavier timber.*

DESCRIPTION: 18cm. Sexes alike. Upperparts olive green, blacker on crown and forehead; face dark with yellowish-white streak from angle of mouth to below eye and large bright yellow ear-tufts; underparts light olive tinged with yellow; wings and tail dark brown, feathers edged with lemon-yellow; bill black; eyes pale grey-blue; legs purplish-grey.

VARIATION: several races have been named but they seem to be of doubtful significance, except perhaps generally darker colouration in southern limits (race *nea*).

HABITAT: rain forest, especially in mountain areas in the north. HABITS: arboreal, feeds among foliage at various heights, active and bold; solitary; sedentary. BREEDING: August–March but mostly September–January in south; nests in thick foliage of trees and shrubs mostly between 2–8m, suspended by rim, cup-shaped with rather untidy external appearance, made of bark, leaves and moss lined with vegetable down and grass; two eggs, white spotted and blotched with shades of dark red. VOICE: penetrating musical staccato notes. FOOD: mostly fruits, also insects and honey.

STATUS: common. TAXONOMY: endemic species.

618 LESSER LEWIN HONEYEATER   *Meliphaga notata* (Gould) 1867
Distribution: Map 224.

RECOGNITION: almost identical with Lewin and Graceful Honeyeaters, *slightly smaller than Lewin,* about 16cm, also looks slightly paler, *mouth streak brighter yellow and yellow ear-tufts rounder* in shape; usually in open timber and mostly in coastal areas where overlaps with Lewin; *notes distinctive.*

HABITAT, etc: very similar to Lewin, they occur together but the Lewin is more frequently in mountain forest and the Lesser Lewin in lowland forest. VOICE: series of clear piercing whistles, each note rising to higher pitch. FOOD: similar to Lewin.

STATUS: common. TAXONOMY: endemic species.

619 GRACEFUL HONEYEATER   *Meliphaga gracilis*   (Gould) 1886
Distribution: Map 224.

RECOGNITION: almost identical with Lewin and Lesser Lewin Honeyeaters but clearly *smaller, 14cm,* also *bill relatively longer and more slender;* voice distinctive.

HABITAT: mostly open forest, sometimes rain forest. HABITS: similar to Lewin. BREEDING: October–February; nests said to be similar to Lewin, but eggs very different; two eggs, rich salmon pink spotted with dark chestnut and purple. VOICE: thin reedy whistle repeated slowly, or short 'click' or 'chip' or 'tick'.

STATUS: fairly common. TAXONOMY: species extending to southern New Guinea and Aru Is.

620 YELLOW HONEYEATER   *Meliphaga flava*   (Gould) 1843
Distribution: Map 225.

RECOGNITION: *mostly yellow, olive-yellow above and lemon-yellow below.*

DESCRIPTION: 17cm. Sexes alike. Upperparts olive-yellow; underparts bright lemon-yellow; dusky streak from base of bill through eye; wings brown, feathers broadly edged with lemon-yellow; bill brownish-black; eyes olive-grey; legs olive-yellow.

HABITAT: open forest especially along rivers and near coasts. HABITS: arboreal, active among flowering trees; solitary or in small feeding parties; sedentary, but fluctuating numbers in certain localities suggests nomadic movements. BREEDING: October–March; nests in trees and bushes suspended by rim from twigs, made of bark and palm fibre bound with cobweb; two eggs, white with pink tinge spotted with reddish-brown and grey. VOICE: loud clear whistling 'whee-a' or 'we-e-ear' or 'cheweer'. FOOD: honey and insects.

STATUS: fairly common. TAXONOMY: endemic species.

621 WHITE-LINED HONEYEATER*   *Meliphaga albilineata*   (White) 1917
Distribution: Map 225.

RECOGNITION: *like Lewin in general appearance but grey-brown with white streak below eye.*

DESCRIPTION: 18cm. Sexes alike. Upperparts grey-brown, darkest on head and neck; underparts dull white, whitest on throat and duskier on breast slightly mottled with grey-brown; broad white streak below eye from base of bill to nape; wings, brown feathers broadly edged

---

*H. L. White named the species White-stripe Honeyeater.

with dull greenish-yellow; bill brownish-black; eyes blue-grey; legs dark grey-brown.

HABITAT: deep wooded sandstone gorges and shrubby slopes. HABITS: arboreal, mostly in dense canopies of shrubs and trees; solitary or in loose flocks when feeding. BREEDING: October–January; nests suspended in outer twigs of trees and shrubs, cup-shaped, an open mesh of vine-like strands bound with cobweb and vegetable cotton; eggs not known. VOICE: loud clear flute-like whistle 'tu-u-u-heer, tu-u-u-in'. FOOD: fruits and seeds.

STATUS: apparently common in restricted habitat. TAXONOMY: endemic species.

622 SINGING HONEYEATER *Meliphaga virescens* (Vieillot) 1817
Distribution: Map 226.

RECOGNITION: *broad black band across face with conspicuous yellow patch below; like Mangrove Honeyeater but throat buffy-white, not yellow; widespread.*

DESCRIPTION: 17–18cm. Sexes alike. Upperparts buff-brown, paler on rump and sometimes tinged with pink; underparts whitish, whitest on sides of throat and on belly, tinged with pinkish-buff on centre of throat and breast, breast sometimes faintly streaked with grey-brown; broad black streak through eye from base of bill and spreading out on side of neck; yellow below eye and on ear-tuft which is tipped white; wings and tail brown, feathers broadly edged sulphur yellow; bill black; eyes dark brown; legs dark grey-brown.

VARIATION: southern populations roughly south of Rockhampton to Lake Torrens to Kalgoorlie to Geraldton, larger and darker with fairly distinct streaks on breast (race *virescens*); northern populations, smaller and paler with barely distinct streaks on breast and sometimes tinge of pink on rump (race *forresti*); other races on Rottnest I and Melville I.

HABITAT: variable, wherever there are trees or bushes, except rain forest. HABITS: adaptable, active and aggressive, usually low down, below about 2–3m and frequently on ground; solitary or small parties; sedentary. BREEDING: August–December, sometimes other months, especially in north; nests in centre of bushes or well hidden low down in tree foliage, suspended from twigs, cup-shaped, roughly and sparsely made of grasses and fibres bound with cobweb and lined with vegetable down; two to three eggs, pale buff or pink lightly spotted with reddish-brown. VOICE: loud clear trilling whistle, also squeaky 'queek' or 'sheek' or chattering 'cr-rook cr-rook'. FOOD: fruit, honey, insects, also said to take eggs.

STATUS: very common. TAXONOMY: endemic species, possibly having close affinity with Mangrove and Varied Honeyeaters.

623 MANGROVE HONEYEATER *Meliphaga fasciogularis* (Gould) 1854
Distribution: Map 226.

RECOGNITION: like Singing Honeyeater in facial pattern, but sometimes white line above black band, also *upperparts dark olive, throat and foreneck yellow (mustard) scalloped with grey-brown, larger, 18–20cm;* more or less confined to mangrove.

HABITAT: mangrove and adjacent thickets, one of the most 'marine' of singing birds. HABITS and BREEDING: similar to Singing Honeyeater. VOICE: flute-like 'wook-e-woow' or melodious 'whit-u-we-u', a series of ascending whistles ending in a flourish.

STATUS: fairly common. TAXONOMY: endemic species, possibly having close affinity with Singing and Varied Honeyeaters.

624 VARIED HONEYEATER *Meliphaga versicolor* (Gould) 1843 Pl 20
Distribution: Map 226.

RECOGNITION: like Singing Honeyeater in facial pattern, but larger, 20cm, upperparts olive-brown with rump and upper tail coverts tawny-olive tinged with yellow; *underparts yellow (mustard) streaked with olive-brown on breast and belly.*

HABITAT, etc: similar to Mangrove Honeyeater; nest recorded as of rather open mesh construction. VOICE: wide range of musical phrases.

STATUS: fairly common. TAXONOMY: race *(versicolor)* extending to New Guinea of species ranging throughout New Guinea and adjacent islands; possibly having close affinity with Mangrove and Singing Honeyeaters.

FUSCOUS AND PALE-YELLOW HONEYEATERS

Some taxonomists regard the Fuscous and Pale-yellow Honeyeaters as races of a single species. Their distributions are contiguous, with a disputed overlap in the Atherton Tableland, and the features of the Fuscous north of the tropic approach those of the Pale-yellow. But the characteristics of both seem to be clearly defined in the critical transitional area and current opinion is that they are separate species or semispecies of a superspecies. It is also possible that the Pale-yellow has as close or closer affinity with the White-plumed Honeyeater.

625 FUSCOUS HONEYEATER *Meliphaga fusca* Gould 1837
Distribution: Map 227.

RECOGNITION: *dull olive-brown, darker above and paler below, no facial markings except dusky ear-tufts tipped with yellow; like Pale-yellow but plumage not distinctly yellow.*

DESCRIPTION: 15cm. Sexes alike. Upperparts dark olive-brown very slightly tinged with yellow on face and forehead; dusky ear-tuft broadly tipped with bright lemon-yellow; throat and breast buff-olive shading to whitish belly; wings and tail grey-brown, feathers broadly edged with greenish-yellow; bill black sometimes with yellow base; eyes brown; legs dark grey-brown.

VARIATION: south of tropic, darker and more olive (race *fusca*); north of tropic, paler and slightly tinged with yellow on foreparts (race *dawsoni*).

HABITAT: open forest. HABITS: arboreal, active in tree foliage at various heights; solitary or small parties; sedentary and locally nomadic, with possible migratory pattern in south. BREEDING: July–December, also recorded other months; nests suspended in tree foliage at various heights, cup-shaped, made of fibres and grass bound with cobweb and lined with soft material; two to three eggs, salmon pink lightly spotted with reddish-brown. VOICE: musical 'kitty-lin-toff-toff-toff' or 'arig-arig-a-taw-taw'. FOOD: insects and honey.

STATUS: fairly common. TAXONOMY: endemic species, possibly forming species or superspecies with Pale-yellow Honeyeater.

626 PALE-YELLOW HONEYEATER *Meliphaga flavescens* (Gould) 1840 Pl 19
Distribution: Map 227.

RECOGNITION: like Fuscous Honeyeater in having plain face and distinct ear pattern—a *black crescent tipped with bright lemon-yellow*—but *plumage distinctly yellow, especially on forehead, face and underparts;* upperparts buff-olive; underparts buff-yellow, brightest on throat and breast.

HABITAT: mainly riverine woods and thickets, and adjacent open forest. HABITS: arboreal, in foliage at various heights; solitary or in loose flocks; sedentary. BREEDING: variable, but mainly August–December; nest and eggs similar to Fuscous Honeyeater. VOICE: loud clear 'porra-cheq, porra-cheu-cheu, chi-porra-cheu, porra-cheu-cheu-cheu', also combinations of short 'twee' (ascending) and longer 'twee' (descending); voice similar to White-plumed Honeyeater but phrases uttered faster and in lower tone. FOOD: insects and honey.

STATUS: common. TAXONOMY: endemic species (except for small population at Port Moresby), or semispecies with or race of Fuscous Honeyeater, but perhaps has close affinity with White-plumed Honeyeater.

627 WHITE-PLUMED HONEYEATER *Meliphaga penicillata* Gould 1837 Pl 19
Distribution: Map 228.

RECOGNITION: like Pale-yellow Honeyeater but with *black crescent-shaped ear mark, a narrow black base to broad white tips;* plumage various shades of greenish-yellow.

VARIATION: Murray–Darling basin, darker and greener—less yellow (race *penicillata*); western plateau, paler and yellower, especially on forehead, face and throat (several races, oldest *carteri*); Eyre Basin, intermediate (race *leilavalensis*).

HABITAT: woodland, especially along rivers and creeks. HABITS and BREEDING: similar to Pale-yellow; peak periods vary with locality and may occur twice in same area. VOICE: variable, some notes like Pale-yellow but slower and higher in pitch, also whistling 'chy-uck-oo-wee' rising and falling in pitch. FOOD: honey and insects.

STATUS: very common. TAXONOMY: endemic species, possibly closely related to Pale-yellow Honeyeater which replaces it in north, and possibly Mallee Honeyeater which more or less replaces it in south.

628 MALLEE HONEYEATER *Meliphaga ornata* (Gould) 1838 Pl 19 Fig p 416
Distribution: Map 230.

RECOGNITION: *dark streaks on dull white underparts, yellow ear-tuft, greenish-yellow crown contrasting with olive-brown back.*

DESCRIPTION: 15cm. Sexes alike. Dark olive-brown back contrasting with greenish-yellow face, crown and upper tail coverts; dusky lores; ear-tufts bright yellow; underparts buffy-white boldly streaked with dark olive-brown on throat and breast; wings and tail black, feathers edged with greenish-yellow; bill black; eyes dark brown; legs grey-brown.

HABITAT: woodland, especially mallee. HABITS: arboreal, active and pugnacious, displays by rising into air from top of tree and singing; solitary or in loose flocks, sometimes quite large; sedentary and nomadic. BREEDING: August–December; nests suspended in low foliage, made mostly of grass and unlined; two to three eggs, white or pink tinged, spotted and blotched with pinkish-brown and grey. VOICE: loud and clear and rather harsh. FOOD: insects and honey.

STATUS: common. TAXONOMY: endemic species, possibly related to White-plumed or Yellow-fronted Honeyeaters.

629 YELLOW-FRONTED HONEYEATER
Meliphaga plumula   (Gould) 1841   Pl 19

Distribution: Map 229.

RECOGNITION: very like the Mallee Honeyeater, with dusky lores, distinguished by *faint (not bold) dark streaks on breast* and by *blackish-brown base to yellow ear-tuft;* where both occur in mallee this species apparently prefers dense clumps of shoots among low trees and the Mallee tall open mallee scrub.

HABITAT: dry woodland, including mallee and mulga, shrubs and shrubby trees along watercourses. HABITS and BREEDING: similar to Mallee, but usually two eggs. VOICE: loud sharp 'it-wirt, wirt, wirt, wirt', wide range of melodious notes some like those of White-plumed and Mallee species. FOOD: insects and honey.

STATUS: fairly common. TAXONOMY: endemic species, possibly related to White-plumed and Mallee Honeyeaters.

Mallee Honeyeater (628)

Purple-gaped Honeyeater (631)

Yellow-faced Honeyeater (630)

630 YELLOW-FACED HONEYEATER   *Meliphaga chrysops*   (Latham) 1801

Distribution: Map 230.

RECOGNITION: *yellow streak below eye ending in white ear-tuft and framed in broad black streaks above and below; otherwise looks greyish, like Fuscous Honeyeater.*

DESCRIPTION: 15cm. Sexes alike. Upperparts dark olive-brown; broad yellow streak across face below eye ending in white ear-tufts and with broad black streaks above and below; breast buff-brown shading to grey-brown on throat and belly and brown on vent; wings and tail brown, feathers edged with greenish-yellow; bill black; eyes dark brown; legs dark grey.

HABITAT: forest and woodland, including mangrove and suburban parks. HABITS: arboreal, but said to feed closer to ground than most honeyeaters although usually sings from high stance; solitary, or small parties or large flocks; mostly sedentary and nomadic in north and mostly migratory in south, departing April–May and returning August–September (large migrating flocks frequently observed in eastern highlands at appropriate season). BREEDING: July–January; nests and eggs similar to others of this group, suspended in low foliage, two pinkish and speckled eggs. VOICE: loud musical 'chick-up' or 'quit-chup' repeated frequently. FOOD: insects, honey and fruit.

STATUS: common. TAXONOMY: endemic species.

631 PURPLE-GAPED HONEYEATER *Meliphaga cratitia* (Gould) 1842   Pl 19
Distribution: Map 231.

RECOGNITION: *broad black band through eye ending in yellow ear-tuft, yellow streak at edge of throat, olive-green above with grey crown, yellowish-olive below (purple streak on face visible only at close range).*

DESCRIPTION: 16cm. Sexes alike. Crown dark grey shading to dark olive-green back and rump, broad black streak through eye ending in yellow ear-tuft, purple or lilac bare skin (or wattle) extending as thin streak from mouth to ear, broad yellow streak at edge of throat; throat and breast pale yellowish-olive becoming paler and more yellow on belly; wings and tail blackish, feathers edged with greenish-yellow; bill black; eyes dark brown; legs dark grey-brown.

VARIATION: throughout most of range, as described (race *cratitia*); Kangaroo I, bare skin of face yellow (race *halmaturina*).

HABITAT: mallee and similar vegetation, sometimes suburban parks. HABITS: arboreal, usually in low branches and bushes, relatively inactive, confident and pugnacious; solitary or in parties or flocks; sedentary and nomadic, sometimes flocking in large numbers to suitable feeding areas. BREEDING: August–December; nests near ground, typical suspended structure with two white or pinkish eggs faintly speckled with red. VOICE: referred to as both pleasing and harsh. FOOD: insects and honey.

STATUS: fairly common but sparsely distributed in isolated populations. TAXONOMY: endemic species.

632 GREY-HEADED HONEYEATER
 Meliphaga keartlandi (North) 1895   Fig p 418
Distribution: Map 231.

RECOGNITION: *grey head contrasting with buff-olive back, blackish face with dark grey ear coverts, yellow throat and patch on neck.*

DESCRIPTION: 15cm. Sexes alike. Forehead and crown grey shading to buff-olive back and yellowish-olive rump and upper tail coverts; broad blackish band through eye ending in grey ear coverts which nearly obscure crescent-shaped yellow patch; underparts buff-yellow, yellower on throat and breast, which have slight dusky streaks, and near white on belly; wings and tail brownish-black, feathers broadly edged with greenish-yellow; bill black; eyes brown; legs pinkish-brown.

HABITAT: gullies in rocky hills of arid savanna. HABITS: lives mostly among bushes and low trees, apparently rather wary; solitary or small parties; sedentary and nomadic. BREEDING: variable, depending on rain, recorded most months from July to April; nests low in trees and bushes, usually suspended and often exposed but well camouflaged, like those of related species, made of bark and cobweb and lined with vegetable down; two eggs, white or pale pink lightly spotted with pale brown. VOICE: very loud 'kwoyt' or 'chee-toyt' repeated. FOOD: insects and honey.

STATUS: common locally. TAXONOMY: endemic species.

633 WHITE-EARED HONEYEATER
 Meliphaga leucotis (Latham) 1801   Fig p 418
Distribution: Map 232.

RECOGNITION: *dark green with grey head, black throat and large white ear patch.*

DESCRIPTION: 20–22cm. Sexes alike. Forehead and crown dark grey streaked black; remainder of upperparts, including edges of wing and tail feathers, dark yellowish-green; face, throat and foreneck black with large white patch on face behind eye; breast and belly pale greenish-yellow with bright yellow blotches, especially on breast; bill black; eyes grey-brown; legs dark grey.

VARIATION: eastern section, as described (race *leucotis*); southwest section, smaller and duller—less yellow in plumage (race *novaenorciae*).

HABITAT: open forest, mallee and heathland. HABITS: arboreal, at various heights but often near ground, wary, but bold when breeding and frequently reported to raid human heads for hair when nest building; solitary or in loose parties or flocks; sedentary and nomadic, sometimes irrupting into areas in large numbers, doubtfully migratory. BREEDING: variable in arid areas, otherwise mainly July–December; nests similar to related species but lined with wool or fur (or human hair!); two to three pink eggs lightly spotted with shades of red. VOICE: loud ringing 'chock' or 'chop' or 'cherry-bob'. FOOD: insects and honey.

STATUS: patchily rare to fairly common. TAXONOMY: endemic species, closely related to Yellow-throated Honeyeater of Tasmania.

Grey-headed Honeyeater (632)   White-eared Honeyeater (633)   Yellow-throated Honeyeater (634)

634 YELLOW-THROATED HONEYEATER   *Meliphaga flavicollis* (Vieillot) 1817
Distribution: Map 232.

RECOGNITION: like mainland White-eared Honeyeater but *throat bright yellow; ear coverts silvery-grey often tipped with yellow;* breast grey; belly pale olive tinged with yellow.

HABITAT: open forests and thickets, suburban gardens. HABITS and BREEDING: similar to White-eared in most respects including use of wool, fur or hair as nest lining; two to three eggs, pinkish-buff lightly spotted with chestnut red. VOICE: variety of melodious warbling notes, also loud 'tonk-tonk'. FOOD: insects and honey.

STATUS: common. TAXONOMY: endemic species, closely related to White-eared Honeyeater.

635 YELLOW-TUFTED HONEYEATER
  Meliphaga melanops   (Latham) 1801   Pl 20
Distribution: Map 233.

RECOGNITION: *yellow crown contrasting with dark olive-brown back and large black face patch, underparts mostly yellow; similar Helmeted Honeyeater has black back, white tipped tail and curled feathers on forehead.*

DESCRIPTION: 18cm. Sexes alike. Forehead to nape greenish-yellow; back dark olive-brown tinged with yellow; face and ear coverts black, ear coverts broadly tipped with golden-yellow; centre of throat blackish streaked with yellow; sides of throat and foreneck bright lemon-yellow extending as streaks on to darker yellowish-olive breast and flanks; centre of belly yellow; wings and tail dark brown, feathers broadly edged with greenish-yellow; bill black; eyes reddish-brown; legs blackish-brown.

HABITAT: open forest and woodland with thick undergrowth. HABITS: arboreal, usually in low vegetation, active and aggressive; sociable, frequently nests in close communities and forms large 'settlements' or scattered populations, also parties tend to 'cluster'; sedentary and locally nomadic. BREEDING: June–December, sometimes other months; nests in low vegetation, often secondary growth on old stumps and fallen branches, suspended, or placed on forks or attached to fern stems, cup-shaped, bulky and made of bark strips and grass and similar material and lined with feathers or vegetable down; two eggs, pale pink, usually spotted and blotched with rich pink. VOICE: melodious trill, harsh 'chop-chop'. FOOD: fruit, honey, insects.

STATUS: fairly common in isolated populations. TAXONOMY: endemic species, closely related to Helmeted Honeyeater.

636 HELMETED HONEYEATER *Meliphaga cassidix* (Gould) 1867 Pl 20
Distribution: Map 233.

RECOGNITION: like Yellow-tufted Honeyeater but *larger, 21cm, feathers of centre of forehead and crown erect and laterally compressed* and anterior feathers curved forward, *back brownish-black,* wing and tail feathers brownish-black with wing feathers edged greenish-yellow and all except central *tail feathers broadly tipped with white,* dusky line from centre of chin and throat curving round to ear coverts; also sexes slightly different, female having less distinct 'helmet', paler upperparts and lighter yellow underparts.

HABITAT: creekside trees and thickets in hill country. HABITS: similar to Yellow-tufted. BREEDING: August–January; nests and eggs similar to Yellow-tufted. VOICE: apparently also similar.

STATUS: rare, in scattered and apparently dwindling populations. TAXONOMY: endemic species, closely related to Yellow-tufted—the two species may not occur together but if reports of hybrids are correct there must be some contact.

637 WHITE-GAPED HONEYEATER *Meliphaga unicolor* (Gould) 1843
Distribution: Map 233.

RECOGNITION: *dull olive-grey with conspicuous white gape.*

DESCRIPTION: 18cm. Sexes alike. Upperparts dull olive-grey with greenish tinge on wings; underparts paler shade of same colour; face dusky with bare skin at gape white, becoming yellow at angle of mouth; bill black; eyes olive-grey; legs dark grey.

HABITAT: mangrove and riverine forests and thickets. HABITS: arboreal, active, aggressive and noisy, cocks tail; mostly solitary; sedentary. BREEDING: September–March or May; nests suspended from forked twigs at various heights, cup-shaped, made of bark strips and fine grass bound with cobweb; two eggs, pale pink blotched with dark pink, chestnut and purple. VOICE: loud flute-like whistle in several notes, meagre 'chip-chirp' like House Sparrow. FOOD: fruits, honey, insects.

STATUS: common. TAXONOMY: endemic species.

638 TAWNY-BREASTED HONEYEATER *Meliphaga flaviventer* (Lesson) 1828

Distribution: Map 233.

RECOGNITION: *dull brown with speckled nape, white and yellow streaks on face, large decurved bill.*

DESCRIPTION: 20cm, with decurved bill 2·5cm. Sexes alike. Upperparts olive-brown, nape flecked with pale grey and wing feathers edged with buff; broad white streak edged with black below eye from mouth to nape; narrow yellow streak below dark grey ear coverts from below white streak at mouth and joining it on nape—yellow streak begins as bare skin and ends as short silky feathers; throat and side of neck pale grey-brown; breast and belly olive-buff; bill black; eyes dark brown; legs dark grey.

HABITAT: mangrove and forest. HABITS: in tree canopy and substage foliage, active and aggressive; solitary or small parties; sedentary. BREEDING: November–February at least; nests suspended in foliage at various heights, cup-shaped, made of bark strips and fibres; two eggs, glossy pinkish-white speckled all over with chestnut. VOICE: (few data) loud noisy whistles. FOOD: fruit, insects, honey.

STATUS: apparently common locally. TAXONOMY: race *(filigera)* of widespread Papuan species, perhaps related to White-Gaped Honeyeater.

Tawny-breasted Honeyeater (638)   Mountain Honeyeater (640)

639 MOTTLED HONEYEATER *Meliphaga macleayana* (Ramsay) 1874   Pl 20

Distribution: Map 234.

RECOGNITION: *black crown and black and white mottled back, yellow ear coverts: rain forest.*

DESCRIPTION: 18cm, with decurved bill 2·5cm. Sexes alike. Forehead to nape olive-black, nape speckled with white; remainder of upperparts blackish-brown blotched and streaked with white and tinged with buff-yellow; lores and ring round eye light chestnut; bare skin below eye yellowish; from base of lower mandible to below eye and ear coverts brownish; ear coverts and pointed tuft behind bright yellow; throat pale olive-grey shading to darker on breast which is finely streaked with white and olive-brown and tinged with buff-yellow; belly blotched olive-brown and olive-black; wings and tail blackish-brown, feathers thinly edged with buff-yellow; bill black (gape white); eyes dark brown; legs dark blue-grey.

HABITAT: rain forest. HABITS: arboreal, in tree foliage at various heights, relatively inactive and shy; mostly solitary; sedentary. BREEDING: October–December; nests suspended in foliage at various heights, cup-shaped, made of fibres and leaves; two eggs, light pinkish-buff speckled with chestnut and violet grey. VOICE: musical 'chewit-che-wew' or 'tweet-your-juice' repeated quickly. FOOD: fruit, honey, insects.

STATUS: fairly common. TAXONOMY: endemic species.

640 MOUNTAIN HONEYEATER *Meliphaga frenata* (Ramsay) 1875

Distribution: Map 235.

RECOGNITION: *mainly blackish-brown, yellow base of bill and patch under eye together with small tuft above black ear coverts form almost continuous yellow band.*

DESCRIPTION: 19cm. Sexes alike. Upperparts blackish-brown darker on head and face; bare skin below and behind eye yellow; small patch of short feathers behind eye speckled black and white; small bright yellow tuft above black ear coverts; underparts greyish-olive, duskier on throat and paler on belly, an indistinct yellowish patch on foreneck; wings and tail blackish-brown, feathers edged with dull green; bill black, basal half bright yellow; eyes blue-grey; legs dark blue-grey.

HABITAT: rain forest. HABITS: arboreal, usually in canopies of high trees, aggressive; solitary or in small loose parties; sedentary and nomadic. BREEDING: September–January; nests in dense foliage, recorded low down, cup-shaped, made of tendrils and twigs and lined with vegetable fibre; two white eggs speckled with grey-brown and deep purple. VOICE: loud 'we-are' and 'wachita', and harsh notes. FOOD: fruit, honey, insects.

STATUS: common. TAXONOMY: endemic species.

Genus MELITHREPTUS

A distinctive endemic group of about seven species. Their principal feature is a blackish head with a white crescent on the nape, except for one species in Tasmania in which the crescent is lacking. Upperparts are greenish-olive to yellowish and underparts whitish. They are fairly small, about 13–15cm, and between them range over most of the continent. There are two species in Tasmania. The others consist of a southern species with sooty-brown head and two groups each of two forms which more or less replace each other and which might be either races or species. The units of each pair have approximately the same geographical relationship, a southeastern form extending into the territory of a northern one along the summit of the Dividing Range in Queensland. One pair, the White-naped and White-throated seem to have reached species status as has the Tasmanian derivative, the Strong-billed Honeyeater; whereas the Black-chinned and Golden-backed might be at an earlier stage of separation. But relatively little is known of how the units of each pair interact, or indeed about their general biology, especially breeding habits; some recorded as nesting communally, especially Brown-headed, White-naped and White-throated Honeyeater.

Key to MELITHREPTUS

[*Note:* the word 'Honeyeater' is omitted.]

1	Head grey-brown	Brown-headed	No 641
2	Head black	3–11	
3	No white on nape; Tasmania	Black-headed	No 647
4	White crescent on nape	5–11	
5	Throat white	7–8	
6	Chin sooty black, throat dusky	9–11	
7	Tip of chin black	White-naped	No 642
8	Tip of chin white	White-throated	No 643
9	Back bright yellow	Golden-backed	No 645
10	Back brownish-yellow	Black-chinned	No 644
11	Back brownish-olive: Tasmania	Strong-billed	No 646

641 BROWN-HEADED HONEYEATER

Melithreptus brevirostris (Vig. & Horsf.) 1827
Distribution: Map 235.

RECOGNITION: *grey-brown crown in east distinctive; in southwest crown darker but buff-olive underparts distinguish from White-naped Honeyeater, the only other species in region, which has pure white underparts.*

DESCRIPTION: 13cm. Sexes alike. Head and face shades of grey-brown with buffy-white crescent on nape; bare skin around eye greenish-blue or dull yellow (seasonal change); back olive-yellow shading to greenish-yellow on rump; underparts pale buff-olive, duskier on chin and whiter on side of throat; wings blackish, feathers narrowly edged with pale buff; tail blackish, feathers edged with greenish-yellow; bill blackish-brown; eyes brown; legs pinkish-brown.

VARIATION: east of Victorian mallee, head pale grey-brown with dark scallops (race *brevirostris*); extreme southwest to about Kalgoorlie, head sooty-brown (race *leucogenys*); Kalgoorlie to Victorian mallee, intermediate (race *augustus*); Kangaroo I, larger bill (race *magnisostris*).

HABITAT: variable, open forest to arid scrub, suburban parks and gardens. HABITS: in foliage of trees and bushes, active and unobtrusive but usually quite vocal; solitary or in small parties when not breeding, moving in close formation from one blossoming tree to another; sedentary and nomadic, doubtfully migratory. BREEDING: June–January; nests suspended from twigs in low trees and bushes, cup-shaped, made of bark strips and lined with fine vegetable fibre; two pink eggs sparsely spotted and with reddish-brown. VOICE: loud musical warbling song, also harsh 'chirp' or 'chick' in flight. FOOD: mainly insects, also honey and blossoms.

STATUS: fairly common. TAXONOMY: endemic species.

642 WHITE-NAPED HONEYEATER *Melithreptus lunatus* (Vieillot) 1802

Distribution: Map 236.

RECOGNITION: *black head with white crescent on nape; like White-throated Honeyeater but where the two species overlap the reddish-orange spot above eye is distinctive, black on chin.*

DESCRIPTION: 14cm. Sexes alike. Crown, face and nape black, black extending to level of lower mandible and on to tip of chin; white crescent on black nape (not extending to eye); bare skin round eye orange or white; back and edges of wing and tail feathers bright olive-green; chin black; throat white; breast and belly dull white; bill black; eyes dark brown; legs purplish-brown.

VARIATION: eastern populations, bare skin round eye reddish-orange (race *lunatus*); extreme southwest, bare skin round eye white above and pale blue below (race *chloropsis*).

HABITAT: open forest and thick woodland. HABITS: arboreal, keeps mostly to high foliage; solitary or in small loose parties; sedentary and nomadic, also migration noted along tops of eastern ranges. BREEDING: July–February; nests suspended in foliage up to at least 15m, cup-shaped, made of interwoven bark strips, grass and other materials, often bound with cobweb; two to three eggs, pale buff or pink dotted with reddish-brown. VOICE: rather harsh chattering 'sherp-sherp' or 'tserp' and single 'tsip' or 'tsit' repeated continuously. FOOD: mostly insects but also honey.

STATUS: common. TAXONOMY: endemic species, apparently closely related to White-throated Honeyeater.

White-naped Honeyeater (642)   White-throated Honeyeater (643)

643 WHITE-THROATED HONEYEATER *Melithreptus albogularis* Gould 1848
Distribution: Map 236.

RECOGNITION: very like White-naped Honeyeater but *white crescent on nape reaches eye, black of face extends only to level of upper mandible, chin white, bare skin round eye bluish-white;* back olive-yellow, yellower on rump.

VARIATION: throughout most of range, as described (race *albogularis*); Kimberley area, slightly smaller and paler (race *subalbogularis*).

HABITAT, etc: similar to White-naped Honeyeater, mostly in lowland in eastern Queensland; doubtfully migratory in extreme south; more extended breeding season in north—records from March to January; nests and eggs similar. VOICE: single high-pitched whistle on a rising note.

STATUS: common. TAXONOMY: species extending across Torres Strait to southeast New Guinea, apparently closely related to White-naped Honeyeater.

644 BLACK-CHINNED HONEYEATER *Melithreptus gularis* (Gould) 1837
Distribution: Map 237.

RECOGNITION: like White-throated Honeyeater but *centre of chin sooty-black shading to dark grey in centre of throat,* bare skin above and round eye pale blue, side of chin and side of throat white, breast and belly pale buff-olive.

HABITAT, etc: similar to White-throated Honeyeater, mainly in forest canopies, apparently fairly gregarious; breeding (not well known) recorded between July and February, nests suspended high up in tree foliage. VOICE: mostly described as loud, varied and melodious. FOOD: insects and honey.

STATUS: rare to fairly common. TAXONOMY: endemic species, perhaps conspecific with Golden-backed Honeyeater.

645 GOLDEN-BACKED HONEYEATER *Melithreptus laetior* (Gould) 1875 Pl 19
Distribution: Map 237.

RECOGNITION: very like Black-chinned Honeyeater but *upperparts golden-yellow*—bright yellow with olive tinge; *bare skin above and around eye bright yellowish-green.*

HABITAT, etc: apparently very similar to Black-chinned Honeyeater—but not well known; breeding said to be during and after rains, one example of communal nesting (five birds to one nest) recorded, one and two eggs noted, pale pinkish-brown with dark spots. VOICE: also similar to Black-chinned, loud melodious song and single sharp note.

STATUS: apparently uncommon. TAXONOMY: endemic species, perhaps conspecific with Black-chinned Honeyeater.

646 STRONG-BILLED HONEYEATER   *Melithreptus validirostris*   (Gould) 1837
Distribution: Map 237.

RECOGNITION: like mainland Black-chinned Honeyeater with black chin and bare skin round eye pale blue, but *back brownish-olive with yellow tinge on rump;* breast pinkish-grey and belly fawn; eyes dark red and legs dull orange.

VARIATION: population on King I has slightly darker underparts (race *kingi*).

HABITAT, etc: similar to Black-chinned but has distinctive habit of hopping up tree trunks and boughs noisily stripping bark in search of insects (hence alternative name 'Bark-bird'); solitary or in flocks. VOICE: loud 'cheep'. FOOD: mostly insects.

STATUS: common. TAXONOMY: endemic species in Tasmania, derived from mainland Black-chinned Honeyeater.

647 BLACK-HEADED HONEYEATER   *Melithreptus affinis*   (Lesson) 1839
Distribution: Map 236.

RECOGNITION: like other melithreptids but *chin and throat wholly black and black patch at side of breast,* bare skin round eye bluish-white; rather smaller, about 13cm, than Strong-billed Honeyeater (the other Tasmanian species) but with similar brownish-olive back.

HABITAT, etc: mostly similar to Strong-billed species but more in open forest and suburban parks, not a bark stripper, possibly more gregarious, even when breeding, which is in October–December, three eggs. VOICE: sharp whistle.

STATUS: common. TAXONOMY: endemic species confined to Tasmania.

Genus ENTOMYZON

The Blue-faced Honeyeater is placed in a genus of its own. It is a large and rather exaggerated edition of the Black-chinned Honeyeater. Many features and characteristics are similar to melithreptids, like digging insects out of bark as found in the Large-billed Honeyeater of Tasmania, and there is little doubt that *Entomyzon* has close affinity with *Melithreptus*.

648 BLUE-FACED HONEYEATER   *Entomyzon cyanotis*   (Latham) 1801   Pl 20
Distribution: Map 238.

RECOGNITION: *black head and throat with white bar on nape and conspicuous patch of purplish-blue on face.*

DESCRIPTION: 25–30cm. Sexes alike. Head, nape and face black, with white crescent on nape, sometimes incomplete, and large area of bare skin round eye, pale blue above and purplish-blue below; back olive-yellow; centre of throat and upper breast dark grey; side of throat and breast white, continuous with white lower breast and belly; wings and tail blackish-brown, feathers edged with bright olive-yellow, tail tipped with white; under shoulder black; centre of underwing varies from pinkish-cinnamon to white; bill pale bluish at base and black at tip; eyes pale yellow; legs dark green.

VARIATION: east of Normanton, concealed patch in wing pinkish-cinnamon and white nape crescent more or less complete; north of Normanton to Cairns smaller and bare face patch large (race *harterti*); south of Normanton to Cairns larger and face patch small (race *cyanotis*); west of Burketown, concealed patch in wing white, centre of flight feathers bright yellow and white nape crescent reduced to patches behind eyes (race *albipennis*).

HABITAT: open forest. HABITS: in tree foliage and bushes, bold and inquisitive, sometimes digs insects and grubs from bark; solitary or in small parties; sedentary and locally nomadic with some evidence of regular seasonal movements. BREEDING: June–January; nests suspended in outer foliage but suitable old nests of other species are frequently adapted, cup-shaped, made of bark strips and lined with grass; two to three eggs, shades of pink blotched and spotted with dark red and purplish-brown. VOICE: musical 'kerleep-kerlow' and harsh 'teew' or 'mew' frequently repeated. FOOD: insects, fruit, honey.

STATUS: common to very common. TAXONOMY: species with one race *(harterti)* extending into southeast New Guinea.

Genus PHILEMON

The friarbird group consists of about seventeen species centred in the northern parts of the Australasian region. There are six species in Australia, apparently fairly recent colonists from both New Guinea and Timor. Friarbirds are distinctive in appearance and have rather harsh or raucous voices. They are relatively large, 25–35cm, with drab brown plumages. Heads have varying amounts of blackish bare skin, wholly bare in the Noisy Friarbird or Leatherhead. Most species have a ridge or knob at the base of the upper mandible and curled feathers on the hind neck.

Key to PHILEMON

1 Face and crown bare	Noisy Friarbird	No 654
2 Face bare, crown feathered	3–8	
3 Bill without ridge or knob	Little Friarbird	No 649
4 Bill with ridge or knob	5–8	
5 Crown buffy	Melville I. Friarbird	No 650
6 Crown silvery	7–8	
7 Over 30cm		
Cape York	Helmeted Friarbird	No 652
Northern Territory	Sandstone Friarbird	No 651
8 Under 28cm	Silver-crowned Friarbird	No 653

FRIARBIRD BILLS

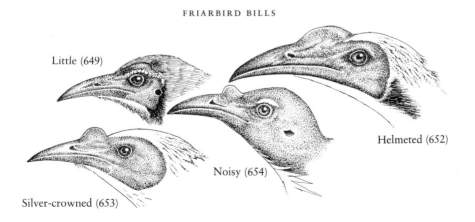

Little (649)

Helmeted (652)

Noisy (654)

Silver-crowned (653)

649 LITTLE FRIARBIRD   *Philemon citreogularis*   (Gould) 1837   Fig p 425

Distribution: Map 239.

RECOGNITION: *drab brown with stout curved bill (without ridge or knob) and bluish-black bare facial skin.*

DESCRIPTION: 25–28cm. Sexes alike. Upperparts dark grey-brown with dull white fringe on nape extending to wide patch on side of neck; bare facial skin blue-black; underparts pale drab, darker on breast and whiter on chin and belly, feathers of chin and throat hairy and silky, breast lightly flecked with white spots; bill black; eyes brown; legs bluish-black. (The *'citreogularis'* is descriptive of young birds which have yellow on foreneck.)

VARIATION: about six variants are currently named, based on slight colour differences and length of wings and bills; they are not well defined.

HABITAT: open forest and well-timbered woodland. HABITS: arboreal, in foliage of trees and bushes; solitary or in small parties; sedentary and nomadic with some indication of regular seasonal movements, especially in south. BREEDING: August–February; nests suspended in outer branches of trees and bushes, usually fairly low, and sometimes over water, cup-shaped, made of bark strips and fibres and lined with grass; two to four eggs, pinkish spotted with shades of reddish-brown. VOICE: loud 'ar-coo', also has musical song. FOOD: fruit, honey, insects.

STATUS: fairly common. TAXONOMY: species extending into southern New Guinea and adjacent islands.

MELVILLE ISLAND AND HELMETED FRIARBIRDS

It is now known that there is a second friarbird in the Arnhemland coastal area including Melville I similar to but distinct from the Melville Island Friarbird. It seems to be racially indistinguishable from *P. buceroides* of Timor. It is possible that there has been a double colonisation and that the Melville I Friarbird arrived first. As the two have not interbred it seems reasonable, as has been suggested, that the Melville Island Friarbird is a valid species. This creates some confusion in the use of common names. The name 'Helmeted' was first used for *P. buceroides* of Timor with a foothold in Arnhemland. It came into use for *P. yorki* when that and other forms were regarded as races of *P. buceroides*. *P. yorki* is now linked (race or semispecies) with *P. novaeguineae*, the New Guinea Friarbird, but as the Cape York bird is widely known as Helmeted Friarbird that name is retained. The race of *P. buceroides* in Arnhemland has been given recently the name Sandstone Friarbird and that is adopted.

650 MELVILLE ISLAND FRIARBIRD   *Philemon gordoni*   Mathews 1912

Distribution: coastal Arnhemland and Melville I.

RECOGNITION: like Little Friarbird but larger, 30cm, *bill has slight but distinct ridge, buffy-white band on hind neck has frilled appearance* due to feathers being curled; like Helmeted Friarbird but smaller, *crown buffy, facial bare skin blue-grey.*

HABITAT: mangroves. HABITS and BREEDING: relatively little known and information may be erroneous because of confusion with Helmeted Friarbird. VOICE: recorded as 'watch-out, watch-out' (first syllable stressed), also 'arrh-won-taw-thraw'.

STATUS: uncertain. TAXONOMY: endemic species, probably an early offshoot from Timor stock.

651 SANDSTONE FRIARBIRD *Philemon buceroides* (Swainson) 1838
Distribution: northern Arnhemland.

RECOGNITION: like Melville I Friarbird but larger, 35cm, *crown silvery, bare facial skin black;* distinguished from commoner Silver-crowned Friarbird by larger size and *whitish frilled band on hind neck.*

HABITAT: dense thickets in sandstone gorges. HABITS and BREEDING: not known except that seen in small flocks and catching insects in flight. VOICE: metallic 'chillanc' (stress on second syllable) and monotonous 'chunk-chunk'.

STATUS: unknown. TAXONOMY: race *(buceroides)* extending to Timor of species widespread in Indonesia.

652 HELMETED FRIARBIRD *Philemon novaeguineae* (Muller) 1842   Fig p 425
Distribution: Map 240.

RECOGNITION: general appearance like Little Friarbird but much larger, about 35cm, *bill has prominent ridge* and *head and neck mostly silvery-white* (feathers have arrowhead shape and are curled on nape) contrasting with drab brown back; very like Silver-crowned Friarbird but larger and bill ridge of different shape; facial bare skin dark grey (leaden).

HABITAT: forest and woodland. HABITS: arboreal, mostly among foliage, noisy and pugnacious, solitary or in small parties; sedentary and locally nomadic. BREEDING: August–February; nests suspended from forks in outer foliage, cup-shaped bulky structure loosely made of bark strips, fibres and grass and lined with fine twigs; three to four eggs, pinkish-white blotched with dark red and purple. VOICE: harsh 'poor-devil, poor-devil' and 'sergeant-major'. FOOD: fruit, honey, insects.

STATUS: common. TAXONOMY: race *(yorki)* of species extending throughout New Guinea and adjacent islands.

653 SILVER-CROWNED FRIARBIRD
  Philemon argenticeps (Gould) 1840   Fig p 425
Distribution: Map 241.

RECOGNITION: almost identical with Helmeted Friarbird but *distinctly smaller, 27cm,* and *bill ridge of slightly different shape* — a ridge ending in knob at basal end.

HABITAT: open forest and woodland. HABITS, etc: apparently very similar to Helmeted Friarbird, but only two eggs. VOICE: not defined other than noisy squawks.

STATUS: common. TAXONOMY: endemic species.

654 NOISY FRIARBIRD *Philemon corniculatus* (Latham) 1790   Fig p 425
Distribution: Map 242.

RECOGNITION: 31–36cm. General appearance like other friarbirds but *head bare and brownish-black* (hence alternative name Leatherhead) and prominent knob at base of upper mandible; chin and throat partly bare; sparse feathers on hind neck whitish and curled; feathers of foreneck and breast long and spear-shaped with dark brown centres.

VARIATION: roughly south of tropic, larger (race *corniculatus*); north of tropic, smaller (race *ellioti*).

HABITAT: open forest and woodland. HABITS, etc: similar to other friarbirds, aggressive, solitary or in noisy parties; sedentary and nomadic with some evidence of regular seasonal movements south of Queensland; two to three eggs, white to salmon-pink, blotched with chestnut and purple. VOICE: loud raucous 'four-o-clock' or 'chok-chok'. FOOD: fruit, honey, insects.

STATUS: common. TAXONOMY: species extending to southeast New Guinea.

Genus PHYLIDONYRIS

This genus now includes *Meliornis* and *Gliciphila*. There are five endemic species and two others in New Caledonia and New Hebrides. They range mainly in southern parts of the continent, including Tasmania, with isolates in the southwest, suggesting that the group is an old established one. The White-fronted Honeyeater is one of few arid-adapted honeyeaters. The species correspond in size with the meliphagids, about 13–17cm. Some have a conspicuous patch of bright yellow on the wing, patches of white on the face and some are boldly streaked in black and white.

Key to PHYLIDONYRIS

[*Note:* the word 'Honeyeater' is omitted.]

1 Forehead tawny, black streak through eye..............	Tawny-crowned	No 659
2 Forehead blackish, patches of white at sides of head and neck	3–8	
3 Face in front of eye white............................	White-fronted	No 658
4 Large patch of yellow in wing	5–8	
5 Broad black crescent at side of breast...................	Crescent	No 655
6 Plumage boldly streaked black and white	7–8	
7 Large white patch below eye..........................	White-cheeked......	No 657
8 Several patches of white on face, eye white	White-eyed.........	No 656

655 CRESCENT HONEYEATER *Phylidonyris pyrrhoptera* (Latham) 1801

Distribution: Map 243.

RECOGNITION: *broad black band on side of breast in front of shoulder, bright yellow in centre of wing, white streak above and behind eye.*

DESCRIPTION: 15cm. Sexes different. *Male:* face and upperparts sooty black; white streak above and behind eye; centre of wing and outer base of tail bright yellow; chin white streaked brown; breast white with broad black band at side; belly dull white; large white spot at tip of outer tail feathers; bill black; eyes red; legs dark grey. *Female:* dusky brown without white above eye, indistinct breast band and yellow of wings and tail much duller.

VARIATION: several rather indefinite races are currently named.

HABITAT: lowland and mountain forest with bushy undergrowth, light scrub with swordgrass. HABITS: among bushes and swordgrass, feeds actively; solitary or in fairly compact nesting groups, in flocks when not breeding; sedentary and nomadic with some regular seasonal movements. BREEDING: July–December; nests low down in bushes, swordgrass, fern clumps, made of bark strips and twigs lined with soft material; two to three eggs, pale pink spotted with dark red and purplish-grey. VOICE: loud 'egypt' repeated, and other shrill notes. FOOD: mostly insects, also honey and fruit.

STATUS: common (Tasmania) to mostly uncommon and patchy elsewhere. TAXONOMY: endemic species.

656 WHITE-EYED HONEYEATER

Phylidonyris novaehollandiae (Latham) 1790 Pl 20
Distribution: Map 244.

RECOGNITION: *like White-cheeked Honeyeater with bold black and white streaks on breast but has white eye (brown in juveniles) and white patches surrounding black face, white tail tip.*

DESCRIPTION: 18cm, with thin decurved bill 2·5cm. Sexes alike. Head and throat mostly black with white stipples on forehead, white streak above and behind eye, white 'moustache', 'beard' of scattered white hairs on throat; white tuft at side of neck; back brownish-black, streaked white on upper back and brown on lower; breast and belly boldly streaked black and white, mostly white on belly; wings and tail blackish with bright yellow patch in centre of wing and outer base of tail, outer tail feathers broadly tipped white; bill and legs black; eyes white.

VARIATION: throughout most of range, as above (race *novaehollandiae*); extreme southwest, bill stouter and longer and white moustache smaller (race *longirostris*); other named races not well defined.

HABITAT: woodland, heath, banksia scrub and swampy thickets. HABITS: mostly in thickets, perches high in trees, active and restless, sometimes catches insects on wing; solitary or in flocks; sedentary and nomadic. BREEDING: variable, nests in bushes below 2m, cup-shaped, loosely made of twigs and bark; two to three eggs, pinkish lightly blotched and spotted with dark red and grey. VOICE: shrill chatter and weak whistle. FOOD: insects, fruit, honey.

STATUS: common. TAXONOMY: endemic species, closely related to White-cheeked Honeyeater.

White-cheeked
Honeyeater (657)

White-eyed
Honeyeater (656)

657 WHITE-CHEEKED HONEYEATER *Phylidonyris nigra* (Bechstein) 1811

Distribution: Map 245.

RECOGNITION: like White-eyed Honeyeater in most respects but white on face consists of *white eyebrow* from lores to nape and *large white tuft below eye, eye brown, no white at tip of tail.*

VARIATION: eastern populations, bill smaller (race *nigra*); western, bill longer (race *gouldii*).

HABITAT, etc: similar to White-eyed Honeyeater but mostly favouring more open habitats and damper heathlands (both sometimes occur together and interbreeding has been recorded); dives with closed wings above nest site then glides to perch at top of bush. VOICE: whistling 'chip-choo-chippy-choo', harsh 'chak-a-chak', melodious 'twee-ee-twee-ee' or rapid 'hee-hee-hee'.

STATUS: mostly uncommon. TAXONOMY: endemic species, closely related to White-eyed Honeyeater.

658 WHITE-FRONTED HONEYEATER *Phylidonyris albifrons* (Gould) 1841
Distribution: Map 246.

RECOGNITION: like White-eyed Honeyeater with bold black and white streaks but distinctive white face pattern; *white band from forehead* (except centre) *to round eye, white moustache, white tips to grey cheeks;* inconspicuous red wattle behind eye; crown and nape blackish lightly scalloped with white; throat blackish speckled white; relatively little yellow in centre of wing.

HABITAT: arid woodland and scrub. HABITS: among tree and shrub foliage, seems rather more wary and elusive than relatives; sometimes catches insects in flight; solitary or in parties; mostly very nomadic, both from regular breeding areas and as wandering groups which settle temporarily to breed wherever conditions suitable, regular seasonal movements uncertain. BREEDING: variable; nests in bushes near ground, cup-shaped, made of bark strips and grass and lined with vegetable down; two to three eggs, pinkish-white spotted with chestnut. VOICE: varied; musical 'tsouee', or metallic 'tchap' or 'tsaap' or 'cheep', or harsh 'truk'; also mimics. FOOD: honey, insects.

STATUS: common. TAXONOMY: endemic species.

659 TAWNY-CROWNED HONEYEATER
Phylidonyris melanops   (Latham) 1801   Pl 19
Distribution: Map 247.

RECOGNITION: *tawny forehead, black band through eye continuous with mottled black band on side of neck and breast.*

DESCRIPTION: 15–16cm. Sexes alike. Forehead reddish-cinnamon; dull white eyebrow; blackish streak from bill through eye and continuous with mottled blackish band on side of neck and breast; upperparts grey-brown streaked blackish-brown in centre of back; underparts dull white; under shoulder reddish-cinnamon; wings and tail blackish-brown, feathers thinly edged with dull white on shoulder and dull yellow in centre of wing; bill black; eyes brown; legs grey.

HABITAT: scrubby heaths and mallee thickets. HABITS: mostly in bush foliage, restless and elusive but quite aggressive, sometimes sings from tops of bushes and makes sudden vertical flights; solitary; sedentary and nomadic, apparently with regular seasonal movements in some areas. BREEDING: variable; nests in bushes close to ground, cup-shaped, roughly made of thick twigs and grass and lined with vegetable down; two eggs, white or pale pink lightly blotched with dark brown. VOICE: musical flute-like notes; ventriloquial. FOOD: insects and honey.

STATUS: uncommon. TAXONOMY: endemic species.

Genus RAMSAYORNIS

Two small, 12cm, drab brown species lacking in distinctive head markings but having the unusual feature of barred breast, distinct in one but only faintly defined in the other. They are associated with wet tropical coastal habitats. The Brown-backed is a New Guinea species extending into Cape York, apparently unmodified; the Bar-breasted is endemic. They have the characteristic, unique among honeyeaters, of building a domed nest.

Key to RAMSAYORNIS

[*Note:* the word 'Honeyeater' is omitted.]

1 Breast boldly barred .... Bar-breasted........ No 660
2 Breast faintly barred; Cape York only .... Brown-backed ...... No 661

660 BAR-BREASTED HONEYEATER *Ramsayornis fasciatus* (Gould) 1843

Distribution: Map 247.

RECOGNITION: *small (12cm), drab brown above, white below with black bars on breast (almost like a small bronze cuckoo).*

DESCRIPTION: 12cm. Sexes alike. Upperparts dark grey-brown scalloped with white on crown and mottled light and dark shades on back; face dull white with thin black lores and black edge of chin; underparts white with broad black bars on breast and streaks on flanks; underwing pale cinnamon; bill dark olive; eyes reddish-brown; legs dull red.

HABITAT: paperbark swamps and adjacent savanna woodland. HABITS: among tree foliage, relatively inactive and wary; solitary or in small parties; sedentary and nomadic, depending on flowering *Melaleuca*. BREEDING: October–March; nests suspended among tree foliage, often over water, dome-shaped with side entrance, made of bark strips and leaves and decorated with pieces of paperbark; three to four eggs, white blotched with reddish-brown. VOICE: sharp high-pitched piping rapidly repeated. FOOD: insects and honey.

STATUS: fairly common. TAXONOMY: endemic species.

Noisy Miner (672)

Bar-breasted
Honeyeater (660)

661 BROWN-BACKED HONEYEATER *Ramsayornis modestus* (Gray) 1858

Distribution: Map 248.

RECOGNITION: *mainly drab brown and featureless; coastal swamps of extreme northeast.*
DESCRIPTION: 11cm. Sexes alike. Face and upperparts buff-brown mottled with darker shades on head and back; thin dull white streak or spot below eye; underparts dull white with faint buff-brown bars on breast and streaks on flanks; underwing pale cinnamon; bill brown; eyes reddish-brown; legs pinkish-brown.
HABITAT: mangrove and tea-tree swamps and adjacent woodland. HABITS: among foliage, solitary breeding or in loose colonies, in small parties at other times; movements not well known but apparently breeding visitor only in south, August–May. BREEDING September–February; nests and eggs similar to Bar-breasted but two to three eggs. VOICE: rapidly repeated 'chit' or 'mick' and chattering 'shee-shee-shee'. FOOD: insects, honey.
STATUS: uncertain but at least fairly common. TAXONOMY: species extending to southern and western New Guinea.

Genus PLECTORHYNCHA

The endemic Striped Honeyeater stands out as a distinct species without obvious connections. Since its discovery it has been kept in a genus of its own. It is relatively large (20–23cm), has foreparts boldly streaked in black and white, is usually solitary and rather noisy.

662 STRIPED HONEYEATER *Plectorhyncha lanceolata* Gould 1838

Distribution: Map 249.

RECOGNITION: *large with black and white streaks on crown and back, white below.*
DESCRIPTION: 20–23cm. Sexes alike. Crown, face and upper back mixed white, pale grey and black, as streaks on crown and face and mottled on back; remainder of upperparts brownish-grey; underparts dull white tinged with buff on belly; on throat and upper breast feathers are long and spiky (lanceolate) with pure white centres, and remainder of underparts have scattered thin brown streaks; bill and legs bluish-black; eyes brown.
HABITAT: woodland, forest, sometimes mangroves. HABITS: among foliage at various heights, sings while hidden in high canopy; usually solitary, rarely in flocks; sedentary and nomadic.
BREEDING: August–January; nests suspended from foliage, cup-shaped, made of grass and fibres and sparingly lined with fine grass; three to four eggs, white evenly speckled with reddish-brown and grey. VOICE: loud and melodious 'chirp-chirp-cherry-cherry'. FOOD: insects, honey.
STATUS: fairly common. TAXONOMY: endemic species.

Genus CONOPOPHILA

An odd collection of four small species (10–15cm), endemic except for the extension of the Rufous-banded into New Guinea and Aru Is. Gould made a separate genus for the Rufous-banded and Red-throated Honeyeaters which have some characteristics in common but are not readily associated with other species. Recently the Grey and Painted Honeyeaters have been added, a course perhaps not widely acceptable. Some claim that the Grey Honey-eater has affinity with silvereyes (Zosteropidae) of which it may be an arid-adapted form.

Key to CONOPOPHILA

[*Note:* the word 'Honeyeater' is omitted.]

1 Throat brownish, breast white......................... Red-throated .... No 664
2 Throat white, breast brownish......................... Rufous-banded...... No 663
3 Underparts white 4–5
4 Black above, yellow patch in wing .... Painted .... No 666
5 Grey above, no yellow in wing......................... Grey .... No 665

663 RUFOUS-BANDED HONEYEATER *Conopophila albogularis* (Gould) 1843
Distribution: Map 250.

RECOGNITION: *reddish-brown breast on white underparts, grey head, bright yellow in centre of wing.*

DESCRIPTION: 12cm. Sexes alike. Crown and face dark grey; remainder of upperparts dark fawn with centre of wing and outer base of tail bright lemon-yellow; throat white; upper breast reddish-brown shading to white on lower breast, belly and flanks; bill dark grey; eyes bright reddish-brown; legs bluish-grey.

HABITAT: mangrove and swamp thickets. HABITS: flits actively among foliage picking insects from leaves and twigs, sometimes catches them in flight; solitary or in small parties; movements not well known but apparently nomadic. BREEDING: October–February; nests usually cup-shaped structures suspended from twig forks; three eggs, white speckled with chestnut. VOICE: thin 'zwee, whit-chi ti' and hard 'zwee' (New Guinea data). FOOD: mostly insects.

STATUS: fairly common. TAXONOMY: species extending to southern New Guinea and Aru Is; Australian populations doubtfully distinct.

664 RED-THROATED HONEYEATER
    Conopophila rufogularis (Gould) 1843   Pl 19
Distribution: Map 251.

RECOGNITION: *reddish-brown throat, bright yellow in centre of wing, crown brown like back (not grey).*

DESCRIPTION: 12cm. Sexes alike. Upperparts fawn, buffier on rump; bright lemon-yellow in centre of wing; face greyish-fawn, greyer at edge of throat; chin and centre of throat reddish-brown; remainder of underparts buffy-white; bill and legs dark grey; eyes olive-grey.

HABITAT: forest and woodland, especially along rivers and creeks. HABITS: among foliage; solitary or in small parties; catches insects on wing low over water; sedentary and nomadic, sometimes with regular seasonal pattern. BREEDING: October–March or later; nests suspended in low foliage at various heights, made of bark and vegetable down and lined with grass; two to three eggs, pinkish-white spotted with dark reddish-brown. VOICE: rasping chatter. FOOD: mainly insects, also honey and fruit.

STATUS: common. TAXONOMY: endemic species.

665 GREY HONEYEATER *Conopophila whitei* (North) 1910   Pl 19
Distribution: Map 252.

RECOGNITION: *small, grey-brown above and whitish below. Very like White-tailed Warbler (488) with which it may be in company, but does not have white eyebrow or white base of tail. Also looks and behaves like silvereye but has only faint grey eyering.*

DESCRIPTION: 11cm. Sexes alike. Face and upperparts grey-brown; faint ash-grey eyering; wing feathers brown edged with olive-yellow; tail dark brown tipped white; underparts dull white, darker on throat and breast; bill and legs black; eyes brown.

HABITAT: arid scrub. HABITS: not well known; recorded as occurring in company with warblers and thornbills. BREEDING: one nest recorded, suspended from tip of low branch, roughly made of horsehair and cobweb; two eggs, white spotted reddish-brown and purplish-grey. VOICE: no certain information. FOOD: known to eat mistletoe berries.

STATUS: apparently rare, but readily overlooked. TAXONOMY: endemic species, affinities still uncertain.

Painted Honeyeater (666)

666 PAINTED HONEYEATER *Conopophila picta* (Gould) 1838

Distribution: Map 252.

RECOGNITION: *black above with bright yellow in centre of wing and base of tail, white below, pinkish bill; associated with mistletoe.*

DESCRIPTION: 15cm. Sexes different. *Male:* face and upperparts jet black, with small patch of white on side of neck, centre of wing bright yellow and inner feathers edged with white, outer base of tail bright yellow; underparts white lightly flecked with black streaks on breast and flanks; bill bright pink tipped brown; eyes light brown; legs black. *Female:* dark areas brownish-black; no black flecks on white underparts.

HABITAT: open forest and woodland. HABITS: usually in trees parasitised with mistletoe, makes distinctive erratic flight above trees; solitary or small family parties or groups of ten to twenty; movements not well understood but irregular occurrences suggest nomadic breeding, selected sites varying according to availability of mistletoe berries. BREEDING: records in period October–March; nests well hidden among outer foliage at about 3–20m, cup-shaped, sparsely made of fibres and grass bound among leaves with cobweb; two eggs, salmon pink speckled with reddish-brown and lilac. VOICE: sing-song whistle 'et-tee' or 'tort-tee' or 'george-eee' mostly uttered in flight, also prattling 'kow-kow-kow'. FOOD: mistletoe berries, perhaps insects.

STATUS: uncertain. TAXONOMY: endemic species; affinities still uncertain.

Genus XANTHOMYZA

The unique features of the endemic Regent Honeyeater has earned for it a genus of its own. In size and distant appearance of boldly mottled black and yellow, it looks rather like a platycercine parrot, but it has a black head, warty face and typical honeyeater bill. In many places it occurs sporadically and seems to be a nomadic breeder.

667 REGENT HONEYEATER *Xanthomyza phrygia* (Shaw) 1794   Pl 20
Distribution: Map 253.

RECOGNITION: *boldly marked in black and yellow, black head and neck.*

DESCRIPTION: 22cm. Sexes alike. Head and neck black; large area of bare warty yellow skin round eye; back and breast mottled black and pale lemon-yellow; belly and under tail coverts pale lemon-yellow; wings and tail black with yellow tips to shoulder feathers, yellow edges to inner wing feathers, yellow centre to outer wing feathers and yellow outer web of all but central pair of tail feathers; bill black; eyes reddish-brown; legs dark grey-brown.

HABITAT: open forest and woodland. HABITS: among tree foliage, sometimes catches insects in flight; solitary or small parties or flocks; highly nomadic even in selection of breeding localities. BREEDING: August–January; nests in trees about 1–8m, in forked branches in dense foliage, cup-shaped, made of bark strips bound with cobweb and lined with soft material; two to three eggs, rich reddish-brown spotted with darker shades. VOICE: tinkling notes, like Bell Miner but softer and less explosive, often 'tink, tink-tink', the rapid double note being in lower tone. FOOD: honey and insects.

STATUS: fairly common. TAXONOMY: endemic species.

Genus CISSOMELA

The endemic Banded Honeyeater has long been placed in company with the Scarlet and Red-headed Honeyeaters in the genus *Myzomela,* but current taxonomic opinion is that it should be on its own and removed to this distant position in the family sequence. The significance of certain plumages is not known. When Gould described the species in 1841 he wrote that birds whose backs were of a 'ferruginous hue' were probably juveniles and perhaps adult females.

668 BANDED HONEYEATER *Cissomela pectoralis* (Gould) 1841   Pl 19
Distribution: Map 253.

RECOGNITION: *mostly black above with white rump, sometimes patches of fawn or cinnamon brown on back; white below with narrow black breast band.*

DESCRIPTION: 12cm. Sexual differences, if any, not clear. Adult plumages of both sexes as follows: face above eye, and upperparts black with rump and upper tail coverts white; face below eye, side of neck and underparts white with narrow black band on upper breast continuous with black back; bill and legs black; eyes blackish-brown. *Immature:* face above eye and crown dark umber brown; back, wings and tail paler brown; yellow patch behind eye; underparts creamy-white with faint dusky breast band.

HABITAT: forest and woodland. HABITS: among foliage, active and aggressive; solitary or in parties or flocks, has been recorded in very large numbers in restricted areas; mostly nomadic, possibly wander to select breeding localities. BREEDING: October–April; nests suspended in foliage, sometimes near ground, cup-shaped, sparsely made of bark strips and tendrils bound with cobweb and lined with soft material; two eggs, pale reddish-buff darker at thick end. VOICE: tinkling twitter. FOOD: honey, insects, blossom.

STATUS: apparently common. TAXONOMY: endemic species of uncertain affinity.

Genus ACANTHORHYNCHUS

The typical awl-shaped honeyeater bill attains its greatest length in the spinebills. This feature and distinctive plumage patterns have relegated them to a genus of their own. They are endemic. The general similarity of the two species and their isolated distributions suggest that they are remnant populations of a once widespread stock. If they are, then their differences, which are quite marked, illustrate the changes which can take place in a relatively short period.

Key to ACANTHORHYNCHUS

1 Crown brown, white eyebrow; west.................... Western Spinebill.... No 670
2 Head and face black; east............................ Eastern Spinebill .... No 669

669 EASTERN SPINEBILL *Acanthorhynchus tenuirostris* (Latham) 1801
Distribution: Map 254.

RECOGNITION: *long thin bill, black head and black band at side of breast, white throat with brown centre.*

DESCRIPTION: 12–15cm, with bill 2·5cm. Sexes slightly different. *Male:* head and face to below eye jet black, more or less continuous with broad black crescent-shaped band on side of breast; narrow cinnamon brown collar shading to grey-brown back; inner wing, rump and upper tail coverts grey; lower face and chin to breast white with large patch in centre of throat reddish-brown to dark umber at lower margin; belly and under tail coverts cinnamon-buff; wings and tail black; outer tail feathers broadly tipped with white; bill black; eyes bright red; legs blackish-brown. *Female:* forehead and crown dark grey, and generally duller.

VARIATION: seven variants currently named on slight differences in size and colour shades, e.g. Tasmania, smaller and much darker (race *dubius*); north Queensland, paler below with less distinct throat patch (race *cairnensis*); South Australia, smaller with head and underparts lighter (race *loftyi*).

HABITAT: from rain forest to heath and suburban gardens. HABITS: among foliage at various heights, active, restless; swift erratic flight with wings making distinct 'frip-frip' sound, hovers beside flowers; solitary or gregarious; sedentary and nomadic with some indication of regular seasonal movements. BREEDING: October–January; nests suspended in foliage of bushes or small trees, cup-shaped, made of bark strips and lined with hair and feathers; two to three eggs, pale buff spotted with chestnut. VOICE: shrill clear whistle, repeated; also soft 'chee-chee-chee'. FOOD: insects and honey.

STATUS: common. TAXONOMY: endemic species; possibly forming superspecies with Western Spinebill.

670 WESTERN SPINEBILL *Acanthorhynchus superciliosus* Gould 1837   Pl 19
Distribution: Map 254.

RECOGNITION: *long bill, brown throat and collar, black band through eye bordered with white.*

DESCRIPTION: 14cm. Sexes different. *Male:* upperparts dark grey-brown with broad cinnamon brown collar joined to brown throat and foreneck; black band through eye with white streak above and white below from edge of throat to chin; brown foreneck bordered with white then black crescentic bands; belly pinkish-buff; outer tail feathers white; bill black; eyes red; legs grey. *Female:* duller; lacks cinnamon collar; underparts wholly pale pinkish-buff with white throat.

HABITAT: woodland and thickets. HABITS: in foliage, often frequenting flowering banksias, explores dead trees for insects, darts restlessly with erratic flight; solitary or in flocks, sometimes congregating in large numbers where food is plentiful; sedentary and nomadic. BREEDING: August–December; nests suspended in foliage below about 5m, cup-shaped, compactly made of bark strips and twigs bound with cobweb and lined with vegetable down; two eggs, white or pale buff spotted with chestnut. VOICE: rather weak 'kleat-kleat'. FOOD: honey and insects.

STATUS: common. TAXONOMY: endemic species; possibly forming superspecies with Eastern Spinebill.

Genus MANORINA

At one time the genus consisted of the Bell Miner but now the Noisy Miner group, recently *Myzantha*, is included. All are endemic. They have in common at least bright yellow bills and legs. Also they are noisily vocal but the tinkling notes of the Bell Miner are one of the most agreeable and unmistakable sounds of southeastern forests. Species of the Noisy Miner group are very alike and stem from the same recent stock but the course and extent of their divergence is not entirely clear. A dark form in a restricted area of the eastern mallee is sometimes linked as a species, Dusky Miner, with a similar dark form in the extreme southwest. Current opinion places the latter as a race of the widespread White-rumped Miner and the former as a species on its own, Black-eared Miner.

Key to MANORINA

1 Mainly green	Bell Miner	No 671
2 Mainly grey and white	3–6	
3 Crown black, forehead white	Noisy Miner	No 672
4 Crown grey, forehead yellowish	5–6	
5 Rump paler than back, mostly white	White-rumped Miner	No 673
6 Rump uniform with back	Black-eared Miner	No 674

671 BELL MINER *Manorina melanophrys* (Latham) 1801   Pl 20

Distribution: Map 255.

RECOGNITION: *tinkling notes, bright yellow bill and legs, olive-green plumage.*

DESCRIPTION: 18cm. Sexes alike. Upperparts mainly dark yellowish-green (olive-green); forehead and edge of throat blackish; lores bright yellow; bare skin below and behind eye orange-red; underparts light greenish-yellow; wings dark brown, outer feathers edged with grey and inner with greenish-yellow; bill and legs bright yellow; eyes dark brown.

HABITAT: dry sclerophyll forest. HABITS: arboreal, often in bushes and saplings, clings to foliage searching under leaves for lerps and other insects, active and aggressive, sidles along branches with head lowered and bill pointing up at another bird; gregarious and sedentary, forms colonies which remain in one small area for many years. BREEDING: July–February; nests suspended from forks in low foliage, cup-shaped, an open mesh of interwoven grass and twigs bound with cobweb and lined with soft material; two to three eggs, pinkish-brown spotted with shades of dark brown and grey. VOICE: a squeaky 'tink', in a colony sounding like a perpetual carillon of fairy bells; also various harsher notes. FOOD: insects mainly, especially lerps.

STATUS: fairly common. TAXONOMY: endemic species.

672 NOISY MINER *Manorina melanocephala* (Latham) 1801   Fig p 431
Distribution: Map 256.

RECOGNITION: *greyish with yellow patch on face and yellow bill and legs; no white on rump.*
DESCRIPTION: 26–28cm. Sexes alike. Upperparts mostly brownish-grey with whitish bars on nape, upper back and side of neck; crown and most of face sooty-black with forehead and lores dull white; bare skin behind eye yellow; underparts pale grey, whitish on throat and belly and lightly barred with dark brown on breast; wings and tail blackish, feathers edged with greenish-yellow and tipped with white; bill and legs yellow; eyes brown.

VARIATION: roughly south of Brisbane, slightly darker with smaller bill (race *melanocephala*); north, slightly paler with larger bill (race *crassirostris*).

HABITAT: woodland, suburban parks. HABITS: arboreal but sometimes on ground, mostly in foliage of trees and bushes, active, inquisitive and aggressive, will harry or attack most other birds, especially predators—a loud clamour of miners usually denotes that a hawk or owl or cat is being 'mobbed'; a notable habit is for one bird to sidle along a branch to another with head dipped and bill pointed up; constantly gregarious, in groups and colonies, most activities are communal; sedentary with nomadic tendencies. BREEDING: variable, but mainly July–December; nests in trees and saplings at about 4–13m, on twig forks, cup-shaped, made of bark, twigs and grass lined with soft material; two to four eggs, deep pink spotted with chestnut and grey. VOICE: variety of mostly harsh notes and phrases, some twenty sounds with distinctive meanings have been determined for birds in one area. FOOD: insects, honey, fruit.

STATUS: common. TAXONOMY: endemic species, closely related to White-rumped Miner.

673 WHITE-RUMPED MINER *Manorina flavigula* (Gould) 1840
Distribution: Map 257.

RECOGNITION: *like Noisy Miner but rump white (in extreme southwest merely paler shade of grey-brown back); crown grey like back; black on face limited to lores, streak under eye and ear coverts; forehead, streak from mouth, small patch on side of neck and chin olive-yellow.*

VARIATION: seven variants currently named, not all of equal distinction—in extreme southwest largest and darkest with rump paler shade of dark grey back (race *obscura*—sometimes regarded as separate species, Dusky Miner, and sometimes as conspecific with Black-eared Miner); northwest, smallest and palest with rump and underparts white (race *lutea*); remainder, various intermediates (race *flavigula*, and others).

HABITAT: dry woodland, especially mallee, scrubby heath. HABITS and BREEDING: similar to Noisy Miner, but in very dry areas at least, frequently feeds on ground insects. VOICE: variable, mostly noisy repetitive squawks and querulous notes. FOOD: insects, honey, fruit.

STATUS: common. TAXONOMY: endemic species, sometimes divided into two species; closely related to Noisy Miner.

674 BLACK-EARED MINER   *Manorina melanotis*   (Wilson) 1911
Distribution: Map 257.

RECOGNITION: like White-rumped Miner, especially southwest race *obscura*, but generally darker and (by original description) black ear-coverts larger, yellow forehead less extensive, belly clear white, bill and bare face patch richer yellow; *rump not paler than back.*

HABITAT: mallee. HABITS, etc: mostly similar to White-rumped Miner which occurs in same area and with which it sometimes flocks; nomadic, apparently within a limited area.

STATUS: fairly common locally. TAXONOMY: endemic species; considered to be sexually isolated offshoot from White-rumped Miner.

Genus ANTHOCHAERA

The Spiny-cheeked Honeyeater, recently in *Acanthogenys,* has a number of characteristics in common with the wattlebirds and current taxonomic opinion places them together in this endemic genus. They are relatively large, about 25–33cm, with the Yellow Wattlebird very large, about 45cm; tails are long and plumages much streaked. There is only one true wattlebird consisting of two semispecies, the Tasmanian Yellow Wattlebird and the Red Wattlebird of the mainland. The Little Wattlebird has no claim to the title.

Key to ANTHOCHAERA

1	Bill pinkish-orange, chin and throat buff	Spiny-cheeked Honeyeater	No 675
2	Bill black, chin white, belly yellow	Yellow Wattlebird	No 678
3	Bill black, chin and throat streaked black and white	4–5	
4	White triangle below eye, belly yellow	Red Wattlebird	No 677
5	Streaked black and white below eye, belly mottled black and white	Little Wattlebird	No 676

675 SPINY-CHEEKED HONEYEATER   *Anthochaera rufogularis*   (Gould) 1830
Distribution: Map 258.

RECOGNITION: *mostly streaked except for plain buff throat, pinkish bill with black tip, broad bands of black and white on face.*

DESCRIPTION: 24–26cm, with tail 13cm. Sexes alike. Upperparts mottled or broadly streaked greyish-olive and brownish-black, greyer and more finely streaked on crown and mostly white tinged with yellow on rump; black bands through eye and at edge of throat, latter widening on side of neck, enclosing white band of bristle-like feathers which extend to patch of very pale yellow mottled with black on side of neck; bare skin under eye and angle of mouth pinkish-orange (like bill); chin to upper breast and underwing plain cinnamon buff; remainder pale yellowish-buff streaked with black, especially on flanks; wings and tail blackish, wing feathers edged with pale yellow and tail tipped with white; bill pinkish-orange with black tip; eyes pale blue; legs dark grey.

HABITAT: woodland to desert scrub. HABITS: arboreal, creeps and clings among foliage, sometimes flies steeply upward then descends with tail spread and uttering loud whistle, swift dipping flight; solitary or in family parties or large wandering flocks; sedentary and nomadic, apparently with some fairly definite seasonal movements. BREEDING: variable, almost any time in suitable conditions, otherwise mainly June–January; nests suspended between twigs, cup-shaped, rough open mesh of tendrils and grass lined with soft material; two to three eggs, white, pale creamy spotted with olive and shades of reddish-brown. VOICE: short 'tock' or 'chuck', various gurgling or guttural notes, loud clear whistle or plaintive pipe, and others. FOOD: insects, fruit, honey.

STATUS: common. TAXONOMY: endemic species.

Red Wattlebird (677)

Spiny-cheeked Honeyeater (675)

676 LITTLE WATTLEBIRD *Anthochaera chrysoptera* (Latham) 1801   Pl 20
Distribution: Map 259.

RECOGNITION: *dark olive-brown streaked and speckled with white; like Red Wattlebird but white streaks below eye and no wattle; harsh voice.*

DESCRIPTION: 27–30cm, with graduated tail about 15cm. Sexes alike. Mainly dark olive-brown streaked and speckled with white, whitest on cheeks and belly; margins of central wing feathers tinged with greenish-yellow and patch of cinnamon rufous visible in extended wing; outer tail feathers broadly tipped with white; bill black; eyes reddish-brown; legs dark grey.

VARIATION: eastern mainland, as above (race *chrysoptera*); southwest population, less white markings—none on crown (race *lunulata*); Tasmania, larger and darker (race *tasmanica*).

HABITAT: open forest and coastal heath, especially with banksias. HABITS: arboreal, usually among foliage, bold and pugnacious, sometimes squawks noisily from high perch while jerking tail and throwing head back; solitary or in scattered companies sometimes including Red Wattlebirds. BREEDING: August–December; nests in small forked branches up to about 4m, frequently in old babbler nests, saucer-shaped and relatively small, rough open mesh of twigs and grass lined with vegetable down; two eggs (one in west), pinkish-buff spotted with reddish-brown and grey. VOICE: loud harsh squawks or cackles, like 'goo-gwar-ruck', accompanied by clattering of mandibles. FOOD: honey, insects, fruit.

STATUS: fairly common. TAXONOMY: endemic species.

677 RED WATTLEBIRD *Anthochaera carunculata* (White) 1790

Distribution: Map 260.

RECOGNITION: *dark olive-grey streaked with white; like Little Wattlebird but white triangle on face and red wattle, yellow on belly; harsh voice.*

DESCRIPTION: 32–35cm, with tail about 16cm. Sexes alike. Forehead to nape and eye level blackish-brown; remainder of upperparts dark olive-grey streaked with white; triangle of silvery-white below eye with large red wattle behind patch; underparts dusky-brown streaked with white except in centre of belly which is pale yellow; wing and tail feathers edged with white, tail feathers broadly tipped with white; patch of cinnamon rufous visible in extended wing; bill black; eyes bright reddish-brown; legs pinkish-brown.

VARIATION: east of Nullarbor Plain, less heavily streaked below and wattle smaller (race *carunculata*); west, more heavily streaked below and wattle larger (race *woodwardi*).

HABITAT: open forest, woodland, suburban parks. HABITS: arboreal, active among foliage, very aggressive and noisy, utters harsh notes with head back and throat extended; solitary or in wandering parties; sedentary and nomadic with definite north–south migratory pattern in west. BREEDING: July–December; nests in trees and bushes, on horizontal branches, saucer-shaped, made of sticks and twigs and lined with soft material; two to three eggs, pinkish-buff spotted or blotched with reddish-brown and grey. VOICE: various loud harsh notes described as hiccupping or gurgling, guttural croak and shrill 'cookay-cook', etc. FOOD: honey, fruit, insects.

STATUS: common to very common. TAXONOMY: endemic species, forming superspecies with Yellow Wattlebird. Straggler in New Zealand.

678 YELLOW WATTLEBIRD *Anthochaera paradoxa* (Daudin) 1800

Distribution: Map 260.

RECOGNITION: like Red Wattlebird in having streaked grey-brown and white plumage, long graduated tail, face wattle and yellow patch on belly; main differences are, larger, 40–45cm with tail 22–25cm, *wattles yellow* and long, 4cm, *forehead to nape broadly streaked* blackish-brown and white, *chin white*.

HABITAT, etc: similar to Red Wattlebird, usually associated with eucalypts anywhere from forest to suburban gardens, sometimes feeds on ground; voice consists of similar raucous and sometimes unpleasant sounds, like someone retching, and uttered apparently with considerable effort with head thrown back.

STATUS: common. TAXONOMY: endemic species, forming superspecies with mainland Red Wattlebird.

Family ESTRILDIDAE

Finches

19(115) species: 14 endemic: 1 introduced

AUSTRALIAN FINCHES BELONG TO a different family to the seed-eating birds of Europe with the same name (see Fringillidae). They are part of a group sometimes included in the large family of weaver-birds (see Ploceidae), especially abundant in Africa, but as they do not weave their nests in the manner of true weavers, and for other reasons, it is now usual to put them in a separate family. It may be noted, however, that the distinctions between the three families referred to above are not clear cut or universally agreed on. The Australian

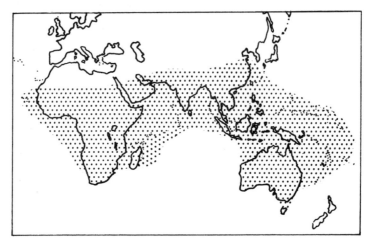

Distribution of ESTRILDIDAE

species belong to two or three main divisions or subfamilies. Those in one group are commonly known as mannikins, and for those in the other, almost entirely Australian, the name grass-finches has been suggested. Finches are small, 12cm or less, with short thick bills (but pointed, not blunt as in pardalotes) and have distinctively patterned and colourfully marked plumages. As their food is mainly grass seeds they frequent a variety of grassy habitats but especially where there are tangles of low bushes suitable for nests. Nests are domed with a side entrance which is sometimes extended into a tunnel; eggs are plain white. As is usual in birds which have a mainly dry diet, most finches must have water and are seldom far from it, indeed some desert species are useful indicators of water-holes.

Key to ESTRILDIDAE

1 Upper tail coverts barred black and white........ Zebra Finch .... No 686
2 Rump blue .... Gouldian Finch .... No 693
3 Rump brown spotted white.................... Plum-headed Finch .... No 692
4 Rump grey-brown like back.................. Pictorella Finch .... No 696
5 Rump and tail golden-yellow 8–10
6 Rump and tail black, upper tail coverts black or
  white 11–16

Genus AEGINTHA

Current opinion places the Red-browed Finch in a genus of its own although previously it was thought to belong to the African waxbills of the genus *Estrilda*. It frequents the well timbered areas of eastern coastal districts. It is similar to the next genus in having a red rump.

679 RED-BROWED FINCH *Aegintha temporalis* (Latham) 1801 Pl 21

Distribution: Map 261.

RECOGNITION: *broad crimson eyebrow and crimson rump, red bill has black stripe above and below.*

DESCRIPTION: 12cm. Sexes alike. Crown and tail grey; back and shoulders yellowish-olive; eyebrow, rump and upper tail coverts crimson; face and side of neck medium grey; throat and breast pale grey tinged with brown; belly greyish-buff; bill red with black stripe above and below; eyes reddish-brown; legs pinkish-brown.

VARIATION: south of Cairns, as above (race *temporalis*); north of Cairns, grey of crown extends to upper back, and back and shoulders yellower (race *minor*).

HABITAT: mangroves, forests and adjacent open country, parks and gardens. HABITS: arboreal but sometimes feeds on ground; gregarious, in loose flocks when not breeding, usually flying low from bush to bush; sedentary with nomadic tendencies. BREEDING: mainly September–November in south and January–April in north; nests in dense bushes, usually between 2 and 4 metres, domed with side tunnel entrance, made of grasses; four to six white eggs. VOICE: high-pitched 'ssitt' or 'ssee', and song consisting of simple variations of these notes. FOOD: seeds, insects when breeding.

STATUS: common, adapted to human settlement; adversely affected by introduced Spice Finch. TAXONOMY: endemic species and genus.

Genus EMBLEMA

A group of four species confined to Australia. Three are called 'firetails' because of their red rumps, but all have this feature—which is not confined to the genus. The Beautiful Firetail is the only finch which has reached Tasmania. It shares with two other species the feature of white spots on black underparts, and as they have separate distributions it suggests that they are of recent origin from the same stock. Except for the painted Finch of the northwest porcupine grass areas, the genus lies mainly south of the tropic.

680 PAINTED FINCH *Emblema picta* Gould 1842   Pl 21
Distribution: Map 262.

RECOGNITION: *scarlet rump, black underparts boldly spotted with white on flanks and blotched with scarlet on centre of belly; associated with porcupine grass in northwest.*

DESCRIPTION: 10cm. Sexes slightly different. *Male:* crown to back and wings dull brown; rump and upper tail coverts scarlet; forehead, face and chin scarlet; throat and foreneck black speckled with scarlet; remainder of underparts black blotched with scarlet in centre of belly and spotted with white on flanks; tail brownish-black; upper mandible black tipped red, lower red with bluish base; eyes white; legs pinkish-brown. *Female:* scarlet in head area limited to face, whole underparts spotted white with very little scarlet on belly.

HABITAT: porcupine grass, especially in rocky localities. HABITS: on or near ground in low bushes; gregarious but flocks small; sedentary and local around permanent waterholes. BREEDING: variable; nests in grass clumps, domed and side entrance without tunnel, roughly made of grasses; three to five white eggs. VOICE: harsh loud 'trut'. FOOD: porcupine grass seeds.

STATUS: probably relatively small population of locally common scattered groups. TAXONOMY: endemic species, probably a close relative of the Red-eared and Beautiful Firetails.

681 RED-EARED FIRETAIL *Emblema oculata* (Quoy & Gaim.) 1830
Distribution: Map 262.

RECOGNITION: *crimson rump, black belly with large white spots; only native finch in extreme southwest.*

DESCRIPTION: 12cm. Sexes alike. Forehead and ring round eye black; ear patch crimson; upperparts olive brown, finely streaked with black on head, finely barred with black on back and wings, broadly barred with black on tail; rump, upper tail coverts and base of outer tail crimson; throat and upper breast pale buff finely barred with black; remainder of underparts black almost obscured by large white spots; bill scarlet; eyes red, bare skin round eye pale blue; legs dark brown.

HABITAT: moist grassy patches in forests. HABITS: on or near ground, seldom alights on ground even when feeding on grass seeds; solitary and sedentary; flight relatively slow and direct. BREEDING: September–January; nests in tree foliage at various heights, large and spherical with long horizontal entrance tunnel, made of tendrils and fresh grass lined with feathers and vegetable down; four to six white eggs. VOICE: sharp low-pitched 'oowee' difficult to localise. FOOD: seeds, insects when breeding.

STATUS: uncommon; adversely affected by human settlement and probably declining. TAXONOMY: endemic species, closely related to Beautiful Firetail and possibly Painted Finch.

682 BEAUTIFUL FIRETAIL *Emblema bella* (Latham) 1801   Pl 21
Distribution: Map 262.

RECOGNITION: *crimson rump, barred plumage; only estrildid finch in Tasmania.*

DESCRIPTION: 12cm. Sexes nearly alike (female has less black in centre of belly). Black forehead continuous with black area round eye; upperparts olive-brown, finely streaked with black on head and finely barred with black on back and wings; rump and upper tail coverts crimson; centre of tail black, sides grey-brown barred with black; underparts grey barred with black, light brownish tinge on throat; vent and under tail coverts black; bill red; eyes reddish-brown, bare skin round eye pale blue; legs pinkish-brown.

HABITAT: scrubby heaths and woodlands. HABITS: in trees and bushes but feeds mainly on ground; solitary, gregarious when not breeding, but only in small flocks; sedentary; flight rapid, direct and low. BREEDING: September–January; nests in trees and bushes usually low down, domed and spherical with long entrance tunnel, made of fresh grass; five to eight white eggs. VOICE: low sharp 'weee', also run of similar notes on descending scale. FOOD: seeds, insects when breeding.

STATUS: uncommon, adversely affected by human settlement. TAXONOMY: endemic species, closely related to Red-eared Firetail and possibly Painted Finch.

683 DIAMOND FIRETAIL *Emblema guttata* (Shaw) 1785   Fig p 446
Distribution: Map 263.

RECOGNITION: *crimson rump, black breast band, white spots on black flanks.*

DESCRIPTION: 11cm. Sexes nearly alike (female has narrower black breast band). Crown, face and hind neck medium grey; lores black; back and wings pale buffy-brown; rump and upper tail coverts crimson; throat to centre of belly white with black band on breast; flanks black boldly spotted with white; tail black; bill crimson, lilac at base; eyes and eyelids crimson; legs dark blue-grey.

HABITAT: various woodlands including mallee. HABITS: arboreal and terrestrial, feeds mostly on ground; solitary but sometimes in small flocks when not breeding; sedentary; elaborate courtship display with male holding grass stem in bill. BREEDING: August–January, or later; nests in trees and bushes, in dense foliage at various heights, domed and spherical with two entrances, one having long tunnel, made of fresh vegetation; five to six white eggs. Records of natural mating with Zebra Finch. VOICE: long 'twooo-heee' rising and falling in pitch. FOOD: seeds, insects when breeding.

STATUS: fairly common, mostly adversely affected by human settlement. TAXONOMY: endemic species.

Genus NEOCHMIA

Of the two species in this genus, one is mainly crimson and the other has a red patch on the rump, like members of the previous genera. Sexes are different in the Crimson Finch but nearly alike in the Star Finch. Both are tropical, the Crimson Finch extending into southern New Guinea.

684 CRIMSON FINCH *Neochmia phaeton* (Homb. & Jacq.) 1841   Pl 21
Distribution: Map 263.

RECOGNITION: *crimson and grey with white spots on flanks, long graduated tail.*

DESCRIPTION: 14cm, with tail 6cm. Sexes different. *Male:* upperparts greyish-olive tinged

Doublebar Finch (687)

Diamond Firetail (683)

with dull crimson on shoulders and centre of back, sometimes blackish or dark grey on crown; face, throat, breast and flanks dull crimson, spotted white on flanks; belly and under-tail coverts black or buffy-white; upper tail dull crimson; bill red, blue at base, or white at base of lower mandible; eyes and legs brownish-yellow. *Female:* similar but with breast pale greyish-olive, flanks grey-brown, belly buffy-white, bill orange.

VARIATION: most of range, belly black and bill mainly red with white at base of lower mandible (race *phaeton*); tip of Cape York, smaller, belly white and base of bill blue (race *albiventer*).

HABITAT: grassy margins of inland waters. HABITS: lives among grasses, feeds while clinging to grass stems; solitary, rarely in small loosely attached flocks; sedentary; tail fanned and flicked up; male holds grass stem in bill in courtship display. BREEDING: January–April; nests in cane grass and pandanus leaves, sometimes domestic buildings (even indoors), domed without tunnel entrance, roughly made of grass and lined with feathers; five to eight white eggs. VOICE: loud continuous 'che-che-che' or 'tsee-tsee-tsee'. FOOD: seeds, insects when breeding.

STATUS: fairly common, adapted to human settlement. TAXONOMY: species with slight extension into southern New Guinea.

685 STAR FINCH *Neochmia ruficauda* (Gould) 1837   Pl 21

Distribution: Map 260.

RECOGNITION: *red mask, white spots on greenish breast and flanks, yellow belly.*

DESCRIPTION: 12cm. Sexes nearly alike (female has smaller mask). Forehead, face and chin crimson, face spotted with white; upperparts yellowish or brownish-olive; upper tail coverts dull scarlet with white spots; central tail feathers dull scarlet, outer black; foreneck, upper breast and flanks yellowish-olive spotted with white; centre of breast and belly yellow; bill scarlet; eyes reddish-orange; legs yellow.

VARIATION: in east, upperparts brownish-olive (race *ruficauda*); in north and northwest, upperparts yellowish-olive (race *clarescens*).

HABITAT: grassy borders of inland waters, especially with clumps of bushes and low trees. HABITS: near ground in grass and bushes, feeds while clinging to grass stems and twigs; gregarious, in large flocks when not breeding; sedentary; drinks by sucking; male carries grass stem in bill in courtship display. VOICE: loud high-pitched 'sseet' or 'ssit' and quicker 'pslit'. FOOD: grass seeds, insects when breeding.

STATUS: fairly common, apparently adversely affected by human settlement. TAXONOMY: endemic species.

Genus POEPHILA

A group of five species of which the Zebra Finch is the commonest and most widespread Australian finch, and the only one of this group extending beyond the continent. All are distinguished by varying amounts of black and white on rump and tail, in the form of bars on the Zebra Finch. The other four belong to the north and east and may be derived from a recent colonist of Zebra Finch stock. The process of divergence is still clearly seen in the Black-throated and Long-tailed Finches (see 'A Poephila Superspecies').

686 ZEBRA FINCH *Poephila guttata* (Vieillot) 1817

Distribution: throughout except forests.

RECOGNITION: *black and white banded rump and upper tail coverts, chestnut flanks with white spots.*

DESCRIPTION: 9cm. Sexes different. *Male:* upperparts pale brownish-grey, greyer on crown and hind neck; rump and long upper tail coverts broadly barred black and white; central tail feathers black, outer dark grey-brown; face white at base of bill, bordered with black and large patch of cinnamon rufous; throat and foreneck finely barred pale grey and black with broad border of black; breast and belly white; flanks chestnut spotted white; bill red; eyes red; legs orange. *Female:* lacks brown on face and flanks, also lacks barring on throat and foreneck, which are pale grey-brown, chin whitish.

HABITAT: woodlands to open dry country with clumps of trees and bushes. HABITS: arboreal, in trees and bushes but often feeds on ground; gregarious, sometimes in large flocks; sedentary, but nomadic in adverse conditions. BREEDING: variable, sometimes continuous or depending on rains; nests in outer foliage of trees and bushes usually low, domed and sometimes with tunnel entrance, roughly made of grass or twigs and lined with feathers or wool—old nests are often patched up and re-used; four to six white eggs, sometimes with pale bluish tinge. Records of natural mating with Diamond Firetail. VOICE: loud 'tia', soft 'tet-tet', hissing 'wssst', also trilling song. FOOD: seeds, insects when breeding.

STATUS: very common, adjusted to human settlement but ousted by Spice Finch. TAXONOMY: race *(castonota)* of species extending to Timor and various Papuan islands.

687 DOUBLEBAR FINCH *Poephila bichenovii* (Vig. & Horsf.) 1827

Distribution: Map 264.

RECOGNITION: *two narrow black bars on white underparts.*

DESCRIPTION: 11cm. Sexes alike. Crown to upper back brownish-grey finely barred with black; centre of back black; rump black or white; tail black; face and throat white with thin black border meeting on forehead and foreneck; breast white with thin black border (borders of throat and breast form the two distinctive black bars); belly pale buff-yellow; wings black spotted white; bill blue-grey; eyes dark brown; legs blue-grey.

VARIATION: east of Burketown, rump white (race *bichenovii*); west of Boroloola, rump black (race *annulosa*); hybrid zone between.

HABITAT: bush savanna. HABITS: arboreal, in trees and bushes but often feeds on ground; gregarious, in loose flocks flying low between bushes and low trees; sedentary. BREEDING: variable but mainly December–March in north and almost any time in south depending on rains; nests in grass clumps, bushes or low in trees, under 3m, domed without entrance tunnel, roughly made of grass and fibres; four white eggs, rarely with small black specks at thick end. VOICE: loud extended 'tiaaat-tiaat' and low 'tat-tat'. FOOD: seeds, insects when breeding.

STATUS: common, adapted to human settlement but being ousted by Spice Finch. TAXONOMY: endemic species.

688 MASKED FINCH   *Poephila personata*   (Gould) 1842   Pl 21

Distribution: Map 265.

RECOGNITION: *white rump, black pointed tail, crown fawn-brown like back.*

DESCRIPTION: 12cm, with pointed tail 6cm. Sexes alike. Black at base of bill forming narrow mask; face below eye white or brown; upperparts pinkish-fawn; rump and upper tail coverts white; tail black; breast and belly pinkish-buff; rear flanks black; vent and under tail coverts white; bill reddish-yellow; eyes reddish-brown; legs red.

VARIATION: west of Leichhardt River, no white on face or foreneck (race *personata*); east of Leichhardt, face below eye white and chin black bordered with white (race *leucotis*).

HABITAT: savanna and open grass plains, often far from water. HABITS: in trees and bushes but feeds mainly on ground; gregarious; sedentary; drinks by sucking. BREEDING: March–May; nests in grass clumps, bushes and trees below about 8m, domed and spherical with entrance tunnel, well made of grass, lined with feathers and vegetable down, frequently contains charcoal; four to six eggs. VOICE: loud 'tiat' and quieter 'twat-twat'. FOOD: seeds, insects when breeding.

STATUS: common, adapted to human settlement. TAXONOMY: endemic species.

A POEPHILA SUPERSPECIES

The Black-throated and Long-tailed Finches illustrate stages in speciation. They are very alike and replace each other but they have a distinct difference in tail shape. It seems clear that they are recently derived from a common stock and have reached the rank of species — but may be regarded as semispecies of a superspecies. The Black-throated Finch also shows an earlier stage of speciation. Northern populations have white upper tail coverts which intergrade with the black upper tail coverts of southern populations. They are now races but may become species.

689 BLACK-THROATED FINCH   *Poephila cincta*   (Gould) 1837

Distribution: Map 266.

RECOGNITION: *short black tail and black bill, black rump and black or white upper tail coverts.*

DESCRIPTION: 10cm. Sexes alike. Crown bluish-grey; hind neck cinnamon or vinous brown shading to grey-brown on back and wings; rump, upper tail coverts and tail black, or part of rump and upper tail coverts white; black of rump extends to underparts to form band on lower belly; face bluish-white; throat black; breast and belly shades of cinnamon and vinous brown; vent and under tail coverts buffy-white; bill black; eyes dark brown; legs reddish-orange.

VARIATION: south of about Townsville to Richmond, upper tail coverts white (race *cincta*); north of about Cairns to Normanton, upper tail coverts black (race *uropygialis*); hybrid zone between; tip of Cape York, breast and belly brown without vinous tinge (race *nigrotecta*).

HABITAT: forests and woodlands with thick ground cover and open water. HABITS: mainly arboreal; solitary or in loosely dispersed breeding colonies, often in small loose flocks when not breeding; male sometimes holds grass stem in bill in courtship display, stretches and contracts neck in rapid bobbing movement of head (unique to this and Long-tailed Finch); drinks by sucking. BREEDING: September–January in south, January–May in north; nests in trees, usually high up, sometimes in holes or under nests of larger species, domed with entrance tunnel, made of grasses; five to nine white eggs. VOICE: loud plaintive 'weet' or 'teeweet', lower pitched than Long-tailed Finch. FOOD: seeds, insects when breeding.

STATUS: fairly common. TAXONOMY: endemic species or semispecies forming superspecies with Long-tailed Finch.

Black-throated Finch (689)

Long-tailed Finch (690)

SEMISPECIES OF A SUPERSPECIES

690 LONG-TAILED FINCH *Poephila acuticauda* (Gould) 1840

Distribution: Map 266.

RECOGNITION: like Black-throated Finch (race *cincta*) with white upper tail coverts, but *tail long and pointed* and *bill red or orange*.

VARIATION: east of about Wyndham, bill orange (race *acuticauda*); west of Wyndham, bill reddish (race *hecki*).

HABITAT, etc: similar to Black-throated Finch but frequents more open country, call note higher pitched.

STATUS and TAXONOMY: similar to Black-throated Finch.

Genus ERYTHRURA

A group of ten species only one of which occurs in Australia. The Blue-faced Finch belongs to New Guinea but has a foothold in the mangroves and rain forests of northern Cape York. It is not well known. It has a red rump like some other finches but is distinguished by a blue face and crown.

691 BLUE-FACED FINCH *Erythrura trichroa* (Kittlitz) 1883   Pl 21

Distribution: Map 267.

RECOGNITION: *mainly green with blue crown and face and reddish rump.*

DESCRIPTION: 12cm. Sexes alike. Forehead to mid-crown and face cobalt blue; back dark grass green; rump and upper tail coverts dull scarlet; underparts pale grass green; flight feathers black edged with green; tail feathers black edged with dull scarlet; bill black; eyes dark brown; legs pale pinkish-buff.

HABITAT: edges of mangroves and rain forest. HABITS: not well known—apparently keeps mainly to bushes and low trees and may be solitary or in small flocks; probably sedentary. BREEDING: scanty information: nests in trees and bushes, domed and inverted pear-shaped, loosely made of moss and fibres; three to six white eggs. FOOD: seeds.

STATUS: not known. TAXONOMY: race *(sigillifera)* extending to New Guinea of species ranging to Celebes and New Hebrides.

Genus AIDEMOSYNE

The Plum-headed Finch may be an early offshoot from the *Erythrura* group which has been isolated long enough in Australia to have evolved features which, it is claimed, justify its being placed in a genus of its own.

692 PLUM-HEADED FINCH *Aidemosyne modesta* (Gould) 1837   Pl 21

Distribution: Map 267.

RECOGNITION: *plum-coloured cap and black tail, olive-brown back.*

DESCRIPTION: 11cm. Sexes nearly alike, female has smaller cap and white chin. Forehead, crown and chin dark reddish-brown (plum); lores black; remainder of upperparts olive-brown with inner wing feathers tipped white and feathers of rump and upper tail coverts barred white at tip; face below eye and underparts white, barred pale olive-brown on face, foreneck and flanks; tail black with white spot near tip of outer feathers; bill black blue-grey at base; eyes dark brown; legs pinkish-brown.

HABITAT: tangle of grass, reeds and bushes along river margins in wooded savanna. HABITS: in low vegetation, feeds while clinging to grass stems or twigs and on ground; solitary or in loose flocks when not breeding, flocks sometimes large and high flying; sedentary or nomadic, depending on water; flight undulating. BREEDING: variable, mainly September–January; nests in grass clumps and bushes, domed without entrance tunnel, made of grass and bound to grass stems or twigs, sometimes lined with feathers; four to seven white eggs. VOICE: high-pitched single or double note and chirping trill. FOOD: seeds, insects when breeding.

STATUS: apparently rare to uncommon. TAXONOMY: endemic species and genus.

Genus CHLOEBIA

Although the relationships of the Gouldian Finch are uncertain there is no doubt about it being the most colourful member of the family and one of the world's most beautiful birds. Currently it is placed in a genus of its own near the *Lonchura* finches, the true mannikins.

693 GOULDIAN FINCH *Chloebia gouldiae* (Gould) 1844   Pl 21
Distribution: Map 268.

RECOGNITION: *lilac breast and blue rump, head colour variable.*

DESCRIPTION: 14cm, with tail 6cm. Sexes alike. Variable head colour—(1) forehead, face and throat black edged with cobalt blue; (2) forehead and face dull crimson edged with black continued to black throat, black encircled with cobalt; (3) similar but forehead and face yellow. All have back green, upper tail coverts cobalt; tail black; breast lilac; belly bright yellow; under tail coverts white; bill whitish, tip red; eyes dark brown; legs yellow.

HABITAT: savanna. HABITS: arboreal, in trees and bushes and feeding in grass, rarely on ground, clings to grass stems or to twigs within reach of grass seed heads; gregarious, in large flocks when not breeding; sedentary and nomadic; drinks by sucking. BREEDING: January–April; nests in holes in trees, usually high up, and in termite mounds, unformed or consisting of some grass fragments; four to eight white eggs. VOICE: variations of soft 'ssit-ssit', but notably silent. FOOD: seeds, insects when breeding.

STATUS: fairly common, not amenable to human settlement and much exploited as cage bird. TAXONOMY: endemic species and genus.

Genus LONCHURA

Sometimes referred to as mannikins, the members of this group of about thirty-four species extend throughout Malaysia, India and Africa. There are three in Australia, mainly in the north, as if recent colonists. The Chestnut-rumped and Yellow-rumped Finches pose a problem in relationship. Where they occur together they interbreed freely but maintain their separate distinctive features; it is estimated that they are in the proportion of two Chestnut-breasted to one Yellow-rumped. One theory is that there is only one species and that it is dimorphic (the Gouldian Finch is polymorphic). Another is that they are colonists of different periods from the same stock which can still interbreed but have features of equal dominance. They are listed here as separate species.

694 CHESTNUT-BREASTED FINCH
     Lonchura castaneothorax (Gould) 1837   Pl 21
Distribution: Map 269.

RECOGNITION: *golden-yellow rump and tail, throat black, breast chestnut.*

DESCRIPTION: 10cm, tail relatively short. Sexes alike. Crown and hind neck mottled light and dark grey-brown; back light cinnamon brown; rump to centre of tail bright orange-yellow, sides of tail blackish-brown; face sooty-black finely streaked with buff; throat black; breast pale chestnut bordered with buff and separated by black bar from dull white belly; flanks barred black and white; under tail coverts black; bill blue-grey; eyes dark brown; legs purplish-grey.

VARIATION: east of Carpentaria, as described (race *castaneothorax*); west of Carpentaria, colours richer and no buff streaks on face (race *assimilis*).

HABITAT: grass and reedy margins of swamps. HABITS: lives among grass and reeds, clings to stalks when feeding, rarely on ground; gregarious, flies high in tight flocks, often in company with Yellow-rumped species; sedentary and nomadic. BREEDING: January–April in north but in any month where rains irregular; nests in grass and reeds attached to and made from vegetation, domed and spherical with side opening; five to six white eggs. VOICE: tinkling bell-like 'teet'. FOOD: seeds, insects when breeding.

STATUS: common and adapted to human settlement. TAXONOMY: species extending to New Guinea; closely related to Yellow-rumped Finch.

695 YELLOW-RUMPED FINCH   *Lonchura flaviprymna*   (Gould) 1845

Distribution: Map 270.

RECOGNITION: like Chestnut-breasted Finch but *face and underparts creamy-buff,* richer buff on breast and whiter on throat and vent; *crown and hind neck plain grey.*

HABITAT, etc: apparently similar to Chestnut-breasted Finch.

STATUS: fairly common (less common than Chestnut-breasted). TAXONOMY: endemic species; closely related to Chestnut-breasted Finch.

696 PICTORELLA FINCH   *Lonchura pectoralis*   (Gould) 1841   Pl 21

Distribution: Map 271.

RECOGNITION: *plain grey-brown above, black throat and white bars on breast.*

DESCRIPTION: 11cm. Sexes alike (but black throat of female is dull not shiny). Upperparts pale grey-brown, slightly darker on head and rump, blackish on tail and some white spots on shoulders; face and throat black edged with pale cinnamon buff; black of throat extends to breast where it is almost obscured by broad white bars; remainder of underparts vinaceous buff with some white markings on flanks; bill blue-grey; eyes dark brown; legs pinkish-buff.

HABITAT: dry savannas, grassy plains and porcupine grass, not necessarily near water. HABITS: mainly terrestrial, feeds on ground but also climbs grass stems; mostly solitary breeding, gregarious at other times; sedentary and nomadic; drinks with rapid sips. BREEDING: January–April; nests on or near ground, in grass tussocks and bushes, domed and bottle-shaped, roughly made of grasses; four to six white eggs. VOICE: loud 'tlit' or 'tleet' or 'teet', also loud 'chip-chip'. FOOD: seeds, also insects when breeding.

STATUS: fairly common. TAXONOMY: endemic species.

Introduced species

697 SPICE FINCH   *Lonchura punctulata*   (Linnaeus) 1788

Distribution: Map 272; continually extending.

RECOGNITION: *golden-yellow rump, chestnut throat, breast and flanks boldly marbled in black and white.*

DESCRIPTION: 10cm. Sexes alike. Head and throat chestnut brown; back and shoulders cinnamon brown, thinly streaked with pale brown; upper tail coverts and edges of tail feathers golden-yellow; breast and flanks boldly marbled black and white; centre of belly whitish; bill black; eyes reddish-brown; legs blue-grey.

HABITAT: bushy savanna. HABITS: mainly arboreal, very adaptable in feeding habits; gregarious, often mixed in flocks with other species; sedentary and nomadic. BREEDING: variable, most months; nests in trees and bushes, usually between 3–7m, domed with short entrance tunnel, strongly made of grass and strips of bark; six to seven white eggs. VOICE: high-pitched 'kit-teee' and sharp 'tret-tret'. FOOD: varied, but seeds mainly, and insects apparently not as essential when breeding as in other finches.

STATUS: common and thriving, sometimes at expense of other finches. TAXONOMY: species ranging from India to Philippines.

Introduced family

Family PLOCEIDAE
Weaverbirds
2(133) species: both introduced

THE TWO SPECIES OF this old world group which have been introduced to Australia belong to one genus, *Passer*, of a fairly distinctive subfamily. It consists of various species denoted by the word 'sparrow'. A general account of the family is unnecessary except to say that the true weavers are distinguished by their elaborately woven nests, suspended among foliage like varied loofah skeletons. Sparrows, by comparison, are inexpert architects and make do with untidy structures crammed into holes and crevices; the House Sparrow is a nuisance when it uses openings under eaves to pile dry grass into attics. But nests are domed with side entrances wherever they are built. Sparrows have thick pointed bills like the estrildine finches and the same seed-eating habits, but they are dull plumaged.

Key to PASSER

1 Crown grey, ear coverts white . . . . House Sparrow . . . . No 698
2 Crown brown, black spot on ear coverts . . . . Tree Sparrow . . . . No 699

698 HOUSE SPARROW *Passer domesticus* (Linnaeus) 1758

Distribution: southeast, from Tasmania to central Queensland and central South Australia, and extending; sporadic occurrences elsewhere especially near ports.

RECOGNITION: *short thick bill, plumage streaked brown and black, male has grey head and black bib.*

DESCRIPTION: 15cm. Sexes different. *Male:* forehead and crown dark grey; nape chestnut, continued as broad band through eye; back and wings boldly streaked brown and black with white bar on shoulder; rump grey; lower face and underparts light grey with black bib from chin to upper breast; tail brown; bill black; eyes brown; legs light brown. *Female:* upperparts brown streaked with black on back and wings; underparts dull white; bill brown.

HABITAT: mostly urban and agriculture. HABITS: arboreal and terrestrial, active, bold and noisy; gregarious; sedentary. BREEDING: variable; nests in holes and crevices in almost any situation, also in tree forks and bushes; domed, roughly made of grass and lined with feathers;

three to six eggs, pale grey spotted with brown. VOICE: various chirruping and cheeping notes. FOOD: omnivorous but seeds mainly.

STATUS: very common and successful colonist.

699 TREE SPARROW *Passer montanus*   (Linnaeus) 1758
Distribution: parts of Victoria, north to about Sydney; doubtfully Tasmania.

RECOGNITION: like House Sparrow but sexes alike, *forehead to nape chestnut, black patch on ear coverts,* black bib smaller (chin and throat only).

HABITAT, etc: similar to House Sparrow but less adapted to human environments; voice more twittery than chirrupy, utters soft 'tek' in flight.

STATUS: uncommon to fairly common colonist.

Introduced family

Family FRINGILLIDAE

Finches

2(125) species: both introduced

THIS FAMILY CONSISTS OF species which first had the name 'finch'. At one time it included the native finches of Australia and elsewhere which are now separated in the family Estrididae. The fringilline finches belong mainly to old world temperate regions. Like the native finches the two colonists introduced to Australia have thick conical bills and feed mostly on seeds extracted from hard husks; they are rarely on the ground. The Goldfinch vies with the Gouldian Finch in striking colour pattern but the Greenfinch is much more sombre. They are gregarious and build well made cup-shaped nests.

Key to FRINGILLIDAE

1 Head red, white and black . . . .   Goldfinch . . . . No 700
2 Head greenish like most of plumage . . . .   Greenfinch . . . . No 701

700 GOLDFINCH *Carduelis carduelis*   (Linnaeus) 1758
Distribution: Map 273.

RECOGNITION: *red mask, white face, broad gold band on wing.*

DESCRIPTION: 12cm. Sexes alike. Forehead to chin scarlet (like mask); remainder of face white; crown to nape and edge of white on face black; back brown; rump and upper tail coverts white; underparts mainly white with pale buff on breast and flanks; wings black with broad yellow central band and flight feathers tipped white; tail black with subterminal white; bill pale yellow; eyes brown; legs pinkish.

HABITAT: urban parks and gardens. HABITS: forages among foliage and especially on the

seeding heads of wasteland plants; gregarious, usually in small parties. BREEDING: October–
February; nests usually in outer branches of trees and bushes, cup-shaped, well made of grass
and fibre and lined with soft material; four to five eggs, pale blue spotted with brown.
VOICE: twittering 'swit-wit'. FOOD: mostly seeds.
STATUS: fairly common to common colonist.

701 GREENFINCH *Chloris chloris* (Linnaeus) 1758

Distribution: mostly Victoria with extensions to other States.

RECOGNITION: *mainly dull green with yellow on wings and base of tail.*

DESCRIPTION: 15cm. Sexes nearly alike, female duller. Mainly olive-green, yellower on rump
and paler and yellower on underparts; base of flight feathers bright yellow making large
patch on extended wing; outer base of tail bright yellow; bill dull white; eyes brown; legs
pale pink.

HABITAT: woodland. HABITS: arboreal, relatively unobtrusive; in small parties; flight undulating. BREEDING: September–January; nests in trees and bushes, made of twigs and fibre and
lined with feathers; four to six eggs, pale blue spotted with brown. VOICE: sharp 'swee-e-e'
and various trilling notes. FOOD: seeds.

STATUS: uncommon colonist but increasing and spreading.

Family STURNIDAE

Starlings

3(110) species: 2 introduced

Distribution: old world; introduced to North America, southern Australia and New Zealand.

SOME MEMBERS OF THIS large and successful family are enterprising colonists on their
own initiative, like species of the genus *Aplonis* which have occupied most Polynesian
islands. Only the Shining Starling has reached Australia, to northeast Queensland, from New
Guinea, but commutes as a breeding visitor. Starlings are typically black plumaged, either
wholly or partially, the black being glossed with iridescent colours. They are gregarious and
noisy, highly adaptable and often more or less omnivorous. The two species introduced to
Australia, the European Starling and Indian Myna, are thriving and extending, often at the
expense of native species.

Key to STURNIDAE

1 Mainly brown, white on wings and tail, bill and legs
  yellow .... Indian Myna .... No 704
2 Plumage black 3–4
3 Bill and legs black; northeast .... Shining Starling .... No 702
4 Bill and legs pale; southeast .... European Starling ..... No 703

Genus APLONIS

A group of about twenty-four species which extends from coastal Bengal to many Polynesian islands. There are five species in New Guinea and one, the Shining Starling, crosses Torres Strait to breed in the rain forests of northeast Queensland. Small numbers are recorded in the non-breeding period which suggests that in time a breeding population may become established as permanent residents.

702 SHINING STARLING *Aplonis metallica* (Temm. & Laug.) 1824   Pl 24

Distribution: Map 275.

RECOGNITION: *glossy black, red eyes, graduated tail; rain forest of northeast.*

DESCRIPTION: 25cm, with sharply graduated tail about 11cm; neck feathers have hackled appearance. Sexes alike. Black highly glossed with purple and green; bill and legs black; eyes red. *Immature:* underparts white streaked with black.

HABITAT: rain forest. HABITS: arboreal, usually in tree canopies but sometimes feeds on ground, flies rapidly, darting among branches or wheeling in large compact flocks above forest; gregarious; migratory, breeding visitor August–May, but some birds apparently sedentary. BREEDING: September–February; nests in colonies high in forest canopy, suspended from bare branches, oval or spherical, domed with side entrance, large and roughly made of tendrils and lined with soft material; three to four eggs, dull white spotted with shades of brown and grey. VOICE: harsh cries (no details). FOOD: fruits, especially nutmeg, also insects. STATUS: common; breeding visitor. TAXONOMY: species extending to New Guinea.

Introduced species

703 EUROPEAN STARLING *Sturnus vulgaris* Linnaeus 1758

Distribution: Map 274.

RECOGNITION: *glossy black often speckled with white, yellow or pale brown bill and legs.*

DESCRIPTION: 20cm, relatively short tail; hackle feathers on throat and foreneck. Sexes alike. Black with iridescent purple and greenish-bronze; fresh plumage speckled, pale buff above and white below; bill yellow (breeding) or dull brown; eyes dark brown; legs reddish-brown.

HABITAT: open country, especially cultivation, and urban localities. HABITS: arboreal and terrestrial, often feeds on ground, digs between grass roots by inserting and opening bill, flight direct and rapid; gregarious, often in large compact flocks which wheel in unison and gather in special roosts; sedentary and nomadic. BREEDING: September–January; nests in holes and crevices in trees and buildings (sometimes ousting other occupants), a rough collection of grass lined with feathers; five to seven eggs, whitish or pale blue. VOICE: varied, mostly rather harsh but sometimes clear whistles, like 'chee-oo-oo'; mimics other birds. FOOD: insects and seeds, also fruit. STATUS: common and thriving.

Introduced species

704 INDIAN MYNA *Acridotheres tristis* (Linnaeus) 1766

Distribution: various eastern localities from northern Tasmania to central Queensland.

RECOGNITION: *chocolate brown with white bar on wing, yellow bill, eyes, legs and face patch.*

DESCRIPTION: 24cm. Sexes alike. Head and neck black with green iridescence; remainder rich tawny brown, paler on underparts; bare skin of face yellow; large white patch in centre of wing; blackish tail tipped with white; bill, eyes and legs yellow.

HABITAT: urban and domestic. HABITS: arboreal and terrestrial, feeds mostly on ground, frequently on or near rubbish dumps and vicinity of stock; active and quarrelsome; gregarious, collects in large noisy roosts, often in urban trees; apparently sedentary. BREEDING: variable, but mainly October–March; nests in holes and crevices, often in buildings, and in dense vegetation, roughly made of grass; three to six eggs, pale blue. VOICE: various sharp and harsh notes and softer chattering. FOOD: fairly omnivorous.

STATUS: common and thriving.

Family ORIOLIDAE

Orioles

4(28) species

THERE IS MUCH SIMILARITY in the species of this distinctive family. It consists of only two genera, the figbirds in addition to orioles, both of which are represented in Australia, each by two species. Many orioles have rich yellow in the plumage which is sometimes modified to green and dullest in the figbirds. Also they are noted for clear flute-like songs

Distribution of ORIOLIDAE

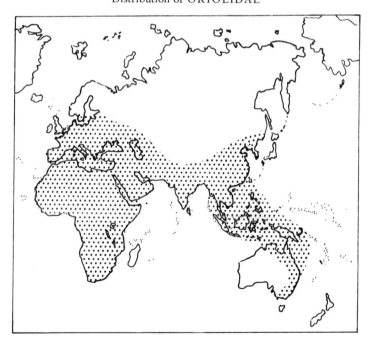

as well as harsh grating calls. They are about 20–30cm in length with fairly long and down-curved bills. They are forest birds and live mainly on soft fruits. None of the four species is endemic and none shows adaptation to Australia's dry habitats. This and their migratory habits suggest they are relatively recent colonists.

Key to ORIOLIDAE

1 Underparts boldly streaked black on white 3–4
2 Underparts mainly green or yellow, sometimes finely streaked 5–8
3 Head and back greenish or greyish-olive . . . . Olive-backed Oriole . . . No 705
4 Head and back brownish
    Shoulders slightly greenish . . . . (♀) Southern Figbird . . . . . . No 707
    Shoulders brownish . . . . (♀) Yellow Figbird . . . . No 708
5 Crown green streaked black . . . . Yellow Oriole . . . . No 706
6 Crown black 7–8
7 Throat grey, breast green . . . . (♂) Southern Figbird . . . . . . No 707
8 Whole underparts bright yellow . . . . (♂) Yellow Figbird . . . . No 708

Genus ORIOLUS

All except four of the family belong to this group. For the most part males are patterned in black and brilliant yellow, but some less well known species are black trimmed with red. When relatively dull in colour, as in the two Australian species, the sexes are nearly alike.

Olive-backed Oriole (705)

705 OLIVE-BACKED ORIOLE *Oriolus sagittatus* (Latham) 1801

Distribution: Map 276.

RECOGNITION: *boldly streaked underparts, upperparts mostly olive-green.*

DESCRIPTION: 25–28cm. Sexes slightly different. *Male:* upperparts shades of olive-green obscurely streaked with black, sometimes greyish on crown, face and throat; underparts white boldly streaked with black and tinged with yellow on flanks; shoulder feathers edged with grey and tipped with white, flight feathers black edged with grey; centre of tail olive-grey, outer feathers blackish edged with grey and large white spot on tip of inner webs; bill orange; eyes red; legs dark blue-grey. *Female:* upperparts more greyish-olive with little green; wing feathers edged with cinnamon and tail spot cinnamon.

VARIATION: west of Leichhardt River, bill smaller and streaks on underparts narrower (race *affinis*); Cape York, bill larger and streaks bolder (race *magnisostris*).

HABITAT: forest and woodland. HABITS: arboreal, usually in tree foliage, often flies high above tree-tops, sometimes catches insects on wing; solitary, but when not breeding usually in small flocks; mainly sedentary in north and mainly migratory in south. BREEDING: September–January; nests suspended in forks of outer foliage (like many honeyeaters), cup-shaped, made of bark strips lined with fine material; two to three eggs, pale buff speckled with shades of dark brown. VOICE: varied, rich and melodious whistles, like 'or-ee-ee', also harsh notes. FOOD: fruit and insects.

STATUS: uncommon to fairly common. TAXONOMY: species extending to southeast New Guinea.

706 YELLOW ORIOLE *Oriolus flavocinctus* (Vigors) 1826 Pl 22
Distribution: Map 277.

RECOGNITION: like Olive-backed Oriole but yellower; *upperparts, throat and breast yellowish-green finely streaked with black; belly yellow;* black wings and tail feathers edged and tipped with pale yellow. Female duller and rather more streaked.

VARIATION: changes in intensity of yellow colour doubtfully associated with distribution.

HABITAT: mostly wet forest and mangroves. HABITS, etc: mainly similar to Green-backed Oriole so far as recorded. VOICE: melodious liquid notes, one recorded as phrase of three notes last being a gurgling sound; also harsh 'chop-chop-chop'.

STATUS: apparently fairly common. TAXONOMY: species extending to Aru Is and southern New Guinea.

Genus SPHECOTHERES
A group of four species, designated as figbirds, belonging to the Australo-Papuan area and distinguished mostly by dull plumage, patch of brightly coloured bare skin on the face and distinct sexual dimorphism.

707 SOUTHERN FIGBIRD *Sphecotheres vieilloti* Vig. & Horsf. 1827
Distribution: Map 278.

RECOGNITION: *male has black crown and red patch on face, female brownish above and boldly streaked below; like Yellow Figbird but dull grey and green below.*

DESCRIPTION: 28cm. Sexes different. *Male:* head and face glossy black, facial bare skin reddish-orange; hind neck, throat and breast grey; back, shoulders and belly yellowish-green, centre of belly pale yellow shading to white vent and under tail coverts; flight feathers black edged with grey; tail black, outer feathers broadly tipped with white; bill black; eyes reddish-brown; legs pale buff. *Female:* face, throat and upperparts brown streaked with darker brown, tinged with olive on shoulders, rump and centre of tail; breast and belly pale buff boldly streaked with dark brown.

VARIATION: apparently some north–south variation but not clearly defined geographically.

HABITAT: forest, woodland, urban fruiting trees. HABITS: arboreal, active and noisy; solitary or parties, sometimes large loose flocks; sedentary and nomadic, apparently also migratory.

BREEDING: October–February; nests in high horizontal forks of tree foliage, flimsy-looking saucer made of twigs and tendrils; three eggs, greenish spotted with dark brown. VOICE: constant sharp chirping, short high-pitched squawk, like European Jackdaw. FOOD: figs and other fruit.

STATUS: fairly common. TAXONOMY: near endemic species, apparently only small population in extreme southeast New Guinea.

708 YELLOW FIGBIRD *Sphecotheres flaviventris*   Gould 1849   Pl 22
Distribution: Map 279.

RECOGNITION: like Southern Figbird but *male has underparts bright yellow,* except for white vent and under tail coverts, and *lacks grey collar;* female has browner upperparts with olive-green limited to tinge on rump and upper tail coverts.

HABITAT, etc: apparently very similar to Southern Figbird, possibly more sedentary, breeding recorded September–March, sometimes nests in small colonies.

STATUS: fairly common. TAXONOMY: near endemic species; one racially distinct population on Kei Is, near Timor.

Family DICRURIDAE

Drongos

1(20) species: endemic

IT SEEMS AS IF in acquiring their distinctive characteristics drongos have obscured their origins; at least taxonomists find difficulty in deciding where to place them on the avian tree. They resemble some species adjacent to their present location in having black plumages with iridescent colours. Some have ornamental head plumes but what distinguishes them best is long tails with fishtail shape. This feature is readily noted for birds frequently perch motionless with drooping tails on low boughs, periodically darting out to catch insects in the manner of some flycatchers. They have robust bills and bristles on the mouth. The only Australian representative, the Spangled Drongo, seems to be a recent colonist.

709 SPANGLED DRONGO *Dicrurus bracteatus*   Gould 1842   Pl 24
Distribution: Map 280.

RECOGNITION: *glossy black, long tail with 'fishtail' fork.*

DESCRIPTION: 28–30cm, with forked tail 15cm. Sexes alike. Black; velvet black on body with blue-green spangles (iridescent spots) on head, neck and breast, oily green iridescence on wings and tail; some white spots on under shoulders; bill black; eyes reddish-brown; legs black.

HABITAT: forest, especially forest edge, mangroves and other heavy timber. HABITS: arboreal, in canopy or low down, often perched upright on low bare branch with tail hanging, and

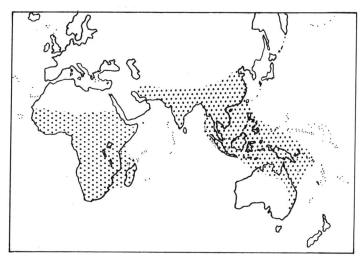

Distribution of DICRURIDAE

darting out to catch insects on wing; solitary or in small parties; sedentary and migratory. BREEDING: September–March, nests in slender horizontal forks of tree foliage, saucer-shaped, open structure of tendrils and fibre; three to four eggs, pale pink spotted with red and purple. VOICE: harsh cackle or chatter, creaking whistle. FOOD: insects.

STATUS: common, rare in south. TAXONOMY: endemic species, partial non-breeding visitor to New Guinea; sometimes regarded as race of wide-ranging *D. hottentottus*.

Family GRALLINIDAE

Mudnest Builders

3(4) species: all endemic

THE FOUR VERY DIFFERENT looking species of this family are linked by certain similarities, especially the habit of building nests of mud. In many other ways the Mudlark and its New Guinea relative differ from the other two and they are given subfamily rank. Although different in appearance, the White-winged Chough and Apostlebird are similar in structure and in some curious aspects of their behaviour. They form very closely attached social units of from about eight to twenty birds, traditionally twelve in the Apostlebird. They do everything together, including nest building and rearing young, and often 'clump' in a tight mass when resting or roosting. It may be noted, however, that this behaviour is also found in wood-swallows and babblers, the White-browed Babbler also being dubbed 'Apostlebird'. The

Apostlebird as now generally accepted has an additional religious connection in its 'clerical grey' plumage. The White-winged Chough is black with some white, like the Pied Currawong but without white at the tip of the tail. The Mudlark is boldly patterned in black and white. It is one of the most ubiquitous and obvious of Australian birds and is well known for its boldness and distinctive 'pee-wee' piping. It is smaller than the magpies with which it is often in company along roadsides.

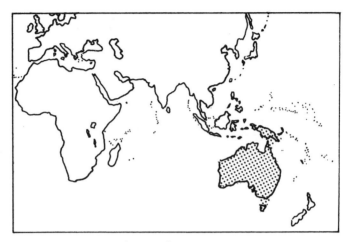

Distribution of GRALLINIDAE

Key to GRALLINIDAE

1 Boldly patterned in black and white . . . . Mudlark . . . . No 710
2 Black with large white patch in wing . . . . White-winged Chough . . . . No 711
3 Dark grey with black tail . . . . Apostlebird . . . . No 712

Genus GRALLINA

A separate genus for the Mudlark. The Torrent Lark of certain New Guinea mountains is sometimes included. The Mudlark builds a cup-shaped mud nest, which limits it to the vicinity of water when breeding. It is a conspicuous pied ground feeder with a piping voice.

710 MUDLARK *Grallina cyanoleuca* (Latham) 1801   Pl 23

Distribution: throughout.

RECOGNITION: *boldly pied, white eye; on ground in open places.*

DESCRIPTION: 25–28cm. Sexes slightly different. *Male:* upperparts mostly black with broad white streak above eye, large white patch on side of neck, broad white band from shoulder to inner wing, and white tips to inner wing feathers, white rump and basal half of tail, narrow white tip to tail; throat and upper breast black; lower breast and belly white; bill dull white; eyes creamy-white; legs black. *Female:* forehead and throat white; white neck patch extends up behind eye; no white patches above or below eye.

HABITAT: open timber of various kinds, suburban parks (mud must be reasonably accessible for nest building). HABITS: arboreal and terrestrial, feeds mostly on ground in open places, common along road margins, movements 'elegant and graceful' (Gould) but flight rather heavy, like plover; readily accepts human settlement, noted for belligerent attacks on reflections in house and car windows; solitary but often in loose sometimes quite large flocks when not breeding; sedentary with some nomadic flock movements. BREEDING: variable, but mostly July–January; nests conspicuously attached to boughs and branches, bowl-shaped, made of mud and grass with soft lining; three to five eggs, white to shades of pink, blotched with purplish-red and violet. VOICE: high-pitched pipe, some notes uttered as duet by sexes, like 'te-he' and 'pee-o-wit', run together as one phrase, accompanied by various wing and body movements. FOOD: insects, but fairly omnivorous.

STATUS: very common. TAXONOMY: endemic species, with one relative in New Guinea.

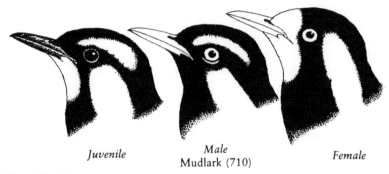

Juvenile　　　*Male*　　　*Female*
Mudlark (710)

Genus CORCORAX

The White-winged Chough is the only member of this genus. It is believed to be more akin to the Apostlebird than to the Mudlark but the affinities of the tree mudnest builders of this family are still an open question.

711 WHITE-WINGED CHOUGH

Corcorax melanorhamphos　(Vieillot) 1817　　　　　　　　Pl 23

Distribution: Map 281.

RECOGNITION: *black with large white patch in wing, no white at tip of tail; in small compact parties.*

DESCRIPTION: 45cm, tail about half, downcurved bill about 4cm. Sexes alike. Black with large area of white conspicuous in extended wing; bill black; eyes reddish-orange (unusual feature is a white eyeball, sometimes noticeable at a distance); legs black.

HABITAT: forest and woodland. HABITS: arboreal and terrestrial, feeds mostly on ground, movements slow and clumsy both on ground and in flight, indulges in tail-fanning display; gregarious and extremely sociable, keeps in small compact parties of about eight consisting of family members as young remain with parents for several years, keeping together even when breeding; indulges in 'anting' behaviour; sedentary and nomadic within fairly restricted area. BREEDING: July–December; nests on horizontal branches, bowl-shaped, made of grass and mud, nests frequently re-used; three to five eggs (larger numbers due to more than one female), whitish spotted with shades of brown and grey. VOICE: harsh grating and piping. FOOD: small animals and insects, also seeds.

STATUS: fairly common. TAXONOMY: endemic species.

Genus STRUTHIDEA

Like the other members of this family the Apostlebird has unusual characteristics and is of uncertain affinity. It has a number of behavioural similarities with the White-winged Chough though in appearance greatly different.

712 APOSTLEBIRD *Struthidea cinerea* Gould 1837   Pl 22

Distribution: Map 282.

RECOGNITION: *dark grey with long black tail; in compact parties which sometimes clump on tree trunks like bees.*

DESCRIPTION: 33cm, tail about half. Sexes alike. Dark grey, slightly paler on head and breast, feathers have pale tips which gives a scalloped or scaly effect; wings brownish; tail black with greenish iridescence; bill and legs black; eyes pearly-white, brown in female.

VARIATION: apparently isolated population in Northern Territory may be distinct (race *dalyi*).

HABITAT: open forest and woodland, country homesteads (sometimes associated with particular vegetation, like pine scrub on Murrumbidgee and lancewood in Northern Territory).

HABITS: arboreal and terrestrial, feeds mostly on ground, actively engages in various social displays, jumps into and up through branches, flies rather heavily for short distances; gregarious, extremely sociable, in parties of about ten to twelve which keep in close contact, even when breeding, sometimes clump together like bees; sedentary or locally nomadic.

BREEDING: August–February; nests on horizontal branches, bowl-shaped, made of mud and grass and lined with grass; four to five eggs (larger numbers due to more than one female); dull white blotched with dark brown and grey. VOICE: loud harsh grating sounds. FOOD: insects and seeds.

STATUS: fairly common. TAXONOMY: endemic species.

Family ARTAMIDAE

Woodswallows

6(10) species: 4 endemic

WOODSWALLOWS ARE NOT RELATED to swallows of the family Hirundinidae, although like them they hawk for insects in the air and some have shallow forked tails. Their connections are obscure. They have bluish-grey bills with black tips like the Cracticidae, brush tipped tongues like honeyeaters and lorikeets*, and the Dusky Woodswallow, possibly other species also, roosts in clusters like the Apostlebird. Although very distinct as a group, the species are uniform in general appearance and habits so that only one genus seems necessary. Differences are mainly in the distribution of plain greys and dusky browns with occasional white patches; only one species has chestnut underparts. They are small, 12–18cm, have pointed wings and sometimes shallow forked tails, and a distinctive 'batwing' shape as

*Tongues often used for sipping nectar.

they gracefully flutter and glide over tree tops and cliffs. They stand in tight rows on bare horizontal branches so that central birds have difficulty in preening; when one darts out the others quickly sidle up to fill the gap. They are typically nomadic and migratory, least so in the Black-faced Woodswallow, and move about in large open flocks. The family is richest in variety in Australia and it might be claimed that it originated there. The four species found elsewhere seem to be recent offshoots from the White-breasted Woodswallow, an Australian species with extensive outside connections. But of course it could equally be claimed that the four to five endemic species may be adapted forms from an early White-breasted colonist stock.

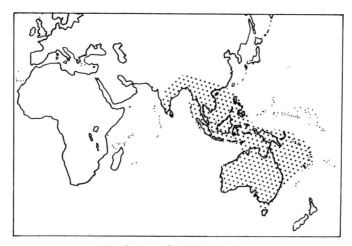

Distribution of ARTAMIDAE

Key to ARTAMIDAE

[*Note:* the word 'Woodswallow' is omitted.]

1 Rump white, tail short	White-breasted	No 713
2 Rump dark, tail medium	3–9	
3 Breast and belly chestnut	White-browed	No 715
4 Breast and belly pale grey	6–7	
5 Breast and belly dark	8–9	
6 Tail grey	Masked	No 714
7 Tail black	Black-faced	No 716
8 White streak in wing	Dusky	No 717
9 No white in wing	Little	No 718

713 WHITE-BREASTED WOODSWALLOW
Artamus leucorhynchus (Linnaeus) 1771

Distribution: Map 283.

RECOGNITION: *white rump and short square tail.*

DESCRIPTION: 17cm; tail relatively short and square; folded wings extend beyond tail; bill short and thick. Sexes alike. Whole head, wings and tail dark grey; lores black; back grey-

Black-faced (716)

White-browed (715)

Dusky (717)

White-breasted (713)

Masked (714)

WOODSWALLOWS

brown; rump, breast and belly white; bill chalky-blue, tip black; eyes dark brown; legs blue-grey.

HABITAT: well timbered places, mainly in coastal areas, especially mangroves in northwest, but further inland in east. HABITS: arboreal, aerial feeder, flutters and glides around tree tops; gregarious, in parties of ten or more, highly sociable, usually perches on bare horizontal boughs in tight packed rows, single birds breaking away to dart out to catch insects, reputed to associate with Mudlark to make use of its old nests; mostly sedentary in northern coasts, nomadic or migratory in south and interior. BREEDING: August–January; nests in tree forks and hollows or old Mudlark nests, cup-shaped, made of grass; three to four eggs, buffy-white spotted and blotched with reddish-brown. VOICE: harsh 'chyek'. FOOD: insects.

STATUS: fairly common. TAXONOMY: race *(leucopygialis)* extending to New Guinea and Moluccas of species ranging from Borneo to Philippines and Fiji.

714 MASKED WOODSWALLOW *Artamus personatus* (Gould) 1841

Distribution: widespread; not Tasmania (recorded on King I) or tip of Cape York.

RECOGNITION: *male has large black mask; female has dusky face and throat, like Black-faced Woodswallow but has grey (not black) tail.*

DESCRIPTION: 18–20cm; tail slightly forked. Sexes different. *Male*: forehead, face and throat black surrounded by white border except on forehead; upperparts grey, darker on crown and paler on rump and tail, tail tipped with white; breast and belly light grey; bill chalky-blue, tip black; eyes dark brown; legs black. *Female*: face and throat dusky shading to dark grey on upper breast and light grey on belly.

HABITAT: mainly inland savanna. HABITS, etc: similar to White-breasted Woodswallow; sometimes feeds on ground; highly nomadic at all seasons, stopping temporarily to breed, October–December, wherever conditions suitable; mostly breeding visitor only south of tropic; often in mixed flocks with other woodswallow species, sometimes accompanied by Crimson Chats; nests usually low down in trees and bushes, shallow cup made of grass and fibre.

STATUS: common. TAXONOMY: endemic species.

715 WHITE-BROWED WOODSWALLOW   *Artamus superciliosus*   (Gould) 1837

Distribution: Map 284.

RECOGNITION: *chestnut breast and belly, white eyebrow of male.*

DESCRIPTION: 18–20cm; tail slightly forked. Sexes different. *Male:* whole head and neck sooty black with broad white eyebrow; back dark grey, blue-grey on rump, wings and tail; tail tipped with white; lower breast and belly chestnut; under wings and under tail whitish; bill chalky-blue, tip black; eyes dark brown; legs black. *Female:* head blue-grey like rest of upperparts, except for black lores; white eyebrow less distinct; breast and belly greyish-chestnut.

HABITAT: variable, mainly savanna. HABITS, etc: similar to White-breasted Woodswallow, highly nomadic, wanders in large flocks often mixed with other woodswallow species, breeding visitor south of tropic. VOICE: high-pitched querulous 'chirp' in flight.

STATUS: common in east, rare elsewhere. TAXONOMY: endemic species.

716 BLACK-FACED WOODSWALLOW   *Artamus cinereus*   (Vieillot) 1817

Distribution: throughout except extreme southeast and Tasmania.

RECOGNITION: *black face patch; like female Masked Woodswallow but crown and throat much paler and rump and tail black (not grey).*

DESCRIPTION: 18cm; tail slightly rounded. Sexes alike. Black round eye to base of bill and tip of chin; crown and back brownish-grey; wings blue-grey, white underneath; rump and tail black, tail with broad white tip; underparts variable (see Variation); bill chalky-blue, tip black; eyes dark brown; legs blue-grey.

VARIATION: centre and northwest, foreneck to belly vinous grey, vent and under tail coverts black, latter sometimes tipped white (race *melanops*); southwest, similar but foreneck to belly more vinous or buffy (race *tregellasi*); east coast south of Townsville, foreneck and upper breast pale vinous grey, lower breast to under tail coverts white (race *hypoleucos*); north of Townsville and Flinders River, similar but vent only black (race *normani*).

HABITAT: savanna woodland (roughly under 50cm rainfall; replaced in higher rainfall areas by Dusky Woodswallow). HABITS, etc: similar to White-breasted Woodswallow; sometimes feeds on ground among grass; much more sedentary ('does not make large concentrated movements after food') but some movements noted; breeds when conditions suitable but mostly August–January. VOICE: twittering 'quet-quet'.

STATUS: common. TAXONOMY: species extending to southeast New Guinea (one form in Timor regarded as conspecific).

717 DUSKY WOODSWALLOW   *Artamus cyanopterus*   (Latham) 1801

Distribution: Map 285.

RECOGNITION: *dark grey-brown with white streak at edge of wing.*

DESCRIPTION: 18cm; shallow forked tail with central feathers slightly extended. Sexes alike. Dark grey-brown, palest on head and breast and darkest on rump and belly; wings and tail blackish, wings with white edge and tail with white tip; bill chalky-blue, tip black; eyes dark brown; legs dark blue-grey.

VARIATION: eastern populations, white on flight feathers 2, 3 and 4 (race *cyanopterus*); southwest population, white on flight feathers 2 and 3 (race *perthi*).

HABITAT: forest and woodland (roughly over 50cm rainfall; replaced in lower rainfall areas by Black-faced Woodswallow). HABITS, etc: similar to White-breasted Woodswallow; habit of resting or roosting in clumps or clusters seems to be most developed in this species, 'bunches' of up to 100 have been recorded; mostly breeding visitor in south, but some apparently sedentary even in Tasmania.

STATUS: common. TAXONOMY: endemic species.

718 LITTLE WOODSWALLOW   *Artamus minor*   Vieillot 1817

Distribution: Map 286.

RECOGNITION: *small and blackish with white tail tip and grey underwing; no white wing streak.*

DESCRIPTION: 12cm; folded wings just reach tip of square tail. Sexes alike. Head and body dark chocolate brown with diffuse sooty-black on forehead, face and throat; wings dark blue-grey, light grey below; rump and tail blue-black, tail with white tip; bill chalky-blue, tip and underside black; eyes dark brown; legs black.

HABITAT: forest to savanna woodland; in southern W.A., near rocky gorges, breakaways and cliffs. HABITS, etc: similar to White-breasted Woodswallow; nomadic but apparently fairly sedentary in some areas; nests in rock crevices and ledges, tree stumps and hollows, as well as in trees and bushes, nests more roughly made than those of other species.

STATUS: fairly common. TAXONOMY: species extending to south New Guinea.

Family CRACTICIDAE
Butcherbirds, Magpies, Currawongs

9(10) species: 7 endemic

MEMBERS OF THIS FAMILY are among the best known of Australian birds. They are found throughout the continent, are medium to large, 25–50cm, mostly black and white, usually bold and at times aggressive, have loud characteristic voices, sometimes harsh but often also tuneful. The voice of the Black-throated Butcherbird in its full volume must consist of the purest tonal notes uttered by any bird, and the most pleasing to the human ear; its less well known subsong is a superb repertoire of varied notes and phrases; but what it says to a goanna or cat is unprintable! Also to hear a magpie 'choir' is a highlight of any Australian experience. By their voices, pied plumages and other characteristics it is sometimes maintained that one genus would be adequate but the species readily fall into three easily recognisable groups. The White-winged Chough might be mistaken for a Pied Currawong but it has no white at the tip of the tail.

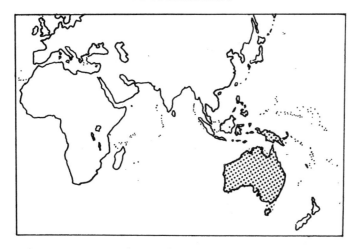

Distribution of CRACTICIDAE

Key to CRACTICIDAE

1 Wholly black	Black Butcherbird	No 722
2 Throat black, belly white	Black-throated Butcherbird	No 719
3 Underparts white		
Back black	Black-backed Butcherbird	No 721
Back grey	Grey Butcherbird	No 720
4 Underparts mainly black	5–7	
5 Collar, back and rump white		
Tail feathers with black shafts (♂)	White-backed Magpie	No 724
Tail feathers with white shafts	Western Magpie	No 725
6 Collar and rump white		
Back grey (♀)	White-backed Magpie	No 724
Back black	Black-backed Magpie	No 723
(♀)	Western Magpie	No 725
7 Upperparts mostly black or grey with white-tipped tail, white in wing and sometimes white on rump	Currawongs	Nos 726–727

Genus CRACTICUS

The butcherbirds were first placed with the original owners of that name, the shrikes (family Laniidae, not in Australia). They have the same habit of frequently taking animal food larger than can be swallowed whole, large insects, especially grasshoppers, and small animals which have to be torn up. This is achieved by means of a sharp black hook at the tip of a large bluish bill. The food is held down by the feet or wedged in a sharp-angled notch or stuck on a spike. They have short legs and hop on the ground but they feed mostly off the ground or carry food into trees to be eaten. They are the smallest group in size, 25–35cm, and pied except for the Black Butcherbird of northeast rain forest.

719 BLACK-THROATED BUTCHERBIRD
Cracticus nigrogularis (Gould) 1837 Pl 23
Distribution: widespread, except in extreme south and tip of Cape York.
RECOGNITION: *boldly pied, with black 'bib' on otherwise white underparts.*

DESCRIPTION: 32–35cm; stout bill with tip sharply hooked. Sexes alike. Whole head to upper breast black (forming a black 'bib'); hindneck white, joined to white lower breast and belly; back black; rump and upper tail coverts white; tail black with broad white tip; wings black with broad white streaks; bill bluish-grey, tip black; eyes black; legs grey. *Immature:* dark areas brownish-black, 'bib' pale buff, buff eyebrow.

VARIATION: mostly north-south size variation—south, larger (race *nigrogularis*); north, smaller (race *picatus*); western birds not clearly distinguished but sometimes recognised (race *kalgoorli*).

HABITAT: woodland, suburban parks. HABITS: arboreal, but sometimes feeds on ground, hops, carries large items of food into trees to be torn up by wedging into forks or impaling on spikes; solitary or in family parties; sedentary. BREEDING: August–December; nests in trees, in vertical forks above about 2m, untidy-looking shallow cup made of twigs and fibres and lined with grass; three to four eggs, shades of pale green or brown spotted with dark brown and black. VOICE: rich variety of loud clear flute-like notes and phrases often uttered in duet and to the accompaniment of elaborate gestures of dipped and erected head and partial wing opening. FOOD: insects and small animals.

STATUS: common. TAXONOMY: endemic species.

720 GREY BUTCHERBIRD *Cracticus torquatus* (Latham) 1801   Pl 23

Distribution: throughout except Cape York north of Palmer River.

RECOGNITION: *all white underparts and white patch in front of eye.*

DESCRIPTION: 28–32cm; stout bill with sharply hooked tip. Sexes alike. Forehead to nape and face black with white lores; white collar joined to white underparts; back bluish-grey; upper tail coverts white; tail black broadly tipped with white; wing blackish-brown with white streak from shoulder to inner wing; bill blue-grey, tip black; eyes blackish; legs bluish-grey. *Immature:* upperparts dark brownish-black mottled with buff, underparts buffy-white.

VARIATION: southeast, back darkest grey (race *torquatus*); northwest, palest (race *argenteus*); remainder, intermediate (race *leucopterus*); Tasmania, largest (race *cinereus*).

HABITAT: most kinds of timber except rain forest. HABITS, etc: similar to Pied Butcherbird, but seems to keep more concealed among foliage, nests generally lower; voice distinctly different, lower pitched and slightly harsher, sudden bursts of loud rollicking phrases sometimes uttered in duet.

STATUS: common. TAXONOMY: endemic species.

721 BLACK-BACKED BUTCHERBIRD *Cracticus mentalis* Salv. & d'Alb. 1876

Distribution: Cape York north of Palmer River.

RECOGNITION: very like Grey Butcherbird but slightly smaller, 25cm, *lores black* (not white), *back black,* rump grey.

HABITAT, etc: similar to Grey Butcherbird, but voice very different.

STATUS: fairly common. TAXONOMY: doubtfully distinct race *(kempi)* of species extending into southeast New Guinea; seems very probable that the Black-backed Butcherbird is merely a melanistic variant of Grey Butcherbird.

722 BLACK BUTCHERBIRD *Cracticus quoyi* (Lesson) 1827   Pl 24
Distribution: Map 287.

RECOGNITION: *all black, also 'rufous' immature phase.*

DESCRIPTION: 32–36cm. Sexes alike but immature dimorphic. *Adult:* black; bill pale blue-grey, tip black; legs black. *Immature:* (1) black; (2) cinnamon brown streaked with black on crown, nape and face, brightest cinnamon on upper tail coverts, palest on underparts, more brownish on wings and tail (commonest in Cooktown to Tully area and may be mated before moulting into black plumage).

VARIATION: Northern Territory population, larger with narrower bill (race *spaldingi*); Cape York, smaller with thicker bill (race *rufescens*).

HABITAT: forest and mangroves. HABITS, etc: apparently similar to Grey Butcherbird; keeps mostly in dense vegetation, feeds on ground in mangroves. VOICE: loud distinctive 'ah-oo-ah' or 'mol-gol-ga' or 'kurr-a-wa' with accent on second syllable, also other more musical phrases. FOOD: crabs included in varied diet.

STATUS: fairly common (at least). TAXONOMY: species with extensions into New Guinea and adjacent islands, and Aru Is.

Grey Butcherbird (720)

White-backed
Magpie (724)

Genus GYMNORHINA

The magpies are intermediate in the family size range, about 35–40cm. They pose a problem for taxonomists to decide whether there is only one species or several. The variants mostly replace each other and some are clearly different. But distinctive patterns and distributions seem curiously confused and the main criterion of a species, that it is reproductively isolated, is not fulfilled. The Black-backed and White-backed Magpies interbreed in northern Victoria and there is a narrow zone of hybrids; in the Alice Springs area the two forms seem to mix but retain their identities; in the southwest the male has a white back and the female a black one. Although it seems that speciation is not complete the solution frequently adopted, and most suitable here, is to recognise three species. At most they are semispecies of a super-species. There is an interesting behavioural variation. In Western Australia the reproductive unit is a group of about six to twenty birds; in the southeast the unit is smaller; and in Queensland at least the unit seems to be the usual pair. Magpies, like butcherbirds, have stout bluish bills with black tips, and although they tear their food in a similar manner the hook is much less distinct; they are mainly ground feeders, with long legs and a walking gait, and dig for grubs and beetles, when a hook might be rather inconvenient.

723 BLACK-BACKED MAGPIE *Gymnorhina tibicen* (Latham) 1801   Pl 23
Distribution: Map 288.

RECOGNITION: *boldly pied, black back; often on ground along roadsides.*

DESCRIPTION: 36–40cm; bill stout and partly hooked. Sexes alike, except that white collar in female is slightly 'dirty'. Mainly black with broad white collar, broad white band from shoulder to inner wing, white rump and tail, except black tip of tail, white vent; shafts of tail feathers black (not white as in Western Magpie); bill bluish-white, tip black; eyes chestnut; legs black. *Immature:* dark areas brownish and mottled.

VARIATION: there is some variation in size in addition to marked changes in amount of white on back but listing races named under each rather dubious species might add confusion rather than clarification.

HABITAT: open timbered areas, pastures, suburban parks and gardens. HABITS, arboreal and terrestrial, roosts and nests in trees but feeds mostly on ground, walks about for long periods; bold, rather aggressive in breeding season, even against humans near nests and young; solitary or loosely gregarious or in closely knit breeding groups (see notes on family); sedentary. BREEDING: July–March, period shortest in south and longest in north; nests in trees, in forks among slender branches, often high up, bowl-shaped, made of twigs and fibres and lined with grass; three eggs, variable, sometimes shades of pale blue or brown spotted and streaked with reddish-brown and dull purple. VOICE: loud chortling warble, more flute than whistle, sometimes interspersed with harsh notes and often uttered in duet with heads vertical and wings partly open; also quiet melodious subsong of very varied phrases. FOOD: omnivorous but mostly insects, especially grasshoppers.

STATUS: very common. TAXONOMY: species or semispecies or race extending to southeast New Guinea; closely related to White-backed and Western Magpies, with which it hybridises.

724 WHITE-BACKED MAGPIE
    Gymnorhina hypoleuca   (Gould) 1837   Pl 23   Fig p 471
Distribution: Map 288.

RECOGNITION: like Black-backed Magpie but *back white,* female has back off-white or pale grey. *(Note:* in some areas, notably from southeast South Australia to southern Northern Territory, this distinction is often not clearly defined; backs may be white or varying widths of black.*)*

HABITAT, etc: similar to Black-backed Magpie, even general tonal quality of voice similar although phrases may be different.

STATUS: very common. TAXONOMY: endemic species, or similar to Black-backed Magpie.

725 WESTERN MAGPIE *Gymnorhina dorsalis* Campbell 1895
Distribution: Map 288.

RECOGNITION: male like White-backed Magpie, female like Black-backed Magpie but *black feathers of upper back have white edges,* both have *white tail feathers with white shafts* (not black).

HABITAT, etc: similar to other magpies, possibly more gregarious and in breeding groups (see notes on family).

STATUS and TAXONOMY: as for White-backed Magpie.

Genus STREPERA
The currawongs are the largest members of the family, 45–50cm. As in other groups bills are large but they are black and only slightly hooked at the tip, as in magpies. They have

relatively long tails. They are mostly dark plumaged, black or grey, with varying amounts of white in the centre and tip of the wings and base of the tail; but all have white tipped tails, a feature which together with less closely gregarious habits distinguishes them from the White-winged Chough. There are at least two species, the Pied Currawong and Grey Currawong, the reservation being that some forms are often listed as species. The two main groups are distinguished thus:

Pied Currawong (726)   Grey Currawong (727)

Pied	Grey
1 Always blackish.	Grey brown to sooty black.
2 Base of tail and under tail coverts white on mainland and black in Tasmania.	Base of tail never white, under tail coverts always white.
3 Bill thicker with well defined hook.	Bill more slender with hook not well defined.
4 Smaller, 45cm.	Larger, 50cm.

726 PIED CURRAWONG *Strepera graculina* (White) 1790   Pl 23

Distribution: Map 289.

RECOGNITION: see note above.

DESCRIPTION: 45cm. Sexes alike. Plumage dull black with varying amounts of white partly concealed in centre of wing, at base of tail and on under tail coverts (sometimes absent); tips of flight feathers usually white and tail feathers always broadly tipped with white; bill and legs black; eyes yellow.

VARIATION: marked differences in bill length and also gradation in amount of white from least in south to most in north: Tasmania, white in wing small (in Tasmanian Grey Currawong distinctly large) and no white at base of tail or on under tail coverts (race *fuliginosa*); Victoria, white in wings and usually at base of tail (race *ashbyi*); New South Wales, more white (race *graculina*); Queensland, maximum white (race *robinsoni*).

HABITAT: forest, suburban patches of large trees. HABITS: arboreal, sometimes feeds on ground turning over sticks and leaves, hops, clambers up trees in jumps, glides or flies rather heavily between trees or to feeding grounds, noisy; loosely gregarious when breeding and in more compact flocks at other times: sedentary. BREEDING: September–March; nests in trees in forks among foliage, bowl-shaped, made of sticks and twigs lined with grass; three to four eggs, shades of brown blotched and lined with darker shades. VOICE: very loud and quite musical variants sounding like 'kurra-wong', also long flute-like whistle and repeated 'wok' and explosive 'whee-ah'. FOOD: omnivorous, including orchard fruits.

STATUS: common. TAXONOMY: endemic species; some forms often listed as separate species, like *fuliginosa* in Tasmania (named Black Jay or Black Currawong).

727 GREY CURRAWONG *Strepera versicolor* (Latham) 1801 Fig p 473
Distribution: Map 290.

RECOGNITION: see notes on genus.

DESCRIPTION: 50cm. Sexes alike. Plumage brownish-grey to brownish-black (more sooty-black than Pied Currawong) with varying amounts of white partly concealed in wing, white tip to tail, white vent and under tail coverts and sometimes white tips to main flight feathers; bill and legs black; eyes yellow.

VARIATION: of the forms listed the most distinctive seem to be—Victoria and New South Wales, palest (race *versicolor*); southeast South Australia, darkest (race *melanoptera*); Tasmania, largest (race *arguta*).

HABITAT: forest and woodland. HABITS and BREEDING: similar to Pied Currawong. VOICE: very different. Some notes likened by Gould to distinct sound of strokes on blacksmith's anvil, variants of 'klink', 'klank' and 'tew' (W.A.)—hence alternative name Bell Magpie; also squeaky notes like cat mewing, and popular name in Western Australia of Squeaker. FOOD: omnivorous, including fruit.

STATUS: common. TAXONOMY: endemic species; the variants listed above are sometimes regarded as species, especially *arguta*, the Black Magpie or Clinking Currawong of Tasmania.

Family PTILONORHYNCHIDAE
Bowerbirds
9(18) species: 7 endemic

BOWERBIRDS SEEM TO HAVE close affinity with birds of paradise but the elaboration of the instinct to display, well developed in both, takes the form of clearing areas on the ground and decorating them in various ways, often with beautifully constructed bowers. Some male bowerbirds do have various kinds of ornamental plumes, but they are not developed to any exaggerated extent. Both families belong essentially to rain forest in the same general region but the *Chlamydera* bowerbirds are adapted to more open habitats. This achievement probably happened only once, with subsequent divergence, for the species are very alike. The three Australian *Chlamydera* replace each other, do not interbreed where they are in proximity and the pattern of their distributions suggests that there have been three colonisations from a single New Guinea source. They have camouflage plumage, drab brown marked with light spots and blotches, like dappled sunlight through the foliage in which the birds often remain hidden. In contrast the males of forest species have varied bright colours. This illustrates the extent to which environment can modify plumage appearance in closely related birds; it seems likely that *Chlamydera* is an offshoot from some gaily coloured forest species, perhaps the Regent Bowerbird of which the female is alike. Of the six species confined to rain forest the Green Catbird is the only one which does not construct a display ground. These cleared areas, made by both forest and woodland species, are not nesting places. Nests are concealed among tree foliage and undergrowth. The Australian representatives of the family are about 23–33cm in length and of average proportions; bills are fairly thick and curved, and deeply notched in the Tooth-billed Catbird or Stagemaker.

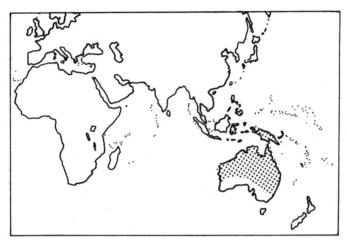

Distribution of PTILONORHYNCHIDAE

Key to PTILONORHYNCHIDAE

1	Wholly violet-black .... (♂)	Satin Bowerbird............	No 733
2	Boldly patterned in black and yellow .... (♂)	Regent Bowerbird	No 732
3	Boldly patterned in gold and yellow .... (♂)	Golden Bowerbird..........	No 731
4	General appearance greenish	6–9	
5	General appearance brownish	10–15	
6	Dull olive-green .... (♀)	Satin Bowerbird............	No 733
7	Bright green	8–9	
8	Crown green like back	Green Catbird	No 728
9	Crown blackish	Spotted Catbird............	No 729
10	Upperparts plain	12–13	
11	Upperparts mottled	14–15	
12	Underparts plain grey .... (♀)	Golden Bowerbird..........	No 731
13	Underparts streaked	Stagemaker................	No 730
14	Nape black .... (♀)	Regent Bowerbird	No 732
15	Nape grey-brown, sometimes violet-pink........	⎰ Spotted Bowerbird	No 734
		⎨ Great Bowerbird	No 735
		⎱ Fawn-breasted Bowerbird	No 736

Genus AILUROEDUS

The green catbirds are probably the most primitive members of the family, or at least they are the only ones which do not construct display grounds. They consist of three species in the present context, for the isolated southern population in Australia is regarded as a separate species or semispecies. These catbirds are plump, about 22–33cm in length, have stout bills and curious mewling calls, like a cat or young baby crying.

728 GREEN CATBIRD *Ailuroedus crassirostris* (Paycull) 1815   Pl 22
Distribution: Map 291.

RECOGNITION: *dark green; rain forests; cat-like calls.*

DESCRIPTION: 33cm. Sexes alike. Upperparts olive-green, nape freckled with white, inner wing feathers and outer tail feathers tipped with white; face mottled black and green; underparts mainly light green spotted with greenish-white, slightly greyer on throat and tinged with buff-yellow on belly; bill pinkish-white; eyes red-brown; legs pinkish-brown.

HABITAT: rain forest. HABITS: (not well known) arboreal; apparently solitary when breeding and in foraging flocks of about fifteen to twenty birds at other times; sedentary. BREEDING: September–December; nests at various heights but often around 4m, in tangle of vines or top of tree fern or similar places, open cup-shaped made of vines and twigs interwoven with leaves and lined with fine fibres; two eggs, creamy white. VOICE: notes uncannily like baby crying or cat mewing; also phrases consisting of sharp clicking and loud guttural sounds usually uttered before sunrise. FOOD: fruits and seeds, chicks fed on insects.

STATUS: fairly common. TAXONOMY: endemic species or semispecies, forming superspecies with Spotted Catbird and other forms in New Guinea.

729 SPOTTED CATBIRD *Ailuroedus melanotis* (Gray) 1858
Distribution: Map 291.

RECOGNITION: like Green Catbird but *smaller, 23cm,* and *head, face and chin black* spotted with grey-brown.

HABITAT, etc: similar to Green Catbird; breeds mostly October–January; voice less like baby or cat and apparently does not use clicking-guttural phase.

STATUS: fairly common TAXONOMY: the two separate populations (see map) are regarded as distinct endemic forms (races *maculosa* and *joanae*) of species in New Guinea and adjacent islands, including Aru Is; forms superspecies with Green Catbird.

Stagemaker (730)   Spotted Catbird (729)

Genus SCENOPOEETUS
A separate genus for the Stagemaker or Tooth-billed Catbird, which seems to be a link between the green catbirds and the bower-building group. The alternative names indicate the bird's principal characteristics, a deep notch near the tip of the bill and the habit of displaying on a cleared space on the forest floor. There is no bower.

730 STAGEMAKER *Scenopoeetes dentirostris* (Ramsay) 1876   Pl 22
Distribution: Map 292.

RECOGNITION: *brownish above, dark streaks on white underparts; mountain rain forest.*

DESCRIPTION: 23cm; short thick curved bill with upper mandible deeply notched near tip. Sexes alike. Upperparts dark olive-brown; underparts buffy-white broadly streaked with dark grey-brown; bill blackish; eyes dark brown; legs dark grey-brown.

HABITAT: mountain rain forest. HABITS: arboreal but displays on ground, 'stage' consists of cleared circular area up to 3m in diameter, decorated each day with fresh green leaves; male perches on special stance near 'stage' and utters 'constant medley of sound'; sedentary. BREEDING: November–December; nests in thick foliage well off ground, saucer-shaped, sparsely made of twigs; two eggs, creamy-brown. VOICE: loud 'chuck', but mostly long repertoire mimicking notes of many other birds. FOOD: mainly leaves cut by toothed bill, also fruit and insects.

STATUS: common in isolated groups. TAXONOMY: endemic species and genus.

Genus PRIONODURA

A separate genus for the endemic Golden Bowerbird. (The name aptly describes the male but it is confusing because it properly belongs to the New Guinea bowerbird *Sericulus aureus* given by Linnaeus.) The Queensland bird of that name is distinctive in its striking sexual dimorphism and in belonging to the 'maypole' building group; the male erects a great mound of twigs round the base and up the trunks of adjacent saplings. The male colour pattern is different to that found in the *Sericulus* group.

731 GOLDEN BOWERBIRD* *Prionodura newtoniana* De Vis 1883

Distribution: Map 293.

RECOGNITION: *male dull gold and bright yellow, female olive-brown above and white below; rain forest.*

DESCRIPTION: 23–26cm. Sexes very different. *Male:* centre of crown, nape, sides of tail and underparts bright orange-yellow; remainder dull golden-brown; many feathers of upperparts and throat have opalescent sheen; bill dark brown; eyes yellowish-white. *Female:* upperparts dark olive-brown; underparts ash-grey.

HABITAT: mountain rain forest. HABITS: arboreal with terrestrial display ground of 'maypole' type; this consists of pyramids of twigs built round two adjacent saplings with cleared area between, there is a bare branch or stick in centre around which both sexes display; area decorated with flowers, usually white, ferns, mosses and berries. BREEDING: October–December; nests in tangled undergrowth near ground, shallow cup made of twigs, leaves and mosses; two white eggs. VOICE: various croaking and rattling sounds but mostly imitations of many other bird voices. FOOD: fruit and insects.

STATUS: common. TAXONOMY: endemic species and genus.

Genus SERICULUS

The species in this group, two in New Guinea and one endemic in Australia, are sexually dimorphic with males having the same basic pattern of black and 'gold'; the *S. aureus* of New Guinea has the original title to the name Golden Bowerbird. The 'gold' areas are a patch of yellow in the wing of varying size and yellow or reddish-orange from crown to mantle, the mantle sometimes extended into an ornamental cape.

---

*A name also used for *Sericulus aureus* of New Guinea.

732 REGENT BOWERBIRD *Sericulus chrysocephalus* (Lewin) 1808   Pl 22
Distribution: Map 293.

RECOGNITION: *male boldly patterned black and orange, female brownish with black patch on nape and throat.*

DESCRIPTION: 23–28cm, male smaller than female. Sexes very different. *Male:* forehead to mantle and large area in centre of wing bright orange-yellow; remainder black; bill and eyes yellow; legs black. *Female:* nape, mantle and centre of throat black; forehead, face and hind neck rusty brown; back and upper breast blackish-brown boldly spotted with dull white; lower breast and belly dull white scalloped with blackish-brown; wings and tail brown; bill and legs blackish-brown; eyes yellow flecked with brown.

HABITAT: rain forest. HABITS: arboreal with terrestrial display ground; constructs avenue-type bower on platform of sticks which harmonises with forest floor, very little decoration (not so neat and elaborate as in Satin Bowerbird), very little vocal accompaniment to display; solitary with some flocking when not breeding; sedentary with local nomadic movement in search of fruit. BREEDING: October–January; nests concealed in vine tangles at medium heights, saucer-shaped, loosely made of twigs; two eggs, dull white or greyish-yellow spotted and vermiculated with reddish-brown and purplish-black. VOICE: soft whisper song and harsh 'te-ar', also accomplished mimic. FOOD: fruit and insects.

STATUS: fairly common. TAXONOMY: endemic species.

Regent Bowerbird (732) *male*   Satin Bowerbird (733) *male*

Genus PTILONORHYNCHUS

A separate genus for the endemic Satin Bowerbird. It is distinguished by extreme sexual dimorphism in which the male is a shiny blue black and has eyes with a curious flashing appearance. The bill is partly feathered at the base in both sexes. The species is one of several in which the bower consists of two parallel rows of elaborately interwoven twigs and the adjacent area decorated with various bright objects. The bower is neater and has more decoration than that of the Regent Bowerbird.

733 SATIN BOWERBIRD *Ptilonorhynchus violaceus* (Vieillot) 1816   Pls 22, 24
Distribution: Map 294.

RECOGNITION: *male violet-black, female olive-green; rain forest.*

DESCRIPTION: 27–33cm; base of bill and nostrils covered by feathers. Sexes very different. *Male:* black with deep violet sheen; bill bluish, tip greenish-yellow, eyes bright gleaming blue edged with red; legs greenish-yellow. *Female:* olive-green, darker above and paler below, tinged with yellow on belly, most of underparts scalloped with blackish-brown.

VARIATION: southern population, larger (race *violaceus*); northern, smaller (race *minor*).
HABITAT: rain forest and adjacent forest with dense ground cover. HABITS: arboreal with terrestrial display ground; males indulge in short swift flights above display area, bower consists of two parallel rows of arched twigs with surrounding cleared area strewn with colourful objects, females attracted to bower where mating takes place, males are promiscuous; gregarious when not breeding, often in flocks of 100 or more; nomadic, sometimes dispersing for long distances. BREEDING: October–December; nests often 100m or more from display ground, in tree foliage or mistletoe bunches, saucer-shaped, made of twigs and leaves; two eggs, creamy-buff, blotched and streaked with dark brown and grey. VOICE: various creaking and hissing sounds, also mimics other birds. FOOD: fruit and insects.
STATUS: common. TAXONOMY: endemic species and genus.

Genus CHLAMYDERA

A group of four species, one endemic to New Guinea, two endemic to Australia and one mostly in New Guinea with a bridge-head in Cape York. They are the only bowerbirds which do not live in rain forest. They belong to open country from woodland to arid savanna with scattered trees. They are very alike and there is little doubt that they originated from the same stock, an offshoot from a forest species; their plumages are basically similar to those of some forest females. It also seems likely that divergence from a forest habitat took place in New Guinea with colonisation of Australia, via Cape York on three occasions. The separation in time would have been long enough for each colonist to evolve differences preventing interbreeding, but they remained competitive with the latest arrival dominant over the previous.

734 SPOTTED BOWERBIRD *Chlamydera maculata* (Gould) 1837   Pl 22
Distribution: Map 295.
RECOGNITION: *blackish-brown boldly spotted with cinnamon brown; like Great Bowerbird but smaller and browner, less grey.*
DESCRIPTION: 27–31cm. Sexes alike. Patch of iridescent violet-pink on nape; crown and face closely mottled dark brown and blackish-brown; hind neck grey-brown; back and shoulders blackish-brown boldly spotted with cinnamon buff; throat and foreneck cinnamon brown mottled with blackish-brown; breast and belly pale buff lightly barred with grey-brown on flanks; wings and tail blackish-brown tipped with buff; bill black; eyes dark brown; legs olive-brown.
VARIATION: eastern population, darker with more conspicuous spots (race *maculata*); western, paler with spots less distinct (race *guttata*—sometimes listed as species).
HABITAT: woodland to arid tree savanna. HABITS: arboreal but has terrestrial display areas; keeps well hidden in trees and not readily detected except by voice; solitary, gregarious when not breeding; sedentary and nomadic; builds avenue-type bower of two rows of interwoven twigs and grass on poorly defined display ground, usually concealed by over-hanging branches and near water, decorated with bleached shells and bones and some colourful objects. BREEDING: October–December but sometimes determined by rains; nests in trees and bushes fairly high and not far from bower, saucer-shaped, made of twigs and lined with grass; two eggs, shades of grey or green with dark vermiculations. VOICE: various hissing and grinding sounds, also mimics other birds. FOOD: fruit, seeds, insects.

STATUS: common. TAXONOMY: endemic species (sometimes divided into two species, Spotted and Western Bowerbirds) closely related to or perhaps forming superspecies with Great and Fawn-breasted Bowerbirds.

735 GREAT BOWERBIRD   *Chlamydera nuchalis*   (Jard. & Selby) 1830

Distribution: Map 295.

RECOGNITION: very like Spotted Bowerbird but larger, 30–33cm, and *all parts of plumage much greyer,* less warm brown, whole underparts buffy-grey; *females sometimes lack iridescent pink patch on nape;* also distribution different.

HABITAT: woodland and open forest (areas with wet season rainfall over about 50cm). HABITS: similar to Spotted Bowerbird in most respects; voice harsh grating and rasping, like cloth being torn, as well as mimicry of other birds.

STATUS: fairly common. TAXONOMY: endemic species; possibly forming superspecies with Spotted and Fawn-breasted Bowerbirds.

736 FAWN-BREASTED BOWERBIRD   *Chlamydera cerviniventris*   Gould 1850

Distribution: Map 295.

RECOGNITION: like Great Bowerbird but much smaller, 23cm, face and throat finely streaked with grey-brown, *breast and belly plain cinnamon buff;* no iridescent violet-pink on nape; crown more or less plain and back only lightly spotted with buffy-white.

HABITAT, etc: similar to Great Bowerbird; frequents low-lying woodland and melaleuca thickets near mangrove swamps; avenue-type bower decorated only with green objects, fragments of leaves, berries and seed-pods; usually one egg, creamy-white with dark vermiculations. VOICE: fairly weak harsh churring as well as mimicry of other birds.

STATUS: probably fairly common. TAXONOMY: species extending to New Guinea; probably forming superspecies with Spotted and Great Bowerbirds.

Great Bowerbird (735)

Family PARADISAEIDAE

Paradisebirds

4(43) species: 3 endemic

BIRDS OF PARADISE ARE forest species closely allied to bowerbirds; there are no sharp distinctions between them. Both have similarities with crows (family Corvidae), particularly in robust build, powerful legs and feet, large bills, greatly elongated and decurved in some paradisebirds, and in their harsh voices and essentially black plumages. Some paradisebirds make display grounds on the forest floor but mostly they have evolved elaborate personal decorations which are displayed in complex acrobatic sequences on selected bare boughs. It is sometimes difficult to accept that the various exaggerated forms of plumes, in many textures and colours, are modified feathers. The four Australian species are among the least decorative. They are about 24–30cm. The sexes are alike in the Manucode but very different in the riflebirds.

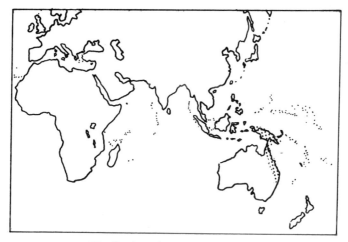

Distribution of PARADISEIDAE

Key to PARADISAEIDAE

1 Black, short thick bill, long square tail	Manucode.................	No 737
2 Black (♂) or brown (♀), long curved bill; male has short square tail	Paradise Riflebird...........	No 738
	Victoria Riflebird...........	No 739
	Magnificent Riflebird	No 740

Genus PHONYGAMMUS

A genus for one of the glossy black manucodes. It is separated from species of the genus *Manucodia* mainly because of its long lanceolate head feathers. The New Guinea section of the species is named Trumpetbird to distinguish it from the true manucodes.

737 MANUCODE *Phonygammus keraudrenii* (Less. & Garn.) 1826   Pl 24
Distribution: Map 292.

RECOGNITION: *glossy black; like Spangled Drongo and Shining Starling but long tail broad and rounded.*

DESCRIPTION: 30cm, with broad tail 14cm; long lanceolate feathers on 'ears' and neck. Sexes alike. Black, with iridescent green on most of body plumage; belly, wings and tail purplish-black; bill and legs black; eyes reddish-orange, less red in female.

HABITAT: rain forest. HABITS: arboreal, active at various heights in tree foliage; apparently solitary, at least only recorded in pairs; movements not well known but thought to be partly migratory. BREEDING: October–January; nests on horizontal forks in foliage, saucer-shaped, sparsely made of interwoven tendrils and twigs and lined with finer material; two eggs, dull white or pinkish, closely streaked with shades of brown and purple. VOICE: trumpet-like guttural squawk. FOOD: fruit and insects.

STATUS: records suggest fairly common. TAXONOMY: race *(gouldii)* of species extending throughout New Guinea and adjacent islands.

Genus PTILORIS

The riflebirds. The Magnificent Riflebird, which spans Torres Strait, is included although it is sometimes listed in a separate genus, *Craspedophora*. Riflebirds are rain forest species of about 24–30cm in length and have short rounded wings. Males are black but readily distinguished from other black forest species by their long decurved bills, sometimes used for probing among bark for insects, and short square tails. Females have similar bills but plumages are brown with dark scallops on pale underparts. Males indulge in elaborate displays, performed on bare horizontal boughs, and in flight their plumage makes a curious 'siffling' sound like rustling silk.

738 PARADISE RIFLEBIRD *Ptiloris paradiseus* Swainson 1825   Pl 22

Distribution: Map 296.

RECOGNITION: *long decurved bill, male glossy black, female brown above, buff below with blackish chevrons.*

DESCRIPTION: 28cm, with tail 5cm. Sexes very different. *Male:* tail relatively short, broad and square; feathers of head and throat short and scale-like; flank feathers elongated into plumes. Plumage black; iridescent purplish-green on crown, centre of throat and foreneck and on central pair of tail feathers; feathers of lower breast and belly broadly tipped with deep olive-green; remainder of plumage velvet black with purplish sheen; bill and legs black; eyes dark brown. *Female:* crown, face and side of neck dark brownish-grey with broad buffy-white eyebrow; remainder of upperparts grey-brown, feathers of wings and tail broadly edged with cinnamon rufous; throat buffy-white; breast and belly cinnamon buff boldly marked with brownish-black chevrons.

HABITAT: rain forest. HABITS: arboreal, often in dense low substage, extracts insects from bark on logs and vertical tree trunks sometimes so vigorously that moss and other debris showers down (looks rather like large babbler or treecreeper), suns and preens on tree tops and takes short flights between trees when 'silken' rustling of male feathers can be heard for long distances; males display on horizontal bare branches; solitary and sedentary. BREEDING: October–December; nests in high tangled foliage, saucer-shaped, made of interwoven growing tendrils and leaves, lined with fine fibres and often decorated with snake skin; two eggs, pinkish-buff streaked with shades of dark brown. VOICE: loud harsh double 'ya-a-a-ss'.

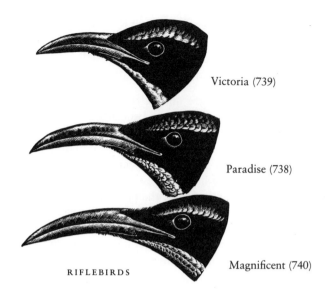

Victoria (739)

Paradise (738)

RIFLEBIRDS

Magnificent (740)

FOOD: fruit and insects.

STATUS: uncommon. TAXONOMY: endemic species; forms species or superspecies with Victoria Riflebird.

739 VICTORIA RIFLEBIRD *Ptiloris victoriae* Gould 1850
Distribution: Map 296.

RECOGNITION: like the Paradise Riflebird but smaller, 24cm; *male has feathers of lower breast and belly with broader olive-green tips completely concealing dull black bases; female has breast and belly richer cinnamon brown with fewer chevron marks.*

HABITAT, etc; similar to Paradise Riflebird; often feeds on ground, turning over leaves and other debris; nests also sometimes decorated with snake skin; voice a rough guttural 'ya-a-rr'.

STATUS: common. TAXONOMY: endemic species, or forming species or superspecies with Paradise Riflebird.

740 MAGNIFICENT RIFLEBIRD *Ptiloris magnificus* (Vieillot) 1819   Pl 24
Distribution: Map 296.

RECOGNITION: like Paradise Riflebird but slightly larger, 30cm; *male differs in having iridescent purplish-green of throat extended to breast and separated from dull purplish-black belly by narrow bands of velvet black and shiny olive-green;* flank feathers extended into long filamentous plumes; *female differs in having upperparts cinnamon brown and tail cinnamon rufous; broad black streak at edge of throat; underparts buffy-white speckled with blackish-brown on throat and upper breast and barred on lower breast and belly.*

HABITAT, etc: apparently very similar to Paradise Riflebird; records of breeding October–February, no record of nests being decorated with snake skin. VOICE: loud 'wheeoo, wheeoo, wheeoo, who-o-o', last in lower tone.

STATUS: apparently fairly common. TAXONOMY: race *(alberti)* of species extending to New Guinea.

Family CORVIDAE

Crows, Ravens

5(100) species: all endemic

MEMBERS OF THIS FAMILY are among the most successful and ubiquitous of birds. They are adaptable and well organised socially. It is widely believed that some are at the present peak of avian evolution, advancing as in the human species along lines of mental development rather than any temporarily successful specialisation. This applies particularly to the genus *Corvus* to which Australian species belong. Australian corvids are readily distinguished from other birds of similar size, about 40–56cm, general appearance and habitat by wholly black plumage, bills and legs; the plumage has a slight purplish sheen; eyes are white in adults and brownish in immatures. They are bold and aggressive but very wary; they fly strongly and in open formation but congregate to feed and roost. Although easily identified as corvids there has been, and may still be, uncertainty as to the number of species. Until recently it was three, currently it is five. All 'crows' are more or less alike to the ordinary observer, and even the experienced student finds difficulty in distinguishing some species except in the hand and then only, it seems, with the aid of a computer. The following notes are based mainly on recent researches by Rowley*. Patient observers may find other ways of distinguishing species.

Key to CORVIDAE

[*Note:* mainly useful for distinguishing birds in the hand.]

1 Throat feathers not specialised; base of body feathers white .... 3–4 (crows)
2 Throat feathers specialised; base of body feathers grey .... 5–6 (ravens)

3 Wings conspicuously 'shuffled' on landing; note short 'uk' or 'ok'.......... Crow

4 Performs elaborate aerobatics; note long 'nark' .... Little Crow
5 Chin partly feathered; throat feathers long and pointed .... Raven
6 Chin wholly feathered; throat feathers short and bifurcate:
    Mainland.. Little Raven
    Only Tasmanian corvid.. Forest Raven

Raven (743)   Little Raven (744)   Crow (741)   Little Crow (742)

CORVID THROAT FEATHERS *(after Rowley)*

---

*I. Rowley, CSIRO *Wildlife Research*, 1970, 15, 27–71.

741 CROW *Corvus cecilae* Mathews 1912
Distribution: Map 297.

RECOGNITION: 48–55cm; *concealed base of body feathers white;* throat feathers relatively narrow and short, pointed or slightly bifurcate; chin wholly feathered; *on landing wings often 'shuffled' in an exaggerated manner;* note short 'uk' or 'ok'.

HABITAT: mainly forest and woodland. HABITS: arboreal and terrestrial; solitary and gregarious but not usually in large flocks; feed and roost together and fly in open formation; wings 'shuffled' in exaggerated manner after landing; mainly sedentary, sometimes nomadic with some indication of migration pattern. BREEDING: most months in some part of range but in any one locality period fairly clearly defined; nests in forked branches of tall tree, often in outer foliage, large and not very substantial structure of sticks and twigs lined with grass and other soft materials; four eggs, pale greenish-blue freckled in varying amounts with shades of dark umber brown. VOICE: short high-pitched nasal 'uk' or 'ok' repeated. FOOD: omnivorous.

STATUS: common. TAXONOMY: endemic species; sometimes regarded as race of *Corvus orru* of New Guinea and other islands.

742 LITTLE CROW *Corvus bennetti* North 1901
Distribution: Map 298.

RECOGNITION: 45–52cm; *concealed base of body feathers white;* throat feathers relatively narrow and short, pointed or slightly bifurcate; chin wholly feathered; *performs elaborate aerobatics;* note long 'nark'.

HABITAT: mostly dry scrub, like mulga, away from tall timber. HABITS: arboreal and terrestrial; solitary and gregarious, sometimes in very large flocks and in company with Little Raven; performs elaborate aerobatics; mainly nomadic. BREEDING: variable, whenever conditions suitable; nests fairly low down in trees and shrubs, sometimes on ground, nests well made of sticks lined with grass and with layer of mud below lining; eggs similar to Crow but smaller. VOICE: high-pitched nasal 'nark' repeated. FOOD: omnivorous.

STATUS: fairly common. TAXONOMY: endemic species.

743 RAVEN *Corvus coronoides* Vig. & Horsf. 1827
Distribution: Map 299.

RECOGNITION: 50–56cm; *concealed base of body feathers grey; throat feathers long, broad and pointed* (lanceolate or 'hackled'), erected in display and when calling; chin feathered only in centre; note long wailing 'aah-aah-aah'.

HABITAT: mostly woodlands, rocky outcrops and coastal dunes. HABITS: arboreal and terrestrial; solitary and gregarious, but only in small flocks, about ten to thirty. BREEDING: June–December; nests high up in tall trees, in main forks, well made of sticks, bark and hair; eggs similar to Crow. VOICE: loud wailing 'aah-aah-aah-r-r', tailing off in 'dying gurgle' in slightly lower pitch in east and rapidly descending pitch in west. FOOD: omnivorous but especially carrion.

STATUS: common. TAXONOMY: endemic species.

744 LITTLE RAVEN *Corvus mellori* Mathews 1912

Distribution: Map 300.

RECOGNITION: 40–45cm; *concealed base of body feathers grey; throat feathers relatively short and bifurcate,* not distinctly 'hackled' and not erectile; *chin wholly feathered;* note guttural 'kar' or 'ark'.

HABITAT: similar to Raven. HABITS: similar to Raven but usually keeps to lower levels in trees and in less prominent situations; flicks wings upwards when calling; post-breeding flocks large and nomadic. BREEDING: apparently similar to Raven but nests usually located at lower levels, under 10m. VOICE: loud guttural 'kar' or 'ark' repeated. FOOD: omnivorous.

STATUS: apparently fairly common. TAXONOMY: endemic species.

745 FOREST RAVEN *Corvus tasmanicus* Mathews 1912

Distribution: Map 300.

RECOGNITION: 50–60cm; *larger than Little Raven with distinctly more massive bill and relatively short tail;* chin rather less completely feathered but much more so than in Raven; otherwise more or less similar to Little Raven; only corvid in Tasmania.

VARIATION: Tasmania and adjacent coastal Victoria, smaller (race *tasmanicus*); Armidale area, N.S.W., larger (race *boreus*).

HABITAT: apparently more heavily wooded areas, including wet sclerophyll forest, also open country and beaches. HABITS: arboreal and terrestrial; solitary and gregarious, sometimes in flocks of up to one hundred. BREEDING: July–September; nests in tree forks, made of sticks; eggs similar to other corvids. VOICE: slow deep 'korr' repeated with final syllable tailing off. FOOD: omnivorous with preference for carrion.

STATUS: common. TAXONOMY: endemic species.

ADDENDA

'RED-RUMPED QUAIL' Attention is drawn to a quail seen a number of times by competent observers, but whose identity, in the absence of a hand held bird, remains in doubt. Field characteristics suggest that it belongs to the Phasianidae and not the Turnicidae.

OCCURRENCE: recorded at Murphy's Creek, near Toowoomba in southeast Queensland. A number of birds remained in the area from December 1929 to April 1930, a few being recorded in October of 1930 (E. A. R. Lord *Emu* 32:127). Subsequently, near Inverramsay, southwest of Toowoomba, up to one hundred birds were recorded during May and June 1959; also in the same area three birds in January 1960 (Lloyd Nielson *Emu* 62:261). Similar birds were recorded from Boonah, Terranora Lakes and Gympie, southeast Queensland.

DESCRIPTION: "In size they appeared to be similar to the King Quail, but did not resemble that bird in colour; they were black, or almost so on the upperparts, except the rump, which was bright red. — — — — underparts (probably) slate or slaty-blue" (Lord). "The most conspicuous feature was a brilliant scarlet-red rump which contrasted vividly with the dark brown, or black, body; there appeared to be short, white, longitudinal stripes on the back. Some birds were lighter in colour than others, and these outnumbered the dark birds by about three to one. A white spot was visible in the region of the eye in the dark individuals, but not in the others" (Nielson).

HABITAT: "They lived principally in the cultivated paddocks, usually in the lucerne crops" (Lord). "In lucerne some 18in in height"; "In a three-acre patch of clover"; "In a paddock overgrown with weeds and self-sown wheat" (Nielson).

HABITS: "When the mower was at work they remained in the standing lucerne until the knife was almost up to them, then rose for a short flight and landed with a dive into the crop" (Lord). "The birds appeared to rest communally during the day in parties of from four to eight birds. On flushing, the birds scattered and flew from 20 to 40 yards before dropping to cover. They proved difficult to flush, and rose beneath one's feet or directly in front of the harvester" (Nielson). Nielson also records correspondence with Lord, who wrote, "I found the birds-with the King Quail in millet and panicum crops, but they had a very decided preference for green lucerne". VOICE: "the call was very much like that of a kitten of the domesticated cat" (Lord). "When flushed they uttered a whistled 'chit'" (Nielson).

COMMENTS: This is not an isolated observation; birds were seen on several occasions and in numbers. They attracted attention because of being different to other species of quail known to the observers, but appeared to have some resemblance to the King Quail. Lord's opinion was that the bird might be a race of that species occurring as a non-breeding migrant.

(continued over)

ASIAN DOWITCHER   *Limnodromas semipalmatus*

Distribution: mainly north and east coasts.

RECOGNITION: very like Bar-tailed Godwit but smaller, 30cm, with *long straight bill;* upperparts grey-brown with dark brown streaks, pale eyebrow, barred rump and tail; folded wings shorter than tail-tip; underparts pale fawn to whitish, especially on chin and flanks, legs dark olive-green.

HABITAT: coastal swamps and mudflaps.

STATUS: fairly common, non-breeding visitor from northern Asia.

REDSHANK   *Tringa totanus*

Distribution: recorded north and northeast coasts.

RECOGNITION: 30cm, like Greenshank but smaller and upperparts more brown than grey, reddish legs and bill, rump and trailing edge of wings white.

HABITAT: coastal swamps and mudflaps.

STATUS: apparently rare, non-breeding visitor from northern hemisphere.

ANALYSIS OF FAMILIES

Number	Family	A	B	C	D	E	F	G	H
1	Casuariidae	4	2	1	–	1	–	–	–
2	Struthionidae	1	–	–	–	–	–	–	–
3	Spheniscidae	18	9	–	–	1	–	8	–
4	Diomedeidae	13	9	–	–	1	–	8	–
5	Procellariidae	60	36	1	–	1	4	30	–
6	Hydrobatidae	21	7	–	–	–	1	6	–
7	Pelecanoididae	4	2	–	–	–	1	1	–
8	Podicipedidae	20	3	1	–	1	1	–	–
9	Pelecanidae	8	1	1	–	–	–	–	–
10	Sulidae	9	4	–	–	1	3	–	–
11	Phalacrocoracidae	31	6	1	–	3	2	–	–
12	Fregatidae	6	2	–	–	–	1	1	–
13	Phaethontidae	3	2	–	–	–	–	2	–
14	Ardeidae	64	15	1	–	4	9	1	–
15	Ciconiidae	17	1	–	–	–	1	–	–
16	Threskiornithidae	32	5	2	–	2	1	–	–
17	Anatidae	147	23	10	4	4	1	2	2
18	Accipitridae	217	17	5	1	7	4	–	–
19	Pandionidae	1	1	–	–	–	1	–	–
20	Falconidae	61	6	2	–	3	1	–	–
21	Megapodidae	13	3	2	–	1	–	–	–
22	Phasianidae	165	7	1	–	1	1	–	4
23	Turnicidae	17	7	6	–	1	–	–	–
24	Gruidae	14	2	1	–	–	1	–	–
25	Rallidae	132	16	3	1	4	6	2	–
26	Otididae	22	1	1	–	–	–	–	–
27	Jacanidae	7	1	–	–	1	–	–	–
28	Rostratulidae	2	1	–	–	–	1	–	–
29	Haematopodidae	3	2	1	–	–	1	–	–
30	Charadriidae	56	17	6	1	1	–	9	–
31	Scolopacidae	70	31	–	–	–	–	31	–
32	Phalaropodidae	3	2	–	–	–	–	2	–
33	Recurvirostridae	7	3	2	–	–	1	–	–
34	Burhinidae	9	2	1	–	–	1	–	–
35	Glareolidae	15	2	1	–	–	–	1	–
36	Stercorariidae	4	4	–	–	–	–	4	–
37	Laridae	80	24	1	–	1	15	7	–
38	Columbidae	289	26	14	–	6	3	–	3
39	Psittacidae	315	55	48	1	6	–	–	–
40	Cuculidae	127	12	3	–	5	3	1	–
41	Tytonodae	10	4	–	–	2	2	–	–
42	Strigidae	120	4	1	–	3	–	–	–
43	Podargidae	12	3	1	–	2	–	–	–
44	Aegothelidae	8	1	–	1	–	–	–	–
45	Caprimulgidae	67	3	1	–	1	1	–	–
46	Apodidae	76	5	–	–	–	1	4	–
47	Alcedinidae	87	10	2	–	7	1	–	–
48	Meropidae	24	1	1	–	–	–	–	–
49	Coraciidae	17	1	–	–	–	1	–	–
50	Pittidae	23	4	1	–	1	1	1	–
51	Menuridae	2	2	2	–	–	–	–	–
52	Atrichornithidae	2	2	2	–	–	–	–	–
53	Alaudidae	75	2	–	–	–	1	–	1
54	Hirundinidae	75	5	3	–	1	–	1	–
55	Motacillidae	48	4	–	–	–	1	3	–
56	Campephagidae	70	7	1	–	5	1	–	–
57	(Pycnonotidae)	109	1	–	–	–	–	–	1
58	Turdidae	?300	5	1	–	1	1	–	2
59	Timaliidae	?280	13	11	–	2	–	–	–
60	Maluridae	?	24	24	–	–	–	–	–
61	Sylviidae	?360	52	43	1	6	2	–	–
62	Muscicapidae	?320	23	13	1	8	1	–	–
63	Monarchidae	?	12	5	1	6	–	–	–
64	Pachycephalidae	?50	20	15	–	5	–	–	–
65	Ephthianuridae	5	5	5	–	–	–	–	–
66	Neosittidae	7	5	5	–	–	–	–	–
67	Climacteridae	8	7	7	–	–	–	–	–
68	Dicaeidae	58	9	8	–	1	–	–	–
69	Nectariniidae	116	1	–	–	1	–	–	–
70	Zosteropidae	?80	4	2	–	1	1	–	–
71	Meliphagidae	170	70	54	–	16	–	–	–
72	Estrildidae	115	19	14	1	3	–	–	1
73	(Ploceidae)	133	2	–	–	–	–	–	2
74	(Fringillidae)	125	2	–	–	–	–	–	2
75	Sturnidae	110	3	–	–	1	–	–	2
76	Oriolidae	28	4	–	2	2	–	–	–
77	Dicruridae	20	1	1	–	–	–	–	–
78	Grallinidae	4	3	3	–	–	–	–	–
79	Artamidae	10	6	4	1	–	1	–	–
80	Cracticidae	10	9	7	–	2	–	–	–
81	Ptilonorhynchidae	18	9	7	–	2	–	–	–
82	Paradisaeidae	43	4	3	–	1	–	–	–
83	Corvidae	100	5	5	–	–	–	–	–

A = Total species (Sum of totals not calculated)
B = Number in Australia (Sum of C–H) 745
C = Endemic species 368
D = Very limited occurrence in southeast New Guinea . . . 16
E = Restricted to Australasian region 136
F = Extending beyond Australasian region 80
G = Non-breeding visitors 125
H = Introduced 20

NOTES ON
ANALYSIS OF FAMILIES

ONLY A FEW SALIENT features of this broad analysis of families are referred to here. The reader may wish to draw other conclusions or take the analysis further by using the data provided in the text. The total number of species in each family, where known with reasonable certainty (but all figures are only approximate), are included to show the relative numbers occurring in Australia. Of the 83 families listed 3 (in brackets) have been introduced. Families sometimes recognised but not shown here are Anhingidae and Pedionomidae; they are included in Phalacrocoracidae and Turnicidae. The muscicapid assemblage Turdidae to Ephthianuridae (numbers 58–65) are sometimes regarded as one family Muscicapidae with the total number of species 1360.

A feature of outstanding interest is the large number of endemic or native species, 383, including about 15 (other than a few regular migrants) with vagrant or limited occurrence in southeast New Guinea. This is nearly 60 per cent of the species which breed in Australia. Of these native species 10 belong to endemic families, Emu, lyrebirds, scrub-birds and chats, and 24 belong to near endemic families, the sittellas, treecreepers, mudnest builders and cracticids. Curiously, among the large families the one best represented is the wader group Scolopacidae with 44 per cent of the world total, but none breeds here. This is 25 per cent of the non-breeding visitors, or 43 per cent of land visitors as distinct from those recorded mostly in offshore waters. Truly, Australia is an attractive resort for these northern hemisphere breeders, perhaps because of almost total lack of local competition from breeding species of the same kind.

As might be expected the honeyeaters are well represented with about 40 per cent of the family and of these nearly 80 per cent are endemic. There is a big drop to the parrots at 17 per cent but with nearly 90 per cent endemism. Ducks are fairly low with only 16 per cent and 40 per cent endemism. Birds of prey and pigeons are not well represented with only about 9 per cent of the world totals but with a high degree of endemism in the pigeons. Pigeons are essentially forest birds but many of those in Australia are species which have adapted to savanna and arid habitats; the bronzewing group probably branched out into various niches from one offshoot of a forest species. Low representation but high endemism is found in crows, estrildine weavers, warblers, babblers and others. Only one lark and one sunbird out of large families have reached the continent and neither have been present long enough to become truly Australian.

SPECIES DISTRIBUTION MAPS

Few changes have been made in the maps as first published. The reason is stated in the Introduction, they are 'simplified patterns of very complex situations'. Many factors influence distribution. For instance, Australian birds are among the most highly nomadic in the world; when not breeding some travel widely in search of food, like honeyeaters which require a constant supply of nectar; and most have an annual flux of surplus numbers which must find new breeding territories if they are to survive, like the Crested Pigeon now settled in new areas where unknown a decade ago. Species also increase and decrease in numbers, or 'pulsate', over periodic cycles, sometimes becoming very numerous, as in the case of the Letterwing Kite, a bird of the arid centre but which several years ago temporarily expanded to such an extent that individuals were recorded as far afield as Melbourne, Stradbroke Is, Derby and Perth; it would be misleading to show its distribution as the whole continent. Then again over a long period some species shrink, like Paradise and Night Parrot, while others thrive, like Cattle Egret and introduced Starling. The maps as shown are a reasonable average of these and other variables.

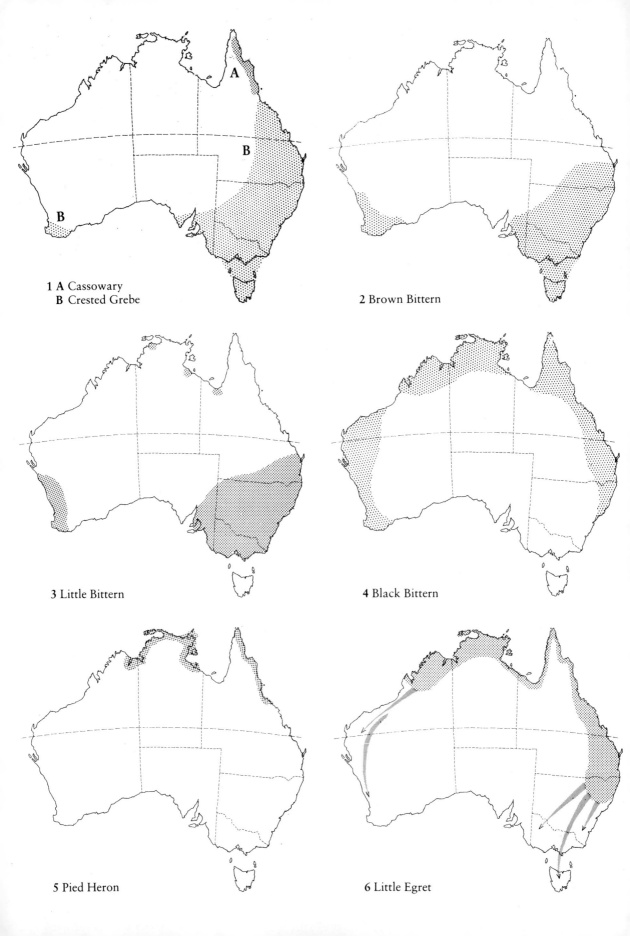

1 A Cassowary
B Crested Grebe

2 Brown Bittern

3 Little Bittern

4 Black Bittern

5 Pied Heron

6 Little Egret

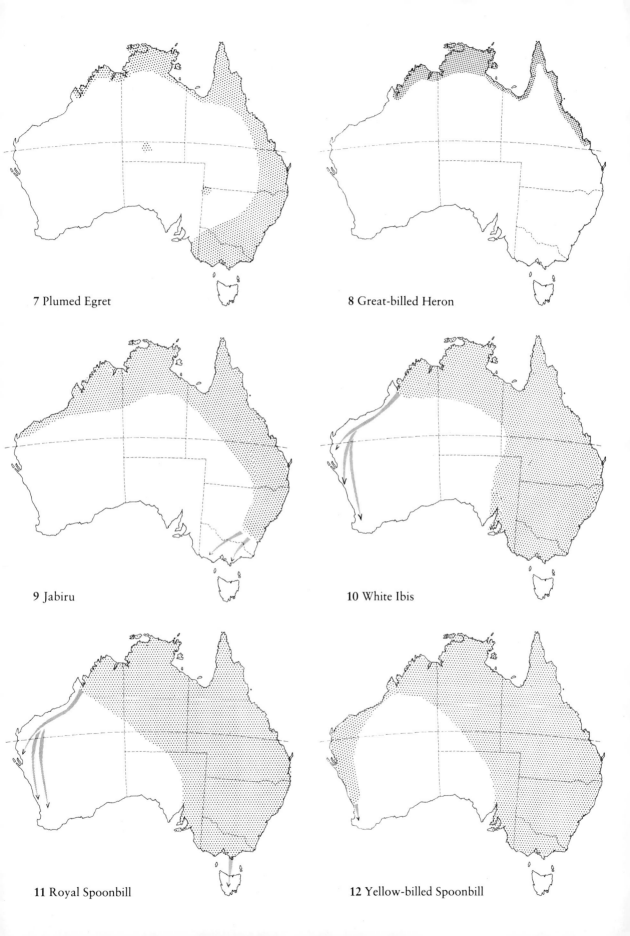

7 Plumed Egret

8 Great-billed Heron

9 Jabiru

10 White Ibis

11 Royal Spoonbill

12 Yellow-billed Spoonbill

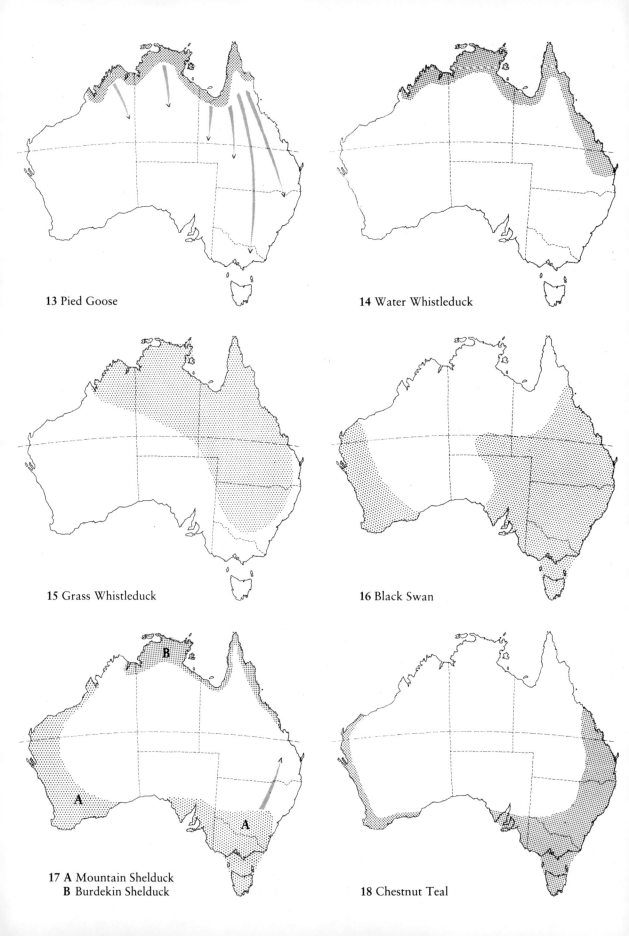

13 Pied Goose

14 Water Whistleduck

15 Grass Whistleduck

16 Black Swan

17 A Mountain Shelduck
   B Burdekin Shelduck

18 Chestnut Teal

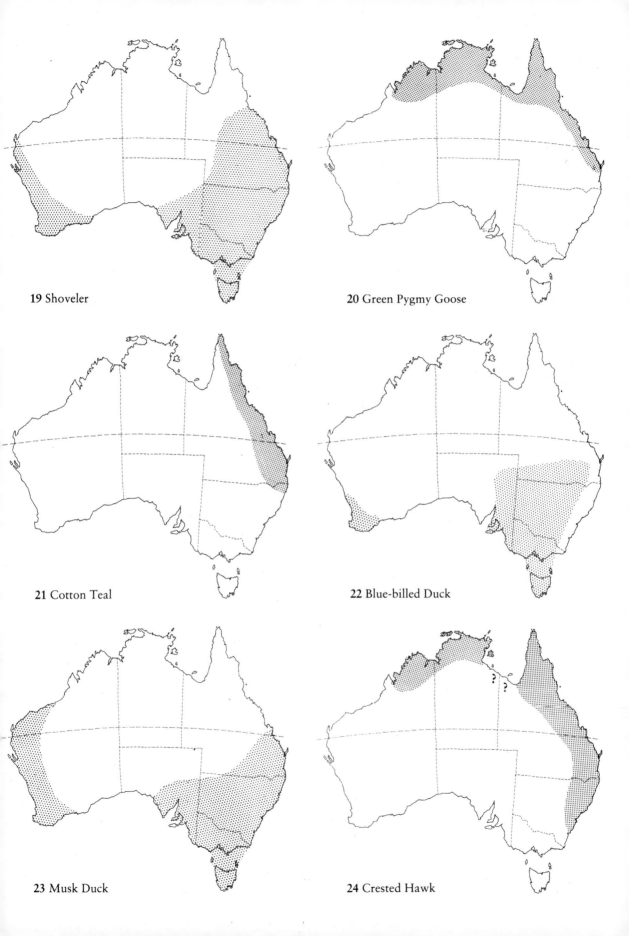

19 Shoveler

20 Green Pygmy Goose

21 Cotton Teal

22 Blue-billed Duck

23 Musk Duck

24 Crested Hawk

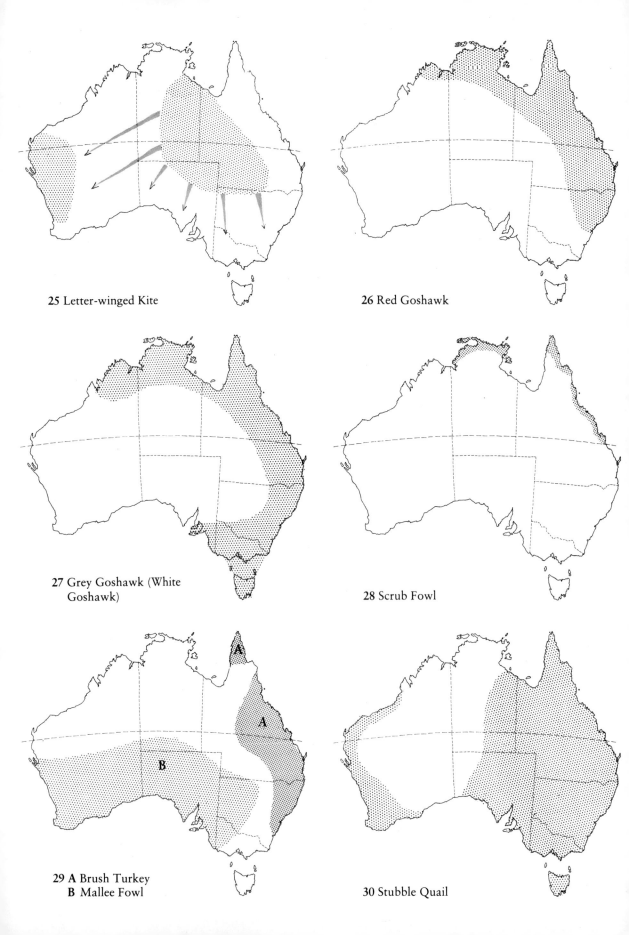

25 Letter-winged Kite

26 Red Goshawk

27 Grey Goshawk (White Goshawk)

28 Scrub Fowl

29 A Brush Turkey
B Mallee Fowl

30 Stubble Quail

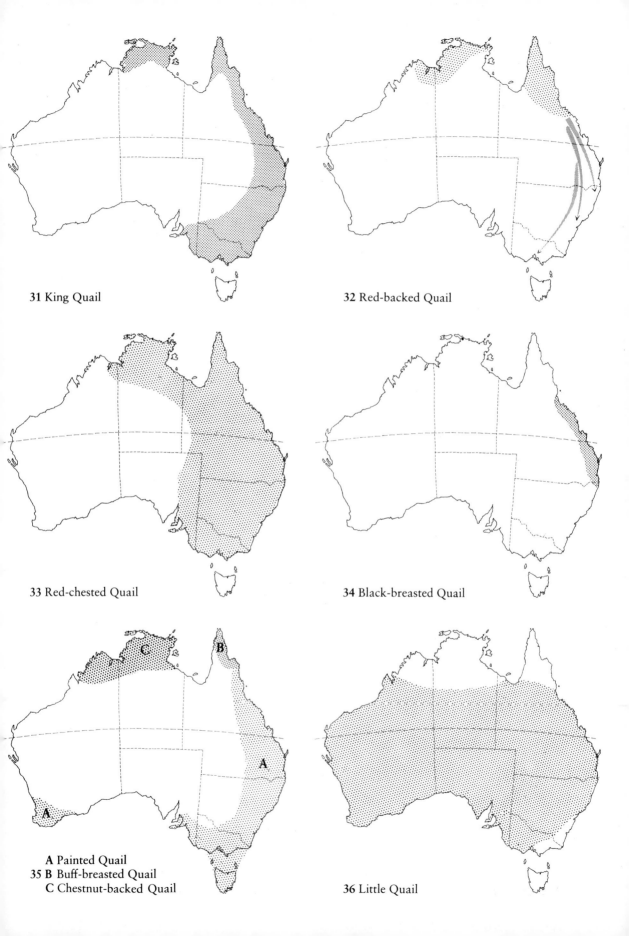

31 King Quail

32 Red-backed Quail

33 Red-chested Quail

34 Black-breasted Quail

A Painted Quail
35 B Buff-breasted Quail
C Chestnut-backed Quail

36 Little Quail

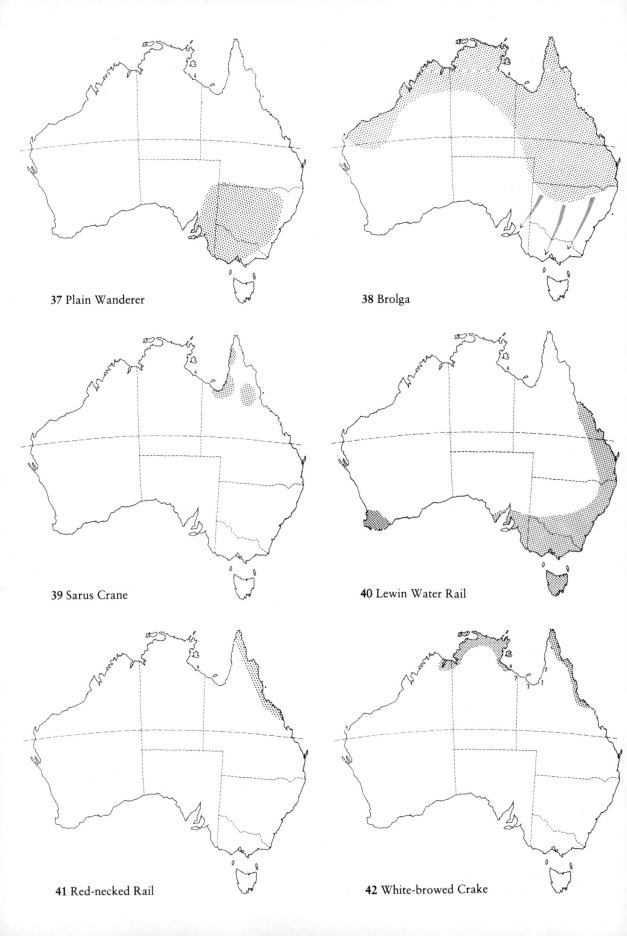

37 Plain Wanderer

38 Brolga

39 Sarus Crane

40 Lewin Water Rail

41 Red-necked Rail

42 White-browed Crake

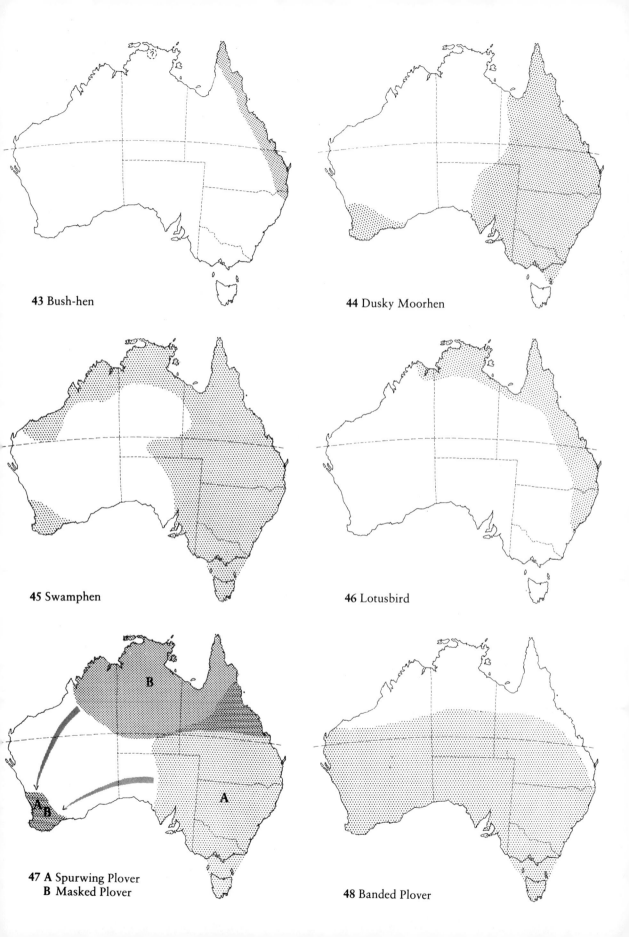

43 Bush-hen

44 Dusky Moorhen

45 Swamphen

46 Lotusbird

47 A Spurwing Plover
B Masked Plover

48 Banded Plover

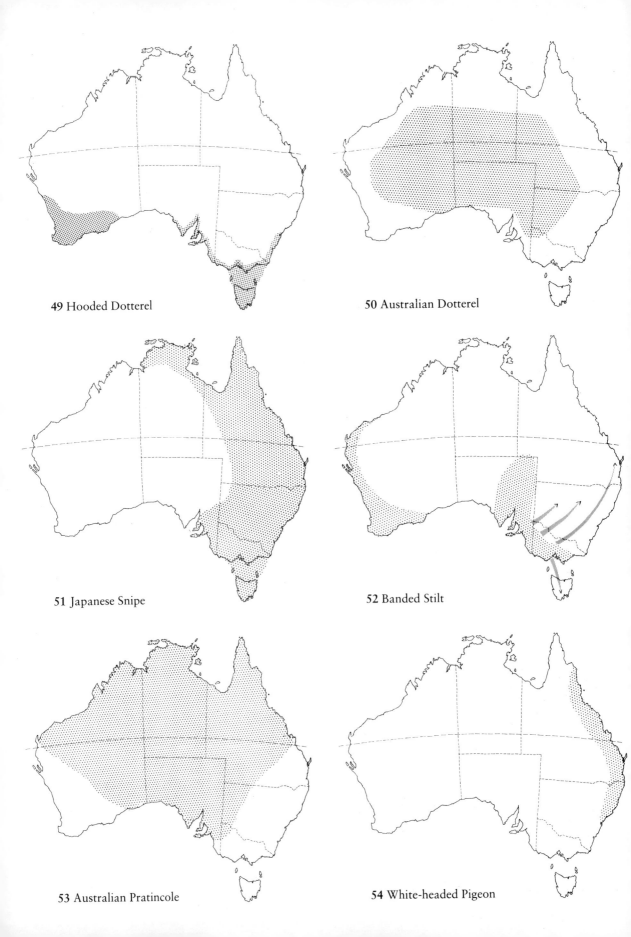

49 Hooded Dotterel

50 Australian Dotterel

51 Japanese Snipe

52 Banded Stilt

53 Australian Pratincole

54 White-headed Pigeon

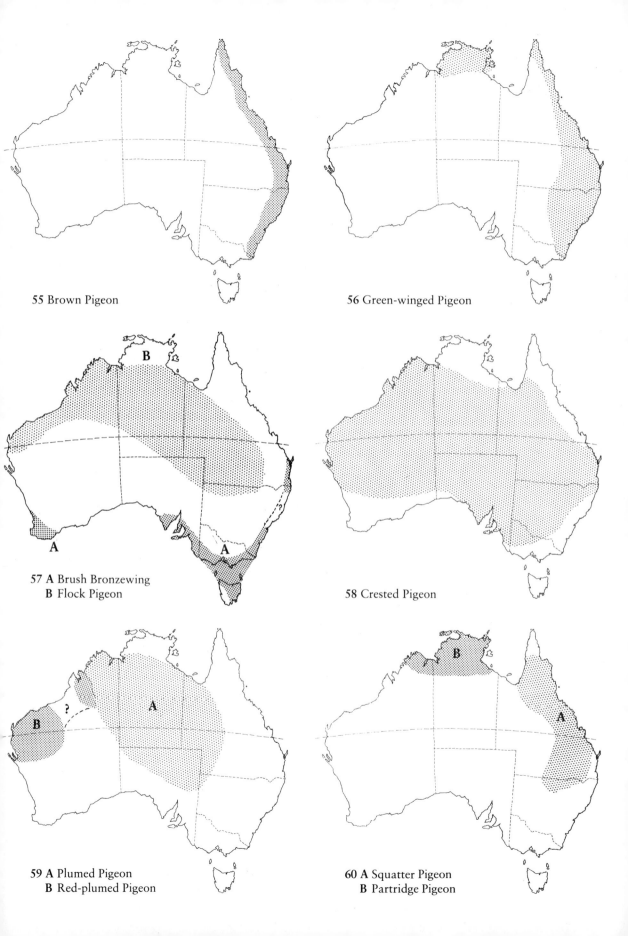

55 Brown Pigeon

56 Green-winged Pigeon

57 **A** Brush Bronzewing
B Flock Pigeon

58 Crested Pigeon

59 **A** Plumed Pigeon
B Red-plumed Pigeon

60 **A** Squatter Pigeon
B Partridge Pigeon

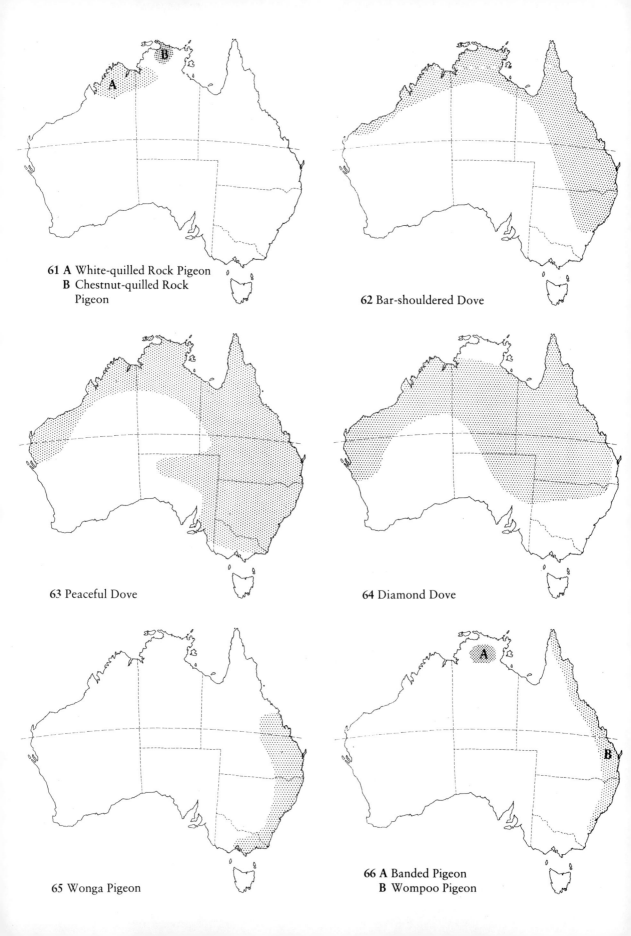

61 A White-quilled Rock Pigeon
B Chestnut-quilled Rock
Pigeon

62 Bar-shouldered Dove

63 Peaceful Dove

64 Diamond Dove

65 Wonga Pigeon

66 A Banded Pigeon
B Wompoo Pigeon

67 Purple-crowned Pigeon

68 Red-crowned Pigeon

69 Torres Strait Pigeon

70 Topknot Pigeon

71 A Rainbow Lorikeet
B Red-collared Lorikeet

72 Scaly-breasted Lorikeet

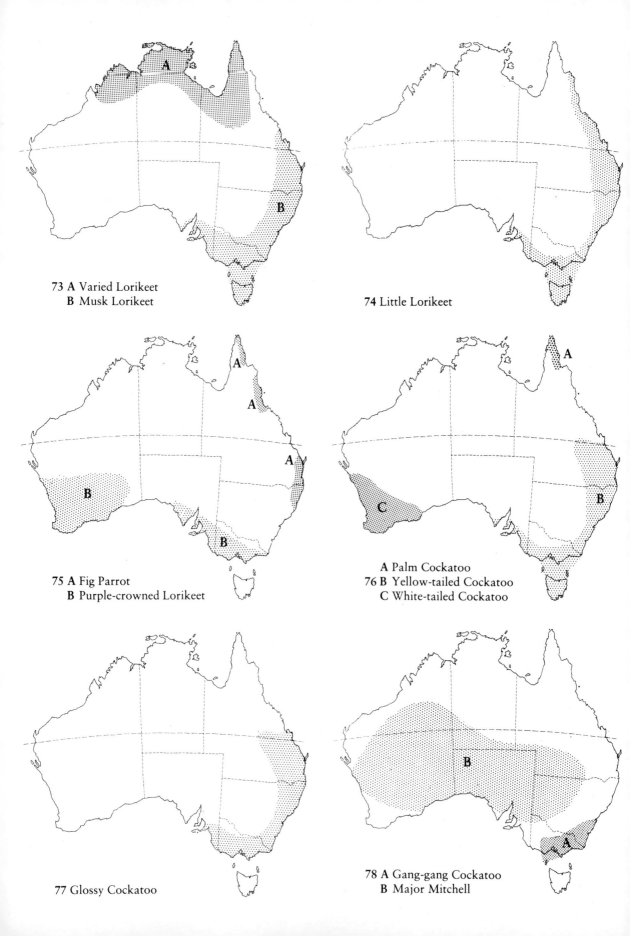

73 **A** Varied Lorikeet
B Musk Lorikeet

74 Little Lorikeet

75 **A** Fig Parrot
B Purple-crowned Lorikeet

A Palm Cockatoo
76 **B** Yellow-tailed Cockatoo
C White-tailed Cockatoo

77 Glossy Cockatoo

78 **A** Gang-gang Cockatoo
B Major Mitchell

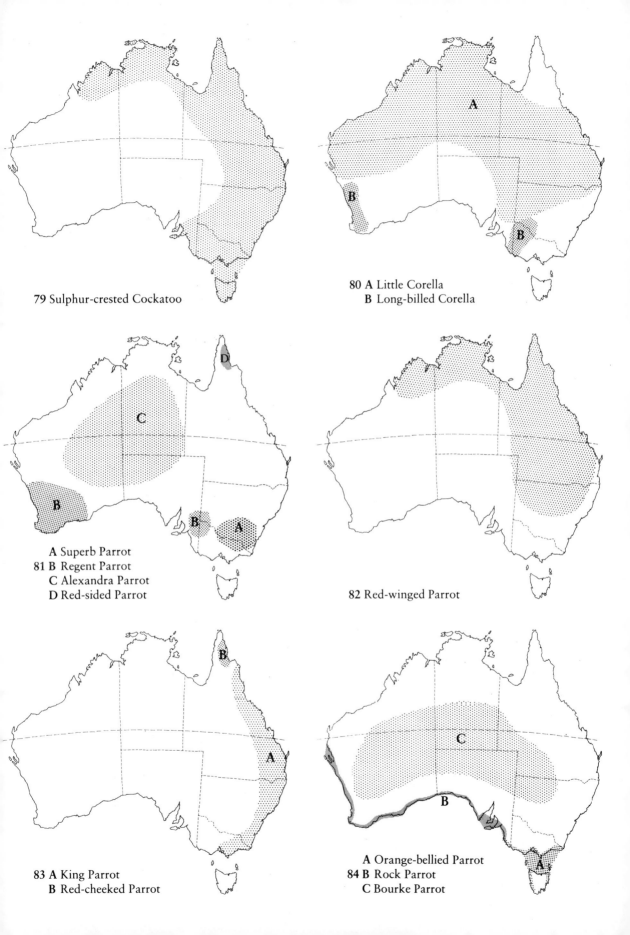

79 Sulphur-crested Cockatoo

80 A Little Corella
B Long-billed Corella

A Superb Parrot
81 B Regent Parrot
C Alexandra Parrot
D Red-sided Parrot

82 Red-winged Parrot

83 A King Parrot
B Red-cheeked Parrot

A Orange-bellied Parrot
84 B Rock Parrot
C Bourke Parrot

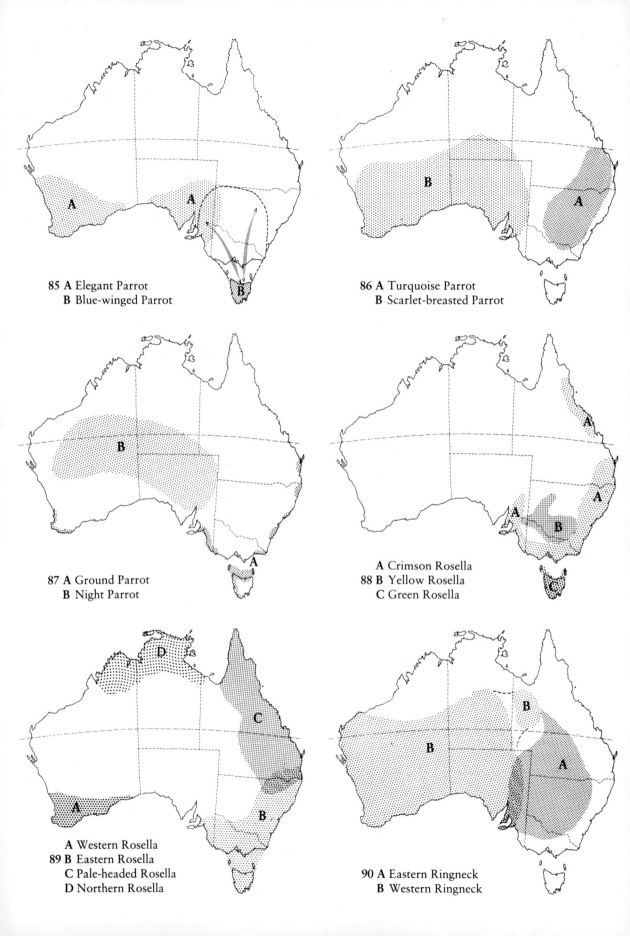

85 **A** Elegant Parrot
   B Blue-winged Parrot

86 **A** Turquoise Parrot
   B Scarlet-breasted Parrot

87 **A** Ground Parrot
   B Night Parrot

A Crimson Rosella
88 **B** Yellow Rosella
   C Green Rosella

A Western Rosella
89 **B** Eastern Rosella
   C Pale-headed Rosella
   D Northern Rosella

90 **A** Eastern Ringneck
   B Western Ringneck

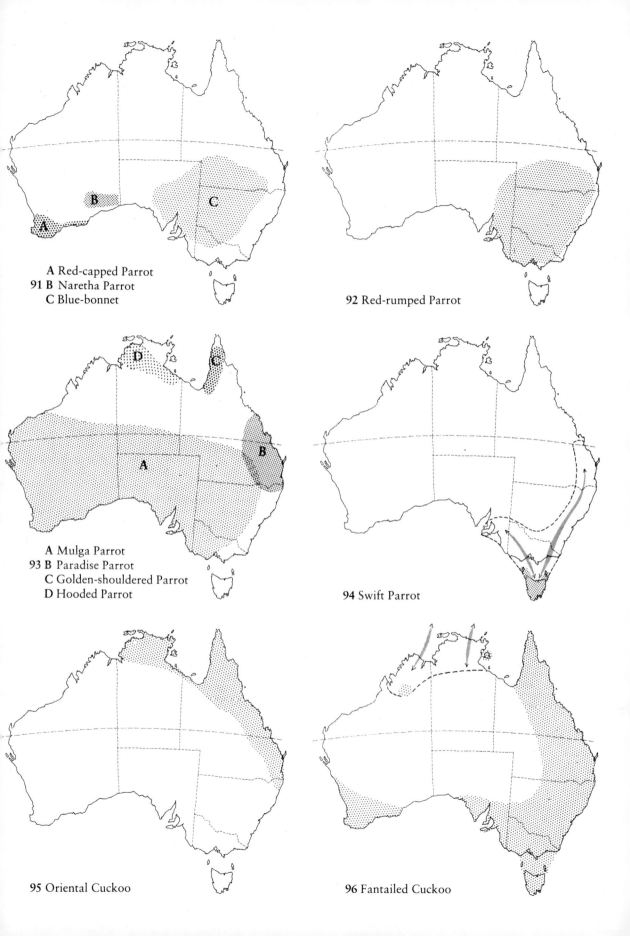

A Red-capped Parrot
91 B Naretha Parrot
C Blue-bonnet

92 Red-rumped Parrot

A Mulga Parrot
93 B Paradise Parrot
C Golden-shouldered Parrot
D Hooded Parrot

94 Swift Parrot

95 Oriental Cuckoo

96 Fantailed Cuckoo

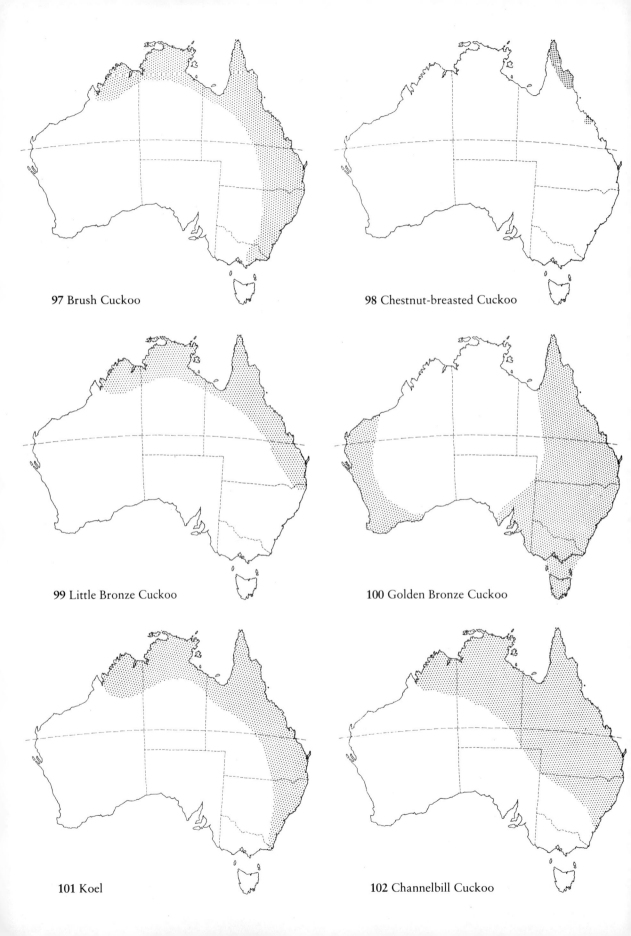

97 Brush Cuckoo

98 Chestnut-breasted Cuckoo

99 Little Bronze Cuckoo

100 Golden Bronze Cuckoo

101 Koel

102 Channelbill Cuckoo

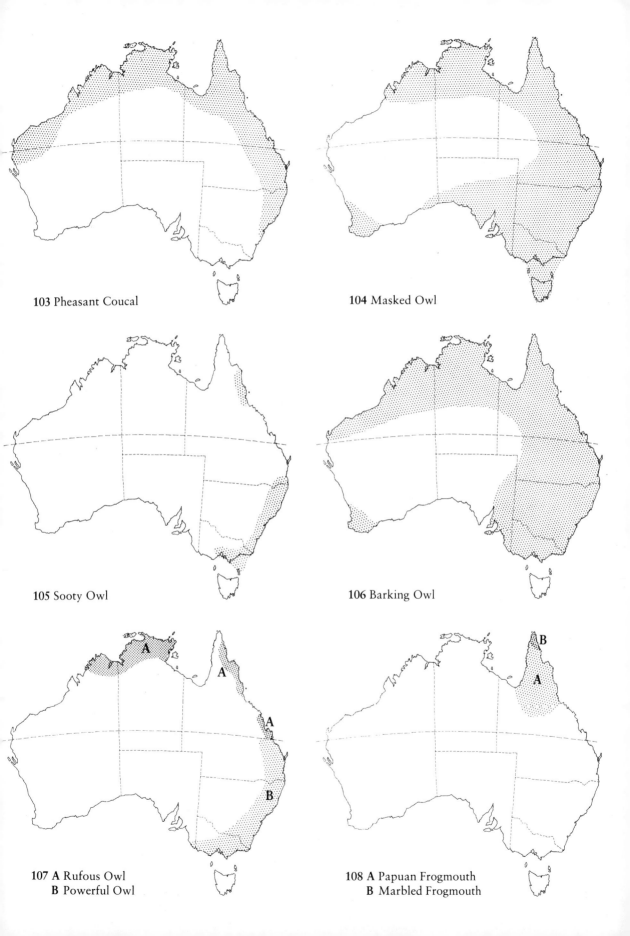

103 Pheasant Coucal

104 Masked Owl

105 Sooty Owl

106 Barking Owl

107 A Rufous Owl
B Powerful Owl

108 A Papuan Frogmouth
B Marbled Frogmouth

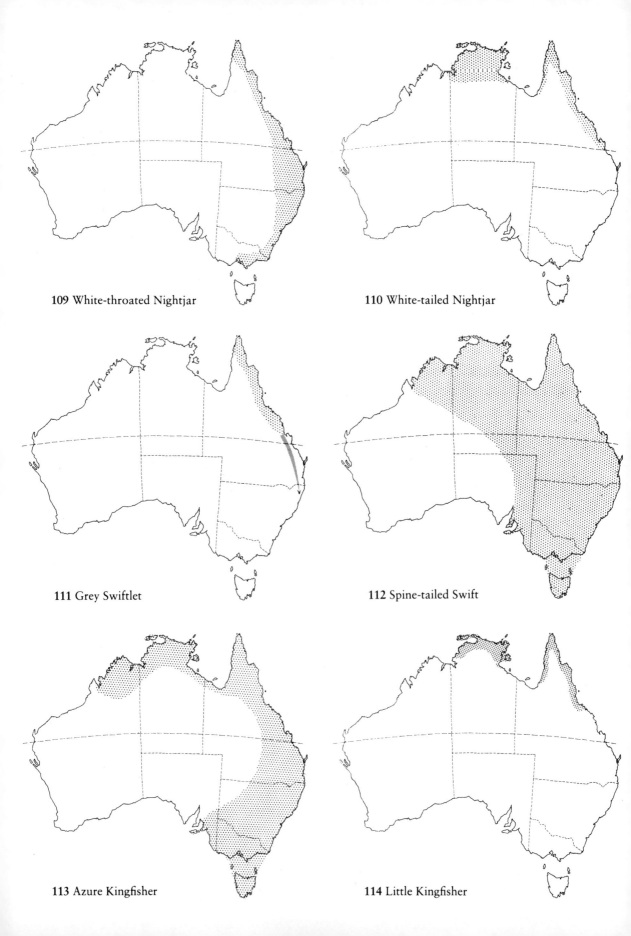

109 White-throated Nightjar

110 White-tailed Nightjar

111 Grey Swiftlet

112 Spine-tailed Swift

113 Azure Kingfisher

114 Little Kingfisher

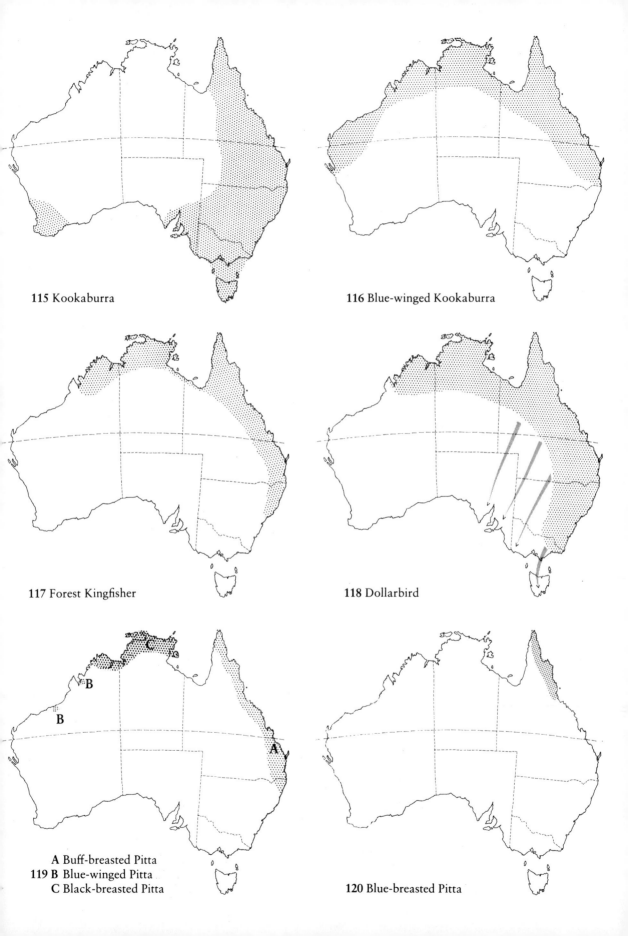

115 Kookaburra

116 Blue-winged Kookaburra

117 Forest Kingfisher

118 Dollarbird

A Buff-breasted Pitta
119 B Blue-winged Pitta
C Black-breasted Pitta

120 Blue-breasted Pitta

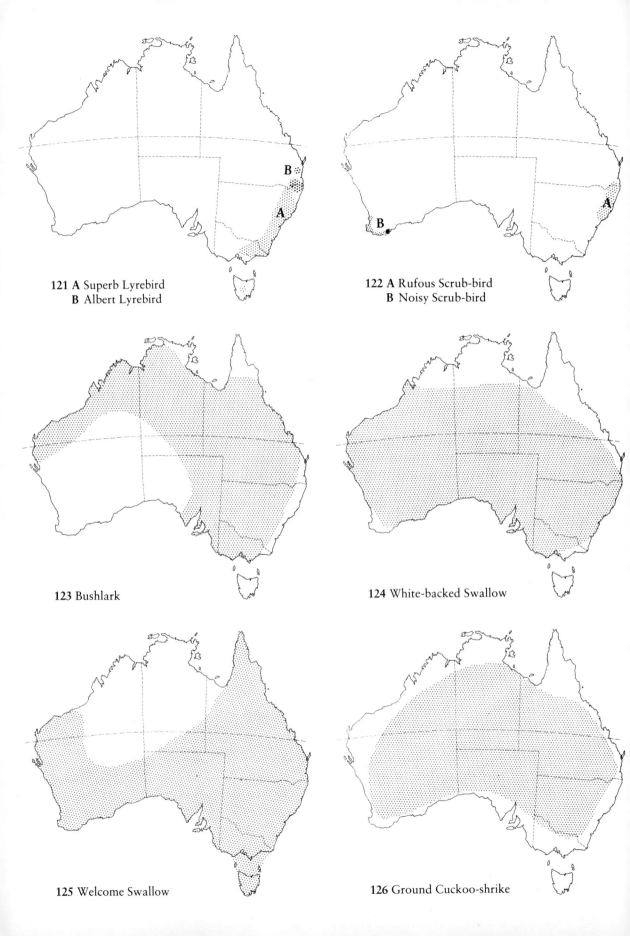

121 A Superb Lyrebird
B Albert Lyrebird

122 A Rufous Scrub-bird
B Noisy Scrub-bird

123 Bushlark

124 White-backed Swallow

125 Welcome Swallow

126 Ground Cuckoo-shrike

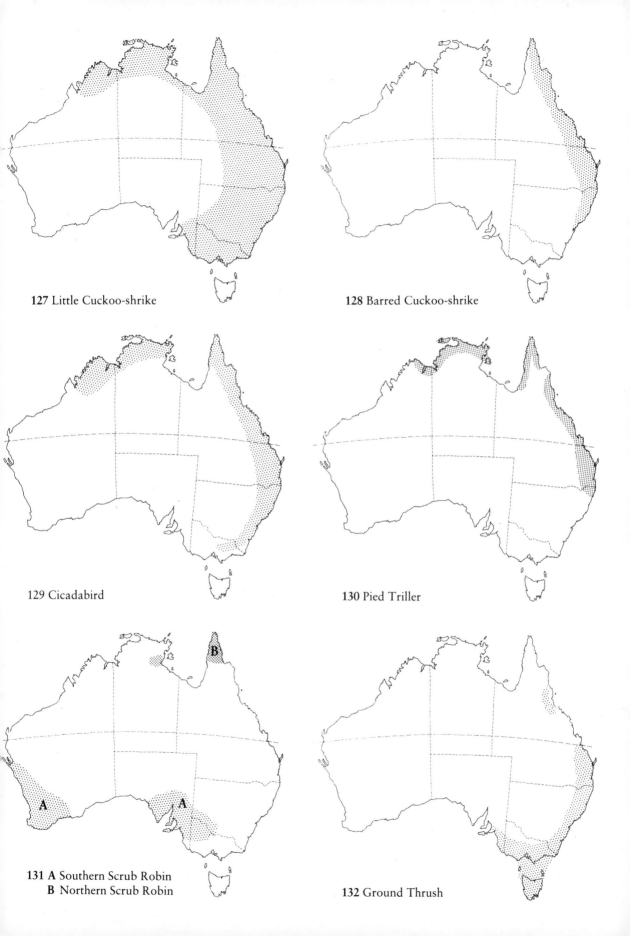

127 Little Cuckoo-shrike

128 Barred Cuckoo-shrike

129 Cicadabird

130 Pied Triller

131 A Southern Scrub Robin
      B Northern Scrub Robin

132 Ground Thrush

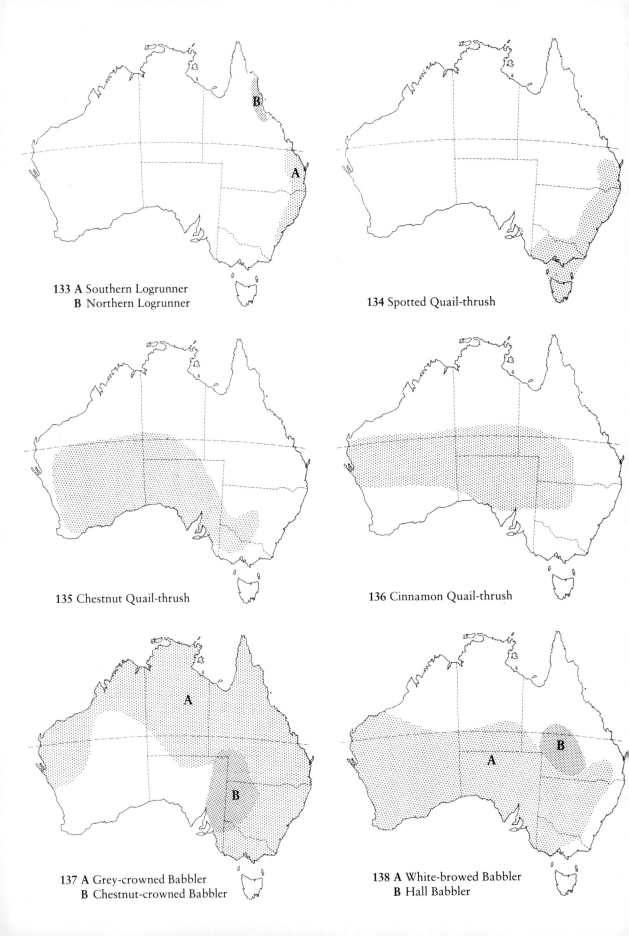

133 **A** Southern Logrunner
    B Northern Logrunner

134 Spotted Quail-thrush

135 Chestnut Quail-thrush

136 Cinnamon Quail-thrush

137 **A** Grey-crowned Babbler
    B Chestnut-crowned Babbler

138 **A** White-browed Babbler
    B Hall Babbler

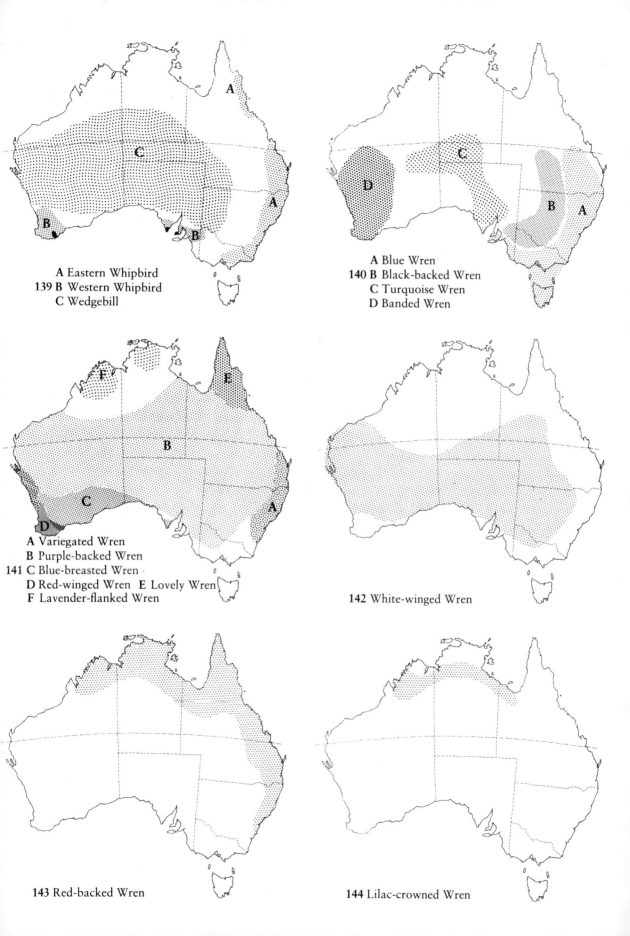

A Eastern Whipbird
139 B Western Whipbird
C Wedgebill

A Blue Wren
140 B Black-backed Wren
C Turquoise Wren
D Banded Wren

A Variegated Wren
B Purple-backed Wren
141 C Blue-breasted Wren
D Red-winged Wren **E** Lovely Wren
F Lavender-flanked Wren

142 White-winged Wren

143 Red-backed Wren

144 Lilac-crowned Wren

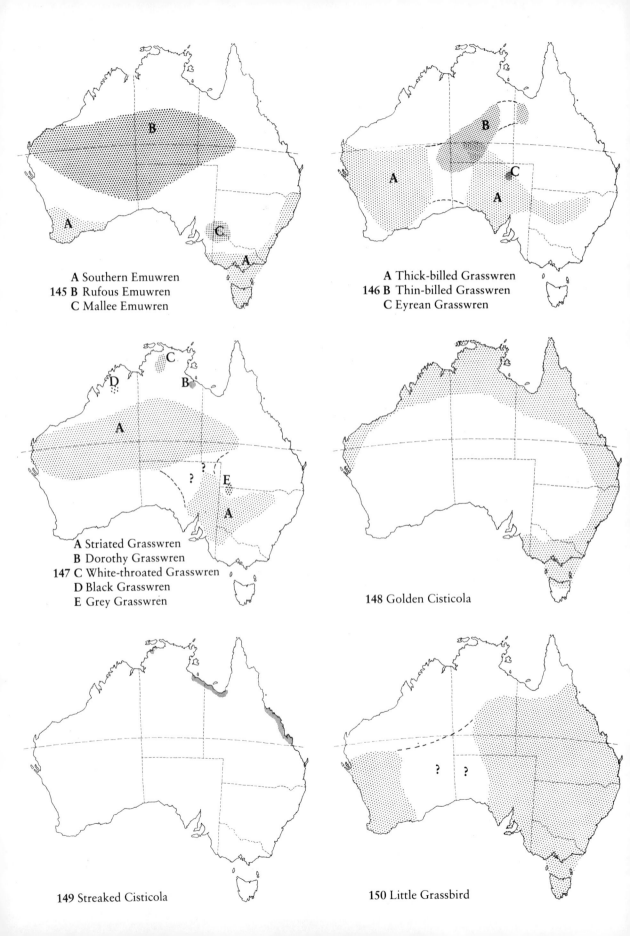

A Southern Emuwren
145 B Rufous Emuwren
C Mallee Emuwren

A Thick-billed Grasswren
146 B Thin-billed Grasswren
C Eyrean Grasswren

A Striated Grasswren
B Dorothy Grasswren
147 C White-throated Grasswren
D Black Grasswren
E Grey Grasswren

148 Golden Cisticola

149 Streaked Cisticola

150 Little Grassbird

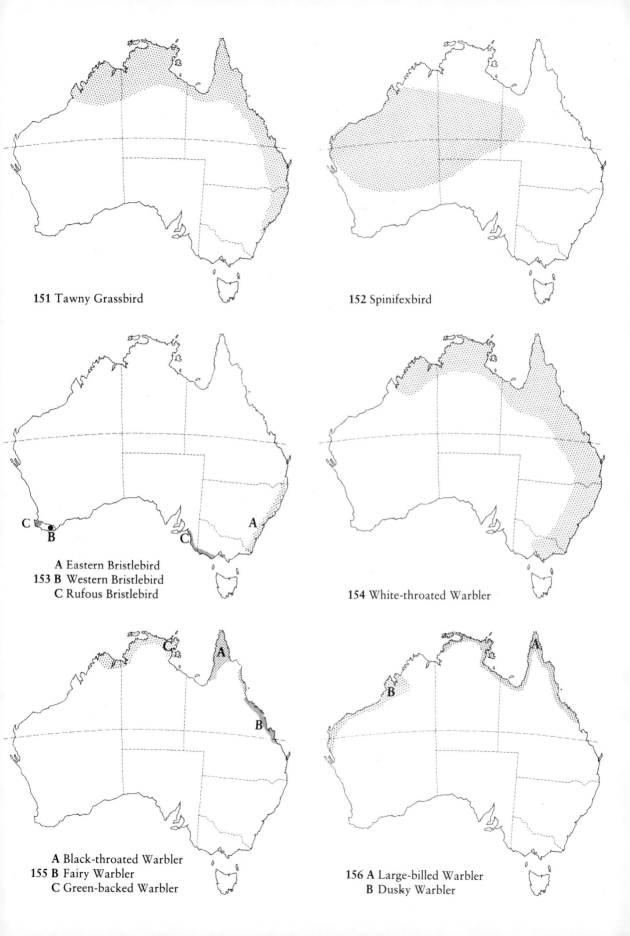

151 Tawny Grassbird

152 Spinifexbird

A Eastern Bristlebird
153 B Western Bristlebird
C Rufous Bristlebird

154 White-throated Warbler

A Black-throated Warbler
155 B Fairy Warbler
C Green-backed Warbler

156 A Large-billed Warbler
B Dusky Warbler

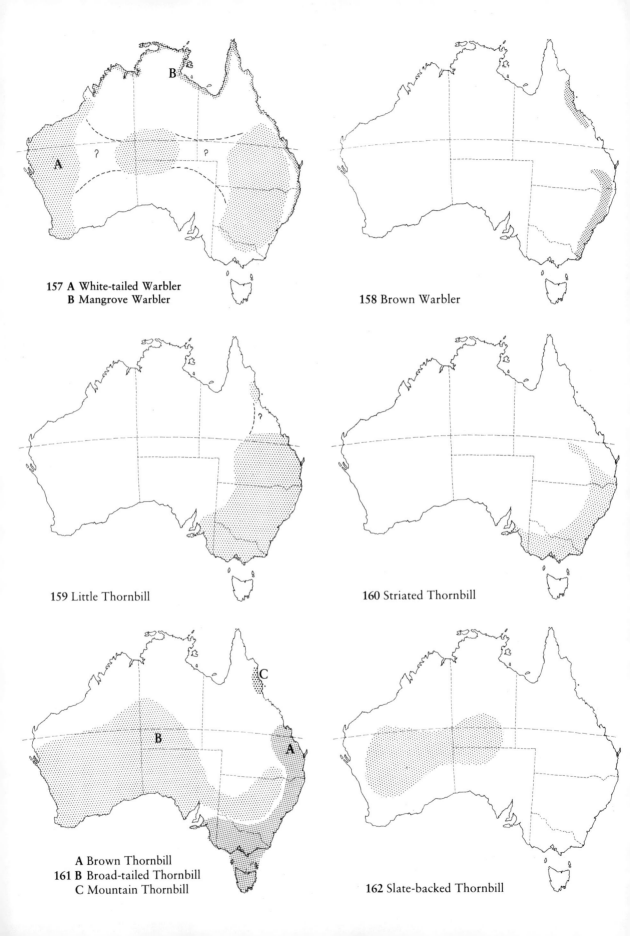

157 A White-tailed Warbler
B Mangrove Warbler

158 Brown Warbler

159 Little Thornbill

160 Striated Thornbill

A Brown Thornbill
161 B Broad-tailed Thornbill
C Mountain Thornbill

162 Slate-backed Thornbill

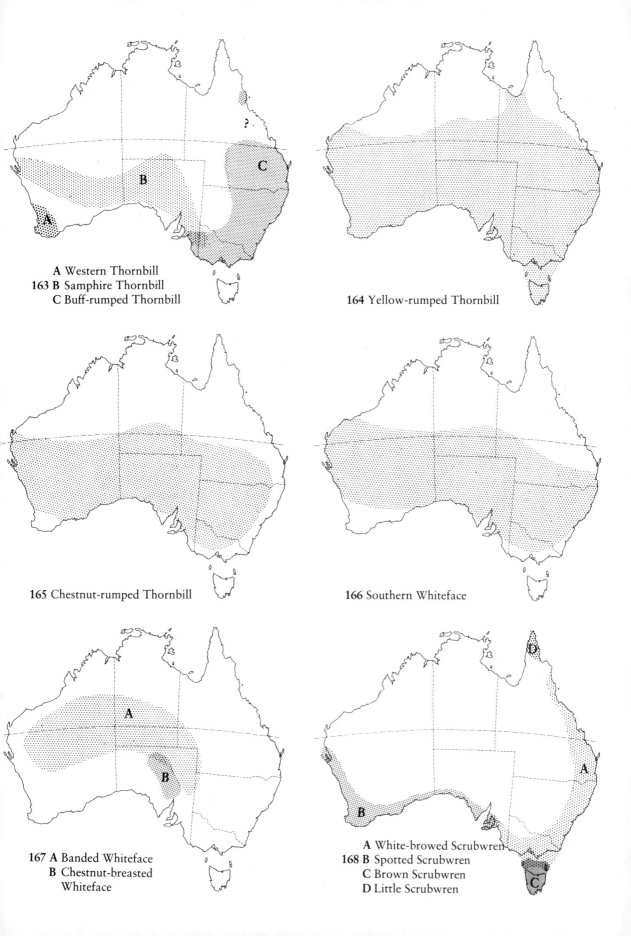

A Western Thornbill
163 B Samphire Thornbill
C Buff-rumped Thornbill

164 Yellow-rumped Thornbill

165 Chestnut-rumped Thornbill

166 Southern Whiteface

167 A Banded Whiteface
B Chestnut-breasted
  Whiteface

A White-browed Scrubwren
168 B Spotted Scrubwren
C Brown Scrubwren
D Little Scrubwren

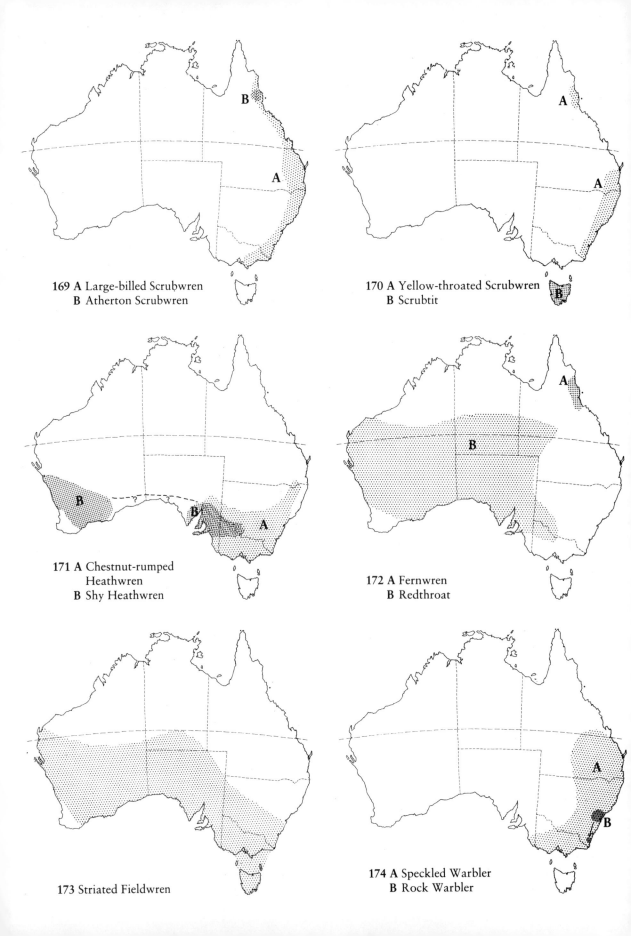

169 A Large-billed Scrubwren
B Atherton Scrubwren

170 A Yellow-throated Scrubwren
B Scrubtit

171 A Chestnut-rumped
Heathwren
B Shy Heathwren

172 A Fernwren
B Redthroat

173 Striated Fieldwren

174 A Speckled Warbler
B Rock Warbler

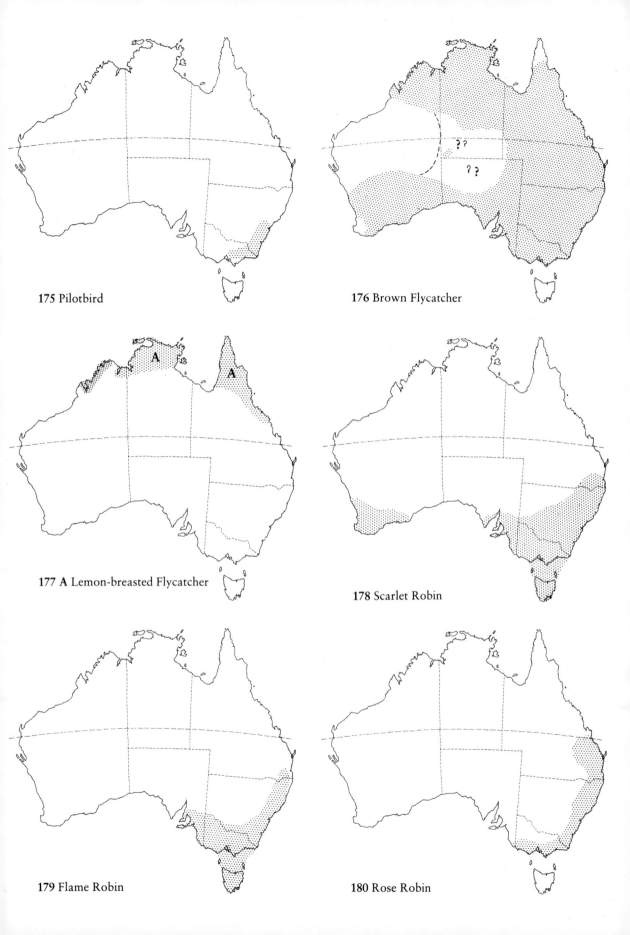

175 Pilotbird

176 Brown Flycatcher

177 A Lemon-breasted Flycatcher

178 Scarlet Robin

179 Flame Robin

180 Rose Robin

181 A Pink Robin
B Grey-headed Robin

182 A White-browed Robin
B Buff-sided Robin

A Eastern Yellow Robin
183 B Western Yellow Robin
C White-breasted Robin

184 A Pale-yellow Robin
B White-faced Robin

185 Grey Fantail

186 Northern Fantail

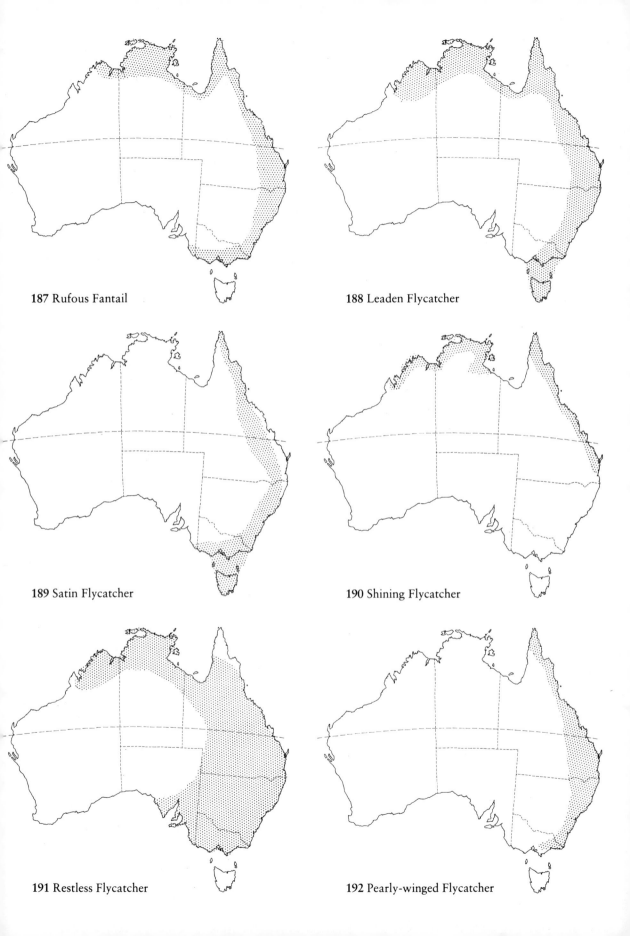

187 Rufous Fantail

188 Leaden Flycatcher

189 Satin Flycatcher

190 Shining Flycatcher

191 Restless Flycatcher

192 Pearly-winged Flycatcher

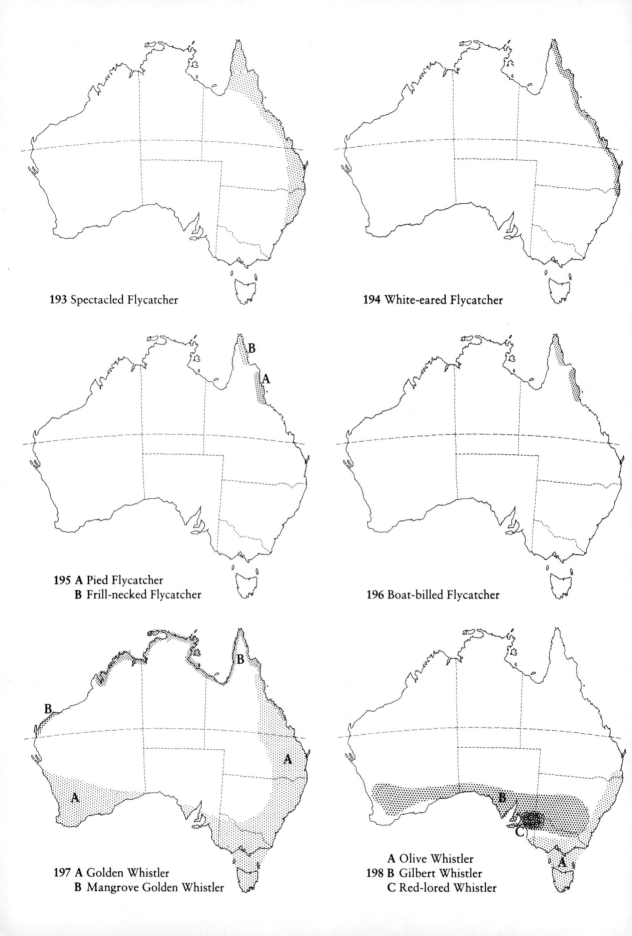

193 Spectacled Flycatcher

194 White-eared Flycatcher

195 A Pied Flycatcher
B Frill-necked Flycatcher

196 Boat-billed Flycatcher

197 A Golden Whistler
B Mangrove Golden Whistler

A Olive Whistler
198 B Gilbert Whistler
C Red-lored Whistler

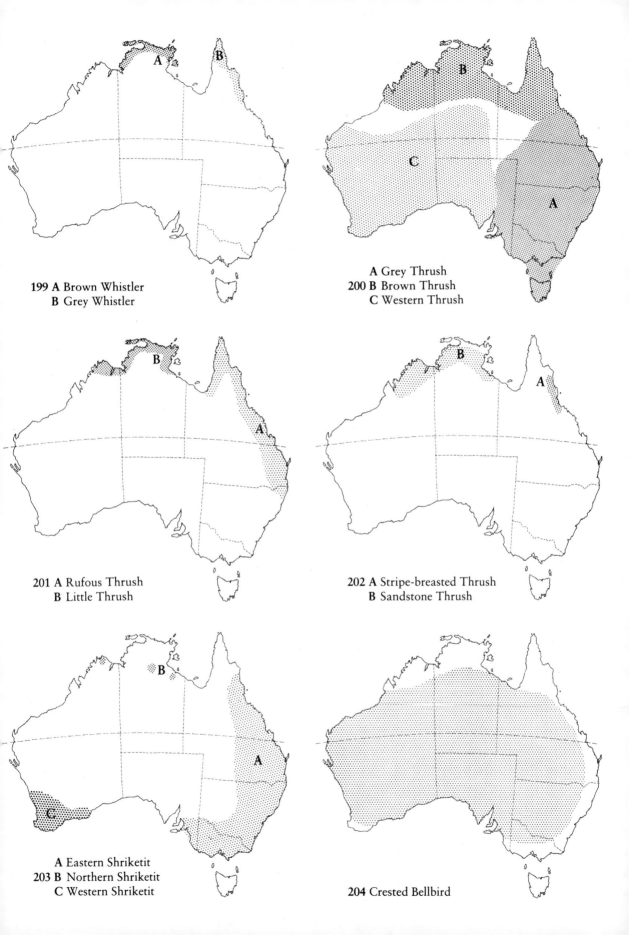

199 **A** Brown Whistler
B Grey Whistler

A Grey Thrush
200 **B** Brown Thrush
C Western Thrush

201 **A** Rufous Thrush
B Little Thrush

202 **A** Stripe-breasted Thrush
B Sandstone Thrush

A Eastern Shriketit
203 **B** Northern Shriketit
C Western Shriketit

204 Crested Bellbird

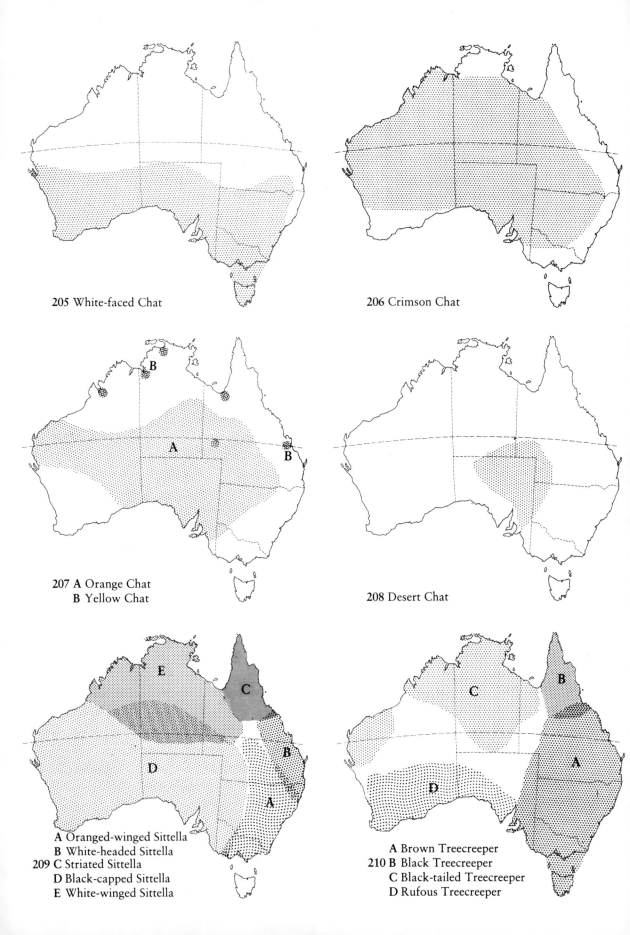

205 White-faced Chat

206 Crimson Chat

207 A Orange Chat
    B Yellow Chat

208 Desert Chat

A Oranged-winged Sittella
B White-headed Sittella
209 C Striated Sittella
D Black-capped Sittella
E White-winged Sittella

A Brown Treecreeper
210 B Black Treecreeper
C Black-tailed Treecreeper
D Rufous Treecreeper

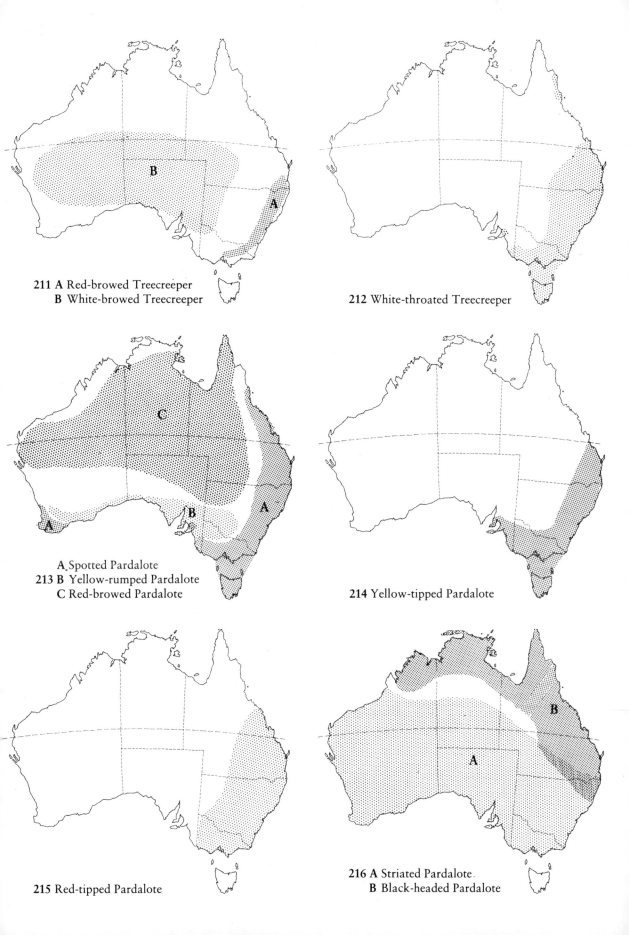

211 A Red-browed Treecreeper
B White-browed Treecreeper

212 White-throated Treecreeper

A Spotted Pardalote
213 B Yellow-rumped Pardalote
C Red-browed Pardalote

214 Yellow-tipped Pardalote

215 Red-tipped Pardalote

216 A Striated Pardalote
B Black-headed Pardalote

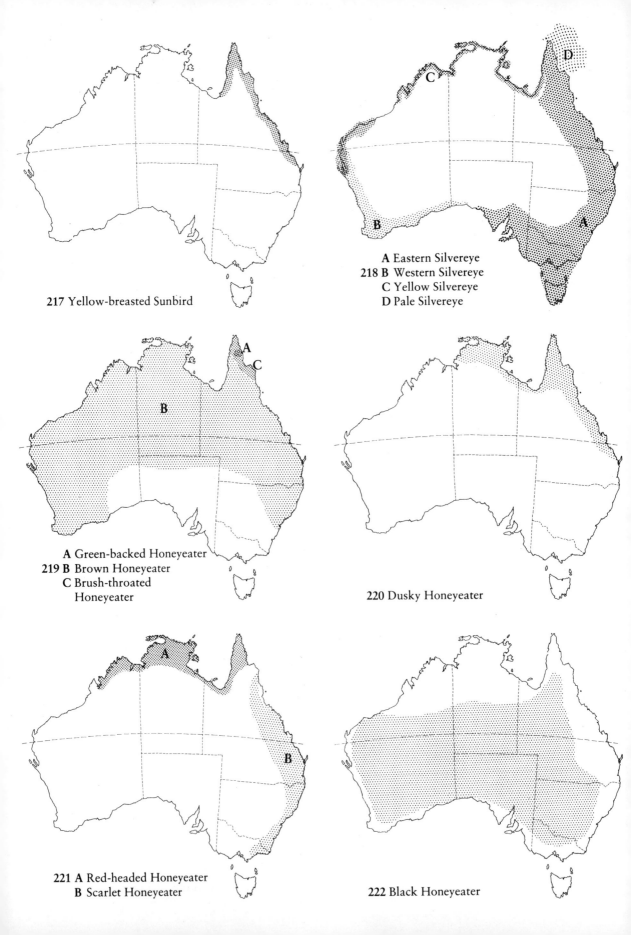

217 Yellow-breasted Sunbird

A Eastern Silvereye
218 B Western Silvereye
C Yellow Silvereye
D Pale Silvereye

A Green-backed Honeyeater
219 B Brown Honeyeater
C Brush-throated
   Honeyeater

220 Dusky Honeyeater

221 A Red-headed Honeyeater
     B Scarlet Honeyeater

222 Black Honeyeater

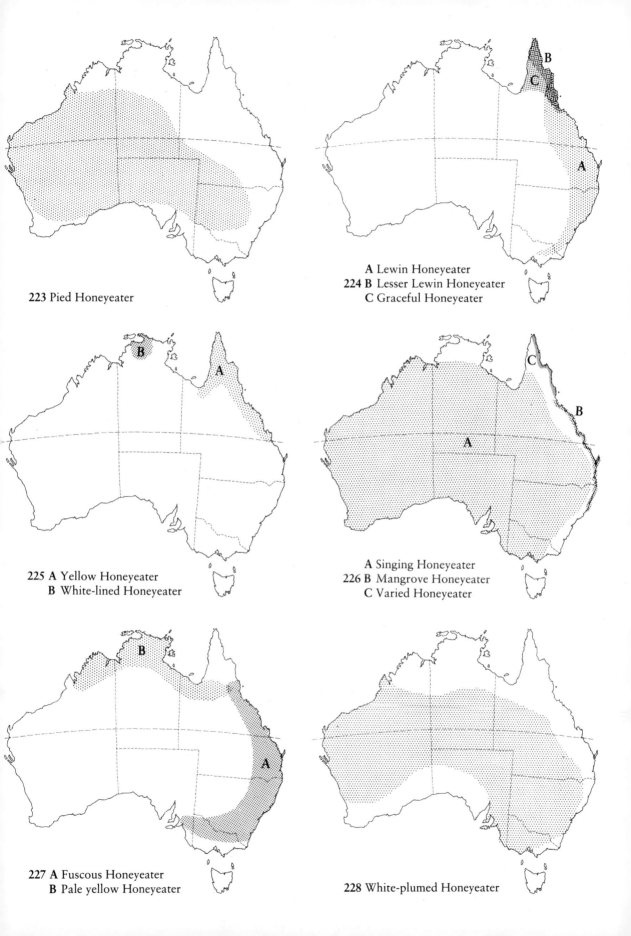

223 Pied Honeyeater

A Lewin Honeyeater
224 B Lesser Lewin Honeyeater
C Graceful Honeyeater

225 A Yellow Honeyeater
B White-lined Honeyeater

A Singing Honeyeater
226 B Mangrove Honeyeater
C Varied Honeyeater

227 A Fuscous Honeyeater
B Pale yellow Honeyeater

228 White-plumed Honeyeater

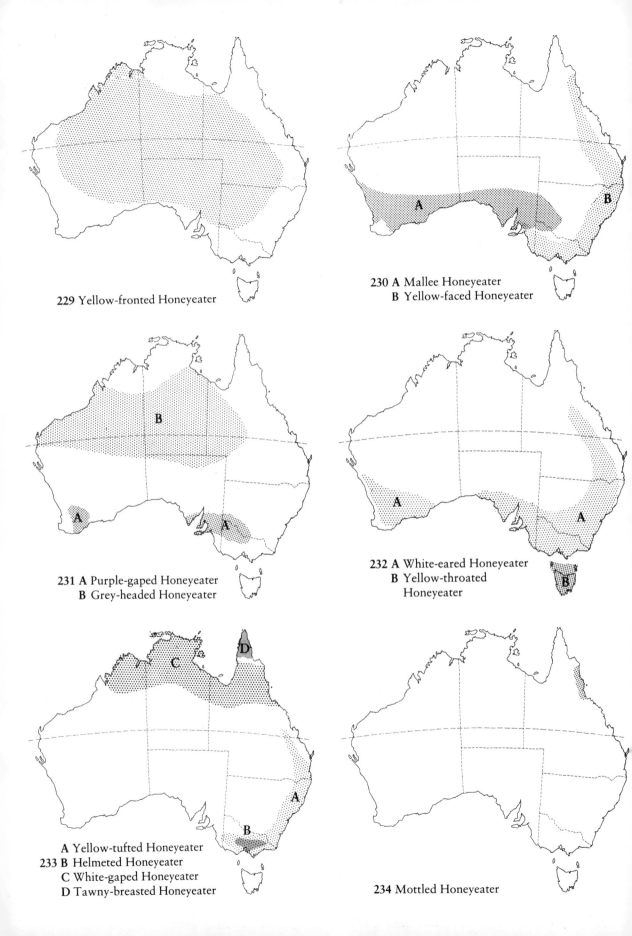

229 Yellow-fronted Honeyeater

230 A Mallee Honeyeater
B Yellow-faced Honeyeater

231 A Purple-gaped Honeyeater
B Grey-headed Honeyeater

232 A White-eared Honeyeater
B Yellow-throated
Honeyeater

A Yellow-tufted Honeyeater
233 B Helmeted Honeyeater
C White-gaped Honeyeater
D Tawny-breasted Honeyeater

234 Mottled Honeyeater

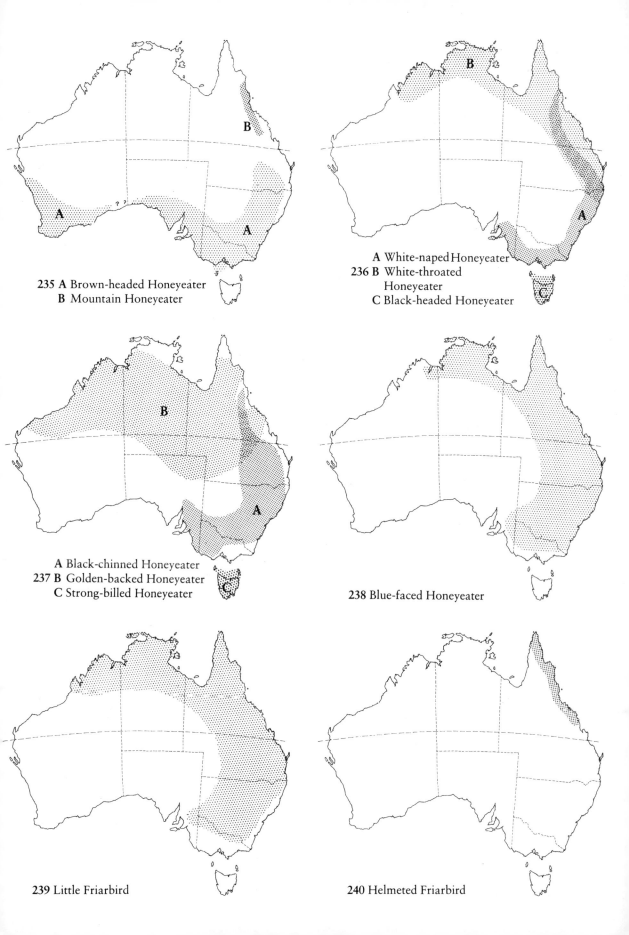

235 A Brown-headed Honeyeater
B Mountain Honeyeater

A White-naped Honeyeater
236 B White-throated
Honeyeater
C Black-headed Honeyeater

A Black-chinned Honeyeater
237 B Golden-backed Honeyeater
C Strong-billed Honeyeater

238 Blue-faced Honeyeater

239 Little Friarbird

240 Helmeted Friarbird

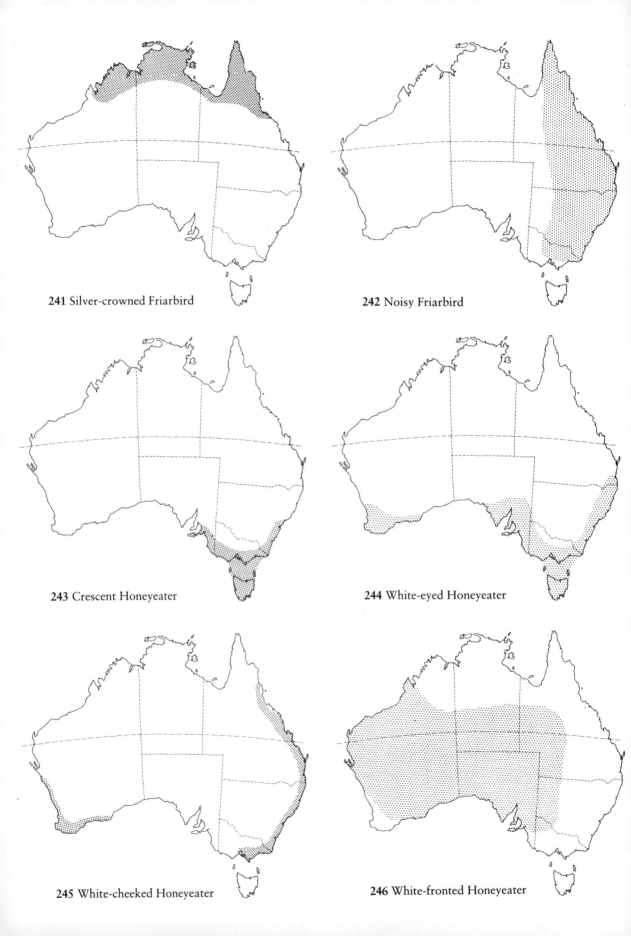

241 Silver-crowned Friarbird

242 Noisy Friarbird

243 Crescent Honeyeater

244 White-eyed Honeyeater

245 White-cheeked Honeyeater

246 White-fronted Honeyeater

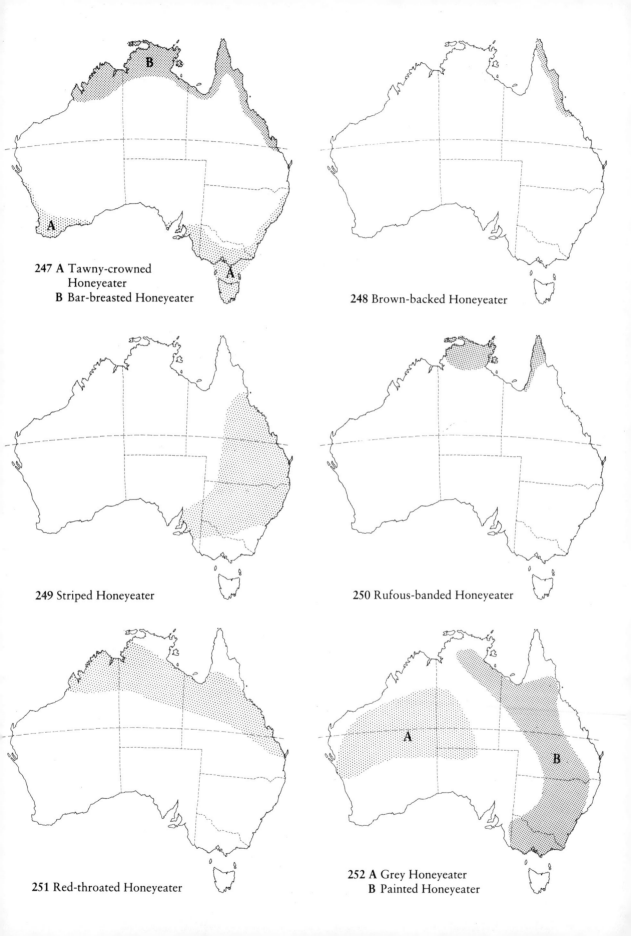

247 A Tawny-crowned
Honeyeater
B Bar-breasted Honeyeater

248 Brown-backed Honeyeater

249 Striped Honeyeater

250 Rufous-banded Honeyeater

251 Red-throated Honeyeater

252 A Grey Honeyeater
B Painted Honeyeater

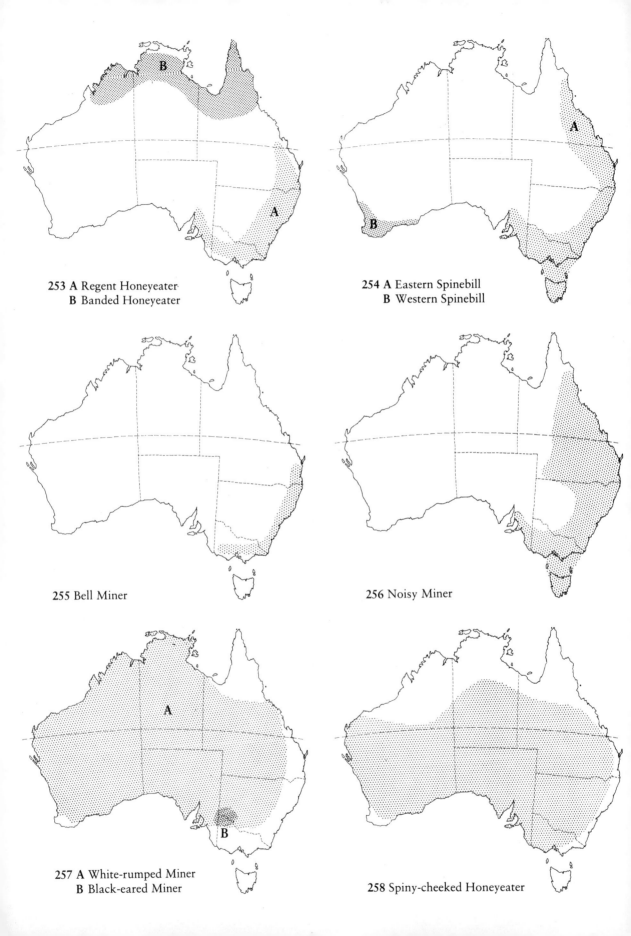

253 A Regent Honeyeater
  B Banded Honeyeater

254 A Eastern Spinebill
  B Western Spinebill

255 Bell Miner

256 Noisy Miner

257 A White-rumped Miner
  B Black-eared Miner

258 Spiny-cheeked Honeyeater

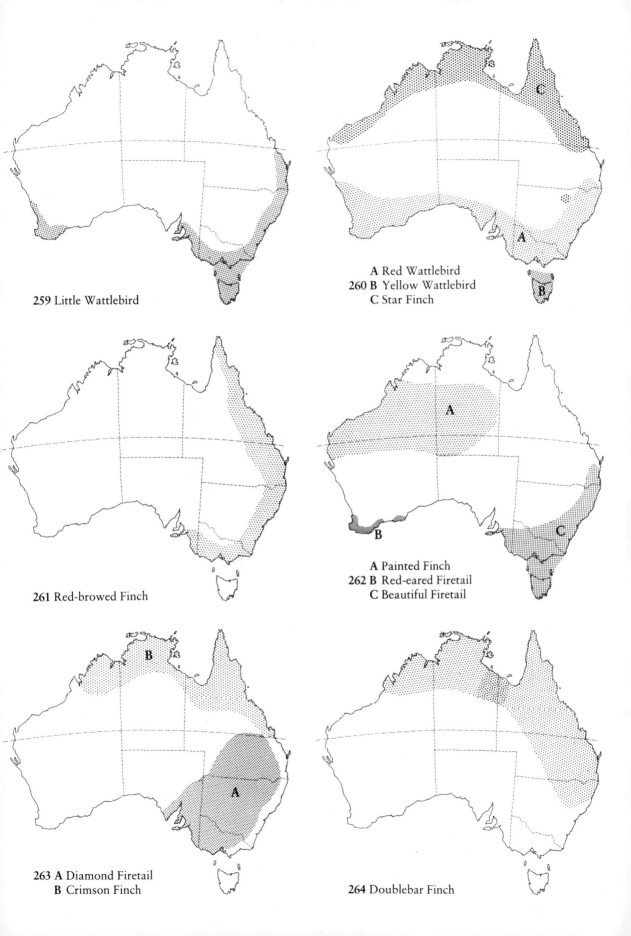

259 Little Wattlebird

A Red Wattlebird
260 B Yellow Wattlebird
C Star Finch

261 Red-browed Finch

A Painted Finch
262 B Red-eared Firetail
C Beautiful Firetail

263 A Diamond Firetail
B Crimson Finch

264 Doublebar Finch

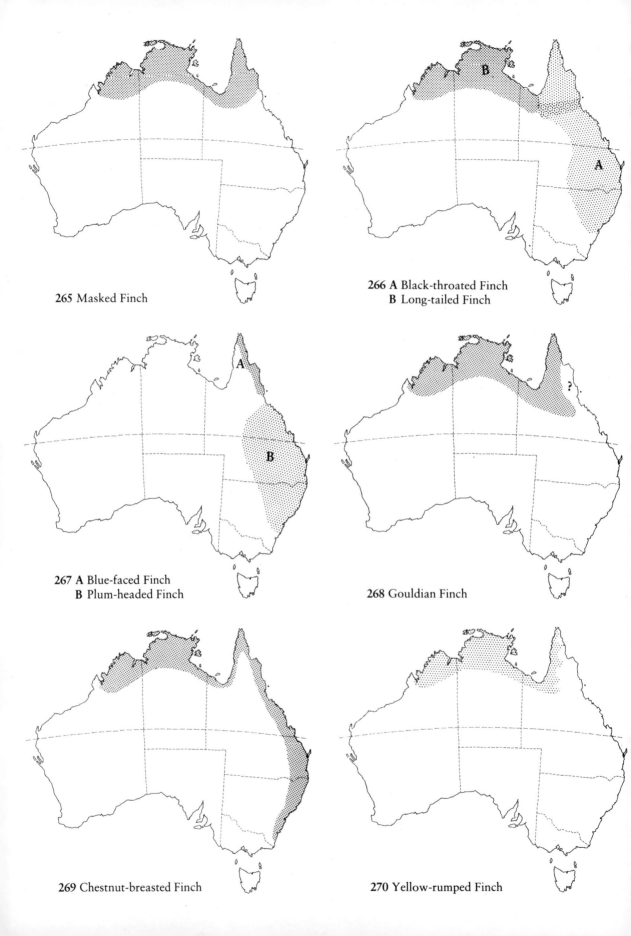

265 Masked Finch

266 A Black-throated Finch
B Long-tailed Finch

267 A Blue-faced Finch
B Plum-headed Finch

268 Gouldian Finch

269 Chestnut-breasted Finch

270 Yellow-rumped Finch

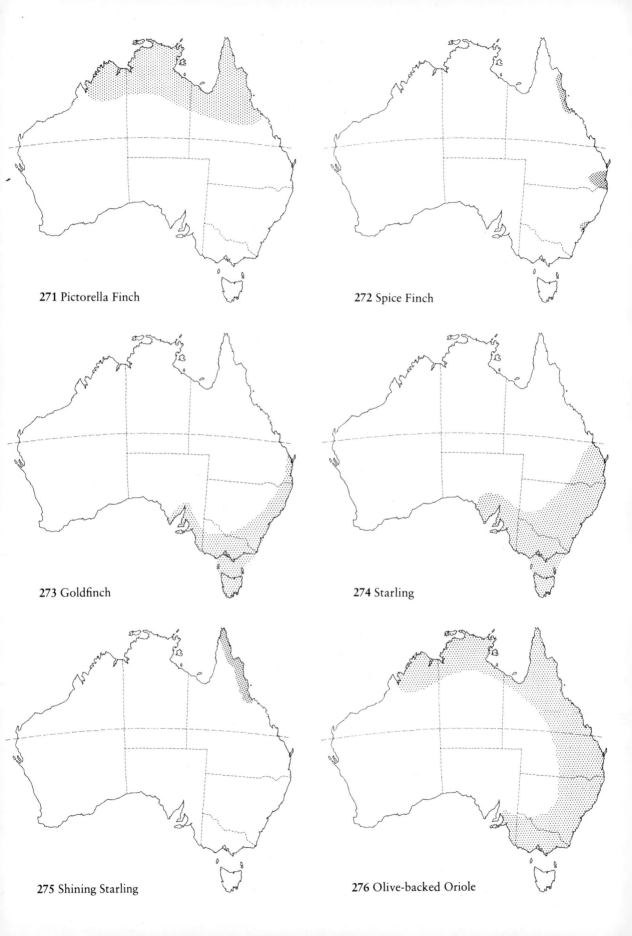

271 Pictorella Finch

272 Spice Finch

273 Goldfinch

274 Starling

275 Shining Starling

276 Olive-backed Oriole

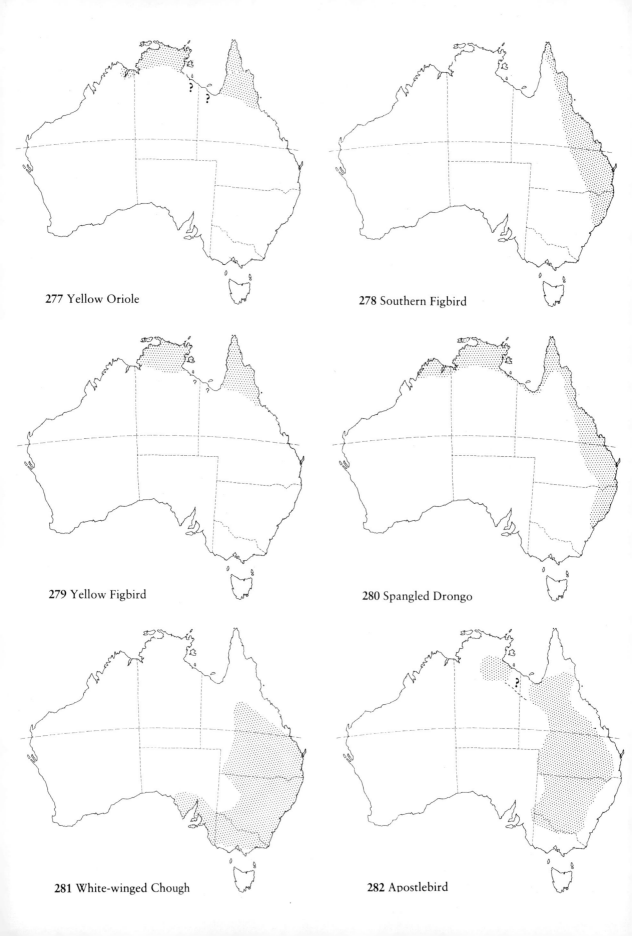

277 Yellow Oriole

278 Southern Figbird

279 Yellow Figbird

280 Spangled Drongo

281 White-winged Chough

282 Apostlebird

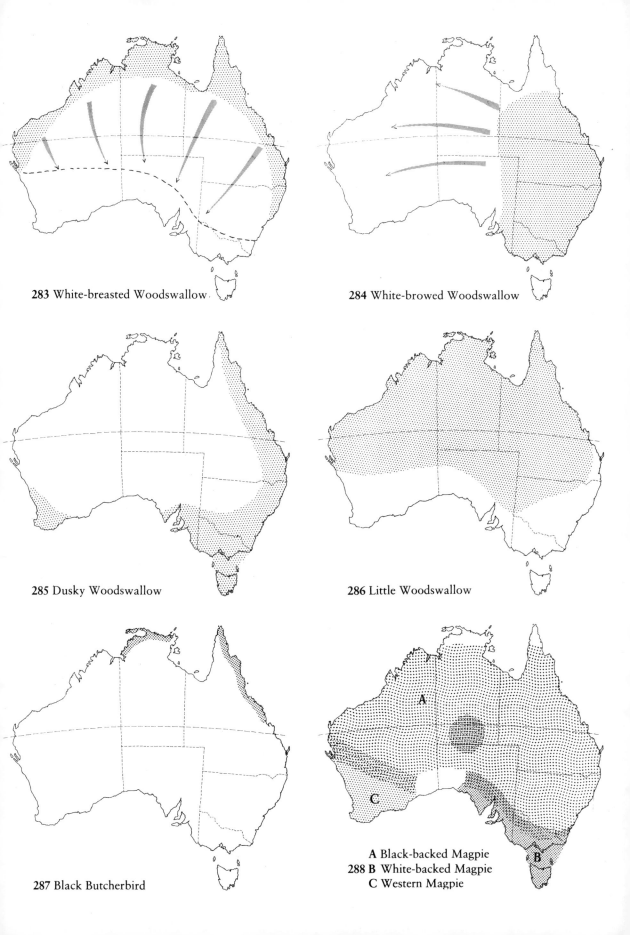

283 White-breasted Woodswallow

284 White-browed Woodswallow

285 Dusky Woodswallow

286 Little Woodswallow

287 Black Butcherbird

A Black-backed Magpie
288 B White-backed Magpie
C Western Magpie

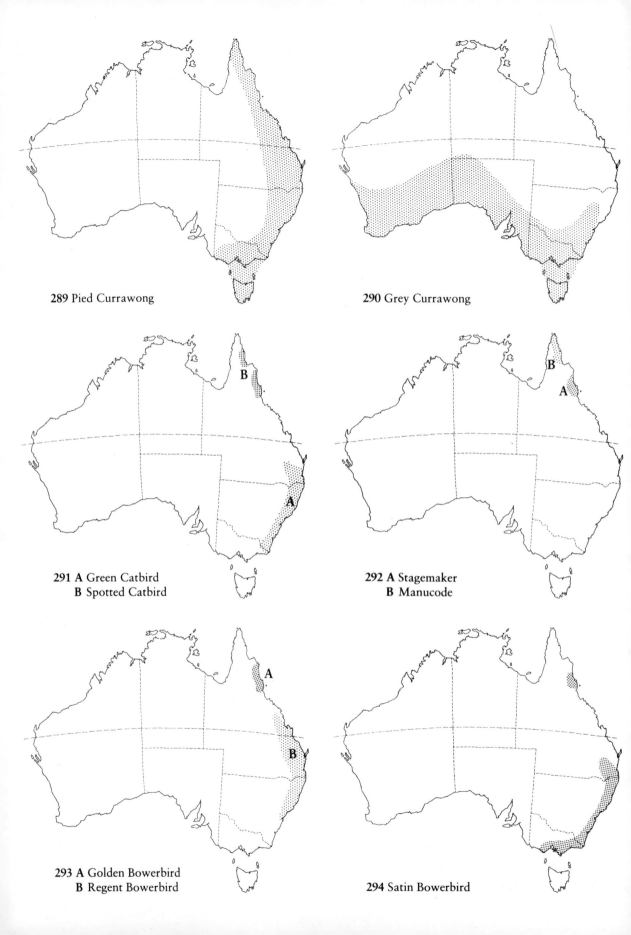

289 Pied Currawong

290 Grey Currawong

291 A Green Catbird
B Spotted Catbird

292 A Stagemaker
B Manucode

293 A Golden Bowerbird
B Regent Bowerbird

294 Satin Bowerbird

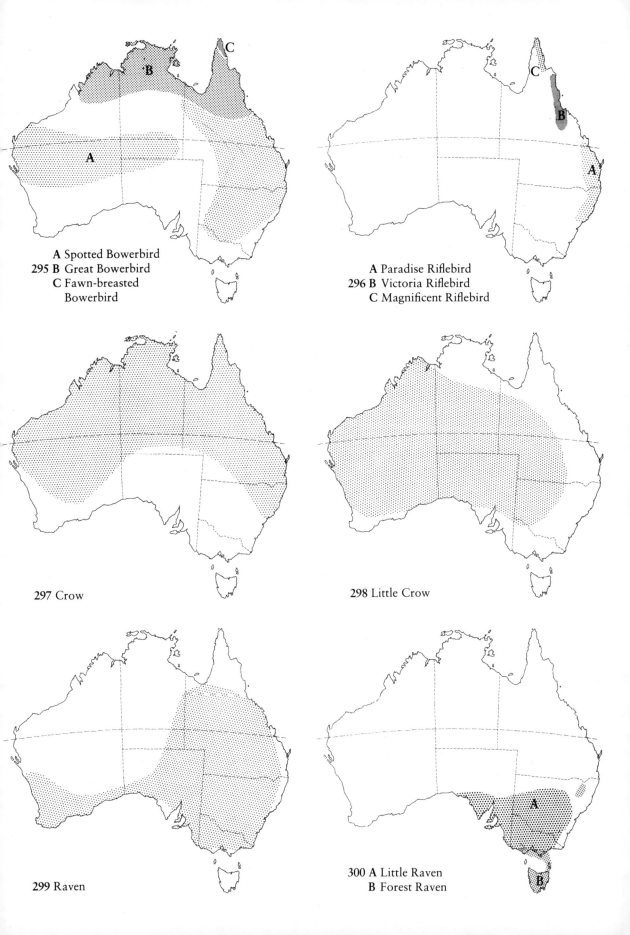

A Spotted Bowerbird
295 B Great Bowerbird
C Fawn-breasted
  Bowerbird

A Paradise Riflebird
296 B Victoria Riflebird
C Magnificent Riflebird

297 Crow

298 Little Crow

299 Raven

300 A Little Raven
   B Forest Raven

INDEX

[Including some alternative common names. There is a comprehensive list of common and scientific names in *An Index of Australian Bird Names*, CSIRO, Canberra, 1969.]